WHAT'S DIFFERENT ABOUT THIS BOOK?

The Handbook of
COLLEGE ENTRANCE EXAMINATIONS

is organized for continuous learning. The day-by-day units of each *language arts* and *mathematics* section begin with the simplest material and progress gradually to a point where you will gain thorough mastery over current testing techniques. This book emphasizes the process of *understanding* rather than rote learning or cramming.

Extended practice with the varied, up-to-date, self-testing material in the book will not only sharpen your ability to perform well on the "boards," but will also make you a better all-around student. You will know the *What* and *Why* of entrance exams—and you will be ready to do your best on *any* exam.

About the Authors

Dr. Stephen Krulik is Assistant Professor of Mathematics Education at Temple University. Dr. Krulik was formerly on the faculty of Hofstra University and has published articles in the professional journals as well as a work in the field of teaching methodology.

Irwin Kaufman teaches mathematics at Lafayette High School. He is a specialist in mathematics for the gifted student and was formerly on the faculty of Brooklyn College. He has written in the field of teaching methodology.

Jerome Shostak is an experienced college advisor, guidance counselor and English teacher. The author of several popular handbooks in language arts, Mr. Shostak is supervisor of Guidance, Board of Education, New York City.

D0423916

The
HANDBOOK
of
COLLEGE
ENTRANCE
EXAMINATIONS

STEPHEN KRULIK
IRWIN KAUFMAN
and JEROME SHOSTAK

A KANGAROO BOOK
PUBLISHED BY POCKET BOOKS NEW YORK

THE HANDBOOK OF COLLEGE ENTRANCE EXAMINATIONS

POCKET BOOK edition published May, 1965

Revised POCKET BOOK edition published March, 1975

This original POCKET BOOK edition is printed from brand-new
plates made from newly set, clear, easy-to-read type.
POCKET BOOK editions are published by
POCKET BOOKS,
a Simon & Schuster Division of
GULF & WESTERN CORPORATION
1230 Avenue of the Americas,
New York, N.Y. 10020.
Trademarks registered in the United States
and other countries.

8987

CONTENTS

The Handbook of
College Entrance Examinations

HOW TO USE THIS BOOK
MOST EFFECTIVELY

The single purpose of this book of examination techniques is to help you to achieve your best score on the competitive College Entrance Examination that you are planning to take. The Inventory and Practice Tests will help you diagnose your strengths and weaknesses. You will then be able to concentrate on the areas in which you could fall down. The Tests of Mastery will evaluate the extent of your growth. The verbal and mathematics tests in Part III will give you the continued drill that leads to maximum results.

1. Daily periods of moderate length with this material are much more productive than are cram sessions at irregular intervals. Take advantage of the day-to-day approach stressed in each section.

2. Vary the material. Intermingle the verbal sections with the mathematics to keep a sharp edge to your level of concentration.

3. Take time out for relaxation—daydreaming, radio listening, television viewing—before you begin that necessarily lonely task of mastering fundamentals. Plan your time so that you complete a full "day's work" in each sitting.

4. Try to work under examination conditions even during your study sessions. Get all of your equipment in advance. Have pens, pencils, scrap paper at your side. Have a watch available so that you learn how to time yourself.

5. Use score averages and time limits to learn how you compare with others. These statistics should also help you to measure your improvement in speed and accuracy.

6. Do not be afraid to repeat a day's work. If you have difficulty in learning a technique, then repeat the basic drill work. Such repetitions lead to mastery.

1

7. Pace yourself. Spend less time on material you find easy so that you can spend more time on the less familiar.

Which Examination?

The skills and techniques emphasized in this book are those measured by all College Entrance Examinations; they are the skills and techniques that are necessary for success in college. To discover which examination you must take, send for the catalogs issued by the colleges in which you are interested. Once you know the name of the test in which you must compete, make certain that you obtain the examination booklet that accompanies the applications. This pamphlet will acquaint you with the specific types of questions which the test will contain. We have tried not to duplicate this material; instead, we have attempted to cover the skills and knowledges upon which these tests are based.

Part I

English: Essential Vocabulary

ESSENTIAL VOCABULARY

Vocabulary controls correlate so closely with ability to succeed in college that every College Entrance Examination attempts to measure the extent of your command over words. The form most frequently used tests your ability to recognize synonyms. Sometimes a word is given and it is followed by four or five words from which you are asked to select the closest synonym. Sometimes a phrase is presented and you are asked to choose the most appropriate synonym for the italicized word.

As in the examinations taken by most candidates, the selection of antonyms rather than of synonyms may be the basic approach. In addition, some of the analogy questions are often based on ability to recognize word families rather than thought relationships. Sentence completion may depend on your understanding the meaning of difficult words rather than on your ability to follow the author's thought pattern. Key questions in reading-comprehension selections may also be out-and-out vocabulary questions. Vocabulary controls are actually part of every one of the tests!

How to Get the Most out of This Section

The material that follows is based on four levels of vocabulary. The key to success on these four levels is based on a methodical approach. Plan to spend time each day. A few minutes daily will bring about best results.

1. Approach each list separately.
2. Check those words that you do not know.
3. Memorize the synonyms, antonyms, and model sentence for each of the words that you do not know.
4. When you think you have a level under control, take *one at a time* the tests that follow. After each test, restudy those words that you missed.

5. After you have completed more than one level, if you still have difficulty with the analogy or sentence-completion techniques, then turn to the sections that explain how to do your best with these types of questions. Also go back to one of the tests on a previous level and retest yourself. The more you memorize the answers, the better your control of the words.

6. Work for accuracy at first. Speed will follow.

BASIC VOCABULARY

Section 1: BASIC LIST

First Day

1. **ABDICATE** to resign, give up   **ant.** claim, defend ♦ When the king *abdicated*, his son succeeded him.

2. **ABRIDGE** to make shorter, make less   **ant.** elongate, enlarge ♦ Unless you *abridge* the film, the children will find it much too long.

3. **ABYSMAL** bottomless, measureless (in a bad sense) ♦ His *abysmal* ignorance of the ways of the world caused him untold misery.

4. **ACCOMPLICE** one who shares in a crime, helper   **ant.** adversary, enemy ♦ His *accomplice* tied up the watchman while the accused allegedly opened the safe.

5. **ACQUIT** to declare not guilty   **ant.** convict, condemn ♦ After the trial, the judge was pleased to be able to *acquit* the defendant.

6. **ADAGE** a well-known proverb, maxim ♦ A famous *adage* is, "An apple a day keeps the doctor away."

7. **ADEPT** expert, skilled   **ant.** bungling, awkward ♦ She is so *adept* at making plausible excuses that we have given up trying to correct her.

8. **ADVERSARY** an opponent, enemy   **ant.** helper, endorser, ally ♦ During World War II, Japan was an *adversary* of the United States.

7

9. AGENDA an order of events ♦ The secretary drew up an *agenda* that included the important matters that had to be discussed during the meeting.

10. ALLAY to relieve, soothe   ant. rouse, agitate ♦ I will *allay* his fears by telling him what happened.

11. ALOOF standoffish, apart   ant. friendly, close ♦ He stood *aloof* from the other employees because he was the son of the owner.

12. AMALGAMATE to consolidate, unite ant. scatter, disintegrate ♦ Rome had followed a deliberate policy of *amalgamating* conquered nations in order to administer them more efficiently.

13. AMEND to improve, correct   ant. impair, corrupt, damage ♦ An advantage of a democracy is that we can *amend* our laws when necessary.

14. ANNIHILATE to destroy completely, exterminate   ant. create, discover ♦ It is difficult to conceive that one hydrogen bomb can *annihilate* almost all of mankind!

15. ANTHROPOLOGIST one who studies the origin and development of mankind ♦ The *anthropologist* spent his summer vacation in Egypt digging in the ruins.

16. APEX the highest point, tip   ant. nadir, bottom ♦ The *apex* of Mt. Everest is the highest point on its peak.

17. APPREHENSIVE anxious, worried; quick to understand ant. confident, cool, nonchalant ♦ What world leader today is not *apprehensive* that some careless hand might trigger the atomic bomb that will end our civilization?

18. ARBITRARY based on one's own wishes, not going by any rule or law, willful   ant. legitimate, lawful ♦ All the constitutional safeguards of individual freedom are endangered when the governor of a state can make decisions that are *arbitrary* and that might, thereby, disregard the other branches of government.

19. ARDUOUS difficult; steep   ant. light, easy, effortless ♦ The soldiers were exhausted after their *arduous* ten-mile hike through the marshland.

20. ARROGANT boastful, very proud   ant. meek, modest, humble ♦ The *arrogant* nobleman disregarded the orders issued by the officials appointed by the people.

21. ARSON the willful burning of property ♦ The insurance company attributed the warehouse fire to *arson* because of the poor financial condition of the warehouse owner's company.

22. ASSAIL to attack with physical force or harsh words **ant.** defend, protect ♦ The people were waiting outside to *assail* the assassin when he left the courtroom.

23. ASSIDUOUS persistent, diligent **ant.** lazy, negligent ♦ Frank claimed that his high average was the result of *assiduous* study and not of good fortune or wishful thinking.

24. ATTRIBUTE to give credit for, ascribe to a cause; an essential quality ♦ We *attribute* the success of the magazine to its feature writers.

25. AUGMENT to increase, make larger **ant.** reduce, decrease ♦ The man took a second job to *augment* his income.

26. AUTHENTIC genuine, true **ant.** counterfeit, false ♦ *Giants in the Earth* seems to give an *authentic* account of the sufferings of the pioneer farmers who settled in the Dakotas.

27. AVOW to declare openly, acknowledge **ant.** contradict, deny ♦ Steve *avowed* that the purpose of his endeavor is to achieve financial gain.

28. AWRY twisted, turned to one side ♦ Their plans went *awry* when they could not start the engine of the automobile.

29. BALMY soothing, fragrant, mild **ant.** rank, musty ♦ The *balmy* summer breeze brought welcome relief to the city dwellers.

30. BANTER to tease, ridicule without malice, jest ♦ Their joy in punning is so great that light *banter* colors even their most serious discussions.

31. BAUBLE a worthless trinket, showy trifle ♦ Can a client tell the sparkling of a diamond from the glitter of a *bauble?*

Second Day

1. BELLIGERENT at war; warlike **ant.** friendly, amicable ♦ The *belligerent* powers in World War I lost millions of men in trench warfare.

2. BERATE to scold, chide ♦ The owner *berated* the driver who had delivered the wrong package to us.

3. BEREAVE to deprive, make desolate by loss (esp. death) ♦ The nation was *bereaved* by the assassination of President Kennedy.

4. BIZARRE grotesque, odd, incongruous   **ant.** conservative, subdued ♦ The costumes of the gypsy women seem *bizarre* to those who are accustomed to quieter colors.

5. BLIGHT a disease in plants that causes them to stop growing and wither; an insect that causes plant disease; anything that destroys or ruins hopes or aims ♦ Last winter most of the tropical plants were ruined by the *blight*.

6. BLUDGEON a short club with one thick heavy end; to strike with a bludgeon; threaten ♦ They are trying to *bludgeon* us into an acceptance of their offer, but I shall not give in to their threats!

7. BOUNTIFUL generous; plentiful   **ant.** stingy, miserly ♦ The *bountiful* king lavished priceless gifts on his favorites.

8. BRANDISH to flourish (as of a sword) ♦ *Brandishing* the whip before him, he walked menacingly toward us.

9. BRUNT the shock of an onslaught, impact ♦ She bore in silence the *brunt* of his scolding.

10. BRUSQUE brisk, abrupt in speech or manner   **ant.** polite, suave ♦ The corporal always spoke in a *brusque* manner when addressing a member of his squad.

11. CACHE a hiding place for food and supplies for future use; to make a cache, put into a cache ♦ The squirrels put their nuts in a *cache* for the long winter ahead.

12. CALLOUS thickened and hardened (as of skin); hardhearted, insensitive   **ant.** tender, gentle ♦ The *callous* employer expected a full day's work from all workers regardless of their state of health.

13. CAPITULATE to surrender on specified terms ♦ Ulysses S. Grant stated that the only terms for *capitulation* were "unconditional surrender."

14. CAPTION the heading of a section or page; heading or title of an illustration; a motion-picture subtitle ♦ You will never get the full significance of his cartoons unless you read the *captions*.

15. CAREEN to tip over on one side, lurch or toss from side to side ◆ The car *careened* out of control and crossed from one side of the road to the other, terrifying those in the automobiles around it.

16. CASCADE a small waterfall; firework imitating a waterfall; to fall or drop as a cascade ◆ When the string broke, the beads *cascaded* to the ground.

17. CAUSTIC able to destroy by chemical action; sarcastic, biting   **ant.** gracious, gentle ◆ Phil's *caustic* comments may have an element of truth in them, but they antagonize the listener into disbelief!

18. CENTENNIAL a hundred years; pertaining to a century ◆ I hope to arrange to attend the *centennial* celebration in honor of the George Washington Bridge.

19. CHASTISE to punish, inflict corporal punishment for the sake of discipline ◆ At times even the mildest of parents will seize some instrument with which to *chastise* an unruly child.

20. CHERUB a heavenly being, an angel; an innocent or lovely child ◆ She may be a beautiful child, but her behavior is anything but that of a *cherub*.

21. CIRCUITOUS roundabout, indirect   **ant.** straight ◆ They took a *circuitous* route home to avoid the busy highway.

22. CLEFT a fissure, crevice, split; divided ◆ The earthquake left a *cleft* in the mountain.

23. CLIQUE an exclusive group, snobbish set ◆ Is there anything more cruel than the few who set themselves up as the *clique* with the sole purpose of excluding others!

24. COERCE to force or compel to act; restrain by force ◆ The only way to *coerce* me into signing this petition would be to put a gun to my head!

25. COLLABORATE to work together (esp. in literature or art); cooperate with the enemy ◆ Rodgers and Hart *collaborated* on many successful musical comedies.

26. COMMODIOUS roomy and comfortable, spacious   **ant.** confined ◆ My two friends found my quarters so *commodious* that they moved in with me.

27. COMPATIBLE congruous, harmonious, able to exist together in harmony   **ant.** uncongenial, antagonistic ♦ When good fortune smiled on him, he moved into quarters more *compatible* with his new station in life.

28. COMPUTE to reckon, calculate, find out by arithmetical work ♦ What method is used to *compute* the distance from one star to another?

29. CONDIMENT a relish, seasoning ♦ Without *condiments*, food would be tasteless to many people.

30. CONDOLENCE sympathy; a message of sympathy   **ant.** congratulation ♦ After her mother's death, Jane received many *condolence* cards.

31. CONNOISSEUR an expert judge or critic (as of art)   **ant.** dabbler, amateur ♦ The *connoisseur* quickly and accurately pointed out the original painting amid the several imitations.

32. CONTEMN to despise, hold in contempt   **ant.** admire, adore, esteem ♦ I *contemn* all hypocrites!

Third Day

1. CONTRIVE to plot, scheme; devise, invent; manage ♦ How he ever *contrived* to arrive on time this morning is beyond me!

2. COQUETTE a flirt ♦ She is a *coquette*, more interested in pleasing her vanity than in finding companionship among the men she works so hard to attract.

3. CORSAIR a pirate, privateer; armed pirate vessel ♦ The *corsairs* roamed the sea in search of smaller vessels that they could capture and loot.

4. COUNTERMAND a contrary order or command; to revoke, cancel ♦ The general *countermanded* the colonel's call for an advance and ordered the troops to dig in.

5. COY bashful, coquettishly shy   **ant.** impudent, brash, pert ♦ I was annoyed by her *coy* unwillingness to accept a gift that she wanted so much.

6. CRONY a pal, chum, close friend ♦ The old man and his *crony* passed the time of the day fishing.

7. **CUISINE** a place where cooking is done; style of cooking; prepared food ♦ Under Pierre's supervision, the *cuisine* at the local motel has achieved an excellent reputation.

8. **CULINARY** pertaining to the kitchen or cooking ♦ The girls took courses in school in the *culinary* arts to prepare for the time when they would cook for their own families.

9. **CURT** abrupt, rudely brief **ant.** voluble, talkative ♦ Strangers thought him rude because he had such a *curt* way of speaking.

10. **DANK** moist and chilly, unpleasantly damp ♦ The *dank* air in the cave gave him a chill.

11. **DEBILITATE** to weaken **ant.** invigorate, refresh ♦ The extreme cold helped to *debilitate* the sick woman even more.

12. **DECREPIT** broken down or weakened by old age **ant.** sturdy, vigorous ♦ The *decrepit* appearance of the neglected house was a blot on the neighborhood.

13. **DEFILE** to make dirty, destroy the purity of, corrupt **ant.** purify, clean ♦ The vandals *defiled* the tombstones in the cemetery by writing on them.

14. **DEGRADATION** a lowering in rank or position **ant.** elevation ♦ Insubordination caused the sergeant's *degradation* to the rank of private.

15. **DELETE** to strike out (something written), omit ♦ The publisher asked the writer to *delete* the insulting passage from his book.

16. **DEMURE** artificially proper, assuming an air of modesty **ant.** brazen ♦ The *demure* young lady refused to say anything on the air.

17. **DEPLETE** to empty, exhaust, drain **ant.** fill, enlarge ♦ Marie Antoinette helped *deplete* the Royal Treasury by squandering money on extravagant trifles.

18. **DERELICT** abandoned; neglectful of duty; a worthless, deserted thing or person ♦ The ragged *derelict* asked the man for money to buy some coffee.

19. **DESTITUTE** lacking necessary things such as food, clothing, and shelter **ant.** prosperous, rich ♦ Only those *destitute* of hope do not try to better their lot.

20. DETONATE to cause to explode with a loud noise ♦ By pressing this button, the sergeant can *detonate* the bombs that would destroy this entire research center.

21. DEVIATE to turn aside, deflect, wander   **ant.** persevere ♦ One should never *deviate* from the path set by one's ideals.

22. DIGRESS to get off the main subject, turn aside, wander ♦ Grandmother could never finish her story as she had a tendency to *digress*.

23. DISBURSE to pay out, expend ♦ My father calls himself the Treasury Department when he *disburses* our allowances on Saturday night.

24. DISCONCERT to embarrass greatly, upset ♦ The speaker was *disconcerted* when he realized that he had left his speech at home.

25. DISHEVELED rumpled, untidy, hanging loosely ♦ When Mrs. Jones saw Tom's *disheveled* appearance, she immediately knew he had been fighting.

26. DISSERTATION a formal discussion, treatise ♦ The committee accepted his *dissertation* on "The Deciduous Trees in the Adirondacks" as partial fulfillment of the requirements for a doctorate.

27. DISSIPATE to spread in different directions, scatter; disappear; spend foolishly   **ant.** accumulate, absorb ♦ The family fortune was *dissipated* quickly by the thoughtless grandchildren.

28. DIVA a prima donna, principal woman opera singer ♦ Joan Sutherland is a famous *diva* in the Metropolitan Opera.

29. DIVEST to strip, rid, free, deprive; force to give up   **ant.** clothe, dress ♦ After his court-martial, the officer was *divested* of all his stripes.

30. DOFF to take off, remove   **ant.** don ♦ A man should always *doff* his hat when the flag goes by.

31. DOTING foolishly fond ♦ The *doting* grandparents gave in to every wish of their only grandchild.

32. DROLL amusingly odd, laughable, funny   **ant.** dull, weighty ♦ The audience enjoyed the comic's *droll* sense of humor.

Fourth Day

1. **EFFACE** to rub out, wipe out; destroy **ant.** retain, renew
♦ Time has *effaced* the inscription on the Civil War monument in the City Square.

2. **EFFIGY** a statue of a person, stuffed image of a person burned or hanged to show hatred ♦ Even to this day, in some sections of England, Guy Fawkes is burned in *effigy* on November 5.

3. **EFFUSIVE** lacking reserve, gushing, too demonstrative **ant.** reserved, quiet ♦ Her greeting was so *effusive* that I began to suspect her sincerity.

4. **ELITE** the choice in a group **ant.** rabble ♦ People trying to better themselves strive to join *elite* groups.

5. **EMBEZZLE** to steal, misappropriate ♦ The official *embezzled* company funds to pay his personal debts.

6. **EMINENT** outstanding, distinguished **ant.** unknown, infamous ♦ Hal's father is an *eminent* astronomer who is in charge of an important space project for the government.

7. **ENCROACH** to intrude, infringe **ant.** withdraw ♦ A good friend will not *encroach* upon his friend's homework time.

8. **ENCUMBER** to burden, hinder **ant.** help, aid ♦ Do not *encumber* your mind with petty annoyances at a time when you must concentrate upon survival.

9. **ENERVATE** to weaken, injure **ant.** strengthen, exhilarate ♦ The child was so *enervated* by the disease that the doctor feared he would catch pneumonia.

10. **EPISTLE** a letter, message ♦ The *epistle* from the bishop to the pastors outlined the part they were to play in the present spiritual crisis.

11. **EPITAPH** words about a person written on a tombstone ♦ The *epitaph* on the tomb of this great scientist reads, "Here lies a man who devoted his life to the betterment of mankind."

12. **EQUIVOCATE** to use expressions of double meaning, hedge ♦ This is the time for you to answer directly and not to *equivocate* if you want them to know just where you stand!

13. ERUDITE learned, educated   **ant.** illiterate, uneducated ♦ The *erudite* professor explained the Theory of Relativity to the select group before him.

14. EULOGIZE to praise very highly   **ant.** insult, slander ♦ The priest *eulogized* the wonderful work that the nun had accomplished during her lifetime.

15. EVINCE to show, display   **ant.** hide, conceal ♦ The little boy *evinced* fear at the sight of the large dog.

16. EXODUS a departure   **ant.** arriving, entrance ♦ On hot summer days there is a general *exodus* from the city to the beaches.

17. EXOTIC from foreign lands, unfamiliar, enticing   **ant.** ordinary, common, native ♦ We viewed many *exotic* costumes worn by delegates to the United Nations.

18. EXTANT in existence   **ant.** extinct ♦ Most of Lincoln's letters are *extant* and on display in museums.

19. EXTINCT no longer in existence   **ant.** extant, current ♦ The pages of history are filled with the names of *extinct* political organizations that died because they did not take the wishes of the people into account.

20. EXTOL to praise highly   **ant.** denounce ♦ A teacher is pleased to *extol* a student who has done his homework well.

21. EXUBERANT overflowing, in high spirits   **ant.** scant, meager; reserved ♦ The *exuberant* crowd sang gaily as it carried the victorious general on eager shoulders through the city streets.

22. FASTIDIOUS very critical, oversensitive   **ant.** gross, uncritical ♦ The *fastidious* housekeeper was almost driven out of her mind by the untidy habits of the children.

23. FELONIOUS injurious, vicious, criminal, wicked   **ant.** helpful, worthy ♦ The members of the teen-age gang were being held for *felonious* assault on the elderly couple who had been hospitalized after the vicious attack on them.

24. FERVID ardent, spirited   **ant.** cool, nonchalant ♦ The *fervid* thanks of the distraught parents made us realize how much the temporary disappearance of the child had upset them.

25. FLAGGING getting tired or weak, drooping ♦ With *flagging* enthusiasm, we continued on despite the unexpected length of the hiking trail.

26. **FLORID** ruddy, highly colored; ornamental and showy **ant.** unobtrusive, colorless, plain ♦ The *florid* complexion of the elderly man caused the physician to check his blood pressure.

27. **FORAY** a raid, plunder ♦ The men made *foray* after *foray* into the valley to carry off the farmers' valuables as booty.

28. **FOUNDER** to be filled with water and to sink; collapse, fail ♦ Without his guidance and leadership, the company soon *foundered* and went into bankruptcy.

29. **FRACAS** a quarrel, noisy fight, brawl ♦ The participants in the *fracas* on the dock were arrested by the police for disturbing the peace.

30. **FREEBOOTER** a pirate, buccaneer ♦ The governor of Porto Bello ordered his fleet to capture at any cost the ship of the *freebooters* who had seized the schooner carrying the gold of the Incas.

31. **FRIVOLOUS** petty, trifling; giddy **ant.** serious, wise, earnest ♦ *Frivolous* remarks are inappropriate during moments of decision.

32. **GAFF** a spear or hook for fish; the upper part of a sail ♦ He used a *gaff* to pull the tuna on board his ship.

Fifth Day

1. **GALLEON** a large, heavy Spanish sailing vessel ♦ Four *galleons* formed the fleet that was to take the plundered gold back to Spain.

2. **GAMUT** scale, range, extent ♦ The supplies ran the *gamut* from applesauce to zinnia seeds.

3. **GAUNTLET** a protective glove used in combat ♦ To meet the challenge, the knight struck his rival across the face with his *gauntlet*.

4. **GAZETTE** a newspaper, an official publication ♦ The story of his amazing feat was told in full in the local *gazette*.

5. **GHASTLY** dreadful, pale, ghostly **ant.** pleasant, mild ♦ I shall never forget the *ghastly* grin on the face of the dead pirate.

6. **GLIB** ~~eloquent,~~ speaking too smoothly **ant.** hesitant, deliberate ♦ The *glib* salesman sold her two air conditioners while she wanted only one.

7. GNOME a dwarf that supposedly lives in the earth and guards precious metals and stones ♦ The *gnome* lived in a cave at the bottom of the ocean, guarding the treasures taken from sunken ships.

8. GOUGE a chisel with a curved blade; to scoop out; cheat, swindle ♦ In order to make the groove deeper, the only tool the carpenter needed was a *gouge*.

9. GRATIS free, without charge   ant. expensive, costly ♦ As a reward, the student who achieved the highest marks was allowed to enter the theater *gratis*.

10. GRIMY dirty, filthy   ant. clean ♦ After he worked in the musty cellar, the man's face and hands were *grimy*.

11. GULLIBLE easily deceived or cheated   ant. experienced, sophisticated ♦ The woman was so *gullible* that she believed every story she heard.

12. HAMLET a small village   ant. metropolis ♦ In the midst of the forest was the little *hamlet* Kulkinville, with a population of 26.

13. HAPLESS unfortunate   ant. lucky ♦ The *hapless* victim of the freak accident was rushed to the hospital.

14. HAUGHTY proud of oneself, scornful of others, arrogant ant. humble, tolerant ♦ The *haughty* airs of the duke did not endear him to the public.

15. HAVEN a place of shelter ♦ The crude shelter in the mountains was a *haven* in the storm.

16. HAWSER a large rope or small cable ♦ A *hawser* is used to tow ships.

17. HONE a stone on which to sharpen razors or tools; to sharpen ♦ In preparation for the debate, Stanley *honed* his wit to a razor's edge.

18. HUMILITY humbleness of mind, lack of pride   ant. vanity ♦ Alex showed the true *humility* of a scholar when he asked his rival to teach him the newer techniques.

19. ICON a sacred image or picture ♦ The walls of the small church were studded with *icons* of saints, each with its guttering candle before it.

20. ILLICIT forbidden, illegal, improper **ant.** legal ♦ How could anyone profit from the *illicit* sale of narcotics!

21. IMBIBE to drink; take into one's mind ♦ The roots of a tree *imbibe* water from the earth.

22. IMPECUNIOUS poor **ant.** wealthy ♦ The *impecunious* couple were unable to scrape together enough money to buy the medicine for their ailing child.

23. IMPERTURBABLE calm, not easily agitated, serene **ant.** touchy, irritable ♦ The *imperturbable* detective continued hour after hour his patient search for the missing button.

24. IMPIOUS irreligious, sinful **ant.** pious, devout, religious ♦ Only a nonbeliever could be guilty of the *impious* act of destroying a prayer book.

25. IMPROVISE to compose or utter without preparation, extemporize ♦ The rescue crew had to *improvise* a stretcher out of poles and a blanket on which to transport the injured miner.

26. INALIENABLE that cannot be given or taken away ♦ The Bill of Rights gives all men the *inalienable* rights of life, liberty, and the pursuit of happiness.

27. INCENSE to enrage; any substance burned to produce a pleasant odor ♦ Her father was so *incensed* by Alice's refusal to assist that he cut off her allowance for two weeks.

28. INCOGNITO unknown; a disguised state or condition ♦ The actress traveled *incognito* to insure her privacy.

29. INCREMENT an increase, addition, gain **ant.** decrease, loss ♦ After being graduated from college, many teachers take additional courses and receive a salary *increment* for their efforts.

30. INDICT to charge with an offense or crime, accuse **ant.** free, liberate, acquit ♦ On the basis of the findings of the Grand Jury, he was *indicted* for accepting bribes.

31. INDOMITABLE unyielding, invincible, unconquerable **ant.** yielding, submissive ♦ Nothing has ever been able to stand in the way of his *indomitable* will to succeed.

32. INEPT out of place, unsuitable, inappropriate **ant.** apt ♦ The chairman's handling of the discussion was so *inept* that the main issues were never expressed.

33. INFRINGE to violate, trespass, intrude   ant. observe, obey, comply with ♦ It is unlawful to *infringe* upon the copyrights of another man.

Sixth Day

1. INHIBIT to restrain, repress; forbid   ant. permit, approve, authorize ♦ A clause in the contract *inhibits* the company from increasing its selling force.

2. INNOVATE to make changes, bring in new ways of doing things ♦ When he assumed the chairmanship, he *innovated* a more thorough inventory system.

3. INSOLVENT bankrupt, moneyless   ant. affluent, monied ♦ When the treasurer could no longer meet the bills, the company was declared *insolvent.*

4. INTER to bury (of people) ♦ The assassinated President was *interred* in Arlington Cemetery.

5. INTERMINABLE endless, infinite   ant. completed; periodic ♦ After what seemed to be an *interminable* wait, the nurse informed him that he was the father of a son.

6. INTRACTABLE stubborn   ant. obedient, docile ♦ The *intractable* child could not be persuaded or threatened into accompanying me.

7. INVETERATE long and firmly established, confirmed in a habit ♦ My father has long been an *inveterate* foe of hypocrisy and double standards.

8. ITINERARY a route, plan of travel; guidebook for travelers ♦ Our *itinerary* through Europe was mapped out for us by an experienced travel agent.

9. JAMB an upright piece forming the side of a doorway or window ♦ By leaning against the door *jamb*, Sam was able to block the entrance into the conference room.

10. JAUNTY easy and lively, sprightly, gay   ant. demure; staid ♦ The army officer walked down the street with a *jaunty* stride on that brisk March day.

11. JEOPARDIZE to risk, endanger ♦ Aerialists constantly *eopardize* their lives while performing high above the heads of the spectators.

12. JOIST one of the parallel pieces of timber to which the boards of a floor or ceiling are attached ♦ The floor of the dance hall rests on reinforced *joists*.

13. KNAVERY trickery, dishonesty ♦ The honest merchant would not resort to *knavery* to sell his goods.

14. LAMINATED made by building up in layers, arranged in thin sheets or layers ♦ Plywood is a good example of *laminated* material.

15. LAUD to praise, commend **ant.** revile, belittle, condemn ♦ The governor *lauded* the boy for his courageous rescue of the children.

16. LEONINE like a lion ♦ Even if a sheep had a *leonine* roar, few who saw it would fear it.

17. LIBRETTO the words of a long musical composition; a book containing the words of that composition ♦ For the Gilbert and Sullivan operettas, which of the two men wrote the *librettos?*

18. LIQUIDATE to settle the accounts of (a business); get rid of; convert to cash ♦ The judge appointed a receiver to *liquidate* the assets of the bankrupt organization.

19. LOATHE to abhor **ant.** love, admire ♦ I truly *loathe* the smell of decaying garbage.

20. LOPE a long, easy stride; to run smoothly ♦ The leopard *loped* tirelessly on the trail of the frightened doe that was racing itself to exhaustion—and death.

21. LUNAR pertaining to the moon ♦ The *lunar* month is shorter than the solar month.

22. MAESTRO an expert, a leader ♦ The *maestro* finally promised to lead the orchestra in the playing of my symphony.

23. MAIM to cripple, damage, mutiliate **ant.** cure, heal Automobiles kill and *maim* thousands of people each year.

24. MALEVOLENT spiteful, evil **ant.** amiable, cordial, kind ♦ The *malevolent* lieutenant did all in his power to cause the dismissal of the captain.

25. MALIGNANT evil, hateful, harmful **ant.** beneficial, kind ♦ Racial hatred is a *malignant* growth that must be removed if a society is to remain democratic.

26. MARITAL matrimonial, wedded ♦ Not once in all these years has this happily wedded man ever broken his *marital* vows.

27. MAXIM a proverb ♦ Who does not know Franklin's famous *maxim* that begins with "Early to bed . . ."?

28. MEANDER to wander aimlessly, wind ♦ The brook *meandered* through the fields in a most irregular path.

29. MÉNAGE a household; the management of a household ♦ How can she appear so calm while managing a business and a *ménage* that includes seven children?

30. MERCANTILE commercial ♦ To my staid old aunt, every business concern is a *mercantile* establishment.

31. MERCENARY hired; greedy; a professional soldier ♦ He is so *mercenary*, he would sell his ideals if the price were right.

32. MIEN manner, appearance, carriage ♦ The princess had a haughty *mien* when addressing her courtiers.

Seventh Day

1. MIRE soft mud; to stick in mud ♦ The wheels were so firmly *mired* in the swamp ooze that the rescue truck could not pull our car out.

2. MISDEMEANOR a not-too-serious breaking of the law ♦ Harold was guilty of a *misdemeanor* when he drove a car with defective brakes.

3. MOMENTOUS important, far-reaching, memorable **ant.** unimportant, trivial ♦ The dropping of the first atomic bomb was a *momentous* event in the history of mankind.

4. MOROSE gloomy, sour, sullen **ant.** cheery ♦ She was tempted to urge him to go back to smoking because he had become so *morose* that she could not endure being in the same room with him.

5. MOUNTEBANK one who sells quick medicines; one who tries to deceive ♦ I shall fight to my dying day all political *mountebanks* who use lies and trickery to gain votes.

6. MUTABLE liable to change, fickle **ant.** set, fixed ♦ Who is the cynical poet who said that women are various and *mutable*?

7. NAPE the back of the neck ♦ Will a cool spoon pressed against the *nape* stop a nosebleed?

8. NETTLE to irk, vex, sting **ant.** please, solace ♦ The loss of the chess game to his former rival *nettled* the world champion.

9. NONPARTISAN not controlled by party spirits or interests; one who does not support any particular party ♦ Mr. Edwards has always been a *nonpartisan* in local politics, favoring the man he thought best regardless of party affiliations.

10. NOVICE a beginner, learner **ant.** master, expert ♦ Only a *novice* would make the mistake of disregarding the advice of an experienced guide.

11. OBESE fat, plump **ant.** slender, scrawny ♦ In later years he became so *obese* that he could scarcely go through the subway turnstiles.

12. OBSOLETE timeworn, out-of-date **ant.** modern, current, new ♦ The two-engined planes are *obsolete* and no longer used by the major airlines.

13. OCULAR having to do with the eyes; the eyepiece of an ocular instrument ♦ The microscope had a broken *ocular*.

14. OFFICIOUS meddling, nosy, pushy, aggressive ♦ The *officious* clerk insisted on reading the instructions aloud to me while I filled out the application.

15. OPIATE anything that quiets, a narcotic ♦ Sleep is the *opiate* of the masses of poor people.

16. ORDINANCE a statute, law, decree ♦ Littering the streets with candy wrappers is a violation of a city *ordinance*.

17. OSTENTATIOUS showy, attracting attention **ant.** timid, shrinking ♦ Mrs. White drove her Cadillac around the neighborhood in an *ostentatious* display of her newly acquired wealth.

18. OSTRACIZE to exclude, exile **ant.** include ♦ The people of the town voted to *ostracize* the man who had betrayed their trust.

19. PALATIAL magnificent, fit for a palace ♦ A corps of gardeners is required to maintain the *palatial* grounds of this estate.

20. PALPABLE apparent, clear **ant.** hidden, concealed ♦ It was such a *palpable* error that carelessness rather than ignorance must have been the cause.

21. PARABLE a short story with a moral ♦ The *parable* that I found most instructive was the one likening the kingdom of heaven to the growth of a mustard seed.

22. PECUNIARY pertaining to money ♦ Since he is in *pecuniary* difficulties, he has taken a temporary part-time job.

23. PEDAGOGUE a teacher ♦ The *pedagogue* made visits to the home of each pupil.

24. PERENNIAL enduring, constant; having a life cycle of more than two years; becoming active again and again   **ant.** fleeting, transient ♦ Since we wanted plants that would survive the winter, we chose *perennials* rather than annuals for our garden.

25. PERPETUATE to keep alive, make perpetual, continue **ant.** terminate, end ♦ A fund for needy students was established to *perpetuate* the memory of the beloved professor.

26. PERT saucy, bold, flippant   **ant.** modest, coy, bashful ♦ The *pert* reply of the saucy youngster brought a smile to the lips of his doting grandparents.

27. PESSIMISM a tendency to see the gloomy, cynical side of things   **ant.** optimism, hope ♦ After so many failures, he viewed everything with *pessimism.*

28. PETULANT peevish, cranky, cross   **ant.** happy, mild ♦ The patient desk clerk listened in sympathetic silence to the *petulant* complaints of the disappointed visitors.

29. PINNACLE the top, apex, peak   **ant.** bottom, nadir ♦ The president-elect had reached the *pinnacle* of his political career!

30. PLACID quiet, gentle, calm   **ant.** ruffled, disturbed ♦ She ranges from being as excitable as a terrier to being as *placid* as a cow!

31. PLAGIARIZE to take and use someone else's work as one's own ♦ The teacher failed the student who had *plagiarized* an essay of Stevenson.

32. PLAINTIVE melancholy, wistful, pathetic, sad   **ant.** happy ♦ The *plaintive* cry of a lonely coyote at night is familiar to all moviegoers.

33. POLL to vote; take the votes of; a voting place ♦ We shall have to *poll* the members before we can take this step.

Eighth Day

1. POTENTATE a ruler, powerful person **ant.** subject ♦ The oriental *potentate* had absolute power over his subjects and the land he allowed them to live on.

2. PRATE foolish or empty talk; to talk on and on ♦ Let him *prate* on about his courage now, but I want to see him in action in an emergency before I pass judgment.

3. PRECOCIOUS showing premature development **ant.** retarded ♦ The very *precocious* boy could play the piano well by the age of four.

4. PREFATORY introductory **ant.** concluding, terminating ♦ The book had a *prefatory* section in which the editor explained the author's intentions.

5. PREVARICATE to lie ♦ Rather than admit his liability, the boy began to *prevaricate*.

6. PRODIGAL lavish, wasteful **ant.** stingy, frugal ♦ My aunt is so *prodigal* with her advice that I dare not tell her any of my plans.

7. PROLIFIC abundant; producing much; producing offspring **ant.** sterile ♦ The starling is so *prolific* that immense flocks now plague sections of New York City.

8. PRONE inclined; lying face down **ant.** upright ♦ The boy's weakened condition made him *prone* to many diseases.

9. PROVIDENT prudent, careful, frugal **ant.** extravagant ♦ A *provident* man would have taken out a larger insurance policy to protect his growing family.

10. PROWESS bravery; superiority of ability **ant.** fear, timidity ♦ Phil's *prowess* as a debater stood him in good stead during the political campaign.

11. PUGNACIOUS belligerent, aggressive **ant.** peaceable, placid ♦ He is so *pugnacious* that he would prefer fighting to eating.

12. PUTREFY to rot, decay **ant.** revive ♦ Who can favor war after viewing the corpses *putrefying* on the blood-drenched battlefield?

13. **PYROMANIAC** an arsonist, one with a persistent compulsion to start fires ♦ The police are looking for the *pyromaniac* who started the fires in the apartment-house basements.

14. **QUAFF** to drink freely ♦ The returning hikers *quaffed* quarts and quarts of milk before they finally quenched their thirst.

15. **QUIRT** a riding whip ♦ He struck the horse with a leather *quirt*.

16. **RABID** insane, mad, frenzied, fanatic   **ant.** sane, normal ♦ Beware of attempting to belittle the efforts of a baseball team in the presence of a *rabid* fan.

17. **RANKLE** to give pain, be sore, cause continual mental anguish or resentment   **ant.** comfort, please ♦ The memory of the humiliating defeat *rankled* him.

18. **REBUT** to disprove, oppose   **ant.** agree, sympathize ♦ The accused demanded equal time to *rebut* the statements of his accuser.

19. **RECALCITRANT** disobedient, resisting   **ant.** docile ♦ The dictator was determined to starve the *recalcitrant* peasants into submission.

20. **RECLUSE** a person who lives shut away from the rest of the world, hermit ♦ For twenty years, the old *recluse* lived in his small house on Main Street, withdrawn from all the affairs of his fellow men.

21. **REFRACTORY** headstrong, stubborn; not yielding to treatment   **ant.** amenable, docile ♦ The *refractory* mule could not be budged from his chosen spot.

22. **REGALE** to delight, entertain   **ant.** vex ♦ The genial host *regaled* his guests with delightful renditions of operatic arias.

23. **RELEVANT** appropriate, proper, apt   **ant.** foreign, unconnected, irrelevant ♦ The questions asked were not *relevant* to the matter under discussion.

24. **REMINISCE** to recall, remember   **ant.** forecast, predict ♦ Once a year, we get together with our former college friends and *reminisce*, recalling the joyous days of our youth.

25. **RESCIND** to call back, cancel, repeal, annul   **ant.** order ♦ They tried to *rescind* the order before it was put into effect.

26. **RESTITUTION** the making good of a loss ♦ Of course, you are expected to make full *restitution* for any damage you cause.

27. **RETRENCH** to cut down, reduce   **ant.** increase, expand ♦ When business slackened, we had to *retrench* and let three assistants go.

28. **REVERT** to go back, return   **ant.** progress, advance ♦ Billy *reverts* to his old habit of biting his nails whenever he is nervous.

29. **REVITALIZE** to renew, strengthen, bring life into again ♦ We invested money in new equipment in a vain attempt to *revitalize* the old company.

30. **RIFT** a split, break, schism ♦ Negotiators were called in to heal the *rift* between labor and management.

31. **RUBBLE** rough, broken stone or bricks ♦ After the air raid, the searchers looked through the *rubble* for survivors.

32. **RUSE** a trick, artifice, device ♦ A favorite *ruse* of the diamond smugglers is to have the gems in a bottle containing a clear liquid.

33. **SAGA** a story of heroic deeds ♦ It is a *saga* that retells the heroic achievements of our founding fathers.

Ninth Day

1. **SANCTITY** purity, sacredness ♦ What political leader ever dared to violate the *sanctity* of human rights!

2. **SCINTILLATING** sparkling, twinkling, shimmering ♦ The *scintillating* remarks of the comedian brought gales of laughter from the youthful audience.

3. **SCRUPULOUS** very careful, exact, conscientious   **ant.** careless; criminal, dishonest ♦ Known for his *scrupulous* sense of fairness, he was our unanimous choice for umpire.

4. **SEDATIVE** soothing; a medicine that relaxes or lessens excitement ♦ The doctor gave his patient a *sedative* to lessen her nervous tension.

5. **SELF-EFFACING** modest, retiring   **ant.** bold, saucy, impertinent ♦ She is so *self-effacing* that she insists on giving her assistants all the credit for whatever is accomplished.

6. SEPULCHER a tomb, grave ♦ The *sepulchers* of the ancient Egyptian kings are in the pyramids.

7. SHOAL a place where the water is shallow; a sandbank which makes the water shallow ♦ The speedboat was caught on the *shoal* during low tide.

8. SIMIAN apelike; an ape or monkey ♦ Do monkeys have a *simian* sense of humor?

9. SLACK loose, lax; not active, dull   ant. active ♦ The rope hung *slack* whenever the boat shifted closer to the dock.

10. SLOTHFUL lazy, indolent   ant. industrious, diligent ♦ You will not find him *slothful* when he is interested in what has to be done.

11. SOLACE comfort, cheer ♦ The respect accorded her husband brought some *solace* to the widow.

12. SOLICITOUS concerned, showing care   ant. unmindful, negligent ♦ The *solicitous* doctor stayed with his patient all night.

13. SOMBER dark, gloomy   ant. light, cheerful ♦ The sunless cold of the winter day matched the *somber* bleakness of his mood when his business failed.

14. SPURIOUS false, sham, counterfeit   ant. genuine, true ♦ The *spurious* coin was easily detected by the treasury agent.

15. STALWART strong and brave, steadfast   ant. weak, timid ♦ The American soldier has always been a *stalwart* defender of democracy.

16. STAMINA endurance, vigor ♦ Does he have the *stamina* to continue once the going becomes difficult?

17. STRIDENT shrill, harsh, creaking   ant. silent, subdued ♦ The *strident* voices of the machines of war were silent for too brief a moment.

18. SUAVE smoothly agreeable or polite, courteous   ant. rough, discourteous ♦ The *suave* young man made a favorable impression on the woman.

19. SUBSTANTIATE to prove, establish by evidence ♦ He was able to *substantiate* that he was the missing heir by producing his birth certificate.

20. SUMPTUOUS costly, magnificent, lavish **ant.** simple, un-adorned ♦ The ambassador was overwhelmed by the *sumptuous* feast prepared in his honor.

21. SUNDRY several, various, numerous ♦ Jonathan dropped *sundry* hints that he wanted a set of trains for Christmas.

22. SUPERSEDE to replace, take the place of ♦ Rockets will eventually *supersede* jet airplanes as a means of transportation.

23. SURMOUNT to rise above, overcome, master **ant.** fail, fall short of ♦ President Roosevelt was able to *surmount* his handi-cap and become the highest official in the United States.

24. SUSTENANCE food, support ♦ What mental *sustenance* is offered by the weekly television programs?

25. SYNTHETIC made artificially **ant.** real, natural ♦ Rayon is a *synthetic* fiber.

26. TANTALIZE to tease by exciting hopes or fears which will not be realized, tempt **ant.** satisfy, comfort ♦ Frequent mirages *tantalized* the thirsty soldiers on their ten-hour march through the heat of the desert.

27. TAUT tightly drawn, stretched; tidy, neat **ant.** loose, slack; disorderly ♦ He pulled the rope *taut* to insure against the horse's rearing up and escaping.

28. TENACIOUS holding fast, cohesive, inseparable **ant.** loose, lax ♦ Fearful of change, he held *tenaciously* to each of his outworn beliefs in a vain hope to stop progress.

29. TEPID lukewarm ♦ The doctor prescribed a *tepid* bath for the man's backache.

30. TERRAIN a tract of land ♦ The rocky *terrain* of the lower Adirondacks is ill-suited for cultivation.

Tenth Day

1. TIMOROUS easily frightened, timid **ant.** confident, as-sured ♦ The *timorous* child cried whenever she saw strangers.

2. TIRADE a long, scolding speech ♦ In a two-hour television program, Castro delivered a *tirade* against the United States.

3. TOXIC poisonous **ant.** harmless, beneficial ♦ The *toxic* fumes of carbon monoxide quickly killed the occupants of the car in the closed garage.

4. TRACTABLE easily managed, docile, obedient **ant.** unruly ◆ Mules are not *tractable* animals.

5. TRAVERSE to go across; something lying across ◆ We were unwilling to *traverse* the desert during the heat of the day.

6. TRICE to haul up and tie with a rope; an instant, a moment ◆ The sailors had to be strong to *trice* up the sails.

7. TRITE worn, commonplace, hackneyed **ant.** fresh, novel ◆ "As good as gold" is a *trite* saying.

8. TRUCULENT savage, cruel, ferocious **ant.** tame, mild ◆ The officer was not intimidated by the *truculent* attitude of the group of boys loitering on the corner.

9. TURNKEY the keeper of a prison ◆ The frantic relatives tried to bribe the *turnkey* to allow the prisoner to escape.

10. TYKE a cur; mischievous child ◆ The *tyke* spilled ink over his mother's dress.

11. UNCOUTH awkward, clumsy, crude **ant.** handsome, courteous ◆ The *uncouth* manners of the stranger embarrassed the children.

12. UNIMPEACHABLE blameless, free from fault **ant.** faulty ◆ He offered us *unimpeachable* evidence of Harold's guilt.

13. UNWITTING unaware, unconscious, unintentional ◆ He was the *unwitting* butt of their cruel joke.

14. UPBRAID to blame, reprove **ant.** praise, commend ◆ The principal called the boy into his office to *upbraid* him for his behavior in class.

15. USURP to seize and hold (power) by force or without right **ant.** restore, reinstate ◆ The prince headed the plot to *usurp* the throne.

16. VALOR courage, bravery **ant.** cowardice ◆ Richard the Lionhearted is known in history for his *valor* on the battlefield.

17. VANGUARD the front part of an army; leaders of a movement ◆ He has always been in the *vanguard* of every movement to promote intercultural understanding.

18. **VERACIOUS** truthful, true **ant.** lying, false ♦ He soon established a reputation for being a *veracious* merchant whose words did not carry double meanings.

19. **VERSATILE** able to do many things well ♦ He proved how *versatile* he is by exchanging roles with each of his fellow actors on successive evenings.

20. **VIANDS** articles of food, provisions ♦ Come ye to the feast and the table shall be laden with delicacies and *viands* from the corners of the earth.

21. **VINDICATE** to clear from suspicion, defend successfully **ant.** slander, calumniate ♦ That he did return our loan promptly was enough to *vindicate* our faith in his integrity.

22. **VIRILE** masculine, manly **ant.** effeminate, puerile ♦ The *virile* backwoodsman was the picture of sturdy manhood.

23. **VIRULENT** very harmful, very poisonous ♦ A most *virulent* form of the dread disease wiped out village after village.

24. **VIVACIOUS** lively, animated, gay **ant.** languid, lifeless ♦ He found the *vivacious* girl able to match wits with him at every turn of a phrase.

25. **VOCIFEROUS** loud and noisy, boisterous **ant.** reserved ♦ The *vociferous* protests of the street peddlers quickly brought the police to the scene of the quarrel.

26. **VOLATILE** evaporating rapidly; fickle, changeable **ant.** heavy, permanent ♦ Who can predict when his *volatile* temper will erupt!

27. **WAN** pale, faint, weak ♦ The patient gave her doctor a *wan* smile as she was wheeled out of the operating room.

28. **WAYWARD** disobedient, willful **ant.** tractable ♦ The only solution that I can see at present is to have him placed in an institution for *wayward* boys.

29. **WILY** cunning, crafty, sly ♦ The *wily* manager kept the true identity of his fighter a secret.

30. **WRANGLE** to quarrel; a noisy or angry dispute ♦ The children *wrangled* over the possession of the ball.

31. **ZEALOUS** eager, earnest, full of zeal **ant.** lazy, sluggish ♦ The *zealous* student took in every word his professor spoke.

Eleventh Day: First Basic-List Practice Test

A. Antonyms

In the space provided, write the letter of the word that is most nearly opposite in meaning to the first word.

1. AMALGAMATE   (a) amend   (b) scatter
(c) compute   (d) unite   (e) equivocate   1. ....

2. EULOGIZE   (a) slander   (b) extol   (c) imbibe
(d) indict   (e) lead   2. ....

3. MALEVOLENT   (a) evil   (b) maligning
(c) amiable   (d) partisan   (e) stationary   3. ....

4. PALPABLE   (a) magnificent   (b) thrilling
(c) concealed   (d) clean   (e) apparent   4. ....

5. POTENTATE   (a) weakness   (b) ability
(c) power   (d) subject   (e) object   5. ....

6. FERVID   (a) healthy   (b) sick   (c) normal
(d) thankful   (e) nonchalant   6. ....

7. GLIB   (a) large   (b) eloquent   (c) deliberate
(d) quick   (e) false   7. ....

8. ILLICIT   (a) married   (b) legal   (c) ordinary
(d) permanent   (e) peaceful   8. ....

9. SOLICITOUS   (a) legal   (b) illegal   (c) negligent
(d) spurious (e) ocular   9. ....

10. SUMPTUOUS   (a) simple   (b) magnificent
(c) ugly   (d) stricken   (e) synthetic   10. ....

11. TENACIOUS   (a) handy   (b) loose   (c) lukewarm
(d) hot   (e) officious   11. ....

12. TRUCULENT   (a) blameless   (b) faulty   (c) mild
(d) muscular   (e) silent   12. ....

13. CIRCUITOUS   (a) square   (b) indirect   (c) short
(d) straight   (e) alternate   13. ....

14. ANNIHILATE   (a) scatter   (b) contrive
(c) create   (d) respect   (e) follow   14. ....

15. ARBITRARY (a) legitimate (b) assiduous
(c) diligent (d) willful (e) capricious   15. ....

16. BOUNTIFUL (a) marine (b) earthy
(c) awarding (d) stingy (e) lovely   16. ....

17. DEGRADATION (a) incline (b) rank (c) saga
(d) height (e) elevation   17. ....

18. DISSIPATE (a) scatter (b) accumulate
(c) please (d) lead (e) cover   18. ....

19. EXOTIC (a) near (b) unfamiliar (c) common
(d) interplanetary (e) stingy   19. ....

20. MAIM (a) drive (b) mutilate (c) cover
(d) heal (e) buy   20. ....

21. OBESE (a) annoying (b) pleasing (c) plump
(d) unpleasant (e) scrawny   21. ....

22. OSTENTATIOUS (a) easterly (b) timid
(c) near (d) distant (e) unfinished   22. ....

23. PLACID (a) marine (b) martial (c) disturbed
(d) lost (e) insular   23. ....

24. PROVIDENT (a) wasteful (b) prudent
(c) painful (d) pleasing (e) rich   24. ....

25. REGALE (a) simple (b) autocratic (c) majestic
(d) choose (e) vex   25. ....

26. INTRACTABLE (a) straight (b) rigid
(c) docile (d) stubborn (e) bent   26. ....

27. SLACK (a) jacket (b) dress (c) active (d) busy
(e) unfilled   27. ....

28. TAUT (a) ignorant (b) learned (c) stretched
(d) tease (e) loose   28. ....

29. TRACTABLE (a) unruly (b) animalistic
(c) docile (d) human (e) musical   29. ....

30. TRITE (a) inexperienced (b) novel (c) open
(d) oral (e) written   30. ....

31. VIVACIOUS (a) deadly (b) magnificent
(c) plaintive (d) vital (e) lifeless   31. ....

32. VOCIFEROUS   (a) silent   (b) threatening
(c) sacrificial   (d) audible   (e) oral   32. ....

33. IMPIOUS   (a) sinful   (b) youthful   (c) religious
(d) deadly   (e) wishful   33. ....

34. INHIBIT   (a) repress   (b) permit   (c) dwell
(d) wander   (e) show   34. ....

35. PUGNACIOUS   (a) aggressive   (b) amateur
(c) peaceful   (d) canine   (e) vital   35. ....

B. Sentence Completion

In the space provided, write the letter of the word that best completes the sentence.

36. He revealed such a(n) .... lack of knowledge that I don't know just where to begin with him!
(a) dank   (b) abysmal   (c) decrepit   (d) destitute   36. ....

37. She is always quoting that .... about a wolf in sheep's clothing.
(a) effigy   (b) foray   (c) diva   (d) adage   37. ....

38. Who drew up the .... for the meeting to be held today?
(a) droll   (b) fracas   (c) agenda   (d) derelict   38. ....

39. How dare they .... the house of worship of others merely because these others are so few in number!
(a) deplete   (b) defile   (c) detonate   (d) delete   39. ....

40. I truly resented his attempts to be .... at a time when we had to make a most important decision.
(a) inalienable   (b) incognito   (c) frivolous
(d) leonine   40. ....

41. Our refusal so .... him that he left the room without saying a word.
(a) perpetuated   (b) incensed   (c) plagiarized
(d) maimed   41. ....

42. The prince who was traveling .... refused to admit his true identity to the inquiring newspapermen.
(a) incognito   (b) palatially   (c) ostentatiously
(d) perennially   42. ....

43. The .... raised his baton, and the members of the orchestra were ready to begin the concert.
(a) mercenary (b) mountebank (c) maestro
(d) pedagogue   43. ....

44. The employer asked him his .... status in an attempt to ascertain the level of salary for which the man would settle.
(a) maxim (b) ménage (c) mercantile (d) marital
                                                         44. ....

45. The visitor .... through the financial district of the big city, gaping at the crowds and the crowded lanes of tall buildings.
(a) mired (b) regaled (c) meandered (d) prated   45. ....

46. What .... can be had by the young widow of the man who was needlessly killed in an avoidable automobile accident!
(a) haven (b) ocular (c) hawser (d) solace   46. ....

47. An older man may have more patience, but he lacks the .... of the younger ones.
(a) stamina (b) humility (c) increment
(d) misdemeanor   47. ....

48. Where will we be able to get the evidence to .... his claim that he had been cheated by the others?
(a) wrangle (b) substantiate (c) inter
(d) innovate   48. ....

49. The .... surrounding the well is so rocky that we could not approach within a mile of it with the car.
(a) terrain (b) pinnacle (c) knavery (d) incense 49. ....

50. The .... venom of the snake paralyzed its victim within less than one second!
(a) volatile (b) wily (c) virulent (d) veracious 50. ....

C. Synonyms

In the space provided, write the letter of the word that is most nearly the same in meaning as the first word.

51. AUTHENTIC (a) solid (b) written (c) oral
(d) genuine (e) consolidated   51. ....

52. BANTER (a) native (b) tease (c) sarcasm
(d) narrate (e) explain   52. ....

53. BRUSQUE   (a) sudden   (b) smooth   (c) exotic
(d) intelligent   (e) blunt   53. ....

54. COMMODIOUS   (a) convenient   (b) limited
(c) roomy   (d) rentable   (e) heavy   54. ....

55. DEFILE   (a) run   (b) irritate   (c) explain
(d) cleanse   (e) corrupt   55. ....

56. FRIVOLOUS   (a) giddy   (b) insincere
(c) cooked   (d) unfair   (e) racy   56. ....

57. NOVICE   (a) star   (b) planet   (c) learner
(d) teacher   (e) player   57. ....

58. REVITALIZE   (a) renew   (b) relive   (c) animate
(d) exhaust   (e) sell   58. ....

59. SLOTHFUL   (a) unclean   (b) sloppy
(c) excitable   (d) lazy   (e) excellent   59. ....

60. GAUNTLET   (a) torture   (b) alley   (c) discussion
(d) armor   (e) glove   60. ....

61. DIVA   (a) athlete   (b) singer   (c) politician
(d) actor   (e) musician   61. ....

62. CURT   (a) abrupt   (b) talkative   (c) silent
(d) headstrong   (e) insulting   62. ....

63. CHASTISE   (a) purify   (b) imprison   (c) reward
(d) beat   (e) complain   63. ....

64. CAUSTIC   (a) related   (b) chemical   (c) flavor
(d) biting   (e) foreign   64. ....

65. BELLIGERENT   (a) lovable   (b) warlike
(c) beautiful   (d) unpleasant   (e) wise   65. ....

66. AVOW   (a) pledge   (b) swear in court
(c) acknowledge   (d) deny   (e) fabricate   66. ....

67. DISSIPATE   (a) destroy   (b) accumulate
(c) scatter   (d) command   (e) build   67. ....

68. EFFUSIVE   (a) gushing   (b) talkative
(c) taciturn   (d) silent   (e) mute   68. ....

69. EVINCE   (a) wash   (b) cleanse   (c) explain
(d) extol   (e) show   69. ....

70. FELONIOUS (a) friendly (b) vicious
(c) sudden (d) provoked (e) foolish   70. ....

71. GOUGE (a) explain (b) hammer (c) squeeze
(d) swindle (e) charge   71. ....

72. ILLICIT (a) dogged (b) open (c) improper
(d) unauthorized (e) insincere   72. ....

73. EXTOL (a) denounce (b) renounce (c) receive
(d) donate (e) praise   73. ....

74. GLIB (a) fluent (b) thick (c) cheap
(d) expensive (e) insincere   74. ....

75. COUNTERMAND (a) supervise (b) serve
(c) contact (d) revoke (e) object   75. ....

76. NETTLE (a) gain (b) collect (c) foretell
(d) lose (e) vex   76. ....

77. OBESE (a) stubborn (b) obnoxious (c) plump
(d) scrawny (e) tractable   77. ....

78. PECUNIARY pertaining to (a) cattle (b) money
(c) pigs (d) autos (e) school   78. ....

79. PROLIFIC (a) abundant (b) rural (c) arboreal
(d) thematic (e) stern   79. ....

80. REGALE (a) majestic (b) democratic
(c) entertain (d) narrate (e) listen   80. ....

81. RUSE (a) dressing (b) device (c) cake (d) fool
(e) intellect   81. ....

82. SOLACE (a) lone (b) soothe (c) confess
(d) befriend (e) conquer   82. ....

83. STRIDENT (a) fast (b) thunderous (c) shrill
(d) angry (e) powerful   83. ....

84. VALOR (a) worth (b) rashness (c) daring
(d) excellence (e) courage   84. ....

85. VIRULENT (a) manly (b) feminine (c) puerile
(d) harmful (e) powerful   85. ....

D. Analogies

In the space provided, write the letter of the set of words that best completes the analogy.

86. STAMINA : HAVEN :: (a) voice : harbor
(b) endurance : shelter   (c) land : sea   (d) quiet :
peaceable   (e) tenderness : vigor   86. ....

87. ABRIDGE : AMALGAMATE :: (a) short : shorter
(b) one : many   (c) span : union   (d) every : none   87. ....

88. MAXIM : ADAGE :: (a) lecture : novel   (b) short
story : play   (c) play : opera   (d) sermon : lecture   88. ....

89. ASSAIL : BERATE :: (a) force : words   (b) book :
gun   (c) soldier : astronaut   (d) object : aim   89. ....

90. CORSAIR : FREEBOOTER :: (a) caption : cascade
(b) hamlet : haven   (c) mercenary : soldier   (d) rift :
ruse   90. ....

91. UNCOUTH : SUAVE :: (a) monster : knight
(b) male : female   (c) legislature : legislative   (d) boor :
gentleman   91. ....

92. DEPLETE : AUGMENT :: (a) capitulate : surrender
(b) doff : don   (c) exuberant : fastidious   (d) morose :
placid   92. ....

93. REMINISCE : MEMORY :: (a) substantiate : fact
(b) solace : soothe   (c) upbraid : fault   (d) wrangle :
cowboy   93. ....

94. TYKE : NOVICE :: (a) man : boy   (b) age :
experience   (c) war : soldier   (d) water : work   94. ....

95. UNIMPEACHABLE : SCRUPULOUS :: (a) good :
bad   (b) bad : good   (c) good : good   (d) bad : bad   95. ....

96. SAGA : PARABLE :: (a) long : short   (b) truth :
fiction   (c) short : long   (d) deeds : moral   96. ....

97. MAIM : HEAL :: (a) morose : sullen
(b) momentous : trivial   (c) impious : religion
(d) humility : enjoy   97. ....

98. DETONATE : DELETE :: (a) touch : hearing
(b) sound : sight   (c) feel : smell   (d) sound : touch   98. ....

99. RECALCITRANT : REFRACTORY :: (a) divest :
doff   (b) encroach : extol   (c) felony : felonious
(d) fastidious : gross   99. ....

100. CURT : BRUSQUE :: (a) rankle : solace
(b) sedative : opiate   (c) destitute : impecunious
(d) gullible : sophisticated   100. ....

Answer Key

A. Antonyms

1. (b)	8. (b)	15. (a)	22. (b)	29. (a)
2. (a)	9. (c)	16. (d)	23. (c)	30. (b)
3. (c)	10. (a)	17. (e)	24. (a)	31. (e)
4. (c)	11. (b)	18. (b)	25. (e) ?	32. (a)
5. (d)	12. (c)	19. (c)	26. (c)	33. (c)
6. (e)	13. (d)	20. (d)	27. (c)	34. (b)
7. (c)	14. (c)	21. (e)	28. (e)	35. (c)

B. Sentence Completion

36. (b)	39. (b)	42. (a)	45. (c)	48. (b)
37. (d)	40. (c)	43. (c)	46. (d)	49. (a)
38. (c)	41. (b)	44. (d)	47. (a)	50. (c)

C. Synonyms

51. (d)	58. (a)	65. (b)	72. (c)	79. (a)
52. (b)	59. (d)	66. (c)	73. (e)	80. (c)
53. (e)	60. (e)	67. (c)	74. (a)	81. (b)
54. (c)	61. (b)	68. (a)	75. (d)	82. (b)
55. (e)	62. (a)	69. (e)	76. (e)	83. (c)
56. (a)	63. (d)	70. (b)	77. (c)	84. (e)
57. (c)	64. (d)	71. (d)	78. (b)	85. (d)

D. Analogies

86. (b)	89. (a)	92. (b)	95. (c)	98. (b)
87. (b)	90. (c)	93. (a)	96. (d)	99. (a)
88. (d)	91. (d)	94. (b)	97. (b)	100. (c)

My Score: Number Right............   Number Wrong............

Clinch by Checking

The purpose of this test was to help you discover which of the words in the Basic List you must concentrate on in order to achieve 100% mastery. Since the list is arranged in alphabetical order, you should have no difficulty in checking back. Mark the words that you missed; these are the ones that should be studied in your next session. Once you have them under control, then you are ready for the Second Basic-List Practice Test.

Twelfth Day: Second Basic-List Practice Test

A. Sentence Completion

In the space provided, write the letter of the word that best completes the sentence.

1. The thieves threatened to torture the old miner if he did not reveal where he .... his gold nuggets.
    (a) detonated   (b) deviated   (c) cached   (d) honed   1. ....

2. The attackers warned that unless the town .... within the next hour they would bomb it out of existence.
    (a) imbibed   (b) capitulated   (c) improvised
    (d) infringed   2. ....

3. The picture of the traffic officer writing on a pad while facing a motorist who is looking up at him from the window of a parked car needed no .... to tell its story to the reader.
    (a) derelict   (b) corsair   (c) coquette   (d) caption   3. ....

4. The doctor suspected that the hollow cough betokened more than just a cough for the patient that had spent so many years working in .... mines.
    (a) dank   (b) authentic   (c) curt   (d) grimy   4. ....

5. Despair and fear had so .... the prisoners that they cowered before their captors.
    (a) gouged   (b) depleted   (c) debilitated
    (d) defiled   5. ....

6. Buy five of the fine products on this shelf, and you will receive a sixth one ....
    (a) detonated   (b) gratis   (c) encumbered
    (d) rescinded   6. ....

7. What .... is available to one who cries out in vain while being tossed on the seas of deep despair?

(a) haven   (b) knavery   (c) fracas   (d) accomplice   **7.** ....

8. Make certain that the frame of the tennis racket is .... to withstand the punishment that it will take in a game.

(a) abridged   (b) destitute   (c) amalgamated
(d) laminated   **8.** ....

9. In vain did the street cat imitate the .... appearance of his cousin as he paced up and down in his cage.

(a) felonious   (b) inept   (c) frivolous   (d) leonine   **9.** ....

10. How disappointed become so many when the .... of a favorite opera is translated into English and the meaning of a favorite aria becomes clear!

(a) maestro   (b) mountebank   (c) libretto
(d) pessimism   **10.** ....

11. The fire marshal suspected .... when the investigation revealed that the forest fire had started in six different places at about the same time.

(a) corsairs   (b) arson   (c) accomplices   (d) rifts   **11.** ....

12. The disappointed man falsely .... his failure to the lack of loyalty among his friends.

(a) effaced   (b) evinced   (c) attributed
(d) revitalized   **12.** ....

13. The names of every player involved in the Black Sox scandal in baseball were .... from the record books.

(a) deleted   (b) inhibited   (c) divested
(d) depleted   **13.** ....

14. The inexperienced speaker was so .... by the heckler that he was unable to continue his remarks.

(a) incensed   (b) disconcerted   (c) infringed
(d) disheveled   **14.** ....

15. Who is the .... who made her reputation by singing the role of Aïda as a last-minute replacement for an ailing singer?

(a) droll   (b) maestro   (c) diva   (d) corsair   **15.** ....

B. Antonyms

In the space provided, write the letter of the word that is most nearly opposite in meaning to the first word.

16. EMINENT (a) past (b) postponed (c) unknown
(d) future (e) misplaced   16. ....

17. ENCROACH (a) withdraw (b) tutor (c) master
(d) infringe (e) indict   17. ....

18. ERUDITE (a) lasting (b) oral (c) exotic
(d) illiterate (e) foreign   18. ....

19. GHASTLY (a) immaterial (b) pleasant (c) solid
(d) clean (e) unbesmirched   19. ....

20. GRIMY (a) humorous (b) sincere (c) toiling
(d) foolish (e) clean   20. ....

21. MUTABLE (a) oral (b) fickle (c) set
(d) stained (e) stellar   21. ....

22. PUTREFY (a) revive (b) spoil (c) conserve
(d) enter (e) descend   22. ....

23. ACCOMPLICE (a) deed (b) thought
(c) adversary (d) police (e) crony   23. ....

24. ACQUIT (a) change (b) articulate (c) behave
(d) convict (e) sing   24. ....

25. ALLAY (a) enemy (b) companion (c) search
(d) worry (e) rouse   25. ....

26. PROLIFIC (a) sterile (b) close (c) offhand
(d) agricultural (e) musical   26. ....

27. RABID (a) animal (b) sane (c) fanciful
(d) extravagant (e) medical   27. ....

28. RANKLE (a) select (b) discard (c) enter
(d) please (e) pun   28. ....

29. STALWART (a) intellectual (b) muscular
(c) weak (d) timid (e) ignorant   29. ....

30. SUAVE (a) cold (b) discernible (c) discontent
(d) disowned (e) discourteous   30. ....

31. SURMOUNT (a) master (b) fail (c) charge
(d) ignore (e) elevate   31. ....

32. TANTALIZE (a) train (b) torture (c) comfort
(d) lead (e) fight   32. ....

33. UNCOUTH   (a) known   (b) handsome
(c) ignorant   (d) timid   (e) fearless   33. ....

34. COMPATIBLE   (a) uncongenial   (b) astronomical
(c) stingy   (d) silent   (e) gracious   34. ....

35. ENCUMBER   (a) enclose   (b) disclose   (c) burden
(d) aid   (e) exaggerate   35. ....

36. GULLIBLE   (a) weak   (b) tall   (c) provincial
(d) sophisticated   (e) extravagant   36. ....

37. HAUGHTY   (a) educated   (b) prejudiced
(c) humble   (d) lovely   (e) plain   37. ....

38. IMPECUNIOUS   (a) genial   (b) wealthy
(c) attractive   (d) shrewd   (e) tense   38. ....

39. IMPERTURBABLE   (a) agitated   (b) quiet
(c) loud   (d) sensitive   (e) commendable   39. ....

40. INDICT   (a) ask   (b) imprison   (c) judge
(d) free   (e) misunderstand   40. ....

41. REBUT   (a) agitate   (b) stop   (c) argue
(d) agree   (e) denounce   41. ....

42. RECALCITRANT   (a) untold   (b) extravagant
(c) obedient   (d) harmonious   (e) distant   42. ....

43. RELEVANT   (a) unseen   (b) unconnected
(c) sane   (d) spiteful   (e) adhesive   43. ....

44. TOXIC   (a) medical   (b) ignorant   (c) tasteful
(d) inelegant   (e) harmless   44. ....

45. UNIMPEACHABLE   (a) biased   (b) delicious
(c) inedible   (d) tasty   (e) organized   45. ....

46. UPBRAID   (a) upset   (b) arrange   (c) execute
(d) anticipate   (e) commend   46. ....

47. VALOR   (a) ugliness   (b) manners   (c) chivalry
(d) cowardice   (e) essence   47. ....

48. VOLATILE   (a) ancient   (b) gaseous   (c) heavy
(d) fickle   (e) admirable   48. ....

49. WAYWARD   (a) untrained   (b) obedient
(c) offensive   (d) mild   (e) certain   49. ....

50. AMEND   (a) damage   (b) edit   (c) shorten
(d) delineate   (e) desire   50. ....

C. Synonyms

In the space provided, write the letter of the word that is most
nearly the same in meaning as the first word.

51. WILY   (a) cooperative   (b) intelligent
(c) offensive   (d) cunning   (e) selfish   51. ....

52. TYKE   (a) child   (b) obstruction   (c) dam
(d) Dutch costume   (e) relative   52. ....

53. WAN   (a) ebb tide   (b) desire   (c) faint
(d) hollow   (e) sickly   53. ....

54. PEDAGOGUE   (a) principal   (b) teacher
(c) pupil   (d) aid   (e) doctor   54. ....

55. MÉNAGE   (a) control   (b) zoo   (c) wild animal
(d) household   (e) supervise   55. ....

56. JOIST   (a) push   (b) fun   (c) discipline
(d) flooring   (e) supports   56. ....

57. INTER   (a) complete   (b) bury   (c) depart
(d) destroy   (e) follow   57. ....

58. INCREMENT   (a) addition   (b) waste
(c) essential   (d) wages   (e) allowance   58. ....

59. INALIENABLE   (a) foreign   (b) domestic
(c) excusable   (d) effortless   (e) essential   59. ....

60. CUISINE   (a) relative   (b) French   (c) food
(d) distant   (e) adhesive   60. ....

61. CONDIMENT   (a) satisfaction   (b) relish
(c) contrariness   (d) execution   (e) salvation   61. ....

62. COMPUTE   (a) add   (b) rival   (c) calculate
(d) delve   (e) design   62. ....

63. DEMURE   (a) object   (b) brazen   (c) offensive
(d) pleasing   (e) modest   63. ....

64. CLIQUE   (a) associates   (b) partners
(c) acquaintances   (d) set   (e) classmates   64. ....

65. LIQUIDATE (a) solve (b) turn to water
(c) bankrupt (d) harass (e) convert to cash   65. ....

66. COERCE (a) restrain (b) associate (c) expel
(d) imprison (e) liberate   66. ....

67. USURP (a) exhaust (b) deplete (c) seize
(d) anticipate (e) evolve   67. ....

68. WRANGLE (a) handle (b) quarrel (c) discuss
(d) compromise (e) beat   68. ....

69. COLLABORATE (a) work together (b) study
(c) examine carefully (d) run together (e) edit   69. ....

70. CHERUB (a) adult (b) happy person (c) angel
(d) religion (e) angle   70. ....

71. BRUNT (a) curt (b) polite (c) offensive
(d) impact (e) dull   71. ....

72. BRANDISH (a) burn (b) create (c) show off
(d) wave (e) excel   72. ....

73. AWRY (a) satisfactory (b) ancient (c) torn
(d) preceding (e) twisted   73. ....

74. RUBBLE (a) destroy (b) wreckage
(c) foundation (d) air raid (e) condition   74. ....

75. SAGA (a) incident (b) anecdote (c) wise man
(d) elder (e) story   75. ....

76. RUSE (a) reddish (b) Communist (c) oriental
(d) western (e) device   76. ....

77. SANCTITY (a) supervision (b) purity
(c) religion (d) excellence (e) whiteness   77. ....

78. SCINTILLATE (a) sparkle (b) demonstrate
(c) reveal (d) thunder (e) storm   78. ....

79. MISDEMEANOR (a) murder (b) highway robbery
(c) error (d) traffic violation (e) injury   79. ....

80. MOUNTEBANK (a) doctor (b) leader
(c) follower (d) patient (e) quack   80. ....

81. NAPE (a) slumber (b) back of neck (c) shoulders
(d) back (e) torso   81. ....

82. OFFICIOUS   (a) meddling   (b) legal   (c) moderate
(d) loyal   (e) unexpected   82. ....

83. SYNTHETIC   (a) cloth   (b) fabric   (c) man-made
(d) shoddy   (e) sturdy   83. ....

84. TEPID   (a) watery   (b) cold   (c) cool
(d) warmish   (e) hot   84. ....

85. SIMIAN   (a) gigantic   (b) sluggish   (c) apelike
(d) oriental   (e) clumsy   85. ....

D. Analogies

In the space provided, write the letter of the set of words that best completes the analogy.

86. ASSIDUOUS : DILIGENT :: BALMY : (a) musty
(b) rank   (c) fragrant   (d) dull   86. ....

87. BAUBLE : VALUABLE :: BLIGHT : (a) bizarre
(b) beneficial   (c) bountiful   (d) compatible   87. ....

88. CUISINE : CULINARY :: (a) dank : cave
(b) payment : disburse   (c) hair : disheveled   (d) derelict :
abandoned   88. ....

89. ICON : IMPIOUS :: (a) increment : lower   (b) law :
indict   (c) jaunt : jaunty   (d) praise : condemn   89. ....

90. LOPE : DISTANCE :: (a) ocular : eyepiece
(b) ordinance : decree   (c) perpetuate : time
(d) plagiarize : copy   90. ....

91. SEDATIVE : OPIATE :: MIRE : (a) enjoyment
(b) terrain   (c) confusion   (d) mud   91. ....

92. IMPROVISE : IMAGINATION :: MEANDER :
(a) stream   (b) obstacle   (c) freedom   (d) wish   92. ....

93. INCENSE : IMPERTURBABLE :: (a) humble :
hapless   (b) rob : pirate   (c) cache : monumental
(d) clique : cherub   93. ....

94. CONDIMENT : PEPPER :: EPISTLE : (a) opera
(b) telegram   (c) essay   (d) libretto   94. ....

95. EXOTIC : COMMON :: ERUDITE : (a) moron
(b) student   (c) illiterate   (d) learned   95. ....

96. SUNDRY : SUMPTUOUS :: (a) one : simple
(b) drink : feast   (c) varied : plain   (d) inexpensive :
costly   96. ....

97. TRACTABLE : UNRULY :: (a) trite : commonplace
(b) truculent : heavy-set   (c) unwitting : bright
(d) veracious : lying   97. ....

98. VIRILE : VIRULENT :: (a) favorable : favorable
(b) unfavorable : unfavorable   (c) unfavorable : favorable
(d) favorable : unfavorable   98. ....

99. VIVACIOUS : VOCIFEROUS :: (a) taciturn :
lifeless   (b) loud : animated   (c) languid : silent
(d) liveliness : shouting   99. ....

100. GNOME : ANTHROPOLOGIST :: (a) man : child
(b) size : occupation   (c) treasure : man   (d) circus :
library   100. ....

Answer Key

A. Sentence Completion

1. (c)	4. (a)	7. (a)	10. (c)	13. (a)
2. (b)	5. (c)	8. (d)	11. (b)	14. (b)
3. (d)	6. (b)	9. (d)	12. (c)	15. (c)

B. Antonyms

16. (c)	23. (c)	30. (e)	37. (c)	44. (e)
17. (a)	24. (d)	31. (b)	38. (b)	45. (a)
18. (d)	25. (e)	32. (c)	39. (a)	46. (e)
19. (b)	26. (a)	33. (b)	40. (d)	47. (d)
20. (e)	27. (b)	34. (a)	41. (d)	48. (c)
21. (c)	28. (d)	35. (d)	42. (c)	49. (b)
22. (a)	29. (c)	36. (d)	43. (b)	50. (a)

C. Synonyms

51. (d)	58. (a)	65. (e)	72. (d)	79. (d)
52. (a)	59. (e)	66. (a)	73. (e)	80. (e)
53. (c)	60. (c)	67. (c)	74. (b)	81. (b)
54. (b)	61. (b)	68. (b)	75. (e)	82. (a)
55. (d)	62. (c)	69. (a)	76. (e)	83. (c)
56. (e)	63. (e)	70. (c)	77. (b)	84. (d)
57. (b)	64. (d)	71. (d)	78. (a)	85. (c)

D. Analogies

86. (c)	89. (a)	92. (c)	95. (c)	98. (d)
87. (b)	90. (c)	93. (c)	96. (a)	99. (c)
88. (d)	91. (d)	94. (b)	97. (d)	100. (b)

My Score: Number Right............ Number Wrong............

Clinch by Checking

The purpose of this test was to help you discover which of the words in the Basic List you must concentrate on in order to achieve 100% mastery. Since the list is arranged in alphabetical order, you should have no difficulty in checking back. Mark the words that you missed; these are the ones that should be studied in your next session. Once you have them under control, then you are ready for the Third Basic-List Practice Test.

Thirteenth Day: Third Basic-List Practice Test

A. Synonyms

In the space provided, write the letter of the word that is most nearly the same in meaning as the first word.

1. BERATE (a) abridge (b) scold (c) praise
(d) lengthen (e) efface   1. ....

2. COQUETTE (a) biscuit (b) cookie (c) chef
(d) flirt (e) knavery   2. ....

3. BEREAVE (a) promote (b) indict (c) deprive
(d) quaff (e) dismiss   3. ....

4. GAMUT (a) range (b) offer (c) style (d) race
(e) child   4. ....

5. BLIGHT (a) pilot (b) course (c) epistle
(d) heavy (e) disease   5. ....

6. PRATE (a) forehead (b) orate (c) chatter
(d) chaste (e) top   6. ....

7. BLUDGEON (a) bird (b) animal (c) mince
(d) club (e) organization   7. ....

8. CAREEN   (a) type of car   (b) drink   (c) game
(d) lurch   (e) dish   8. ....

9. CENTENNIAL   (a) guard   (b) 100 years
(c) soldier   (d) quarterly   (e) semi-annual   9. ....

10. DISBURSE   (a) expend   (b) solace   (c) delete
(d) deviate   (e) delve   10. ....

11. CRONY   (a) small animal   (b) poet   (c) ancestor
(d) weak   (e) pal   11. ....

12. DECREPIT   (a) ruined   (b) destroyed   (c) sturdy
(d) broken down   (e) active   12. ....

13. DESTITUTE   (a) residence   (b) charity
(c) penniless   (d) without friends   (e) envious   13. ....

14. DIGRESS   (a) clothing   (b) wander   (c) wonder
(d) explain   (e) write   14. ....

15. EXTANT   (a) size   (b) length   (c) decent
(d) visible   (e) existing   15. ....

16. FASTIDIOUS   (a) critical   (b) sharp   (c) simple
(d) elaborate   (e) crucial   16. ....

17. FLAGGING   (a) decorating   (b) drooping
(c) interesting   (d) dull   (e) timid   17. ....

18. GAFF   (a) fun   (b) hook   (c) florid
(d) anthropologist   (e) noisy   18. ....

19. FLORID   (a) state   (b) municipal   (c) colorless
(d) sentimental   (e) ruddy   19. ....

20. MIRE   (a) praise   (b) sell   (c) mud   (d) small
object   (e) instrument   20. ....

21. JAMB   (a) side   (b) cover   (c) door   (d) knob
(e) screen   21. ....

22. FORAY   (a) imprisonment   (b) roller   (c) plunge
(d) raid   (e) perpetual   22. ....

23. MERCANTILE   (a) bargain   (b) expensive
(c) dear   (d) commercial   (e) oral   23. ....

24. MIEN   (a) gentle   (b) coarse   (c) stingy   (d) proud
(e) manner   24. ....

25. FOUNDER (a) establish (b) fish (c) fail
(d) collect (e) follow   25. ....

26. KNAVERY (a) cutlery (b) trickery
(c) cleverness (d) wisdom (e) napery   26. ....

27. FRACAS (a) friendliness (b) curiosity
(c) complaining (d) brawl (e) foreign   27. ....

28. QUAFF (a) odd (b) eat (c) drink (d) feast
(e) perform   28. ....

29. RECLUSE (a) celebrity (b) hermit (c) secretive
(d) open (e) famous   29. ....

30. FREEBOOTER (a) friend (b) enemy (c) sailor
(d) officer (e) pirate   30. ....

31. GAZETTE (a) epistle (b) telescope (c) editor
(d) propaganda (e) newspaper   31. ....

32. GNOME (a) recognizable (b) averaged
(c) official (d) dwarf (e) municipality   32. ....

33. HAMLET (a) village (b) actor (c) hero
(d) villain (e) writer   33. ....

34. PLAINTIVE (a) complaining (b) melancholy
(c) simple (d) elaborate (e) talkative   34. ....

35. RIFT (a) mound (b) snow (c) split
(d) appropriate (e) type of boat   35. ....

B. Sentence Completion

In the space provided, write the letter of the word that best completes the sentence.

36. Beneath their light ...., the onlookers sensed a readiness to take offense and a willingness to use blows rather than words.
(a) berating (b) banter (c) adage (d) assailing   36. ....

37. How could he throw away the chance of becoming a surgeon for the .... of success as a summer-resort comedian?
(a) fracas (b) hawser (c) gazette (d) bauble   37. ....

38. How she ever .... to get him to attend the meeting is a secret to me!
(a) contrived   (b) abdicated   (c) bereaved
(d) countermanded   38. ....

39. I still do not know the fundamental difference between a(n) .... and a highway robber other than for a difference in means of transportation.
(a) anthropologist   (b) agenda   (c) corsair
(d) accomplice   39. ....

40. Navy divers attempted to raise the .... which had sunk and was now blocking the only channel into the harbor.
(a) derelict   (b) effigy   (c) gnome   (d) rift   40. ....

41. The failure of the business left the family so .... that they had to seek public assistance.
(a) inveterate   (b) mercenary   (c) destitute
(d) maimed   41. ....

42. Once all of the men were out of the blasting area, the engineer gave the signal for the charges to be ....
(a) jambed   (b) detonated   (c) laminated
(d) interred   42. ....

43. The most hated man in the district was the local landlord who inevitably had the reputation of being one born to .... the poor.
(a) gouge   (b) joist   (c) jeopardize   (d) laud   43. ....

44. The barber .... the razor before stropping it.
(a) liquidated   (b) innovated   (c) loathed
(d) honed   44. ....

45. The young Erasmus went from university to university in his eager desire to .... knowledge.
(a) imbibe   (b) indict   (c) mire   (d) improvise   45. ....

46. The hungry coyote .... across the prairie in pursuit of prey.
(a) enervated   (b) abridged   (c) loped
(d) infringed   46. ....

47. The .... dust brought back by the astronaut was examined in the laboratory to discover its composition.
(a) lunar   (b) jaunty   (c) momentous
(d) frivolous   47. ....

48. He was so lacking in originality and inventiveness that he governed all of his decisions not on the needs of the individual situation but on the applicability of one of the dozen or so .... that he had faith in.
  (a) freebooters   (b) maxims   (c) epistles   (d) gaffs   48. ....

49. I can have no respect for a person who is so .... that he allows monetary gain and not ideals to formulate his basic attitudes.
  (a) obese   (b) malevolent   (c) nonpartisan
  (d) mercenary   49. ....

50. Wisely, since he had little interest in .... matters and really wanted to devote all of his time to the problems that arose in the laboratory, he left all business transactions to his capable partner.
  (a) palpable   (b) pecuniary   (c) officious
  (d) mercantile   50. ....

C. Analogies

In the space provided, write the letter of the set of words that best completes the analogy.

51. MOROSE : MUTABLE :: (a) cheerful : injured
(b) mild : severe   (c) spiteful : likable   (d) gloomy : fickle   51. ....

52. COQUETTE : MERCENARY :: (a) male : female
(b) flirt : money   (c) woman : man   (d) genial : greedy   52. ....

53. MOUNTEBANK : RUSE :: (a) corsair : foray
(b) gnome : treasure   (c) hamlet : town   (d) haven : storm   53. ....

54. HONE : INNOVATE :: (a) interminable : endless
(b) dull : ineffective   (c) provident : careless   (d) excellent : new   54. ....

55. MEANDER : CIRCUITOUS :: (a) contemn : enjoyable   (b) chastise : punishment   (c) acquit : guilty
(d) glib : fluent   55. ....

56. LAUD : COMMEND :: (a) disconcert : embarrass
(b) revile : praise   (c) enervate : operate   (d) enter : surmount   56. ....

57. TAUT : TRUCULENT :: (a) book : mood
(b) hawser : bully   (c) uncouth : unimpeachable
(d) viands : ostentatious   57. ....

58. OBESE : FLORID :: (a) man : plant   (b) fat : fate
(c) build : complexion   (d) grimy : dirt   58. ....

59. NOVICE : PREFATORY :: (a) first : last   (b) early :
first   (c) skier : writer   (d) man : statement   59. ....

60. APEX : PINNACLE :: (a) mountain : sail
(b) galleon : frigate   (c) misdemeanor : marital   (d) eye :
ocular   60. ....

61. EXTANT : EXTINCT :: (a) compatible :
antagonistic   (b) degradation : insult   (c) destitute :
penniless   (d) disheveled : clothing   61. ....

62. PREVARICATE : EQUIVOCATE :: (a) more : less
(b) same : opposite   (c) equal : equal   (d) less : more 62. ....

63. GOUGE : GLIB :: (a) fair : unfair   (b) chisel :
tongue   (c) fast : slow   (d) dig : smooth   63. ....

64. STRIDENT : PALPABLE :: (a) quiet : clear
(b) hearing : touch   (c) sight : sound   (d) perennial :
enduring   64. ....

65. PYROMANIAC : ARSON :: (a) poll : voting place
(b) potentate : rule   (c) quaff : drinker   (d) fighter :
prowess   65. ....

D. Antonyms

In the space provided, write the letter of the word that is most
nearly opposite in meaning to the first word.

66. BRUSQUE   (a) long   (b) polite   (c) blunt
(d) abrupt   (e) following   66. ....

67. HAPLESS   (a) hopeful   (b) helpful   (c) rich
(d) fortunate   (e) poor   67. ....

68. INFRINGE   (a) obey   (b) decorate   (c) destroy
(d) delete   (e) uncover   68. ....

69. NOVICE   (a) apprentice   (b) timer   (c) teacher
(d) author   (e) reader   69. ....

70. PERT (a) pretty (b) plain (c) flippant (d) old
(e) bashful   70. ....

71. PETULANT (a) happy (b) leading (c) annoyed
(d) previous (e) peevish   71. ....

72. PINNACLE (a) sail (b) body (c) flag
(d) bottom (e) deck   72. ....

73. REMINISCE (a) refer (b) predict (c) focus
(d) scatter (e) herd   73. ....

74. SELF-EFFACING (a) creative (b) parasite
(c) efficient (d) saucy (e) retiring   74. ....

75. ABDICATE (a) announce (b) denounce
(c) elope (d) claim (e) clarify   75. ....

76. ALOOF (a) down (b) friendly (c) quiet
(d) clamorous (e) exotic   76. ....

77. ARROGANT (a) claim (b) dispute (c) meek
(d) alert (e) inactive   77. ....

78. BALMY (a) peaceable (b) flagrant (c) locked
(d) sensitive (e) rank   78. ....

79. DEVIATE (a) persevere (b) abnormal
(c) ascending (d) falling (e) agree   79. ....

80. INTERMINABLE (a) flowing (b) exceptionable
(c) average (d) completed (e) fine   80. ....

81. LOATHE (a) accelerate (b) feel (c) linger
(d) abhor (e) admire   81. ....

82. MOMENTOUS (a) lasting (b) trivial (c) slight
(d) decisive (e) mutable   82. ....

83. OSTRACIZE (a) include (b) sell (c) make
(d) encourage (e) plague   83. ....

84. PRECOCIOUS (a) baked (b) retarded (c) alert
(d) late (e) postponed   84. ....

85. PRODIGAL (a) unwonted (b) unknown
(c) unforgettable (d) frugal (e) frenzied   85. ....

86. SLOTHFUL   (a) filled   (b) vacant   (c) entire
(d) interested   (e) diligent   86. ....

87. APPREHENSIVE   (a) grotesque   (b) nonchalant
(c) free   (d) captured   (e) dense   87. ....

88. ARDUOUS   (a) effortless   (b) arrogant
(c) defensive   (d) burnt   (e) steep   88. ....

89. COMMODIOUS   (a) cruel   (b) kind   (c) limited
(d) lively   (e) listless   89. ....

90. DOFF   (a) enter   (b) conceive   (c) wear   (d) don
(e) late   90. ....

91. EVINCE   (a) defeat   (b) win   (c) conceal
(d) horrify   (e) find   91. ....

92. EXTOL   (a) denounce   (b) astonish   (c) redeem
(d) enter   (e) remain silent   92. ....

93. HUMILITY   (a) care   (b) concern   (c) foolishness
(d) vanity   (e) design   93. ....

94. MOROSE   (a) large   (b) cheerful   (c) cheerless
(d) minute   (e) dour   94. ....

95. PERENNIAL   (a) unpleasant   (b) flowery
(c) plain   (d) cheap   (e) fleeting   95. ....

96. REFRACTORY   (a) clear   (b) dense   (c) docile
(d) obvious   (e) noisy   96. ....

97. SOMBER   (a) cheerful   (b) serious   (c) talkative
(d) nonsensical   (e) prior   97. ....

98. SPURIOUS   (a) uneven   (b) shameful   (c) lazy
(d) genuine   (e) lasting   98. ....

99. STRIDENT   (a) afoot   (b) subdued   (c) ruined
(d) mounted   (e) protective   99. ....

100. ABRIDGE   (a) destroy   (b) study   (c) annotate
(d) envisage   (e) enlarge   100. ....

Answer Key

A. Synonyms

1. (b)	8. (d)	15. (e)	22. (d)	29. (b)
2. (d)	9. (b)	16. (a)	23. (d)	30. (e)
3. (c)	10. (a)	17. (b)	24. (e)	31. (e)
4. (a)	11. (e)	18. (b)	25. (c)	32. (d)
5. (e)	12. (d)	19. (e)	26. (b)	33. (a)
6. (d)	13. (c)	20. (c)	27. (d)	34. (b)
7. (d)	14. (b)	21. (a)	28. (c)	35. (c)

B. Sentence Completion

36. (b)	39. (c)	42. (b)	45. (a)	48. (b)
37. (d)	40. (a)	43. (a)	46. (c)	49. (d)
38. (a)	41. (c)	44. (d)	47. (a)	50. (b)

C. Analogies

51. (d)	54. (b)	57. (b)	60. (b)	63. (b)
52. (c)	55. (d)	58. (c)	61. (a)	64. (b)
53. (a)	56. (a)	59. (d)	62. (c)	65. (b)

D. Antonyms

66. (b)	73. (b)	80. (d)	87. (b)	94. (b)
67. (d)	74. (d)	81. (e)	88. (a)	95. (e)
68. (a)	75. (d)	82. (b)	89. (c)	96. (c)
69. (c)	76. (b)	83. (a)	90. (d)	97. (a)
70. (e)	77. (c)	84. (b)	91. (c)	98. (d)
71. (a)	78. (e)	85. (d)	92. (a)	99. (b)
72. (d)	79. (a)	86. (e)	93. (d)	100. (e)

My Score: Number Right.............   Number Wrong.............

Clinch by Checking

The purpose of this test was to help you discover which of the words in the Basic List you must concentrate on in order to achieve 100% mastery. Since the list is arranged in alphabetical order, you should have no difficulty in checking back. Mark the words that you missed; these are the ones that should be studied in your next session. Once you have them under control, then you are ready for the Fourth Basic-List Practice Test.

Fourteenth Day: Fourth Basic-List Practice Test

A. Analogies

In the space provided, write the letter of the set of words that best completes the analogy.

1. EFFUSIVE : RESERVED :: (a) people : population
(b) elite : rabble   (c) eminent : outstanding
(d) encroaching : elegant   1. ....

2. EMBEZZLE : JEOPARDIZE :: (a) money : life
(b) right : wrong   (c) bank : valley   (d) emblem : donkey
                                                   2. ....

3. FRACAS : PUGNACIOUS :: (a) destitute : money
(b) doff : clothing   (c) tirade : quarrelsome   (d) ship : founder   3. ....

4. EPISTLE : HAND :: (a) anthropologist : science
(b) condiment : pepper   (c) cache : gold   (d) tirade : tongue   (e) freebooter : leg   4. ....

5. EPITAPH : MAXIM :: (a) fool : knavery   (b) many : one   (c) one : many   (d) perpetual : everlasting   5. ....

6. TRICE : TEPID   (a) three : one   (b) ocean : sea
(c) ounce : pound   (d) hot : cold   (e) time : temperature   6. ....

7. VANGUARD : TURNKEY :: (a) front : rear
(b) auto : lock   (c) storage : road   (d) army : prison
(e) keeper : scout   7. ....

8. SUAVE : VERACIOUS :: (a) courteous : truthful
(b) smooth : greedy   (c) man : child   (d) action : deed 8. ....

9. CULINARY : VIANDS :: (a) fear : potentate
(b) run : gamut   (c) libretto : composer   (d) devil : malevolent   (e) legal : ordinance   9. ....

10. VINDICATE : SLANDER :: (a) puerile : virile
(b) wrangle : quarrel   (c) tantalize : satisfy   (d) rescind : replace   (e) regale : kingly   10. ....

11. LEONINE : LUNAR :: (a) cat : mouse   (b) leopard : sun   (c) loud : soft   (d) lion : moon   (e) cruel : large   11. ....

12. ACCOMPLICE : ADVERSARY :: (a) freebooter ;
corsair (b) crony : competition (c) friend : rival
(d) jamb : joist   12. ....

13. COUNTERMAND : RESCIND :: (a) amalgamate :
unite (b) avow : deny (c) punishment : chastise
(d) curt : talkative   13. ....

14. SEPULCHER : INTER :: (a) agenda : meeting
(b) exist : annihilate (c) apex : mountain (d) cache :
hide   14. ....

15. CONDOLENCE : BEREAVE :: (a) plot : contrive
(b) disbelief : equivocate (c) gaff : hook (d) gazette :
newspaper   15. ....

B. Synonyms

In the space provided, write the letter of the word that is most
nearly the same in meaning as the first word.

16. SUNDRY   (a) religious   (b) drink   (c) several
(d) selected   (e) weak   16. ....

17. SUSTENANCE   (a) support   (b) cooperation
(c) condition   (d) education   (e) wish   17. ....

18. TIMOROUS   (a) assured   (b) negative   (c) weak
(d) timid   (e) trembling   18. ....

19. TIRADE   (a) ceremony   (b) eulogy   (c) commerce
(d) line   (e) scolding   19. ....

20. OPIATE   (a) dream   (b) narcotic   (c) power
(d) sensation   (e) illegal act   20. ....

21. EQUIVOCATE   (a) expel   (b) shout   (c) discuss
(d) hedge   (e) confess   21. ....

22. ORDINANCE   (a) usual action   (b) decision
(c) statue   (d) section   (e) statute   22. ....

23. TRAVERSE   (a) cross   (b) lie   (c) imperil
(d) journey   (e) expand   23. ....

24. SHOAL   (a) strengthen   (b) peninsula   (c) shallow
(d) inlet   (e) harbor   24. ....

25. SEPULCHER   (a) secluded spot   (b) statue
(c) integration   (d) grave   (e) monument   25. ....

26. RETRENCH   (a) dig in   (b) retreat   (c) reduce
(d) mold   (e) excel   26. ....

27. QUIRT   (a) joke   (b) peculiarity   (c) whip
(d) pole   (e) story   27. ....

28. SCRUPULOUS   (a) criminal   (b) conscientious
(c) hypocritical   (d) careless   (e) worn   28. ....

29. RESTITUTION   (a) success   (b) restoration
(c) damage   (d) wealth   (e) material   29. ....

30. SEDATIVE   (a) excitement   (b) friend
(c) secretion   (d) medicine   (e) injection   30. ....

31. PYROMANIAC   (a) liar   (b) arsonist   (c) insane
person   (d) doctor   (e) attendant   31. ....

32. OCULAR   (a) aural   (b) oral   (c) auditory
(d) vital   (e) visual   32. ....

33. PARABLE   (a) equality   (b) essential   (c) story
(d) lecture   (e) morale   33. ....

34. NONPARTISAN   (a) independent   (b) follower
(c) supporter   (d) leader   (e) rebel   34. ....

35. PESSIMISM   (a) foolishness   (b) wisdom
(c) happiness   (d) dullness   (e) hopelessness   35. ....

36. PLAGIARIZE   (a) write   (b) sell   (c) steal   (d) act
(e) confer   36. ....

37. POLL   (a) bird   (b) vote   (c) elect   (d) nominate
(e) tally   37. ....

38. ICON   (a) building   (b) area   (c) square
(d) picture   (e) book   38. ....

39. PREVARICATE   (a) own   (b) confess   (c) lie
(d) extol   (e) exaggerate   39. ....

40. PRONE   (a) sitting   (b) erect   (c) inclined
(d) short   (e) squat   40. ....

41. HAWSER   (a) cable   (b) car   (c) vessel   (d) hoist
(e) animal   41. ....

42. COUNTERMAND   (a) meet   (b) revoke
(c) attend   (d) revile   (e) battle   42. ....

43. DEPLETE   (a) demand   (b) exhaust   (c) envelop
(d) cover   (e) uncover   43. ....

44. DISHEVELED   (a) mussed   (b) bald   (c) unclean
(d) used   (e) straight   44. ....

45. DISSERTATION   (a) treatise   (b) treat
(c) selection   (d) parable   (e) essay   45. ....

46. DIVEST   (a) stripe   (b) clothe   (c) deprive
(d) arrest   (e) burn   46. ....

47. DOTING   (a) silly   (b) fond   (c) fighting
(d) peaceful   (e) wise   47. ....

48. EFFACE   (a) erase   (b) paint   (c) portray
(d) steal   (e) upset   48. ....

49. DROLL   (a) dully   (b) toylike   (c) funny   (d) large
(e) mythical character   49. ....

50. EFFIGY   (a) article   (b) game   (c) monument
(d) stuffed figure   (e) doll   50. ....

C. Antonyms

In the space provided, write the letter of the word that is most
nearly opposite in meaning to the first word.

51. ADEPT   (a) unfortunate   (b) bungling   (c) skilled
(d) lucky   (e) honored   51. ....

52. ADVERSARY   (a) ally   (b) judge   (c) jury
(d) counsel   (e) executor   52. ....

53. AUGMENT   (a) settle   (b) discuss   (c) reduce
(d) enslave   (e) dissolve   53. ....

54. CONDOLENCE   (a) sorrow   (b) superiority
(c) congratulation   (d) envy   (e) wish   54. ....

55. CONNOISSEUR   (a) extra   (b) lawyer
(c) representative   (d) dabbler   (e) teacher   55. ....

56. ENERVATE   (a) antagonize   (b) injure   (c) extol
(d) elaborate   (e) strengthen   56. ....

57. EXODUS (a) entrance (b) condemnation
(c) excellence (d) development (e) house   57. ....

58. EXTINCT (a) unknown (b) current
(c) disgraced (d) honored (e) inevitable   58. ....

59. EXUBERANT (a) sharp (b) foreign
(c) domestic (d) declared (e) meager   59. ....

60. INDOMITABLE (a) stubborn (b) noisy
(c) proud (d) submissive (e) taut   60. ....

61. INEPT (a) careful (b) competent (c) clean
(d) handsome (e) intelligent   61. ....

62. INSOLVENT (a) easy (b) understandable
(c) logical (d) wealthy (e) commercial   62. ....

63. JAUNTY (a) staid (b) lovely (c) ugly
(d) talkative (e) harsh   63. ....

64. LAUD (a) master (b) destroy (c) condemn
(d) govern (e) compose   64. ....

65. MALIGNANT (a) surgical (b) clever (c) deep
(d) beneficial (e) adept   65. ....

66. NETTLE (a) plant (b) harvest (c) vex
(d) gather (e) please   66. ....

67. OBSOLETE (a) thin (b) stingy (c) current
(d) unmechanical (e) automatic   67. ....

68. APEX (a) culture (b) light (c) ignorance
(d) bottom (e) censure   68. ....

69. ASSAIL (a) defend (b) ashore (c) attack
(d) announce (e) denounce   69. ....

70. ASSIDUOUS (a) ignorant (b) brilliant
(c) negligent (d) stubborn (e) uneasy   70. ....

71. AUTHENTIC (a) oral (b) shameful (c) contrary
(d) total (e) counterfeit   71. ....

72. AVOW (a) deny (b) promise (c) announce
(d) nullify (e) resolve   72. ....

73. BELLIGERENT (a) rural (b) friendly (c) lying
(d) biased (e) raw   73. ....

74. BIZARRE   (a) expensive   (b) handmade
(c) conservative   (d) odd   (e) unaffected   74. ....

75. CALLOUS   (a) salty   (b) harsh   (c) tanned
(d) tender   (e) famous   75. ....

76. CAUSTIC   (a) quiet   (b) boisterous
(c) inelegant   (d) unpleasant   (e) gracious   76. ....

77. CONTEMN   (a) judge   (b) misjudge   (c) esteem
(d) elect   (e) reject   77. ....

78. COY   (a) impudent   (b) shy   (c) pertinent
(d) loud   (e) accidental   78. ....

79. CURT   (a) clever   (b) talkative   (c) attentive
(d) inattentive   (e) askance   79. ....

80. PERPETUATE   (a) create   (b) laud   (c) cultivate
(d) terminate   (e) reply   80. ....

81. PREFATORY   (a) original   (b) concluding
(c) derivative   (d) additional   (e) essential   81. ....

82. PROWESS   (a) manly   (b) muscular   (c) fortitude
(d) rear   (e) timidity   82. ....

83. RETRENCH   (a) expand   (b) elevate   (c) destroy
(d) pacify   (e) emend   83. ....

84. ZEALOUS   (a) earnest   (b) navigable   (c) sluggish
(d) calm   (e) alert   84. ....

85. VIRILE   (a) sturdy   (b) exhausted   (c) effeminate
(d) exaggerated   (e) slow   85. ....

D. Sentence Completion

In the space provided, write the letter of the word that best completes the sentence.

86. We shall have to .... some device to help us raise the boat out of the mud.
(a) laud   (b) nettle   (c) improvise   (d) perpetuate   86. ....

87. When I assume control, I shall .... no new system, but I shall attempt to make the old one more efficient.
(a) innovate   (b) loathe   (c) poll   (d) prevaricate   87. ....

88. Unfortunately, he has the reputation for being a(n) ....
cynic, and I do not think that he will come to our assistance.
(a) nonpartisan (b) obese (c) mutable
(d) inveterate   88. ....

89. Our .... shall include side trips to Arlington Cemetery
and Monticello when we travel through the Washington area.
(a) prefatory (b) itinerary (c) recluse (d) mien 89. ....

90. Your reluctance to accept his advice may .... our entire
plan!
(a) jeopardize (b) lope (c) revert (d) maim   90. ....

91. The one sure way to .... this entire industry is to place in
key positions young men with new ideas.
(a) imbibe (b) innovate (c) revitalize (d) gouge 91. ....

92. One who studies fossilized remains to discover the historical
development of man is a(n) ....
(a) anthropologist (b) gnome (c) pessimist
(d) mercenary   92. ....

93. Hidden from view behind the .... is a large cave.
(a) mire (b) cascade (c) misdemeanor (d) ordinance
                                                  93. ....

94. Overcome by the miracle of his escape from injury, the
parents of the mischievous child forgot to .... him for disobeying their instructions.
(a) ostracize (b) rebut (c) regale (d) chastise 94. ....

95. The district attorney will attempt to prove they had ....
intent when they surrounded the elderly couple.
(a) felonious (b) flagging (c) grimy (d) hapless 95. ....

96. Once the mayor is made aware of the unfortunate results of
this order, I am certain that he will .... it immediately.
(a) contrive (b) rescind (c) contemn
(d) compute   96. ....

97. When the Board of Directors realized that age had robbed
him of his ability to make decisions, they advertised for someone
to .... him.
(a) vindicate (b) wrangle (c) supersede
(d) nettle   97. ....

98. In his desire to make a profit, he was the .... ally of the very men whose business tactics he had decried.
(a) unwitting   (b) malignant   (c) morose
(d) commodious   98. ....

99. The model of a(n) .... that he built is so realistic that you can almost hear commands shouted up to the men in the rigging.
(a) cherub   (b) cache   (c) caption   (d) galleon   99. ....

100. Had his .... not been made of meshed steel, the blow of the mace would have forced the sword from his hand.
(a) gauntlet   (b) haven   (c) gazette   (d) joist   100. ....

Answer Key

A. Analogies

1. (b)	4. (d)	7. (d)	10. (c)	13. (a)
2. (a)	5. (c)	8. (a)	11. (d)	14. (d)
3. (c)	6. (e)	9. (e)	12. (c)	15. (b)

B. Synonyms

16. (c)	23. (a)	30. (d)	37. (b)	44. (a)
17. (a)	24. (c)	31. (b)	38. (d)	45. (a)
18. (d)	25. (d)	32. (e)	39. (c)	46. (c)
19. (e)	26. (c)	33. (c)	40. (c)	47. (b)
20. (b)	27. (c)	34. (a)	41. (a)	48. (a)
21. (d)	28. (b)	35. (e)	42. (b)	49. (c)
22. (e)	29. (b)	36. (c)	43. (b)	50. (d)

C. Antonyms

51. (b)	58. (b)	65. (d)	72. (a)	79. (b)
52. (a)	59. (e)	66. (e)	73. (b)	80. (d)
53. (c)	60. (d)	67. (c)	74. (c)	81. (b)
54. (c)	61. (b)	68. (d)	75. (d)	82. (e)
55. (d)	62. (d)	69. (a)	76. (e)	83. (a)
56. (e)	63. (a)	70. (c)	77. (c)	84. (c)
57. (a)	64. (c)	71. (e)	78. (a)	85. (c)

D. Sentence Completion

86. (c)	89. (b)	92. (a)	95. (a)	98. (a)
87. (a)	90. (a)	93. (b)	96. (b)	99. (d)
88. (d)	91. (c)	94. (d)	97. (c)	100. (a)

My Score: Number Right............   Number Wrong............

Clinch by Checking

The purpose of this test was to help you discover which of the words in the Basic List you must concentrate on in order to achieve 100% mastery. Since the list is arranged in alphabetical order, you should have no difficulty in checking back. Mark the words that you missed; these are the ones that should be studied in your next session. Once you have them under control, then you are ready for the Lower-Junior List.

LOWER-JUNIOR VOCABULARY

Section 2: LOWER-JUNIOR LIST

First Day

1. ABOMINATE to detest **ant.** love ♦ Men of good will *abominate* dictators and exploiters.

2. ABSTEMIOUS moderate, sparing **ant.** overindulgent, uncontrolled ♦ Harold proved that he was an *abstemious* smoker when his package of cigarettes lasted him two months.

3. ACCLIMATE to adjust to, accustom ♦ You will need several days in order to become *acclimated* to the unusually high humidity in this area.

4. ACCORD to agree; agreement, harmony **ant.** oppose, argue; strife ♦ The leaders were in *accord* about which direction to take.

5. ACME peak, summit **ant.** depth, nadir ♦ Many people feel that a baseball player reaches the *acme* of his skill when he bats .400.

6. ACTUATE to put into action, influence to act **ant.** deter, hinder ♦ The waterwheel was *actuated* by the force of the current under pressure.

7. ADMONISH to advise; warn; dissuade **ant.** praise, acclaim, applaud ♦ Part of a teacher's job is to *admonish* a student whose performance is unsatisfactory.

8. ADULTERATE to mix, debase **ant.** purify, refine ♦ A painter may try to save money by *adulterating* his paint with quantities of water.

9. **AGAPE** openmouthed in surprise **ant.** blasé ♦ The youngster stood *agape* when he saw his new red truck.

10. **ALIENATE** to make unfriendly or hostile **ant.** unite, join ♦ A thoughtless remark can do more to *alienate* a sensitive friend than can an overt act of hostility.

11. **ALLEGE** to state, declare (without proof) **ant.** repudiate, deny ♦ The prosecutor *alleged* that the accused was guilty of embezzlement.

12. **ALTRUISTIC** unselfish, thoughtful **ant.** egoistic, selfish ♦ The *altruistic* landowner allowed the Hiking Club to build trails over his land so that others could enjoy its beauty.

13. **AMULET** something worn as a magic charm against evil or harm ♦ The witch doctor wore an *amulet* around his neck to protect him from evil spirits.

14. **ANNOTATE** to supply with notes, make comments on, explain ♦ In the *annotated* edition of *Hamlet*, the editor added an interesting note explaining the meaning of "coil."

15. **ANTIPATHY** a strong feeling of dislike **ant.** sympathy, affection ♦ The people of the United States have always had a strong feeling of *antipathy* for poverty.

16. **APATHETIC** indifferent, lacking feeling **ant.** alert, awakened, watchful ♦ So long as the public remains *apathetic*, gangs will roam the streets and molest citizens while passers-by hurry along.

17. **APPEASE** to satisfy, quiet, pacify **ant.** aggravate, annoy ♦ The mother tried to *appease* her son by promising to take him to the zoo later in the day.

18. **APPROBATION** approval, praise **ant.** condemnation ♦ The President's speech won the immediate *approbation* of the leaders in his party.

19. **ARDENT** eager, enthusiastic **ant.** apathetic, cool ♦ Peter is such an *ardent* Yankee fan that he knows the life history of every man who has ever played on that team.

20. **ARIA** a melody usually for a soloist with accompaniment ♦ Rise Stevens received a standing ovation for her rendition of that *aria!*

21. ARTLESS lacking skill; natural; without trickery **ant.** artful, crafty, cunning ♦ Not suspecting a trap, we fell for his seemingly *artless* request for advice.

22. ASPIRE to be ambitious, seek **ant.** stoop, grovel ♦ How long have I *aspired* to no avail to reach success!

23. ATONE to repent ♦ How can he expect me to *atone* for an act that I did not commit?

24. ATTRITION wear due to friction or rubbing **ant.** increase, enlargement ♦ How many years of constant *attrition* will reduce pebbles in a stream to sand?

25. AUGUR to predict from omens, foretell ♦ To the superstitious, even a flight of birds can *augur* good or ill.

26. AVARICE greed **ant.** generosity, extravagance ♦ He is so consumed by *avarice* that he forced his dearest friend into bankruptcy in order to increase his own wealth!

27. AVID very eager, greedy **ant.** indifferent, unwilling ♦ Edna has such an *avid* thirst for knowledge that all her spare moments are devoted to reading.

28. AXIOMATIC self-evident, generally accepted ♦ That personal happiness cannot be based on the misery of others is accepted as *axiomatic* by most people.

29. BALUSTRADE a handrail with balusters on a stairway or balcony ♦ She made her grand entrance from the top of the stairs with one hand on the *balustrade*.

30. BARB a sharp point projecting backward, as on an arrowhead or fishhook; one of the growths from the shaft of a feather ♦ Jerry filed the *barbs* off the tip of the hook so that he would not injure any fish he caught.

31. BARRISTER in England, one permitted to present a case in court; in the United States, an attorney ♦ The solicitor recommended the *barrister* who would present our case in court.

Second Day

1. BELLICOSE warlike, quarrelsome **ant.** peaceful, pacific ♦ The intoxicated man was in such a *bellicose* mood that he was put into a cell to keep him from harming others.

2. **BENIGHTED** overcome or surrounded by darkness; ignorant **ant.** enlightened ♦ The *benighted* peasants of the Middle Ages were very superstitious.

3. **BIAS** a slanting or oblique line; prejudice, partiality ♦ When material is cut on a *bias*, the pair of scissors snips diagonally across the weave.

4. **BILIOUS** having too much bile; bad-tempered, cross **ant.** amiable, good-natured ♦ I cringe every time the *bilious* old man shouts my name!

5. **BLASPHEMOUS** positively irreverent, profane, impious ♦ The villagers ostracized the shepherd for his *blasphemous* utterances in church.

6. **BOGUS** spurious, counterfeit **ant.** real, genuine ♦ The FBI warned the merchants in the area to be on the lookout for checks issued by the *bogus* count.

7. **BOOR** a rough, rustic person; a rude, awkward, ill-mannered individual **ant.** gentleman ♦ He is such a *boor* that he does not even realize how much he spoils with his loudmouthed quarreling and disregard of the rights of others.

8. **BRAVADO** a pretense of bravery, defiantly reckless action **ant.** modesty, shyness ♦ His offer to assist us was more out of *bravado* than the desire to see justice done.

9. **BRAZEN** of or like brass; harsh and piercing; shameless; to behave with an impudent swagger **ant.** bashful, shy ♦ The *brazen* thief had offered to sell us our own clothing at half price!

10. **BUMPTIOUS** self-assertive, disagreeably conceited, arrogant **ant.** modest ♦ The *bumptious* youth so antagonized the group with his acts of selfishness that no one offered him friendship.

11. **BURLY** big and strong, husky **ant.** lank, lean, skinny ♦ The *burly* wrestler pinned his weaker opponent down on the mat.

12. **CAJOLE** to coax or persuade with flattery ♦ The nurse tried to *cajole* the child into eating and promised to tell him a story during the meal.

13. **CANT** a hypocritical speech; terms used by some particular group; insincere, trite talk ♦ The man infuriated the crowd with his *cant* against democracy.

14. **CAPRICIOUS** inclined to change abruptly and unreasonably, whimsical; faultfinding   **ant.** steadfast, faithful   ♦ The *capricious* director was so unpredictable that the actors found themselves ever unable to please him.

15. **CARICATURE** a picture or description that exaggerates a person's peculiarities or traits; to draw such a picture   ♦ The *caricatures* of Winston Churchill always stressed the cigar in a pudgy hand.

16. **CASTIGATE** to punish, chastise   **ant.** reward, praise ♦ The editors *castigated* the Senator in the pages of their journals for his attack on their stand.

17. **CATHOLIC** universal, general, liberal   **ant.** narrow, provincial, parochial ♦ Lucy's taste in poetry is *catholic;* she enjoys good poetry whether it is modern or not.

18. **CHAFE** to rub so as to make warm; make sore by rubbing; be angry or irritable; an injury caused by friction ♦ The rough wool of the scarf so *chafed* his neck that he had to apply an ointment to the irritated area.
chafe at the bit—to be impatient

19. **CHARY** cautious, careful   **ant.** reckless, careless ♦ The burnt child will be *chary* of fires.

20. **CHURLISH** ungracious, surly, ill-mannered, crude   **ant.** courtly, civil, polite ♦ The *churlish* remarks hurled at the speaker made him sense how much the group despised him.

21. **CIRCUMVENT** to get the better of, outwit; surround   **ant.** promote, advance ♦ That one remark that the plotter had carelessly let slip by enabled the warden to *circumvent* the planned escape.

22. **CLEMENCY** mercy, mildness   **ant.** rigor, severity, harshness ♦ The lawyer asked the judge to show *clemency* for his client because of his youth.

23. **CLICHÉ** a trite or hackneyed phrase or literary expression ♦ Any clever or apt phrase can become a *cliché* if it is used too often or given too many applications.

24. **COGENT** clear and forceful, convincing   **ant.** weak, ineffectual ♦ The lawyer's *cogent* arguments convinced the jury of his client's innocence.

25. COLLUSION a secret agreement for a fraudulent or evil purpose ♦ The judge is investigating the charge that the divorce was obtained by the *collusion* of the husband and his wife.

26. COMELY of pleasing person and manner, attractive, proper **ant.** ugly, homely, plain ♦ Helen was chosen to head the reception committee because of her *comely* appearance and tactful manner.

27. COMPLEMENT that which completes; the whole personnel of a vessel ♦ The ship had been so understaffed that twelve men had to be added to its *complement*.

28. CONCILIATE to win the favor or good opinion of, soothe **ant.** antagonize, incite ♦ After the quarrel, Alice tried to *conciliate* Jerry with a present.

29. CONCOCT to cook things together, prepare by mixing; devise, as a plan or scheme ♦ The woman *concocted* a new dish made out of tuna fish and rice.

30. CONCUR to coincide, unite in expression of opinion or in action, agree **ant.** disagree, fight ♦ Several opposing forces *concurred* in bringing about the rise of Adolph Hitler.

31. CONSECRATE to set apart as sacred, dedicate to God **ant.** desecrate, profane, violate ♦ Many of the executives of the UN have *consecrated* their lives to the betterment of mankind.

32. CONTENTIOUS quarrelsome **ant.** peaceable, obliging ♦ He is so *contentious* that I am tired of his constant search for a quarrel.

Third Day

1. CONTRABAND goods forbidden by law to be exported or imported, smuggled merchandise ♦ The Coast Guard seized the shipment of *contraband* that had been smuggled into the country.

2. CONVIVIAL pertaining to a feast, festive, gay, sociable **ant.** reserved, serious ♦ In the *convivial* atmosphere of the country club, Allison threw off his cares and became a lively participant.

3. CORPULENT fat **ant.** lean ♦ Mr. Five-by-five is a short, *corpulent* person.

4. COVENANT an agreement formally made; to make a formal agreement ♦ It is unlawful for a deed to contain a *covenant* restricting the sale of property to people of a specific race or creed.

5. COWER to sink down, trembling with fear, cringe ♦ The frightened child *cowered* at the sight of the stick in the bully's hand.

6. CRAVEN a coward; cowardly, base   **ant.** brave ♦ How can he live with such a *craven* fear of others?

7. CRITERION a standard of criticism or judgment ♦ What *criterion* do you use to judge the sincerity of others?

8. CURRY a spice; to comb; dress leather; seek or gain by flattery ♦ None of your soft words will ever *curry* one bit of favor from me!

9. CURTAIL to shorten, abridge   **ant.** prolong, extend ♦ He had to *curtail* his extracurricular activities to catch up with his homework.

10. DAUNT to frighten, intimidate, horrify   **ant.** encourage, rally ♦ The perils of the mountain did not *daunt* the mountain climber.

11. DEBASE to lessen the value of, degrade   **ant.** elevate, improve ♦ Should television programs that *debase* the literary taste of the public be kept off the air?

12. DEFAMATION slander, libel   **ant.** praise ♦ He sued the newspaper columnist for *defamation* of character.

13. DEFRAY to pay the costs or expenses   **ant.** disown, disavow ♦ He had to raise his price in order to *defray* the costs of advertising.

14. DEFUNCT dead, extinct   **ant.** alive, extant ♦ The stock of the *defunct* company was worthless.

15. DELINEATE to trace the outline of; describe in words ♦ The President went to the people to *delineate* his position on the crucial issue.

16. DEMISE death   **ant.** birth ♦ The *demise* of the popular leader was a great shock to his followers.

17. DEPREDATION an act of plundering, robbery ♦ The *depredations* of the crooked politicians brought the town to bankruptcy.

18. DERIDE to ridicule, taunt   **ant.** encourage, comfort ♦ The girl *derided* every attempt by her brother to prove his ability as a musician.

19. **DESECRATE** to treat or use without respect ♦ The barbarians *desecrated* places of worship by using them as stables and barns.

20. **DIABOLICAL** very cruel or wicked, devilish **ant.** angelic ♦ The sadist dreamed up *diabolical* methods of torture for his victims.

21. **DIADEM** a crown, an ornamental band of cloth that used to be worn as a crown ♦ Miss America wore a diamond *diadem* at her "coronation."

22. **DIFFIDENT** lacking in self-confidence, timid **ant.** brazen, confident ♦ The *diffident* boy was unwilling to speak from the stage.

23. **DILEMMA** a situation causing one to choose between two evils, a difficult choice ♦ How do you solve the *dilemma* of whether to cheat on a test or take the chance of failing?

24. **DISCERNIBLE** capable of being seen clearly **ant.** invisible ♦ The difference between the forgery and the original was not *discernible* to the eye of the dealer.

25. **DISPARAGE** to belittle, discredit **ant.** praise, acclaim ♦ The critic *disparaged* the novel by saying that it was good—for a first attempt.

26. **DISPARATE** different, unlike **ant.** comparable, similar ♦ Because of the *disparate* cultures from which they came, the two people found it difficult to adjust to each other.

27. **DISSOLUTE** living an evil life, immoral ♦ Soon even the *dissolute* life of a playboy offered him no escape from his fears.

28. **DIURNAL** daily, belonging to the daytime; lasting a day **ant.** nocturnal ♦ How many years has the Earth rolled around in its *diurnal* course?

29. **DOGGED** stubborn, persistent, determined **ant.** undecided, faltering ♦ With *dogged* determination to pass, the freshman studied way into the night.

30. **DOGMATIC** doctrinal, positive; asserting opinions as if one were the highest authority; asserted without proof **ant.** uncertain, doubtful ♦ His opponents were reluctant to disagree with the man because he was so *dogmatic* in his assertions.

31. **DORMANT** sleeping, inactive **ant.** active ♦ The volcano remained *dormant* for ten years before becoming active again.

Fourth Day

1. DROSS waste material, rubbish; the waste that comes to the surface of melting metals ♦ All is *dross* if my efforts rob me of the respect of family and friends.

2. EGREGIOUS remarkably bad ♦ His *egregious* blunder caused the failure of our entire campaign.

3. ÉLAN enthusiasm, spirit   **ant.** dullness ♦ We all admire the *élan* with which the Three Musketeers approached the tasks set for them by the Queen.

4. ELUCIDATE to clarify, point out   **ant.** confuse ♦ When the student's answer was not clearly understood by the class, the teacher asked him to *elucidate*.

5. EMACIATED lean, wasting away of flesh   **ant.** well-fed ♦ When the prisoners were released from the concentration camps, their *emaciated* appearance was horrifying.

6. EMBELLISH to adorn, beautify   **ant.** simplify ♦ Why does he insist on *embellishing* his stories with so many really unnecessary details?

7. EMISSARY a go-between, representative ♦ A president often sends a member of his cabinet as an *emissary* to foreign nations.

8. ENAMORED in love, captivated   **ant.** repulsed ♦ Many young men are *enamored* with the idea of becoming well-known heroes.

9. ENHANCE to make more of or add to, intensify   **ant.** detract, lessen ♦ The woman's new hairdo seemed to *enhance* her appearance.

10. ENNUI boredom   **ant.** enthusiasm ♦ Tom's joy in worthwhile activities kept him from the *ennui* that consumed the less active patients in the convalescent home.

11. EPICURE one who is discriminating; one who is pleasure-loving about food ♦ An unusually fine restaurant will attract an *epicure* from anyplace in the world.

12. EQUABLE calm, little-changing   **ant.** changeable, varied ♦ The *equable* temperature of this island where it is 70° all year round makes it an ideal place in which to live.

13. EQUANIMITY composure, calmness of the mind ♦ The philosopher accepts his failures with great *equanimity*.

14. ESTRANGED made unfriendly, kept apart, alienated **ant.** attracted, allied ♦ The Civil War kept brothers *estranged*.

15. EUPHONIOUS having a pleasant sound **ant.** harsh, discordant ♦ He found the name Millicent Miller so *euphonious* that he repeated it aloud several times just to enjoy the pleasure of its sound.

16. EXEMPLARY serving as a model or example ♦ The judge acted in an *exemplary* fashion when he fined his own son for careless driving.

17. EXONERATE to free from blame, declare or prove blameless **ant.** accuse ♦ The jury *exonerated* the defendant and the judge set him free.

18. EXPEDITE to hurry along, accelerate **ant.** delay, retard ♦ Airplanes *expedite* travel to all parts of the world today.

19. EXPIATE to atone for, make amends for ♦ His pangs of conscience were so great that he cried in vain for a chance to *expiate* his crime.

20. EXTENUATE to weaken, partially excuse **ant.** blame ♦ What *extenuating* circumstances could there be to justify his cruel disregard of our welfare and safety?

21. EXTRANEOUS foreign, not belonging **ant.** inherent, relevant ♦ Water is rarely so pure that it is free from *extraneous* matter.

22. FABRICATE to build, devise, plan, invent **ant.** destroy ♦ Where shall I be able to find someone who can help me to disprove this horrid tale that he *fabricated?*

23. FEASIBLE possible, workable, plausible **ant.** impractical ♦ His plan seemed so *feasible* that we offered to assist in putting it into effect.

24. FELICITOUS appropriate, aptly expressed, well-worded **ant.** awkward, inappropriate ♦ She has the happy faculty of being able to express her thoughts in remarks so *felicitous* that she is constantly being quoted.

25. FIASCO a failure, breakdown   ant. success ♦ The Bay of Pigs invasion ended in a *fiasco*, destroying all hope of liberating Cuba.

26. FLAIL to beat, thrash; swing aimlessly; an instrument used for threshing ♦ In vain did the victim *flail* the surface of the mud with his hands as he was slowly sucked under.

27. FLOTSAM parts of a wreck found floating on water ♦ The waters of the nearby beach were filled with *flotsam*, the remains of the fishing fleet destroyed by the tidal wave.

28. FOMENT to promote, foster; stir up, arouse   ant. quell, suppress, restrain ♦ He tried to *foment* trouble among the crew.

29. FORESTALL to anticipate, prevent by doing something beforehand ♦ To *forestall* criticism, he wrote a long note to justify his actions.

30. FRAUGHT loaded, filled   ant. empty ♦ The situation is *fraught* with possibilities for the ambitious man who is willing to take risks.

31. FRESHET a flood caused by rain or melted snow, a rushing of water ♦ The western stream bed, dry and rocky minutes before, now directed the *freshet* that threatened to destroy all in its path.

32. FROWSY dirty, messy, untidy   ant. neat, clean, tidy ♦ The *frowsy* woman did not seem overwhelmed by the lack of cleanliness and neatness in the cabin she and her children called home.

Fifth Day

1. FURTIVE stealthy, clandestine, sly   ant. open ♦ A *furtive* glance showed that no one was watching him.

2. GALA festive, happy   ant. sad ♦ The wedding was a *gala* affair.

3. GARNER to gather, store   ant. scatter, discard ♦ The farmer *garners* the wheat at harvest time.

4. GAUNT thin, scraggly; looking grim, desolate   ant. stout, husky ♦ After a long winter of scant supplies, the *gaunt* survivors were overjoyed at the sight of the feast spread before them.

5. GERIATRICS that phase of medicine dealing with the elderly   ant. pediatrics ♦ The doctor decided to study *geriatrics* as a specialty in order to better understand the process of aging.

6. **GIBBET** a gallows ♦ The man was hanged from the *gibbet* set in the public square for all to see.

7. **GLEAN** to gather little by little ♦ How can we *glean* the truth from such contradictory testimony?

8. **GLUTTON** a greedy eater ♦ The fat man released his frustrations by becoming a *glutton*—ever hungry and ever eating.

9. **GOURMET** someone who enjoys fine foods for their own sake ♦ The *gourmet* sampled each of the sauces with a deliberate, leisurely regard for the full values in each.

10. **GRAPHIC** vivid, pictorial, picturesque **ant.** vague ♦ He wrote a *graphic* description of the look on the face of a young child watching a clown at the circus.

11. **GRUELING** very tiring, tormenting, exhausting ♦ The ten-hour hike up Mount Marcy proved a *grueling* experience for those who were not in their top physical condition.

12. **HAGGARD** tired, exhausted **ant.** healthy, exuberant ♦ I shall never forget the *haggard* expression on the faces of the parents of the kidnapped child after their long hours of futile waiting.

13. **HALLOWED** sacred, honored as sacred **ant.** desecrated ♦ The President's speech referred to this ground as *hallowed* by the blood of those who died here defending our nation.

14. **HARROW** a heavy frame with teeth like a plow; to hurt, wound; to torment, vex **ant.** soothe ♦ Being locked in the cage with a rattlesnake was the most *harrowing* experience I ever had.

15. **HIBERNATE** to spend the winter sleeping ♦ The life processes seem to approach a halt when the bear *hibernates* in his winter cave.

16. **HISTRIONIC** dramatic, theatrical, melodramatic, artificial ♦ My sympathies were not aroused by her *histrionic* announcement of her great loss.

17. **HOLOCAUST** utter destruction by fire (esp. of animals or human beings), great destruction ♦ The man was sickened by the pictures he saw of the *holocaust* caused by one A-bomb exploded over the city.

18. **HOMAGE** reverence, respect ♦ Many people go to Arlington Cemetery to pay *homage* to our war dead.

19. HOVER to hang about; waver, be in an uncertain condition ◆ The helicopter *hovered* over the place where the boat had gone down.

20. HYPOTHETICAL assumed, of or involving a hypothesis **ant.** certain, proved ◆ The man used a *hypothetical* situation to illustrate his point.

21. IGNOBLE without honor, mean, base   **ant.** ennobled, refined, splendid ◆ He is fated to be remembered as the *ignoble* wretch who failed to deliver the message to Romeo.

22. IMMACULATE pure, without a spot   **ant.** impure, defiled ◆ She prides herself on keeping her kitchen so *immaculate* that even the dishes shine.

23. IMPASSE a deadlock, blind alley ◆ The *impasse* between labor and management was broken by the arbitrator.

24. IMPENITENT without regret, shame, or remorse; not penitent   **ant.** contrite ◆ The *impenitent* killer was led to the gallows still shouting that he had no regrets for what he had done.

25. IMPLACABLE unyielding, unrelenting, not to be appeased **ant.** lenient, tolerant ◆ Ambition, unless controlled, can be an *implacable* force leading to self-destruction.

26. IMPUTE to attribute, ascribe, charge   **ant.** defend, justify ◆ I still cannot understand how you can *impute* such base motives to me!

27. INCARCERATE to imprison   **ant.** liberate ◆ Unless he can raise the money for bail, he will be *incarcerated* until the trial.

28. INCESSANT continual, ceaseless, unending   **ant.** intermittent, occasional ◆ The *incessant* warning blasts from the foghorns of the tugs in the thick fog kept Henry awake for hours.

29. INCLEMENT rough, stormy, harsh   **ant.** pleasant, mild ◆ The *inclement* weather caused us to postpone the picnic to another day.

30. INCREDULOUS skeptical, doubting   **ant.** believing, accepting ◆ Children today are *incredulous* about wizards and goblins.

31. INDEFATIGABLE untiring ◆ The *indefatigable* fingers of the typist continued to press out the finished copy hour after hour.

32. **INDUBITABLE** certain, unquestionable **ant.** questionable, doubtful ♦ Lowered grades are the *indubitable* results of loss of determination or interest.

Sixth Day

1. **INFAMOUS** known to be very wicked, shameful, corrupt; notorious **ant.** virtuous ♦ Benedict Arnold is *infamous* for his treachery.

2. **INGENIOUS** clever, inventive; cleverly planned and made **ant.** unskillful, incompetent ♦ When will the *ingenious* minds that created the H-bomb discover ways of controlling its destructive powers?

3. **INIMICAL** unfriendly, hostile; harmful ♦ I am *inimical* to any organization that favors racial or religious inequality.

4. **INNOCUOUS** harmless **ant.** injurious ♦ His remark seemed so *innocuous* that I was astonished by her angry reply.

5. **INSIPID** without taste or flavor; dull, colorless **ant.** tasty, pungent; lively, interesting ♦ The *insipid* remarks of the visitor infuriated the guide into silence.

6. **INTANGIBLE** not capable of being touched; not grasped by the mind **ant.** perceptible ♦ One of the *intangible* assets of a company is its good will.

7. **INTERMITTENT** occasional, periodic **ant.** continual, constant ♦ The silence on the battlefield was broken by *intermittent* sounds of gunfire.

8. **INTREPID** fearless, bold **ant.** timid ♦ The *intrepid* soldier crept through the enemy lines and singlehandedly blew up their supply depot.

9. **IOTA** a very small part or quantity ♦ There was not one *iota* of truth in the girl's story.

10. **IRIDESCENT** changing colors; displaying colors like those of the rainbow ♦ The *iridescent* dome of the soap bubble sailed majestically down the stream.

11. **JADED** worn out, weary; dulled from continual use **ant.** refreshed, renewed ♦ What could seem new or novel to the *jaded* eye of one who claims that he has seen all and been everywhere?

12. **JOCULAR** funny, joking　**ant.** grave, serious ♦ The *jocular* mood of the group resulted in slaughtered jokes and puns.

13. **JUXTAPOSE** to put side by side, place close together　**ant.** separate ♦ Even when the two signatures were *juxtaposed*, I could not tell my own from the forged copy.

14. **KNELL** the sound of a bell rung after death; a mournful sound; to ring slowly ♦ His refusal to join us rung the *knell* of our high hopes.

15. **LACKADAISICAL** pretending to be tired; apathetic, spiritless　**ant.** energetic, lively ♦ The bored students followed directions in so *lackadaisical* a manner that the teacher was certain that nothing was being done correctly.

16. **LARGESS** a generous gift, generous giving ♦ The disappointed waiter openly commented on the amount I had given him as compared with the *largess* of the spendthrift.

17. **LATENT** hidden, present but not active　**ant.** apparent, evident ♦ The *latent* intelligence of the boy showed up when he entered high school.

18. **LETHARGIC** very drowsy, sluggish　**ant.** lively, vigorous ♦ The injection had made the patient so *lethargic* that he answered the questions very slowly and in monosyllables.

19. **LIEU** place, stead ♦ The woman used margarine in *lieu* of butter.

20. **LITHE** supple, bending easily　**ant.** stiff, rigid, clumsy ♦ In order to be an acrobat, one must have a *lithe* body.

21. **LONGEVITY** long life ♦ Science has increased the *longevity* of modern man by many decades.

22. **LOQUACIOUS** fond of talking　**ant.** reticent, quiet ♦ The *loquacious* guide did not stop his chatter even when we were in transit from one room to another.

23. **LURID** sensational; ghastly; lighted up with a glare　**ant.** commonplace, ordinary ♦ Gossip spread all the *lurid* details of the scandal.

24. **MAELSTROM** a whirlpool of air, thought, or water ♦ A ship, once caught in a *maelstrom*, is soon sucked down to the bottom of the ocean.

25. **MAGNATE** a great or important man ♦ This powerful *magnate* owns several chemical plants.

26. **MALIGN** to blacken, besmirch, revile   **ant.** defend, praise ♦ The slanderers had so *maligned* his character that he moved out of the neighborhood.

27. **MARAUDER** a raider, plunderer ♦ The night *marauders* ransacked the entire village.

28. **MAUSOLEUM** a large, artistic tomb ♦ The family *mausoleum* contained the bodies of six generations.

29. **MEDIATE** to connect, be a go-between ♦ The delegate offered to *mediate* the dispute between the rival manufacturers.

30. **MELEE** a confused fight or battle ♦ The two street gangs met in a wild, free-swinging *melee* that was soon broken up by the police.

31. **MENDACIOUS** lying, false   **ant.** truthful, reliable ♦ One can never rely on the reports of a man who has been branded as *mendacious*.

32. **MENDICANT** begging; a beggar ♦ Allen suggested to the *mendicant* that he seek a job rather than alms.

Seventh Day

1. **METTLE** spirit, stamina, courage   **ant.** fear, timidity ♦ The coming battle will be the true test of the *mettle* of each soldier.

2. **MILITATE** to fight, act, operate (against) ♦ His inability to accept responsibility *militated* against his being appointed chairman of the committee.

3. **MISANTHROPE** a cynic; churl; one who hates mankind ♦ The *misanthrope*, rejecting society and all the works of man, became a hermit.

4. **MODULATE** to regulate, soften; change a key or tone **ant.** aggravate ♦ Alex *modulated* his voice when he realized that the person to whom he was addressing his complaint was the president of the company.

5. **MOLLIFY** to lessen, soften, appease, soothe   **ant.** enrage, incite ♦ Whenever she became angry, we could always *mollify* her with flattery.

6. **MORTIFY** to shame, humiliate; make gangrenous; punish by fasting ◆ The father was so *mortified* at the child's behavior that he slapped him in the presence of company.

7. **MURKY** obscure, dark, gloomy   **ant.** clear, bright ◆ The *murky* waters of the pool in the cave hid many fish in its depths.

8. **NAÏVETÉ** an unspoiled freshness, artlessness   **ant.** sophistication ◆ The young girl exhibited an honesty and a *naïveté* that were very becoming.

9. **NATAL** pertaining to one's birth ◆ Of course, your day of birth is your *natal* day.

10. **NEOPHYTE** a novice, beginner   **ant.** expert ◆ In order to speed up his initial learning period, the *neophyte* was assigned to assist the head laboratory aide.

11. **NONCOMMITTAL** not saying yes or no   **ant.** opinionated ◆ When asked his opinion, the commentator tried to be *noncommittal* and replied, "This really is a difficult situation!"

12. **NOSTALGIA** a homesickness, longing for something far away or long ago ◆ He was filled with *nostalgia* for the days long since past when he had parents to guide him.

13. **OAF** a nitwit, numbskull   **ant.** sage ◆ The boy's clumsy behavior made everyone think he was an *oaf*.

14. **OBSTREPEROUS** boisterous, noisy   **ant.** restrained, quiet ◆ The teacher threatened to send the *obstreperous* youngster to the dean unless he quieted down and behaved himself.

15. **OCCULT** secret, mysterious   **ant.** obvious ◆ One of the *occult* sciences is astrology.

16. **OMNIVOROUS** eating every kind of food—both meat and vegetable; fond of all things ◆ Paul is such an *omnivorous* reader that he reads even encyclopedias and telephone directories.

17. **ONSLAUGHT** a rigorous attack ◆ The Arabs' *onslaught* on the settlement was repulsed by its defenders.

18. **OPULENCE** wealth, abundance   **ant.** poverty, lack ◆ As evidence of his *opulence*, he had a different limousine for each day of the week.

19. **OSTENSIBLE** evident, apparent   **ant.** unknown, concealed ◆ The young man's *ostensible* purpose was to have an interview with the owner, but he really wanted to make the acquaintance of the owner's secretary.

20. **OVERT** obvious, open, evident **ant.** concealed ♦ The principal did not dare ignore this *overt* act of insubordination and fired the clerk right then and there.

21. **PALETTE** a board used by artists to hold paints ♦ An artist often mixes paints on his *palette*.

22. **PANACEA** a cure-all ♦ Will man ever discover a *panacea* that will cleanse us of fear and anger?

23. **PARADOX** a statement that seems to contradict itself; an enigma, inconsistency ♦ One of the *paradoxes* of art is that the old becomes new in the hands of genius.

24. **PARSIMONIOUS** stingy, tight **ant.** profuse, lavish ♦ Forced to live within the limits of his pension, he became so *parsimonious* that he devoted most of his energy to devising schemes for saving pennies.

25. **PEDANTIC** displaying excessive knowledge; tediously learned ♦ The man bored everyone with his *pedantic* interest in the minutest details of every issue.

26. **PERDITION** the loss of one's soul, damnation; hell; utter loss ♦ How many times in our prayers have we sent the tyrant's soul to *perdition!*

27. **PERPETRATE** to commit a bad or foolish deed ♦ Macbeth *perpetrated* the murder of the king in order to gain the throne for himself.

28. **PERTINACIOUS** resolute, tenacious, obstinate ♦ Once he sets his mind on doing something, he is as *pertinacious* as the proverbial bulldog.

29. **PETRIFY** to terrify; turn to stone ♦ The sight of the villain seemed to *petrify* the children.

30. **PHENOMENON** a fact that can be observed; something unusual ♦ An eclipse is one of Nature's many observable *phenomena*.

31. **PIQUANT** spirited, clever; sharp; spicy **ant.** tasteless; dull, bland ♦ The food was served with a *piquant* sauce to flavor it.

32. **PLATITUDE** a banality, cliché, dull remark ♦ The valedictorian did not miss even the *platitude* about graduation being both a beginning and an ending.

Eighth Day

1. PLAUSIBLE believable, credible, reasonable **ant.** impossible, unbelievable ♦ His arguments sounded so *plausible* that even I believed him.

2. PODIUM a platform, rostrum ♦ The conductor mounted the *podium* to lead the symphony orchestra.

3. POSTHUMOUS after death **ant.** prenatal ♦ The medal was a *posthumous* award given to the children and widow of the heroic policeman.

4. POTPOURRI a mixture, medley ♦ Lunch was a *potpourri* of odds and ends.

5. PRECEPT a doctrine, rule, law ♦ He followed all the *precepts* laid down by his predecessors but failed because he did not adjust to the changing times.

6. PREDATORY inclined to robbery or plundering; preying upon other animals **ant.** law-abiding ♦ *Predatory* bands roamed the countryside in search of unarmed travelers.

7. PRELATE a clergyman of high rank ♦ The *prelates* met to select a new leader for their religious group.

8. PRIMORDIAL primitive, original **ant.** modern, new ♦ The Earth as we know it evolved from a *primordial* gaseous mass.

9. PRODIGIOUS huge **ant.** minute ♦ The child had such a *prodigious* memory that he was able by the age of five to memorize the entire Old Testament.

10. PROMULGATE to announce officially, publish, spread far and wide **ant.** conceal, hide ♦ The dictator *promulgated* a series of decrees to prevent any further riots.

11. PROPITIATE to appease, conciliate **ant.** anger, aggravate ♦ The child tried to *propitiate*, with a gift of flowers, the gods who had brought so much rain to the village.

12. PROPRIETY fitness, proper behavior ♦ *Propriety* demands that a man open the door for a woman.

13. PROXY an agent, deputy ♦ I made Dave my *proxy* so that he could vote for me at the meeting.

14. PUNGENT tart, biting **ant.** sweet, bland ♦ The *pungent* odor of ammonia warned us that the refrigeration system was defective.

15. PUSILLANIMOUS timid, weak   **ant.** brave, courageous ♦ The *pusillanimous* wretch cringed in the corner when the bully threatened him.

16. QUAGMIRE soft, muddy ground ♦ During the rainy season, the roads turned into *quagmires*, seas of mud that marooned us in our huts.

17. QUALMS misgivings, doubts   **ant.** certainties ♦ We felt some *qualms* about swimming at the beach when the lifeguard was not on duty.

18. QUIRK a sudden twist; a peculiar mannerism ♦ What *quirk* of fate sent you down Kings Highway just when I needed you most!

19. QUIZZICAL odd, queer, comical, teasing   **ant.** serious ♦ The boy wore a *quizzical* smile as he listened to the endless lecture aimed at him for an offense he had not committed.

20. RAMPANT wild, violent, unruly   **ant.** calm, moderate ♦ Malaria ran *rampant* through the village and left death's calling card in every household.

21. RATIONALIZE to make excuses ♦ Instead of facing the facts and causes, Milton too often *rationalizes* and finds the fault in everyone but himself.

22. RECANT to recall, take back   **ant.** endorse, sanction ♦ The threat of torture forced Galileo to *recant* what his scientific research had told him was the truth.

23. RECTIFY to fix   **ant.** destroy, spoil ♦ It was not too difficult to *rectify* the bookkeeper's error.

24. REDRESS to repair, remedy, amend; a correction, reformation ♦ We shall seek *redress* in the law courts if they do not satisfy our demands at once.

25. RELEGATE to send down, banish   **ant.** call up, invite ♦ Because of his unreliability, he was *relegated* to a minor role in our subsequent productions.

26. REMUNERATION a reward, pay ♦ Your gratitude is the only *remuneration* that I shall want once the task is completed.

27. REPARTEE a witty reply; such replies collectively ♦ When Lloyd and Lou are at their best, the *repartee* is so brilliant that the very words seemed to glitter.

28. REPREHENSIBLE deserving blame ♦ Your cowardly silence at a time when you could have cleared my name was most *reprehensible*.

29. RESUSCITATE to revive, bring back to life   ant. kill ♦ The lifeguard tried in vain to *resuscitate* the victim of the drowning.

30. RETRIBUTION a deserved punishment ♦ Frieda was convinced that her loss of the money was in some way *retribution* for the unkindness she had shown us.

31. RETROACTIVE acting upon what is past   ant. postdated ♦ This *retroactive* law is so unfair; it applies to events that had occurred before the law was passed.

32. RIBALD mocking, indecent, offensive in speech, uncouth ant. refined, courteous ♦ The sailors passed the hours singing *ribald* songs.

Ninth Day

1. ROTE a repetition of forms or phrases, often without attention to their meaning ♦ He had learned the formulas by *rote*, and although he could repeat them correctly, he could not derive meaning from any of them.

2. RUDIMENTARY elementary, undeveloped ♦ The boy learned the *rudimentary* principles of flying in his first few lessons.

3. RUTHLESS cruel, brutal   ant. kind, tender ♦ The *ruthless* burglars took all the money in the orphanage.

4. SALIENT easily seen, prominent, outstanding, conspicuous ant. insignificant ♦ The automatic pilot was the one *salient* feature that attracted most attention to the model plane.

5. SARDONIC very sarcastic, heartless ♦ With a *sardonic* smile, he offered me the pen when it had run out of ink.

6. SCION a descendant, heir; a bud or branch cut for planting, a shoot or twig ♦ The *scion* of a prominent family was married to a debutante on Sunday.

7. SECULAR worldly, temporal ♦ The nun gave up *secular* life when she entered the convent.

8. SEDITIOUS stirring up discontent; disloyal, insubordinate **ant.** loyal, obedient ♦ Tom Paine's writings were *seditious* in that they encouraged rebellion against the British.

9. SENILITY old age, decrepitude, dotage **ant.** youth ♦ Suffering from *senility*, the old woman became very forgetful.

10. SERRATED notched like the edge of a saw **ant.** smooth ♦ Bread can be sliced more easily with a knife that has a *serrated* cutting edge.

11. SERVILE obsequious, fawning; of or pertaining to slaves **ant.** authoritative ♦ How can he enjoy the *servile* flattery of his underlings?

12. SIDEREAL pertaining to the stars ♦ A *sidereal* day is measured by the apparent motion of fixed stars.

13. SKITTISH easily frightened, nervous, changeable; coy ♦ The *skittish* horse reared when he heard the screech of brakes.

14. SLEAZY flimsy ♦ The *sleazy* material of the jacket soon ripped in several places.

15. SLUGGARD a lazy, sluggish person ♦ Be not the *sluggard* who is always almost but never quite the bird who gets the worm.

16. SONOROUS deep-toned, rich (in sound) ♦ The *sonorous* prose of the orator wove verbal images in praise of our defenders.

17. SORDID filthy, foul; mean, base ♦ The detective needed all the *sordid* details of the murder.

18. SPORADIC scattered, infrequent, isolated **ant.** clustered ♦ The silence was broken by *sporadic* gunfire in the distance.

19. STEADFAST firmly fixed, staunch **ant.** unreliable, capricious ♦ Canada is a *steadfast* ally of the United States.

20. STEALTHY done secretly, sly **ant.** open ♦ The boy tried to cheat by casting *stealthy* glances at his neighbor's paper.

21. STRIATED striped, streaked ♦ Rather than a solid color, she chose a gay, *striated* pattern with alternate, diagonal stripes of yellow and green.

22. STUPEFY to make stupid, dull, or senseless; astound, daze ♦ We stood in gawking silence, *stupefied* by the magnitude of the destruction caused by the blast.

23. SUBTERFUGE a trick or excuse used to escape something unpleasant ♦ An experienced supervisor can see through the various *subterfuges* others employ in order to avoid responsibility.

24. SUCCULENT juicy ♦ What is more tasty than a ripe, *succulent* peach?

25. SUPERFICIAL of the surface **ant.** deep, profound; radical ♦ The doctor dressed the man's *superficial* burns at the scene of the fire and then sent him home.

26. SUPINE lying flat on the back, reclining, prostrate **ant.** prone, erect ♦ The referee hovered over the *supine* boxer as he counted him out.

27. SURFEIT an excess or superabundance **ant.** scarcity ♦ One can get a stomach-ache from a *surfeit* of food.

28. SYLVAN of or in the woods ♦ The elves danced in their *sylvan* hiding place.

29. TACIT silent, implied, understood **ant.** explicit ♦ His willingness to lend us the car was *tacit* approval of our plan.

30. TACTILE having to do with touch ♦ The blind man had to rely almost completely on his *tactile* sense.

31. TANTAMOUNT equivalent **ant.** different ♦ Such an action would be *tantamount* to admitting defeat.

32. TEMPORIZE to evade immediate action; effect a compromise ♦ In an attempt to gain time, we *temporized* by agreeing to have a committee investigate his claims.

33. TERRESTRIAL of the earth; of land as opposed to water; living on the ground as opposed to in the air, water, or trees **ant.** celestial, heavenly ♦ None of the *terrestrial* animals could live on the airless surface of the moon.

Tenth Day

1. TERSE brief and to the point, compact **ant.** profuse ♦ His *terse* statement wasted no words in telling us just what his position was in this matter.

2. THERAPEUTIC having to do with the treating or curing of disease ♦ The *therapeutic* value of a drug can be determined only after long, exhaustive tests.

3. **TITANIC** of great size, strength, or power **ant.** minute, fragile ♦ Through the United Nations, the nations of the world have been making a *titanic* effort to erase disease from the face of the earth.

4. **TRANSCEND** to go beyond, surpass, excel ♦ Man's inability to control the passions of war fills me with a sorrow that *transcends* all other sorrows.

5. **TRANSGRESS** to sin, break a law; go beyond (limits) ♦ His boisterous remarks *transgress* the limits of good taste.

6. **TRAVAIL** to labor with pain, toil; suffer pangs of childbirth ♦ Through the long hours of *travail*, I never lost faith in our ability to accomplish our ultimate aim.

7. **TROTH** a promise, pledge; faithfulness, loyalty; truth ♦ The Knights of the Round Table pledged their *troth* to King Arthur.

8. **TRYST** an appointment to meet at a certain time and place; place of meeting ♦ Overlook Drive is the favorite *trysting* place for young couples.

9. **TURBID** muddy, thick, unclear **ant.** lucid, transparent ♦ Arnold spoke of the "*turbid* ebb and flow of human misery."

10. **TURBULENCE** a disorder, commotion **ant.** serenity ♦ The *turbulence* of the flooding waters filled the hearts of the onlookers with fear and dismay.

11. **TURGID** swollen, bloated; bombastic ♦ Living woody tissue is *turgid* with sap.

12. **UNBRIDLED** not having a bridle on; uncontrolled ♦ In an *unbridled* rage, the drunkard smashed all of the movable furniture.

13. **UNDULATE** to move in waves; have a wavy surface ♦ The *undulating* breezes made the tall grass roll and ripple.

14. **UNREMITTING** never stopping, maintaining steadily **ant.** intermittent ♦ The line soon began to weaken and stretch under the *unremitting* pressure to which we subjected it.

15. **URBAN** of or pertaining to cities or towns ♦ She was very unhappy with *urban* living since she had been brought up on a farm.

16. VACILLATE to waver in mind or opinion, fluctuate ♦ The President did not *vacillate* under the pressure of public opinion.

17. VALIDATE to make valid, confirm, support by authority **ant.** invalidate ♦ The woman waited impatiently for the official to *validate* her passport.

18. VENERABLE respected, sage, time-honored, worthy of reverence **ant.** inexperienced ♦ The *venerable* old man was the worthy leader of the community.

19. VERBIAGE the use of too many words; an abundance of useless words ♦ His message was so full of *verbiage* that we spent ten minutes in learning that he had said "Yes!"

20. VERBOSE wordy **ant.** terse, laconic ♦ His narrative contained many interesting asides, yet it was not *verbose*.

21. VERTIGO dizziness, giddiness ♦ Do you too suffer from *vertigo* when looking down from a great height?

22. VINDICTIVE bearing a grudge, given to or prompted by revenge ♦ His *vindictive* attempts to punish us for the supposed slight made me realize how bitter he was.

23. VISCOUS sticky, thick like syrup or glue ♦ The oil turned *viscous* as the temperature dropped.

24. VITIATE to spoil, render faulty; destroy the legal force of; debase **ant.** aid, improve ♦ Party jealousies *vitiated* our attempts to unseat the dictatorial district leader.

25. VITUPERATIVE bitterly abusive, reviling ♦ His *vituperative* attack filled with insulting references to his opponent was in very bad taste.

26. VOLUBLE having a great flow of words, garrulous **ant.** curt ♦ The more he drank, the more *voluble* he became and the more he embroidered the tale of his recent exploits.

27. VORACIOUS greedy in eating, ravenous ♦ Jerry is so *voracious* a reader that he spends a minimum of six hours a day with his beloved books.

28. WARY cautious, careful **ant.** careless, rash ♦ The child was taught to be *wary* of strangers.

29. WHEEDLE to persuade by flattery, coax ♦ The young girl tried to *wheedle* her father into giving her an increase in allowance.

30. WHIT a very small bit, smallest particle ♦ I am not a *whit* concerned about his whereabouts at present.

31. WONT accustomed; a custom or habit ♦ I was *wont* to rise at six o'clock every morning.

32. ZENITH the highest point; culmination **ant.** nadir ♦ When he was elected President of the United States, he reached the *zenith* of his political career.

Eleventh Day: First Lower-Junior List Practice Test

A. Antonyms

In the space provided, write the letter of the word that is most nearly opposite in meaning to the first word.

1. **ABOMINATE** (a) detest (b) love (c) destroy (d) create (e) snow   1. ....

2. **CHARY** (a) raw (b) burned (c) reckless (d) computed (e) known   2. ....

3. **CONCILIATE** (a) bury (b) loiter (c) organize (d) judge (e) antagonize   3. ....

4. **DORMANT** (a) sleeping (b) window (c) open (d) active (e) inert   4. ....

5. **EXONERATE** (a) accuse (b) weigh (c) flee (d) honor (e) disgruntle   5. ....

6. **PUNGENT** (a) bland (b) oriental (c) simple (d) undeveloped (e) tart   6. ....

7. **SUPERFICIAL** (a) exceptional (b) turgid (c) profound (d) therapeutic (e) dull   7. ....

8. **SUPINE** (a) odorous (b) prone (c) lethargic (d) secondary (e) excellent   8. ....

9. **LETHARGIC** (a) drowsy (b) sensitive (c) lively (d) bright (e) hurt   9. ....

10. **PUSILLANIMOUS** (a) courageous (b) strong (c) towering (d) lowly (e) honest   10. ....

11. **RECTIFY** (a) adjust (b) add (c) distrust (d) spoil (e) spell   11. ....

12. DOGGED   (a) canine   (b) faltering   (c) spirited
(d) willing   (e) cold   12. ....

13. COMELY   (a) opportune   (b) early   (c) detailed
(d) plain   (e) pleasant   13. ....

14. CASTIGATE   (a) reward   (b) imprison
(c) liberate   (d) accept   (e) reject   14. ....

15. ABSTEMIOUS   (a) athletic   (b) religious
(c) moderate   (d) impious   (e) uncontrolled   15. ....

16. ASPIRE   (a) control   (b) curse   (c) stoop
(d) explain   (e) call   16. ....

17. ENAMORED   (a) lovable   (b) repulsed
(c) extolled   (d) excited   (e) loved   17. ....

18. EQUABLE   (a) assuring   (b) insuring   (c) risky
(d) untold   (e) changeable   18. ....

19. JADED   (a) renewed   (b) satiated   (c) cheap
(d) adorned   (e) expensive   19. ....

20. NONCOMMITTAL   (a) innocent   (b) intelligent
(c) slow   (d) opinionated   (e) quiet   20. ....

21. BRAVADO   (a) courage   (b) cowardice
(c) modesty   (d) ignorance   (e) poverty   21. ....

22. TURBID   (a) twisted   (b) clear   (c) dry
(d) meddled   (e) sensational   22. ....

23. VERBOSE   (a) oral   (b) concise   (c) written
(d) understood   (e) open   23. ....

24. ZENITH   (a) pinnacle   (b) horizon   (c) base
(d) corporation   (e) visual   24. ....

25. PLAUSIBLE   (a) impossible   (b) crude   (c) greedy
(d) unselfish   (e) ordinary   25. ....

26. RECANT   (a) sing   (b) lecture   (c) listen
(d) describe   (e) admit   26. ....

27. RESUSCITATE   (a) acknowledge   (b) deny
(c) kill   (d) develop   (e) renounce   27. ....

28. RUTHLESS   (a) anonymous   (b) tender   (c) rich
(d) unfriendly   (e) stingy   28. ....

29. MENDACIOUS (a) veracious (b) stealing
(c) begging (d) sensible (e) understandable   29. ....

30. MODULATE (a) regulate (b) soften (c) excite
(d) aggravate (e) answer   30. ....

31. MOLLIFY (a) depart (b) help (c) hinder
(d) abet (e) anger   31. ....

32. OSTENSIBLE (a) witty (b) serious
(c) concealed (d) excellent (e) sharp   32. ....

33. LACKADAISICAL (a) wealthy (b) lively
(c) extant (d) talkative (e) capable   33. ....

34. SALIENT (a) trivial (b) stationary (c) stellar
(d) bland (e) delectable   34. ....

35. BILIOUS (a) sick (b) cross (c) crude
(d) elegant (e) good-natured   35. ....

B. Sentence Completion

In the space provided, write the letter of the word that best
completes the sentence.

36. The traitor attempted to .... dissension among the
soldiers so that they would not do their jobs with the precision
necessary for the success of the enterprise.
(a) juxtapose (b) foment (c) relegate (d) surfeit 36. ....

37. In .... of the assignment to be done by the other members
of the class, Margie was put in charge of the entertainment
committee.
(a) fulfillment (b) acceptance (c) lieu
(d) deference   37. ....

38. I often cannot tell the difference between the ...., with
its smudges and globs of variegated colors, and the finished
product that is supposed to grace the wall of a museum or home.
(a) palette (b) abstraction (c) barb (d) amulet 38. ....

39. In that he has been warned repeatedly that his actions have
endangered the safety of the other members of the group, I shall
have no .... about reporting him to the authorities the next
time he violates the waterfront regulations.
(a) desire (b) willingness (c) fears (d) qualms 39. ....

40. I become so impatient whenever Phyllis decides to .... the efforts of others who are courageous enough to be willing to try while she is just sitting back and criticizing!

(a) disparage   (b) glean   (c) praise   (d) mediate   40. ....

41. The .... parents of the injured youth visited him separately, and requested that the family doctor be kept fully informed of the boy's progress.

(a) estranged   (b) impenitent   (c) frantic
(d) indubitable   41. ....

42. The only way to .... arguments is to discuss long in advance with the entire group just what the problems to be faced are and what course of action should be assumed.

(a) settle   (b) forestall   (c) judge   (d) appease   42. ....

43. In vain did the old man seek some way of passing on to his children the invaluable bits of wisdom that he had .... through the years.

(a) alleged   (b) concocted   (c) abominated
(d) garnered   43. ....

44. The team of surgeons seemed .... as they progressed steadily, step by step, through the long and complicated procedures of the delicate operation.

(a) altruistic   (b) comely   (c) indefatigable
(d) furtive   44. ....

45. During the influenza epidemic, my mother insisted on my wearing around my neck a small bag filled with camphor as a(n) .... to protect me from the disease.

(a) approbation   (b) amulet   (c) medicine
(d) attrition   45. ....

46. The superior court ruled that the judge had been .... in favor of one of the witnesses, and therefore a new trial was ordered.

(a) avid   (b) axiomatic   (c) biased   (d) bellicose   46. ....

47. His willingness to meet people and talk with them did much to .... the reputation of the young singing star.

(a) chafe   (b) damage   (c) circumvent
(d) enhance   47. ....

48. The leaders of the party, certain that their favorite had the resilience and imagination to come out ahead, viewed with .... the obstacles that the opposition had placed in his path.

(a) alarm   (b) clemency   (c) equanimity
(d) collusion   48. ....

49. The blind .... pleading for alms outside the wall of the town had once been a powerful knight, but the infirmities of old age and the disloyalty of former friends had reduced him to the lowest level of existence.

(a) singer   (b) neophyte   (c) mendicant
(d) augur   49. ....

50. The arms of the helicopter .... the air in wide circles as the machine hovered over the tops of the trees.

(a) pushed   (b) imputed   (c) flailed   (d) sought   50. ....

C. Synonyms

In the space provided, write the letter of the word that is most nearly the same in meaning as the first word.

51. SCION   (a) eastern   (b) religious   (c) descendant
(d) prince   (e) parent   51. ....

52. REPREHENSIBLE   (a) blameworthy
(b) cowardly   (c) understanding   (d) dull
(e) captive   52. ....

53. PROPRIETY   (a) fitness   (b) ownership   (c) lease
(d) manner   (e) excellence   53. ....

54. PHENOMENON   (a) disaster   (b) good fortune
(c) science   (d) fast   (e) proof   54. ....

55. NATAL   (a) swimming   (b) marine   (c) birth
(d) culminating   (e) beginning   55. ....

56. MORTIFY   (a) stone   (b) humiliate   (c) harden
(d) fool   (e) hurt   56. ....

57. TACTILE   able to be   (a) seen   (b) touched
(c) heard   (d) hurt   (e) taught   57. ....

58. UNBRIDLED   (a) not controlled   (b) untrained
(c) understood   (d) stupid   (e) sharp   58. ....

59. URBAN   (a) singular   (b) musical
(c) municipal   (d) national   (e) universal   59. ....

60. VERBIAGE   (a) disease   (b) use of too many words
(c) aristocracy   (d) filled with useless details
(e) lack of value   60. ....

61. SYLVAN   (a) American   (b) Dutch   (c) peaceful
(d) forest   (e) old-fashioned   61. ....

62. TEMPORIZE (a) time (b) train (c) delude
(d) aid (e) delay   62. ....

63. SURFEIT (a) injure (b) excess (c) satisfy
(d) repair (e) retain   63. ....

64. MISANTHROPE (a) cynic (b) leader
(c) follower (d) optimist (e) student   64. ....

65. MILITATE (a) arm (b) defeat (c) oppose
(d) argue (e) strengthen   65. ....

66. IMPUTE (a) defend (b) consider (c) explain
(d) emphasize (e) charge   66. ....

67. HALLOWED (a) sacred (b) described
(c) praised (d) condemned (e) protected   67. ....

68. HARROW (a) educate (b) wound
(c) circumscribe (d) elevate (e) plan   68. ....

69. SONOROUS (a) rich (b) elderly (c) religious
(d) thin (e) audible   69. ....

70. TRANSGRESS (a) walk (b) sin (c) wander
(d) hope (e) injure   70. ....

71. TRAVAIL (a) visit (b) train (c) envisage
(d) toil (e) excite   71. ....

72. VITUPERATIVE (a) mild (b) talkative
(c) abusive (d) finicky (e) exacting   72. ....

73. STRIATED (a) striped (b) stained (c) muscular
(d) voluntary (e) involuntary   73. ....

74. STEALTHY (a) rich (b) sparse (c) open
(d) abandoned (e) sly   74. ....

75. GOURMET one who (a) eats much (b) eats little
(c) eats for enjoyment (d) prepares fancy dishes
(e) owns a restaurant   75. ....

76. GLUTTON one who (a) eats much (b) eats little
(c) eats for enjoyment (d) prepares fancy dishes
(e) owns a restaurant   76. ....

77. FRESHET (a) deodorant (b) flood (c) insult
(d) spring (e) mansion   77. ....

78. FLOTSAM (a) raft (b) ship (c) boat
(d) wreckage (e) booty   78. ....

79. EXPIATE (a) atone (b) maim (c) modulate
(d) mediate (e) suffer   79. ....

80. VERTIGO (a) truth (b) falsity (c) dizziness
(d) altitude (e) risk   80. ....

81. VINDICTIVE (a) losing (b) victorious
(c) narrating (d) vivid (e) vengeful   81. ....

82. TROTH (a) pledge (b) placement (c) marriage
(d) engagement (e) description   82. ....

83. SECULAR (a) clerical (b) worldly
(c) wise (d) sophisticated (e) political   83. ....

84. SARDONIC (a) foreign (b) clever (c) sarcastic
(d) understanding (e) genial   84. ....

85. ACCLIMATE (a) forecast (b) dress (c) develop
(d) accustom (e) acquire   85. ....

D. Analogies

In the space provided, write the letter of the set of words that best completes the analogy.

86. LITHE : ACROBAT :: (a) longevity : child
(b) experience : neophyte (c) obstreperous : enemy
(d) parsimonious : miser   86. ....

87. POTPOURRI : PODIUM :: (a) medley : platform
(b) speaker : actor (c) tune : speech (d) action :
noise   87. ....

88. SORDID : INCLEMENT :: (a) inexpensive : severe
(b) wholesome : pleasant (c) foul : weather (d) varied :
harsh   88. ....

89. AVARICE : AVID :: (a) food : grueling (b) whip :
flail (c) persistence : dogged (d) dilemma : decision 89. ....

90. DEFUNCT : DEMISE :: (a) noun : noun (b) verb :
verb (c) adjective : noun (d) adjective : adjective   90. ....

91. PANACEA : MENDICANT :: (a) medicine : lie
(b) cure : beggar (c) doctor : lawyer (d) indoors :
outdoors   91. ....

92. TURBID : MURKY :: (a) clear : unclear
(b) unclear : clear (c) clear : clear (d) unclear :
unclear   92. ....

93. LATENT : INNOCUOUS :: (a) evident : harmful
(b) hidden : injurious   (c) healthy : known   (d) apparent :
wholesome   93. ....

94. GLUTTON : GOURMET :: (a) favorable :
unfavorable   (b) unfavorable : favorable   (c) favorable :
favorable   (d) unfavorable : unfavorable   94. ....

95. EXPEDITE : DELAY :: (a) deride : journey
(b) delineate : book   (c) cower : execute   (d) extenuate :
blame   95. ....

96. EXPIATE : ATONE :: (a) forestall : prevent
(b) incarcerate : liberate   (c) infamous : virtuous
(d) ingenious : incompetent   96. ....

97. CORPULENT : EMACIATED :: (a) vitamins :
minerals   (b) healthy : ill   (c) fat : lean   (d) elephant :
giraffe   97. ....

98. PLATITUDE : PARADOX :: (a) clever : dull
(b) wordy : terse   (c) clear : confusing   (d) ancient :
modern   98. ....

99. SARDONIC : HEARTLESS :: (a) seditious : loyal
(b) supine : prone   (c) viscous : watery   (d) mendacious :
false   99. ....

100. ZENITH : ACME :: (a) second : first   (b) last : first
(c) first : second   (d) first : first   100. ....

Answer Key

A. Antonyms

1. (b)	8. (b)	15. (e)	22. (b)	29. (a)
2. (c)	9. (c)	16. (c)	23. (b)	30. (d)
3. (e)	10. (a)	17. (b)	24. (c)	31. (e)
4. (d)	11. (d)	18. (e)	25. (a)	32. (c)
5. (a)	12. (b)	19. (a)	26. (e)	33. (b)
6. (a)	13. (d)	20. (d)	27. (c)	34. (a)
7. (c)	14. (a)	21. (c)	28. (b)	35. (e)

B. Sentence Completion

36. (b)	39. (d)	42. (b)	45. (b)	48. (c)
37. (c)	40. (a)	43. (d)	46. (c)	49. (c)
38. (a)	41. (a)	44. (c)	47. (d)	50. (a)

C. Synonyms

51. (c)	58. (a)	65. (c)	72. (c)	79. (a)
52. (a)	59. (c)	66. (e)	73. (a)	80. (c)
53. (a)	60. (b)	67. (a)	74. (e)	81. (e)
54. (d)	61. (d)	68. (b)	75. (c)	82. (a)
55. (c)	62. (e)	69. (a)	76. (a)	83. (b)
56. (b)	63. (b)	70. (b)	77. (b)	84. (c)
57. (b)	64. (a)	71. (d)	78. (d)	85. (d)

D. Analogies

86. (d)	89. (c)	92. (d)	95. (d)	98. (c)
87. (a)	90. (c)	93. (a)	96. (b)	99. (d)
88. (b)	91. (b)	94. (b)	97. (c)	100. (d)

My Score: Number Right............ Number Wrong............

Clinch by Checking

The purpose of this test was to help you discover which of the words in the Lower-Junior List you must concentrate on in order to achieve 100% mastery. Since the list is arranged in alphabetical order, you should have no difficulty in checking back. Mark the words that you missed; these are the ones that should be studied in your next session. Once you have them under control, then you are ready for the Second Lower-Junior List Practice Test.

Twelfth Day: Second Lower-Junior List Practice Test

A. Sentence Completion

In the space provided, write the letter of the word that best completes the sentence.

1. What child has not thrilled to the idea of sliding down the .... in an old-fashioned mansion with a central staircase!
(a) gibbet   (b) maelstrom   (c) balustrade
(d) melee

1. ....

2. Harold controlled his temper when he realized that the .... that George was throwing at him were the result of a temporary jealousy that would subside once George analyzed his own feelings.
(a) magnates   (b) barbs   (c) marauder
(d) mausoleum   2. ....

3. How can he dare claim that there was .... of character in remarks that were based on provable facts?
(a) defamation   (b) phenomenon   (c) perdition
(d) propriety   3. ....

4. Men of good will in generations to come will wonder how the rest of the world countenanced Hitler's .... plans to murder millions of women and children.
(a) pungent   (b) sonorous   (c) rudimentary
(d) diabolical   4. ....

5. It is a restaurant that attracts the .... rather than the glutton, for, while the portions are small, each dish is prepared to exacting standards set by its famous chef.
(a) epicure   (b) fiasco   (c) steadfast   (d) flotsam   5. ....

6. If there are any points that are not crystal clear to you, now is the time for you to demand that we ....
(a) modulate   (b) elucidate   (c) flail   (d) curtail   6. ....

7. After fourteen hours of fruitless search in the sub-zero cold near the summit of Prospect Mountain, the .... volunteers returned to the headquarters of the rescue team.
(a) emaciated   (b) obstreperous   (c) haggard
(d) parsimonious   7. ....

8. His dream was so vivid that he screamed aloud as the row-boat raced into the ever-narrowing circles of the .... that would eventually suck the boat under.
(a) maelstrom   (b) onslaught   (c) opulence
(d) palette   8. ....

9. Only a madman would attempt to .... such a fraud in this day and age and expect to be able to enjoy the fruits of his trickery.
(a) cajole   (b) concur   (c) brazen   (d) perpetrate   9. ....

10. The .... look on the faces of the onlookers told the youngster that they had enjoyed and not resented his little act.
(a) sardonic   (b) titanic   (c) quizzical
(d) reprehensible   10. ....

11. If he sincerely feels that he does not want to join us in this enterprise, then I for one refuse to pressure or .... him into becoming part of the group.
(a) exonerate   (b) castigate   (c) cajole   (d) cower   11. ....

12. The dean threatened to .... all athletic activities in the school if the students persisted in their unsportsmanlike activities during games with New Utrecht, Midwood's traditional rival.
(a) curtail   (b) hibernate   (c) concoct
(d) propitiate   12. ....

13. If there is anything that I can do to .... your request for a leave of absence, please do not hesitate to ask me.
(a) abominate   (b) admonish   (c) augur
(d) expedite   13. ....

14. Three days of steady rain turned the valley into a .... that held fast to any vehicle that the High Command was foolish enough to order into action.
(a) flotsam   (b) quagmire   (c) gibbet
(d) mausoleum   14. ....

15. Of course your .... will be commensurate with the increased responsibility that you will assume once you are in charge of the entire project.
(a) remuneration   (b) flotsam   (c) repartee
(d) defamation   15. ....

B. Analogies

In the space provided, write the letter of the set of words that best completes the analogy.

16. NONCOMMITTAL : OPINIONATED ::
(a) pertinacious : resolute   (b) plausible : impossible
(c) primordial : primate   (d) succulent : edible   16. ....

17. TITANIC : SIZE :: (a) venerable : age   (b) verbiage : grammar   (c) salient : weight   (d) retroactive : past   17. ....

18. TRYST : TROTH :: (a) money : promise   (b) time : place   (c) place : pledge   (d) conscience : awareness   18. ....

19. PERPETRATE : VALIDATE :: (a) commit : confirm   (b) deed : mortgage   (c) outlast : end
(d) develop : destroy   19. ....

20. LOQUACIOUS : VOLUBLE :: (a) much : little
(b) too little : too much   (c) too much : too little
(d) too much : too much   20. ....

21. EGREGIOUS : INFAMOUS :: (a) good : good
(b) bad : bad   (c) bad : good   (d) good : bad   21. ....

22. GLEAN : HOLOCAUST :: (a) little : much
(b) quick : slow   (c) before : after   (d) good fortune :
disaster   22. ....

23. FROWSY : LETHARGIC :: (a) sluggish : messy
(b) neat : drowsy   (c) trim : lively   (d) dress : color   23. ....

24. DEBASE : CARICATURE :: (a) less : more
(b) over : above   (c) insult : sarcasm   (d) foreign :
artistic   24. ....

25. EUPHONIOUS : GAUNT :: (a) hearing : sound
(b) tall : thin   (c) sound : sight   (d) feel : sight   25. ....

26. LURID : MALIGN :: (a) defend : sensational
(b) startling : blacken   (c) lively : revile   (d) ghastly :
sarcasm   26. ....

27. OSTENSIBLE : OVERT :: (a) exceptional : usual
(b) fiery : ardent   (c) evident : obvious   (d) concealed :
open   27. ....

28. GIBBET : DIADEM :: (a) criminal : queen
(b) judge : ruler   (c) male : female   (d) rope : band   28. ....

29. BOGUS : ALTRUISTIC :: (a) spurious : unselfish
(b) count : saint   (c) one : many   (d) counterfeit :
egoistic   29. ....

30. DAUNT : INTIMIDATE :: (a) defray : fight
(b) desecrate : respect   (c) flail : thrash   (d) hibernate :
winterize   30. ....

31. IMPENITENT : IMPLACABLE :: (a) willing : unwilling   (b) soft : hard   (c) unwilling : willing   (d) hard :
hard   31. ....

32. STEALTHY : SUPERFICIAL :: (a) open : revealed
(b) sly : profound   (c) open : deep   (d) thief : actor   32. ....

33. TEMPORIZE : COMPROMISE :: (a) wont : activity
(b) wheedle : flattery   (c) stupefy : dazzle   (d) militate :
uniform   33. ....

34. TANTAMOUNT : SERVILE :: (a) equal : unequal
(b) equal : equal   (c) unequal : unequal   (d) unequal :
equal   34. ....

35. PRECEPT : PRELATE :: (a) instructor : instruction
(b) law : student   (c) doctrine : official   (d) political :
religious   35. ....

C. Antonyms

In the space provided, write the letter of the word that is most
nearly opposite in meaning to the first word.

36. ACCORD   (a) loosen   (b) tight   (c) argue
(d) distill   (e) expel   36. ....

37. BOGUS   (a) genuine   (b) dry   (c) arid   (d) fertile
(e) poor   37. ....

38. FRAUGHT   (a) perilous   (b) sagacious   (c) safe
(d) empty   (e) wise   38. ....

39. GARNER   (a) disturb   (b) store   (c) elect
(d) select   (e) scatter   39. ....

40. GRAPHIC   (a) pictorial   (b) lifeless   (c) educated
(d) wishful   (e) drawn   40. ....

41. PARSIMONIOUS   (a) lavish   (b) poor
(c) impious   (d) supine   (e) pusillanimous   41. ....

42. PREDATORY   (a) lethargic   (b) superficial
(c) law-abiding   (d) well-developed   (e) exact   42. ....

43. VENERABLE   (a) respectable   (b) inexperienced
(c) lovable   (d) ugly   (e) dead   43. ....

44. VOLUBLE   (a) roomy   (b) narrow   (c) dormant
(d) curt   (e) talkative   44. ....

45. WARY   (a) chary   (b) clever   (c) righteous
(d) wrong   (e) rash   45. ....

46. PROPITIATE   (a) pray   (b) anger   (c) appeal
(d) deny   (e) excel   46. ....

47. PROMULGATE   (a) punish   (b) govern
(c) conceal   (d) sing   (e) refuse   47. ....

48. OCCULT   (a) obvious   (b) ceremonial
(c) mystical   (d) wordy   (e) western   48. ....

49. JOCULAR   (a) noisy   (b) loud   (c) soft
(d) pungent   (e) grave   49. ....

50. FELICITOUS   (a) sad   (b) clumsy   (c) foolish
(d) stupid   (e) safe   50. ....

51. EXTENUATE   (a) blame   (b) thicken   (c) excuse
(d) organize   (e) order   51. ....

52. DOGMATIC   (a) victorious   (b) defeated
(c) angelic   (d) loud   (e) doubtful   52. ....

53. EGREGIOUS   (a) erroneous   (b) correct
(c) notable   (d) legal   (e) awful   53. ....

54. FIASCO   (a) felonious   (b) success   (c) foreigner
(d) peace   (e) fight   54. ....

55. BRAVADO   (a) coward   (b) slipperiness
(c) modesty   (d) bullheaded   (e) shame   55. ....

56. IGNOBLE   (a) splendid   (b) common
(c) conservative   (d) democratic   (e) coming   56. ....

57. LOQUACIOUS   (a) decent   (b) reticent
(c) constructive   (d) joyful   (e) serious   57. ....

58. PIQUANT   (a) selected   (b) common   (c) spicy
(d) tasteless   (e) stocky   58. ....

59. RETROACTIVE   (a) sluggish   (b) recorded
(c) postdated   (d) sterile   (e) passive   59. ....

60. TACIT   (a) impolite   (b) untouchable
(c) additional   (d) explicit   (e) written   60. ....

61. IMMACULATE   (a) orderly   (b) impure
(c) modest   (d) wild   (e) unknown   61. ....

62. IMPENITENT   (a) free   (b) imprisoned
(c) registered   (d) on trial   (e) remorseful   62. ....

63. INCESSANT   (a) quiet   (b) occasional   (c) dull
(d) disorderly   (e) aural   63. ....

64. **LATENT** (a) evident (b) old (c) paint
(d) removable (e) flat   64. ....

65. **MURKY** (a) obscure (b) stormy (c) peaceful
(d) clear (e) deep   65. ....

66. **NEOPHYTE** (a) novice (b) customer (c) animal
(d) article for sale (e) expert   66. ....

67. **PRODIGIOUS** (a) wonderful (b) ordinary
(c) small (d) menacing (e) abiding   67. ....

68. **SEDITIOUS** (a) foreign (b) loyal (c) ancient
(d) revolutionary (e) British   68. ....

69. **SPORADIC** (a) flying (b) stationary (c) grouped
(d) isolated (e) dangerous   69. ....

70. **STEADFAST** (a) sloping (b) muddy (c) tall
(d) unreliable (e) wasted   70. ....

D. Synonyms

In the space provided, write the letter of the word that is most nearly the same in meaning as the first word.

71. **VITIATE** (a) enliven (b) kill (c) spoil
(d) honor (e) insult   71. ....

72. **VISCOUS** (a) royal (b) sick (c) mature
(d) sticky (e) black   72. ....

73. **TERSE** (a) tense (b) brief (c) loud
(d) understandable (e) recent   73. ....

74. **TERRESTRIAL** (a) universal (b) animal
(c) vegetable (d) aquatic (e) of land   74. ....

75. **ANTIPATHY** (a) dislike (b) sympathy
(c) oversight (d) signal (e) present   75. ....

76. **APPEASE** (a) aggravate (b) quiet (c) cook
(d) feed (e) entertain   76. ....

77. **BARRISTER** (a) stare (b) stairwell
(c) staircase (d) doorway (e) lawyer   77. ....

78. **AXIOMATIC** (a) self-evident (b) mathematical
(c) logical (d) false (e) secret   78. ....

79. BLASPHEMOUS   (a) loud   (b) dangerous
(c) irreverent   (d) irrelevant   (e) irritating   79. ....

80. AUGUR   (a) tool   (b) predict   (c) explain
(d) force   (e) enlarge   80. ....

81. CANT   (a) tilt   (b) gallop   (c) singer   (d) leader
(e) talk   81. ....

82. ATTRITION   (a) enlargement   (b) discussion
(c) erosion   (d) garment   (e) dullness   82. ....

83. CARICATURE   (a) quality   (b) ego   (c) humor
(d) exaggeration   (e) painting   83. ....

84. ATONE   (a) pacify   (b) repent   (c) pray
(d) explain   (e) aid   84. ....

85. CATHOLIC   (a) universal   (b) eastern
(c) western   (d) European   (e) sectarian   85. ....

86. ARTLESS   (a) dull   (b) foolish   (c) crafty
(d) slow   (e) natural   86. ....

87. CLICHÉ   (a) person   (b) deed   (c) scene
(d) remark   (e) object   87. ....

88. DAUNT   (a) tease   (b) test   (c) frighten   (d) dare
(e) escape   88. ....

89. HISTRIONIC   (a) sick   (b) loud   (c) ancient
(d) praiseworthy   (e) melodramatic   89. ....

90. DROSS   (a) polish   (b) waste   (c) danger
(d) excess   (e) surface   90. ....

91. CURRY   (a) Indian   (b) vegetable   (c) spice
(d) fruit   (e) meat   91. ....

92. ARDENT   (a) eager   (b) tall   (c) handsome
(d) weak   (e) thorough   92. ....

93. COLLUSION   (a) violence   (b) plotting
(c) accident   (d) safety   (e) advice   93. ....

94. COMPLEMENT   (a) personnel   (b) praise
(c) number   (d) noun   (e) syntax   94. ....

95. DELINEATE   (a) publish   (b) write   (c) praise
(d) outline   (e) read   95. ....

96. HOMAGE   (a) repeat   (b) dues   (c) respect
(d) toll   (e) salary   96. ....

97. DIURNAL (a) daily (b) fatal (c) everlasting
(d) weak (e) medical   97. ....

98. HOVER (a) clean (b) waver (c) wager (d) rule
(e) criticize   98. ....

99. DISSOLUTE (a) sickly (b) determined
(c) uncertain (d) painted (e) immoral   99. ....

100. MAGNATE (a) attraction (b) politician
(c) leader (d) metal (e) machine   100. ....

Answer Key

A. Sentence Completion

1. (c)	4. (d)	7. (c)	10. (c)	13. (d)
2. (b)	5. (a)	8. (a)	11. (c)	14. (b)
3. (a)	6. (b)	9. (d)	12. (a)	15. (a)

B. Analogies

16. (b)	20. (d)	24. (a)	28. (d)	32. (c)
17. (a)	21. (b)	25. (c)	29. (a)	33. (b)
18. (c)	22. (a)	26. (b)	30. (c)	34. (a)
19. (a)	23. (c)	27. (c)	31. (d)	35. (c)

C. Antonyms

36. (c)	43. (b)	50. (b)	57. (b)	64. (a)
37. (a)	44. (d)	51. (a)	58. (d)	65. (e)
38. (d)	45. (e)	52. (e)	59. (c)	66. (e)
39. (e)	46. (b)	53. (c)	60. (d)	67. (c)
40. (b)	47. (c)	54. (b)	61. (b)	68. (b)
41. (a)	48. (a)	55. (c)	62. (e)	69. (c)
42. (c)	49. (e)	56. (a)	63. (b)	70. (d)

D. Synonyms

71. (c)	77. (e)	83. (d)	89. (e)	95. (d)
72. (d)	78. (a)	84. (b)	90. (b)	96. (c)
73. (b)	79. (c)	85. (a)	91. (c)	97. (a)
74. (e)	80. (b)	86. (e)	92. (a)	98. (b)
75. (a)	81. (e)	87. (d)	93. (b)	99. (e)
76. (b)	82. (c)	88. (c)	94. (a)	100. (c)

My Score: Number Right............ Number Wrong............

Clinch by Checking

The purpose of this test was to help you discover which of the words in the Lower-Junior List you must concentrate on in order to achieve 100% mastery. Since the list is arranged in alphabetical order, you should have no difficulty in checking back. Mark the words that you missed; these are the ones that should be studied in your next session. Once you have them under control, then you are ready for the Third Lower-Junior List Practice Test.

Thirteenth Day: Third Lower-Junior List Practice Test

A. Synonyms

In the space provided, write the letter of the word that is most nearly the same in meaning as the first word.

1. DIFFIDENT   (a) confident   (b) same
(c) exceptional   (d) timid   (e) timeless   1. ....

2. DISPARATE   (a) different   (b) comparable
(c) whole   (d) clear   (e) unfair   2. ....

3. EMISSARY   (a) ejection   (b) permit
(c) representative   (d) follower   (e) leader   3. ....

4. EUPHONIOUS   (a) beautiful
(b) pleasant-sounding   (c) harsh   (d) ugly   (e) even   4. ....

5. EXEMPLARY   (a) model   (b) defined   (c) refined
(d) confined   (e) singular   5. ....

6. JUXTAPOSE   (a) expose   (b) condemn   (c) guess
(d) destroy   (e) put side by side   6. ....

7. KNELL   (a) execute   (b) mourn   (c) ring   (d) tell
(e) told   7. ....

8. LARGESS   (a) immensity   (b) generosity
(c) excellence   (d) nobility   (e) dreaminess   8. ....

9. NOSTALGIA   (a) illness   (b) stickiness
(c) plant life   (d) longing   (e) stain   9. ....

10. OMNIVOROUS   (a) all-powerful   (b) all-knowing
(c) all-seeing   (d) in love with all things
(e) eating every kind of food   10. ....

11. PANACEA (a) fear (b) pride (c) cure-all
(d) musical (e) forest   11. ....

12. PERDITION (a) damnation (b) safety
(c) conflagration (d) loss (e) development   12. ....

13. REPARTEE (a) divorced person (b) witty answer
(c) dead person (d) leader (e) winner   13. ....

14. SIDEREAL (a) stellar (b) lunar (c) earthy
(d) solar (e) planetary   14. ....

15. THERAPEUTIC (a) surgical (b) medical
(c) hospital (d) curative (e) destructive   15. ....

16. UNREMITTING (a) postponed (b) safe
(c) stubborn (d) silent (e) endless   16. ....

17. VACILLATE (a) be a coward (b) waver
(c) wane (d) wish (e) quiet   17. ....

18. WHEEDLE (a) turn (b) straighten (c) coax
(d) train (e) spoil   18. ....

19. WONT (a) custom (b) dress (c) desire
(d) volunteer (e) refusal   19. ....

20. TURGID (a) theatrical (b) willing (c) untold
(d) swollen (e) plain   20. ....

21. SUBTERFUGE (a) passageway (b) trick
(c) reluctance (d) present (e) castle   21. ....

22. STUPEFY (a) explain (b) attack (c) astound
(d) cleanse (e) besmirch   22. ....

23. RETRIBUTION (a) compensation (b) reward
(c) punishment (d) verdict (e) action   23. ....

24. PROXY (a) nearness (b) heir (c) employer
(d) deputy (e) ticket   24. ....

25. PRELATE (a) deceased (b) promoted
(c) religious (d) clerk (e) clergyman   25. ....

26. ONSLAUGHT (a) execution (b) attack
(c) victory (d) defeat (e) result   26. ....

27. MELEE (a) dessert (b) farmland (c) opinion
(d) fight (e) native   27. ....

28. LONGEVITY   (a) long time   (b) long life
(c) long history   (d) longing   (e) long war   28. ....

29. IRIDESCENT   (a) growing larger   (b) challenging
(c) changing colors   (d) risky   (e) emitting rays   29. ....

30. SKITTISH   (a) dramatic   (b) childish   (c) short
(d) vocal   (e) coy   30. ....

31. SLUGGARD   (a) pugilist   (b) manager
(c) lazy person   (d) insect   (e) animal   31. ....

32. TRANSCEND   (a) rise   (b) descend   (c) retell
(d) retail   (e) excel   32. ....

33. VALIDATE   (a) confirm   (b) weaken   (c) sell
(d) betray   (e) extol   33. ....

34. WHIT   (a) cleverness   (b) insult   (c) dust   (d) bit
(e) serious   34. ....

35. SENILITY   (a) wisdom   (b) old age
(c) experience   (d) service   (e) falseness   35. ....

B. Analogies

In the space provided, write the letter of the set of words that
best completes the analogy.

36. MISANTHROPE : HATER :: (a) palette : paint
(b) remuneration : pay   (c) repartee : dullard
(d) barrister : defendant   36. ....

37. CAPRICIOUS : STEADFAST :: COGENT :
(a) clear   (b) ineffectual   (c) obvious   (d) unknown 37. ....

38. ACCORD : AGREEMENT :: APPROBATION :
(a) condemnation   (b) acceptance   (c) approval
(d) applause   38. ....

39. BRAZEN : DIFFIDENT :: (a) bumptious : forward
(b) catholic : provincial   (c) curtail : prolong
(d) dormant : inactive   39. ....

40. GALA : ENAMORED :: (a) celebration : romance
(b) gay : fated   (c) event : people   (d) brief : lasting   40. ....

41. EXTRANEOUS : INHERENT :: FEASIBLE :
(a) impractical   (b) profitable   (c) workable
(d) tricky   41. ....

42. FRESHET : LARGESS :: (a) short : large
(b) dangerous : generous   (c) sudden : gradual
(d) height : weight   42. ....

43. SERRATED : NOTCHED :: (a) mountain range :
valley   (b) pass : valley   (c) skyscraper : mansion
(d) saw : file   43. ....

44. OPULENCE : PARSIMONIOUS :: (a) much : little
(b) poor : rich   (c) lack : lavish   (d) all : none   44. ....

45. SALIENT : TRIVIAL :: HALLOWED :
(a) desecrated   (b) sacred   (c) honorable
(d) ceremonial   45. ....

46. BELLICOSE : BELLIGERENT :: (a) ignoble :
refined   (b) immaculate : holy   (c) incessant : loud
(d) incredulous : doubting   46. ....

47. MODULATE : MOLLIFY :: MORTIFY : (a) praise
(b) injure   (c) fast   (d) humiliate   47. ....

48. HAGGARD : LOOKS :: INSIPID : (a) actions
(b) appearance   (c) taste   (d) customs   48. ....

49. QUAGMIRE : MAELSTROM :: (a) mud : water
(b) safe : dangerous   (c) slow : swift   (d) usual :
rare   49. ....

50. NAIVETÉ : NOSTALGIA :: (a) fresh : homesick
(b) one : many   (c) female : male   (d) young : old   50. ....

C. Antonyms

In the space provided, write the letter of the word that is most
nearly opposite in meaning to the first word.

51. INCARCERATE   (a) kill   (b) liberate   (c) install
(d) expel   (e) believe   51. ....

52. BENIGHTED   (a) honored   (b) disgraced
(c) lowly   (d) enlightened   (e) light   52. ....

53. COGENT   (a) weak   (b) convincing   (c) automatic
(d) selfish   (e) insular   53. ....

54. HALLOWED   (a) desecrated   (b) consecrated
(c) full   (d) empty   (e) improved   54. ....

55. CONVIVIAL (a) unintelligible (b) oral
(c) reserved (d) dead (e) deadly   55. ....

56. FROWSY (a) alert (b) clean (c) quiet
(d) troublesome (e) graphic   56. ....

57. IMPLACABLE (a) voluble (b) predatory
(c) lenient (d) extreme (e) modern   57. ....

58. OAF (a) meal (b) earth (c) saga (d) millionaire
(e) sage   58. ....

59. OBSTREPEROUS (a) restrained (b) clammy
(c) wasteful (d) neat (e) dorsal   59. ....

60. POSTHUMOUS (a) written (b) oral
(c) subdued (d) prenatal (e) premature   60. ....

61. PRIMORDIAL (a) savage (b) modern (c) last
(d) first (e) foremost   61. ....

62. QUIZZICAL (a) clear (b) serious (c) sociable
(d) angry (e) stating   62. ....

63. RAMPANT (a) moderate (b) hostile (c) friendly
(d) subordinate (e) violent   63. ....

64. DEFUNCT (a) extinct (b) distinct (c) alive
(d) instinctive (e) constrictive   64. ....

65. DEFAMATION (a) attack (b) order (c) law
(d) column (e) praise   65. ....

66. CORPULENT (a) organized (b) legal
(c) personal (d) thin (e) useful   66. ....

67. CIRCUMVENT (a) air (b) suffocate
(c) promote (d) emote (e) remove   67. ....

68. BRAZEN (a) bashful (b) ugly (c) wooden
(d) metallic (e) solid   68. ....

69. AVARICE (a) relative (b) generosity
(c) honesty (d) corruption (e) goodness   69. ....

70. ALLEGE (a) deny (b) declare (c) legalize
(d) suppose (e) arrest   70. ....

71. INCLEMENT (a) conditional (b) charitable
(c) selfish (d) ordinary (e) mild   71. ....

72. INCREDULOUS (a) sincere (b) doubting
(c) believing (d) faithless (e) firm   72. ....

73. NAÏVETÉ (a) ugliness (b) old age
(c) studiousness (d) sophistication (e) despair   73. ....

74. OPULENCE (a) marine (b) poverty
(c) intelligence (d) bad luck (e) abundance   74. ....

75. PRECEPT (a) doctrine (b) rule (c) counsel
(d) council (e) principal   75. ....

76. RELEGATE (a) invite (b) banish (c) brand
(d) excuse (e) exercise   76. ....

77. RIBALD (a) neat (b) bright (c) rough
(d) wrinkled (e) refined   77. ....

78. SERRATED (a) toothed (b) smooth (c) violent
(d) brazen (e) wary   78. ....

79. SERVILE (a) leading (b) ardent (c) loyal
(d) authoritative (e) slavish   79. ....

80. CRAVEN (a) undesirable (b) courageous
(c) silent (d) modest (e) boastful   80. ....

81. CONTENTIOUS (a) empty (b) bold (c) trifling
(d) peaceable (e) heavy   81. ....

82. AVID (a) sane (b) blue (c) unwilling
(d) bedecked (e) warm   82. ....

83. BELLICOSE (a) answerable (b) unpleasant
(c) talkative (d) silent (e) pacific   83. ....

84. BOOR (a) entertain (b) gentleman (c) salesman
(d) manufacturer (e) magician   84. ....

85. BURLY (a) lank (b) masculine (c) childish
(d) pleasing (e) ugly   85. ....

D. Sentence Completion

In the space provided, write the letter of the word that best completes the sentence.

86. When a(n) .... was reached in the negotiations, the company sent in its top executives to use their skill to overcome the obstacles.
(a) defamation (b) impasse (c) volubility
(d) agreement   86. ....

87. The .... swept in from the sea and ransacked the unguarded village.
(a) marauders   (b) misanthropes   (c) barbs
(d) typhoon   87. ....

88. The gas-station operator decided to test the .... of his opposition by instituting a price war.
(a) intelligence   (b) finances   (c) mettle
(d) excellence   88. ....

89. I so enjoyed several of the .... in Mozart's *Magic Flute* that I intend to buy the records of the opera.
(a) apexes   (b) arias   (c) actors   (d) monologues   89. ....

90. The Pilgrim Fathers signed a(n) .... on board the *Mayflower* so that they could present a united front against foreseeable hazards.
(a) analysis   (b) bond   (c) covenant   (d) expiation   90. ....

91. Rather than .... in fear at the thought of the destructiveness of the hydrogen bomb, we should take action to see that it is outlawed but for peaceful uses.
(a) shout   (b) laugh   (c) exonerate   (d) cower   91. ....

92. She has the knack of being able to .... the simplest of meals with extras that make it the repast of an epicure.
(a) embellish   (b) describe   (c) cook   (d) extenuate   92. ....

93. When the teen-ager complained of ...., his astute adviser interested him in several hobbies.
(a) flailing   (b) ennui   (c) flotsam   (d) headaches   93. ....

94. In that he had become extremely interested in the welfare of our older citizens, he decided to specialize in ....
(a) geriatrics   (b) orthopedics   (c) pediatrics
(d) orthodontia   94. ....

95. I shall never be able to understand how anyone could have been so filled with morbid curiosity that he would visit the crossroads to view the bodies of neighbors hanging from a ....
(a) yard arm   (b) gibbet   (c) gibbon
(d) tree stump   95. ....

96. What little information we could .... from his hysterical ravings was passed on immediately to the intelligence officers.
(a) disparage   (b) chafe   (c) glean   (d) wring   96. ....

97. The most .... experience I have ever had in school has been to take three tests in a row!
(a) histrionic   (b) enlightening   (c) grueling
(d) instructional

97. ....

98. I think it unfair for him to state—even facetiously—that students find the classrooms the most suitable place to .... in during the long period of time between summer vacations.
(a) hibernate   (b) grow   (c) study   (d) hover

98. ....

99. The placement of unfriendly troops so close to our borders is .... to our national interests, and we shall take counter-measures if they are not withdrawn within the next two hours.
(a) innocuous   (b) favorable   (c) frightening
(d) inimical

99. ....

100. Unfortunately, my knowledge of the basic theories is so .... that I could not apply them to the problem facing us, and I had to call in an expert to assist.
(a) rudimentary   (b) complex   (c) advanced
(d) servile

100. ....

Answer Key

A. Synonyms

1. (d)	8. (b)	15. (d)	22. (c)	29. (c)
2. (a)	9. (d)	16. (e)	23. (c)	30. (e)
3. (c)	10. (e)	17. (b)	24. (d)	31. (c)
4. (b)	11. (c)	18. (c)	25. (e)	32. (e)
5. (a)	12. (a)	19. (a)	26. (b)	33. (a)
6. (e)	13. (b)	20. (d)	27. (d)	34. (d)
7. (c)	14. (a)	21. (b)	28. (b)	35. (b)

B. Analogies

36. (d)	39. (b)	42. (b)	45. (a)	48. (c)
37. (b)	40. (c)	43. (d)	46. (d)	49. (a)
38. (c)	41. (a)	44. (c)	47. (d)	50. (a)

C. Antonyms

51. (b)	58. (e)	65. (e)	72. (c)	79. (d)
52. (d)	59. (a)	66. (d)	73. (d)	80. (b)
53. (a)	60. (d)	67. (c)	74. (b)	81. (d)
54. (a)	61. (b)	68. (a)	75. (c)	82. (c)
55. (c)	62. (b)	69. (b)	76. (a)	83. (e)
56. (b)	63. (a)	70. (a)	77. (e)	84. (b)
57. (c)	64. (c)	71. (e)	78. (b)	85. (a)

D. Sentence Completion

86. (b)	89. (b)	92. (a)	95. (b)	98. (a)
87. (a)	90. (c)	93. (b)	96. (d)	99. (d)
88. (c)	91. (d)	94. (a)	97. (c)	100. (a)

My Score: Number Right............   Number Wrong............

Clinch by Checking

The purpose of this test was to help you discover which of the words in the Lower-Junior List you must concentrate on in order to achieve 100% mastery. Since the list is arranged in alphabetical order, you should have no difficulty in checking back. Mark the words that you missed; these are the ones that should be studied in your next session. Once you have them under control, then you are ready for the Fourth Lower-Junior List Practice Test.

Fourteenth Day: Fourth Lower-Junior List Practice Test

A. Analogies

In the space provided, write the letter of the set of words that best completes the analogy.

1. PETRIFY : TERRIFY :: (a) impute : justify
(b) garner : storage   (c) embellish : adorn   (d) disparage :
applaud   1. ....

2. CLICHÉ : WORDS :: (a) collusion : action
(b) comely : bus   (c) balustrade : stairs   (d) approbation :
threat   2. ....

3. WARY : CHARY :: (a) cautious : bold   (b) weak : weal   (c) confident : certain   (d) careful : cautious   3. ....

4. POSTHUMOUS : NATAL :: (a) before : after (b) after : later   (c) soon : late   (d) evening : morning   4. ....

5. BRAZEN : DIABOLICAL :: (a) approval : approval (b) disapproval : disapproval   (c) approval : disapproval (d) disapproval : approval   5. ....

6. BURLY : FURTIVE :: (a) sight : sound   (b) forest : city   (c) tall : short   (d) size : manner   6. ....

7. WHIT : IOTA :: (a) small : large   (b) smaller : larger (c) larger : smaller   (d) small : small   7. ....

8. SLUGGARD : LACKADAISICAL :: (a) magnate : iron   (b) rainbow : iridescent   (c) friend : loquacious (d) lurid : detail   8. ....

9. ANTIPATHY : APATHETIC :: (a) aria : soprano (b) salesman : bilious   (c) avarice : avid   (d) clemency : harsh   9. ....

10. CONTENTIOUS : CONVIVIAL :: (a) peaceable : gay   (b) festive : argumentative   (c) quarrelsome : sociable (d) court : bar   10. ....

11. CRAVEN : INTREPID :: (a) boor : churlish (b) epicure : food   (c) repartee : dull   (d) drunkard : abstemious   11. ....

12. CAJOLE : CASTIGATE :: (a) flatter : punish (b) reward : penalty   (c) praise : soften   (d) action : reaction   12. ....

13. LOQUACIOUS : VOLUBLE :: (a) sight : hearing (b) sound : sound   (c) sound : taste   (d) taste : sight   13. ....

14. MARAUDER : MAGNATE :: (a) follower : leader (b) illegal : illegal   (c) legal : illegal   (d) illegal : legal   14. ....

15. NEOPHYTE : PROXY :: (a) old : new   (b) new : old   (c) beginner : substitute   (d) apprentice : master   15. ....

B. Synonyms

In the space provided, write the letter of the word that is most nearly the same in meaning as the first word.

16. MAUSOLEUM   (a) cemetery   (b) tomb
(c) monument   (d) guard   (e) coffin   16. ....

17. DISCERNIBLE   (a) visible   (b) extinguishable
(c) light   (d) dim   (e) past   17. ....

18. CONCOCT   (a) sew   (b) build   (c) explain
(d) cook   (e) eat   18. ....

19. APPROBATION   (a) condemnation
(b) acceptance   (c) approval   (d) guidance
(e) resignation   19. ....

20. CONTRABAND   (a) label   (b) rival goods
(c) edible goods   (d) smuggled goods
(e) manufactured articles   20. ....

21. DEBASE   (a) found   (b) founder   (c) destroy
(d) improved   (e) lessen   21. ....

22. CRITERION   (a) standard   (b) theater   (c) drama
(d) writer   (e) excellence   22. ....

23. DEPREDATION   (a) merchandise   (b) robbery
(c) trickery   (d) kidnaping   (e) selling   23. ....

24. MEDIATE   (a) correct   (b) decide   (c) condemn
(d) connect   (e) explain   24. ....

25. PARADOX   (a) lake   (b) suggestion
(c) inconsistency   (d) tale   (e) moral   25. ....

26. DILEMMA   (a) deed   (b) choice   (c) statement
(d) person   (e) object   26. ....

27. PEDANTIC   (a) authoritative   (b) ignorant
(c) wise   (d) foolish   (e) learned   27. ....

28. DIADEM   (a) crown   (b) dress   (c) necklace
(d) belt   (e) buckle   28. ....

29. PERTINACIOUS   (a) slow   (b) stubborn
(c) clever   (d) tricky   (e) legal   29. ....

30. DESECRATE   (a) regard highly   (b) simplify
(c) enter   (d) treat disrespectfully
(e) develop for the use of others   30. ....

31. PETRIFY (a) shield (b) astonish (c) terrify
(d) cover (e) damage   31. ....

32. QUIRK (a) wish (b) whip (c) desire
(d) reference (e) mannerism   32. ....

33. RATIONALIZE (a) be logical (b) excuse
(c) extol (d) condemn (e) satirize   33. ....

34. REDRESS (a) speak to (b) register (c) rustle
(d) exercise (e) remedy   34. ....

35. TRYST (a) embrace (b) violation
(c) appointment (d) party (e) parkway   35. ....

36. TURBULENCE (a) twisting (b) revolt (c) quiet
(d) arrest (e) disorder   36. ....

37. UNBRIDLED (a) uncontrolled (b) slow
(c) furious (d) arrested (e) wild   37. ....

38. UNDULATE (a) move quickly (b) hesitate
(c) move in waves (d) be violent (e) praise   38. ....

39. VORACIOUS (a) hungry (b) cranky
(c) ferocious (d) sly (e) greedy   39. ....

40. ABOMINATE (a) respect (b) cold
(c) mountainous (d) enter (e) hate   40. ....

41. FELICITOUS (a) jubilant (b) appropriate
(c) old (d) modern (e) courtly   41. ....

42. IMPASSE (a) railroad (b) bridge (c) deadlock
(d) argument (e) fight   42. ....

43. PIQUANT (a) impertinent (b) dull
(c) resourceful (d) spicy (e) tangential   43. ....

44. RECANT (a) retell (b) relay (c) recall
(d) remake (e) restore   44. ....

45. GLEAN (a) gather (b) shine (c) escape
(d) help (e) hinder   45. ....

46. IGNOBLE (a) rare (b) real (c) democratic
(d) base (e) bright   46. ....

47. INTREPID (a) exploratory (b) fine
(c) sarcastic (d) dangerous (e) bold   47. ....

48. MAELSTROM   (a) swimming pool   (b) dock
(c) whirlpool   (d) mix-up   (e) disaster   48. ....

49. RUDIMENTARY   (a) delicate   (b) elementary
(c) regional   (d) geographic   (e) raw   49. ....

50. TURBID   (a) whirling   (b) electrical
(c) dangerous   (d) muddy   (e) frightened   50. ....

C. Sentence Completion

In the space provided, write the letter of the word that best
completes the sentence.

51. The .... fabric shredded the moment the force of the
wind put it to a test of strength.
   (a) decorated   (b) expensive   (c) fine   (d) sleazy   51. ....

52. It was a(n) .... tale of foolish hopes, undisciplined efforts,
and insufficient training for the necessary tasks.
   (a) sordid   (b) unnecessary   (c) usual
   (d) sporadic   52. ....

53. The starving prisoner played the game of planning the
number of .... steaks he would consume on the day of his
liberation.
   (a) inedible   (b) raw   (c) succulent   (d) sardonic   53. ....

54. His counsel refused to allow him to issue the statement that
—in his opinion—was .... a confession of guilt.
   (a) tantamount to   (b) as ruthless as   (c) interpreted as
   (d) as vindictive as   54. ....

55. The .... wave came in from the sea as a wall of water
fifty feet high, destroying everything in its path.
   (a) turbid   (b) undulating   (c) unremitting
   (d) titanic   55. ....

56. Since he had memorized the basic functions of the machinery
by ...., he lacked an understanding of the principles underlying its operation and was unable to adjust it to meet changing
demands.
   (a) rote   (b) items   (c) operations   (d) criteria   56. ....

57. May I ask you to .... my copy of the report so that I will
have no difficulty in understanding any of the technical words
it includes.
   (a) annotate   (b) develop   (c) aspire   (d) debase   57. ....

58. In order to bring back circulation into his numbed hands, the rescue worker used a piece of rough cloth to .... the skin.
(a) soothe (b) chafe (c) cajole (d) cover   58. ....

59. Alan finally .... some explanation that he hoped would be acceptable to the visitors and then entered the room.
(a) alleged (b) discovered (c) concocted
(d) concurred   59. ....

60. To .... the expenses involved in sending the Olympic team to compete in Tokyo, the committee sponsored the sale of emblems.
(a) disparage (b) deride (c) expedite (d) defray 60. ....

61. The .... patients began to gain weight when the new drug enabled their bodies to absorb proteins once again.
(a) rescued (b) tortured (c) determined
(d) emaciated   61. ....

62. The forest fire, unchecked for days, created a .... in its wake, a devastated area so vast that the nation will take years to recover from its destructive force.
(a) scene (b) holocaust (c) maelstrom
(d) spectacle   62. ....

63. She is such a trusting soul that there is never even a(n) .... of suspicion or doubt in her reaction to people.
(a) statement (b) ounce (c) iota (d) action   63. ....

64. The leader of the choral group stood on a(n) .... so that he could be seen by every member.
(a) redress (b) podium (c) accord
(d) balustrade   64. ....

65. The story is such a .... of old plots that I could predict the outcome of every episode.
(a) potpourri (b) precept (c) copy (d) resultant 65. ....

D. Antonyms

In the space provided, write the letter of the word that is most nearly opposite in meaning to the first word.

66. ACME (a) disgrace (b) fiasco (c) depth
(d) lethargy (e) exoneration   66. ....

67. ACTUATE (a) count (b) discount (c) deter
(d) exempt (e) exercise   67. ....

68. DEMISE　(a) hiring　(b) birth　(c) relief
(d) order　(e) descent　　　　　　　　　　68. ....

69. DERIDE　(a) encourage　(b) mount　(c) guide
(d) garner　(e) rectify　　　　　　　　　　69. ....

70. EXTRANEOUS　(a) interior　(b) inherent
(c) inviting　(d) extra　(e) older　　　　　70. ....

71. FABRICATE　(a) narrate　(b) read
(c) construct　(d) wreck　(e) raise　　　　71. ....

72. GALA　(a) decorative　(b) simple　(c) legal
(d) religious　(e) sad　　　　　　　　　　72. ....

73. HYPOTHETICAL　(a) problematical　(b) false
(c) extra　(d) essential　(e) certain　　　　73. ....

74. FEASIBLE　(a) edible　(b) inedible
(c) impractical　(d) wily　(e) wise　　　　74. ....

75. GAUNT　(a) hungry　(b) thirsty　(c) tame
(d) husky　(e) short　　　　　　　　　　75. ....

76. FURTIVE　(a) clean　(b) open　(c) clandestine
(d) protective　(e) fast　　　　　　　　　76. ....

77. INDUBITABLE　(a) single　(b) lonely　(c) artistic
(d) doubtful　(e) sentimental　　　　　　77. ....

78. LITHE　(a) tall　(b) squat　(c) bent　(d) new
(e) rigid　　　　　　　　　　　　　　　78. ....

79. INTREPID　(a) endless　(b) short　(c) shallow
(d) timid　(e) facing　　　　　　　　　　79. ....

80. LURID　(a) commonplace　(b) stolid　(c) soiled
(d) dim　(e) likable　　　　　　　　　　80. ....

81. INTANGIBLE　(a) intact　(b) ghastly
(c) perceptible　(d) capable　(e) tangential　81. ....

82. MALIGN　(a) steal　(b) praise　(c) deride
(d) actuate　(e) develop　　　　　　　　82. ....

83. INSIPID　(a) pungent　(b) frozen　(c) watery
(d) tacit　(e) extraneous　　　　　　　　83. ....

84. OVERT　(a) obvious　(b) lazy　(c) industrious
(d) manageable　(e) concealed　　　　　　84. ....

85. INNOCUOUS   (a) ocular   (b) auditory
(c) injurious   (d) having insight   (e) daily   85. ....

86. PLATITUDE   (a) relish dish   (b) witty saying
(c) race horse   (d) tale   (e) tension   86. ....

87. INGENIOUS   (a) sophisticated   (b) simple
(c) incompetent   (d) clear   (e) quick   87. ....

88. INFAMOUS   (a) executed   (b) working
(c) notorious   (d) traitorous   (e) virtuous   88. ....

89. ELAN   (a) lifelessness   (b) masculine   (c) adult
(d) spirit   (e) earthliness   89. ....

90. ADMONISH   (a) displease   (b) applaud
(c) astonish   (d) entertain   (e) fabricate   90. ....

91. CAPRICIOUS   (a) centered   (b) abrupt
(c) readable   (d) steadfast   (e) open   91. ....

92. ADULTERATE   (a) age   (b) freshen   (c) develop
(d) disclaim   (e) purify   92. ....

93. CHURLISH   (a) musical   (b) easy   (c) courtly
(d) surly   (e) grateful   93. ....

94. AGAPE   (a) blasé   (b) tepid   (c) curled
(d) gala   (e) feasible   94. ....

95. CLEMENCY   (a) learned   (b) severity   (c) ill
(d) mildness   (e) fairness   95. ....

96. ALIENATE   (a) naturalize   (b) solve   (c) unite
(d) beat   (e) resign   96. ....

97. CONCUR   (a) coincide   (b) extenuate
(c) promulgate   (d) disagree   (e) accept   97. ....

98. ALTRUISTIC   (a) singular   (b) conceited
(c) dexterous   (d) harmonious   (e) jocular   98. ....

99. CONSECRATE   (a) pray   (b) violate   (c) beg
(d) order   (e) cancel   99. ....

100. APATHETIC   (a) selfish   (b) egregious
(c) ignoble   (d) incessant   (e) alert   100. ....

Answer Key

A. Analogies

1. (c)	4. (a)	7. (d)	10. (c)	13. (b)
2. (a)	5. (b)	8. (b)	11. (d)	14. (d)
3. (d)	6. (d)	9. (d)	12. (a)	15. (c)

B. Synonyms

16. (b)	23. (b)	30. (d)	37. (a)	44. (c)
17. (a)	24. (d)	31. (c)	38. (c)	45. (a)
18. (d)	25. (c)	32. (e)	39. (e)	46. (d)
19. (c)	26. (b)	33. (b)	40. (e)	47. (e)
20. (d)	27. (e)	34. (e)	41. (b)	48. (c)
21. (e)	28. (a)	35. (c)	42. (c)	49. (b)
22. (a)	29. (b)	36. (e)	43. (d)	50. (d)

C. Sentence Completion

51. (d)	54. (a)	57. (a)	60. (d)	63. (c)
52. (a)	55. (d)	58. (b)	61. (d)	64. (b)
53. (c)	56. (a)	59. (c)	62. (b)	65. (a)

D. Antonyms

66. (c)	73. (e)	80. (a)	87. (c)	94. (a)
67. (c)	74. (c)	81. (c)	88. (e)	95. (b)
68. (b)	75. (d)	82. (b)	89. (a)	96. (c)
69. (a)	76. (b)	83. (a)	90. (b)	97. (d)
70. (b)	77. (d)	84. (e)	91. (d)	98. (b)
71. (d)	78. (e)	85. (c)	92. (e)	99. (b)
72. (e)	79. (d)	86. (b)	93. (c)	100. (e)

My Score: Number Right............ Number Wrong............

Clinch by Checking

The purpose of this test was to help you discover which of the words in the Lower-Junior List you must concentrate on in order to achieve 100% mastery. Since the list is arranged in alphabetical order, you should have no difficulty in checking back. Mark the words that you missed; these are the ones that should be studied in your next session. Once you have them under control, then you are ready for the Upper-Junior List.

UPPER-JUNIOR VOCABULARY

Section 3: UPPER-JUNIOR LIST

First Day

1. ABHOR to hate, despise, dislike **ant.** love, admire ♦ I have learned to *abhor* selfish acts that hurt others.

2. ABSCOND to run off, flee, disappear **ant.** remain ♦ The police soon caught the clerk who had attempted to *abscond* with the company's funds.

3. ABUT to border (on), touch at the end ♦ Since our lawn *abuts* the highway, the children are forbidden to play there.

4. ACCOST to greet, approach **ant.** avoid, ignore ♦ The child had been trained never to speak to a stranger who *accosted* him.

5. ACQUIESCE to agree, submit quietly, accept without making objections **ant.** object, disagree ♦ The girls were happy to *acquiesce* to their escorts' choice of restaurants.

6. ACRID sharp, bitter to taste or smell **ant.** fragrant ♦ The *acrid* odor of burning leaves penetrated the entire neighborhood in autumn.

7. ADULATION excessive flattery or praise **ant.** condemnation ♦ I shall never understand the *adulation* youth showers on the popular singer of the moment.

8. AFFABLE kindly, gracious **ant.** reserved, curt ♦ Despite his power and wealth, he takes great pains to be *affable* and gracious to everyone.

125

9. AFFRONT to insult, offend **ant.** please, honor ♦ The teacher refused to be *affronted* by the crude insults of the frightened child.

10. AGHAST struck with horror   **ant.** unmoved ♦ The woman stood *aghast* as she saw the child run in front of a car.

11. ALLEVIATE to relieve, remove   **ant.** intensify, aggravate ♦ He took aspirin to *alleviate* the toothache.

12. AMELIORATE to improve, help   **ant.** worsen ♦ The only way to *ameliorate* conditions in their home is to find a better-paying job for the father.

13. AMORPHOUS formless, shapeless **ant.** formed ♦ The *amorphous* ghost was able to elongate into a wisp and slip out through the keyhole.

14. ANIMOSITY a violent hatred, ill will, active dislike   **ant.** affection, liking ♦ How can such *animosity* exist between two sisters?

15. ANTITHESIS a contrast of ideas, direct opposite ♦ The *antithesis* of light is dark.

16. APERTURE an opening, gap ♦ We were able to see part of the doctor's office by looking through the *aperture* created by the partly opened door.

17. APPOSITE suitable, proper, fitting   **ant.** awkward, random ♦ He has the knack of being able to choose an illustration so *apposite* that his audience grasps immediately the point he is trying to make clear.

18. APROPOS fitting, to the point   **ant.** unsuitable, improper ♦ Now that the matter has come up, I should like to tell an anecdote that is most *apropos*.

19. ARBOREAL of trees; living in or among trees ♦ Most monkeys are *arboreal*, seldom leaving the protection of the height from the ground afforded by the branches of the trees.

20. ARID dry, dull, barren   **ant.** alive, fertile ♦ The *arid* sections of the southwestern United States resemble the Sahara Desert.

21. ARTIFICE a trick, artful or crafty device; trickery ♦ The experienced dean of boys saw through every *artifice* Alan had used to avoid doing his schoolwork.

22. ASKEW awry, placed to one side   **ant.** straight ♦ Because you did not measure accurately, the seam on this skirt runs *askew*.

23. ASSUAGE to soften, pacify, calm   **ant.** intensify, excite ♦ We attempted to *assuage* Betty's hurt feelings by making her the center of attention.

24. AUGER a tool used for boring holes in wood ♦ The carpenter used an *auger* to make a hole for the wire to pass through the plywood.

25. AUGUST impressive, having dignity, majestic   **ant.** unimposing ♦ The dignified group of *august* elders of the village deliberated the fate of the deposed leader.

26. AUTONOMOUS self-governed ♦ The British Commonwealth consisted of *autonomous* nations banded together for mutual benefits.

27. AVIARY an enclosure for keeping live birds ♦ Many birds of varied species are kept in the same large cage in the *aviary*.

28. AZURE the clear blue sky; blue like the sky ♦ The *azure* sky made the billowing shapes of the thunderhead cloud seem of the purest white.

29. BANAL commonplace, trite   **ant.** original, fresh, new ♦ The reviewer criticized the plot as being very *banal*, as being so trite that it would not be used for a television western.

30. BANEFUL poisonous, ruinous   **ant.** beneficial, healthful ♦ He stated that those TV programs that provided such a *baneful* atmosphere in which to develop young minds should be forced off the air.

31. BATTEN a strip of wood for fastening edges; to fasten such strips; make or become fat ♦ The moment the threat of a storm appeared, the cry of "*Batten* down the hatches!" could be heard aboard the sailing vessels of old.

Second Day

1. BEGUILE to deceive, mislead; charm or delight; pass time pleasantly ♦ They spoke of a man-eating monster that *beguiled* the hunters into the woods by imitating the cry of a child in distress.

2. BENEDICTION a blessing; asking for divine blessing at the end of a church service   **ant.** curse ♦ The rabbi, the priest, and the minister intoned the *benediction* at the end of the meeting as the assembled multitude prayed silently for peace.

3. BETROTH to promise in marriage ♦ In some countries it is customary to *betroth* one's daughter to a boy at a very young age.

4. BIBLIOPHILE a lover of books, particularly one who collects them ♦ A *bibliophile* would enjoy browsing through a secondhand bookstore.

5. BLATANT noisy, coarse; flashy, gaudy   **ant.** reserved, prudent ♦ Mr. Motz denounced the intruders as *blatant* strangers accustomed to being noisy rowdies.

6. BLITHE joyous, gay   **ant.** morose, sullen, glum ♦ The singing, dancing children, so *blithe* in spirit, filled the hearts of their parents with joy.

7. BONDAGE slavery   **ant.** freedom ♦ They that are ignorant are in deeper *bondage* than are those held in chains.

8. BOVINE dull and patient like an ox, slow, stupid   **ant.** bright ♦ The doctor suspected that the *bovine* characteristics of the slow-moving, slow-witted man were the results of a glandular deficiency.

9. BREVITY shortness of time; conciseness of expression ♦ The sermons of the popular minister were noted for their *brevity* and directness; he did not take long to call a spade a spade.

10. BUFFOON a clown, professional jester ♦ I refuse to play the *buffoon* every time he wants to laugh at someone.

11. BURNISH a gloss produced by rubbing; to polish by friction ♦ On Friday nights the *burnished* brass of the candlesticks shone like mirrors.

12. CADAVEROUS corpselike, pale, haggard   **ant.** plump ♦ The prisoners of war, *cadaverous* after the months of short rations, were rushed to the hospital.

13. CALUMNIATE to bring false and malicious accusations against, slander   **ant.** praise, defend ♦ The woman was tried for slander because she had tried to *calumniate* her neighbor.

14. **CARAFE** an ornamental glass water bottle, decanter ♦ The nurse filled the *carafe* with ice water and placed it on the night-table.

15. **CARNIVOROUS** flesh-eating ♦ Lions and tigers are *carnivorous* in that they feed on the flesh of other animals.

16. **CARRION** decayed or decaying flesh; feeding on such flesh ♦ The prospector knew that if he stopped walking and sat down, he would be *carrion* in a short time for the vultures sailing overhead.

17. **CATACLYSM** a catastrophe that changes the earth's surface (esp. a devastating flood); a great upheaval in the social order ♦ The hydrogen bomb is capable of creating a *cataclysm* that could destroy our civilization.

18. **CENSURE** blame, harsh criticism; to condemn, criticize severely **ant.** praise, compliment ♦ The coach *censured* the captain for having revealed team plans to the reporters without first consulting the press manager.

19. **CHAGRIN** distress caused by disappointment or humiliation ♦ Much to her *chagrin*, Nancy did not win the spelling bee.

20. **CHOLERIC** bilious, irritable, quick-tempered **ant.** placid, calm ♦ The *choleric* old man lost his temper when the children became noisy.

21. **CIRCUMSPECT** watchful on all sides, cautious **ant.** rash, reckless, daring ♦ He who would be respected as a judge must be *circumspect* in his dealings with all men lest the charge of favoritism be leveled at him.

22. **CITADEL** the fortified part of a city, fortification, place of retreat ♦ Our cities must be *citadels* of democracy in which the rights of all our citizens are fully protected.

23. **CLEMENT** lenient, merciful, mild **ant.** harsh, barbarous ♦ The *clement* ruler pardoned the captured rebels when their plot had been foiled.

24. **COGITATE** to think over, consider with care ♦ Mr. Pepper spent ten minutes *cogitating* before he expressed his opinion.

25. **COGNOMEN** a family name, last name ♦ One branch of the family is known under the *cognomen* of Smith.

26. COMMISERATE to feel or express sympathy or pity for ♦ One had to *commiserate* with the poor widows in their desperate plight.

27. COMPLACENT contented, self-satisfied ♦ He wore a *complacent* smile as he looked around and saw the many comforts his money had bought him.

28. CONCLAVE a secret meeting; meeting of cardinals to elect a pope ♦ The political leaders met in *conclave* in a last desperate attempt to prevent an open split in the party.

29. CONCOMITANT something attendant upon another thing; an attendant circumstance; accompanying, attending ♦ Must obligation always be a *concomitant* of leadership?

30. CONJECTURE a guess, surmise; to guess, surmise ♦ Who our next President will be can only be *conjectured* until the ballots are counted.

31. CONSTITUENT a necessary part; one who follows and votes for an elected officer of the State; necessary or serving as a part or an element of a compound; empowered to elect ♦ Milk, syrup, malt, and ice cream are *constituent* parts of a malted.

32. CONTIGUOUS touching, near, adjoining ♦ He calls that long line of *contiguous* one-family homes a horizontal apartment house.

Third Day

1. CONTRITE penitent, thoroughly sorry, showing deep regret ♦ The *contrite* boy apologized to his mother for being so careless.

2. CONVERSE to talk; the opposite or reverse ♦ What is the *converse* of "The sum of the angles of all three-sided figures is 180 degrees"?

3. CORROBORATE to confirm; support **ant.** reject, deny, invalidate ♦ The lawyer asked for a witness to *corroborate* his client's statements.

4. COTERIE a social set or circle ♦ Martha and her *coterie* meet often at the edge of the pool to discuss the events of the day.

5. COVETOUS desiring enviously that which belongs to another ♦ The Joneses were *covetous* of the Smiths' car and yearned to own one similar to it.

6. CREDULOUS inclined to trust or believe too easily, easily deceived ♦ The *credulous* old man actually believed the fantastic tale that the practical joker had told him.

7. CRYPTIC hidden, secret; having a hidden meaning ♦ Margie spent many minutes trying to find some meaning in Harold's *cryptic* statement about tending to your own goldfish.

8. CULPABLE deserving of blame, faulty, guilty **ant.** blameless ♦ If anything happens to the cattle while you are in charge, I shall hold you *culpable*.

9. DAIS a raised platform at one end of a hall or room ♦ There were many dignitaries on the *dais* at the luncheon honoring the President.

10. DEARTH a scarcity, lack; famine ♦ The only thing that would dismay my brother would be living in an area where there was a *dearth* of ice cream.

11. DEBONAIR gay, cheerful; courteous **ant.** awkward, clumsy ♦ Women thought the bachelor was very *debonair* with his easy graciousness and charming smile.

12. DECOROUS well-behaved, dignified, proper ♦ On Sunday afternoons, in our best clothing, the entire family would take that *decorous* stroll through the neighborhood.

13. DEFT skillful, clever **ant.** awkward, inept ♦ The *deft* surgeon saved many lives.

14. DELECTABLE very pleasing, delightful, delicious **ant.** offensive, loathesome ♦ The fruit cup was *delectable* to the eye as well as to the palate.

15. DEMAGOGUE a popular leader who stirs up the people by appealing to their prejudices ♦ Hitler was a *demagogue*, an evil star that led to madness and destruction.

16. DEMEAN to lower in dignity, humble; behave or conduct oneself poorly ♦ The college student would not *demean* himself by cheating.

17. DERANGED disturbed, insane, demented   **ant.** sane, rational ♦ The *deranged* man escaped from the mental hospital.

18. DESCRY to catch sight of, discern ♦ The hunter could not *descry* the flying duck because of the setting sun.

19. DEVIOUS winding, twisting, roundabout; going astray **ant.** straightforward ♦ He was able to escape the man following him by taking a *devious* route through side streets.

20. DEXTEROUS having or showing skill in using the hands or body   **ant.** clumsy, awkward ♦ Under the *dexterous* hands of the sculptor, a statue soon emerged from the slab of stone.

21. DIDACTIC intended to instruct; too much inclined to teach others ♦ The *didactic* youngster insisted on teaching us how to do the crossword puzzle.

22. DIFFUSE spread out in order to cover a larger surface; wordy; to mix together by spreading into one another   **ant.** compact, concise ♦ The fan quickly *diffused* into the outer air the unpleasant odors of the chemicals.

23. DILETTANTE a lover of the fine arts; dabbler in the arts, trifler ♦ His interest in painting is that of a *dilettante* and not that of one who is searching for a depth of understanding.

24. DISCONSOLATE without hope, unhappy   **ant.** cheerful, optimistic ♦ The coach was *disconsolate* when his team lost a 7–6 game to a weaker team.

25. DISCURSIVE wandering or shifting from one subject to another, rambling ♦ The speech was so *discursive* that I could not tell just what the speaker was trying to bring out.

26. DISSEMINATE to spread about ♦ The missionaries went to Africa to *disseminate* their beliefs among the natives.

27. DISTRAUGHT in a state of mental conflict, crazed   **ant.** collected, cool ♦ After the accident, the *distraught* woman wandered about looking for her husband.

28. DIVERGENT different, varying, contrary   **ant.** similar, identical ♦ The members of the Board of Education had *divergent* opinions on how to deal with the latest school crisis.

29. DOLOROUS mournful, sorrowful, grievous, painful ♦ The child uttered a *dolorous* cry as she stood over the broken doll.

30. DOLT a dull, stupid person ♦ His explanation was so clear that only a *dolt* would have misunderstood!

31. DOUR gloomy, sullen ♦ The *dour* look on the old man's face prevented his son from joking with him.

Fourth Day

1. DUBIOUS doubtful, uncertain; of questionable character **ant.** certain, positive ♦ He achieved a *dubious* success when he lost Mr. Bellafiore's support while winning his point.

2. EDICT a public order or command by some authority, decree ♦ During the rioting, the governor issued an *edict* setting an eight o'clock curfew for all citizens.

3. EDIFY to improve morally, instruct (esp. religiously) ♦ My aunt always recommends TV programs that she is certain will be *edifying* and will make a better person of me.

4. EFFICACIOUS producing desired results, effective **ant.** powerless, useless ♦ The Salk vaccine has proved to be *efficacious* in the prevention of polio.

5. EFFRONTERY boldness, impudence **ant.** modesty, humility ♦ Paul had the *effrontery* to ask me to help him after he had refused to lend me lunch money.

6. EMEND to improve, correct **ant.** corrupt, spoil ♦ Now that the translation has proved faulty, you shall have to *emend* your quotations.

7. EMULATE to imitate; compete with ♦ Many boys try to *emulate* their fathers by studying for the same profession.

8. ENCYCLOPEDIC possessing a wide range of information **ant.** narrow, parochial ♦ He seemed to have an *encyclopedic* command of knowledge as he answered detailed questions from many varied fields.

9. ENGROSS to monopolize, occupy, absorb **ant.** distract, repel ♦ Science fiction books can so *engross* the reader's attention that he becomes unaware of his surroundings.

10. ENSUE to follow, result **ant.** precede ♦ Such confusion must ever *ensue* when one man attempts to do the work of twenty.

11. EPHEMERAL very short-lived, fleeting   **ant.** durable ♦ A beautiful sunset is an *ephemeral* event.

12. EPITHET a descriptive phrase ♦ The *epithet* most applied to Abraham Lincoln is that of "Honest Abe."

13. EQUITABLE impartial, fair   **ant.** unjust ♦ The decision to divide the profits evenly among the partners was an *equitable* one.

14. ESOTERIC private, secret, understood by few ♦ The symbols used by the physicist to explain the formation of the elements seemed *esoteric* and very puzzling to the student of literature.

15. EUPHEMISM mild words to express a harsh statement ♦ One may use "not very intelligent" as a *euphemism* in describing a moronic-minded individual.

16. EXACERBATE to irritate, make more intense or bitter   **ant.** soothe, lessen ♦ Phil's unwillingness to listen to her suggestions *exacerbated* Helen.

17. EXPATIATE to write or talk at length ♦ The barker *expatiated* upon the unusual qualities of the exhibition inside the huge tent.

18. EXPEND to spend, use up   **ant.** save ♦ The runner *expended* all his energy in the race and collapsed at the end.

19. EXPUNGE to erase, remove   **ant.** imprint, stamp ♦ The teacher was directed to *expunge* the student's test mark from his permanent records.

20. EXTEMPORANEOUS offhand, done without preparation   **ant.** prepared, premeditated ♦ A political leader must be able to make *extemporaneous* speeches whenever the occasion arises during a tour of his precincts.

21. EXTRICATE to free, liberate, release   **ant.** hamper, impede, obstruct ♦ How will I ever be able to *extricate* the car from that pool of mud?

22. FACETIOUS humorous, lightly joking   **ant.** solemn, sad ♦ Helen objected to Paula's *facetious* comments on her dancing ability.

23. FALLIBLE liable to be deceived or make a mistake ♦ A person who makes hasty decisions is apt to be *fallible* in his judgments.

24. **FERRET** to hunt, search; a member of the weasel family ♦ The Texas Police and the FBI were given the task of *ferreting* out the assassin.

25. **FINITE** having boundaries or limits **ant.** endless, infinite ♦ Man's understanding is *finite*—his imagination unbounded.

26. **FLAMBOYANT** striking, flashy, gaudy **ant.** quiet, restrained ♦ The *flamboyant* display of colors in his tie caused all who saw it to gasp.

27. **FOIST** to impose on someone, palm off ♦ He tried to *foist* the worthless stock on his trusting neighbors.

28. **FORBEARANCE** patience, control ♦ The police showed great *forbearance* when they refused to react to the taunts of the crowd that followed as they marched the prisoner off to jail.

29. **FORENSIC** legal; suitable for public debate ♦ His *forensic* style of speech was more appropriate in the debating halls than in the living room of his own home.

30. **FORTITUDE** courage, endurance **ant.** weakness, cowardice ♦ With great *fortitude*, the men accepted the humiliating terms of defeat, vowing that they would rise again and make the enemy regret its cruelty.

31. **FRITTER** to waste a little at a time on petty things; a small cake ♦ The boy *frittered* away his youth on useless projects.

Fifth Day

1. **FROND** a leaf of a fern or palm tree ♦ I studied with amazement the intricate designs in the *frond* of the fern that I had picked while walking through the woods.

2. **FRUITION** a coming to fulfillment, realization; producing of fruit; pleasure from possession ♦ The *fruition* of his dream —a new office—finally came into being!

3. **GAMBOL** to frolic; jump and skip about in play **ant.** work ♦ After a long winter of confinement indoors, the children *gamboled* and shouted in the parks on this first fine spring day.

4. **GARNISH** to embellish, adorn, beautify **ant.** spoil, mar ♦ They would *garnish* the cake with candy roses.

5. GARRULOUS talking too much, loquacious **ant.** silent, taciturn ◆ The *garrulous* old man insisted on telling us the entire story of how he came to settle in Luzern.

6. GERMANE closely related, pertinent, relevant **ant.** foreign, alien, extraneous ◆ The point he made is extremely interesting, but not *germane* to the issue at hand.

7. GIST the meaning, essence, main point ◆ The *gist* of his message was that his men would come to our aid.

8. GLUT to stuff, fill, gorge **ant.** abstain, fast ◆ The girls *glutted* themselves with cookies, candy, and cake at the party.

9. GNARLED rugged, bent, knotty **ant.** delicate, smooth ◆ The old woman's hands were *gnarled* and wrinkled.

10. GOURMAND an individual who is fond of good eating in large quantities ◆ The man who was a *gourmand* spent all his time in the best restaurants in Italy.

11. GRATUITOUS free, granted without obligation; uncalled for **ant.** warranted, requested ◆ His *gratuitous* advice, unrequested and deeply sarcastic, antagonized the members of the committee.

12. GRISLY frightful, horrible, ghastly **ant.** pleasant, agreeable ◆ The headless corpse was a *grisly* sight.

13. HACKNEYED overused, trite **ant.** fresh, original, novel ◆ "Black as coal" is a *hackneyed* comparison.

14. HALCYON content, calm **ant.** disturbed, turbulent, stormy ◆ We were lulled into a feeling of peace during those *halcyon* days of summer when man and nature seemed in harmony.

15. HARANGUE a noisy speech; to give such a speech ◆ How could I listen in silence to his hypocritical *harangue* on the advantages of being unselfish?

16. HEW to chop, cut, cleave; make or shape by cutting or chopping ◆ The lumberjack can *hew* a log faster than you can pick up the pieces.

17. HIATUS a gap, empty space ◆ The pause between games was a welcome *hiatus*.

18. HIERARCHY a group of persons or things arranged in order ◆ He is so high in the official *hierarchy* that he rates two secretaries of his own.

19. HOMESPUN made at home; plain, not polished **ant.** finished, sophisticated ♦ Her *homespun* clothes seemed out of place in the ducal palace.

20. HYPOCHONDRIAC a person who thinks he is ill when he is not; self-tormenter; pessimist ♦ The *hypochondriac* was positive that he was the victim of the same illnesses that beset his friends.

21. HYPOTHESIS something assumed for the purpose of argument; supposition, postulate, unproved theory **ant.** certainty, fact ♦ The police are working on the *hypothesis* that only an intruder could have stolen the jewels.

22. IGNOMINIOUS disgraceful, humiliating, shameful **ant.** reputable, worthy ♦ Paul sulked for hours after he went down in *ignominious* defeat in three straight sets: 6–1, 6–1, 6–1.

23. IMPALE to pierce through with a stake; make helpless as if fixed on a stake ♦ Her angry glance *impaled* the terrified child to the spot.

24. IMPASSIVE apathetic, without emotion or feeling, unmoved **ant.** responsive, sympathetic ♦ The jury listened with *impassive* faces to the case against the murderer.

25. IMPERIOUS arrogant, haughty, dictatorial **ant.** subservient, servile ♦ Who would dare to stand up and oppose the *imperious* will of a dreaded dictator!

26. IMPROMPTU offhand, without previous preparation, extemporaneous **ant.** rehearsed, premeditated ♦ The surprised guest made an *impromptu* speech on juvenile delinquency.

27. IMPUNITY freedom from punishment or harm ♦ One cannot tease a strange dog with *impunity*.

28. INANE empty, silly, pointless, absurd **ant.** meaningful ♦ Her *inane* remarks about the weather were an attempt to fill in an awkward pause in the conversation.

29. INCARNATE embodied in flesh; put into an actual form ♦ He is the devil *incarnate* when he pursues his evil ways.

30. INCISIVE cutting, sharp, biting **ant.** dull; vague ♦ The *incisive* commands issued by the general set the emergency plan in motion as quickly as possible.

31. INCOMPATIBLE not able to live or act together peaceably; inconsistent **ant.** harmonious ♦ Since their basic interests were

so different, we were pleased that they decided that they were *incompatible* and ceased going steady.

32. INDEMNIFY to repay, make good, compensate for damage, recompense ♦ The court made the man *indemnify* his landlady for her losses.

Sixth Day

1. INDIGENT poor, needy ant. wealthy ♦ His many *indigent* relatives flocked to his home when news of his winning the lottery was announced.

2. INEXORABLE unyielding, relentless; severe ant. merciful; lenient ♦ Has anyone ever been able to determine the *inexorable* limitations of human understanding?

3. INGENUOUS frank, candid, sincere ant. cunning, tricky, subtle ♦ Only an *ingenuous* youngster would reveal so much of his inner thought to a stranger.

4. INIQUITOUS very wicked, sinful, unjust ant. innocent, pure, honest ♦ The *iniquitous* practices of the hate-mongers must be exposed at every turn.

5. INNUENDO an indirect hint or suggestion about somebody ♦ The woman slurred her rival by using *innuendos*, never making a direct attack that could be answered.

6. INSURGENT rising in revolt; a rebel ♦ The *insurgent* troops were ruthlessly mowed down by their former comrades-in-arms.

7. INTEMPERATE lacking in self-control; drinking too much intoxicating liquid; severe ant. sober, temperate, abstinent ♦ One who practices moderation in all things will not become *intemperate*.

8. INTIMATE to hint, suggest, allude ♦ *Intimating* that he knew more than he was willing to reveal, Jules suggested that we postpone action for a few hours.

9. INUNDATE to overflow, flood ♦ The mayor's office was *inundated* by letters of protest the day after he proposed to close the city's parks.

10. INVIDIOUS likely to arouse ill will, provoking, troublesome ant. pleasant, gratifying ♦ Comparisons can be *invidious* when too many of the factors involved are overlooked.

11. IRASCIBLE irritable **ant.** good-natured, calm ♦ The *irascible* old gentleman almost bit my head off because I had mumbled my *good morning*.

12. JAUNDICED having a soured state of mind caused by jealousy, envy, etc.; suffering from jaundice ♦ Nothing appealed to Norman's *jaundiced* eye the day after his bitter quarrel with Paul.

13. JOCOSE playful, humorous **ant.** serious, grave ♦ The *jocose* remarks of the toastmaster brought smiles to the faces of the diners, and the eating to a halt.

14. KEN a range, domain; range of sight or knowledge ♦ Are there any secrets of the universe that are beyond the *ken* of man's apprehension?

15. LACONIC concise, using few words **ant.** verbose, wordy ♦ The general was so *laconic* that I spent many minutes mulling over his few precious words trying to absorb their full import.

16. LAGGARD a loiterer, person who lags; slow, falling behind **ant.** prompt, vigilant ♦ Nelson has been so *laggard* in his payments that the installment company threatened to repossess his car.

17. LASCIVIOUS feeling or causing lust **ant.** chaste, pure ♦ In order to protect their escorts, the girls pretended not to hear the *lascivious* remarks of the ruffians and hurried into the cab.

18. LAVE to wash, bathe; flow along or against ♦ The water of the Atlantic *laves* the eastern coast of North America.

19. LEXICON a dictionary (esp. of an ancient language) ♦ Is there a *lexicon* that defines current slang terms?

20. LIBELOUS making injurious statements about a person on purpose; containing such statements ♦ Quentin Reynolds sued Westbrook Pegler for making *libelous* statements about him in his newspaper column.

21. LINGUISTICS having to do with languages or the study of them ♦ Because of his intense interest in languages, he plans to major in *linguistics*.

22. LITIGATE to contest in a lawsuit, carry on a lawsuit ♦ You would need more money than you now possess in order to *litigate* this matter, especially since it would most likely be appealed to the Supreme Court.

23. **LUGUBRIOUS** sad, mournful   **ant.** happy, joyful ♦ The *lugubrious* tone in which she announced the death of the parakeet caused us to smirk rather than to sorrow.

24. **MACHETE** a large, heavy knife ♦ The guide used his *machete* to cut a path through the heavy undergrowth in the jungle.

25. **MADRIGAL** a song with several parts; poem set to music ♦ The choral group sang a Christmas *madrigal* in three-part harmony.

26. **MAGNANIMOUS** generous, noble, lofty   **ant.** selfish, corrupt, mean ♦ The *magnanimous* king pardoned the captured rebels and allowed them to go home to their families.

27. **MALEFACTOR** an evildoer, wrongdoer   **ant.** exemplar, model ♦ The justice of the peace swore war eternal on all *malefactors* in his district.

28. **MANDATORY** compulsory, containing a command   **ant.** voluntary ♦ To serve in the army is a *mandatory* obligation of both men and women in many countries.

29. **MAUDLIN** sentimental, emotional ♦ The drunkard became *maudlin* and wept beery tears as he told of the sorrows of his ever-faithful wife.

30. **MAVERICK** an unmarked stray; independent ♦ Many western senators have been *mavericks* who disregarded the party line when it opposed supporting bills they favored.

31. **MEMENTO** something serving as a reminder, souvenir ♦ The shell fragment in my right thigh is the *memento* I brought home from Italy during World War II.

32. **MEMORIALIZE** to present a memorial to ♦ The President authorized the issuance of a postage stamp to *memorialize* the discovery of insulin.

Seventh Day

1. **MENTOR** a teacher, advisor ♦ Mr. Squire had hoped that his own former teacher would serve as his son's *mentor* during the crucial freshman year.

2. **METICULOUS** careful about detail, precise, scrupulous **ant.** sloppy, careless ♦ The schoolteacher was so *meticulous* in her marking that she rated each paper two times.

3. MIRAGE a scene of something not really there ♦ Your hope that he will finally reform is a *mirage*, a false base upon which to build your plans for the future.

4. MISCREANT a wretch, villain   **ant.** model, hero ♦ When the *miscreant* was finally apprehended, he was quickly placed behind bars.

5. MODICUM a small quantity of work, minimum ♦ A *modicum* of effort is all that is needed to make the machine do the work.

6. MORIBUND dying, coming to an end ♦ Is democracy *moribund* as claimed by the Communists and is the future theirs alone?

7. MOTLEY a mixture of different things; assorted, heterogeneous   **ant.** uniform, homogeneous ♦ The crew of the ship was a *motley* bunch—all ages, all sizes, all nationalities.

8. MUNDANE worldly, earthly   **ant.** heavenly ♦ How can so saintly a person concern herself with such *mundane* matters as weekly allowances!

9. MYRIAD a large number, many   **ant.** few ♦ There are *myriad* pleasures awaiting one at a World's Fair.

10. NEBULOUS hazy, vague, cloudlike, confused   **ant.** clear ♦ His plan was so *nebulous* that we appointed a committee to help him clarify it.

11. NIGGARDLY miserly, stingy   **ant.** generous, liberal, bountiful ♦ The boy received what he considered a *niggardly* tip from the rich man of the town.

12. NONENTITY a thing or person of little importance   **ant.** celebrity ♦ I shall never understand why they picked such a *nonentity* to be our guest speaker.

13. NOXIOUS harmful, dangerous, poisonous   **ant.** harmless ♦ The fumes of the *noxious* gas snuffed out the lives of the trapped miners.

14. OBSEQUIOUS enslaved, servile   **ant.** defiant ♦ Ben could become an *obsequious* employee, fawning over his superiors.

15. OBTUSE blunt; insensitive   **ant.** sharp; sensitive ♦ Jack was too *obtuse* to see the advantages in our suggestions.

16. ODORIFEROUS giving out a smell (esp. a fragrant odor) ♦ The *odoriferous* spring flowers filled the garden with their fragrance.

17. OMNIPOTENT having all power, almighty ♦ During the twentieth century, the scientist assumed the role of the *omnipotent* discoverer who could do anything that the gods of old were supposedly able to do.

18. ONEROUS burdensome, difficult, irksome **ant.** easy, light, trivial ♦ Feeding eight people and taking care of the household chores has been my *onerous* duty for the past four summers.

19. ORNATE decorated, embellished, adorned **ant.** simple, austere ♦ On holidays, the natives wear very *ornate* robes, decorated with lacework that describes events in their country's history.

20. OSCILLATE to fluctuate, waver **ant.** stabilize ♦ The needle of the indicator *oscillated* between good and excellent, revealing that the tube had been capable of functioning properly.

21. PALATABLE pleasing to taste; agreeable **ant.** distasteful ♦ The food served here is not elaborate, but you will find it most *palatable*.

22. PALLID colorless, pale **ant.** colorful ♦ The red dress looked striking on the girl because it contrasted so with her *pallid* complexion.

23. PANDEMONIUM an uproar, racket; place of wild disorder or lawless confusion ♦ The convention hall was filled with *pandemonium* when the chairman shouted his resignation into the microphone.

24. PARAMOUNT supreme, eminent, principal **ant.** minor, trivial ♦ Winning the war was the *paramount* goal of the army.

25. PATHOS a feeling of sadness or pity **ant.** joy ♦ We were filled with *pathos* as we watched Oedipus bring about his own destruction.

26. PENCHANT an inclination ♦ Anna was able to satisfy her *penchant* for taking long walks during her stay at Lake Lucerne, which is surrounded by miles of hiking trails.

27. PERMEATE to spread through, saturate, drench ♦ The smell of freshly cut grass *permeates* the air all around the house.

28. PERSONABLE pleasant, amiable **ant.** miserable ♦ The social director, who was very *personable*, had no difficulty in putting the guests at their ease.

29. PERUSE to read carefully, study ♦ The bridge player needed some time to *peruse* his hand.

30. PERVERSE contrary, stubborn **ant.** docile ♦ The *perverse* child did whatever he was told not to do!

31. PHILANTHROPIST one who loves mankind; one who is benevolent **ant.** misanthrope, cynic ♦ The *philanthropist* donated large sums of money to many charitable institutions.

32. PILLAGE to plunder, loot; robbery **ant.** repair ♦ The pirates *pillaged* the towns along the seacoast.

Eighth Day

1. PITHY full of substance or meaning **ant.** empty ♦ The *pithy* remarks of the instructor gave his students much to think about.

2. PLACATE to soothe, make peaceful **ant.** arouse, annoy, enrage ♦ He tried to *placate* the customer by offering him a large discount.

3. POLITIC prudent, cunning, wary **ant.** dull, stupid, blundering ♦ I don't think that his decision was as *politic* as he thinks it to be, in that he did antagonize his immediate superior.

4. POSEUR (POSER) an affected person ♦ The *poseur* made me lose my patience when he insisted that art was born with Picasso.

5. POULTICE a soft mass of herbs, etc., applied to a sore part of the body ♦ My mother has a recipe for a hot *poultice* that is a sure cure for a toothache.

6. PRECLUDE to prevent, make impossible **ant.** permit ♦ Being foreign-born *precluded* Ira's ever becoming President of the United States.

7. PREDESTINED settled beforehand, preordained **ant.** voluntary ♦ Feeling that he was *predestined* to succeed, Aaron did little to assure his reaching his goals.

8. PREPOSTEROUS unbelievable, nonsensical **ant.** reasonable, believable ♦ I never saw anything more *preposterous* than Milton's trying to be serious while still dressed in his clown's costume.

9. PRESENTIMENT a foreboding, intuition ♦ The man felt a *presentiment* of danger approaching and checked the position of his gun.

10. PROCRASTINATE to delay, put things off, defer **ant.** proceed, advance ♦ When an unpleasant task awaits us, we often *procrastinate*, hoping to avoid the inevitable through delay.

11. PROGENY offspring, descendants **ant.** antecedents, parents ♦ The duck proudly led her *progeny* in a line down to the pond.

12. PROGNOSTICATE to forecast, predict ♦ The analyst *prognosticated* a drop in the stock market by the end of the week.

13. PROPITIOUS favorable, pleasing **ant.** unfavorable, antagonistic ♦ The soothsayer announced a *propitious* day, favorable for the wedding.

14. PSEUDONYM a pen name, alias ♦ If you wanted to hide your identity, what *pseudonym* would you use?

15. PULCHRITUDE beauty, grace **ant.** ugliness, repulsiveness ♦ The model was an example of feminine *pulchritude*.

16. PUTATIVE commonly regarded, supposed ♦ The *putative* heir to the fortune assumed control of the business during the emergency.

17. QUELL to stop, put down, quiet **ant.** promote, stimulate ♦ The governor ordered the state militia to rush to the city to *quell* the riots.

18. QUERULOUS fretful, touchy **ant.** cheerful ♦ How long must I be patient with her *querulous* tone and never-ending complaints?

19. QUIESCENT still, resting, serene **ant.** active, dynamic ♦ How can I remain *quiescent* when my heart bubbles over with joy?

20. QUIXOTIC imaginary, romantically idealistic, not practical **ant.** realistic, possible ♦ To insist on a pardon for all involved in the rioting would have required *quixotic* courage.

21. RANCOR spite, hatred, malice **ant.** friendship, affection
♦ The losing candidate was so filled with *rancor* that he did not congratulate the man who had defeated him.

22. RAUCOUS hoarse, harsh, loud **ant.** quiet, sweet-sounding
♦ The *raucous* cries of the crow broke the silence in the grove.

23. RECIPIENT a person who receives something **ant.** sender, giver, donor ♦ It is better to be the donor than the *recipient* of charity.

24. RECURRENT occurring again ♦ A back condition can be a *recurrent* illness.

25. REDUNDANT extra; repetitious **ant.** concise, terse ♦ The word *again* is *redundant* in the phrase *to repeat again.*

26. REITERATE to repeat, redo ♦ In vain did the prisoner *reiterate* his request for an interpreter.

27. REPLETE full, stuffed **ant.** starved, empty ♦ The report was so *replete* with details that we soon lost sight of the main issues.

28. REPLICA a copy, reproduction ♦ They displayed a *replica* of the "Santa Maria" in honor of Columbus Day.

29. REPUGNANT antagonistic, hostile, distasteful **ant.** pleasing; allied ♦ I find his insincerity most *repugnant*.

30. RESPITE a reprieve, pause, delay **ant.** continuation, extension ♦ The pause for lunch was the only *respite* in the all-day march.

31. RESURGENT tending to rise again ♦ The police were alerted to the possibility of a *resurgent* crime wave with the increase of visitors to the city.

32. RETROSPECT thinking of the past ♦ In *retrospect*, I now know that we certainly knew so little at that time!

33. REVERBERATE to echo back; reflect (light or heat); resound ♦ The sound of a bullet *reverberated* through the hills.

Ninth Day

1. RIFE common, prevalent, widespread, abundant **ant.** insufficient ♦ During the Cuban crisis, the air was *rife* with rumors of invasion.

2. RUEFUL unhappy, sorrowful, pathetic. **ant.** cheerful ♦
There was a *rueful* expression on the face of the girl on whose
dress the ice cream had been spilled.

3. SAGACIOUS shrewd, astute   **ant.** dull, thick, stupid ♦
Even his most *sagacious* advisers had not foreseen the possibility
of such deception!

4. SALUBRIOUS healthful   **ant.** diseased ♦ The month spent
in the *salubrious* climate of Lake Lucerne brought the color of
health back into his cheeks.

5. SATE to satisfy fully, supply with more than enough ♦ Two
weeks of volunteer work in the emergency room of the hospital
quickly *sated* Sarah's urge for excitement.

6. SCURRILOUS joking coarsely, abusive, vulgar, offensive
ant. refined ♦ The *scurrilous* article by the journalist caused the
actor to sue for libel.

7. SEDENTARY used to sitting still much of the time,
inactive   **ant.** active ♦ People engaged in *sedentary* occupations
need planned, daily exercise to avoid becoming flabby.

8. SEDULOUS diligent, industrious   **ant.** inactive, lazy ♦
We were so flattered by their *sedulous* attention to our wants.

9. SENTENTIOUS meaningful, saying much in few words ♦
The *sententious* maxims of old say so much in so few words.

10. SERAPHIC angelic ♦ The *seraphic* smile on the face of
the Madonna filled the onlookers with a sense of peace.

11. SHAMBLES a place of butchery or great bloodshed ♦
The cloudburst made a *shambles* of the tiny village, having poured
death and destruction into each street.

12. SIMULATE to pretend, imitate, resemble ♦ It is very
difficult to *simulate* the atmosphere of outer space.

13. SLAKE to satisfy; quench; put out (a fire) ♦ You will
slake their curiosity only when you learn to discuss your plans
with them beforehand.

14. SLATTERNLY untidy, slovenly   **ant.** neat ♦ As they grew
older, the children resented the *slatternly* appearance of the
housekeeper.

15. SLOVENLY untidy, careless in dress, appearance, habits, work, etc. **ant.** neat, careful ♦ The *slovenly* manner in which the dinner was served made us feel unwanted.

16. SOLILOQUY a speech made by an actor to himself when he's alone on the stage, monologue ♦ I enjoyed most the *soliloquy* in which Macbeth debates with himself whether he should murder to satisfy his ambitions.

17. SOMNOLENT sleepy, drowsy, lethargic **ant.** alert ♦ The *somnolent* child did not protest as he was undressed and put to bed.

18. SQUALID degraded, dirty, poor **ant.** clean, pure ♦ The *squalid* homes of the migrants were a disgrace to the community.

19. SQUEAMISH finicky; easily shocked or turned sick; slightly sick at one's stomach ♦ A doctor cannot have a *squeamish* stomach in his profession.

20. STIPEND a salary, fixed pay ♦ The *stipend* paid to federal employees is usually lower than that paid by private industry to workers.

21. STRIDENT producing a shrill, grating sound **ant.** melodious ♦ The *strident* sound of crickets prevented the man from sleeping.

22. SUBJUGATE to conquer, subdue, overthrow ♦ The aim of the dictator is to *subjugate* each of the surrounding countries, one at a time.

23. SUBSERVIENT submissive, subordinate **ant.** superior ♦ The employer expected all his workers to be *subservient* to him.

24. SUCCINCT concise, terse **ant.** talkative, wordy ♦ The note was so *succinct* that we had to weigh very carefully the meaning of each word.

25. SUPERFLUOUS needless, excess **ant.** necessary, essential ♦ We usually shun *superfluous* words when sending a telegram.

26. SUPPOSITITIOUS counterfeit, questionable **ant.** real, actual ♦ The *supposititious* heir to the estate was soon exposed by the facts uncovered during the trial.

27. SURMISE to guess, conjecture ♦ I can only *surmise* that he was absent from school because he was sick.

28. SYCOPHANT a selfish flatterer; parasite **ant.** master, ruler ♦ The vain duke was constantly surrounded by a swarm of *sycophants*, all attempting to gain his favor with their fawning flattery.

29. TACITURN speaking very little, reticent, secretive **ant.** loquacious, garrulous ♦ The *taciturn* farmer answered each of my questions with a nod of his head.

30. TANGIBLE concrete, real **ant.** unfounded, insubstantial ♦ The lawyer could offer no *tangible* proof of his client's innocence.

31. TEDIUM tiresomeness, wearisomeness ♦ I can never endure the *tedium* of waiting even ten minutes while she is in a store shopping.

32. TEMERITY rashness, reckless boldness **ant.** timidity ♦ And he had the *temerity* to question my answer!

33. TESTY impatient, peevish **ant.** patient ♦ The supervisor became more and more *testy* as the tired workers became less productive.

34. TETHER a rope or chain by which an animal is fastened ♦ The cow broke her *tether* and wandered through the fields.

Tenth Day

1. TOME a book (esp. a large, heavy one) ♦ Who can decipher the *tomes* that contain the mystical incantations of the magicians of old?

2. TORPID inactive, numb, apathetic **ant.** active ♦ In the *torpid* state brought on by the drug, Evan cannot think or move.

3. TRANSIENT brief, fleeting; a visitor who stays for a short time **ant.** permanent, perpetual ♦ The motels along the highway depend on *transient* trade.

4. TRANSLUCENT letting light through, but not transparent ♦ The man saw only their silhouettes through the *translucent* glass.

5. TREK a journey; stage of a journey between one stopping place and the next; to travel slowly by any means ♦ Many pioneers made the long, painful *trek* across the prairies.

6. TREMULOUS quivering, trembling; timid **ant.** steady ♦ The *tremulous* voice of the old beggar could scarcely be heard above the din of the market place.

7. TRILOGY three plays, novels, etc., which fit together to make a related series ♦ *Prometheus Bound* is the first of the three plays in the *trilogy* written by Euripides.

8. TUMID swollen, pompous, ostentatious **ant.** shrunken, deflated ♦ The *tumid* style, with many high-sounding words to develop single thoughts, tires me to the brink of boredom.

9. TUTELAGE guardianship, instruction ♦ Under the *tutelage* of his professor, the student became well acquainted with the history of the Civil War.

10. TYRO a novice, beginner in learning something **ant.** master, teacher, expert ♦ Only a *tyro* would disregard such a fundamental rule of safety.

11. UNCTUOUS oily, greasy; too smooth **ant.** brusque ♦ We could not but smile at the *unctuous* remarks of the assistant who was so painstakingly imitating his master, the undertaker.

12. UNKEMPT untidy, neglected **ant.** neat, fastidious ♦ The *unkempt* garden, so long neglected, slowly gained its former orderliness under her constant care.

13. UNTENABLE incapable of being defended ♦ The loss of the fortress on our flank left our forces in an *untenable* position, and the high command ordered that we fall back to the second line of defense.

14. URBANE courteous, refined, smoothly polite **ant.** uncouth, rough ♦ The *urbane* young man stood in sharp contrast to the street ruffians.

15. VACUOUS empty; showing no intelligence **ant.** full, replete ♦ The *vacuous* expression on the boy's face showed that he did not comprehend the lecture.

16. VEGETATE to grow as plants do; live indolently ♦ I refuse to *vegetate* in a sleepy mountain village when life can be so full and variable in a large city.

17. VEHEMENT showing strong feeling, forceful, violent **ant.** weak ♦ You should have been less *vehement* and more understanding in your criticism.

18. VERBATIM word for word   **ant.** summarized, digested ♦ The newspaper printed the pastor's Sunday sermon *verbatim.*

19. VERNAL pertaining to spring; belonging to youth ♦ This year I could scarcely wait for the appearance of the first flowers in the *vernal* woods.

20. VICISSITUDES changes in circumstance, variations ♦ He accepted philosophically the *vicissitudes* of fortune that made him wealthy at one time and penniless soon thereafter.

21. VILIFY to speak evil of, slander, malign   **ant.** defend, extol, praise ♦ The editor used every foul trick of his trade to *vilify* the candidate whom he could not control.

22. VISCID sticky, very thick like glue   **ant.** watery ♦ I unfortunately put my hand right on top of a *viscid* glob of pine sap.

23. VITRIOLIC bitterly sharp   **ant.** soft, sweet ♦ The victim of his *vitriolic* verbal attack cringed before the bitterness of the assault.

24. VULNERABLE capable of being wounded, open to attack ♦ Most people are *vulnerable* to criticism.

25. WANTON heartless, wild, reckless; not moral, not chaste **ant.** restrained, serious ♦ The *wanton* boy tied cans to the dog's tail.

26. WASTREL a waster; good-for-nothing ♦ The *wastrel* discovered all too late that money is the prime requisite for a life devoted to pleasure only.

27. WEND to direct (oneself), go, pass ♦ Someday I shall *wend* my way along a path leading to contentment.

28. WHIMSICAL fanciful; odd in appearance ♦ The *whimsical* appearance of the old man made us feel that we were in the presence of a leprechaun.

29. WIZENED shriveled, withered ♦ The *wizened* face of the old man had as many wrinkles as a dried-up apple!

30. WRIT something written; a formal order directing a person to do or to avoid doing something ♦ It is against the law to hold a man without a *writ* of habeas corpus.

31. ZEALOT a fanatic, enthusiast ♦ The *zealots* stormed the car of the infidel and threatened to kill him for having dared to step into their temple.

Eleventh Day: First Upper-Junior List Practice Test

A. Antonyms

In the space provided, write the letter of the word that is most nearly opposite in meaning to the first word.

1. ABHOR   (a) dislike   (b) adhere   (c) admire
(d) adjoin   (e) defer   1. ....

2. DELECTABLE   (a) indecent   (b) offensive
(c) coarse   (d) antagonistic   (e) joyful   2. ....

3. EMEND   (a) sew   (b) rip   (c) ripe   (d) spoil
(e) edit   3. ....

4. NEBULOUS   (a) vague   (b) fast   (c) dark
(d) vast   (e) clear   4. ....

5. TACITURN   (a) talkative   (b) pleasing
(c) enraged   (d) pleased   (e) smooth   5. ....

6. DIVERGENT   (a) identical   (b) quarrelsome
(c) peaceful   (d) gay   (e) serious   6. ....

7. GAMBOL   (a) try   (b) risk   (c) win   (d) lose
(e) work   7. ....

8. DERANGED   (a) orderly   (b) sane   (c) urban
(d) rural   (e) grazing   8. ....

9. EXTRICATE   (a) liberate   (b) delve   (c) destroy
(d) hamper   (e) relive   9. ....

10. QUIXOTIC   (a) foreign   (b) domestic   (c) realistic
(d) cowardly   (e) vain   10. ....

11. FINITE   (a) fixed   (b) artless   (c) arid
(d) reasonable   (e) endless   11. ....

12. PERSONABLE   (a) objective   (b) sensible
(c) ugly   (d) miserable   (e) subjective   12. ....

13. QUIESCENT   (a) serene   (b) noisy   (c) active
(d) healthy   (e) young   13. ....

14. SUPPOSITITIOUS   (a) actual   (b) assumed
(c) false   (d) standard   (e) rare   14. ....

15. TUMID   (a) short   (b) curt   (c) curious
(d) definite   (e) deflated   15. ....

16. EXTEMPORANEOUS   (a) dated   (b) ancient
(c) prepared   (d) oral   (e) written   16. ....

17. ACCOST   (a) avoid   (b) border   (c) raid
(d) price   (e) sell   17. ....

18. BANAL   (a) acceptable   (b) original   (c) severe
(d) stormy   (e) peaceable   18. ....

19. LACONIC   (a) native   (b) patriotic   (c) past
(d) wordy   (e) clever   19. ....

20. PERVERSE   (a) spoiled   (b) docile   (c) straight
(d) tortured   (e) learned   20. ....

21. SUPERFLUOUS   (a) fast   (b) sluggish
(c) essential   (d) deep   (e) humble   21. ....

22. TORPID   (a) active   (b) apathetic   (c) antagonistic
(d) agonizing   (e) deep   22. ....

23. FORTITUDE   (a) strength   (b) cowardice
(c) error   (d) leadership   (e) curse   23. ....

24. DEXTEROUS   (a) swift   (b) lazy   (c) short
(d) awkward   (e) accepted   24. ....

25. BLATANT   (a) obvious   (b) unknown   (c) curable
(d) giddy   (e) prudent   25. ....

26. GERMANE   (a) forged   (b) domestic   (c) foreign
(d) forgivable   (e) poor   26. ....

27. PITHY   (a) empty   (b) wise   (c) sudden   (d) close
(e) ancient   27. ....

28. INTIMATE   (a) close   (b) hint   (c) stir
(d) declare   (e) antagonize   28. ....

29. SUCCINCT   (a) muddy   (b) wordy
(c) extravagant   (d) stingy   (e) loose   29. ....

30. VACUOUS   (a) full   (b) childish   (c) dull
(d) stainless   (e) quick   30. ....

31. RANCOR   (a) disorder   (b) friendship   (c) folly
(d) wisdom   (e) anger   31. ....

32. SALUBRIOUS   (a) proud   (b) wise   (c) clumsy
(d) tall   (e) diseased   32. ....

33. UNCTUOUS   (a) brusque   (b) slow   (c) wordy
(d) sterile   (e) stern   33. ....

34. BENEDICTION   (a) prayer   (b) curse   (c) advice
(d) warning   (e) rite   34. ....

35. ACQUIESCE   (a) stop   (b) follow   (c) object
(d) assent   (e) accentuate   35. ....

B. Sentence Completion

In the space provided, write the letter of the word that best completes the sentence.

36. The political leader decided to poll his .... before declaring his position on the controversial issue.
(a) poseurs   (b) sycophants   (c) shambles
(d) constituents   36. ....

37. The lookout high on the mast of the sailing vessel struggled long to .... the nationality of the ship that was following it at a distance.
(a) burnish   (b) descry   (c) accost   (d) converse   37. ....

38. Henry is so low in the .... of governmental officials that he often despairs of ever rising to prominence.
(a) stipend   (b) trek   (c) hierarchy
(d) vicissitudes   38. ....

39. Because of his growing interest in words, Paul bought an authoritative ....
(a) madrigal   (b) lexicon   (c) maverick
(d) mentor   39. ....

40. If only he could use a .... of the intelligence that I am positive he possesses!
(a) bondage   (b) modicum   (c) brevity
(d) concomitant   40. ....

41. He is so .... in his approach that he stresses the moral lesson rather than the insights or enjoyment that the reader should expect from all forms of literature.
(a) ignominious   (b) magnanimous   (c) didactic
(d) inane   41. ....

42. His intense devotion led the people to add the .... *the Confessor* to King Edward's name during his lifetime.
(a) epithet   (b) malefactor   (c) maverick
(d) palatable   42. ....

43. To the chagrin of the engineers, even the mighty machines of automation can be .... if they are not set on the right track from the very beginning of an operation.
(a) pallid   (b) quiescent   (c) ornate   (d) fallible   43. ....

44. I pledge that I shall devote myself wholly to the task ahead, and I shall never rest until I have .... the man who is guilty of this horrible deed.
(a) harangued   (b) hewed   (c) ferreted out
(d) oscillated   44. ....

45. Only a .... can justify his eating such quantities in the best of restaurants so frequently!
(a) gourmand   (b) poultice   (c) rancor
(d) progeny   45. ....

46. In that I could never afford to buy original statuary, I have resigned myself to owning .... of some of the most famous modern sculptures.
(a) replicas   (b) edicts   (c) coteries   (d) citadels   46. ....

47. The relatives looked on in dismay as the .... squandered in a few short years the inheritance that it had taken his parents a lifetime to accumulate.
(a) dolt   (b) wastrel   (c) batten
(d) philanthropist   47. ....

48. Only a .... would claim that no one but those who agree with him and have accepted the same faith should be allowed to live in peace.
(a) maverick   (b) memento   (c) zealot
(d) mentor   48. ....

49. Arthur claims that we can assume any .... so long as our purpose is not to violate the law.
(a) mirage   (b) pseudonym   (c) fortitude
(d) forbearance   49. ....

50. The .... manner of the former aristocrat annoyed his associates and made them unwilling to cooperate with him.
(a) omnipotent   (b) onerous   (c) noxious
(d) imperious   50. ....

C. Analogies

In the space provided, write the letter of the set of words that best completes the analogy.

51. OBTUSE : DUBIOUS :: (a) man : deed
(b) sensitive : certain   (c) doubt : idea   (d) objectionable :
questionable   51. ....

52. CARNIVOROUS : LION :: (a) cataclysm :
devastating   (b) homespun : human   (c) benevolent :
philanthropist   (d) predestined : fate   52. ....

53. HIERARCHY : LEXICON :: (a) order : details
(b) time : book   (c) importance : alphabet   (d) word :
meaning   53. ....

54. CONCOMITANT : HALCYON ::
(a) accompanying : calm   (b) friend : disturbed
(c) event : place   (d) lone : stormy   54. ....

55. EUPHEMISM : SHAMBLES :: (a) witty : serious
(b) unreal : warlike   (c) pleasanter : bloody
(d) well : run   55. ....

56. GLUT : GORGE :: (a) memorialize : forget
(b) permeate : saturate   (c) placate : annoy
(d) surmise : set   56. ....

57. TETHER : ROPE :: TREK : (a) army   (b) torture
(c) war   (d) journey   57. ....

58. TUTELAGE : TYRO :: (a) teacher : instruction
(b) teacher : pupil   (c) reverberate : echo
(d) obstruction : laggard   58. ....

59. DOLT : SAGACIOUS :: (a) youth : debonair
(b) dilettante : scholarly   (c) malefactor : evil
(d) gourmand : hungry   59. ....

60. MODICUM : MYRIAD :: (a) great : small
(b) little : many   (c) slight : light   (d) earthy : stellar   60. ....

61. SLOVENLY : METICULOUS :: (a) careful : sloppy
(b) dirty : pleasant   (c) scrupulous : neat   (d) weak :
strong   61. ....

62. RAUCOUS : ODORIFEROUS :: (a) pleasant :
unpleasant   (b) unpleasant : pleasant   (c) pleasant :
pleasant   (d) unpleasant : unpleasant   62. ....

63. REDUNDANT : REPETITIOUS :: (a) replete :
personable   (b) gratuitous : insulting   (c) garrulous :
talkative   (d) fallible : weak   63. ....

64. ABHOR : ALLEVIATE :: (a) stick : weaken
(b) like : intensify   (c) love : relieve   (d) remove :
hate   64. ....

65. BOVINE : INDIGENT :: (a) intelligence : money
(b) light : wealthy   (c) rural : angry   (d) slow :
pleased   65. ....

D. Synonyms

In the space provided, write the letter of the word that is
most nearly the same in meaning as the first word.

66. SLAKE   (a) wet   (b) stoke   (c) quench   (d) steal
(e) lend   66. ....

67. TOME   (a) explosive   (b) volume   (c) area
(d) weight   (e) lore   67. ....

68. TRANSLUCENT   (a) foreign
(b) partly transparent   (c) completely opaque
(d) clear   (e) visible   68. ....

69. MIRAGE   (a) review   (b) game   (c) illusion
(d) illumination   (e) water   69. ....

70. GOURMAND   (a) eater   (b) walker   (c) talker
(d) worker   (e) employer   70. ....

71. FORENSIC   (a) tall   (b) reserved   (c) static
(d) forceful   (e) legal   71. ....

72. COTERIE   (a) descendants   (b) followers
(c) public   (d) circle   (e) dance   72. ....

73. CONSTITUENT   (a) laws   (b) essential part
(c) partner   (d) candidate   (e) officer   73. ....

74. DOLOROUS   (a) financial   (b) clever   (c) slow
(d) extra   (e) mournful   74. ....

75. EMULATE   (a) imitate   (b) order   (c) explain
(d) lead   (e) accept   75. ....

76. ESOTERIC (a) essential (b) snobbish (c) violent
(d) secret (e) immense   76. ....

77. IRASCIBLE (a) related (b) irritable (c) cute
(d) placid (e) intelligent   77. ....

78. LEXICON (a) encyclopedia (b) book of maps
(c) magazine (d) book of photographs
(e) dictionary   78. ....

79. MENTOR (a) aide (b) skill (c) parent
(d) student (e) adviser   79. ....

80. PHILANTHROPIST (a) wastrel (b) scoundrel
(c) manager (d) benefactor (e) worker   80. ....

81. SOLILOQUY (a) speech (b) lecture (c) flight
(d) article (e) actor   81. ....

82. TREMULOUS (a) great (b) massive
(c) quivering (d) acidic (e) sensitive   82. ....

83. VEHEMENT (a) controlled (b) actual
(c) truthful (d) mild (e) forceful   83. ....

84. VICISSITUDES (a) events (b) deeds
(c) thoughts (d) variations (e) flights   84. ....

85. VITRIOLIC (a) loud (b) sweet (c) sharp
(d) clever (e) sudden   85. ....

86. WASTREL (a) container (b) leftovers
(c) spendthrift (d) son (e) parent   86. ....

87. DOLT (a) wizard (b) expert (c) scholar
(d) dullard (e) teacher   87. ....

88. DIDACTIC (a) instructive (b) completed
(c) undone (d) risky (e) rash   88. ....

89. CRYPTIC (a) low (b) buried (c) silent
(d) hidden (e) complete   89. ....

90. CREDULOUS (a) concerned (b) acceptable
(c) lowly (d) believing (e) crafty   90. ....

91. DAIS (a) time (b) platform (c) section (d) pit
(e) orchestra   91. ....

92. COVETOUS (a) hidden (b) open (c) excellent
(d) anxious (e) envious   92. ....

93. LITIGATE   (a) lighten   (b) assure   (c) sue
(d) control   (e) contest   93. ....

94. MACHETE   (a) knife   (b) soldier   (c) native
(d) tree   (e) vine   94. ....

95. PILLAGE   (a) amass   (b) extract   (c) charge
(d) examine   (e) plunder   95. ....

96. PSEUDONYM   (a) false foot   (b) false name
(c) friend   (d) quack   (e) specialist   96. ....

97. SQUEAMISH   (a) sensible   (b) tricky   (c) finicky
(d) stolid   (e) strapping   97. ....

98. SURMISE   (a) rise   (b) fall   (c) top
(d) determine   (e) guess   98. ....

99. TREK   (a) coach   (b) guide   (c) train
(d) journey   (e) safari   99. ....

100. ZEALOT   (a) animal   (b) hunter
(c) mysterious person   (d) fanatic   (e) hermit   100. ....

Answer Key

A. Antonyms

1. (c)	8. (b)	15. (e)	22. (a)	29. (b)
2. (b)	9. (d)	16. (c)	23. (b)	30. (a)
3. (d)	10. (d)	17. (a)	24. (d)	31. (b)
4. (e)	11. (e)	18. (b)	25. (e)	32. (e)
5. (a)	12. (d)	19. (d)	26. (c)	33. (a)
6. (a)	13. (c)	20. (b)	27. (a)	34. (b)
7. (e)	14. (a)	21. (c)	28. (d)	35. (c)

B. Sentence Completion

36. (d)	39. (b)	42. (a)	45. (a)	48. (c)
37. (b)	40. (b)	43. (d)	46. (a)	49. (b)
38. (c)	41. (c)	44. (c)	47. (b)	50. (d)

C. Analogies

51. (b)	54. (a)	57. (d)	60. (b)	63. (c)
52. (c)	55. (c)	58. (d)	61. (a)	64. (b)
53. (c)	56. (b)	59. (c)	62. (b)	65. (a)

D. Synonyms

66. (c)	73. (b)	80. (d)	87. (d)	94. (a)
67. (b)	74. (e)	81. (a)	88. (a)	95. (e)
68. (b)	75. (a)	82. (c)	89. (d)	96. (b)
69. (c)	76. (d)	83. (e)	90. (d)	97. (c)
70. (a)	77. (b)	84. (d)	91. (b)	98. (e)
71. (e)	78. (e)	85. (c)	92. (e)	99. (d)
72. (d)	79. (e)	86. (c)	93. (e)	100. (d)

My Score: Number Right............ Number Wrong............

Clinch by Checking

The purpose of this test was to help you discover which of the words in the Upper-Junior List you must concentrate on in order to achieve 100% mastery. Since the list is arranged in alphabetical order, you should have no difficulty in checking back. Mark the words that you missed; these are the ones that should be studied in your next session. Once you have them under control, then you are ready for the Second Upper-Junior List Practice Test.

Twelfth Day: Second Upper-Junior List Practice Test

A. Sentence Completion

In the space provided, write the letter of the word that best completes the sentence.

1. The cashier who had attempted to .... with the company's money was quickly apprehended by the police.
(a) permeate   (b) abscond   (c) emend   (d) peruse   1. ....

2. When their candidate suddenly became ill, the party chieftains held a(n) .... to determine the successor.
(a) aperture   (b) auger   (c) conclave
(d) forbearance   2. ....

3. She .... so much of her time and energy in planning the conference that she had too little time to prepare her speech of welcome.
(a) expended   (b) inundated   (c) expatiated
(d) foisted   3. ....

4. When he disagrees with you, he becomes so .... that you just cannot explain anything to him!
(a) apposite (b) august (c) obtuse (d) facetious   4. ....

5. As I look at the chain of events in ...., I can now see how easily we could have been the victims rather than the victors.
(a) surmise (b) retrospect (c) pillage (d) rancor   5. ....

6. The .... visitor studiously avoided any mention of her recent loss.
(a) blithe (b) clement (c) bovine (d) politic   6. ....

7. My point of view is so well known that I need not .... my opposition to this measure at this time.
(a) demean (b) diffuse (c) reiterate (d) hew   7. ....

8. If you are ever to reach the top, you must learn to .... your emotions and allow your reason to make your decisions for you.
(a) subjugate (b) calumniate (c) impale
(d) indemnify   8. ....

9. As the day of the test arrived, we regretted that we had .... away our precious study time in an unsuccessful search for the missing puppy.
(a) abutted (b) burnished (c) buffooned
(d) frittered   9. ....

10. As a(n) .... he had learned many of the techniques of the artist, but he had never had the patience to perfect his controls.
(a) dilettante (b) artifice (c) cognomen
(d) benediction   10. ....

11. The .... attempted to seize the local television station so that they could issue a call to arms to all their followers.
(a) myriads (b) insurgents (c) recipients
(d) philanthropists   11. ....

12. In the study of ...., the emphasis is not on what usage is right or wrong, but on what level is a given expression appropriate.
(a) hypotheses (b) demagogues (c) linguistics
(d) concomitants   12. ....

13. The sound of the hammering .... through the empty building.
(a) cogitated (b) accosted (c) battened
(d) reverberated   13. ....

14. Buried in the .... long since lost to history are the hopes and sorrows of countless writers of old.
(a) bibliophiles (b) carrions (c) tomes
(d) cataclysm   14. ....

15. He had .... so long away from men and ideas that he had lost his ability to focus sharply on a social issue.
(a) surmised (b) vegetated (c) subjugated
(d) deranged   15. ....

B. Antonyms

In the space provided, write the letter of the word that is most nearly opposite in meaning to the first word.

16. ACRID (a) tasty (b) delicate (c) coarse
(d) bitter (e) blunt   16. ....

17. DISCONSOLATE (a) lonely (b) crowded
(c) hopeful (d) servile (e) trying   17. ....

18. METICULOUS (a) assigned (b) careless
(c) daring (d) dense (e) shallow   18. ....

19. RAUCOUS (a) finished (b) skillful (c) distant
(d) aquatic (e) quiet   19. ....

20. SUBSERVIENT (a) excellent (b) distant
(c) certain (d) superior (e) alterable   20. ....

21. LAGGARD (a) vigilant (b) slow (c) scab
(d) proud (e) brave   21. ....

22. FLAMBOYANT (a) burning (b) quiet
(c) extinguished (d) famous (e) silent   22. ....

23. CADAVEROUS (a) slain (b) sudden
(c) studious (d) dissected (e) plump   23. ....

24. ADULATION (a) abuse (b) purity
(c) personality (d) fickleness (e) stain   24. ....

25. AFFABLE (a) gracious (b) curt (c) false
(d) lifelike (e) factual   25. ....

26. WANTON (a) uncertain (b) extra (c) restrained
(d) solvable (e) unclean   26. ....

27. SLOVENLY   (a) flowing   (b) slow   (c) sad
(d) neat   (e) cagily   27. ....

28. INANE   (a) exterior   (b) expressive   (c) oral
(d) messy   (e) cold   28. ....

29. DEFT   (a) vague   (b) broken   (c) complete
(d) untold   (e) awkward   29. ....

30. CLEMENT   (a) accidental   (b) harsh   (c) low
(d) noble   (e) solid   30. ....

31. DISTRAUGHT   (a) collected   (b) striated
(c) straight   (d) uneven   (e) last   31. ....

32. GARNISH   (a) eat   (b) sell   (c) seize   (d) spoil
(e) address   32. ....

33. CALUMNIATE   (a) whiten   (b) darken   (c) praise
(d) steal   (e) exhort   33. ....

34. AFFRONT   (a) backward   (b) aside   (c) request
(d) demand   (e) honor   34. ....

35. AUGUST   (a) wintry   (b) unimpressive
(c) invisible   (d) artful   (e) stern   35. ....

36. DUBIOUS   (a) certain   (b) single   (c) actual
(d) fictional   (e) fortunate   36. ....

37. EFFRONTERY   (a) van   (b) aftermath
(c) staidness   (d) modesty   (e) station   37. ....

38. MOTLEY   (a) uniform   (b) colorless   (c) coiled
(d) few   (e) massive   38. ....

39. MUNDANE   (a) trivial   (b) heavenly
(c) discursive   (d) definite   (e) foolish   39. ....

40. SEDENTARY   (a) clerical   (b) physical   (c) active
(d) spoiled   (e) fair   40. ....

41. VERBATIM   (a) oral   (b) written   (c) long
(d) summarized   (e) tedious   41. ....

42. VILIFY   (a) extol   (b) exceed   (c) expedite
(d) exit   (e) except   42. ....

43. FACETIOUS   (a) true   (b) solemn   (c) witty
(d) dull   (e) tense   43. ....

44. GARRULOUS (a) quarrelsome (b) extensive
(c) silent (d) positive (e) balmy   44. ....

45. GLUT (a) satisfy (b) fast (c) excel (d) abstract
(e) accept   45. ....

46. PALLID (a) full (b) colorful (c) distorted
(d) disdainful (e) errant   46. ....

47. PARAMOUNT (a) minor (b) dramatic (c) dull
(d) excellent (e) gray   47. ....

48. PLACATE (a) destroy (b) accept (c) accede
(d) deny (e) annoy   48. ....

49. SAGACIOUS (a) sick (b) dull (c) thin
(d) flabby (e) rigid   49. ....

50. TYRO (a) failure (b) tenant (c) expert
(d) accident (e) mountaineer   50. ....

C. Synonyms

In the space provided, write the letter of the word that is
most nearly the same in meaning as the first word.

51. IMPERIOUS (a) needed (b) selfish (c) stupid
(d) arrogant (e) wily   51. ....

52. INNUENDO (a) entrance (b) dismissal (c) actor
(d) role (e) hint   52. ....

53. LAVE (a) praise (b) bathe (c) answer
(d) knock (e) detail   53. ....

54. MEMENTO (a) speed (b) weight (c) souvenir
(d) time (e) celerity   54. ....

55. ONEROUS (a) burdensome (b) sweet
(c) ordinary (d) routine (e) rare   55. ....

56. PALATABLE (a) quiet (b) tasty (c) visible
(d) touchable (e) smooth   56. ....

57. PATHOS (a) silliness (b) drama (c) struggle
(d) tragedy (e) pity   57. ....

58. REPLICA (a) original (b) copy (c) book
(d) statue (e) painting   58. ....

59. SENTENTIOUS   (a) trivial   (b) meaningful
(c) essential   (d) wordy   (e) serious   59. ....

60. REVERBERATE   (a) shoot   (b) wound   (c) echo
(d) reply   (e) thunder   60. ....

61. PANDEMONIUM   (a) uproar   (b) dance hall
(c) lecture room   (d) auditorium   (e) underworld   61. ....

62. IMPROMPTU   (a) rehearsed   (b) professional
(c) crude   (d) mediocre   (e) offhand   62. ....

63. MADRIGAL   (a) singer   (b) chorus   (c) conductor
(d) song   (e) symphony   63. ....

64. PENCHANT   (a) allowance   (b) income
(c) inclination   (d) lantern   (e) necklace   64. ....

65. SERAPHIC   (a) holy   (b) angelic   (c) daily
(d) written   (e) sarcastic   65. ....

66. VEGETATE   (a) cultivate   (b) plant   (c) sow
(d) grow   (e) support   66. ....

67. DEARTH   (a) end   (b) rival   (c) soil   (d) scarcity
(e) mildness   67. ....

68. CONTRITE   (a) healthy   (b) sorry   (c) attempt
(d) tempting   (e) repulsive   68. ....

69. AGHAST   (a) manufactured   (b) approved
(c) wholesome   (d) fatal   (e) horrified   69. ....

70. CARAFE   (a) utensil   (b) bottle   (c) water
(d) liquor   (e) implement   70. ....

71. SHAMBLES   (a) walk   (b) conflict
(c) slaughterhouse   (d) armies   (e) hills   71. ....

72. RESURGENT   (a) writing again   (b) talking again
(c) receding   (d) rising again   (e) defeating again 72. ....

73. MODICUM   (a) trivia   (b) theme   (c) home
(d) minimum   (e) domestic   73. ....

74. ORNATE   (a) possessed   (b) old   (c) simple
(d) majestic   (e) decorated   74. ....

75. HARANGUE   (a) defend strongly   (b) speak loudly
(c) attack vigorously   (d) loiter   (e) reside   75. ....

76. CITADEL (a) small city (b) river (c) folly
(d) shopping center (e) fortification   76. ....

77. CATACLYSM (a) disaster (b) rush (c) destiny
(d) conclusion (e) explosion   77. ....

78. BIBLIOPHILE (a) writer (b) publisher (c) editor
(d) collector (e) reader   78. ....

79. ABUT (a) argue (b) prove false (c) aid
(d) border (e) co-operate   79. ....

80. COMPLACENT (a) difficult (b) contented
(c) servile (d) vile (e) annoyed   80. ....

81. HEW (a) chop (b) manage (c) accent (d) deny
(e) contain   81. ....

82. INUNDATE (a) enter (b) displace (c) occupy
(d) flood (e) destroy   82. ....

83. OSCILLATE (a) weave (b) waver (c) standardize
(d) filter (e) shine   83. ....

84. PERMEATE (a) accentuate (b) dispel
(c) inoculate (d) drench (e) dry   84. ....

85. SIMULATE (a) request (b) imitate (c) urge
(d) lessen (e) educate   85. ....

D. Analogies

In the space provided, write the letter of the set of words that
best completes the analogy.

86. ADULATION : AFFRONT :: (a) excess :
progression (b) abuse : honor (c) praise : insult
(d) spoil : offend   86. ....

87. IMPERIOUS : IGNOMINIOUS :: (a) pride :
ignorance (b) height : depth (c) error : sin
(d) servant : reputation   87. ....

88. EXTEMPORANEOUS : IMPROMPTU ::
(a) planned : unplanned (b) unplanned : unplanned
(c) planned : planned (d) unplanned : planned 88. ....

89. INTIMATE : INUNDATE :: (a) over : under
(b) little : much (c) much : little (d) close : distant 89. ....

90. MORIBUND : LUGUBRIOUS :: (a) fast : slow
(b) sick : sad   (c) reviving : happy   (d) dying :
taciturn   90. ....

91. SUPERFLUOUS : ESSENTIAL ::
SUPPOSITITIOUS : (a) absent   (b) false   (c) actual
(d) answerable   91. ....

92. SYCOPHANT : RECIPIENT :: (a) weakling : donor
(b) animal : artist   (c) instrument : article   (d) flatterer :
receiver   92. ....

93. MISCREANT : MALEFACTOR :: MAVERICK :
(a) follower   (b) independent   (c) sheep   (d) cow   93. ....

94. INVIDIOUS : IRASCIBLE :: PROVOKING :
(a) brazen   (b) laggard   (c) indigent   (d) choleric   94. ....

95. COMPLACENT : DEFT :: (a) contented : skillful
(b) sight : sound   (c) willing : awkward   (d) discontent :
clever   95. ....

96. EMEND : IMPROVE :: EMULATE : (a) lead
(b) rebel   (c) follow   (d) imitate   96. ....

97. EXACERBATE : SOOTHE :: FRITTER : (a) cook
(b) bake   (c) save   (d) destroy   97. ....

98. INCISIVE : INCOMPATIBLE :: (a) dull :
harmonious   (b) sharp : consistent   (c) vague : competent
(d) peaceable : cutting   98. ....

99. INGENIOUS : OMNIPOTENT :: (a) all : none
(b) sincere : almighty   (c) clever : all-seeing   (d) dull :
weak   99. ....

100. POLITIC : PREPOSTEROUS :: (a) democratic :
modest   (b) loud : long   (c) stupid : reasonable
(d) current : nonsensical   100. ....

Answer Key

A. Sentence Completion

1. (b)	4. (c)	7. (c)	10. (a)	13. (d)
2. (c)	5. (b)	8. (a)	11. (b)	14. (c)
3. (a)	6. (d)	9. (d)	12. (c)	15. (b)

B. Antonyms

16. (a)	23. (e)	30. (b)	37. (d)	44. (c)
17. (c)	24. (a)	31. (a)	38. (a)	45. (b)
18. (b)	25. (b)	32. (d)	39. (b)	46. (b)
19. (e)	26. (c)	33. (c)	40. (c)	47. (a)
20. (d)	27. (d)	34. (e)	41. (d)	48. (e)
21. (a)	28. (b)	35. (b)	42. (a)	49. (b)
22. (b)	29. (e)	36. (a)	43. (b)	50. (c)

C. Synonyms

51. (d)	58. (b)	65. (b)	72. (d)	79. (d)
52. (e)	59. (b)	66. (d)	73. (d)	80. (b)
53. (b)	60. (c)	67. (d)	74. (e)	81. (a)
54. (c)	61. (a)	68. (b)	75. (b)	82. (d)
55. (a)	62. (e)	69. (e)	76. (e)	83. (b)
56. (b)	63. (d)	70. (b)	77. (a)	84. (d)
57. (e)	64. (c)	71. (c)	78. (d)	85. (b)

D. Analogies

86. (c)	89. (b)	92. (d)	95. (a)	98. (a)
87. (a)	90. (c)	93. (b)	96. (d)	99. (b)
88. (b)	91. (c)	94. (d)	97. (c)	100. (c)

My Score: Number Right............ Number Wrong............

Clinch by Checking

The purpose of this test was to help you discover which of the words in the Upper-Junior List you must concentrate on in order to achieve 100% mastery. Since the list is arranged in alphabetical order, you should have no difficulty in checking back. Mark the words that you missed; these are the ones that should be studied in your next session. Once you have them under control, then you are ready for the Third Upper-Junior List Practice Test.

Thirteenth Day: Third Upper-Junior List Practice Test

A. Synonyms

In the space provided, write the letter of the word that is most nearly the same in meaning as the first word.

1. AMORPHOUS   (a) formed   (b) shapeless   (c) tall
(d) ruined   (e) unborn   1. ....

2. BANEFUL   (a) rich   (b) sealed   (c) cruel
(d) poisonous   (e) simple   2. ....

3. CARNIVOROUS   (a) majestic   (b) cruising
(c) flesh-eating   (d) vegetarian   (e) ferocious   3. ....

4. CRYPTIC   (a) praising   (b) critical   (c) ordinary
(d) hidden   (e) short   4. ....

5. EDICT   (a) statement   (b) call   (c) plea   (d) plan
(e) command   5. ....

6. FROND   (a) leaf   (b) fore   (c) stern   (d) stem
(e) root   6. ....

7. IMPUNITY   (a) future   (b) without money
(c) freedom from punishment   (d) fear of reprisal
(e) unfortunate   7. ....

8. MAUDLIN   (a) sentimental   (b) well   (c) terrified
(d) easy   (e) tender   8. ....

9. MORIBUND   (a) trivial   (b) dying   (c) fatal
(d) harmful   (e) quiet   9. ....

10. ODORIFEROUS   (a) fragrant   (b) flagrant   (c) fluid
(d) flowery   (e) flowing   10. ....

11. OMNIPOTENT   (a) all-knowing   (b) all-seeing
(c) all-important   (d) all-powerful   (e) all-hearing   11. ....

12. PROGNOSTICATE   (a) diagnose   (b) forecast
(c) analyze   (d) summarize   (e) inspect   12. ....

13. RESPITE   (a) pause   (b) solution   (c) respect
(d) hatred   (e) ill will   13. ....

14. SATE   (a) deceive   (b) receive   (c) relieve
(d) satisfy   (e) blow   14. ....

15. STRIDENT (a) boasting (b) slight (c) menacing
(d) distant (e) shrill   15. ....

16. QUIXOTIC (a) rapid (b) imaginary (c) slow
(d) firm (e) infirm   16. ....

17. TEDIUM (a) worry (b) tiresomeness (c) joy
(d) folly (e) speed   17. ....

18. VISCID (a) angry (b) outrageous (c) foolish
(d) hateful (e) thick   18. ....

19. WHIMSICAL (a) fanciful (b) serious (c) tragic
(d) satirical (e) old   19. ....

20. ANTITHESIS (a) relative (b) author (c) contrast
(d) solution (e) wish   20. ....

21. HIATUS (a) cough (b) illness (c) spare
(d) fruit (e) gap   21. ....

22. INDEMNIFY (a) point out (b) repay (c) sell
(d) defend (e) attack   22. ....

23. JAUNDICED (a) healthy (b) suspicious
(c) prejudiced (d) sweet (e) objective   23. ....

24. INTEMPERATE (a) cold (b) fast (c) abstinent
(d) uncontrolled (e) vicious   24. ....

25. KEN (a) smell (b) strictness (c) range
(d) ability (e) learning   25. ....

26. POSEUR a person who is (a) ill (b) a professional
(c) an artist (d) affected (e) a leader   26. ....

27. TESTY (a) impatient (b) careless (c) loud
(d) sensitive (e) stern   27. ....

28. PUTATIVE (a) reckless (b) factual
(c) antagonistic (d) original (e) supposed   28. ....

29. HYPOCHONDRIAC a person who (a) is very rich
(b) is very charitable (c) is dull (d) torments himself
(e) experiments much   29. ....

30. INCARNATE (a) wasted (b) embodied
(c) emboldened (d) embalmed (e) empty   30. ....

31. PRECLUDE (a) organize (b) ruin (c) solve
(d) present (e) prevent   31. ....

32. TETHER   (a) revoke   (b) cultivate   (c) harvest
(d) chain   (e) liberate   32. ....

33. TRILOGY   (a) book   (b) three related plays
(c) three sections of a train   (d) three-part song
(e) three-motored plane   33. ....

34. UNTENABLE   (a) unwanted   (b) unseen
(c) indefensible   (d) unworthy   (e) invincible   34. ....

35. VULNERABLE   (a) untidy   (b) neat   (c) weak
(d) open to attack   (e) fortified   35. ....

B. Analogies

In the space provided, write the letter of the set of words that best completes the analogy.

36. DEVIOUS : DISTRAUGHT :: (a) dolorous : joy
(b) winding : crazed   (c) accidental : incidental
(d) collected : straightforward   36. ....

37. EQUITABLE : EFFICACIOUS :: IMPARTIAL :
(a) powerless   (b) ineffectual   (c) effective
(d) maimed   37. ....

38. MOTLEY : TESTY :: UNIFORM : (a) peevish
(b) loud   (c) placid   (d) anxious   38. ....

39. QUIESCENT : STRIDENT :: WANTON :
(a) ordinary   (b) intelligent   (c) restrained
(d) vulnerable   39. ....

40. INIQUITOUS : IMPASSIVE :: INNOCENT :
(a) responsible   (b) living   (c) covetous
(d) extemporaneous   40. ....

41. GIST : ESSENCE :: (a) hiatus : time   (b) memento :
souvenir   (c) zealot : reform   (d) writ : order   41. ....

42. UNKEMPT : UNTENABLE :: (a) tie : money
(b) appearance : position   (c) order : clasp   (d) riches :
heir   42. ....

43. TUMID : SUCCINCT :: (a) much : little   (b) least :
most   (c) ill : well   (d) swollen : wordy   43. ....

44. SQUALID : SERAPHIC :: (a) soiled : clean
(b) degraded : heavenly   (c) low : loud   (d) anticipatory :
eventual   44. ....

45. PERVERSE : DISCONSOLATE :: (a) docile :
childish   (b) hopeful : stubborn   (c) contrary : unhappy
(d) mild : optimistic   45. ....

46. DELECTABLE : BITTER :: CULPABLE : (a) heavy
(b) sincere   (c) truthful   (d) blameless   46. ....

47. CORROBORATE : CONFIRM :: PLACATE :
(a) arouse   (b) soothe   (c) empower   (d) assign   47. ....

48. EXPATIATE : EDIFY :: (a) expand : improve
(b) spare : moralize   (c) listen : teach   (d) lecture :
building   48. ....

49. DERANGED : DEMENTED :: DISCURSIVE :
(a) brief   (b) long   (c) pointed   (d) rambling   49. ....

50. DECOROUS : PROPER :: RESURGENT :
(a) falling   (b) rebelling   (c) peaceful
(d) rising again   50. ....

C. Antonyms

In the space provided, write the letter of the word that is most
nearly opposite in meaning to the first word.

51. SOMNOLENT   (a) active   (b) suspicious   (c) inert
(d) workable   (e) wrong   51. ....

52. RUEFUL   (a) empty   (b) cheerful   (c) awkward
(d) trembling   (e) sad   52. ....

53. NOXIOUS   (a) harmless   (b) nightly   (c) daily
(d) eternal   (e) wordy   53. ....

54. MALEFACTOR   (a) buyer   (b) miser   (c) model
(d) prisoner   (e) warden   54. ....

55. INVIDIOUS   (a) pleasant   (b) unselfish   (c) quiet
(d) total   (e) frightened   55. ....

56. NONENTITY   (a) victory   (b) debt   (c) loser
(d) failure   (e) celebrity   56. ....

57. INGENUOUS   (a) young   (b) old   (c) dull
(d) cunning   (e) clever   57. ....

58. CORROBORATE   (a) explain   (b) refrain
(c) deny   (d) confuse   (e) confess   58. ....

59. HYPOTHESIS   (a) claim   (b) evidence
(c) authority   (d) idea   (e) ideal   59. ....

60. INCISIVE   (a) choleric   (b) efficacious
(c) culpable   (d) vague   (e) chewing   60. ....

61. RIFE   (a) insufficient   (b) better   (c) worse
(d) alien   (e) wet   61. ....

62. REPUGNANT   (a) peaceful   (b) stern
(c) pleasing   (d) wasteful   (e) expensive   62. ....

63. SEDULOUS   (a) human   (b) humane
(c) scandalous   (d) inactive   (e) model   63. ....

64. REPLETE   (a) sharp   (b) empty   (c) stuffy
(d) stable   (e) sorry   64. ....

65. QUERULOUS   (a) cheap   (b) turning   (c) sour
(d) cheerful   (e) questioning   65. ....

66. PULCHRITUDE   (a) ugliness   (b) haste
(c) contest   (d) judge   (e) carnival   66. ....

67. PROPITIOUS   (a) leasing   (b) illegal
(c) unfavorable   (d) unkempt   (e) recent   67. ....

68. MISCREANT   (a) jailer   (b) hero   (c) cult
(d) deed   (e) credit   68. ....

69. QUELL   (a) incite · (b) lengthen   (c) drive
(d) torture   (e) squash   69. ....

70. RECIPIENT   (a) donor   (b) adulation   (c) merger
(d) prow   (e) purser   70. ....

71. SLATTERNLY   (a) straight   (b) curved
(c) distant   (d) neat   (e) hungry   71. ....

72. TANGIBLE   (a) tactless   (b) clumsy
(c) unfounded   (d) fair   (e) touchy   72. ....

73. DIFFUSE   (a) slight   (b) thin   (c) conclusive
(d) compact   (e) conscious   73. ....

74. EXACERBATE   (a) accede   (b) soothe   (c) recess
(d) conclude   (e) depart   74. ....

75. INIQUITOUS   (a) innocent   (b) rash   (c) cautious
(d) worthy   (e) charitable   75. ....

76. EXPEND   (a) deliver   (b) drop   (c) save
(d) tease   (e) yell   76. ....

77. INTEMPERATE   (a) tropical   (b) terse   (c) sober
(d) choleric   (e) stingy   77. ....

78. PROCRASTINATE   (a) accede   (b) accent
(c) advise   (d) advance   (e) lessen   78. ....

79. RECURRENT   (a) strong   (b) weak
(c) automatic   (d) drastic   (e) continuous   79. ....

80. AMELIORATE   (a) worsen   (b) deject   (c) deter
(d) demand   (e) weld   80. ....

81. REDUNDANT   (a) straight   (b) strained
(c) weak   (d) wrong   (e) terse   81. ....

82. ANIMOSITY   (a) spirit   (b) desire   (c) defense
(d) affection   (e) disorder   82. ....

83. APROPOS   (a) recent   (b) individual
(c) indefinite   (d) unsuitable   (e) apt   83. ....

84. TEMERITY   (a) decency   (b) caution   (c) strength
(d) weakness   (e) cowardice   84. ....

85. ARID   (a) odorous   (b) dull   (c) ill   (d) damp
(e) dark   85. ....

D. Sentence Completion

In the space provided, write the letter of the word that best completes the sentence.

86. The .... leaves felt the cold blast of the autumn wind and rustled their protest.
(a) covetous   (b) delectable   (c) tremulous
(d) credulous   86. ....

87. Under the .... of the chairman of the science department, Philip prepared for the scholarship examination.
(a) tutelage   (b) coterie   (c) demean   (d) edict   87. ....

88. As the March winds swept mercilessly through the valley, the inhabitants longed for the warmth of the .... sun and the reappearance of the early flowers that announced the coming of the milder seasons.
(a) bovine   (b) vernal   (c) clement   (d) ephemeral   88. ....

89. The .... comments of the merciless critic made the playwright wince and shudder.

(a) affable   (b) vitriolic   (c) apposite   (d) blithe   89. ....

90. I plan to follow the river as it .... its way through unknown lands down to the distant sea.

(a) litigates   (b) abuts   (c) absconds   (d) wends   90. ....

91. Paul claims that *mortician* is merely a .... for the older word *undertaker*.

(a) euphemism   (b) seraphic   (c) soliloquy
(d) shambles   91. ....

92. He has spoken for so long that I hope that someone can tell me very briefly the .... of his remarks.

(a) stipend   (b) gist   (c) vicissitudes   (d) writ   92. ....

93. We gazed in awe at the .... roots of the tree that had entwined around the boulder and had split the mass of rock in several places.

(a) repugnant   (b) resurgent   (c) sagacious
(d) gnarled   93. ....

94. The crowd at the station turned out to be so large that the candidate felt obligated to deliver a(n) .... speech.

(a) impromptu   (b) personable   (c) nebulous
(d) perverse   94. ....

95. The doctor brought a copy of the .... statement to his lawyer and asked him to consider what steps should be taken to put a stop to such insults.

(a) mandatory   (b) meticulous   (c) libelous
(d) pallid   95. ....

96. He was so .... in his denials that we finally began to suspect that he might be protesting just a wee bit too much.

(a) choleric   (b) equitable   (c) circumspect
(d) vehement   96. ....

97. The .... student nurse had hoped that she would not be assigned to the emergency ward until she had more experience.

(a) grisly   (b) impassive   (c) squeamish
(d) imperious   97. ....

98. I finally resigned when I realized that the anger of the .... employer would be a constant factor in our relationship.

(a) irascible   (b) acrid   (c) mandatory
(d) maudlin   98. ....

99. I have .... all the time and money that I care to on your impractical schemes!
(a) glutted (b) expended (c) acquiesced
(d) alleviated   99. ....

100. The jet plane left an ominous white streak across the .... sky as it raced upward and westward.
(a) banal (b) dolorous (c) azure (d) finite   100. ....

Answer Key

A. Synonyms

1. (b)	8. (a)	15. (e)	22. (b)	29. (d)
2. (d)	9. (b)	16. (b)	23. (c)	30. (b)
3. (c)	10. (a)	17. (b)	24. (d)	31. (d)
4. (d)	11. (c)	18. (e)	25. (c)	32. (d)
5. (e)	12. (b)	19. (a)	26. (d)	33. (e)
6. (a)	13. (a)	20. (c)	27. (a)	34. (e)
7. (c)	14. (d)	21. (e)	28. (e)	35. (d)

B. Analogies

36. (b)	39. (c)	42. (b)	45. (c)	48. (a)
37. (c)	40. (a)	43. (a)	46. (d)	49. (d)
38. (c)	41. (d)	44. (b)	47. (b)	50. (d)

C. Antonyms

51. (a)	58. (c)	65. (d)	72. (c)	79. (e)
52. (b)	59. (b)	66. (a)	73. (d)	80. (a)
53. (a)	60. (d)	67. (c)	74. (b)	81. (e)
54. (c)	61. (a)	68. (b)	75. (a)	82. (d)
55. (a)	62. (c)	69. (a)	76. (c)	83. (d)
56. (e)	63. (d)	70. (a)	77. (c)	84. (b)
57. (d)	64. (b)	71. (d)	78. (d)	85. (d)

D. Sentence Completion

86. (c)	89. (b)	92. (b)	95. (c)	98. (a)
87. (a)	90. (d)	93. (d)	96. (d)	99. (b)
88. (b)	91. (a)	94. (a)	97. (c)	100. (c)

My Score: Number Right............ Number Wrong............

Clinch by Checking

The purpose of this test was to help you discover which of the words in the Upper-Junior List you must concentrate on in order to achieve 100% mastery. Since the list is arranged in alphabetical order, you should have no difficulty in checking back. Mark the words that you missed; these are the ones that should be studied in your next session. Once you have them under control, then you are ready for the Fourth Upper-Junior List Practice Test.

Fourteenth Day: Fourth Upper-Junior List Practice Test

A. Analogies

In the space provided, write the letter of the set of words that best completes the analogy.

1. ANTITHESIS : APPOSITE :: (a) hate : contrast
(b) relative : unrelated (c) ideal : practical (d) contrast : suitable   1. ....

2. COGITATE : DESCRY :: (a) thought : sight
(b) idea : sound (c) praise : complaint (d) reason : purpose   2. ....

3. COGNOMEN : EPITHET :: (a) given name : title
(b) nickname : thought (c) family name : descriptive phrase (d) nickname : given name   3. ....

4. ARTIFICE : AUGER :: (a) honest : industrious
(b) trick : tool (c) truce : hole (d) manufactured : homemade   4. ....

5. ASKEW : STRAIGHT :: (a) lugubrious : sad
(b) linguistics : tongue (c) succinct : wordy (d) ornate : wealthy   5. ....

6. WEND : BETROTH :: (a) book : word (b) walk : promise (c) litigate : maudlin (d) mention : quell   6. ....

7. CONCLAVE : POULTICE :: (a) man : bird
(b) close : noisy (c) open : irritating (d) diplomatic : articulate   7. ....

8. EXPUNGE : ADD :: (a) lave : clear
(b) procrastinate : oppose   (c) vegetate : reap
(d) conjecture : know   8. ....

9. AFFABLE : VITRIOLIC :: (a) pleasant : childish
(b) exceptional : heavy   (c) agreeable : bitter
(d) manner : food   9. ....

10. ARBOREAL : AVIARY :: (a) twig : bee   (b) leaf :
feather   (c) water : height   (d) treelike : cage   10. ....

11. BEGUILE : DECEPTION :: (a) future :
prognosticate   (b) sky : azure   (c) bless : benediction
(d) act : aperture   11. ....

12. BATTEN : CARRION :: (a) wood : flesh
(b) cotton : vulture   (c) fasten : destroy   (d) choose :
pick   12. ....

13. GNARLED : WIZENED :: (a) hand : face
(b) feature : tree   (c) trunk : leaf   (d) smooth : old   13. ....

14. LIBELOUS : PREDESTINED :: (a) free : known
(b) injurious : fated   (c) apt : possible   (d) unnecessary :
necessary   14. ....

15. DOUR : FACETIOUS :: (a) dull : witty   (b) gray :
blue   (c) heavy : light   (d) gloomy : humorous   15. ....

B. Synonyms

In the space provided, write the letter of the word that is most
nearly the same in meaning as the first word.

16. ASSUAGE   (a) insult   (b) deny   (c) accuse
(d) pacify   (e) appall   16. ....

17. DISSEMINATE   (a) publish   (b) contract
(c) advise   (d) sow   (e) crowd   17. ....

18. CONTIGUOUS   (a) decent   (b) near   (c) tall
(d) raw   (e) deep   18. ....

19. AUTONOMOUS   (a) self-propelled
(b) self-centered   (c) automatic   (d) self-governed
(e) compulsive   19. ....

20. BATTEN   (a) fatten   (b) obtain   (c) clothe
(d) storm   (e) pacify   20. ....

21. DOUR   (a) sweet   (b) foreign   (c) ghostly
(d) fearful   (e) sullen   21. ....

22. PREPOSTEROUS   (a) sensible   (b) nonsensical
(c) great   (d) small   (e) trivial   22. ....

23. FRUITION   (a) joy   (b) solution   (c) realization
(d) heaviness   (e) seed   23. ....

24. PRESENTIMENT   (a) timeliness   (b) foreboding
(c) forecast   (d) obscurity   (e) past   24. ....

25. ENGROSS   (a) monopolize   (b) total   (c) profit
(d) lose   (e) sell   25. ....

26. FOIST   (a) elevate   (b) accept   (c) impose
(d) resign   (e) rely   26. ....

27. ENCYCLOPEDIC   (a) informational   (b) learned
(c) deep   (d) varied   (e) oral   27. ....

28. WIZENED   (a) irritable   (b) ripe   (c) raw
(d) spiteful   (e) shriveled   28. ....

29. PROGENY   (a) parents   (b) offspring
(c) ancestors   (d) sons   (e) relatives   29. ....

30. WRIT   (a) concept   (b) ceremony   (c) civilian
(d) legalism   (e) order   30. ....

31. EDIFY   (a) instruct   (b) deliver   (c) lecture
(d) organize   (e) chastise   31. ....

32. COMMISERATE   (a) torture   (b) enjoy   (c) pity
(d) foretell   (e) execute   32. ....

33. BONDAGE   (a) money   (b) credit   (c) debit
(d) jailer   (e) slavery   33. ....

34. CHAGRIN   (a) charge   (b) humiliation
(c) humility   (d) anger   (e) resentment   34. ....

35. INSURGENT   (a) follower   (b) leader
(c) autocrat   (d) dictator   (e) rebel   35. ....

36. ABSCOND   (a) kill   (b) escape   (c) follow
(d) flee   (e) arrest   36. ....

37. ANIMOSITY   (a) liveliness   (b) giddiness
(c) hatred   (d) evil   (e) love   37. ....

38. BEGUILE   (a) deceive   (b) play   (c) entertain
(d) follow   (e) understand   38. ....

39. BURNISH   (a) destroy   (b) polish   (c) create
(d) use   (e) erode   39. ....

40. CONVERSE   (a) listen   (b) opposite   (c) oppose
(d) unify   (e) turn   40. ....

41. DEMAGOGUE   (a) dictator   (b) fascist   (c) king
(d) leader   (e) president   41. ....

42. DISCURSIVE   (a) positive   (b) influential
(c) poor   (d) silent   (e) wandering   42. ....

43. EDICT   (a) portion   (b) lawyer   (c) vote
(d) suggestion   (e) decree   43. ....

44. EQUITABLE   (a) imported   (b) insurable
(c) protective   (d) fair   (e) fast   44. ....

45. EXPATIATE   (a) except   (b) address   (c) lecture
(d) expand   (e) extirpate   45. ....

46. FERRET   (a) insect   (b) animal   (c) building
(d) weapon   (e) dart   46. ....

47. FORBEARANCE   (a) thin   (b) furry   (c) trusting
(d) gentleness   (e) patience   47. ....

48. GIST   (a) grain   (b) commotion   (c) essence
(d) dispute   (e) peace   48. ....

49. GNARLED   (a) difficult   (b) knotty   (c) old
(d) tired   (e) tiresome   49. ....

50. IMPALE   (a) pierce   (b) whiten   (c) tan
(d) embarrass   (e) destroy   50. ....

C. Sentence Completion

In the space provided, write the letter of the word that best completes the sentence.

51. .... broke loose in the theater when the lion on the stage escaped from its cage.
   (a) hierarchy   (b) pandemonium   (c) aperture
   (d) artifice   51. ....

52. Do you really believe that you were .... to become President of the United States?
(a) cogitated   (b) absconded   (c) predestined
(d) abhorred   52. ....

53. The .... remarks of the speaker angered the audience, and many of them spoke to their neighbors in defense of the victim of the attack.
(a) scurrilous   (b) equitable   (c) esoteric
(d) contrite   53. ....

54. The instructor delights in being .... and in making us think through to obtain the full meaning of his statements.
(a) homespun   (b) apposite   (c) sententious
(d) askew   54. ....

55. I refuse to .... an interest in something about which I am so indifferent.
(a) slake   (b) impale   (c) memorialize
(d) simulate   55. ....

56. The .... inhabitants of the grove—the bluejays—scolded the hikers for intruding on their privacy.
(a) decorous   (b) credulous   (c) arboreal
(d) devious   56. ....

57. The nurse filled the .... with ice water and left it on the small table within easy reach of the patient.
(a) auger   (b) aviary   (c) benediction   (d) carafe   57. ....

58. What his real reason was for appearing so generous is something that I can only ....
(a) expend   (b) conjecture   (c) expunge
(d) censure   58. ....

59. Those who stand by and do not interfere when youngsters commit malicious mischief are just as .... as the wrongdoers.
(a) culpable   (b) garrulous   (c) choleric
(d) complacent   59. ....

60. If you want to find fault with what I do or for what I stand, state your objection openly and frankly; do not use .... that cannot be answered or faced squarely.
(a) insurgents   (b) hypotheses   (c) penchants
(d) innuendoes   60. ....

61. The visiting dignitary was given a standing ovation by the assembled diplomats as he walked slowly toward his seat of honor on the ....
(a) machete (b) dais (c) myriad (d) penchant   61. ....

62. If I ever succeed in perfecting my automated composition writer, I am certain that there shall be no .... of clients for its services.
(a) dearth (b) modicum (c) pathos
(d) divergent   62. ....

63. The speaker was so .... that I soon lost sight of the main points that he had planned to make.
(a) aghast (b) cadaverous (c) discursive
(d) gratuitous   63. ....

64. The self-conscious teen-ager desperately attempted to .... the calm sophistication of his older brother.
(a) emulate (b) ameliorate (c) betroth
(d) subjugate   64. ....

65. As a result of his long experience as a member of the debating team, Arthur developed a .... ability that, unfortunately, spilled over into his discussions with his parents.
(a) garrulous (b) hackneyed (c) forensic
(d) lugubrious   65. ....

D. Antonyms

In the space provided, write the letter of the word that is most nearly opposite in meaning to the first word.

66. CENSURE (a) neglect (b) commend
(c) command (d) refuse (e) enumerate   66. ....

67. CULPABLE (a) blameless (b) senseless
(c) askew (d) quixotic (e) false   67. ....

68. DEBONAIR (a) modern (b) old-fashioned
(c) awkward (d) regent (e) arid   68. ....

69. EFFICACIOUS (a) powerful (b) light (c) dense
(d) trained (e) powerless   69. ....

70. ENSUE (a) confound (b) refuse (c) precede
(d) exceed (e) concede   70. ....

71. GRATUITOUS   (a) ungrateful   (b) requested
(c) renewed   (d) fortunate   (e) simple   71. ....

72. HACKNEYED   (a) fresh   (b) driven   (c) tame
(d) wild   (e) odorous   72. ....

73. ALLEVIATE   (a) raise   (b) depress   (c) aggravate
(d) answer   (e) control   73. ....

74. CHOLERIC   (a) cool   (b) placid   (c) extra
(d) forward   (e) foreign   74. ....

75. DEVIOUS   (a) evil   (b) beneficial   (c) bent
(d) cold   (e) straightforward   75. ....

76. EQUITABLE   (a) free   (b) unjust   (c) insured
(d) risky   (e) rank   76. ....

77. GRISLY   (a) agreeable   (b) awkward   (c) old
(d) white   (e) fancy   77. ....

78. HOMESPUN   (a) handmade   (b) crude
(c) finished   (d) lettered   (e) locked   78. ....

79. IGNOMINIOUS   (a) ugly   (b) darned   (c) untold
(d) reputable   (e) skilled   79. ....

80. INDIGENT   (a) calm   (b) angry   (c) telegraphic
(d) written   (e) wealthy   80. ....

81. JOCOSE   (a) sensible   (b) serious   (c) silent
(d) truthful   (e) trusting   81. ....

82. LASCIVIOUS   (a) chaste   (b) choice   (c) coarse
(d) relative   (e) dreary   82. ....

83. LUGUBRIOUS   (a) dry   (b) tragic   (c) joyful
(d) soft   (e) refined   83. ....

84. MAGNANIMOUS   (a) big   (b) tiny   (c) torn
(d) mighty   (e) selfish   84. ....

85. MANDATORY   (a) ordered   (b) voluntary
(c) frequent   (d) rare   (e) fancy   85. ....

86. CIRCUMSPECT   (a) round   (b) narrow
(c) reckless   (d) ordinary   (e) tall   86. ....

87. EPHEMERAL   (a) durable   (b) daily   (c) stern
(d) sturdy   (e) straight   87. ....

88. HALCYON   (a) tight   (b) sterile   (c) stormy
(d) unknown   (e) flighty   88. ....

89. IMPASSIVE   (a) penetrable   (b) penitent
(c) laggard   (d) affable   (e) responsive   89. ....

90. INCOMPATIBLE   (a) married   (b) loud
(c) lovable   (d) harmonious   (e) offside   90. ....

91. INEXORABLE   (a) single   (b) lenient   (c) lost
(d) harsh   (e) recent   91. ....

92. MYRIAD   (a) near   (b) controlled   (c) few
(d) dim   (e) brief   92. ....

93. IRASCIBLE   (a) awkward   (b) good-natured
(c) insane   (d) loud   (e) unfair   93. ....

94. NIGGARDLY   (a) generous   (b) stingy
(c) distant   (d) southern   (e) domestic   94. ....

95. OBSEQUIOUS   (a) sensible   (b) standard
(c) defiant   (d) definite   (e) whimsical   95. ....

96. VILIFY   (a) injure   (b) repair   (c) defend
(d) refuse   (e) contend   96. ....

97. URBANE   (a) rash   (b) uncouth   (c) content
(d) restless   (e) romantic   97. ....

98. TRANSIENT   (a) pleasing   (b) antisocial
(c) exterior   (d) motel   (e) permanent   98. ....

99. SYCOPHANT   (a) soldier   (b) marine
(c) commander   (d) parasite   (e) client   99. ....

100. SQUALID   (a) young   (b) pure   (c) ill   (d) short
(e) unknown   100. ....

Answer Key

A. Analogies

1. (d)	4. (b)	7. (c)	10. (d)	13. (a)
2. (a)	5. (c)	8. (d)	11. (c)	14. (b)
3. (c)	6. (b)	9. (c)	12. (a)	15. (d)

B. Synonyms

16. (d)	23. (c)	30. (e)	37. (c)	44. (d)
17. (a)	24. (b)	31. (a)	38. (a)	45. (d)
18. (b)	25. (a)	32. (c)	39. (b)	46. (b)
19. (d)	26. (c)	33. (e)	40. (b)	47. (e)
20. (a)	27. (d)	34. (e)	41. (d)	48. (c)
21. (e)	28. (e)	35. (e)	42. (e)	49. (b)
22. (b)	29. (b)	36. (d)	43. (e)	50. (a)

C. Sentence Completion

51. (b)	54. (c)	57. (d)	60. (d)	63. (c)
52. (c)	55. (d)	58. (b)	61. (b)	64. (a)
53. (a)	56. (c)	59. (a)	62. (a)	65. (c)

D. Antonyms

66. (b)	73. (c)	80. (e)	87. (a)	94. (a)
67. (a)	74. (b)	81. (b)	88. (c)	95. (c)
68. (c)	75. (e)	82. (a)	89. (e)	96. (c)
69. (e)	76. (b)	83. (c)	90. (d)	97. (b)
70. (c)	77. (a)	84. (e)	91. (b)	98. (e)
71. (b)	78. (c)	85. (b)	92. (c)	99. (c)
72. (a)	79. (d)	86. (c)	93. (b)	100. (b)

My Score: Number Right............   Number Wrong............

SENIOR VOCABULARY

Section 4: Senior List

First Day

1. ABJECT wretched, low, mean **ant.** noble, proud ♦ The *abject* poverty of the slum dwellers robbed them of joy and hope.

2. ABSOLVE to pardon, release, free from blame **ant.** accuse, convict ♦ No jury's verdict can *absolve* an accused with a guilty conscience.

3. ABSTRUSE hard to understand, obscure, profound **ant.** simple, clear ♦ His talk on the theory of numbers was so *abstruse* that few in the audience were able to follow him.

4. ACCRUE to accumulate, increase **ant.** decrease, dwindle ♦ Leave-time will *accrue* to soldiers for each month spent in the armed forces.

5. ACOUSTICS the science of sound; quality of sound in an auditorium, room, etc. ♦ George says that the *acoustics* at the Lincoln Center in New York are so good that a person sitting in the last row can hear a pin drop on the stage.

6. ACRIMONIOUS sharp or bitter in temper, language, or manner **ant.** good-natured, peaceable ♦ The argument became more and more *acrimonious* as tempers grew shorter.

7. ADAMANT firm, unyielding, stubborn **ant.** submissive ♦ The father remained *adamant* in his refusal to soften the punishment for such disobedience.

8. ADVENTITIOUS accidental; added from outside **ant.** natural, normal ♦ The botanist could not explain why the *adventitious* roots had begun to grow out of the upper stem of the plant.

9. AFFLUENT abundant; wealthy **ant.** destitute ♦ The *affluent* nations of the world contribute toward the betterment of the lot of the people in less-fortunate countries.

10. ALACRITY quick willingness, eager readiness **ant.** laziness; indifference ♦ The raw recruits soon learned to obey with *alacrity* the orders of the drill sergeant.

11. ALTERCATION an angry dispute, controversy **ant.** accord, agreement ♦ It is not unusual for a candidate to have an *altercation* with his political rival.

12. AMENABLE open to suggestions, docile, obedient **ant.** independent; stubborn ♦ The President was very popular because he was *amenable* to advice.

13. ANATHEMA a solemn curse; anything greatly disliked ♦ Her name has been an *anathema* to Milton ever since she refused to help.

14. ANIMADVERSION adverse criticism, blame, censure **ant.** approbation, praise ♦ John's *animadversions* hurt me more than did all the jibes of the professional critics.

15. ANOMALY an irregularity, abnormality, departure from the common rule ♦ A bird such as the ostrich is an *anomaly* in that it cannot fly.

16. APLOMB assurance, poise **ant.** shyness; bewilderment ♦ Ignoring with admirable *aplomb* that he had been caught breaking a minor regulation, he insisted on being treated as an equal by the school guard.

17. APPELLATION a name, title; act of calling by name ♦ "Jackie" was the *appellation* applied by the newspapermen to Mrs. Kennedy when she was our First Lady.

18. ARBITER a person chosen to decide a dispute ♦ Both labor and management must approve first of the man who would act as *arbiter* in this dispute over wages.

19. ARCHAIC ancient, old-fashioned **ant.** modern, fresh ♦ Time makes both language and customs *archaic*, relics of a past era.

20. ARRAIGN to bring to court for trial; accuse, charge **ant.** discharge, pardon, free ♦ Since formal charges have been made against Mr. Allison, he will be *arraigned* next week.

21. ASCETIC one who retires from the world and devotes himself to a life of severe discipline; rigidly abstinent, austere ♦ The *ascetic* had fasted so often in order to have more time for his devotions that he seemed all skin and bones.

22. ASCRIBE to attribute, assign ♦ I can only *ascribe* his actions to a jealous desire to prevent anyone else from getting what he himself could not.

23. ASSEVERATE to state in a positive manner   ant. contradict, refute ♦ The accused *asseverated* his innocence every time he was led out of his cell.

24. ATTENUATE to make thin; weaken, reduce   ant. enlarge, increase ♦ The wire was *attenuated* by being forced through successively smaller holes.

25. AUSPICIOUS having promise of success, favorable   ant. adverse; ill-omened ♦ Having achieved so high a mark on the first test, I felt that I had made an *auspicious* beginning for the new term.

26. AVER to affirm positively, assert   ant. contradict, deny ♦ How can he *aver* that we saw him when we had never been there!

27. AVERSE unwilling, reluctant   ant. inclined ♦ Alice has always been *averse* to letting others copy her homework.

28. BAGATELLE a trifle; game played with balls or marbles and a cue on a board ♦ How can you call this a mere *bagatelle* when I find it so alarming?

29. BALEFUL deadly, harmful, evil   ant. beneficial, wholesome ♦ Under the *baleful* urging of the witch doctor, the villagers doomed the three youths to death by stoning.

30. BARRAGE a screen of gunfire covering the advance of troops; prolonged attack of words or blows ♦ The *barrage* of words that greeted the latecomer made him cringe in silence.

31. BASTION an angular projection from a fortification affording crossfire on attackers; any strong defense ♦ No longer is our shoreline a *bastion* to protect us from an invading enemy.

Second Day

1. BEATIFIC blissful, very happy ♦ Which painter has captured the *beatific* smile of the blessed?

2. BENIGN having a kind or gentle disposition; favorably disposed; mild, not dangerous   **ant.** malignant, menacing ♦ She was relieved to find that her tumor was *benign.*

3. BERSERK in a frenzy or state of violent rage   **ant.** calm ♦ The men went *berserk* and destroyed the entire village when their leader was killed by a sniper's bullet.

4. BLANDISH to flatter; coax ♦ With many a *blandishing* remark, he tried in vain to persuade me to do the errand for him.

5. BLAZON to display ostentatiously; show in heraldry, as a family history; a shield; showy display ♦ Columbus unfurled the Spanish flag in a *blazon* of glory when he landed in the New World.

6. BODE to be a bad omen; wait or await; the past tense of *bide* ♦ Their silence *bodes* us no good!

7. BOMBASTIC pompous, extravagant, flowery (of talk)   **ant.** sincere; severe ♦ He is so *bombastic* that instead of a simple "yes" of agreement, he runs thirty or forty polysyllables into a five-minute speech of affirmation!

8. BOWDLERIZE to mutilate, as a text, by cutting out passages deemed objectionable ♦ The vegetarian *bowdlerized* the text by deleting all references to meat eating.

9. BROCHURE a treatise put out in pamphlet form ♦ The State issued a *brochure* outlining the most popular trails up Mount Marcy.

10. BUCOLIC rural, pastoral   **ant.** urbane; sophisticated ♦ The *bucolic* poet could see no beauty outside that of plant life.

11. BUTTRESS to supply with supports; to support; any support ♦ They placed sandbags behind the dike to *buttress* it against the rising waters.

12. CACOPHONY an unpleasant or discordant sound   **ant.** harmony ♦ Modern music often uses *cacophony* rather than harmony to develop contemporary themes.

13. CALLOW unfledged (of a bird); young and inexperienced (of a person)   **ant.** full-fledged, mature ♦ *Callow* youth has only his faith and determination to pit against the experience of the mature.

14. CAPTIOUS ready to criticize or find fault   **ant.** appreciative ♦ The *captious* critic was all too quick to condemn the inexperienced actor.

15. **CARNAGE** a heap of bloody slaughtered bodies, massacre ♦ Who could view the *carnage* of the battlefield with calm acceptance?

16. **CARPING** picky, meticulous, faultfinding **ant.** complimentary, approving ♦ I could never work with anyone who could be so *carping* in her criticism, so willing to blame, so ready to judge others.

17. **CAVIL** a specious objection, quibble; to find flaws in; raise baseless or fussy objections ♦ The purpose of this committee is not to *cavil* over petty differences but to investigate basic causes.

18. **CELERITY** promptness, speed **ant.** leisureliness, slowness ♦ He worked with such remarkable *celerity* that he always accomplished much more than anyone else in the office.

19. **CHARLATAN** a quack, pretender to knowledge not possessed, impostor ♦ He is a vicious *charlatan* who preys on the ignorance and vanity of those who are willing to believe his absurd claims.

20. **CHICANERY** trickery, subterfuge, fraud **ant.** honesty ♦ Dishonest lawyers sometimes use *chicanery* to win their suits.

21. **CIRCUMSCRIBE** to enclose within fixed bounds, surround, limit ♦ The actions of youth are *circumscribed* by the code of behavior set by their elders.

22. **CLANDESTINE** secret, under cover **ant.** open ♦ The conspirators held *clandestine* meetings to plot the overthrow of the government.

23. **CLOY** to weary by too much; to be too sweet, too rich ♦ His appetite was soon *cloyed* by the overrichness of the malt drink.

24. **COGNIZANT** aware of, informed **ant.** ignorant, unknowing ♦ The king was *cognizant* of the plot to overthrow his government.

25. **COLLATE** to compare critically, as two manuscripts; bring material together ♦ After they gathered the material from the polls, the men would *collate* this material with results of other polls.

26. **COMMEND** to praise, name as worthy, entrust **ant.** blame, censure ♦ The mother called the baby sitter to *commend* her for her excellent care of the child.

27. COMPASSION sorrow for the sufferings of others, pity **ant.** indifference, mercilessness ♦ The man had *compassion* for the hurt bird and nursed it back to health.

28. COMPUNCTION remorse, regret ♦ I am so annoyed that I would—without any *compunction*—refuse to assist him in any way.

29. CONDIGN deserved, fitting   **ant.** inappropriate ♦ Edna's definition of *condign* punishment is a punitive measure that is appropriate to the misdeed.

30. CONDONE to find excuses for, overlook (as a fault) ♦ One cannot *condone* the killing of a child.

31. CONSUMMATE perfect; to complete, finish   **ant.** crude, rough ♦ Heifetz was one of the *consummate* violinists of our time.

32. CONTINGENT a quota, as of troops; proportionate share; accidental occurrence; depending, accidental, possible but not certain ♦ I would not want my being given the part to be *contingent* on anything other than on my ability.

33. CONVERSANT aware of, familiar with, proficient in   **ant.** ignorant ♦ Anyone who was *conversant* with the world of teen-agers would never have been sarcastic at that crucial moment.

Third Day

1. CONVEYANCE any vehicle in which persons or things are carried; transfer of property ownership ♦ Trains are a dependable means of public *conveyance*.

2. COPIOUS abundant, plentiful   **ant.** meager, scant ♦ He takes such *copious* notes that he writes two pages for each page of text that he reads.

3. COVERT a woolen fabric, frequently waterproofed; thicket; hiding place for game; hidden, concealed, furtive   **ant.** open, plain ♦ The shy boy attempted a *covert* glance at the girl as they walked past each other.

4. CRASS dull, stupid; gross, coarse   **ant.** brilliant; sensitive ♦ Such *crass* ignorance seems never to have been exposed to the light of understanding.

5. CREDENCE belief, faith, trust ♦ One should never give *credence* to malicious gossip.

6. **CRUX** anything difficult to explain; important or critical point. The *crux* of the difficulty is Harold's lack of faith in other people.

7. **CULL** to pick over and remove the unfit ♦ Martha went to the bin to *cull* whatever good ones remained among the winter apples.

8. **CURSORY** hasty, superficial, without attention to details **ant.** complete, detailed, painstaking ♦ After a *cursory* reading of the note, Rose realized that Paul had refused her offer.

9. **DEBACLE** a sudden disaster, downfall ♦ In the *debacle* that followed the unexpected defeat of the loyalist troops, many a promising young officer lost his life.

10. **DECIDUOUS** falling off at a particular season or stage of growth; shedding leaves annually ♦ We know that Winter has left his calling card when the leaves of the *deciduous* trees flutter to the ground.

11. **DECORUM** good taste in action and speech **ant.** indecency ♦ There never could be a breach of *decorum* in the household of this most proper of men.

12. **DEFECTION** desertion; falling away from loyalty ♦ The stand of the Presidential candidate caused so many *defections* from the party that it faces almost certain defeat in the coming elections.

13. **DEIGN** to condescend, stoop ♦ The statesmen would never *deign* to reply to such petty criticism.

14. **DELETERIOUS** harmful, injurious **ant.** beneficial, wholesome ♦ Smoking is *deleterious* to good health.

15. **DEMUR** to hesitate, object **ant.** accept, admit ♦ I do not think that he would *demur* at contributing to this cause!

16. **DEPRECATE** to express strong disapproval of, disapprove **ant.** endorse, approve ♦ Many people *deprecate* the tendency of popular comedians to resort solely to slapstick and buffoonery.

17. **DEROGATORY** disparaging, belittling **ant.** complimentary ♦ The author could not forgive the critic the *derogatory* remarks in the review of his play.

18. **DESICCATE** to dry thoroughly; preserve by drying **ant.** soak ♦ A *desiccated* plum is called a prune.

19. **DESULTORY** jumping from one thing to another, cursory, superficial   **ant.** steady, constant ♦ An advantage to his *desultory* style is that he is able to cover many disconnected topics by jumping from one to another at will.

20. **DIAPHANOUS** transparent   **ant.** opaque ♦ She wore a *diaphanous* scarf to protect herself from the night chill and yet not hide the richness of her gown.

21. **DILATORY** not prompt, causing delay   **ant.** diligent ♦ Mr. Jones received a warning from the telephone company that he was *dilatory* in his payments.

22. **DISAVOW** to deny that one knows about or is responsible for, disclaim ♦ The young man *disavowed* any connection with the group that had stolen the car.

23. **DISCOMFIT** to overthrow completely, defeat; frustrate; embarrass greatly; confuse ♦ Mr. Scher was completely *discomfited* when he realized he was no match for Gladys in this game of wits.

24. **DISCRETE** separate, distinct ♦ Living matter consists of *discrete* units like particles of salt and not a continuum like sea water.

25. **DISSEMBLE** to hide one's feelings, thoughts, etc.; pretend, feign, disguise   **ant.** uncover, unveil, disclose ♦ It is difficult to *dissemble* one's boredom when a play is too wordy.

26. **DISSIMULATE** to disguise or hide under a pretense, hide the truth ♦ The student found it hard to *dissimulate* his lack of knowledge in the class.

27. **DISTRAIT** absent-minded, inattentive   **ant.** alert, sharp ♦ A professor is often portrayed as a *distrait* person who becomes so deeply involved in thought that he loses awareness of external realities.

28. **DOSSIER** a collection of documents or papers about some subject ♦ The aide delivered the *dossier* on internal affairs to the ambassador.

29. **DOTAGE** a weak-minded and childish condition caused by old age   **ant.** infancy ♦ He must be in his *dotage* if he expects us to believe that tale!

30. **DOUGHTY** brave, valiant, hardy   **ant.** cowardly ♦ The *doughty* knights served King Arthur well.

Fourth Day

1. DULCET soothing (esp. to the ear) **ant.** harsh ♦ The *dulcet* tones of Guy Lombardo's band caused many a young couple to dance during the mid-years of the twentieth century.

2. DUPLICITY deceitfulness, treachery **ant.** honesty, loyalty ♦ I never thought that you could be guilty of such *duplicity*, praising me to my face and condemning me to my friends.

3. DURESS compulsion; imprisonment ♦ The confession was not valid because the man claimed he had signed it under *duress*.

4. EBULLIENT overflowing with excitement, very enthusiastic ♦ Ellen was so *ebullient* at the idea of forming the club that she could not stop talking about it whenever we met.

5. EFFETE exhausted; spent and sterile ♦ The plotters called the government *effete*, one incapable of meeting any of the current emergencies.

6. EMBROIL to involve ♦ I was sorry that I became *embroiled* in Harold's argument with the teacher.

7. EMOLLIENT a medicine that soothes surface tissue ♦ The doctor applied an *emollient* to soothe the pain and to soften the skin of his chapped hands.

8. ENCOMIUM praise, commendation **ant.** denunciation ♦ The valedictorian received *encomium* from her parents for her speech to the graduating class.

9. ENJOIN to direct, advise; prohibit **ant.** allow ♦ A court injunction will *enjoin* a publisher from selling a particular book.

10. ENTHRALL to charm, captivate, enchant **ant.** repulse ♦ The TV programs based on the adventures of hardy Western cowboys *enthrall* many a youngster.

11. EPILOGUE a part at the end of a book or play **ant.** prologue ♦ The *epilogue* to the play was spoken by the stage manager after the curtain had been closed.

12. EPITOME a digest, brief summary, essence **ant.** enlargement, expansion ♦ Sir Galahad was the *epitome* of chivalry.

13. EQUIVOCAL ambiguous, having more than one meaning **ant.** clear, obvious ♦ His *equivocal* reply to our question left us as confused as before.

14. ESCHEW to avoid, stay away from   ant. seek, catch ♦ To achieve excellence, you must learn to *eschew* the paths that lead to second-best.

15. EVANESCENT vanishing, disappearing   ant. perpetual, durable ♦ She was disturbed by the *evanescent* glimmer of a thought that had barely reached her consciousness before it disappeared.

16. EXCORIATE to denounce strongly; chafe   ant. praise ♦ The speaker *excoriated* those who would keep the facts from the voting public.

17. EXPEDIENT useful; advisable, convenient; guided by self-interest   ant. harmful ♦ His parents felt that it would not be *expedient* for them to visit him during the week of examinations.

18. EXPEDITIOUS speedy, fast, prompt   ant. slow; inconvenient ♦ Helicopters provided the most *expeditious* means for moving the troops to the besieged area.

19. EXPOSTULATE to reason (with); protest   ant. acquiesce, accept ♦ Hoping to veer his younger brother from a path of self-destruction, the older brother *expostulated* with the boy.

20. EXTIRPATE to destroy, remove totally   ant. revive; create ♦ Racial prejudice must be *extirpated* if we are to survive as a democracy.

21. FALLACIOUS deceptive, misleading   ant. valid, sound ♦ The evidence submitted by the defense attorney proved many of the statements of the star witness to be *fallacious*.

22. FALLOW uncultivated; untrained   ant. used ♦ The farmer allowed one-fourth of his land to lie *fallow* each year to enable the grass to renew the minerals in the soil.

23. FATUOUS stupid but self-satisfied   ant. sensible, judicious ♦ The *fatuous* spectator continued to ask questions that revealed his complete lack of understanding of the process he was viewing.

24. FETID foul-smelling, rank   ant. aromatic, fragrant ♦ A *fetid* smell arose from the stagnant pool.

25. FETTER to chain or manacle, restrain   ant. liberate, free ♦ The prisoners were *fettered* by their ankles in a line.

26. FIAT a decree, order ♦ The dictator replaced government by constitution with rule by *fiat*.

27. FLACCID limp, weak, flabby   **ant.** firm, solid, strong ♦ A person who exercises infrequently has *flaccid* muscles.

28. FOIBLE a small weak point in character; weak point   **ant.** merit, virtue ♦ Each of us can bear to hear his *foibles* exposed—but not his faults.

29. FOREBODING a feeling of something bad about to happen ♦ With an ever-increasing sense of *foreboding* oppressing her, the mother of the missing child waited for the inevitable telephone call.

30. FORTUITOUS accidental, happening by chance   **ant.** planned, rehearsed ♦ Our meeting on a street in Rome on a hot July day was most *fortuitous* since we had lost contact with each other years before.

31. FRACTIOUS cross, unruly, peevish   **ant.** even-tempered; obedient ♦ The substitute teacher sent several of the *fractious* children to the dean before she was able to maintain order in the classroom.

Fifth Day

1. FRAILTY a weakness, imperfection   **ant.** strength ♦ Human *frailty* prevents the discovery of a "perfect" person.

2. FROWARD willful, contrary   **ant.** docile, agreeable, obedient ♦ The *froward* child was given the nickname "Muley" for very obvious reasons.

3. FULSOME coarse, gross; displeasing because of excess   **ant.** pleasant; fitting ♦ Because of his tendency to exaggerate, his praise was so *fulsome* that the audience felt he was an insincere flatterer.

4. GAINSAY to deny, contradict   **ant.** reaffirm; agree ♦ No one will *gainsay* that you were within your rights to do what you did.

5. GARISH loud, glaring, showy   **ant.** sober, quiet, somber ♦ The gypsy in her *garish* dress—all blue and purple and orange—was easily followed through the crowd.

6. GAUCHE clumsy, awkward; tactless   **ant.** skillful ♦ The boy was very *gauche* in his attempt to make a date.

7. GENOCIDE the systematic extermination of a whole people or nation ♦ May the world never forget the horror felt when Hitler practiced *genocide* to rid the world of groups he disliked.

8. GIBE to jeer, scoff, sneer   **ant.** praise, exalt ♦ The taunts and *gibes* of his former friends cut deeply into the conscience of the accused traitor.

9. GLOAMING dusk, twilight   **ant.** dawn ♦ In our area we prefer to use the term *twilight* rather than *dusk* or *gloaming*.

10. GOSSAMER light and thin; thin thread   **ant.** heavy, thick ♦ Like a *gossamer* thread spun by the spider, the rescue rope slithered down the side of the canyon.

11. GRANDILOQUENT using high-flown, flowery language ♦ The speech of the *grandiloquent* orator contained too many references and words dimly understood by the audience.

12. GRANDIOSE showy, pompous, imposing   **ant.** plain, simple ♦ The family was in debt because they tried to live in a *grandiose* manner.

13. GUILE cunning, deceit; deceitful talk or conduct   **ant.** honesty; frankness ♦ *Guile* and trickery rather than honesty and frankness were the practice when Harold sold his goods to the nearby farmers.

14. HABILIMENTS clothing, dress ♦ Attractive *habiliments* enhance one's appearance.

15. HAP chance, luck   **ant.** destiny ♦ Thomas Hardy brought the word *hap* back into the language when he used it to mean a force working against the wishes of the individual.

16. HARBINGER that which goes ahead to announce another's coming ♦ Falling leaves are the *harbingers* of winter.

17. HEINOUS wicked, hateful ♦ His crime was so *heinous* that even his fellow prisoners avoided him.

18. HERESY a belief different from the accepted one   **ant.** conformity ♦ The nonconformist was charged with *heresy* and was thrown out of the party.

19. HETEROGENEOUS varied, mixed   **ant.** homogeneous, alike ♦ The interests of the group were so *heterogeneous* that the members had very little in common.

20. HOMILY a sermon, serious moral talk ♦ The preacher prayed fervently that his congregation would take to heart his *homily* on the need to respect the rights of all others.

21. HYPERBOLE an exaggeration for effect ♦ Writers often for humor effect *hyperboles* such as "a skyscraper hinged to let the moon go by."

22. ICONOCLAST a person who attacks beliefs or institutions which he thinks are wrong or foolish, a rebel ♦ Mencken was an *iconoclast* who attacked the moral standards of the smug middle class of his day.

23. IDIOSYNCRASY a personal peculiarity or mannerism ♦ Helen's *idiosyncrasy* is to turn over the plates to see where they were made.

24. IMMUTABLE unchangeable, never varying ♦ In this universe of change, only change itself seems *immutable*.

25. IMPECCABLE faultless, perfect **ant.** defective ♦ Despite his foreign background, the professor spoke *impeccable* English—without any trace of an accent.

26. IMPERVIOUS not allowing a thing to pass through, impenetrable **ant.** open, susceptible ♦ His coat had been treated to make it *impervious* to water.

27. IMPORTUNE to ask repeatedly or urgently ♦ The widow *importuned* the judge to show mercy on her only son.

28. IMPROVIDENT not thrifty; lacking foresight, careless **ant.** thrifty, stingy ♦ The *improvident* young couple spent so much money for the open roadster that they had to eat sparingly for four months.

29. INADVERTENT inattentive, negligent, due to oversight **ant.** conscious, aware ♦ The *inadvertent* omission of a word made the meaning of the sentence unclear.

30. INCENDIARY having to do with the malicious setting of property on fire; deliberately stirring up strife or rebellion; designed to cause fires; pyromaniac, arsonist ♦ The Allies set the enemy city on fire with *incendiary* bombs.

31. INCIPIENT in an early stage, initial, just beginning **ant.** final, mature ♦ The surgeon advised the immediate removal of the *incipient* tumor, removal before it would grow large enough to be dangerous.

32. INCUMBENT lying upon; pressing, urgent; the holder of an office **ant.** exempt, immune ♦ The *incumbent* Senator was favored over his challenger at the polls.

33. INCURSION an invasion, raid, sudden attack ♦ Forts were built along the border to discourage enemy *incursions*.

Sixth Day

1. INDIGENOUS native, born or originating in the region or country where found   **ant.** imported, foreign, alien ♦ Polar bears are *indigenous* to the Arctic region.

2. INEFFABLE inexpressible, too great to be described in words ♦ Who can describe the *ineffable* beauty in the face of a smiling child?

3. INGRATIATE to bring (oneself) into favor, get into the good graces of ♦ He tried to *ingratiate* himself into the group by treating the boys to sodas.

4. INNATE natural, inborn, inbred   **ant.** external; acquired ♦ The *innate* weakness in his plan was evident to us from the very start.

5. INORDINATE excessive, profuse   **ant.** moderate; insufficient ♦ The *inordinate* demands of the exacting employer caused me to quit within a few days.

6. INSATIABLE very greedy, that cannot be satisfied ♦ King Midas had an *insatiable* lust for gold.

7. INTELLIGENTSIA persons representing the superior intelligence or enlightened opinion of a century ♦ The *intelligentsia* of the school formed the Culture Club in the hope of raising the standards of their classmates.

8. INTIMIDATE to frighten, threaten   **ant.** encourage, inspire ♦ I refuse to be *intimidated* by your threats of violence!

9. INURE to accustom; be useful ♦ We became so *inured* to her insults that they effected little change in our behavior.

10. INVECTIVE a violent attack in words; censure, abuse   **ant.** approval, sanction ♦ In an article filled with *invective* and lashing attacks, the reporter brought out into the open the corruption that he had uncovered in the local government.

11. INVEIGH to make a bitter attack in words ♦ The minister *inveighed* against selfishness that caused so much grief to others.

12. JARGON meaningless talk, slang; talk containing a mixture of languages; specialized vocabulary and idiom of a group ♦

I was not able to understand what the two reporters were saying, as they shouted in the *jargon* of their trade.

13. JUNKET a pleasure trip; excursion by an official paid for out of public funds; feast, picnic; type of dessert ♦ When a Congressman goes on a *junket* to Europe, does the government pay the bill for his wife and secretary if they accompany him?

14. JUNTO a political faction; group of plotters ♦ The ruling *junto* in this small country will remain in power only as long as it has the support of the army.

15. KILN a furnace for burning, baking, or drying something ♦ The potter placed in the *kiln* the clay pieces that he had just fashioned so that he could fire them.

16. LAMBENT moving lightly over a surface without burning it; playing lightly and brilliantly over a subject; radiant, brilliant **ant.** dull ♦ The only light in the room was that of the *lambent* rays of the candle flickering softly on the table.

17. LAMPOON a piece of writing that ridicules and attacks a person; satire; to attack or ridicule **ant.** applause, praise, tribute ♦ The humor magazine *lampooned* the high seriousness that characterized the members of the New Jazz cult.

18. LASSITUDE a weariness of body or mind, feeling of weakness, fatigue **ant.** liveliness, vigor ♦ The intense physical strain left the candidate with a feeling of *lassitude*, and he sat on the bench for almost an hour before he could summon enough energy to leave.

19. LEVITY a lightness of mind or behavior, gaiety **ant.** gravity, austerity ♦ The professor refused to allow any phase of the serious question to be treated with *levity*.

20. LIAISON a connection between parts of an army to get cooperation; unlawful relationship between a man and a woman ♦ Jonathan acted as *liaison* officer because of his thorough command of French.

21. LIMPID clear, transparent **ant.** turbid, muddy, obscure ♦ The boy could see the bottom of the pool through the *limpid* water.

22. LOATH averse, unwilling **ant.** anxious, eager ♦ The boy was *loath* to leave his friends even though bedtime had arrived.

23. LUMINOUS bright, shining, glowing; clear ant. dim, dark; obscure ♦ His statement was so *luminous* that the entire matter now seemed clear and easily understood.

24. MACABRE gruesome, grim, horrible ant. pleasant ♦ It was a *macabre* tale of torture, death, and destruction.

25. MACHINATION a scheme, evil-plotting ♦ The chieftain attributed his defeat in battle to the *machinations* of his hated rival.

26. MAGNILOQUENT using big words and flowery language ♦ The *magniloquent* utterances of the orator almost made us forget the simplicity of the man whose virtues he was extolling.

27. MALAPROPISM a wrong word or expression, one incorrectly used ♦ People who unintentionally misuse a big word are guilty of a *malapropism*.

28. MALINGERER one who pretends to be ill in order to escape duty or work ♦ The officer accused Hugh of being a *malingerer* when Hugh claimed that he had a headache and could not stand guard.

29. MARTINET someone who upholds strict discipline ♦ Our new teacher is such a *martinet* that we dare not think of whispering during Quiet Period.

30. MAUVE a soft purple ♦ Dare I wear a *mauve* tie to blend with a violet-colored shirt?

31. MAWKISH overly sentimental; sickening ♦ He so exaggerated the sense of sorrow in his *mawkish* remarks that I was almost sick to my stomach.

32. MELLIFLUOUS sweetly flowing, smooth ant. rough ♦ What can sound more *mellifluous* to a hungry teen-ager than "Dinner is ready!"?

33. MENIAL servile, lowly ant. high, important ♦ Washing floors is considered a *menial* task by many.

Seventh Day

1. METE to give each his due, distribute ♦ How can a judge *mete* out justice when he himself accepts bribes?

2. MINCING putting on airs or a refined manner; with affected elegance or daintiness **ant.** coarse, common, gross ♦ The audience tittered at the *mincing* walk of the courtier.

3. MISCHANCE misfortune, bad luck ♦ Did you by some *mischance* forget to hand your homework in on time?

4. MITIGATE to abate, soften, mollify **ant.** aggravate ♦ Warm clothing and good health are the only means that I know for *mitigating* the severity of winter.

5. MOOT debatable **ant.** definite ♦ Whether he really agreed to the arrangement is a *moot* question that shall never be answered.

6. MOTE a speck, as of dust ♦ You are but as a *mote* in the eye of eternity, so do not assume arrogance and pride!

7. MULCT to deprive, cheat; punish ♦ The clever card-shark tried to *mulct* him of his money.

8. NADIR the lowest point **ant.** apex, peak ♦ The derelict's fortunes were at their *nadir* when he could find no shelter for the night in the slums of the town.

9. NEFARIOUS wicked, sinful **ant.** good, virtuous ♦ Who will take them to account for this *nefarious* neglect of their aged parents?

10. NOMINAL formal, named; low-priced; insignificant **ant.** costly, expensive ♦ For a *nominal* sum, the gypsy will tell you your fortune.

11. NONPAREIL having no equal ♦ We intend to incorporate the word *nonpareil* in our title since the book will truly be without equal.

12. NUANCE a slight variation, shade of difference ♦ Only an expert could be fully aware of the *nuances* in expression that make one of his essays better written than another.

13. OBDURATE obstinate, stubborn, headstrong **ant.** yielding; tender ♦ Despite the appeals of Vickie's many neighbors, the landlord was *obdurate* in his refusal to delay her eviction.

14. OBVIATE to avoid; remove; prevent **ant.** seek; cause ♦ The manager told him that resigning would *obviate* his being fired.

15. ODIOUS hateful, repulsive **ant.** pleasing, attractive ♦ The swamp water is so brackish, so *odious* to the senses!

16. OMNISCIENT all-knowing ♦ The oracle was an *omniscient* prophet in ancient Greece, capable of foretelling events in any field of human endeavor.

17. ONUS a burden, responsibility ♦ When the refrigerator needed repairs, I refused to have placed on me the *onus* of finding someone to fix it.

18. OPPORTUNE fortunate, well-chosen ant. ill-timed; inappropriate ♦ The fighter unfortunately chose as an *opportune* moment to press his attack the time when his opponent had gained his second wind.

19. OPPROBRIOUS hateful; scandalous; scornful, abusive ♦ They called him a coward and a thief, *opprobrious* names for one held in such high esteem by his colleagues.

20. PAEAN a song of joy, triumph, or praise ♦ The angry whine of the saws cutting down the once lovely grove of stately elms was a *paean* of triumph sung by ugliness while once more conquering in the name of progress.

21. PALLIATE to make appear less serious, lessen without curing; excuse ♦ At no time did I ever try to conceal or *palliate* his errors.

22. PARAGON a pattern, model, ideal ♦ The priest was a *paragon* of goodness.

23. PARIAH an outcast ant. representative; paragon ♦ Phyllis became the village *pariah*, shunned by all, when her traitorous act became known.

24. PAUCITY a lack, scarcity, dearth ant. fullness ♦ To compensate for his *paucity* of ideas, he formed a committee to assist him.

25. PENURIOUS destitute; stingy ant. luxurious, abundant ♦ Our neighbor is so *penurious* that his unwillingness to part with his money has led strangers to offer him financial assistance.

26. PERFUNCTORY indifferent; mechanical; superficial ant. careful ♦ The mechanic gave the typewriter such a *perfunctory* examination that he did not notice the missing key.

27. PERNICIOUS destructive, deadly; mischievous ant. pure, wholesome, harmless ♦ Smoking is a *pernicious* habit that is hard to break once acquired.

28. PERSPICACIOUS keen, penetrating, astute **ant.** dull ♦ The *perspicacious* psychologist quickly had a keen insight into the man's personality difficulties.

29. PERVADE to spread throughout ♦ A deep sense of peace *pervaded* the happy valley.

30. PETTISH peevish, cross ♦ The *pettish* replies of the slighted child caused his older brother to smirk.

31. PHLEGMATIC dull, indifferent, sluggish **ant.** lively, keen ♦ He is so *phlegmatic* that nothing ever gets him excited!

32. PIQUE resentment, wounded pride; to anger **ant.** please, amuse, satisfy ♦ He rushed out of the meeting room in a *pique* when he wasn't elected.

Eighth Day

1. PITTANCE a small amount or share ♦ The boy considered his small allowance as a mere *pittance* compared with what he wanted.

2. POIGNANT sharp in taste or smell; acute, piercing ♦ The sight of the letter written to him by his mother so many years ago flooded his mind with *poignant* memories of days that had been.

3. PORTENTOUS ominous, threatening, warning ♦ The loud thunder was a *portentous* omen, a warning of evil to come.

4. PRAGMATIC worldly; practical ♦ Harold is so filled with common sense that he constantly looks for the *pragmatic* rather than for the ideal solution to a problem.

5. PRECARIOUS doubtful, uncertain, risky **ant.** certain, assured ♦ As a substitute teacher, his position is so *precarious* that he never knows how much he will earn in any given month.

6. PREDILECTION a preference, liking **ant.** aversion, dislike ♦ When selecting fabrics, I have a definite *predilection* for any material colored blue.

7. PREPONDERATE to be greater than something else, be more important ♦ In April, rainy weather *preponderates* over sunny weather.

8. PREROGATIVE a right or privilege ♦ It is a woman's *prerogative* to change her mind.

9. PROCLIVITY an inclination ♦ I decided to see my former doctor and discuss with him my *proclivity* toward evading the truth.

10. PROFLIGATE recklessly wasteful; wicked, depraved, sinful **ant.** virtuous, upright; conserving ♦ He was so *profligate* of his energy that it seemed as though he felt his youth would last forever.

11. PROPENSITY a natural inclination **ant.** dislike ♦ Most boys seem to have a *propensity* for playing baseball.

12. PROSAIC ordinary, unexciting **ant.** unusual ♦ How can he appear so content in such a *prosaic* and commonplace occupation?

13. PUERILE boyish, inexperienced, immature **ant.** experienced, mature ♦ It is *puerile* for a grown man to act so hurt over an insignificant remark.

14. PUNCTILIOUS formal; exact, precise **ant.** careless, heedless ♦ She is so *punctilious* in her observance of the rules of etiquette!

15. PURPORT the essence, meaning; to claim ♦ The statement was *purported* to have originated in the President's office.

16. QUANDARY a dilemma, predicament ♦ We were in a *quandary* as to how we would ever be able to leave on time.

17. QUEUE a line of people, autos, etc.; a braid of hair ♦ There was a *queue* of automobiles waiting for the ferry.

18. QUINTESSENCE the purest form; purest example ♦ Dressed for the Senior Prom, Margie was the *quintessence* of youthful loveliness to her parents.

19. RAILLERY light, good-natured ridicule or satire; teasing ♦ How long must I continue to smile when all of the *raillery* centers on my attempts to play golf!

20. RAMIFY to branch, spread ♦ The results of this decision *ramify* in so many directions that I do not know where it will all end.

21. RAPACIOUS grasping, greedy, thievish, plundering **ant.** charitable ♦ Like *rapacious* birds of prey, the pirates swooped down on the village and plundered it of all its wealth.

22. **RECONDITE** learned, profound **ant.** familiar ♦ The point of law involved is so *recondite* that it is of interest only to the scholarly.

23. **REDOLENT** fragrant; smelling (of), suggestive (of) **ant.** malodorous ♦ The rope was *redolent* of tar, reminding us of our days on the sailing boat.

24. **REDOUBTABLE** feared, dreaded **ant.** loved; fearful ♦ Harold has such a reputation as a *redoubtable* debater that his opponents are often tongue-tied and ill-at-ease from the moment they see him.

25. **REFULGENT** splendid; shining brightly **ant.** ordinary; dull ♦ The diamond necklace was *refulgent* in the sunlight and was emitting colored sparks that dazzled the onlooker.

26. **REMISS** neglectful, slack, careless **ant.** careful, scrupulous ♦ I would be *remiss* in my duties if I did not punish you for breaking this rule!

27. **REMONSTRATE** to object; criticize **ant.** commend, laud ♦ In vain did his well-meaning friends *remonstrate* with Jack on the dangerous experiment he was conducting.

28. **REQUITAL** a payment, return ♦ What *requital* do the gods have in store for one who so cruelly murdered the innocent?

29. **RESOLUTE** steady, firm, persevering **ant.** weak, unsteady, afraid ♦ Alan was *resolute* in his determination to end the reign of terror of the bully.

30. **RESTIVE** uneasy, restless; unruly **ant.** quiet, peaceful ♦ Helen took the reins of the *restive* horse, thinking that she could control him.

31. **RETROGRESS** to decline, relapse, go backward **ant.** progress ♦ Since they haven't practiced, they have *retrogressed* and know less now than before.

32. **REVULSION** a sudden change or reaction (of feelings); disgust **ant.** pleasure ♦ Tom was filled with *revulsion* at the sight of Henry's cheating the old man.

Ninth Day

1. **ROTUND** round, plump, circular **ant.** thin ♦ The *rotund* little man had trouble finding clothes to fit him properly.

2. RUMINATE to chew the cud; think, reflect ♦ He sat staring into the fire and *ruminating* on the events of the past few hours.

3. SACRILEGIOUS insulting to sacred things, impious, desecrating ant. reverent ♦ It is *sacrilegious* to defile church property.

4. SALLOW having a yellow complexion, pallid ant. ruddy ♦ No one could spend hours in the sun and not lose a *sallow* complexion.

5. SATIATE to satisfy fully, supply with too much ♦ After his tonsillectomy, Arthur so *satiated* his appetite for ice cream that for weeks after recovering he could not even bear to see a picture of any.

6. SCOURGE to whip, lash, strap; punish; something that causes great trouble or misfortune ♦ Dr. Salk erased the *scourge* of polio.

7. SEDATE quiet, serious ant. wild, lively, gay ♦ The *sedate* young lady spent all her free time reading.

8. SEEMLY proper, fitting, becoming ant. unseemly, indecent ♦ It is not *seemly* for girls to come to school in slacks.

9. SEMBLANCE appearance; likeness ♦ The modern portrait here bears no *semblance* to its model.

10. SEQUESTER to remove from public use; seize by authority ♦ The district attorney asked for a court order to *sequester* the firm's records.

11. SERRIED crowded very closely together ♦ The soldiers in *serried* lines filed proudly before the reviewing stand.

12. SINECURE an easy job that usually pays well ♦ If you think being manager of a ball team is a *sinecure*, I'd like you to try it just for one day!

13. SINUOUS having many curves; indirect ant. unswerving; straightforward ♦ The driver had to be careful with his steering while driving on the *sinuous* mountain roads.

14. SLOUGH old skin shed or cast off (usually by a snake); a place full of soft, deep mud; swamp; to discard (a losing card) ♦ The rattlesnake slowly moved away from his *slough*.

15. SOJOURN to stay for a time, visit; a brief stay ♦ During his brief *sojourn* in Israel, he visited many areas mentioned in the Bible.

16. SPATE a flood; very heavy downpour of rain; sudden outburst ♦ Such a *spate* of words issued from the gossip's lips that I was certain I would never get away.

17. SPECIOUS seeming reasonable, but not really so **ant.** demonstrable, confirmed ♦ Helen saw quickly through Don's *specious* arguments.

18. SPECTRAL ghostly ♦ Washington Irving's headless horseman seemed to be a *spectral* figure.

19. SQUIB a broken firecracker; sharp sarcasm ♦ The pugilist threatened to punch the nose of the columnist for the *squib* in which the writer questioned the fighter's level of intelligence.

20. STENTORIAN very loud, powerful in sound **ant.** low, modulated ♦ Over the loud-speaker came the *stentorian* voice of the conductor announcing the next stop.

21. STRICTURE a critical remark; unhealthy narrowing of some duct of the body **ant.** praise, commendation ♦ Few are the youths who can accept with good grace the *strictures* of a friend, regardless of how wise the criticism may be.

22. STRINGENT strict, severe **ant.** liberal, easygoing ♦ In many states there are *stringent* laws against jaywalking.

23. SUBLIMATE to purify, refine; channel ♦ The wise teacher invented games that taught the children to *sublimate* their selfish impulses into socially worthwhile channels.

24. SUNDER to separate, divide, break **ant.** link, unite ♦ What time has *sundered* in sorrow, man is often powerless to bring together again.

25. SUPERCILIOUS haughty, disdainful, showing scorn because of a feeling of superiority **ant.** humble ♦ The *supercilious* actress brushed past her admirers without a smile.

26. SUPPLIANT beseeching, asking humbly; a person who asks humbly ♦ The penniless father sent a *suppliant* letter to his more fortunate brother pleading for help for his family.

27. SURREPTITIOUS secret, acting or done in a secret way **ant.** frank, open ♦ I discovered where she kept the *surreptitious* hoard of candy that made a farce of her dieting efforts.

28. SURVEILLANCE supervision, watch kept over a person ♦ The police kept their prime suspect under constant *surveillance*.

29. SYNDROME the characteristic pattern of a disease; accompanying pattern ♦ The examining physician quickly recognized the rash as part of the scarlet-fever *syndrome*.

30. TALISMAN a charm, lucky piece; stone engraved with figures that are supposed to have magical powers ♦ She wore the old Indian penny on a string around her neck as a *talisman* to ward off evil.

31. TAWDRY gaudy, flashy, cheap, garish **ant.** elegant ♦ The *tawdry* display excited the imagination of the naïve teen-ager.

32. TEMERARIOUS rash, reckless, foolhardy **ant.** timid, cautious ♦ The *temerarious* band of adventurers tried to take the citadel by surprise when they launched their attack in midwinter.

33. TENUOUS thin, slender, flimsy **ant.** dense ♦ During the long illness, the *tenuous* thread of life threatened to snap at every moment of crisis.

34. TERMAGANT a violent, quarreling woman; violent, quarreling, scolding ♦ The voice of our landlady, the *termagant* of the neighborhood, constantly assailed our ears as she quarreled with her cronies on the front doorstep.

Tenth Day

1. THESAURUS a treasury; book of synonyms ♦ I plan to look in the *thesaurus* for a synonym for *thanks* that will best fit this sentence.

2. TOADY a fawning flatterer ♦ He was a *toady* in the presence of the rich and influential and a bully when surrounded by his employees.

3. TORTUOUS full of twists, turns, or bends **ant.** straight, unbending ♦ The *tortuous* path followed the meanderings of the stream through the long valley.

4. TRANSMUTE to change from one substance or form into another ♦ The successful writer *transmutes* his personal and private agonies into something universal and impersonal.

5. TRAVESTY a parody, burlesque, imitation that makes a serious thing look ridiculous ♦ What a *travesty* on justice was the trial afforded the victim of the lynching mob's fury!

6. TRENCHANT sharp, keen, cutting **ant.** weak, feeble ♦ I deeply appreciate his *trenchant* analysis and evaluation of my work!

7. TREPIDATION fear, fright, trembling **ant.** bravery ♦ He faced the dangerous operation with a feeling of *trepidation*.

8. TUMBREL a cart that carried prisoners to be executed ♦ Marie Antoinette rode in a *tumbrel* to her execution.

9. UBIQUITOUS present everywhere, or seeming to be so ♦ The *ubiquitous* butler anticipated his employer's every move.

10. UMBRAGE resentment; suspicion that one has been slighted; offense **ant.** sympathy ♦ He took *umbrage* at the teacher's curt dismissal of his efforts.

11. UNCONSCIONABLE unreasonable; excessive; not guided by conscience **ant.** moderate; appropriate ♦ I resigned from the position because of his *unconscionable* demands on my time.

12. UNGAINLY awkward, clumsy **ant.** graceful ♦ The *ungainly* girl blossomed into a beautiful young woman.

13. UNTOWARD unfavorable, unfortunate **ant.** lucky ♦ Provided nothing *untoward* occurs, our success is assured!

14. UNWONTED not usual; not accustomed **ant.** common ♦ I had the *unwonted* joy of achieving the highest mark in the mathematics test.

15. VAGARY a whim; extravagant notion ♦ I was unable to comprehend the *vagaries* of his inventive mind.

16. VAPID dull, bland, lifeless **ant.** spicy ♦ This *vapid* novel presents the dull life of dull people in dull prose.

17. VENAL willing to sell one's services or influence, open to bribes, corruptible **ant.** pure, honest ♦ The *venal* politicians sold their votes to the highest bidders.

18. VENIAL pardonable, excusable **ant.** inexcusable, unpardonable ♦ He was guilty of no more than the *venial* indiscretions of youth.

19. VERDANT green; inexperienced ♦ The pasture was covered with the *verdant* grass of early spring.

20. VICARIOUS taking the place of another; done or suffered for another ♦ The child received *vicarious* thrills by reading adventure stories.

21. VIRAGO a bad-tempered or scolding woman, termagant ♦ Who can long endure a woman turned *virago*, a loudmouthed, foul-tongued scold!

22. VIRTUOSO one skilled in the methods of an art (esp. music) ♦ Only a *virtuoso* such as Millstein could have played the solo part in that concerto with such assurance and ease.

23. VISIONARY not practical; existing only in one's imagination; a dreamer, one who is not practical ♦ I hope that no other would-be dictator has *visionary* schemes for world conquest in my lifetime.

24. VOUCHSAFE to be willing to grant or give, concede ♦ The stubborn prisoner *vouchsafed* no reply to his interrogators.

25. WAGGISH funny, fond of making jokes, playful **ant.** serious, sober ♦ Never critical, he always displays a *waggish* good humor as the base of his remarks.

26. WAIVE to relinquish, defer, put aside **ant.** demand, claim ♦ The author was willing to *waive* the royalties on his book for a flat sum of money.

27. WELTER to wallow or roll, as in mud; commotion, confusion ♦ The mass of people have for too long *weltered* in shocking ignorance.

28. WHET to sharpen by rubbing; make keen or eager ♦ Just the mention of roast beef was enough to *whet* the boy's appetite.

29. WINSOME pleasant, attractive, charming **ant.** repulsive ♦ The *winsome* young girl had little difficulty in winning the favor of our host.

30. WREAK to give, work off (feelings, desires, etc.); inflict ♦ The gods shall *wreak* their vengeance on you for such blasphemy!

31. ZANY a clown, fool, comedian ◆ You do not have to act the part of a *zany* all the time!

Eleventh Day: First Senior-List Practice Test

A. Antonyms

In the space provided, write the letter of the word that is most nearly opposite in meaning to the given word.

1. CARPING (a) hunting (b) netting (c) meticulous (d) approving (e) questionable 1. ....

2. DISSEMBLE (a) disclose (b) gather (c) scatter (d) orate (e) enact 2. ....

3. FOIBLE (a) tale (b) nonfiction (c) virtue (d) open (e) willingness 3. ....

4. INDIGENOUS (a) wealthy (b) alien (c) poor (d) operating (e) mediocre 4. ....

5. LOATH (a) love (b) childish (c) doting (d) wooden (e) eager 5. ....

6. SEDATE (a) wild (b) quiet (c) medical (d) surgical (e) physiological 6. ....

7. STENTORIAN (a) soundproof (b) low (c) impolite (d) sarcastic (e) injurious 7. ....

8. HERESY (a) conformity (b) masculine (c) feminine (d) trial (e) guilt 8. ....

9. EXCORIATE (a) police (b) find (c) build (d) praise (e) elevate 9. ....

10. INCIPIENT (a) foolish (b) ordinary (c) wise (d) final (e) discarded 10. ....

11. ABJECT (a) aim (b) poor (c) noble (d) accept (e) reject 11. ....

12. CACOPHONY (a) ugliness (b) harmony (c) pleasure (d) folly (e) hardness 12. ....

13. GRANDIOSE (a) small (b) gigantic (c) plain (d) defeated (e) eroded 13. ....

14. LAMPOON   (a) applause   (b) lantern
(c) darkness   (d) glimmer   (e) ray   14. ....

15. LEVITY   (a) sincerity   (b) hypocrisy
(c) musicianship   (d) gravity   (e) nonsense   15. ....

16. OPPORTUNE   (a) rich   (b) inappropriate   (c) late
(d) futile   (e) scholarly   16. ....

17. SINUOUS   (a) dull   (b) shining   (c) spinning
(d) unpleasing   (e) straightforward   17. ....

18. UMBRAGE   (a) resentment   (b) suspicion
(c) sympathy   (d) cover   (e) sunlight   18. ....

19. UNWONTED   (a) usual   (b) disliked   (c) dull
(d) pleasurable   (e) painful   19. ....

20. VAPID   (a) slow   (b) spicy   (c) sullen
(d) praiseworthy   (e) thunderous   20. ....

21. CURSORY   (a) complimentary   (b) intentional
(c) exact   (d) foreign   (e) oral   21. ....

22. ANIMADVERSION   (a) vegetable   (b) blame
(c) sense   (d) praise   (e) originality   22. ....

23. ABSOLVE   (a) thicken   (b) catch   (c) execute
(d) imprison   (e) blame   23. ....

24. BALEFUL   (a) ugly   (b) light   (c) overweight
(d) beneficial   (e) actual   24. ....

25. CELERITY   (a) anonymity   (b) slowness
(c) emphasis   (d) harm   (e) desirability   25. ....

26. EXPOSTULATE   (a) accept   (b) drive   (c) guide
(d) enter   (e) prearrange   26. ....

27. GIBE   (a) pardon   (b) destroy   (c) praise
(d) request   (e) sneer   27. ....

28. INNATE   (a) exterior   (b) external
(c) extraordinary   (d) excitable   (e) extant   28. ....

29. MELLIFLUOUS   (a) rude   (b) rotten
(c) righteous   (d) rightful   (e) rough   29. ....

30. MINCING   (a) long   (b) clever   (c) dull
(d) coarse   (e) affected   30. ....

31. PENURIOUS   (a) luxurious   (b) uncomfortable
(c) modest   (d) fitting   (e) false   31. ....

32. REDOLENT   (a) forgetful   (b) malcontent
(c) malodorous   (d) complex   (e) wholesale   32. ....

33. SPECIOUS   (a) ordinary   (b) exceptional   (c) true
(d) profound   (e) seldom   33. ....

34. UNCONSCIONABLE   (a) material   (b) moral
(c) flimsy   (d) modest   (e) possible   34. ....

35. VENAL   (a) fishing   (b) pardonable
(c) unavoidable   (d) unwanted   (e) pure   35. ....

B. Sentence Completion

In the space provided, write the letter of the word that best completes the sentence.

36. The men were so .... after being without food for seventy-two hours that the doctors injected fluids intravenously into their bodies.
(a) mitigated   (b) importuned   (c) desiccated
(d) extirpated   36. ....

37. The only way to improve the .... of this hall is to install three permanent speakers along the front wall.
(a) acoustics   (b) appellation   (c) conveyance
(d) cacophony   37. ....

38. The leaves of the .... trees turned orange and red and yellow before they fluttered to the ground at the end of the autumn season.
(a) redolent   (b) deciduous   (c) consummate
(d) dilatory   38. ....

39. Nothing is sacred to the .... who attacks any belief or institution having a weakness that he can detect.
(a) zany   (b) visionary   (c) iconoclast
(d) supercilious   39. ....

40. The .... had been a humble cart used by farmers before it soared into history as the executioner's wagon.
(a) fiat   (b) incumbent   (c) encomium
(d) tumbrel   40. ....

41. In that the promise had been made under ...., Harold felt that it could be broken.
(a) pittance   (b) duress   (c) predilection
(d) trepidation   41. ....

42. The crime of .... brought the methods of modern-day big business into the execution chamber.
(a) semblance   (b) sinecure   (c) quintessence
(d) genocide   42. ....

43. What parent is so .... that he can predict the daydreams of his offspring?
(a) omniscient   (b) perfunctory   (c) phlegmatic
(d) penurious   43. ....

44. I place the .... of our failure right where it belongs, on your shoulders!
(a) purport   (b) quandary   (c) onus   (d) paucity   44. ....

45. The song of the lark as it soared ever upward and out of sight was a .... of joy.
(a) paragon   (b) paean   (c) pariah   (d) nonpareil   45. ....

46. When exposed by the doctor, the .... calmly admitted that he was willing to resort to any trickery to avoid unpleasant tasks.
(a) blazon   (b) anomaly   (c) malingerer
(d) encomium   46. ....

47. The sight of the .... suit of armor in the case in the museum brought the sound of jousts to the ears of the enchanted boy.
(a) refulgent   (b) fulsome   (c) discrete
(d) adventitious   47. ....

48. The old man prayed that the time would never come when his curiosity would be ....
(a) flaccid   (b) ebullient   (c) absolved
(d) satiated   48. ....

49. Any .... between the truth and the story that he has just told us is purely coincidental.
(a) lampoon   (b) requital   (c) semblance
(d) proclivity   49. ....

50. The .... forest was the home of the migrant tribes during the hot summer days.
(a) seemly   (b) archaic   (c) amenable
(d) verdant   50. ....

C. Synonyms

In the space provided, write the letter of the word that is most nearly the same in meaning as the first word.

51. ARBITER (a) defendant (b) juror (c) lawyer (d) accused (e) judge   51. ....

52. HABILIMENTS (a) food (b) manner (c) dress (d) speech (e) trade   52. ....

53. HEINOUS (a) hateful (b) strong (c) germane (d) refined (e) crude   53. ....

54. ICONOCLAST (a) student (b) professor (c) idol (d) rebel (e) remnant   54. ....

55. INTELLIGENTSIA (a) dupes (b) intellectuals (c) writers (d) politicians (e) actors   55. ....

56. JARGON (a) nonsense (b) reasoning (c) slang (d) dish (e) patriot   56. ....

57. MAGNILOQUENT (a) loud (b) silent (c) talkative (d) audible (e) flowery   57. ....

58. PREROGATIVE (a) request (b) right (c) error (d) rejection (e) characteristic   58. ....

59. PERVADE (a) conquer (b) accept (c) spoil (d) spread (e) commit   59. ....

60. RAILLERY (a) fence (b) attack (c) turn (d) satire (e) warning   60. ....

61. ASCRIBE (a) edit (b) create (c) copy (d) publish (e) assign   61. ....

62. ASSEVERATE (a) see (b) hear (c) read (d) state (e) understand   62. ....

63. DISCRETE (a) certain (b) separate (c) modest (d) bold (e) tepid   63. ....

64. DISSIMULATE (a) smile (b) evade (c) pretend (d) request (e) answer   64. ....

65. DOSSIER (a) document (b) order (c) ruling (d) sentence (e) declaration   65. ....

66. VIRAGO (a) fool (b) scholar (c) scold (d) secretary (e) owner   66. ....

67. VICARIOUS   (a) distant   (b) substitute
(c) literal   (d) fortunate   (e) evil   67. ....

68. TRAVESTY   (a) thought   (b) tragedy   (c) heresy
(d) burlesque   (e) barrage   68. ....

69. TOADY   (a) insect   (b) animal   (c) bird
(d) machine   (e) person   69. ....

70. TERMAGANT   (a) man   (b) woman   (c) infant
(d) youth   (e) child   70. ....

71. SURVEILLANCE   (a) watch   (b) accuse
(c) suspect   (d) arrest   (e) arraign   71. ....

72. SYNDROME   (a) diagnosis   (b) illness
(c) pattern   (d) prognosis   (e) medication   72. ....

73. SUPPLIANT   (a) bent   (b) pleader   (c) prayer
(d) priest   (e) temple   73. ....

74. SUBLIMATE   (a) explain   (b) reveal
(c) condemn   (d) elevate   (e) purify   74. ....

75. PERSPICACIOUS   (a) eventual   (b) astute
(c) clear   (d) dull   (e) vanishing   75. ....

76. PARIAH   (a) friend   (b) follower   (c) executioner
(d) outcast   (e) beggar   76. ....

77. INCENDIARY   (a) belligerent   (b) pilot
(c) navigator   (d) bombardier   (e) arsonist   77. ....

78. ENJOIN   (a) connect   (b) prohibit   (c) enlist
(d) enlarge   (e) encourage   78. ....

79. EFFETE   (a) damaged   (b) whole   (c) ruinous
(d) modern   (e) spent   79. ....

80. COVERT   (a) thicket   (b) quill   (c) fiber
(d) blanket   (e) canoe   80. ....

81. COLLATE   (a) enter   (b) attend   (c) compare
(d) design   (e) publish   81. ....

82. CIRCUMSCRIBE   (a) foretell   (b) limit
(c) extend   (d) include   (e) recast   82. ....

83. BLAZON   (a) risk   (b) rush   (c) cover
(d) display   (e) desire   83. ....

84. BLANDISH (a) wave (b) explain (c) discover
(d) hide (e) coax   84. ....

85. BASTION (a) deferment (b) soldier (c) defense
(d) reinforcement (e) entry   85. ....

D. Analogies

In the space provided, write the letter of the set of words that best completes the analogy.

86. BAGATELLE : TRIFLE :: COVERT : (a) field
(b) open (c) thicket (d) design   86. ....

87. DEPRECATE : DEROGATORY ::
EXPOSTULATE : (a) reason (b) opposing (c) praising
(d) acquiescent   87. ....

88. FRACTIOUS : FATUOUS :: (a) forward : froward
(b) fulsome : praiseworthy (c) docile : satisfying
(d) cross : stupid   88. ....

89. CONVEYANCE : TUMBREL :: (a) incumbent :
mayor (b) incursion : incident (c) junto : plotters
(d) liaison : conference   89. ....

90. FALLACIOUS : SPECIOUS :: SURREPTITIOUS :
(a) sudden (b) frank (c) secret (d) violent   90. ....

91. EBULLIENT : ENTHUSIASTIC :: EFFETE :
(a) unfinished (b) fatal (c) mild (d) exhausted 91. ....

92. DISSEMBLE : FEELINGS :: DISSIMULATE :
(a) truth (b) clothing (c) mentality (d) opposite 92. ....

93. DISTRAIT : ALERT :: DULCET : (a) loving
(b) harsh (c) clever (d) sweet   93. ....

94. DIAPHANOUS : LIMPID :: (a) cloth : water
(b) clear : muddy (c) camera : bulb (d) light :
flabby   94. ....

95. ASSEVERATE : STATE :: ATTENUATE:
(a) watch (b) count (c) weaken (d) destroy   95. ....

96. MALAPROPISM : MAUVE :: (a) accident :
sensation (b) time : costume (c) illness : envy
(d) word : color   96. ....

97. PROFLIGATE : UNCONSCIONABLE ::
MENIAL : (a) kind   (b) lasting   (c) noble
(d) servile   97. ....

98. EXCORIATE : DENOUNCE :: INTIMIDATE :
(a) aid   (b) threaten   (c) encourage   (d) weaken   98. ....

99. MAGNILOQUENT : LUMINOUS :: (a) much :
little   (b) one : many   (c) many : much   (d) weak :
strong   99. ....

100. PERVADE : SPREAD :: (a) enjoin : prohibit
(b) cull : reject   (c) circumscribe : autograph   (d) accrue :
violence   100. ....

Answer Key

A. Antonyms

1. (d)	8. (a)	15. (d)	22. (d)	29. (e)
2. (a)	9. (d)	16. (b)	23. (e)	30. (d)
3. (c)	10. (d)	17. (e)	24. (d)	31. (a)
4. (b)	11. (c)	18. (e)	25. (b)	32. (c)
5. (e)	12. (b)	19. (a)	26. (a)	33. (c)
6. (a)	13. (c)	20. (b)	27. (c)	34. (d)
7. (b)	14. (a)	21. (c)	28. (b)	35. (e)

B. Sentence Completion

36. (c)	39. (c)	42. (d)	45. (b)	48. (d)
37. (a)	40. (d)	43. (a)	46. (c)	49. (c)
38. (b)	41. (b)	44. (c)	47. (a)	50. (d)

C. Synonyms

51. (e)	58. (b)	65. (a)	72. (c)	79. (e)
52. (c)	59. (d)	66. (c)	73. (b)	80. (a)
53. (a)	60. (d)	67. (b)	74. (e)	81. (c)
54. (d)	61. (e)	68. (d)	75. (b)	82. (b)
55. (b)	62. (d)	69. (e)	76. (d)	83. (d)
56. (c)	63. (b)	70. (b)	77. (e)	84. (e)
57. (e)	64. (c)	71. (a)	78. (b)	85. (c)

D. Analogies

86. (c)	89. (d)	92. (a)	95. (c)	98. (b)
87. (b)	90. (c)	93. (b)	96. (d)	99. (c)
88. (d)	91. (d)	94. (a)	97. (d)	100. (a)

My Score: Number Right............ Number Wrong............

Clinch by Checking

The purpose of this test was to help you discover which of the words in the Senior List you must concentrate on in order to achieve 100% mastery. Since the list is arranged in alphabetical order, you should have no difficulty in checking back. Mark the words that you missed; these are the ones that should be studied in your next session. Once you have them under control, then you are ready for the Second Senior-List Practice Test.

Twelfth Day: Second Senior-List Practice Test

A. Sentence Completion

In the space provided, write the letter of the word that best completes the sentence.

1. The critic felt that if the editor had to .... the text of the manuscript to such an extent that the messages of the author were lost, then the material should have been either printed as it originally was or rejected by the publisher in the first place.
(a) excoriate   (b) gainsay   (c) bowdlerize
(d) importune   1. ....

2. I sent for a copy of the .... in which he describes the full effects of radiation.
(a) foible   (b) brochure   (c) genocide   (d) gossamer   2. ....

3. Inasmuch as he has insisted on disobeying instructions, I have no .... against rating him unsatisfactory in my next report.
(a) compunctions   (b) frailty   (c) habiliments
(d) idiosyncrasy   3. ....

4. The first .... of the UN force will arrive on the war-torn island by this afternoon.
(a) harbinger   (b) contingent   (c) heresy
(d) incipient   4. ....

5. I refuse to become .... in a quarrel between a brother and a sister.
(a) embroiled   (b) incumbent   (c) improvident
(d) incendiary   5. ....

6. Starlings, which had been .... to Japan, are now so prevalent in the northern United States that they have replaced the English sparrows and robins in most of our cities.
(a) baleful   (b) captious   (c) aplomb
(d) indigenous   6. ....

7. A look of .... joy spread over the face of the saintly hermit as he recited his articles of faith.
(a) ineffable   (b) anomaly   (c) ascetic
(d) clandestine   7. ....

8. The gossip had such a(n) .... lust for newsy tidbits that she barely had time to do her household chores.
(a) evanescent   (b) insatiable   (c) expedient
(d) flaccid   8. ....

9. The businessmen joined the .... set up by the army colonels to overthrow the unsympathetic president.
(a) junto   (b) barrage   (c) alacrity   (d) acoustics   9. ....

10. The molten metal was taken out of the .... and was poured into the molds.
(a) nadir   (b) bagatelle   (c) decorum   (d) kiln   10. ....

11. Why are we so willing to put up with the .... of our friends though we resent those of our brothers and sisters?
(a) foibles   (b) junkets   (c) gibes   (d) pittances   11. ....

12. How could you be so taken in by the .... praise of a flatterer whose only interest is in the generous gifts of money he extracts from your purse?
(a) portentous   (b) precarious   (c) fulsome
(d) pragmatic   12. ....

13. To take full advantage of the tide, we set sail in the .... rather than at dawn, the customary time in this port.
(a) predilection   (b) gloaming   (c) proclivity
(d) wreak   13. ....

14. I still do not know what was to be considered more ....—
the crime he committed or the punishment meted out to him by the angry citizens.
(a) profligate   (b) serried   (c) prosaic   (d) heinous   14. ....

15. With each ...., the Moors became bolder until a large-scale assault was launched to wipe out the defenses of all the cities in the province.
(a) incursion   (b) invective   (c) machination
(d) malapropism   15. ....

B. Antonyms

In the space provided, write the letter of the word that is most nearly opposite in meaning to the first word.

16. WAGGISH   (a) motionless   (b) silent   (c) serious
(d) silly   (e) momentary   16. ....

17. DISTRAIT   (a) alert   (b) relevant   (c) upset
(d) calm   (e) absent   17. ....

18. ENCOMIUM   (a) exit   (b) rebuff   (c) illness
(d) wealth   (e) attack   18. ....

19. FORTUITOUS   (a) bad   (b) late   (c) playful
(d) rehearsed   (e) told   19. ....

20. DESULTORY   (a) praising   (b) jumpy   (c) light
(d) slight   (e) steady   20. ....

21. MENIAL   (a) feminine   (b) special   (c) accidental
(d) sweet   (e) thoughtful   21. ....

22. MITIGATE   (a) aggravate   (b) favor   (c) impress
(d) extol   (e) disclaim   22. ....

23. PAUCITY   (a) stupidity   (b) misfortune
(c) power   (d) gracefulness   (e) fullness   23. ....

24. PROSAIC   (a) verse   (b) gracious   (c) talented
(d) unusual   (e) fashionable   24. ....

25. REDOUBTABLE   (a) feared   (b) protected
(c) loved   (d) hated   (e) inferior   25. ....

26. SEEMLY   (a) timely   (b) dated   (c) unwanted
(d) indecent   (e) clean   26. ....

27. SUPERCILIOUS   (a) essential   (b) humble
(c) ordinary   (d) rare   (e) scorched   27. ....

28. VENIAL   (a) unpardonable   (b) cheap   (c) pure
(d) accepted   (e) honorable   28. ....

29. LUMINOUS   (a) inoperative   (b) careless
(c) old-fashioned   (d) dim   (e) extant   29. ....

30. INVECTIVE   (a) co-operation   (b) violence
(c) approval   (d) mildness   (e) judgment   30. ....

31. GUILE   (a) hate   (b) love   (c) quietude
(d) authority   (e) honesty   31. ....

32. GAUCHE   (a) right   (b) skillful   (c) wrong
(d) French   (e) fast   32. ....

33. FALLACIOUS   (a) truthful   (b) sensible
(c) sensitive   (d) common   (e) musical   33. ....

34. EVANESCENT   (a) past   (b) appalling
(c) durable   (d) vague   (e) loud   34. ....

35. DOTAGE   (a) massiveness   (b) infancy
(c) maturity   (d) sunrise   (e) sunset   35. ....

36. DILATORY   (a) slow   (b) rapid   (c) rich
(d) poor   (e) industrious   36. ....

37. ENTHRALL   (a) free   (b) tease   (c) repulse
(d) annoy   (e) torture   37. ....

38. ADAMANT   (a) clever   (b) submissive
(c) stubborn   (d) wild   (e) tame   38. ....

39. FETID   (a) raw   (b) completed   (c) unreal
(d) aromatic   (e) fond   39. ....

40. MOOT   (a) clear   (b) clean   (c) detailed
(d) headgear   (e) tame   40. ....

41. NEFARIOUS   (a) concise   (b) incipient
(c) unwonted   (d) actual   (e) virtuous   41. ....

42. PROFLIGATE   (a) amateur   (b) liberal
(c) virtuous   (d) religious   (e) scant   42. ....

43. PUERILE   (a) fast   (b) mature   (c) insipid
(d) insolent   (e) polite   43. ....

44. REMISS   (a) absent   (b) willing   (c) cagey
(d) careful   (e) spoiled   44. ....

45. RETROGRESS   (a) progress   (b) struggle
(c) succeed   (d) flag   (e) obey   45. ....

46. STRICTURE   (a) loosening   (b) regulation
(c) praise   (d) injury   (e) request   46. ....

47. TRENCHANT   (a) deep   (b) shallow   (c) certain
(d) open   (e) weak   47. ....

48. WAIVE   (a) stabilize   (b) demand   (c) push
(d) direct   (e) determine   48. ....

49. WINSOME   (a) losing   (b) loose   (c) rich
(d) entire   (e) repulsive   49. ....

50. ODIOUS   (a) fragrant   (b) pleasing   (c) old
(d) patriotic   (e) smooth   50. ....

C. Analogies

In the space provided, write the letter of the set of words that
best completes the analogy.

51. DISCRETE : EXPEDIENT :: (a) sensible :
convenient   (b) separate : advisable   (c) sedate : incipient
(d) vapid : cursory   51. ....

52. VIRAGO : TERMAGANT :: (a) loud : soft
(b) calm : violent   (c) burst : barrage   (d) scolding :
scolding   52. ....

53. UNGAINLY : GRACEFUL :: (a) untoward :
auspicious   (b) callow : unfledged   (c) cognizant : legal
(d) deciduous : contingent   53. ....

54. EXPOSTULATE : PROTEST :: (a) fetter : judge
(b) inveigh : free   (c) mitigate : mollify   (d) obviate :
cure   54. ....

55. GRANDIOSE : BOMBASTIC :: (a) plain : ornate
(b) pompous : flowery   (c) covert : cross   (d) dilatory :
impeccable   55. ....

56. EQUIVOCAL : EPITOME :: (a) incipient : epilogue
(b) effete : habiliments   (c) dulcet : tone   (d) ambiguous :
summary   56. ....

57. REDOUBTABLE : DOUGHTY :: (a) coward :
craven   (b) barrier : dynamiter   (c) enemy : champion
(d) questioning : raw   57. ....

58. SINUOUS : TORTUOUS :: (a) muscle : path
(b) wisdom : turn   (c) direction : cruelty   (d) straight :
unbending   58. ....

59. STRINGENT : SUPERCILIOUS :: (a) severe :
disdainful   (b) sharp : trivial   (c) stingy : liberal
(d) straight : superior   59. ....

60. TOADY : SUPPLIANT :: (a) leader : worshiper
(b) general : corporal   (c) private : captive   (d) flattery :
prayer   60. ....

61. VAGARY : IDIOSYNCRASY :: (a) tramp : ideal
(b) synonym : antonym   (c) whim : mannerism
(d) public : personal   61. ....

62. WINSOME : STENTORIAN :: (a) appearance :
tone   (b) loud-speaker : beauty   (c) gambler : conductor
(d) belle : whistle   62. ....

63. OBDURATE : ODIOUS :: (a) hard : soft
(b) headstrong : repulsive   (c) harsh : hate   (d) long :
love   63. ....

64. AVERSE : BALEFUL :: (a) good : bad
(b) opposite : heavy   (c) bad : worse   (d) sympathetic :
evil   64. ....

65. BASTION : BUTTRESS :: (a) veal : lamb
(b) animal : vegetable   (c) bake : fry   (d) defense :
support   65. ....

D. Synonyms

In the space provided, write the letter of the word that is most
nearly the same in meaning as the first word.

66. DUPLICITY   (a) duplication   (b) treachery
(c) example   (d) finery   (e) leadership   66. ....

67. HYPERBOLE   (a) microscopic animal
(b) excellence   (c) exaggeration   (d) feature
(e) essence   67. ....

68. MALAPROPISM   (a) wrong word   (b) wrong deed
(c) wrong person   (d) wrong idea   (e) wrong diagnosis
                                                       68. ....

69. **MARTINET** (a) bird (b) soldier
(c) disciplinarian (d) teacher (e) student   69. ....

70. **MAUVE** (a) soft (b) cloth (c) green (d) red
(e) purple   70. ....

71. **PAEAN** (a) thunder (b) lightning (c) song
(d) challenge (e) poem   71. ....

72. **MAWKISH** (a) gawky (b) sentimental
(c) deadly (d) long (e) tiresome   72. ....

73. **NOMINAL** (a) early (b) insignificant
(c) financial (d) orderly (e) thin   73. ....

74. **NONPAREIL** (a) uneven (b) unsung
(c) unequaled (d) unwanted (e) untold   74. ....

75. **PALLIATE** (a) appall (b) appease (c) excuse
(d) extend (e) exit   75. ....

76. **PROPENSITY** (a) inclination (b) ownership
(c) distaste (d) training (e) mark   76. ....

77. **RAMIFY** (a) rage (b) fade (c) branch
(d) fasten (e) embroil   77. ....

78. **RAPACIOUS** (a) clever (b) kind (c) wandering
(d) thievish (e) thick   78. ....

79. **RECONDITE** (a) superficial (b) unknown
(c) scientific (d) profound (e) mediocre   79. ....

80. **REVULSION** (a) disgust (b) turn (c) exchange
(d) attack (e) fear   80. ....

81. **SALLOW** (a) low (b) learned (c) waxy
(d) wont (e) pallid   81. ....

82. **SATIATE** (a) scorn (b) attack (c) empty
(d) foil (e) full   82. ....

83. **SEQUESTER** (a) steal (b) seize (c) authorize
(d) enjoin (e) follow   83. ....

84. **TALISMAN** (a) charm (b) follower (c) knight
(d) serf (e) spear   84. ....

85. SERRIED   (a) torn   (b) crowded   (c) separate
(d) vacant   (e) wounded   85. ....

86. ROTUND   (a) center   (b) tall   (c) plump
(d) thick   (e) weighty   86. ....

87. SLOUGH   (a) heap   (b) shed   (c) wet   (d) attack
(e) wonder   87. ....

88. SOJOURN   (a) trek   (b) slick   (c) mud   (d) stay
(e) food   88. ....

89. SQUIB   (a) fish   (b) monster   (c) drug
(d) paste   (e) remark   89. ....

90. UBIQUITOUS   (a) questioning   (b) irreligious
(c) omnipresent   (d) local   (e) wan   90. ....

91. VERDANT   (a) old   (b) inexperienced   (c) yellow
(d) showery   (e) showy   91. ....

92. WELTER   (a) wound   (b) scar   (c) conversation
(d) confusion   (e) song   92. ....

93. DURESS   (a) extent   (b) compulsion   (c) torture
(d) award   (e) demand   93. ....

94. CONVEYANCE   (a) order   (b) speed   (c) vehicle
(d) chair   (e) airport   94. ....

95. BERSERK   (a) turban   (b) frenzied   (c) ordered
(d) beret   (e) tam   95. ....

96. BAGATELLE   (a) container   (b) document
(c) candy   (d) trifle   (e) desert   96. ....

97. AVERSE   (a) unwilling   (b) turned   (c) following
(d) adamant   (e) coarse   97. ....

98. ASCETIC   (a) bitter   (b) acid   (c) hermetic
(d) hermit   (e) scavenger   98. ....

99. EMOLLIENT   (a) meal   (b) instrument
(c) soothing medicine   (d) part of a suit of armor
(e) shaving cream   99. ....

100. IDIOSYNCRASY   (a) ideal   (b) pattern
(c) personality   (d) clothing   (e) mannerism   100. ....

Answer Key

A. Sentence Completion

1. (c)	4. (b)	7. (a)	10. (d)	13. (b)
2. (b)	5. (a)	8. (b)	11. (a)	14. (d)
3. (a)	6. (d)	9. (a)	12. (c)	15. (a)

B. Antonyms

16. (c)	23. (e)	30. (c)	37. (c)	44. (d)
17. (a)	24. (d)	31. (e)	38. (b)	45. (a)
18. (b)	25. (c)	32. (b)	39. (d)	46. (c)
19. (d)	26. (d)	33. (a)	40. (a)	47. (e)
20. (e)	27. (b)	34. (c)	41. (e)	48. (b)
21. (b)	28. (a)	35. (b)	42. (c)	49. (e)
22. (a)	29. (d)	36. (e)	43. (b)	50. (b)

C. Analogies

51. (b)	54. (c)	57. (c)	60. (d)	63. (b)
52. (d)	55. (b)	58. (d)	61. (c)	64. (c)
53. (a)	56. (d)	59. (a)	62. (a)	65. (d)

D. Synonyms

66. (b)	73. (b)	80. (a)	87. (b)	94. (c)
67. (c)	74. (c)	81. (e)	88. (d)	95. (b)
68. (a)	75. (c)	82. (e)	89. (e)	96. (d)
69. (c)	76. (a)	83. (b)	90. (c)	97. (a)
70. (e)	77. (c)	84. (a)	91. (b)	98. (d)
71. (c)	78. (d)	85. (b)	92. (d)	99. (c)
72. (b)	79. (d)	86. (c)	93. (b)	100. (e)

My Score: Number Right............. Number Wrong.............

Clinch by Checking

The purpose of this test was to help you discover which of the words in the Senior List you must concentrate on in order to achieve 100% mastery. Since the list is arranged in alphabetical order, you should have no difficulty in checking back. Mark the words that you missed; these are the ones that should be studied in your next session. Once you have them under control, then you are ready for the Third Senior-List Practice Test.

Thirteenth Day: Third Senior-List Practice Test

A. Synonyms

In the space provided, write the letter of the word that is most nearly the same in meaning as the first word.

1. BEATIFIC   (a) defeated   (b) scornful   (c) blissful
(d) reasonable   (e) clever   1. ....

2. ANATHEMA   (a) blessing   (b) curse   (c) wish
(d) folly   (e) idea   2. ....

3. ATTENUATE   (a) weaken   (b) careful   (c) attend
(d) regulate   (e) examine   3. ....

4. BENIGN   (a) mean   (b) regal   (c) menacing
(d) mild   (e) healthy   4. ....

5. CARNAGE   (a) battle   (b) message   (c) diet
(d) menu   (e) massacre   5. ....

6. DEBACLE   (a) finances   (b) dance   (c) foreigner
(d) answer   (e) downfall   6. ....

7. DIAPHANOUS   (a) transparent   (b) weak
(c) sturdy   (d) scientific   (e) spidery   7. ....

8. DISAVOW   (a) urge   (b) broadcast   (c) deny
(d) allow   (e) confess   8. ....

9. EBULLIENT   (a) exacting   (b) flowery   (c) fluid
(d) enthusiastic   (e) wan   9. ....

10. ANOMALY   (a) pattern   (b) irregularity
(c) name   (d) statue   (e) height   10. ....

11. BROCHURE   (a) container   (b) article   (c) series
(d) pamphlet   (e) lecture   11. ....

12. CAVIL   (a) national   (b) municipal   (c) quibble
(d) flow   (e) answer   12. ....

13. DEFECTION   (a) desertion   (b) fault   (c) exit
(d) elopement   (e) resignation   13. ....

14. FALLOW   (a) unseen   (b) unified   (c) old
(d) discarded   (e) uncultivated   14. ....

15. PREPONDERATE (a) urge (b) order
(c) outweigh (d) outlast (e) stand   15. ....

16. PURPORT (a) harbor (b) claim (c) hint
(d) understanding (e) sell   16. ....

17. QUANDARY (a) time element (b) entrance
(c) dilemma (d) child (e) animal   17. ....

18. ZANY (a) idea (b) clue (c) common sense
(d) truth (e) clown   18. ....

19. WREAK (a) destroy (b) build (c) attack
(d) inflict (e) toil   19. ....

20. WHET (a) soil (b) sharpen (c) steel (d) repair
(e) satisfy   20. ....

21. VOUCHSAFE (a) spoil (b) solve (c) urge
(d) earn (e) concede   21. ....

22. VIRTUOSO (a) musician (b) carpenter
(c) teacher (d) painter (e) pupil   22. ....

23. UNTOWARD (a) reversal (b) unfortunate
(c) unknown (d) ill (e) future   23. ....

24. TREPIDATION (a) joy (b) wish (c) sorrow
(d) fear (e) following   24. ....

25. SPECTRAL (a) huge (b) refined (c) fortunate
(d) ugly (e) ghostly   25. ....

26. SPATE (a) oral rendition (b) flood (c) disaster
(d) fire (e) rage   26. ....

27. REQUITAL (a) return (b) order (c) revenge
(d) extra (e) love   27. ....

28. REMONSTRATE (a) show (b) watch (c) spy
(d) praise (e) criticize   28. ....

29. QUINTESSENCE (a) least (b) most (c) first
(d) purest (e) weakest   29. ....

30. PUNCTILIOUS (a) critical (b) exact (c) fast
(d) slow (e) cautious   30. ....

31. PARAGON (a) rival (b) captain (c) player
(d) ideal (e) sport   31. ....

32. NUANCE   (a) replacement   (b) variation
(c) shadow   (d) relative   (e) thinness   32. ....

33. MULCT   (a) deprive   (b) sell   (c) write
(d) farm   (e) act   33. ....

34. MISCHANCE   (a) matron   (b) misfortune
(c) war   (d) catastrophe   (e) error   34. ....

35. LIAISON   (a) officer   (b) illegal   (c) connection
(d) comfort   (e) pain   35. ....

B. Analogies

In the space provided, write the letter of the set of words that
best completes the analogy.

36. UBIQUITOUS : OXYGEN :: (a) tortuous : cruelty
(b) sacrilegious : worship   (c) poignant : sorrow
(d) nadir : peak   36. ....

37. FIAT : DICTATOR :: (a) sports car : student
(b) theory : intelligentsia   (c) duty : onus   (d) nonpareil :
beauty   37. ....

38. PHLEGMATIC : CRASS :: (a) speed : knowledge
(b) illness : wealth   (c) fatigue : poverty   (d) power :
control   38. ....

39. INCUMBENT : PIQUE :: (a) action : instrument
(b) time : area   (c) man : emotion   (d) position :
personality   39. ....

40. INEFFABLE : PITTANCE :: (a) dull : debacle
(b) inexpressible : smallness   (c) derogatory : anathema
(d) slim : diaphanous   40. ....

41. TUMBREL : QUEUE :: (a) old : modern
(b) driver : driven   (c) sedan : cabriolet   (d) block :
counter   41. ....

42. SEMBLANCE : LIKENESS :: (a) harbinger :
messenger   (b) heresy : conformity   (c) idiosyncrasy :
ideal   (d) invective : speech   42. ....

43. INNATE : INDIGENOUS :: (a) interior : exterior
(b) natural : native   (c) foreign : poor   (d) superfluous :
alien   43. ....

44. GIBE : LAMPOON :: (a) writer : speaker
(b) victim : object   (c) praise : tribute   (d) word :
bulb   44. ....

45. CLANDESTINE : SURREPTITIOUS ::
(a) carping : captious   (b) praise : criticism   (c) sharp :
harsh   (d) vague : definite   45. ....

46. DEMUR : DISAVOW :: (a) accept : reject
(b) reject : accept   (c) accept : accept   (d) reject :
reject   46. ....

47. REFULGENT : FULSOME :: (a) favorable :
unfavorable   (b) unfavorable : unfavorable
(c) favorable : favorable   (d) unfavorable : favorable   47. ....

48. SQUIB : WAGGISH :: (a) talisman : charming
(b) jewelry : tawdry   (c) humorous : zany   (d) virtuoso :
skilled   48. ....

49. FETID : RANK :: (a) name : order   (b) promotion :
authority   (c) bad : bad   (d) full : foul   49. ....

50. ENCOMIUM : STRICTURE :: (a) emollient : salve
(b) dotage : age   (c) indecency : decorum
(d) compassion : indifference   50. ....

C. Sentence Completion

In the space provided, write the letter of the word that best
completes the sentence.

51. Even though you may wear the .... of a man of peace,
the anger in your heart will make your sword the sword of
vengeance, not the symbol of inner strength.
(a) levity   (b) onus   (c) pique   (d) habiliments   51. ....

52. If one speaks constantly in .... there is little danger that
others will take literally any of what is said.
(a) hyperboles   (b) mischances   (c) nonpareils
(d) nuances   52. ....

53. The only way in which you will be able to .... yourself
into his good graces will be by devoting your energy and time to
the betterment of your fellow townspeople.
(a) absolve   (b) accrue   (c) ingratiate   (d) arraign   53. ....

54. I do think that I shall never become .... to the blasts of icy air that sweep down Main Street during wintry school mornings.
(a) inured   (b) loath   (c) asseverated
(d) cognizant   54. ....

55. The principal .... against the practices of businessmen who sold cigarettes to minors.
(a) cloyed   (b) disavowed   (c) inveighed
(d) embroiled   55. ....

56. Whether we could survive a second attack is a .... question that I should not like to put to the test.
(a) portentous   (b) moot   (c) precarious
(d) profligate   56. ....

57. Sitting in the rocker, Alice watched lazily while the .... danced in the sunlight that streaked into the room through the lace curtains.
(a) motes   (b) semblances   (c) predilections
(d) sinecures   57. ....

58. The day is gone when the city treasury can be .... of its tax money by a shrewd politician.
(a) scourged   (b) wreaked   (c) sloughed
(d) mulcted   58. ....

59. Although Mr. Anderson is the .... head of the group, the power is all in the hands of Sue, the treasurer.
(a) nominal   (b) perfunctory   (c) pernicious
(d) perspicacious   59. ....

60. While history can find some kind words for dictators of the past, in our democratic age the word *dictator* has become a(n) .... term.
(a) pettish   (b) poignant   (c) fulsome
(d) opprobrious   60. ....

61. The necklace of bear claws that the youthful warrior wore around his neck as a(n) .... to give him added strength in times of emergency deflected the enemy arrow, and thus saved his life.
(a) duplicity   (b) emollient   (c) talisman
(d) heresy   61. ....

62. In search for the exact word to fit the sentence, Joel pored for hours over the ...., searching through various word families for the term he required.
(a) thesaurus   (b) nuance   (c) nadir
(d) conveyance   62. ....

63. The trail did not make a beeline up the hillside but followed the .... bed of a brook that wandered seemingly aimlessly over the rocks.
(a) unconscionable   (b) odious   (c) opprobrious
(d) tortuous   63. ....

64. The psychologist attempted to .... his insights into his own reactions and thereby into paths along which he could lead others.
(a) vouchsafe   (b) transmute   (c) waive   (d) whet 64. ....

65. Theories of present-day scientists point to the .... hydrogen atom as the basis of all matter.
(a) ubiquitous   (b) ungainly   (c) untoward
(d) unwonted   65. ....

D. Antonyms

In the space provided, write the letter of the word that is most nearly opposite in meaning to the first word.

66. EXTIRPATE   (a) censure   (b) create   (c) correct
(d) follow   (e) find   66. ....

67. FETTER   (a) annoy   (b) liberate   (c) starve
(d) decay   (e) declare   67. ....

68. GAINSAY   (a) lose   (b) resign   (c) volunteer
(d) agree   (e) defeat   68. ....

69. FULSOME   (a) empty   (b) past   (c) obsolete
(d) fine   (e) fitting   69. ....

70. FATUOUS   (a) sensible   (b) thin   (c) stuffed
(d) smug   (e) daring   70. ....

71. EXPEDIENT   (a) conventional   (b) rare   (c) stout
(d) judicious   (e) injurious   71. ....

72. ADVENTITIOUS   (a) timid   (b) stark   (c) natural
(d) unseen   (e) prosaic   72. ....

73. CONDONE   (a) fitting   (b) imprison   (c) excel
(d) reject   (e) accuse   73. ....

74. DEROGATORY   (a) indecent   (b) complimentary
(c) full   (d) detrimental   (e) pure   74. ....

75. EPITOME   (a) height   (b) decision   (c) essence
(d) expansion   (e) exercise   75. ....

76. FLACCID   (a) firm   (b) thin   (c) active   (d) lost
(e) certain   76. ....

77. INORDINATE   (a) slanted   (b) selective
(c) massive   (d) major   (e) insufficient   77. ....

78. LASSITUDE   (a) permission   (b) reluctance
(c) disobedience   (d) vigor   (e) anger   78. ....

79. MACABRE   (a) oral   (b) pleasant   (c) deadly
(d) lively   (e) uncertain   79. ....

80. NADIR   (a) nymph   (b) dwarf   (c) apex
(d) sentinel   (e) mountain   80. ....

81. OBDURATE   (a) coarse   (b) definite   (c) stricken
(d) tender   (e) tense   81. ....

82. PERFUNCTORY   (a) usual   (b) rare   (c) famous
(d) anonymous   (e) careful   82. ....

83. AFFLUENT   (a) destitute   (b) furious   (c) furtive
(d) finicky   (e) dilatory   83. ....

84. DESICCATE   (a) scorn   (b) escape   (c) eradicate
(d) soak   (e) steal   84. ....

85. EQUIVOCAL   (a) complaining   (b) obvious
(c) vast   (d) vigilant   (e) furious   85. ....

86. ALACRITY   (a) loneliness   (b) gusto   (c) distaste
(d) avowal   (e) indifference   86. ....

87. DULCET   (a) rash   (b) timid   (c) sinuous
(d) harsh   (e) ignorant   87. ....

88. DOUGHTY   (a) cowardly   (b) slow   (c) sweet
(d) pedestrian   (e) usual   88. ....

89. ESCHEW   (a) digest   (b) seek   (c) enjoy
(d) dislike   (e) vow   89. ....

90. FRACTIOUS   (a) whole   (b) maimed   (c) rough
(d) balmy   (e) mild   90. ....

91. GARISH   (a) dressing   (b) entree   (c) essential
(d) sober   (e) foreign   91. ....

92. FROWARD   (a) infantile   (b) ignorant   (c) docile
(d) smiling   (e) sensible   92. ....

93. IMPERVIOUS   (a) humble   (b) penetrable
(c) stubborn   (d) stern   (e) stylish   93. ....

94. INTIMIDATE   (a) encourage   (b) dazzle
(c) drain   (d) drop   (e) retain   94. ....

95. LIMPID   (a) rigid   (b) righteous   (c) muddy
(d) alive   (e) sullen   95. ....

96. OBVIATE   (a) crooked   (b) curve   (c) call
(d) cause   (e) worry   96. ....

97. PERNICIOUS   (a) harmless   (b) good-natured
(c) bright   (d) sanitary   (e) certain   97. ....

98. TAWDRY   (a) elevated   (b) foreign   (c) domestic
(d) elegant   (e) flashy   98. ....

99. TEMERARIOUS   (a) rash   (b) cautious   (c) flat
(d) depressed   (e) warlike   99. ....

100. TENUOUS   (a) hard   (b) harsh   (c) dense
(d) tall   (e) heavenly   100. ....

Answer Key

A. Synonyms

1. (c)	8. (c)	15. (c)	22. (a)	29. (d)
2. (b)	9. (d)	16. (b)	23. (b)	30. (b)
3. (a)	10. (b)	17. (c)	24. (d)	31. (d)
4. (d)	11. (d)	18. (e)	25. (e)	32. (b)
5. (e)	12. (c)	19. (d)	26. (b)	33. (a)
6. (e)	13. (a)	20. (b)	27. (a)	34. (b)
7. (a)	14. (e)	21. (e)	28. (e)	35. (c)

B. Analogies

36. (c)	39. (c)	42. (a)	45. (a)	48. (d)
37. (b)	40. (b)	43. (b)	46. (d)	49. (c)
38. (a)	41. (d)	44. (c)	47. (a)	50. (d)

C. Sentence Completion

51. (d)	54. (a)	57. (a)	60. (d)	63. (d)
52. (a)	55. (c)	58. (d)	61. (c)	64. (b)
53. (c)	56. (b)	59. (a)	62. (a)	65. (a)

D. Antonyms

66. (b)	73. (e)	80. (c)	87. (e)	94. (a)
67. (b)	74. (b)	81. (d)	88. (a)	95. (c)
68. (d)	75. (d)	82. (e)	89. (b)	96. (d)
69. (e)	76. (a)	83. (a)	90. (e)	97. (a)
70. (a)	77. (e)	84. (d)	91. (d)	98. (d)
71. (e)	78. (d)	85. (b)	92. (c)	99. (b)
72. (c)	79. (b)	86. (e)	93. (b)	100. (c)

My Score: Number Right............   Number Wrong............

Clinch by Checking

The purpose of this test was to help you discover which of the words in the Senior List you must concentrate on in order to achieve 100% mastery. Since the list is arranged in alphabetical order, you should have no difficulty in checking back. Mark the words that you missed; these are the ones that should be studied in your next session. Once you have them under control, then you are ready for the Fourth Senior-List Practice Test.

Fourteenth Day: Fourth Senior-List Practice Test

A. Analogies

In the space provided, write the letter of the set of words that best completes the analogy.

1. EMBROIL : FIGHT :: (a) disavow : order
(b) attenuate : strengthen   (c) rich : affluent   (d) christen :
appellation   1. ....

2. CLOY : WEARY :: (a) condign : fitting
(b) conversant : unusual   (c) deciduous : definite
(d) fatuous : sensible   2. ....

3. IMPORTUNE : ORDER :: (a) dissemble : organize
(b) ingratiate : irritate   (c) inure : accustom
(d) lampoon : illustrate   3. ....

4. DELETERIOUS : DEROGATORY ::
(a) wholesale : belittling   (b) complaint : illness
(c) harmful : belittling   (d) erasure : remark   4. ....

5. MALINGERER : MARTINET :: (a) soft : hard
(b) pretense : strictness   (c) carefulness : cruelty
(d) young : old   5. ....

6. OMNISCIENT : AFFLUENT :: (a) soldier :
mechanic   (b) power : law   (c) knowledge : wealth
(d) astronomy : psychology   6. ....

7. PORTENTOUS : PRECARIOUS :: (a) favorable :
unfavorable   (b) unfavorable : favorable
(c) unfavorable : unfavorable   (d) favorable :
favorable   7. ....

8. PRAGMATIC : VISIONARY :: (a) worldly :
ascetic   (b) bucolic : child   (c) musical : cacophony
(d) pity : compassion   8. ....

9. CHARLATAN : CHICANERY :: (a) judge :
compunction   (b) contingent : emergency   (c) deserter :
defection   (d) custom : decorum   9. ....

10. DESULTORY : SUPERFICIAL :: (a) fallow : rich
(b) flaccid : linen   (c) grandiloquent : severe
(d) heterogeneous : varied   10. ....

11. INCURSION : MACHINATION :: (a) reality :
dream   (b) event : engine   (c) raid : scheme   (d) plot :
attack   11. ....

12. MOTE : PETTISH :: (a) rapid : slow   (b) dot : cross
(c) large : small   (d) tiny : big   12. ....

13. PREDILECTION : PROCLIVITY :: (a) attract :
repel   (b) repel : repel   (c) repel : attract   (d) attract :
attract   13. ....

14. SINECURE : THESAURUS :: (a) position : article
(b) activity : word   (c) job : book   (d) man : volume   14. ....

15. TRANSMUTE : WREAK :: (a) send : receive
(b) change : inflict   (c) horrify : conflict   (d) build :
destroy   15. ....

B. Synonyms

In the space provided, write the letter of the word that is most
nearly the same in meaning as the first word.

16. KILN   (a) skirt   (b) pottery   (c) wheel
(d) furnace   (e) form   16. ....

17. JUNKET   (a) feed   (b) trip   (c) noise   (d) spoon
(e) vapor   17. ....

18. INSATIABLE   (a) quiet   (b) talkative   (c) dead
(d) cruel   (e) greedy   18. ....

19. HAP   (a) luck   (b) gay   (c) sadness   (d) future
(e) weakness   19. ....

20. GRANDILOQUENT   (a) purpose   (b) deed
(c) thought   (d) language   (e) activity   20. ....

21. GLOAMING   (a) happy   (b) envious   (c) dusk
(d) dawn   (e) daytime   21. ....

22. FRAILTY   (a) girlishness   (b) evil   (c) strength
(d) torture   (e) weakness   22. ....

23. APPELLATION   (a) order   (b) name   (c) legend
(d) feature   (e) contents   23. ....

24. BARRAGE   (a) barter   (b) order   (c) massacre
(d) thunder   (e) attack   24. ....

25. CHARLATAN   (a) leader   (b) thief   (c) impostor
(d) specialist   (e) coach   25. ....

26. DEIGN   (a) order   (b) hate   (c) stoop   (d) steal
(e) praise   26. ....

27. DECIDUOUS   (a) fatal   (b) autocratic   (c) strong
(d) fickle   (e) shedding   27. ....

28. CULL (a) select (b) row (c) command (d) obey
(e) cultivate   28. ....

29. REFULGENT (a) dull (b) dutiful (c) new
(d) shining (e) repaired   29. ....

30. SCOURGE (a) kill (b) honor (c) retell
(d) anger (e) whip   30. ....

31. TORTUOUS (a) painful (b) bending
(c) powerful (d) organized (e) rioting   31. ....

32. VAGARY (a) hobo (b) whim (c) actor
(d) writer (e) director   32. ....

33. METE (a) feast (b) fast (c) drill (d) deign
(e) distribute   33. ....

34. LAMBENT (a) radiant (b) mild (c) sheeplike
(d) violent (e) playful   34. ....

35. JUNTO (a) bird (b) insect (c) group
(d) leader (e) follower   35. ....

36. INVEIGH (a) consider (b) reject (c) narrate
(d) attack (e) exist   36. ....

37. IMMUTABLE (a) silent (b) talkative
(c) wishful (d) ruling (e) unchangeable   37. ....

38. HOMILY (a) nest (b) sermon (c) endorsement
(d) lectern (e) lecture   38. ....

39. HARBINGER (a) enemy (b) messenger
(c) alien (d) aviator (e) bird   39. ....

40. GENOCIDE (a) ceremony (b) honor
(c) heritage (d) massacre (e) harm   40. ....

41. FOREBODING (a) warning (b) notice
(c) trigger (d) fortunate (e) eventual   41. ....

42. EPILOGUE (a) notice (b) addition (c) play
(d) act (e) scene   42. ....

43. DISCOMFIT (a) ease (b) expel (c) accept
(d) refuse (e) defeat   43. ....

44. CRUX (a) essence (b) nutriment (c) trouble
(d) music (e) horror   44. ....

45. CREDENCE   (a) truth   (b) faith   (c) fortune
(d) evil   (e) wish   45. ....

46. CHICANERY   (a) fringe   (b) drink   (c) order
(d) trickery   (e) spice   46. ....

47. BUTTRESS   (a) support   (b) oil   (c) repair
(d) command   (e) bomb   47. ....

48. BODE   (a) promise evil   (b) wave good-by
(c) sell cheaply   (d) wash lightly   (e) save   48. ....

49. AVER   (a) deny   (b) heat   (c) strengthen
(d) apply   (e) assert   49. ....

50. AUSPICIOUS   (a) elegant   (b) expensive
(c) favorable   (d) weak   (e) foreign   50. ....

C. Antonyms

In the space provided, write the letter of the word that is most nearly opposite in meaning to the first word.

51. ABSTRUSE   (a) soft   (b) simple   (c) complex
(d) compound   (e) ordinary   51. ....

52. ACCRUE   (a) dwindle   (b) die   (c) soften
(d) join   (e) resign   52. ....

53. ACRIMONIOUS   (a) tough   (b) pungent   (c) tall
(d) good-natured   (e) bleak   53. ....

54. ARCHAIC   (a) mature   (b) childish   (c) timely
(d) concerned   (e) modern   54. ....

55. BUCOLIC   (a) well   (b) sickly   (c) infantile
(d) exact   (e) urbane   55. ....

56. CALLOW   (a) injured   (b) mature   (c) major
(d) guide   (e) finishing   56. ....

57. BOMBASTIC   (a) cloth   (b) soft   (c) solid
(d) certain   (e) unadorned   57. ....

58. ARRAIGN   (a) scatter   (b) extol   (c) excoriate
(d) free   (e) loathe   58. ....

59. CAPTIOUS   (a) appreciative   (b) free   (c) exposed
(d) faint   (e) fancied   59. ....

60. COPIOUS (a) curt (b) desultory (c) meager
d) fortuitous (e) incipient 60. ....

61. DEMUR (a) bold (b) timid (c) accept
d) hesitate (e) counsel 61. ....

62. GOSSAMER (a) thick (b) fatal (c) beneficial
d) tall (e) artistic 62. ....

63. HETEROGENEOUS (a) mediocre (b) decent
c) identical (d) varied (e) vague 63. ....

64. DEPRECATE (a) accept (b) approve (c) select
d) design (e) reject 64. ....

65. CRASS (a) brilliant (b) earthy (c) animal
d) thin (e) expert 65. ....

66. CONVERSANT (a) lecture (b) listening
c) ignorant (d) studious (e) wishful 66. ....

67. ADAMANT (a) selective (b) gross
c) deferential (d) determined (e) yielding 67. ....

68. APLOMB (a) depth (b) seal (c) shallowness
d) carefulness (e) shyness 68. ....

69. CLANDESTINE (a) illegal (b) open (c) paced
d) wise (e) sensitive 69. ....

70. COGNIZANT (a) ignorant (b) unknown
c) trust (d) insensitive (e) weary 70. ....

71. DECORUM (a) elegance (b) indecency
c) knowledge (d) encomium (e) stricture 71. ....

72. IMPECCABLE (a) liberal (b) stingy
c) defective (d) dull (e) intense 72. ....

73. RESOLUTE (a) menial (b) menacing
c) slavish (d) stylish (e) afraid 73. ....

74. STRINGENT (a) serious (b) heavy
c) easygoing (d) dried (e) drooping 74. ....

75. SUNDER (a) order (b) ordain (c) link
d) send (e) refer 75. ....

76. SURREPTITIOUS (a) anticipated (b) open
c) perfect (d) rough (e) noisy 76. ....

77. RESTIVE   (a) quiet   (b) sleepy   (c) sleazy
(d) desultory   (e) feared   77. ....

78. INADVERTENT   (a) unknown   (b) careless
(c) serviceable   (d) conscious   (e) trivial   78. ....

79. IMPROVIDENT   (a) foreign   (b) extravagant
(c) thoughtful   (d) cantankerous   (e) thrifty   79. ....

80. DELETERIOUS   (a) overt   (b) beneficial
(c) thickening   (d) appearing   (e) fading   80. ....

81. CONSUMMATE   (a) crude   (b) complete
(c) polished   (d) total   (e) traitorous   81. ....

82. COMPASSION   (a) indifference   (b) conscience
(c) pity   (d) playfulness   (e) judgment   82. ....

83. AMENABLE   (a) feminine   (b) maternal
(c) paternal   (d) stubborn   (e) evasive   83. ....

84. COMMEND   (a) select   (b) reject   (c) reserve
(d) join   (e) warn   84. ....

85. ALTERCATION   (a) creation   (b) agreement
(c) adjustment   (d) justice   (e) injustice   85. ....

D. Sentence Completion

In the space provided, write the letter of the word that best completes the sentence.

86. He told us just enough to .... our curiosity but not enough for us to be able to guess the outcome.
(a) fetter   (b) importune   (c) whet   (d) gibe   86. ....

87. The bully .... his annoyance and anger on his unfortunate followers, who took their punishment with yells and screeches of pain.
(a) intimidated   (b) wreaked   (c) inured
(d) lampooned   87. ....

88. The judge .... him from visiting the home of the children until the investigator's report had been read and evaluated.
(a) obviated   (b) palliated   (c) mitigated
(d) enjoined   88. ....

89. In the ...., the author has the characters describe just how each of them would have wanted the play to end.
(a) epilogue (b) paragon (c) pariah (d) pique   89. ....

90. A mind that has been allowed to lie .... too long loses its ability to view with sharpness and clarity.
(a) pettish (b) fallow (c) phlegmatic
(d) pragmatic   90. ....

91. You will find no one more .... than he in observing every regulation down to the most minute detail.
(a) redoubtable (b) clandestine (c) punctilious
(d) beatific   91. ....

92. During wartime, there would be long .... of civilians in front of stores supplying consumers' goods.
(a) queues (b) idiosyncrasies (c) fiats
(d) habiliments   92. ....

93. The .... figure of Mr. Roly Poly graced the children's page of the Sunday-newspaper supplement for many years.
(a) ebullient (b) froward (c) carping (d) rotund   93. ....

94. Things have been happening too quickly for me to be able to put them together into a meaningful sequence; I need time to .... before I can even discuss what has been happening.
(a) expostulate (b) disavow (c) blandish
(d) ruminate   94. ....

95. They called Fulton an impractical .... for proposing to harness steam to move power wheels on a steamboat.
(a) charlatan (b) visionary (c) welter (d) oaf   95. ....

96. Milton declared that he would not be .... to allowing us to use his boat for the fishing trip if we took him along!
(a) sacrilegious (b) sinuous (c) averse
(d) specious   96. ....

97. The candidate did not wilt under the .... of questions fired at him by the reporters; indeed, he kept his composure and sense of humor while answering each in order with an admirable forthrightness.
(a) barrage (b) vagary (c) umbrage
(d) proclivity   97. ....

98. When the besiegers found their slain comrades, they went .... and killed all the native prisoners.
(a) flaccid (b) berserk (c) precarious
(d) visionary   98. ....

99. When so generous an offer comes from one from whom we
did not expect any mercy, we dare not .... over petty details.
  (a) excoriate   (b) cavil   (c) extirpate
  (d) intimidate   99. ....

100. Since she did not .... to answer my note, I shall not feel
obligated to assist her in preparing for the test.
  (a) dissemble   (b) demur   (c) eschew   (d) deign   100. ....

Answer Key

A. Analogies

1. (d)	4. (c)	7. (c)	10. (d)	13. (d)
2. (a)	5. (b)	8. (a)	11. (c)	14. (c)
3. (b)	6. (c)	9. (c)	12. (b)	15. (b)

B. Synonyms

16. (d)	23. (b)	30. (e)	37. (e)	44. (a)
17. (b)	24. (e)	31. (b)	38. (b)	45. (b)
18. (e)	25. (c)	32. (b)	39. (b)	46. (d)
19. (a)	26. (c)	33. (e)	40. (d)	47. (a)
20. (d)	27. (e)	34. (a)	41. (a)	48. (a)
21. (c)	28. (a)	35. (c)	42. (b)	49. (e)
22. (e)	29. (d)	36. (d)	43. (e)	50. (c)

C. Antonyms

51. (b)	58. (d)	65. (a)	72. (c)	79. (e)
52. (a)	59. (a)	66. (c)	73. (e)	80. (b)
53. (d)	60. (c)	67. (e)	74. (c)	81. (a)
54. (d)	61. (c)	68. (e)	75. (c)	82. (a)
55. (e)	62. (a)	69. (b)	76. (b)	83. (d)
56. (b)	63. (c)	70. (a)	77. (a)	84. (e)
57. (e)	64. (b)	71. (b)	78. (d)	85. (b)

D. Sentence Completion

86. (c)	89. (a)	92. (a)	95. (b)	98. (b)
87. (b)	90. (b)	93. (d)	96. (c)	99. (b)
88. (d)	91. (c)	94. (d)	97. (a)	100. (d)

My Score: Number Right............ Number Wrong............

Clinch by Checking

The purpose of this test was to help you discover which of the words in the Senior List you must concentrate on in order to achieve 100% mastery. Since the list is arranged in alphabetical order, you should have no difficulty in checking back. Mark the words that you missed; these are the ones that should be studied in your next session.

COMPLETING THE COMPARISON

Section 5: COMPLETING THE COMPARISON

The examination makers long ago concluded that there is a close connection between ability to do well in school and ability to complete their comparison questions. Very few indeed are the nationwide tests in language ability that do not include analogies. Because of the popularity of this type of question, the student who has developed the technique of handling them has a distinct advantage over those who ordinarily just muddle through the analogy section of a test. The initial analysis and the day-by-day exercises that follow should help you to achieve maximum grades every time you meet this type of question.

What is the extent of your command over questions requiring you to choose the correct word or phrase to complete the comparison? Take the Inventory Test that follows and find out!

First Day: Inventory Test

Time at Start ....

In the space provided, write the letter of the set of words that best completes the analogy.

1. TRAIN : WAIL :: (a) real : artificial (b) sign : sound (c) wind : howl (d) blubber : child (e) man : nature

1. ....

2. BAKER : COBBLER :: (a) pan : pot (b) cake : pancake (c) yeast : thread (d) spatula : wrench (e) cap : apron

2. ....

3. ELEPHANTINE : MASS :: (a) insipid : taste
(b) sound : muffled   (c) varnished : truth   (d) glossy :
shape   (e) sun : bright   3. ....

4. VETERINARIAN : MULE :: (a) purse : book
(b) one : all   (c) internist : men   (d) student : teachers
(e) general : soldier   4. ....

5. HOUSEHOLDER : HOUSEWORKER ::
(a) worker : foreman   (b) clay : ink   (c) factual :
fictional   (d) rich : poor   (e) employer : employee   5. ....

6. HAND : BANANA :: (a) bunch : drapes   (b) arm :
warfare   (c) seed : corn   (d) clump : grass   (e) brace :
suspenders   6. ....

7. PICTURE : FRAME :: (a) fence : field   (b) pie :
meringue   (c) bread : crust   (d) jacket : lapel
(e) cupcake : cup   7. ....

8. YES : NO :: (a) frequently : rarely   (b) often :
sometimes   (c) maybe : perhaps   (d) ever : never
(e) can : may   8. ....

9. WATER : LIFE :: (a) rudder : ship   (b) gasoline :
automobile   (c) printed page : student   (d) radio :
announcer   (e) uniform : soldier   9. ....

10. NOTCH : RAVINE :: (a) ditch : gully   (b) belt :
gun   (c) book : volume   (d) handle : bullet   (e) bridge :
support   10. ....

11. GUILD : TRADE UNION :: (a) ancient : medieval
(b) medieval : modern   (c) recent : old   (d) liquid :
solid   (e) see : hear   11. ....

12. CAPTION : PICTURE :: (a) article : grammar
(b) John Bull : England   (c) prescription : medicine
(d) vertical file : library   (e) blurb : book   12. ....

13. CASANOVA : ROMEO :: (a) female : male
(b) many : one   (c) one : many   (d) female : female
(e) male : female   13. ....

14. HUG : CHUCK :: (a) love : like   (b) embrace :
squeeze   (c) waist : chin   (d) love : anger   (e) caress :
hurt   14. ....

15. FURLOUGH : SOLDIER :: (a) truancy : student
(b) coffee break : worker   (c) teacher : sabbatical
(d) liberty : sailor   (e) French leave : actor   15. ....

16. CHESTNUT : AUBURN :: (a) tree : blacksmith
(b) area : region   (c) canary : tawny   (d) type : title
(e) shoe : heel   16. ....

17. BOUND : FORWARD :: (a) jump : skid   (b) lurch :
flounce   (c) dart : slow   (d) lunge : backward   (e) zoom :
upward   17. ....

18. NUPTIALS : DIVORCE :: (a) groom : respondent
(b) bliss : reality   (c) judge : minister   (d) honeymoon :
wedlock   (e) ceremony : law court   18. ....

19. MINOR : FOUNDLING :: (a) boy : child   (b) tot :
tyke   (c) ore : shipwreck   (d) ward : orphan   (e) pick :
money   19. ....

20. CABIN : COMPARTMENT :: (a) wood : metal
(b) ship : train   (c) small : large   (d) country : city
(e) large : small   20. ....

Time at End ....   *Total Number of Minutes Elapsed* ....

Answer Key

1. (c)	5. (e)	9. (b)	13. (b)	17. (e)
2. (c)	6. (d)	10. (a)	14. (c)	18. (a)
3. (a)	7. (c)	11. (b)	15. (d)	19. (d)
4. (c)	8. (d)	12. (e)	16. (c)	20. (b)

My Score: Number Right............   Number Wrong............

Comparing with Others

	Time	Number Correct
Elite	12 minutes	20
Superior	15–17 minutes	17–19
Average	20 minutes	15–16
Below Average	21–24 minutes	11–14
Weak	25–30 minutes	8–10

Clinch by Checking

The purpose in your taking this test was twofold: to discover your level of competency and to discover how much time you need to handle just such questions. The results become meaningful not only when you compare your efforts with those of other students, but also when you compare your present score and the amount of time spent in taking this test with the results after you have done the daily exercises that follow. Remember that if you want to bring your results up to the best you are capable of, you must first know what you are doing and then, through practice and more practice, increase your speed.

Regardless of how well you did, the exercises that follow will give you the day-by-day sharpening that means best results.

Second Day: Gaining Exam Know-How

Taking A Closer Look

Sometimes the answer to an analogy or a comparison question depends upon your knowing the meaning of the key words. Sometimes the answer depends upon your being able to discover the operational or functional relationship between familiar words. However, regardless of the level of the words involved, the technique of answering the question remains the same. What is the best way to approach this type of question? Let us begin by analyzing a typical question.

Before looking at the analysis that follows, read the exercise below, and write your own answer in the space provided.

GALLEY : PANTRY :: (a) house : ship   (b) cook : chef
(c) picture : pie   (d) cook : store   (e) slave : captain

Answer ...d.......

Analysis

(c) *picture : pie*   Although a pie can be found in a pantry, pictures are usually hung in galleries, not in galleys. Only half of the analogy could hold.

(e) *slave : captain*   Although in days of old slaves were used on ships called galleys, there is no connection between a captain and a pantry. Only half of the analogy could hold.

(b) *cook : chef* One can cook in a galley or be a cook or chef in the galley. Usually the person in the galley is called a cook and not a chef. Nevertheless, both men would make use of a pantry. Therefore no clear lines of demarcation can be drawn between these.

(a) *house : ship* A pantry is usually found in a house while a galley would be in a ship. This answer, however, is wrong inasmuch as the choices have been reversed, a usual trap for the unwary!

(d) *cook : store* We usually think of *cook* as a person and *store* as a place, but if we consider both words as verbs, then one *cooks* in a galley and *stores* goods in a pantry. This, therefore, must be the correct answer.

Such careful analysis is always necessary for this type of question. It is planned to test your ability to handle and to manipulate words and their meanings. To do this, you cannot afford to skim or to skip. You must read with extreme care.

For Highest Marks

1. Glance at the first pair quickly. If you find the comparison a simple one, look through the choices and select the one that you consider correct.

2. Do not jump to any conclusions! You must train yourself, even if you are positive that your choice is correct, not to skip any of the others. You may very easily have chosen a *good* answer, but one of the ones that you failed to examine may have been the *better* or *best* answer!

3. Use the cues in the choices themselves to help you to eliminate the obviously wrong ones. Often one of the two items is inappropriate, thus eliminating both. Sometimes the items are correct but in reversed order. THESE ARE WRONG!

4. If all the words are familiar ones, then look for the unusual use of one or more of them. Ever be alert to the varied meanings that each of the words can have.

5. If you find that there are too many difficult words in the question, then don't waste time. Go on to the next. You can always come back to this one later, if there is time.

6. If all the words are familiar and you still cannot find the key to the comparison, then go on to the next. Plan to come back to this one soon. By the time you come back, your mind will have worked out the answer for you!

7. Don't fill in random answers for those analogies that you did not fathom or did not have time to complete. Remember that the penalty for guessing can be too great. If you have been able to eliminate two or three of the choices, then an educated guess would not be amiss. Once you have guessed, do not change it unless you have reason based on fact to do so. If you have four or more, however, to choose from, it is better to leave the answer blank and go on to the next. If time permits, then you can come back to this troublesome one and reread it with a different perspective.

The tests that follow will give you the practice that should lead to your achieving maximum results in the examination. Study the initial analysis. Then take the test. Do not rush through it. Speed will come after accuracy. Your first task is to develop a technique that results in correct answers; speed will follow. Analyze each of your wrong answers to discover why you went astray. If necessary, after an interim of a few weeks, take the same tests over again, not to recall the correct answers, but to recall the techniques that produce correct answers at your maximum rate of reading speed.

Third Day: Analysis and Practice Test

A Closer Look

Before looking at the analysis that follows, read the exercise below, and write your own answer in the space provided.

NIBBLE : SNACK :: (a) consume : diet (b) breakfast : juice (c) luxuriate : lunch (d) order : lunch (e) gorge : feast

Answer ℰ.........

Analysis

(b) *breakfast : juice* Both *snack* and *juice* refer to food, but *nibble* and *breakfast* are unrelated.

(d) *order : lunch* Lunch and *snack* refer to meals, but *nibble* and *order* are unrelated.

(c) *luxuriate : lunch* Whereas we nibble a snack, we do not always luxuriate while eating lunch. Lunch is usually a sparse meal.

We are left with (a) *consume : diet* and (e) *gorge : feast*. Of the two, (e) *gorge : feast* is closer, since *nibble* describes how one eats a snack and *gorge* describes how one eats a feast. *Consume* and *diet* are much more general than the others.

Practice Test

Time at Start ....

In the space provided, write the letters of the set of words that best completes the analogy.

1. SOLDIER : BARRACKS :: (a) climber : cabana
(b) trapper : igloo (c) mountaineer : chalet (d) life :
biosphere (e) Indian : hogan   1. ....

2. WAKE : SPOOR :: (a) early : late (b) cruiser :
lion (c) unpleasant : scant (d) alert : sleepy
(e) mourner : money   2. ....

3. DISGRUNTLED : SATISFACTION :: (a) surly :
disagreeable (b) glum : silence (c) sullen : talk
(d) irritable : temperament (e) moody : ability   3. ....

4. RECTANGLE : CIRCLE :: (a) parking lot : drive
(b) square : cylinder (c) dollar : nickel
(d) quadrilateral : cigarette (e) printing : stamping 4. ....

5. CHISEL : STONE :: (a) saw : wood (b) emery :
grinding (c) power : tools (d) pilot : rudder
(e) scalpel : flesh   5. ....

6. CHIDE : REVILE :: (a) torture : whip (b) word :
deed (c) revenge : avenge (d) chasten : crucify
(e) flog : beat   6. ....

7. FUR : SEAL :: (a) hide : steer (b) skin : man
(c) lid : put (d) scales : cod (e) metal : ore   7. ....

8. FLAKE : SNOW :: (a) bullet : gun (b) grain : wood
(c) rifle : pellet (d) perspiration : droplet (e) drop :
rain   8. ....

9. SHAMPOO : HAIR :: (a) clothing : soak
(b) gargle : throat   (c) glow : lamp   (d) soap : dirt
(e) missionary : jungle   9. ....

10. GREEN GAGE : DELICIOUS :: (a) sharp : mellow
(b) pear : peach   (c) raw : ripe   (d) plum : apple
(e) tart : sweet   10. ....

11. SMUG : FEELING :: (a) tidy : ship   (b) snow :
landscape   (c) deed : thoughtfulness   (d) prim :
appearance   (e) picture : photograph   11. ....

12. POLLUTED : DINGY :: (a) grime : smudge
(b) messy : littered   (c) water : boat   (d) germ : white
(e) food : mud   12. ....

13. STAR : CONSTELLATION :: (a) ship : plan
(b) continent : nation   (c) island : archipelago
(d) offspring : parent   (e) eyepiece : telescope   13. ....

14. MONUMENTAL : MASSIVE :: (a) statue : bridge
(b) large : substantial   (c) imposing : bulky
(d) medicine : surgery   (e) knowledge : lore   14. ....

15. RIGIDITY : IRON :: (a) pliability : copper
(b) elasticity : nickel   (c) rubber : inflexibility
(d) visibility : glass   (e) clarity : writing   15. ....

Time at End ....   *Minutes Elapsed* ....
                                              Average Time 12 *Minutes*

Answer Key for this test is on page 270.

My Score: Number Right ...4.......   *Number Wrong* ....
             Average Number Right 13

Fourth Day: Analysis and Practice Test

A Closer Look

Before looking at the analysis that follows, read the exercise
below, and write your own answer in the space provided.

POUT : SNARL :: (a) anger : rage   (b) lip : teeth   (c) sound :
silence   (d) brief : long   (e) intense : lax   Answer ....a......

Analysis

(d) *brief : long* This is incorrect because the original pair has no time-element difference.

(a) *anger : rage* While *snarl* could signify rage, *pout* is not associated with anger.

(e) *intense : lax* If anything, this is a reversal. *Snarl* implies something intense, while *pout* could imply something less than intense.

(c) *sound : silence* This is a reversal: To snarl is to produce sound; to pout is to make an expression, usually, silently.

(b) *lip : teeth* The lips do reveal a pout, and the teeth are prominent in a snarl. This is the only possible answer.

Practice Test

Time at Start ....

In the space provided, write the letter of the set of words that best completes the analogy.

1. DECADE : CENTURY :: (a) penny : dime
(b) quarter : dollar   (c) dime : dollar   (d) nickel :
quarter   (e) nickel : dollar   1: ....

2. BLACK SHEEP : LAMB :: (a) foreign : domestic
(b) stew : chop   (c) experienced : inexperienced
(d) tender : tough   (e) bad : innocent   2. ....

3. GUST : BLAST :: (a) taste : sound   (b) dynamite :
wind   (c) blaze : glow   (d) tame : wild   (e) sudden :
violent   3. ....

4. FALLACY : REASONING :: (a) error : calculation
(b) lapse : error   (c) errata : speech   (d) pitfall : oversight
(e) fluff : acting   4. ....

5. DEMI : HALF :: (a) quad : twin   (b) tri- : triangle
(c) quint : babies   (d) duo : twofold   (e) treble :
quadruped   5. ....

6. ASPHALT : PAVEMENT :: (a) dress : silk
(b) hide : cover   (c) aluminum : foil   (d) engine : motor
(e) spelling : sentence   6. ....

7. CALORIE : WEIGHT :: (a) gram : pound (b) day :
year (c) clock : time (d) temperature : thermometer
(e) inch : length   7. ....

8. DICTIONARY : STUDENT :: (a) book : scholar
(b) telephone directory : secretary (c) recipe : cook
(d) guidebook : tourist (e) sugar : ice cream   8. ....

9. SWARTHY : ASHEN :: (a) dark : light (b) useful :
waste (c) new : old (d) condition : color (e) ill :
healthy   9. ....

10. FROWN : BROW :: (a) boil : feelings (b) chafe :
anger (c) flounce : movement (d) blaze : intensity
(e) glower : eyes   10. ....

11. LEVEL : MASON :: (a) lathe : carpenter
(b) tripod : photographer (c) siren : ambulance
(d) book : librarian (e) glove : hand   11. ....

12. INMATE : NATIVE :: (a) stranger : owner
(b) permanent : temporary (c) prison : country
(d) tenement : farm (e) inhabitant : dweller   12. ....

13. BEGRUDGE : LOATHE :: (a) food : conduct
(b) friend : enemy (c) hate : dislike (d) envy : disgust
(e) feel : sense   13. ....

14. DRONE : PARASITE :: (a) bee : ant (b) harmful :
harmless (c) noisy : silent (d) sponge : leech
(e) assistant : helper   14. ....

15. HABITAT : HABITATION :: (a) area : dwelling
(b) place : lodging (c) animal : plant (d) plant : animal
(e) mountain : plateau   15. ....

Time at End ....   *Minutes Elapsed* ....
                                        Average Time 14 *Minutes*

Answer Key for this test is on page 270.

My Score: *Number Right* ....   *Number Wrong* ....
             Average Number Right 12

Fifth Day: Analysis and Practice Test

A Closer Look

Before looking at the analysis that follows, read the exercise below, and write your own answer in the space provided.

JUDGE : LAW :: (a) teacher : student   (b) editor **:** news   (c) manager : boxer   (d) principal : school (e) warden : prisoner   Answer ....

Analysis

The first word of all the choices deals with people. Therefore the key to the answer is in the second word of each comparison. Since the second word (*law*) is not a person, we can eliminate (c) *manager : boxer*, (a) *teacher : student*, and (e) *warden : prisoner*. This leaves (b) *editor : news* and (d) *principal : school*. We can eliminate (d) *principal : school* because *school*—as a noun —is a place while *law* is an abstraction. We are left with (b) *editor : news*, and as the judge interprets the law, so the editor interprets the news. Therefore (b) *editor : news* is the correct answer.

Practice Test

Time at Start ....

In the space provided, write the letter of the set of words that best completes the analogy.

1. BANTER : GOOD-NATURED :: (a) scoff **:** ridicule   (b) sneer : scorn   (c) spurn : contemptuous (d) flout : sincere   (e) disdain : respectful   1. ....

2. LAND OF THE MIDNIGHT SUN : CATHAY **::** (a) Japan : Russia   (b) Switzerland : Ireland   (c) Sweden **:** India   (d) Norway : China   (e) Canada : Mexico   2. ....

3. NIBBLE : NIP :: (a) large : small   (b) cat : rat (c) much : little   (d) gentle : sharp   (e) snake : dog   3. ....

4. VOLUME : AREA :: (a) weight : size (b) floor space : business   (c) cube : square   (d) aviator **:** astronaut   (e) plane : height   4. ....

5. CUTOFF VALVE : FUSE :: (a) tire : firecracker
(b) pressure : current   (c) boiler : dynamite   (d) water :
steam   (e) metal : liquid   5. ....

6. PLAGIARIZE : EMBEZZLE :: (a) take : steal
(b) idea : money   (c) clerk : author   (d) copyright :
patent   (e) modern : recent   6. ....

7. TIRE : RIM :: (a) circumference : circle   (b) valve :
tube   (c) spout : neck   (d) ring : finger   (e) eraser :
pencil   7. ....

8. PRIMARY : TERTIARY :: (a) muscle : energy
(b) second : fourth   (c) first : fifth   (d) sixth : seventh
(e) specific : universal   8. ....

9. TAVERN : CAFETERIA :: (a) country : city
(b) slow : fast   (c) liquor : self-service   (d) expensive :
moderate   (e) diner : night club   9. ....

10. SNUB : ACTION :: (a) flout : offend   (b) taunt :
remark   (c) offend : intentional   (d) insult : insolence
(e) slap : praise   10. ....

11. BARNACLE : SHIP :: (a) soil : farm   (b) leaves :
tree   (c) lichen : rock   (d) dust : furniture   (e) pod :
pea   11. ....

12. CENTIMETER : METER :: (a) hundred : one
(b) all : part   (c) penny : dollar   (d) century : decade
(e) science : instrument   12. ....

13. TIDE : WATER :: (a) cloud : color   (b) canyon :
river   (c) bomb : destruction   (d) paper : white
(e) breeze : air   13. ....

14. DYE : PAINT :: (a) pigment : color   (b) in : on
(c) discolor : color   (d) tint : tarnish   (e) artificial :
real   14. ....

15. COLLEGE : UNIVERSITY :: (a) high : low
(b) higher : high   (c) many : one   (d) one : many
(e) school : institution   15. ....

Time at End ....   *Minutes Elapsed* ....
                                         Average Time 18 *Minutes*

Answer Key for this test is on page 270.

My Score: Number Right ....   *Number Wrong* ....
            Average Number Right 11

Sixth Day: Analysis and Practice Test

A Closer Look

Before looking at the analysis that follows, read the exercise below, and write your own answer in the space provided.

INFINITESIMAL : MINUTE :: (a) less : more   (b) big :
bigger   (c) more : less   (d) time : size   (e) hour : second
Answer ....

Analysis

(d) *time : size*   At best, this could be a reversal.

(e) *hour : second* is similar to (c) *more : less*, in that both go from "larger" to "smaller." *Infinitesimal : minute*, however, goes from something smaller to something larger.

Both (a) *less : more* and (b) *big : bigger*, also imply going from smaller to larger. The word *less*, though, implies "smallness" more than does the word *big*. Therefore (a) *less : more* is a better choice than (b) *big : bigger*.

Practice Test

Time at Start ....

In the space provided, write the letter of the set of words that best completes the analogy.

1. FINE : FLOGGING :: (a) grate : coarse
(b) money : beating   (c) punish : hurting   (d) coarse :
signaling   (e) grand : usual   1. ....

2. GROPE : HAND :: (a) cord : twine   (b) hurry :
loiter   (c) ear : hear   (d) paint : brush   (e) visualize :
mind   2. ....

3. SCOUR : MOP :: (a) sweep : clean   (b) rub : wipe
(c) wet : dry   (d) brush : vacuum   (e) swab : dust   3. ....

4. HUMILIATE : PRIDE :: (a) mortify : shamefaced
(b) hug : annoyance   (c) indignity : injury   (d) outrage :
unbearable   (e) humble : dignity   4. ....

5. LOFT : MANUFACTURE :: (a) temple : worship
(b) arsenal : magazine   (c) skyscraper : lofty
(d) terminal : fly   (e) tenement : slums   5. ....

6. ENDORSE : INSCRIBE :: (a) product : check
(b) top : bottom   (c) back : front   (d) front : back
(e) bottom : top   6. ....

7. CLUTTERED : GLUTTED :: (a) noisy : silent
(b) confused : excess   (c) spoken : written   (d) disorder :
burned out   (e) filled : untidy   7. ....

8. AUDITORY : TACTILE :: (a) pianist : diplomat
(b) stethoscope : radar   (c) loud : prickly   (d) pupil :
orator   (e) eye : ear   8. ....

9. RUST : IRON :: (a) pit : peach   (b) nail : finger
(c) chrome : bumper   (d) barnacle : ship   (e) skin :
bone   9. ....

10. CLOUD : WIND :: (a) man : peace   (b) action :
impulse   (c) lure : line   (d) fish : bait   (e) flotsam :
current   10. ....

11. ELEGY : ANTHEM :: (a) churchyard : yardarm
(b) poem : ballad   (c) sadness : patriotism   (d) England :
America   (e) single : many   11. ....

12. SQUARE : CUBE :: (a) two : three   (b) food :
person   (c) shelf : bin   (d) subject : object   (e) street :
boulevard   12. ....

13. REGATTA : ROWER :: (a) bout : wrestling
(b) match : racket   (c) derby : promoter   (d) runner :
timer   (e) steeplechase : jockey   13. ....

14. DEPTH : PLUMB LINE :: (a) style : designer
(b) contents : gauge   (c) quality : weighing scale
(d) time : hour   (e) color : age   14. ....

15. REVEILLE : A.M. :: (a) danger : foghorn
(b) P.M. : taps   (c) beacon : fire   (d) tattoo : battle
(e) semaphore : code   15. ....

Time at End ....   *Minutes Elapsed* ....
                                  Average Time 14 *Minutes*

Answer Key for this test is on page 270.

My Score: Number Right ....   *Number Wrong* ....
            Average Number Right 13

Seventh Day: Analysis and Practice Test

A Closer Look

Before looking at the analysis that follows, read the exercise below, and write your own answer in the space provided.

ARBOREAL : BLUEJAY :: (a) gregarious : apes (b) whale : marine (c) amphibious : rabbit (d) aquatic : cod (e) terrestrial : frog   Answer ....

Analysis

(b) *whale : marine* This is a reversal.

(c) *amphibious : rabbit* The rabbit is not an animal that lives on both land and water, as implied in the meaning of *amphibious*.

(e) *terrestrial : frog* The frog lives on both land and water. *Terrestrial* refers to land only.

We are left with (a) *gregarious : apes* and (c) *aquatic : cod*. Apes do tend to live together; therefore they are gregarious. Cod live in water and thus are aquatic. Since *arboreal* refers to "where" and not "how," (d) *aquatic : cod* is the correct answer.

Practice Test

Time at Start ....

In the space provided, write the letter of the set of words that best completes the analogy.

1. AEROBIC : AIR :: (a) aniline : dye
(b) microscopic : microbes (c) aseptic : germs
(d) protozoa : animals (e) germ : disease   1. ....

2. INFANT : MAN :: (a) eagle : eaglet (b) duckling : swan (c) chick : pullet (d) squab : pigeon
(e) gosling : swan   2. ....

3. RESPECT : PARTNER :: (a) hostility : army
(b) desire : aim (c) anger : duel (d) accuracy : shooting
(e) admiration : ideal   3. ....

4. ARSENAL : BATTLE :: (a) courtroom : judge
(b) warehouse : sale (c) room : furniture (d) garage : truck (e) stall : cow   4. ....

5. LINK : CHAIN :: (a) sentence : paragraph (b) leaf : tree (c) strand : rope (d) editor : newspaper (e) plot : story   5. ....

6. BOAR : PIG :: (a) leopard : tiger (b) stallion : horse (c) dog : collie (d) island : mainland (e) talking : eating   6. ....

7. SQUARE : CIRCLE :: (a) old-fashioned : new (b) avenue : park (c) tower : cone (d) cube : sphere (e) rectangle : quadrilateral   7. ....

8. BRASH : SLAPDASH :: (a) young : old (b) reckless : careless (c) serious : comic (d) swift : slow (e) hurried : hasty   8. ....

9. DOOR : ROOM :: (a) outlet : socket (b) foyer : apartment (c) vault : valuable (d) house : exit (e) flap : tent   9. ....

10. BUD : SHOOT :: (a) plant : animal (b) missile : meadow (c) new : rapid (d) burr : callous (e) beer : bamboo   10. ....

11. EMIGRATION : IMMIGRANT :: (a) entry : foreigner (b) exit : newcomer (c) judge : jury (d) nativity : visitor (e) departure : entrance   11. ....

12. WORSTED : SUIT :: (a) cloth : clothing (b) jacket : style (c) satin : velvet (d) alpaca : overcoat (e) gingham : gown   12. ....

13. CANINE : MASTIFF :: (a) basset : hound (b) lion : tiger (c) dog : animal (d) cat : kitten (e) feline : Persian   13. ....

14. SEPTEMBER : NOVEMBER :: (a) summer : winter (b) brown : red (c) seven : nine (d) wet : dry (e) vacation : work   14. ....

15. WORD : SENTENCE :: (a) minute : second (b) color : painting (c) platform : dais (d) note : phrase (e) line : sculptor   15. ....

Time at End ....   *Minutes Elapsed* ....
                                 Average Time 11 *Minutes*

Answer Key for this test is on page 270.

My Score: *Number Right* ....   *Number Wrong* ....
             Average Number Right 13

Eighth Day: Analysis and Practice Test

A Closer Look

Before looking at the analysis that follows, read the exercise below, and write your own answer in the space provided.

SELDOM : FREQUENTLY :: (a) never : always (b) rarely : often (c) sometimes : occasionally (d) ever : constantly (e) continuous : continual   Answer ....

Analysis

The relationship sought is one of time. Neither *seldom* nor *frequently* is an extreme word; however, *seldom* has a slight negative quality, while *frequently* has a slight positive one.

Therefore (a) *never : always*, both words being without exception, can be eliminated. For the same reason, (d) *ever : constantly* can be eliminated. Since *continuous* in (e) *continuous : continual* implies uninterrupted, this pair can be eliminated.

(c) *sometimes : occasionally* These synonyms are too close in meaning. At best, they present a reversal of quality.

(b) *rarely : often* gives us two synonyms in the correct order—negative to positive. This, then, is the correct answer.

Practice Test

Time at Start ....

In the space provided, write the letter of the set of words that best completes the analogy.

1. DELUGE : RAIN :: (a) mountain : rock
(b) tornado : wind (c) hurricane : damage (d) swamp :
trees (e) book : words   1. ....

2. RECIPE : COOK :: (a) cure : remedy
(b) chemicals : pharmacist (c) formula : chemist
(d) book : publisher (e) author : idea   2. ....

3. KILN : BRICKS :: (a) wheel : pottery
(b) assignment : homework (c) typewriter : author
(d) canvas : artist (e) oven : bread   3. ....

4. RAKE : HOE :: (a) fork : knife (b) shovel :
pitchfork (c) spoon : spatula (d) grass : corn
(e) pull : tug   4. ....

5. BLOOD : ARTERY :: (a) gasoline : carburetor
(b) electricity : wire   (c) pipe : water   (d) spigot : barrel
(e) faucet : flow   5. ....

6. WHITTLE : CAMEO :: (a) amateur : professional
(b) chisel : knife   (c) cut : grind   (d) wood : stone
(e) sculpture : painting   6. ....

7. MURAL : DIADEM :: (a) wall : head   (b) female :
male   (c) paint : plant   (d) art : science   (e) view :
vision   7. ....

8. BEACON : ALARM :: (a) sound : sound   (b) light :
light   (c) safety : fear   (d) light : sound   (e) aviation :
car   8. ....

9. CORONET : ENSIGN :: (a) magazine : soldier
(b) sign : officer   (c) nobility : rank   (d) badge : medal
(e) label : flag   9. ....

10. MASSIVE : SOGGY :: (a) heavy : light   (b) slow :
wet   (c) many : few   (d) car : boat   (e) big : moist   10. ....

11. QUADRILATERAL : OCTAGON :: (a) square :
rectangle   (b) triangle : hexagon   (c) pentagon : triangle
(d) equilateral : square   (e) triangle : cone   11. ....

12. COMPUTER : CALCULATION :: (a) typewriter :
words   (b) auditor : accounts   (c) teletype :
communication   (d) mathematics : arithmetic
(e) automation : individuation   12. ....

13. COMMISSION : OFFICER :: (a) compensation :
salesman   (b) bonus : worker   (c) general : admiral
(d) license : driver   (e) rank : file   13. ....

14. DIVIDEND : INTEREST :: (a) owner : creditor
(b) stock : business   (c) bonds : stocks   (d) book :
painting   (e) factory : store   14. ....

15. LOFT : GARRET :: (a) capacious : narrow
(b) cellar : vault   (c) saloon : rotunda   (d) den : library
(e) immense : ample   15. ....

Time at End ....   *Minutes Elapsed* ....
                                     Average Time 16 *Minutes*

Answer Key for this test is on page 271.

My Score: Number Right ....   *Number Wrong* ....
            Average Number Right 11

Ninth Day: Analysis and Practice Test

A Closer Look

Before looking at the analysis that follows, read the exercise below, and write your own answer in the space provided.

SPAN : STRIDE :: (a) hand : foot   (b) bridge : street
(c) year : time   (d) horse : stretch   (e) radius : diameter

Answer ....

Analysis

(b) *bridge : street*   While a bridge has a span, stride is unrelated to street.

(c) *year : time*   One can span the years, but stride is unrelated to time.

(e) *radius : diameter*   There is no relationship between these words and the given pair.

We are left with (a) *hand : foot* and (d) *horse : stretch*. In some countries the size of a horse is measured in spans while a stretch results in a stride. However (a) *hand : foot* has a much closer set of relationships with the given pair. Span is the action done by a hand, while stride is the action done by a foot. Therefore (a) *hand : foot* is the correct answer.

Practice Test

Time at Start ....

In the space provided, write the letter of the set of words that best completes the analogy.

1. EXECUTE : LYNCH :: (a) rope : electricity
(b) illegal : legal   (c) swift : painful   (d) try : trial
(e) gas chamber : tree   1. ....

2. PATENT : PRODUCT :: (a) book : copyright
(b) law : right to vote   (c) judge : attorney   (d) money :
profit   (e) time : material   2. ....

3. ACTOR : STAGE :: (a) musician : pit
(b) audience : balcony   (c) prompter : script
(d) gridiron : fullback   (e) policeman : beat   3. ....

4. CIRCLE : SPHERE :: (a) one : two   (b) two : three
(c) foot : square foot   (d) length : depth   (e) one : three
                                                    4. ....

5. BROTHER : SISTER :: (a) mother : grandmother (b) mother : father   (c) aunt : uncle   (d) son : son-in-law (e) cousin : cousin   5. ....

6. TREE : FOREST :: (a) wall : room   (b) voice : chorus   (c) flower : meadow   (d) flour : bread (e) conductor : orchestra   6. ....

7. CHILD : MAN :: (a) lamb : sheep   (b) mouse : rat (c) spore : seed   (d) roe : deer   (e) bud : flower   7. ....

8. JEALOUSY : ANGER :: (a) love : hate   (b) poor : wealthy   (c) emotion : reason   (d) action : reaction (e) green : red   8. ....

9. MUTTON : SHEEP :: (a) sow : pig   (b) cow : heifer (c) steak : rib   (d) veal : steer   (e) old : young   9. ....

10. TEAM : COACH :: (a) association : president (b) Congress : Cabinet   (c) sergeant : squad   (d) navy : admiral   (e) army : private   10. ....

11. IMPULSE : NERVE FIBER :: (a) water : sound (b) electricity : copper   (c) light : battery   (d) touch : finger   (e) horror : fright   11. ....

12. MARRIAGE : BACHELOR :: (a) automobile : mechanic   (b) steeplejack : skyscraper   (c) money : miser (d) contract : free-lance writer   (e) happiness : loneliness
                                                                            12. ....

13. COVE : INLET :: (a) island : sea   (b) pilot : ship (c) lobby : entrance   (d) gamble : insure   (e) bay : ocean
                                                                            13. ....

14. FORSAKE : RELINQUISH :: (a) abduct : reduce (b) accept : abdicate   (c) time : hour   (d) injury : sue (e) loathe : detest   14. ....

15. CLINIC : ILLNESS :: (a) nurse : doctor (b) patient : cure   (c) school : ignorance   (d) sickness : infirm   (e) ward : building   15. ....

Time at End ....   *Minutes Elapsed* ....
                                    Average Time 12 *Minutes*

Answer Key for this test is on page 271.

My Score: *Number Right* ....   *Number Wrong* ....
             Average Number Right 13

Tenth Day: Analysis and Practice Test

A Closer Look

Before looking at the analysis that follows, read the exercise below, and write your own answer in the space provided.

LIVERY : SERVANT :: (a) robe : judge (b) sackcloth : civilian (c) soldier : uniform (d) apron : worker (e) medieval : modern   Answer ....

Analysis

(c) *soldier : uniform* is a reversal, and thus is wrong.

(b) *sackcloth : civilian* is true only in times of national disaster and mourning, and therefore cannot be accepted as being as typical as is livery to servant.

(c) *medieval : modern* offers a contrast that is not evident in the given pair.

We are then left with (a) *robe : judge* and (d) *apron : worker*. The correct answer can be selected on the basis of which of these comparisons holds true as frequently as servants wear livery. The answer, then, is (a) *robe : judge*.

Practice Test

Time at Start ....

In the space provided, write the letter of the set of words that best completes the following analogy.

1. ROOF : BUILDING :: (a) vault : arch (b) ceiling : room (c) spire : church (d) attic : house (e) marquee : theater   1. ....

2. SHRILL : THUNDEROUS :: (a) flute : drum (b) blast : pedal (c) high : low (d) hard : high (e) thrill : fear   2. ....

3. TROUSSEAU : ENSEMBLE :: (a) young : older (b) formal : informal (c) many : one (d) expensive : reasonable (e) one : many   3. ....

4. CRAG : LEDGE :: (a) high : low (b) dangerous : safe (c) rocky : grassy (d) goat : cattle (e) steep : flat   4. ....

5. CHAPTER : BOOK :: (a) joint : finger (b) ticket : admission (c) suit : jacket (d) vase : lamp (e) stub : check   5. ....

6. VACCINATION : DISEASE :: (a) cold : infection (b) temperature : comfort (c) injection : allergy (d) refrigeration : decay (e) job : security   6. ....

7. ACROSS-THE-BOARD : SELECTIVE :: (a) each : other (b) every : few (c) uniform : same (d) some : several (e) all : none   7. ....

8. SWATCH : CLOTH :: (a) sew : darn (b) morsel : bite (c) stitch : rip (d) sample : line (e) miniature : full-scale   8. ....

9. VARSITY : SQUAD :: (a) freshman : senior (b) eligible : ineligible (c) best : poorest (d) player : participant (e) part : whole   9. ....

10. SNEER : SCORN :: (a) smile : freedom (b) scowl : gloom (c) pout : pleasure (d) pain : grimace (e) deadpan : expression   10. ....

11. COWLICK : FOREHEAD :: (a) beard : chin (b) frizzle : curl (c) neck : queue (d) wig : bald spot (e) fur : animal   11. ....

12. APRON : STAGE :: (a) porch : house (b) attic : roof (c) driveway : garage (d) miter : bishop (e) pavement : street   12. ....

13. BRISTLE : BRAID :: (a) tousled : shaggy (b) trained : untrained (c) short : long (d) shaved : unshaved (e) soft : tough   13. ....

14. AUBURN : RED :: (a) tow-haired : dark (b) grizzled : gray (c) sandy : white (d) carroty : blond (e) light : fair-haired   14. ....

15. MUSTACHE : UPPER LIP :: (a) Vandyke : lips (b) mutton chops : chin (c) sideburns : cheeks (d) imperial : upper lip (e) goatee : chin   15. ....

Time at End ....   *Minutes Elapsed* ....
                                    Average Time 17 *Minutes*

Answer Key for this test is on page 271.

My Score: *Number Right* ....   *Number Wrong* ....
             Average Number Right 12

Eleventh Day: Test of Mastery

Time at Start ....

In the space provided, write the letter of the set of words that best completes the analogy.

1. PROLOGUE : PLAY :: (a) thinking : planning
(b) scene : act   (c) live : cast   (d) preface : book
(e) work : fun   1. ....

2. BATTERY : CANNON :: (a) fleet : ship   (b) fish :
school   (c) mammal : man   (d) power : vessel
(e) reserve : destructive   2. ....

3. BOLD : RASH :: (a) right : wrong   (b) vicious :
cruel   (c) temperate : moderate   (d) teen-ager :
adolescent   (e) courageous : foolhardy   3. ....

4. PYRAMID : CUBE :: (a) rectangle : pentagon
(b) triangle : prism   (c) disc : sphere   (d) ancient :
modern   (e) large : small   4. ....

5. EAGLE : THE UNITED STATES :: (a) rocket : space
(b) lion : Great Britain   (c) Soviet Russia : bear
(d) elephant : Africa   (e) empire : New York   5. ....

6. LEATHER : AWL :: (a) painter : canvas   (b) dress :
rayon   (c) stone : chisel   (d) needle : cloth   (e) typing :
ribbon   6. ....

7. HIVE : BEES :: (a) brood : wildcats   (b) kennel :
kittens   (c) drove : cattle   (d) fold : goats   (e) aviary :
birds   7. ....

8. CENTAUR : HORSE :: (a) Pan : goat   (b) Siren :
tree   (c) Sphinx : dog   (d) satyr : reed   (e) mermaid :
woman   8. ....

9. MERLIN : KING ARTHUR :: (a) medicine man :
Indian   (b) magician : sideshow   (c) Aladdin : lamp
(d) Africa : witch doctor   (e) voodoo : Haitian   9. ....

10. SURNAME : GIVEN NAME :: (a) individual :
family   (b) family : individual   (c) family : family
(d) individual : individual   (e) nickname : pen name   10. ....

11. PACKED : SATURATED :: (a) 100% : 80%
(b) 100% : 20%   (c) 80% : 100%   (d) 20% : 100%
(e) 90% : 90%   11. ....

12. JANUARY : WINTER :: (a) leaves : spring
(b) April : rain   (c) September : fall   (d) July : summer
(e) time : season   12. ....

13. PEN : PIG :: (a) pasture : sheep   (b) corral : horse
(c) cage : bear   (d) cell : nucleus   (e) animal : zoo   13. ....

14. NOVEL : FICTION :: (a) act : farce   (b) prose :
poetry   (c) story : nonfiction   (d) poem : epic   (e) play :
drama   14. ....

15. ENGRAVE : FRINGE :: (a) in : edge   (b) over :
border   (c) light : serious   (d) on : over   (e) tassel : ring
                                                          15. ....

16. BROOCH : LOCKET :: (a) diamond : gold
(b) luxury : necessity   (c) pin : chain   (d) ornament :
storage   (e) neck : chest   16. ....

17. LANDSCAPE : PORTRAIT :: (a) watercolor : oils
(b) painting : picture   (c) lifeless : living   (d) pastoral :
caricature   (e) mural : mosaic   17. ....

18. STAR : UNDERSTUDY :: (a) player : scholar
(b) regular : substitute   (c) trouper : impersonator
(d) coach : captain   (e) varsity : scrub   18. ....

19. SHUTTER : VEIL :: (a) horror : tragedy
(b) camera : fact   (c) widow : photographer   (d) winter :
holiday   (e) cover : obscure   19. ....

20. CLERICAL : TECHNICAL :: (a) book : machine
(b) entry : item   (c) foreman : manager   (d) entry :
blueprint   (e) typist : keypunch operator   20. ....

Time at End ....   *Minutes Elapsed* ....

Answer Key for this test is on page 271.

My Score: Number Right ....   *Number Wrong* ....

Comparing with Others

	Time	Number Correct
Elite	13 minutes	20
Superior	14–16 minutes	17–19
Average	19 minutes	15–16
Below Average	20–23 minutes	11–14
Weak	24–30 minutes	8–10

Section 5   Completing the Comparison

Answer Key

Third Day   **Page 251**

1. (e)	4. (c)	7. (d)	10. (d)	13. (c)
2. (b)	5. (e)	8. (e)	11. (d)	14. (c)
3. (c)	6. (d)	9. (b)	12. (a)	15. (a)

Fourth Day   **Page 253**

1. (c)	4. (a)	7. (e)	10. (e)	13. (d)
2. (e)	5. (d)	8. (d)	11. (b)	14. (d)
3. (e)	6. (c)	9. (a)	12. (c)	15. (a)

Fifth Day   **Page 256**

1. (c)	4. (c)	7. (d)	10. (b)	13. (e)
2. (d)	5. (b)	8. (b)	11. (c)	14. (b)
3. (d)	6. (b)	9. (c)	12. (c)	15. (d)

Sixth Day   **Page 258**

1. (b)	4. (e)	7. (b)	10. (e)	13. (e)
2. (e)	5. (a)	8. (c)	11. (c)	14. (b)
3. (b)	6. (c)	9. (d)	12. (a)	15. (d)

Seventh Day   **Page 260**

1. (c)	4. (b)	7. (d)	10. (c)	13. (e)
2. (d)	5. (a)	8. (b)	11. (b)	14. (c)
3. (e)	6. (b)	9. (e)	12. (d)	15. (d)

Eighth Day   **Page 262**

1. (b)	4. (a)	7. (a)	10. (e)	13. (d)
2. (c)	5. (b)	8. (d)	11. (b)	14. (a)
3. (e)	6. (d)	9. (c)	12. (c)	15. (b)

Ninth Day   **Page 264**

1. (e)	4. (b)	7. (a)	10. (d)	13. (c)
2. (b)	5. (e)	8. (e)	11. (b)	14. (e)
3. (a)	6. (b)	9. (d)	12. (d)	15. (c)

Tenth Day   **Page 266**

1. (b)	4. (e)	7. (b)	10. (b)	13. (c)
2. (c)	5. (a)	8. (d)	11. (a)	14. (b)
3. (c)	6. (d)	9. (e)	12. (a)	15. (e)

Eleventh Day   **Page 268**

1. (d)	5. (b)	9. (a)	13. (b)	17. (d)
2. (a)	6. (c)	10. (b)	14. (e)	18. (b)
3. (e)	7. (e)	11. (c)	15. (a)	19. (e)
4. (a)	8. (a)	12. (d)	16. (c)	20. (d)

READING FOR FULL COMPREHENSION

Section 6: READING FOR FULL COMPREHENSION

The reading-comprehension section of the Verbal Test consists of passages selected from standard reading matter. Each selection is followed by questions based on its content. The reader may be asked to select from a list of five possibilities the one that he considers the most suitable title. He may be asked to identify the important details or ideas in the selection; or he may be asked to apply the knowledge gained from such reading.

The material is based on the type of passages that you will be called on to read and digest in courses given for the freshman and sophomore levels in college. Fundamentally, then, what is being evaluated is your ability to do the reading found in typical English, social studies, and science textbooks.

While the questions may prove, occasionally, to be truly searching, the approach in general is not one planned to trap the unwary reader. Those who have done wide and systematic reading are rarely those who find the going tough in the reading-comprehension section.

The best preparation for this part of the examination, then, is reading widely and regularly. You must be familiar with the techniques of the short-story writer, the novelist, and the biographer. Your weekly reading fare should include magazines containing articles in the sciences and social sciences. You should spend time daily in digesting the opinions found on the editorial page of the newspaper. As you come across unfamiliar terms, you must develop some methodical approach to them. Some students look up each one and then study a few each day. Others list all, but concentrate on only one or two at a time. You, too, must discover the way to the mature reading habits that are necessary for success on the Verbal Test and in college.

The tests and exercises which follow cannot bring you to the reading level that is reached only through a long-range reading program on an ever-maturing level. There are, however, certain techniques that must be mastered for maximum scores on reading-comprehension tests. Control of these techniques will mean that you will reveal your best on such tests. This section should lead you to such mastery.

How well prepared are you now for the reading-comprehension section of the College Entrance Examination? Take the Inventory Test that follows and find out!

First Day: Inventory Test

Time at Start ....

Read each selection below; and in each space provided, write the letter of the word or set of words that best completes the statement.

In the degree in which I have been privileged to know the intimate secrets of hearts, I ever more realize how great a part is played in the lives of men and women by some little concealed germ of abnormality. For the most part they are occupied in the task of stifling and crushing these germs, treating them like weeds in their gardens. There is another and better way, even though more difficult and more perilous. Instead of trying to suppress the weeds that can never be killed, they may be cultivated into useful or beautiful flowers. For it is impossible to conceive of any impulse in a human heart which cannot be transformed into Truth or into Beauty or into Love.

1. The basic concept in this selection concerns itself with (a) geniuses (b) freaks (c) differences (d) beauty (e) truth.   **1.** ....

2. According to this article, most people (a) are glad to be different (b) are ashamed to be different (c) cultivate flowers (d) avoid weeds (e) have impulses.   **2.** ....

3. The author is a(n) (a) cynic (b) pessimist (c) optimist (d) nature lover (e) none of these.   **3.** ....

4. The author would praise the person who (a) stutters (b) admits his errors (c) loves mankind (d) hates war (e) admits his faults.   **4.** ....

5. An idea *not* developed in this article is that (a) there are many styles for the architecture of the soul   (b) talents must be guided, not thwarted   (c) people exaggerate their similarities   (d) it is dangerous to develop one's individuality   (e) defects can lead to valuable accomplishments.   5. ....

Distance in truth produces in idea the same effect as in real perspective. Objects are softened, rounded, and rendered doubly graceful. The harsher and more ordinary points of character are melted down, and those by which it is remembered are the more striking outlines that mark sublimity, grace, or beauty. There are mists, too, as in the natural horizon, to conceal what is less pleasing in distant objects; and there are happy lights to stream in full glory upon those points which can profit by brilliant illumination.

6. The article deals with (a) a main cause of distortion   (b) a means of enjoying painting   (c) distance and illumination (d) grace and light   (e) objects in reality and in art.   6. ....

7. Men will most often agree (a) after a good night's sleep (b) during an event   (c) when the truth is pointed out to them (d) if they have good characters   (e) if they are well trained.
                                                                                       7. ....

8. With the passage of time we forget (a) happy times   (b) perspective   (c) distant objects   (d) unimportant details (e) unpleasant details.   8. ....

9. The happy lights result from (a) forgetfulness   (b) training (c) skill in painting   (d) artificiality   (e) desire to distort.
                                                                                       9. ....

10. A close-up would reveal (a) things as they really are   (b) the effects of perspective   (c) basic ideas   (d) graceful lines (e) ugliness.   10. ....

The chickadee has a scientific name twice as big as he is, *Parus atricapillus*, but there isn't another bird in the woodland or dooryard that rates as much respect and affection, especially at this time of year.

Actually, the chickadee is one of the smallest of our familiar winter birds, weighing only a little more than a first-class letter. And a good half of that weight is feathers; he can fluff himself, on a cold day, to the size of a fat sparrow. Yet he is one of the most adept of all birds on the wing. His wings can beat thirty times a second and, though he can't fly backward, he can hover and he can fly straight up.

All birds live at high speed, physiologically, but Mr. Chick is a sprinter even among his own kind. His tiny heart beats five hundred times a minute when he is asleep and double that rate when he is awake and active. His normal temperature, 108 degrees, would be a fatal fever for any human being. His metabolism is terrific—he needs a winter diet of about his own weight in food each day. That is one reason he is so eternally busy, so incredibly hungry.

There he is, Mr. Chick, a mere fleck of feathered life, gay, jaunty, gregarious, chipper even in a snowstorm, singing even in zero weather. He rates a salute, and hereby gets one.

11. A statement *not* true of the chickadee is that (a) he does not migrate   (b) he can remain in one spot while beating his wings in mid-air   (c) he doesn't seem to mind cold weather   (d) he is a friendly bird   (e) he is about the size of an ordinary sparrow

11. ....

12. This article was written during (a) wintertime   (b) the spring (c) the autumn   (d) summertime (e) none of the above times.

12. ....

13. The chickadee eats (a) more food during the winter than during the summer   (b) less food than most birds   (c) more food than most birds   (d) less food during the winter than during the summer   (e) at a comparative rate not mentioned in this article.

13. ....

14. A statement *not* made in the article is that (a) the chickadee cannot fly backward   (b) his rate of breathing is faster than that of man   (c) his heartbeat during the daytime is about one thousand times a minute   (d) he can make himself appear to be much bigger than he really is   (e) he enjoys traveling in flocks.

14. ....

15. The author (a) feeds chickadees   (b) has written a book about birds   (c) is a scientist   (d) admires chickadees (e) is famous.

15. ....

In the early years of this century it seemed timely that the direct pressure of large advertisers, as, for instance, department stores, might affect the press with bias. Probably that danger is decreasing; but today we are faced with a new menace to the freedom of the press, a menace in this country vastly more acute than the menace from government. And this menace may come through the pressure not of one group of advertisers but of a wide sector of newspaper advertisers. These advertising agencies undertake to protect their clients from what the clients and agents may regard as real dangers from inimical social, political, or industrial influences. As advisers the advertising agencies may exercise unbelievably powerful pressure upon the newspapers. There is grave danger that in the coming decade, as social, industrial, and economic problems become more and more acute, this capacity for organized control of newspaper opinion by the political advisers of national advertisers may constitute a major threat to a free press.

16. The most serious threat that the writer sees is that (a) the government would suppress news (b) the press would lose its influence (c) department stores would refuse to advertise (d) freedom would be lost (e) outsiders could tell the editors what to print.   16. ....

17. The danger foreseen by the author is (a) as old as newspapers (b) sixty years old   (c) going to decrease   (d) going to increase in the next ten years   (e) controllable.   17. ....

18. The advertising agencies (a) own the newspapers   (b) advise the advertisers   (c) write the advertisements   (d) buy the advertisements   (e) are a wide sector.   18. ....

19. *Not* discussed in the article is the (a) consumer   (b) management   (c) government official   (d) political consultant (e) business executive.   19. ....

20. This article could *not* have been written in (a) twentieth-century United States (b) nineteenth-century England (c) twentieth-century Russia   (d) nineteenth-century United States (e) twentiety-century France.   20. ....

Time at End ....   *Minutes Elapsed* ....

Answer Key

1. (c)	5. (c)	9. (a)	13. (e)	17. (d)
2. (b)	6. (a)	10. (a)	14. (b)	18. (b)
3. (c)	7. (b)	11. (e)	15. (d)	19. (a)
4. (e)	8. (e)	12. (a)	16. (e)	20. (c)

My Score: Number Right............ Number Wrong............

Comparing with Others

	Time	Number Correct
Elite	14 minutes	20
Superior	17 minutes	18–19
Average	21–23 minutes	15–17
Below Average	26–29 minutes	11–14
Weak	30–35 minutes	6–10

Clinch by Checking

The purpose in your taking this Inventory Test was to discover your level of competency in reading this type of material and to discover how much time you need to handle such questions. The results become meaningful not only when you compare your efforts with those of other students, but also when you compare your present score and the amount of time spent in taking this test with the results after you have done the daily exercises that follow. No one can ask you to do better than your best! These exercises will help to bring you up to that level by giving you the day-by-day sharpening that means best results.

Second Day: Gaining Exam Know-How

A Closer Look

Most of us find some reading-comprehension passages easier to understand than others. The key lies in the types of reading to which we are accustomed. The student who has done much reading in science will find selections in that area comparatively simple. The student who has spent time delving into books on philosophy will not be stumped by passages on that level of abstract thinking. The more we have read in an area, the more confident we feel when faced with similar material. Regardless, however, of the area from which a selection is taken, the technique of answering the questions remains the same. You must over-come your initial reaction to the subject matter before you. Familiarity may cause overconfidence and careless reading; material from fields new to you may rob you of the self-assurance that you need for concentration on the task at hand. Therefore, let us begin with the basic question: What is the best approach to *any* reading question? Our first step will be to analyze typical questions.

Before looking at the analysis that follows, read the exercise below, and write your own answers in the spaces provided.

The assembly line has not been an unmixed blessing. For one thing, it discouraged the old traditions of pride of craftsmanship. Two engineers named Arnold and Faurote, who wrote a classic study called "Ford Methods and the Ford Shops" in 1915, observed: "The Ford Company has no use for experience, in the working ranks anyway. It desires and prefers machine-tool operators who have nothing to unlearn, who . . . will simply do as they are told to do, over and over again, from bell-time to bell-time."

A deeper complaint was that the line dehumanized the worker. Henry Ford observed: "The idea is that a man must not be hurried in his work—he must have every second necessary but not a single unnecessary second." The results of treating men like machines were satirized by Charlie Chaplin in "Modern Times" and by the French movie director René Clair in "A Nous la Liberté." They were seen more grimly in years of often bloody strikes.

However, the worst abuses of the assembly line have been remedied in recent years. Its future lies in another direction. The concept of a steady flow from raw materials to finished product—perfected through years of experience with the assembly line—is essential to automation. If the human problems of the new technological age can be worked out, the assembly line may yet fulfill Ford's ambition of fifty years ago to "lift . . . drudgery off flesh and blood and lay it on steel and motors."

1. According to the article, Henry Ford (a) mistrusted machines   (b) did not trust his workers   (c) disregarded the effects of the assembly line on his workers   (d) felt that man and machines must operate as a single unit   (c) made his fortune from exploiting his fellow men.   1. ....

2. "Modern Times" (a) praised the Ford methods   (b) was a biography of Ford   (c) was made in France   (d) was written in 1915   (e) was none of the above.   2. ....

3. The main point made in this article is that (a) the assembly line almost dehumanized the workers   (b) Henry Ford revolutionized the automobile industry   (c) the assembly line is a necessary step in automation   (d) the assembly line led to strikes   (e) the assembly line may eventually be a blessing rather than a curse to the working man.   3. ....

Analysis

These three questions are typical of the types of questions found on most College Entrance Examinations. The first one is based on *inference*. The facts are not stated explicitly in the text. The reader must use the facts in the passage and carry them a logical step further to obtain the correct answer.

The second question is the easiest one of all to handle. The facts are stated in the passage. The reader must find the correct reference in this *factual* question.

The third question is based on the reader's following the development of thought in the passage and being able to realize just what the author's main point was. This question, since it demands understanding of the entire selection, is often called a *title* question.

Question 1 (*Inference Question*)

(a) *mistrusted machines* This is wrong because Ford was accused of "treating men like machines."

(b) *did not trust his workers* This may or may not be true, but no statement in the paragraph points in this direction.

(e) *made his fortune from exploiting his fellow men* This may or may not be true, but no statement in the selection hints at such a conclusion.

(c) *disregarded the effects of the assembly line on his workers* In one respect this statement may be true, inasmuch as Ford was accused of allowing the assembly line to dehumanize the workers; yet, in that he did time the efforts of his workers, he did show concern.

(d) *felt that man and machines must operate as a single unit* This is better than statement (c) since each of the quotations, especially the last, points in this direction. This statement (d) is therefore the correct one.

Question 2 (*Factual Question*)

(a) *praised the Ford methods* The film "satirized," not praised them.

(b) *was a biography of Ford* The film dealt with "treating men like machines." No mention is made of its being a biography.

(c) *was made in France*   "A Nous la Liberté" was made by a French director. No mention is made of where "Modern Times" was made.

(d) *was written in 1915*   Arnold and Faurote's book was written in 1915. No mention is made of when "Modern Times" was written.

(e) *was none of the above*   This is the only possible answer, since we have eliminated all the others.

Question 3 (Title Question)

(b) *Henry Ford revolutionized the automobile industry*   No mention is made of this in the selection.

(a) *the assembly line almost dehumanized the workers*   This is developed in the second paragraph only.

(d) *the assembly line led to strikes*   This is developed in the last sentence of the second paragraph only.

(c) *the assembly line is a necessary step in automation*   This is developed in the last paragraph only.

(e) *the assembly line may eventually be a blessing rather than a curse to the working man*   This is correct, for the thought development from paragraph to paragraph leads to this conclusion.

For Highest Marks

A. Through Handling the Selection Correctly

1. This is a test in reading a selection. You can speed up the process through practice, but there is no short cut. Do *not* turn to the questions first. Doing so may give you a distorted view of the main ideas of the selection.

2. Read the selection through quickly the first time in order to find out with just what area of learning it deals.

3. Then read the selection carefully, phrase by phrase, idea by idea. If the selection seems difficult, then read it with care a second and a third time. No one is going to mark you on the number of times you had to read the selection. The only thing that really counts is reaching the correct answers.

4. When reading analytically, be sensitive to such key words as *therefore, as a result, for example, for one thing, if, occasionally,*

frequently, in my opinion, on the other hand. These are the words that help you to follow the author's train of thought.

5. If one selection proves too difficult, don't fret over it for a long period of time. Go to the next, complete that one, and then return to the difficult one. Very often, your mind will have painlessly untied the knots for you. When you return to the selection, you will often find that it has become relatively simple!

6. Don't allow pangs of panic or nervousness to rob you of the ability to concentrate. If you think of facing the selections before you and nothing else, panic and nervousness will leave you. The main path of understanding is reached through concentration; don't let anything get in your way!

7. Look for the examples and illustrative phrases that the author plants in order to help you. Very often the example will clarify the entire meaning of a paragraph.

8. If it will help you in your thinking, underline lightly the key phrases in each paragraph.

B. Through Attention to the Questions

1. Do *not* turn to the questions first. The answers lie in the selection; read that before looking at the questions.

2. Usually, it is better to take the questions in order. The answer arrived at for the first one may help with the second.

3. The information for questions should be in the selection itself, not in your previous knowledge. Your ability to read, and not what you know, is being tested.

4. Do not rely upon what you remember of the contents of the selection. Turn back constantly to the selection to verify your thinking.

5. Each question has been written with four or five possible completions. Each one is a possible answer. Use the process of elimination to narrow down the field. Sometimes you will be left with only one answer that could be correct! Always reread the selection to check even this one!

6. Make certain that you examine each of the possible completions. The one that you skip could easily be the best choice of answers. You may have selected one that is highly possible, but the one that you missed could be a more logical one!

7. If it will help you to become more methodical, then draw a light line through the letter of each choice that you eliminate. This will make the remaining ones stand out for better consideration.

8. In the final elimination process, favor the statement that is more specific to the selection over the one that is too general.

However, do not reach the guessing stage before you have eliminated as many as possible of the choices that you feel are definitely incorrect.

The tests that follow will give you the practice that should lead to your achieving maximum results in the reading-comprehension selections. Study the initial analysis. Then take the test. Do not rush through it. Speed will follow. Analyze each of your wrong answers to discover why you went astray. If necessary, after an interim of a few weeks, take the same tests over again, not to recall the correct answers, but to recall the techniques that produce correct answers at your maximum rate of speed. These tests will help you to develop the necessary sense of urgency that leads to concentration without loss of credits caused by undue rushing.

Third Day: Analysis and Practice Test

A Closer Look

Before looking at the analysis that follows, read the exercise below, and write your own answer in the space provided.

For combating racism before it sinks its poison fangs deep in our body politic, the scientist has both a special motive and a special responsibility. His motive comes from the fact that when personal liberty disappears, scientific liberty also disappears. His responsibility comes from the fact that only he can give the people the truth. Only he can clean out the falsities which have been masquerading under the name of science in our colleges, our high schools, and our public prints. Only he can show how groundless are the claims that one race, one nation, or one class has any God-given right to rule.

The selection does *not* explain (a) to what the poison fangs belong (b) what the role of the scientist should be (c) what racism is (d) how the scientist discovers the truth (e) why the scientist must combat racism.   Answer ....

Analysis

The Selection

The two key words are *racism* and *scientist*. The most important sentence, the one that contains the main idea and is the topic sentence, is the last one. Once the reader realizes the importance of that sentence, the ideas of the selection come through clearly. Learn to look for the topic sentence in each of the selections in this practice test.

The Question (Factual)

(a) *to what the poison fangs belong*   The author does tell us that racism has poison fangs.

(b) *what the role of the scientist should be*   He does tell us that the scientist can "give the people the truth."

(c) *what racism is*   His last sentence defines racism.

(e) *why the scientist must combat racism*   He does state that "when personal liberty disappears, scientific liberty also disappears."

(d) *how the scientist discovers the truth*   By re-examining each sentence, we see that nowhere in the selection does he explain how the scientist discovers truths. This, therefore, is the correct answer.

Practice Test

Time at Start ....

Read each selection below; and in each space provided, write the letter of the word or set of words that best completes the statement.

Microbes affect man's life in many ways, from the day of his birth to the day of his death, and even thereafter, since they attack and destroy his mortal remains. Microbes are always with us, in our food and our bodies, in our clothing and in our habitation, in the soil under our feet, and in the water we drink and bathe in. They are always ready to help us or to destroy us. Only circumstances decide which it shall be.

It is usually not recognized that for every injurious or parasitic microbe there are dozens of beneficial ones. Without the latter, there would be no bread to eat nor wine to drink, no fertile soils and no potable waters, no clothing and no sanitation. One can visualize no form of higher life without the existence of the microbes. They are the universal scavengers. They keep in constant circulation the chemical elements which are so essential to the continuation of plant and animal life.

1. The underlying realization developed in this selection is that (a) some microbes are harmful   (b) microbes have their own life

cycle   (c) microbes are effective   (d) microbes are essential to the continuance of life   (e) microbes aid man in his progress.

1. ....

2. The purpose of the author was to (a) make people more aware of how beneficial microbes can be   (b) make people sensitive to the presence of microbes   (c) summarize present knowledge   (d) show the reader how important scientists are   (e) protect the reader from harmful microbes.   2. ....

3. An aspect of microbiology *not* touched in this article is (a) man's attempts to control microbes   (b) man's knowledge of microbes   (c) yeast's role in fermentation   (d) the microbes of disease   (e) what gives water a distinct flavor.   3. ....

4. A basic assumption made in the article is that (a) microbes destroy more than they build   (b) man knows very little about microbes   (c) microbes will eventually destroy all other forms of life   (d) man will eventually control all microbes   (e) microbes are a lower form of life.   4. ....

5. Disease microbes attack healthy, living organisms (a) to destroy them   (b) to make certain that the life cycle continues (c) to survive   (d) to weaken them   (e) for none of the above reasons.   5. ....

Tyrants use their power against the people in three ways. The first is that they strive that those under their mastery be ever ignorant and timorous, because when they are such, they may not be bold to rise against them, nor to resist their wills; and the second is that their victims be not kindly and united among themselves, in such wise that they trust not one another; and the third way is that they strive to make them poor, and to put them upon great undertakings which they can never finish, whereby they may have so much harm that it may never come into their hearts to devise anything against their ruler.

6. Tyrants could not exist under (a) fascism   (b) democracy (c) republicanism   (d) dictatorships   (e) autocracy.   6. ....

7. A tyrant would be opposed to (a) undeclared war   (b) the UN   (c) book burning   (d) uncontrolled production of atomic weaponry   (e) construction of giant dams.   7. ....

8. The tyrants ruled because (a) they were capable leaders of the people   (b) they had strong armies to suppress revolts (c) the people loved and admired them   (d) the people elected them   (e) they tricked the people.   8. ....

9. A tyrant would favor the type of education that (a) taught each man a useful trade   (b) taught the worth of the individual (c) stressed racial superiority   (d) taught the arts of war (e) stressed physical fitness.   9. ....

10. Tyrants believed that (a) right makes might   (b) science can lead to progress   (c) poverty can be eradicated   (d) propaganda is a powerful weapon   (e) the people were fools.
                                                                                10. ....

The business classes are conservative, on the whole, but such a conservative bent is, of course, not peculiar to them. These occupations are not the only ones whose reasoning prevailingly moves on a conventional plane. Indeed, the intellectual captivity of other classes, such as soldiers, politicians, the clergy, and men of fashion, moves on a plane of still older conventions; so that if the training given by business employments is to be characterized as conservative, that given by these other, more archaic employments should be called reactionary. Extreme conventionalization means extreme conservatism. Conservatism means the maintenance of convention already in force. On this head, therefore, the discipline of modern business life may be said simply to retain something of the complexion which marks the life of the higher barbarian culture, at the same time that it has not retained the disciplinary force of the barbarian culture in so high a state of preservation as some of the occupations just named.

11. A businessman tends to be conservative because (a) other businessmen are conservative   (b) business thrives best in least change   (c) governments control business trends   (d) he is peculiar   (e) he tends to be reasonable.   11. ....

12. The difference in attitude of a businessman and a soldier results from (a) age of occupation   (b) training   (c) life needs (d) forces in modern society
(e) attitude of the people.   12. ....

13. The word *barbarian* as used in this selection refers to (a) the cruelty of the invaders   (b) the business practices of the invaders (c) the military might of an older generation   (d) a period of culture   (e) aristocracy.   13. ....

14. An idea *not* developed by the author in this selection is that (a) a minister tends to be more conservative than does the owner of a department store   (b) the more traditions we follow, the more conservative we become   (c) many of the beliefs of our politicians can be traced back to the times of the nomadic tribes

(d) as a storekeeper grows older, he grows even more conservative   (e) a reactionary is prisoner to tradition.   14. ....

15. The author believes that (a) a man's occupation and
not his personality decides his politics   (b) there are exceptions
to all generalizations   (c) social classes change their points
of view   (d) conservatives can easily become reactionaries
(e) reactionaries are dangerous to the progress of govern-
ment.   15. ....

It is a truth universally acknowledged that a single man in
possession of a good fortune must be in want of a wife.

However little known the feelings or views of such a man may
be on his first entering a neighborhood, this truth is so well fixed
in the minds of the surrounding families that he is considered as
the rightful property of some one or other of their daughters.

"My dear Mr. Bennet," said his lady to him one day, "have you
heard that Netherfield Park is let at last?"

Mr. Bennet replied that he had not.

"But it is," returned she; "for Mrs. Long has just been here,
and she told me all about it."

Mr. Bennet made no answer.

"Do not you want to know who has taken it?" cried his wife
impatiently.

"You want to tell me, and I have no objection to hearing it."
This was invitation enough.

"Why, my dear, you must know, Mrs. Long says that Netherfield is taken by a young man of large fortune from the north of
England."

"What's his name?"

"Bingley."

"Is he married or single?"

"Oh! single, my dear, to be sure! A single man of large fortune;
four or five thousand a year. What a fine thing for our girls!"

"How so? How can it affect them?"

"My dear Mr. Bennet," replied his wife, "how can you be so
tiresome! You must know that I am thinking of his marrying one
of them."

"Is that his design in settling here?"

"Design! Nonsense, how can you talk so! But it is very likely
that he may fall in love with one of them, and therefore you must
visit him as soon as he comes."

16. The dialogue in the selection (a) is filled with suspense
(b) illustrates the ideas in the initial two paragraphs   (c) shows

how desperate both parents were   (d) reveals Mr. Bingley's
character   (e) took place over a long period of time.   16. ....

17. Mrs. Bennet was *not* interested in Mr. Bingley's (a) marital
status   (b) presence in the neighborhood   (c) annual
income   (d) original home   (e) personality.   17. ....

18. Mr. Bennet spoke little because (a) his wife did not give him
a chance to ask questions   (b) he was so disgusted   (c) he did not
want to be interrupted   (d) his wife needed no prompting
(e) he did not want to interrupt his wife.   18. ....

19. Mrs. Bennet was impatient with Mr. Bennet because
(a) he was teasing her   (b) he was so slow to understand her
(c) he did not offer to meet Mr. Bingley   (d) he did not love
his daughters   (e) he was unconcerned.   19. ....

20. A statement that is not true is that (a) Mrs. Bennet was concentrating on the problem of finding a husband for her daughters
(b) Mrs. Long was a gossip   (c) Mr. Bingley had already met the
Bennet girls   (d) Netherfield Park was an estate
(e) Mrs. Bennet was all excited by the news.   20. ....

Time at End ....   *Minutes Elapsed* ....
                                          Average Time 18 *Minutes*

Answer Key for this test is on page 320.

My Score: *Number Right* ....   *Number Wrong* ....
               Average Number Right 14

Fourth Day: Analysis and Practice Test

A Closer Look

Before looking at the analysis that follows, read the selection
below, and write your own answer in the space provided.

Children are principally the creatures of example—whatever
surrounding adults do, they will do. If we strike them, they will
strike each other. If they see us attempting to govern each other,
they will imitate the same barbarism. If we habitually admit the
right of sovereignty in each other and in them, they will become
equally respectful of our rights and of each other's. All these
propositions are probably self-evident, yet not one of them is

practicable under the present mixture of the interests and responsibilities between adults and between parents and children. To solve the problem of education, children must be surrounded with equity and must be equitably treated, and each and every one, parent or child, must be understood to be an individual, and must have his or her individual rights equitably respected.

The author of this selection does *not* believe that (a) adults at present handle children poorly   (b) children learn through doing (c) children are creative in their actions most of the time (d) adults help children to develop their own sense of self-esteem (e) adults are the source of a child's attitude toward others.

Answer ....

Analysis

The Selection

The key to this selection lies in your understanding of the sentence that begins: "All these propositions are . . . " Up to this point, the author has stated some obvious realizations about children. In the key sentence he points out that the most important item in the training of children is none of the above. The additional realizations that he then states in the last sentence— the need for fairness and the need for each child's being accepted as an individual—are most important of all. This, then, is a selection in which ideas are presented in increasing order of importance. The reader must be able to follow the thought sequence if he is to grasp the author's full intent.

The Question (Factual)

(a) *adults at present handle children poorly*   The author is not discussing whether parents are or are not handling their children properly. He stresses that if parents are to handle their children properly, then certain attitudes should be in evidence. Therefore, the reader cannot tell whether the author does or does not believe in this statement.

(b) *children learn through doing*   Since imitating is doing, the author does believe in this statement.

(d) *adults help children to develop their own sense of self-esteem* The author does believe in this, since he urges adults to understand each child as an individual.

(e) *adults are the source of a child's attitude toward others* The author does believe in this, since he stresses that children imitate the attitudes of the adults around them.

(c) *children are creative in their actions most of the time* Since, as he claims, they are "creatures of example," they are imitative, not creative. This, therefore, is the best answer.

Practice Test

Time at Start ....

Read each selection below; and in each space provided, write the letter of the word or set of words that best completes the statement.

But to conclude: The question before the court and you, gentlemen of the jury, is not of small nor [of] private concern, it is not the cause of a poor printer, nor of New York alone, which you are now trying. No! It may in its consequence affect every freeman that lives under a British government on the main of America. It is the best cause. It is the cause of liberty; and I make no doubt but your upright conduct, this day, will not only entitle you to the love and esteem of your fellow-citizens, but every man who prefers freedom to a life of slavery will bless and honor you as men who have baffled the attempt of tyranny; and by an impartial and uncorrupt verdict, have laid a noble foundation for securing to ourselves, our posterity, and our neighbors, that to which nature and the laws of our country have given us a right—the liberty, both of exposing and opposing arbitrary power (in these parts of the world, at least), by speaking and writing.

1. The statement that is not true of the contents of this selection is (a) the speaker is the prosecuting attorney (b) the case took place before the American Revolution (c) the lawyer was summarizing his principal arguments (d) the lawyer used flattery in his statements (e) the case took place in one of the Colonies.   1. ....

2. The attorney appealed to his listeners' (a) religious beliefs (b) love of good government (c) loyalty to the King (d) hatred of tyranny (e) knowledge of reading.   2. ....

3. An argument that the attorney used was that (a) their decision had world-wide significance (b) their decision would affect

all British subjects   (c) the cause of justice demanded an acquittal
(d) their decision would affect the lives of their children
(e) the love and esteem of their family was at stake.   3. ....

4. The case most likely involved (a) libel   (b) the laws of
slander   (c) freedom of the press   (d) rebellion
(e) the right to bear arms.   4. ....

5. The "arbitrary power" referred to was that of the (a) judge
(b) attorney   (c) accused   (d) jury   (e) Crown.
                                                           5. ....

It is bad to be oppressed by a minority, but it is worse to be
oppressed by a majority. For there is a reserve of latent power in
the masses, which if it is called into play, the minority can seldom
resist. But from the absolute will of an entire people, there is no
appeal, no redemption, no refuge but treason.

6. The author favors (a) oppression   (b) treason   (c) rule of
the minority   (d) rule of the majority   (e) none of these.
                                                           6. ....

7. The author believes that (a) the majority cannot make
mistakes   (b) the minority ruler cannot afford to disregard the
majority   (c) the strength of the people favors the minority
(d) a dictatorship is doomed to failure   (e) reserve power
always wins.   7. ....

8. This statement was most likely written by one who (a) feared
democracy   (b) feared dictatorships   (c) favored communism
(d) lived in a democracy   (e) lived under a king.
                                                           8. ....

9. The statement of Lincoln that is applicable to this selection
is the one in which he says (a) that God must love the common
man since He made so many of them   (b) that the people have the
right to overthrow the government   (c) that our government is a
monument to the men who sacrificed their lives to preserve it
(d) that all men are brothers   (e) none of the above.
                                                           9. ....

I long to hear that you have declared an independency. And in
the new code of laws which I suppose it will be necessary for you
to make, I desire you would remember the ladies, and be more
generous and favorable to them than your ancestors. . . . If particular care and attention are not paid to the ladies, we are deter-

mined to foment a rebellion and will not hold ourselves bound by any laws in which we have no voice or representation.

10. This statement was most likely written by (a) the wife of a UN delegate (b) the wife of a President of the United States (c) a general in the British army (d) someone living in Colonial America (e) a Daughter of the American Revolution.

10. ....

11. The author (a) appeals to the emotions of the reader by asking for kindness (b) tries to reason with the reader (c) threatens the reader (d) appeals to the reader's sense of fairness (e) does none of the above. 11. ....

12. The author wants women to have (a) the right to vote (b) a voice in the government (c) equality with men (d) more politeness shown them (e) more respect shown them

12. ....

It is quite right that there should be a heavy duty on cards; not only on moral grounds; not only because they act on a social party like a torpedo, silencing the merry voice and numbing the play of the features; not only to fill the hunger of the public purse, which is always empty, however much you may put into it; but also because every pack of cards is a malicious libel on courts, and on the world seeing that the trumpery with number one at the head is the best part of them, and that it gives kings and queens no other companions than knaves.

13. The author wrote this article (a) with tongue in cheek (b) in anger (c) with bitterness (d) with moral indignation (e) to reform people. 13. ....

14. An advantage to card playing that he does not mention is that (a) the tax supplies the government with needed money (b) people who play are not forced to make polite conversation (c) with card playing, time can pass pleasantly for many people (d) people who play cards do not have to search for humorous things to say (e) it lowers respect paid to nobility.

14. ....

15. The card not mentioned but referred to is the (a) ace (b) queen of spades (c) ten (d) jack (e) deuce.

15. ....

Mr. Pickwick and his three friends struck into the footpath across the fields and walked briskly away, leaving Mr. Weller and the fat boy confronted together for the first time. Sam looked at the fat boy with great astonishment, but without saying a word; and began to stow the luggage rapidly away in the cart, while the fat boy stood quietly by, and seemed to think it a very interesting sort of thing to see Mr. Weller working by himself.

"There," said Sam, throwing in the last carpetbag. "There you are!"

"Yes," said the fat boy, in a very satisfied tone, "there they are."

"Vell, young twenty stun," said Sam, "you're a nice speciment of a prize boy, you are!"

"Thank'ee," said the fat boy.

"You ain't got nothin' on your mind as makes you fret yourself, have you?" inquired Sam.

"Not as I knows on," replied the fat boy.

"I should rayther ha' thought to look at you, that you was a laboring under an unrequited attachment to some young woman," said Sam.

The fat boy shook his head.

"Vell," said Sam, "I'm glad to hear it. Do you ever drink anythin'?"

"I like eating, better," replied the boy.

"Ah," said Sam, "I should ha' supposed that; but what I mean is, should you like a drop of anythin' as'd warm you? but I suppose you never was cold, with all them elastic fixtures, was you?"

"Sometimes," replied the boy; "and I like a drop of something when it's good."

"Oh, you do, do you?" said Sam. "Come this way, then!"

16. Sam Weller was (a) Mr. Pickwick's host (b) the fat boy's helper (c) owner of the luggage (d) one of Mr. Pickwick's friends (e) none of the above.   16. ....

17. The author intended the fat boy as (a) an object lesson (b) an object of ridicule (c) a clinical study (d) a humorous character (e) a pathetic character.   17. ....

18. A statement that is *not* true is that (a) Sam did not resent that the fat boy did not help him with the luggage (b) Sam was disgusted by the sight of the boy's unhealthy fatness (c) the hard work made Sam very thirsty (d) the boy did not mind having people stare at him (e) Sam treated the boy as a curiosity.   18. ....

19. Sam's theories of causes for overweight did *not* include (a) overeating   (b) an unhappy love affair   (c) gnawing worries (d) mental anguish   (e) glandular disturbance.

19. ....

20. Sam invited the boy to join him because (a) Sam was lonely (b) Sam wanted to see how the boy would eat   (c) Sam wanted to make up for the questions he had asked the boy   (d) Sam wanted to repay him for his assistance   (e) it was the polite thing to do.

20. ....

Time at End ....   *Minutes Elapsed* ....
                                   Average Time 20 *Minutes*

Answer Key for this test is on page 320.

My Score: Number Right ....   *Number Wrong* ....
            Average Number Right 13

Fifth Day: Analysis and Practice Test

A Closer Look

Before looking at the analysis that follows, read the exercise below, and then write your own answer in the space provided.

To divest either politics or religion of ceremony is the most certain method of bringing either into contempt. —The weak must have their inducements to admiration as well as the wise; and it is the business of a sensible government to impress all ranks with a sense of subordination whether this be effected by a diamond buckle, a virtuous edict, a sumptuary law, or a glass necklace.

The author would *not* approve of (a) special uniforms for high-ranking officers in the army   (b) bigger offices for more important officials in the State Department   (c) swearing in of the President by the head of the Supreme Court   (d) a 21-gun salute for a visiting foreign official   (e) eliminating the salute to officers in the Armed Services.   Answer ....

Analysis

The Selection

The difficulty in the selection lies in its seeming simplicity. Only when you try to find the key phrase that ties the ideas into a unity do you realize that there is an ever-widening series of concepts in this selection rather than an amplification of one. Usually, the best way to handle such a selection is to make certain that you understand the full meaning of each of the thought-groups; then turn to the questions to see in which direction the examiner expects your thinking to go. Constant rereading of each question is the technique that leads to best results with such a paragraph.

The Question (Implication)

(a) *special uniforms for high-ranking officers in the army* and (b) *bigger offices for more important officials in the State Department* both stress "a sense of subordination" that would be approved of by the author.

(c) *swearing in of the President by the head of the Supreme Court* and (d) *a 21-gun salute for a visiting foreign official* are ceremonials that would induce admiration of the weak; therefore the author would approve.

(e) *eliminating the salute to officers in the Armed Services* would take away some of the "sense of subordination," and if so, the author would, therefore, object. This, then, is the correct answer.

Practice Test

Time at Start ....

Read each selection below; and in each space provided, write the letter of the word or set of words that best completes the statement.

Art is this intense form of individualism that makes the public try to exercise over it an authority that is as immoral as it is ridiculous, and as corrupting as it is contemptible. It is not quite their fault. The public has always, and in every age, been badly brought up. They are continually asking Art to be popular, to please their want of taste, to flatter their absurd vanity, to tell them what they have been told before, to show them what they ought to be tired of seeing, to amuse them when they feel heavy after eating too much, and to distract their thoughts when they are wearied of their own stupidity. Now Art should never try to be popular. The public should try to make itself artistic.

1. The artist must learn (a) to please the popular taste   (b) to avoid pleasing the public   (c) to avoid criticism   (d) to express himself   (e) the universal fundamentals of art.   1. ....

2. The author does *not* explain (a) why people make fun of truly modern art   (b) why people buy truly modern art   (c) why the work of one artist is different from that of another   (d) what the people want of their artists   (e) why the public expects the wrong things of their artists.   2. ....

3. The blame for the poor taste of the public belongs mainly on the (a) artist   (b) critic   (c) quality of paintings available (d) schools   (e) public itself.   3. ....

4. To be a popular success an artist must (a) be artistic (b) never try to please the public   (c) educate the public   (d) disregard his own inner drives   (e) be contemptuous.

4. ....

5. An artist will move to Greenwich Village (a) to avoid being influenced by public pressures   (b) because the rent is so much cheaper there   (c) because of the many scenes there that he can paint   (d) to gain the attention of the public   (e) to show his contempt for society.   5. ....

My main thesis is that a social system is kept together by the blind force of instinctive actions, and of instinctive emotions clustered around habits and prejudices. It is therefore not true that any advance in the scale of culture inevitably tends to the preservation of society. On the whole, the contrary is more often the case, and any survey of nature confirms this conclusion. A new element in life renders in many ways the operation of the old instincts unsuitable. Mankind misses its opportunities, and its failures are a fair target for ironic criticism. But the fact that reason too often fails does not give fair ground for the hysterical conclusion that it never succeeds.

6. In order that a government remain stable and avoid revolution, (a) the lot of the common people must constantly be bettered (b) unfair laws and practices must be abolished   (c) no reforms

should be effected   (d) the scale of wages should be raised
(e) control of the army and navy is essential.   6. ....

7. Any change in governmental regulations (a) is doomed to
failure   (b) must have some weakness   (c) is better than none
(d) is worth trying if only to let the people know that the government has their interests at heart   (e) is unsuitable.
7. ....

8. A person's habits (a) cannot be changed   (b) can be changed
through wise and careful planning   (c) involve strong, unlearned
reactions   (d) should not be tampered with   (e) grow out
of the social system.   8. ....

9. Letters of protest from the public to officials concerning
recent legislation (a) contain hysterical conclusions   (b) reveal
their pride and interest in government   (c) show resentment
against change   (d) attack the personalities of the officials
(e) should not be heeded.   9. ....

10. The author of this selection is (a) a conservative opposed
to change   (b) an aristocrat who fears the public reaction
(c) a social historian who does not trust instincts   (d) a progressive who favors change   (e) none of the above.   10. ....

In the course of our experiments we have administered over
seventy-five doses of extract from degenerated pancreatic tissue
to ten different diabetic animals. Since the extract has always produced a reduction of the percentage sugar of the blood and of the
sugar excreted in the urine, we feel justified in stating that this
extract contains the internal secretion of the pancreas. Some of
our more recent experiments, which are not yet completed, give,
in addition to still more conclusive evidence regarding sugar-re-
taining power of diabetic animals treated with extract, some
interesting facts regarding the chemical nature of the active
principle of the internal secretion. These results, together with a
study of the respiratory exchange in diabetic animals before and
after administration of extract, will be reported in a subsequent
communication.

We have always observed a distinct improvement in the clinical
condition of diabetic dogs after administration of extract of
degenerated pancreas, but it is very obvious that the results of our
experimental work, as reported in this paper, do not at present

justify the therapeutic administration of degenerated gland extracts to cases of diabetes mellitus in the clinic.

11. The experimenters were (a) enthusiastic about the results (b) cautious about the results   (c) conclusive about their results (d) dejected by their results   (e) secretive about their results.   11. ....

12. At this point in the study, (a) insulin had been discovered (b) experiments had been carried on in hospital clinics on human beings   (c) the effects of insulin had been noted   (d) the experiments were to be abandoned   (e) the type of additional experimentation to be carried on in the future was not determined.   12. ....

13. This extract did *not* (a) cure the disease   (b) lower the amount of sugar in the blood   (c) have a prolonged effect   (d) increase the body's ability to retain sugar   (e) bring about improvement in the animal's physical condition.   13. ....

14. A major reason why human subjects would be a future consideration is that (a) the experimenters were filled with doubts (b) too many variables had been discovered   (c) such experimentation is against the law   (d) too few animals had been involved   (e) permission had to be granted.   14. ....

15. A basic premise *not* made by the experimenters was that (a) diabetes in dogs was caused by one major factor   (b) diabetes in dogs was similar to that found in human beings   (c) the pancreatic extract was the same in all instances   (d) the disease was caused by a germ.   15. ....

When hapless Phaëthon looked down upon the earth, now spreading in vast extent beneath him, he grew pale and his knees shook with terror. In spite of the glare all around him, the sight of his eyes grew dim. He wished he had never touched his father's horses, never learned his parentage, never prevailed in his request. He is borne along like a vessel that flies before a tempest, when the pilot can do no more and betakes himself to his prayers. What shall he do? Much of the heavenly road is left behind, but more remains before. He turns his eyes from one direction to the other; now to the goal whence he began his course, now to the realms of sunset which he is not destined to reach. He loses his self-command, and knows not what to do—whether to draw tight the reins or throw them loose; he forgets the names of the horses.

He sees with terror the monstrous forms scattered over the surface of heaven. Here the Scorpion extended his two great arms, with his tail and crooked claws stretching over two signs of the zodiac. When the boy beheld him, reeking with poison and menacing with his fangs, his courage failed, and the reins fell from his hands. The horses, when they felt them loose on their backs, dashed headlong, and unrestrained went off into unknown regions of the sky, in among the stars, hurling the chariot over the pathless places, now in high heaven, now down almost to the earth. The moon saw with astonishment her brother's chariot running beneath her own. The clouds begin to smoke, and the mountain tops take fire; the fields are parched with heat, the plants wither, the trees with their leafy branches burn, the harvest is ablaze! The forest-clad mountains burn, Athos and Taurus and Tmolus and Ete; Ida, once celebrated for fountains, but now all dry.

16. This ride took place during (a) winter   (b) summer
(c) autumn   (d) spring   (e) more than one season.   16. ....

17. Phaëthon had chosen to drive the horses of the (a) heavens
(b) sun   (c) gods   (d) moon   (e) earth.   17. ....

18. A statement not true of Phaëthon is (a) he was the son of
a god   (b) his father had commanded him to the task   (c) he
allowed the horses to stray off their accustomed path   (d) he had
not driven the horses before   (e) he had received no
training for the task.   18. ....

19. Phaëthon lost self-control when (a) he saw the immensity of
the heavens   (b) the sun rose   (c) he saw the destruction that
was occurring   (d) he neared the mountains   (e) he neared
the stars.   19. ....

20. All this happened to Phaëthon and earth because (a) his
father listened to him   (b) Phaëthon was impetuous   (c) a boy
was given a man's job   (d) it was decreed by fate   (e) they
had both sinned.   20. ....

Time at End ....   *Minutes Elapsed* ....
                                              Average Time 17 *Minutes*

Answer Key for this test is on page 320.

My Score: *Number Right* ....   *Number Wrong* ....
              Average Number Right 15

Sixth Day: Analysis and Practice Test

A Closer Look

Before looking at the analysis that follows, read the exercise below, and then write your own answer in the space provided.

Doubt is the vestibule which all must pass before they can enter the temple of wisdom. When we are in doubt and puzzle out the truth by our own exertions, we have gained something that will stay by us and will serve us again. But if to avoid the trouble of the search we avail ourselves of the superior information of a friend, such knowledge will not remain with us; we have not bought but borrowed.

The author believes that (a) we learn most rapidly through observation   (b) we learn best through teaching others   (c) understanding is reached through skepticism rather than through acceptance   (d) there is only one way to gain knowledge   (e) we should be neither a borrower nor a lender of knowledge.   Answer ....

Analysis

The Selection

The key to the significance of the passage is in the word *vestibule*. The reader must envisage a passageway or hallway. He must realize that the author does not want the word in its most literal sense as a physical structure. He must see that it is to be taken figuratively. The first sentence then becomes the topic sentence, having the other two sentences explaining and amplifying its meaning. Fortunately, in this instance, even if the reader did not know the meaning of the word *vestibule*, he could deduce it from the rest of the sentence—a technique that must be used often by the taker of examinations.

The Question (Factual)

(a) *we learn most rapidly through observation* Nowhere in the selection does the author discuss speed.

(b) *we learn best through teaching others* The author discusses learning *from* others and not teaching others.

(e) *we should be neither a borrower nor a lender of knowledge*
While this idea seems well phrased, the author did not discuss what we should do with the knowledge we obtain.

At this point we are left with (c) *understanding is reached through skepticism rather than through acceptance* and (d) *there is only one way to gain knowledge.* Choice (d) is open to two interpretations. When the author mentions the inferior method—through listening to others—of gaining knowledge, he is stating that there are at least *two* approaches to knowledge; therefore (d) would be wrong. However, (d) could also mean that there is only one *true* way to gain knowledge; then (d) would be correct. Choice (c), on the other hand, includes the word *skepticism.* If you know that it means *doubting,* then you would have little difficulty in seeing that (c) summarizes the author's main point. Since (d) is open to two interpretations and (c) to only one, the latter must be the correct answer.

Practice Test

Time at Start ....

Read each selection below; and in each space provided, write the letter of the word or set of words that best completes the statement.

The leader who in order to hold his power suppresses every superiority, does away with good men, forbids education and light, controls every movement of the citizens and, keeping them under perpetual servitude, wants them to grow accustomed to baseness and cowardice, has his spies everywhere to listen to what is said in the meetings, and spreads dissension and calumny among the citizens and impoverishes them, is obliged to make war in order to keep his subjects occupied and impose on them permanent need of a chief.

1. The type of leader described here would usually be called
(a) the president   (b) the king   (c) aristocratic
(d) benevolent   (e) dictator.   1. ....

2. Such a leader does *not* need (a) loyalty   (b) a large army
(c) control of the newspapers   (d) propaganda
(e) secret police.   2. ....

3. His government remains in power through (a) corruption (b) international cowardice (c) fear (d) mass murders (e) elections.   3. ....

4. A device that such a leader would *not* use would be (a) using a large portion of the population to build roads (b) spreading distrust of religion different from one's own (c) destroying all libraries (d) having Peace Corps representatives go among his people (e) accusing the country's top scientists of treason.   4. ....

5. War that such a leader would *not* advocate would be against (a) his strong neighbors (b) ignorance (c) learning (d) disease (e) poverty.   5. ....

Where ends are agreed, the only questions left are those of means, and these are not political but technical, that is to say, capable of being settled by experts or machines like arguments between engineers or doctors. That is why those who put their faith in some immense, world-transforming phenomenon, like the final triumph of reason or the proletarian revolution, must believe that all political and moral problems can thereby be turned into technological ones. That is the meaning of St. Simon's famous phrase about "replacing the government of persons by the administration of things," and the Marxist prophecies about the withering away of the state and the beginning of the true history of humanity.

6. The author presupposes that engineers do not discuss (a) theories (b) application of theories (c) particulars (d) technological advantages (e) phenomena.   6. ....

7. Governments are necessary because (a) people differ   (b) society can function best under such organizations   (c) chaos would result without such controls   (d) they are traditional (e) men's goals in life differ.   7. ....

8. The author agrees with the communists that (a) the proletariat will finally triumph (b) capitalism is doomed to failure in the near future (c) governments are proof of political imperfection (d) technology is important (e) reason can triumph over emotion.   8. ....

9. The writer is opposed to (a) true communism (b) democracy (c) fascism (d) revolution (e) we cannot tell from this selection.   9. ....

10. The author favors (a) government by engineers   (b) less and less government   (c) a return to reason   (d) agreement on aims   (e) we cannot tell from this selection.   10. ....

Microciona is one of that large class of monaxonid sponges which lack definite shape and in which the number of oscula is correlated simply with the size of the mass. While we may look on such a mass from the phylogenetic standpoint as a corm, we speak of it as an individual. Yet it is an individual of which with the stroke of a knife we can make two. Or conversely it is an individual which may be made to fuse with another, the two forming one. To such a mass the ordinary idea of the individual is not applicable. It is only a mass large or small having the characteristic organs and tissues of the species but in which the shape of the whole and the number of the organs are indefinite. As with the adult, so with the lumps of regenerative tissue. They have no definiteness of shape or size, and their structure is only definite insofar as the histological character of the syncytial mass is fixed for the species. A tiny lump may metamorphose into a sponge, or may first fuse with many such lumps, the aggregate also producing but a single sponge although a larger one. In a word, we are not dealing with embryonic bodies of complicated organization but with a reproductive or regenerative tissue which we may start on its upward path of differentiation in almost any desired quantity. A striking illustration of this nature of the material is afforded by the following experiment. The tissue in the shape of tiny lumps was poured out in such wise that it formed continuous sheets about one millimeter thick. Such sheets were then cut into pieces, each about one cubic millimeter. These were hung in bolting-cloth bags in an outside live-box. Some of the pieces in spite of such rough handling metamorphosed into functional sponges.

11. A single sponge may (a) result from a single cell   (b) result from the combining of two small sponges   (c) result from the dividing of one sponge into two or more   (d) consist of two or more individual sponges living together   (e) survive being cut in half.   11. ....

12. An organism is identified as a sponge by (a) its characteristic organs   (b) its habitat   (c) its shape   (d) its flexibility (e) the type of cells it contains   12. ....

13. The purpose of the experiment was to show (a) how un-differentiated the sponge cells are   (b) how quickly the sponge

can regenerate   (c) the simplicity of the sponge   (d) where the
sponge can be grown   (e) what single sponge cells
are like.   13. ....

14. The sponge differs from fish in that the sponge (a) cannot
survive under water   (b) has an indefinite number of body
organs   (c) gains oxygen from the water   (d) does not
grow in size.   14. ....

15. The sponge differs from higher animals in that (a) it does
not reproduce   (b) it lacks specialized tissue   (c) it can regenerate differentiated cells   (d) any of its reproductive cells can
differentiate   (e) it has a limited number of functioning
parts.   15. ....

We had been talking about the masters who had achieved but
a single masterpiece—the artists and poets who but once in
their lives had known the divine afflatus and touched the high
level of perfection. Our host had shown us a charming little
cabinet picture by a printer whose name we had never heard, and
who, after this single spasmodic bid for fame, had appeared to
relapse into obscurity and mediocrity. There was some discussion
as to the frequency of this inconsequence; during which I noted
H—— sit silent, finishing his cigar with a meditative air and
looking at the picture, which was being handed around the table.
"I don't know how common a case it is," he said at last,
"but I've seen it. I've known a poor fellow who painted his one
masterpiece, and who"—he added with a smile—"didn't even
paint that. He made his bid for fame and missed it."
We all know H—— for a clever man who had seen much of
men and manners and had a great stock of reminiscences.
Someone immediately questioned him further, and while I was
engrossed with the raptures of my neighbor over the precious
object in circulation he was induced to tell his tale. If I were to
doubt whether it would bear repeating, I should only have to
remember how that charming woman our hostess, who had
left the table, ventured back, in rustling rose-color, to pronounce
our lingering a want of gallantry, and then finding us under the
spell, sank into her chair in spite of our cigars and heard the
story out so graciously that when the catastrophe was reached,
she glanced across and showed me a tear in each of her beautiful eyes.

16. The story that followed (a) was about the painter of the
small picture owned by the host   (b) was about H——   (c) dealt

with an incident in the life of the author   (d) was about one whom the others knew   (e) ended in tragedy.   16. ....

17. The author's purpose in this selection was to (a) arouse the reader's curiosity   (b) set the scene of the story   (c) describe the main characters   (d) describe H——   (e) prove his point.   17. ....

18. The hostess rejoined her guests (a) to be polite   (b) to hear the story   (c) to find out what had been delaying them   (d) to sit with them   (e) for none of the above reasons.   18. ....

19. The group had been discussing (a) amateur artists   (b) men who had been fortunate enough to create one work of art   (c) failures in art   (d) artists who had created only one work of art   (e) how often artists fail.   19. ....

20. A statement that would *not* be true of the people in the selection is that (a) the hostess was moved by the story that was told   (b) the author urged the telling of the story   (c) the group had just finished their dinner   (d) the host skillfully started the discussion   (e) H—— was well known as a teller of tales.   20. ....

Time at End ....   *Minutes Elapsed* ....
                                 Average Time 22 Minutes

Answer Key for this test is on page 320.

My Score: Number Right ....   *Number Wrong* ....
             Average Number Right 14

Seventh Day: Analysis and Practice Test

A Closer Look

Before looking at the analysis that follows, read the exercise below, and then write your own answer in the space provided.

Did you ever hear of a man who had striven all his life faithfully and singly toward an object, and in no measure obtained it? If a man constantly aspires, is he not elevated? Did ever a man try heroism, magnanimity, truth, sincerity, and find that there was no advantage in them—that it was a vain endeavor?

A restatement of the basic idea of the selection is (a) the attempt and not the achievement should be the measure of success (b) all is not lost if you continue to have hope (c) we must be thankful even for small things (d) nothing ventured, nothing gained (e) the means as well as the end helps to measure of achievement.   Answer ....

Analysis

The Selection

The key to the understanding of this selection lies in the reader's realization of the meaning of *in no measure*, a phrase implying that a goal can be reached partially. All the traits mentioned—heroism, magnanimity, and so on—are ones admired by society; therefore, if we search without trickery or falsehood, we gain, even if we do not win all.

The Question (Title)

(b) *all is not lost if you continue to have hope* Hope is not listed among the admired traits. The selection does not deal with hope at all.

(d) *nothing ventured, nothing gained* The advantage of being willing to try something is *not* under discussion.

(a) *the attempt and not the achievement should be the measure of success* This possibility goes too far. The method of attempt should be given some success-value, but not all of it.

(c) *we must be thankful even for small things* The term *small things* is not defined. The sentence thus has too loose a meaning to apply to this selection.

(e) *the means as well as the end helps to measure of achievement* This possibility can apply to good as well as to evil; the selection stresses the good only. Since, however, this is the one answer that is most nearly correct, this is the one that must be selected.

Practice Test

Time at Start ....

Read each selection below; and in each space provided, write the letter of the word or set of words that best completes the statement.

"I have considered the structure of all volant animals, and find the folding continuity of the bat's wings most easily accommodated to the human form. Upon this model I shall begin my task tomorrow, and in a year expect to tower into the air beyond the malice or pursuit of man. But I will work only on this condition, that the art shall not be divulged, and that you shall not require me to make wings for any but ourselves."

"Why," said Rasselas, "should you envy others so great an advantage? All skill ought to be exerted for universal good; every man has owed much to others, and ought to repay the kindness that he has received."

"If men were all virtuous," returned the artist, "I should with great alacrity teach them all to fly. But what would be the security of the good, if the bad could at pleasure invade them from the sky? Against an army sailing through the clouds neither wall, nor mountains, nor seas, could afford any security. A flight of northern savages might hover in the wind, and light at once with irresistible violence upon the capital of a fruitful region that was rolling under them. Even this valley, the retreat of princes, the abode of happiness, might be violated by the sudden descent of some of the naked nations that swarm on the coast of the southern sea."

1. The artist plans to (a) draw pictures of flying bats (b) fly with Rasselas (c) fight off the savages along the coast (d) attack the people in the North (e) raise an army. 1. ....

2. The artist (a) has faith in his own ability but not in that of his fellow men (b) is determined to study science (c) trusts Rasselas (d) already knows the secret of flight (e) is pessimistic about his chances to prevent war. 2. ....

3. This conversation took place (a) in a southern valley (b) high in the northern mountains (c) in a rich agricultural area (d) in an area protected by surrounding mountains (e) along the seacoast. 3. ....

4. The artist did not foresee (a) guided missiles (b) the air raids of World War II (c) paratroopers (d) undeclared war (e) an airborne invasion of England.   4. ....

5. The artist's point of view differs from Rasselas' because (a) Rasselas is against all progress that can benefit a minority (b) Rasselas has faith in the brotherhood of man (c) Rasselas trusts people with evil intentions (d) the artist is against all progress that benefits only a minority (e) the artist trusts his fellow men.   5. ....

To one of middle age the countenance was that of a young man, though a youth might hardly have seen any necessity for the term of immaturity. But it was really one of those faces which convey less the idea of so many years as its age than of so much experience as its store.

The face was well shaped, even excellently. But the mind within was beginning to use it as a mere waste table whereon to trace its idiosyncrasies as they developed themselves. The beauty here visible would in no long time be ruthlessly overrun by its parasite, thought, which might just as well have fed upon a plainer exterior where there was nothing it could harm. Had Heaven preserved him from a wearing habit of meditation, people would have said, "A handsome man." Had his brain unfolded under sharper contours they would have said, "A thoughtful man." But an inner strenuousness was preying upon an outer symmetry, and they rated his look as singular.

Hence people who began by beholding him ended by perusing him. He already showed that thought is a disease of flesh, and indirectly bore evidence that ideal physical beauty is incompatible with emotional development and a full recognition of the coil of things.

6. The writer (a) was mocking the character he described (b) envied this character (c) set this character up as a bad example (d) pitied the character he was writing about (e) disliked the character he described.   6. ....

7. The person described was, most likely, (a) 10 years old (b) 20 years old (c) 40 years old (d) 60 years old (e) an infant.   7. ....

8. The author feels that (a) life is a tragedy to those who think (b) thought leads to development (c) intelligence and beauty are necessary and vital (d) thought is a bad disease.   8. ....

9. The character described was (a) a philosopher   (b) plain looking   (c) still handsome   (d) a parasite   (e) ill.

9. ....

10. People would look twice at the person described because (a) he was a stranger   (b) of his troubled look   (c) he was so good-looking   (d) he was so plain-looking   (e) he was an important leader.

10. ....

We cannot for a moment admit that by simply applying an unpopular or obloquious name to men, whether that name be anarchist or socialist, capitalist or vagabond, republican or democrat, an officer can be justified in depriving men of rights guaranteed by the fundamental law, and can break up their meeting, can club, search and imprison them, not for what they have done, but for what he, in his wisdom, or his prejudice, or his caprice, fears they might do.

If this principle were once admitted, there is no limit to its application. While it is sought to apply it to one class today, it could be applied to any other class tomorrow, and a precedent made in one case would be sure to be cited and acted on in another and a political party, for the time being in power, could prevent its opponents from meeting and put them in jail.

11. This selection most likely was excerpted from (a) a newspaper article   (b) a novel   (c) a high-school textbook (d) an interview   (e) a legal decision.

11. ....

12. The writer of this statement would most likely agree that (a) communism can overthrow our government   (b) Communists should not be allowed to run for office   (c) Communists should not be allowed to hold open meetings   (d) Communists should be punished for breaking laws   (e) Communists should be protected from themselves.

12. ....

13. The officer referred to in the selection is (a) a club official (b) a political leader   (c) a congressman   (d) head of the government   (e) a policeman.

13. ....

14. A fundamental principle recognized by the writer is (a) that men must be able to preserve their rights   (b) that citizens have equal rights in the eyes of the law   (c) that officers have their own prejudices   (d) that an anarchist may be right (e) none of the above.

14. ....

15. The writer feels that an officer does not have the right to
(a) judge others (b) arrest others (c) fear others
(d) uphold the law (e) attend meetings. 15. ....

I must again repeat that constant touch with the people is
bringing me to believe that there are very few ignorant among
them. The ordinary citizen is better posted than the average
Senator or Congressman—the reason is that they read more
current literature. In this connection I see only one danger—
and it is a grave danger—the purchase by corporations which
have "interests to protect," and by enormously wealthy men who
have ambitions to serve, of so many newspapers. Newspapers
thus owned give the people only such information as will help
their owners, suppressing all information that might injure them,
on the one hand; and on the other hand, giving them information that will help the owners. This, of course, poisons the source
of the people's information, and so far as their influence goes,
makes them a good deal worse than ignorant, because it makes
them misinformed.

16. The writer praises the citizenry because (a) they refuse to
be misinformed (b) they see through fraud and deceit (c) they
keep up with the affairs of the day (d) they vote
intelligently (e) they tell their leaders what to do. 16. ....

17. The writer would object if (a) the local newspaper broadcast the news over the district television station (b) the workers
on a newspaper owned it cooperatively (c) the local paper
subscribed to a nationwide news agency (d) several small newspapers combined their news-gathering facilities (e) Sears
or Montgomery Ward bought a newspaper chain 17. ....

18. The people are in true danger when (a) they are unable
to get an unbiased account of the news events (b) their legislative representatives disregard the interest of the people (c) the
enemy threatens from without (d) businessmen run advertisements in the local newspapers (e) newspapers are owned
by the wrong people. 18. ....

19. A basic principle accepted by the writer is that (a) given
the facts, most people choose not too wisely (b) management
runs business primarily for its own interests (c) newspapers
mislead people (d) wealthy people cannot be trusted (e) our
Senators are too busy to keep up with current events.
19. ....

20. The writer is most likely one who believes in (a) democracy
(b) fascism   (c) republicanism   (d) authoritarianism
(e) rule by kings.   20. ....

Time at End ....   *Minutes Elapsed* ....
                                                    Average Time 19 *Minutes*

Answer Key for this test is on page 320.

My Score: *Number Right* ....   *Number Wrong* ....
              Average Number Right 15

Eighth Day: Intensive Reading Practice Test 1

Each of the tests for the next five days is planned to give you
an opportunity to do a thorough analysis of one or two reading
selections. You will find that you can do your best with the
questions if you constantly turn to the selection to support your
choice of answer.

Time at Start ....

Read the selection below; and in each space provided, write
the letter of the word or set of words that best completes the
statement.

You must know, then, that there are two methods of fighting,
the one by law, the other by force; the first method is that of
men, the second of beasts; but as the first method is often
insufficient, one must have recourse to the second. It is therefore
necessary for a prince to know well how to use both the beast
and the man. This was covertly taught to rulers by ancient
writers, who relate how Achilles and many others of those ancient
princes were given to Chiron the centaur to be brought up and
educated under his discipline. The parable of this semi-animal,
semi-human teacher is meant to indicate that a prince must know
how to use both natures, and that the one without the other is
not durable.

A prince, being thus obliged to know well how to act as a
beast, must imitate the fox, and the lion, for the lion cannot
protect himself from traps, and the fox cannot defend himself
from wolves. Those that wish to be only lions do not understand
this. Therefore, a prudent ruler ought not to keep faith when

by doing so it would be against his interest, and when the reasons which made him bind himself no longer exist. If men were all good, this precept would not be a good one; but as they are bad, and would not observe their faith with you, so you are not bound to keep faith with them. Nor have legitimate grounds ever failed a prince who wished to show colorable excuse for the non-fulfillment of his promise. Of this one could furnish an infinite number of examples, and show how many times peace has been broken, and how many promises rendered worthless, by the faithlessness of princes, and those that have best been able to imitate the fox have succeeded best. But it is necessary to be able to disguise this character well, and to be a great feigner and dissembler, and men are so simple and so ready to obey present necessities, that the one who deceives will always find those who allow themselves to be deceived.

1. The writer of the article does not believe that (a) right makes might (b) the truth makes men free (c) people can protect themselves (d) princes are human (e) leaders have to be consistent.   1. ....

2. The writer uses the word *prince* to designate (a) anyone in power (b) duly elected officials (c) sons of kings (d) aristocrats (e) dictators.   2. ....

3. The weakness in the lion is (a) that he is too trusting (b) his strength (c) his reliance on force (d) his lack of intelligence (e) his desire to rule.   3. ....

4. The fox, in this selection, is (a) admired for his trickery (b) pitied for his wiles (c) condemned for his lack of prudence (d) considered worthless (e) no match for the lion.   4. ....

5. The writer agreed with Hitler that (a) there are inferior races (b) there is one group destined to govern all others (c) force can conquer the world (d) people will believe big lies (e) people exist for the benefit of the state.   5. ....

6. The writer warns that (a) successful leaders must have faith in the people (b) successful leaders must have principle to guide their actions (c) successful leaders are cheats and liars (d) successful leaders must be prudent (e) truth is the best guide for leaders.   6. ....

7. The head of a modern democracy would (a) approve of the ideas found in this selection (b) say that the approach advocated

in this selection is necessary in a political campaign if you want to be successful   (c) say that this approach is correct for dealing in foreign affairs   (d) condemn the approach because it reveals a lack of faith in people   (e) condemn this approach because it can never be successful.   7. ....

8. The suggested measure of success of a prince is (a) how many lies he tells   (b) how many promises he breaks   (c) how long he rules   (d) how many people believe him   (e) how wealthy he becomes.   8. ....

9. The writer would approve if an unsuccessful political candidate (a) promised to try again next time   (b) threatened his opponent   (c) shot his opponent at a political rally   (d) overthrew the government by force   (e) told the people the truth about his opponent.   9. ....

10. The people ruled by such a prince (a) are very fortunate since he can protect them so well   (b) can be kept under control only by force   (c) enjoy democratic privileges   (d) believe what they read in the papers   (e) trust the prince.   10. ....

Time at End ....   *Minutes Elapsed* ....
                                                   Average Time 12 *Minutes*

Answer Key for this test is on page 320.

My Score: *Number Right* ....   *Number Wrong* ....
              Average Number Right 7

Ninth Day: Intensive Reading Practice Test 2

Time at Start ....

Read each selection below; and in each space provided, write the letter of the word or set of words that best completes the statement.

If anything indicates the imperfect state of our knowledge of the intimate structure of plants, it is the divergence of opinion of naturalists on the subject. The source of this diversity of opinion lies in the extreme difficulty of observation which cannot be done without the aid of the microscope, and which consequently is susceptible to manifold errors, practically impossible to avoid in using this instrument. To obtain a good idea of the form of an object, one must examine it on all sides; moreover, the sense of sight must be supplemented by touch. Now with the microscope, one sees objects from one side only and the sense of touch is entirely lacking. A host of optical illusions increase the difficulties of investigation. Various refractions of light rays make parts that are really transparent appear opaque, and convey the impression of forms and structures that have no real existence. A space more transparent than the parts that surround it gives the appearance of an opening, and if the transparency is perfect, it is impossible to decide whether one is dealing with a free aperture or an opening closed by a transparent membrane.

1. The tone of this selection can best be characterized as (a) condemnatory (b) objective (c) opinionated (d) laudatory (e) inquisitive. 1. ....

2. Naturalists have difficulty in (a) using microscopes (b) interpreting what they see (c) forming satisfactory opinions (d) finding good microscopes (e) stating what they see.
2. ....

3. Research workers need to touch objects in order to (a) understand their structure (b) understand their texture (c) develop a sense of depth (d) gain an idea of the size of the plant (e) interpret temperature changes. 3. ....

4. The cause of many false impressions is (a) reflected light (b) weak light rays (c) transparent light rays (d) overpowering light (e) undirected light. 4. ....

5. The scientists' difficulties could be overcome if (a) microscopes were more powerful (b) microscopic particles were more definite in shape (c) two images could be seen at the same time under the microscope (d) the colleges could train research workers better (e) photographs could be taken. 5. ....

The people who believe most that our greatness and welfare are proved by our being very rich, and who most give their lives and thoughts to becoming rich, are just the very people whom we call Philistines. Culture says, "Consider these people, then, their way of life, their habits, their manners, the very tones of their voices; look at them attentively; observe the literature they read, the things which give them pleasure, the words which come from out of their mouths, the thoughts which make the furniture of their minds: would any amount of wealth be worth having with the condition that one has to become just like these people by having it?" And thus culture begets a dissatisfaction which is of the highest possible value in stemming the common tide of men's thoughts in a wealthy and industrial community; and which may save the future, as one may hope, from being vulgarized, even if it cannot save the present.

6. The writer of the article (a) condemns Philistines   (b) praises Philistines   (c) envies Philistines   (d) is a Philistine (e) urges people to become Philistines.   6. ....

7. The Philistines define *success* in terms of (a) knowledge gained   (b) people helped   (c) religious inner security (d) money in the bank   (e) understanding gained.   7. ....

8. *Culture* as used by the writer (a) describes Philistinism (b) is opposed to Philistinism   (c) is based on literature (d) leads to dissatisfaction   (e) protects the populace from the wealthy.   8. ....

9. The weakness in Philistinism, as seen by the writer, (a) is its stress on materialism   (b) is never stated   (c) is its disregard of human values   (d) is its emphasis on eternals   (e) is its disregard of other people.   9. ....

10. The term *culture* as used by the writer is (a) the best that has been said or thought by man   (b) a process   (c) a state of being   (d) a way of thought   (e) a set of standards.
          10. ....

Time at End ....   *Minutes Elapsed* ....
                              Average Time 9 Minutes

Answer Key for this test is on page 321.

My Score: Number Right ....   *Number Wrong* ....
          Average Number Right 8

Tenth Day: Intensive Reading Practice Test 3

Time at Start ....

Read the selection below; and in each space provided, write the letter of the word or set of words that best completes the statement.

A teacher is always obliged to steer his own bark through a densely packed mass of other people's lives grinding together around him like floes in a crowded ice-field. At the beginning of each year when there were many parents to be seen, Timothy Hulme was all but crushed by the impact on him of the innumerable disasters, triumphs, hopes, hardships, successes, despairs, problems he was expected on a moment's notice to share, alleviate, solve. He envied and pitied people not teachers who had only their own lives to live. He turned incessantly at top speed from parents, satisfied and dissatisfied, to teachers, to students, to booksellers, to plumbers, to salesmen—making important decisions based on nothing better than snap-judgments, guessing at what he needed to know, making mistakes and brazenly acting on them, leaping to half-baked conclusions and sticking to them because a conclusion of some sort was at that moment needed more than wisdom. During the first two weeks of the Academy year Mr. Hulme was not a man with insoluble problems of his own but an administrator, the picket fence of detail standing between him and the dark formless abyss of personal life.

1. Mr. Hulme's main occupation was that of (a) writer (b) parent (c) head of a school (d) teacher in a private school (e) student.   1. ....

2. Mr. Hulme was (a) overwhelmed by his responsibilities (b) unable to find satisfying answers (c) impressed by the necessity for making decisions (d) unhappy at his job (e) unwilling to lead.   2. ....

3. Mr. Hulme was (a) weak (b) stubborn (c) intelligent (d) devoted (e) flexible.   3. ....

4. The writer of the article (a) admired Mr. Hulme (b) despised Mr. Hulme (c) was Mr. Hulme himself (d) was critical of Mr. Hulme (e) worked for Mr. Hulme.   4. ....

5. The tone of the article is (a) gloomy (b) gay (c) satirical (d) frenzied (e) quarrelsome.   5. ....

6. Mr. Hulme justified decisions based on his ignorance by claiming that (a) his salary was too low (b) he was poorly trained (c) he was learning (d) he disliked his job (e) he had no choice.   6. ....

7. An advantage to Mr. Hulme was that (a) he could feel important (b) he was able to help people (c) he could forget himself (d) he was able to get the school going smoothly (e) he was appreciated.   7. ....

8. The weakness in Mr. Hulme's position was that (a) he could do little reflective thinking (b) he had to make decisions (c) his decisions could not be reversed   (d) he had to listen to others all day   (e) he had little power to act.   8. ....

9. The school that employed Mr. Hulme was most likely (a) a private, one-teacher academy (b) situated in a large city (c) one that employed many teachers   (d) a very large academy   (e) a small-sized school.   9. ....

10. This selection (a) condemns our school system   (b) praises the academy system   (c) reveals the work day of a school head (d) asks the reader to sympathize with school heads (e) calls for reform.   10. ....

Time at End ....   *Minutes Elapsed* ....
                                             Average Time 11 *Minutes*

Answer Key for this test is on page 321.

My Score: *Number Right* ....   *Number Wrong* ....
              Average Number Right 6

Eleventh Day: Intensive Reading Practice Test 4

Time at Start ....

Read the selection below; and in each space provided, write the letter of the word or set of words that best completes the statement.

> So all day long the noise of battle roll'd
> Among the mountains by the winter sea;
> Until King Arthur's Table, man by man,
> Had fall'n in Lyonnesse about their lord,
> King Arthur. Then, because his wound was deep,
> The bold Sir Bedevere uplifted him,
> And bore him to a chapel nigh the field,
> A broken chancel with a broken cross,
> That stood on a dark strait of barren land:
> On one side lay the Ocean, and on one
> Lay a great water, and the moon was full.

1. In this battle, (a) King Arthur was defeated   (b) the diners died   (c) the Round Table came to an end   (d) the men fought well   (e) many men died.   ·   1. ....

2. At this point in the battle (a) King Arthur had died (b) Bedevere was wounded (c) Arthur was carried from the battle-field (d) Arthur had surrendered (e) the enemy had fled.

2. ....

3. Sir Bedevere was (a) Arthur's valet (b) one of the Knights of the Round Table (c) a loyal follower of Arthur (d) one of the enemy (e) leader of the opposition. 3. ....

4. The battle took place (a) outside the chapel (b) on a beach (c) in London (d) outside Arthur's castle (e) near Lyonnesse. 4. ....

5. The tone of this selection is one of (a) melancholy (b) defiance (c) gaiety (d) mockery (e) hysteria. 5. ....

6. The description of the chapel stresses (a) pageantry (b) desolation (c) loyalty (d) religious faith (e) determination. 6. ....

7. The last six lines emphasize (a) silence (b) color (c) the horrors of war (d) the bravery of the knights (e) the greatness of King Arthur. 7. ....

8. This scene does not highlight (a) Arthur's suffering (b) the end of an era (c) the loyalty of the Knights of the Round Table (d) the pitiless light of the moon (e) the loss of faith.

8. ....

9. "A broken chancel with a broken cross" could also describe (a) the chapel (b) Sir Bedevere (c) King Arthur (d) England (e) the Round Table and its knights 9. ....

10. Sir Bedevere took Arthur to the chapel (a) to prepare for the burial (b) to protect him from the enemy (c) to wait for reinforcements (d) for consolation (e) to give him a chance to recover. 10. ....

Time at End .... *Minutes Elapsed* ....
Average Time 11 *Minutes*

Answer Key for this test is on page 321.

My Score: *Number Right* .... *Number Wrong* ....
Average Number Right 8

Twelfth Day: Intensive Reading Practice Test 5

Time at Start ....

Read each selection below; and in each space provided, write the letter of the word or set of words that best completes the statement.

> Toiling, rejoicing, sorrowing,
> Onward through life he goes;
> Each morning sees some task begin,
> Each evening sees it close;
> Something attempted, something done,
> Has earned a night's repose.
>
> Thanks, thanks to thee, my worthy friend,
> For the lesson thou has taught!
> Thus at the flaming forge of life
> Our fortunes must be wrought;
> Thus on its sounding anvil shaped
> Each burning deed and thought.

1. These lines most likely come from a poem describing (a) a doctor   (b) a teacher   (c) a blacksmith   (d) a business leader   (e) a student.   1. ....

2. The "worthy friend" is (a) nature   (b) religion (c) work   (d) the anvil   (e) none of these.   2. ....

3. The secret of life that the poet learned is that (a) we must do useful things each day   (b) we must plan ahead   (c) we must think out our problems   (d) we need a philosophy of life (e) we must learn to help others.   3. ....

4. We sleep well when we (a) plan well   (b) have great ambitions   (c) have accomplished what we have planned (d) work hard, play hard   (e) reach the end of the road.   4. ....

5. The author's purpose was (a) to moralize   (b) to reveal beauty   (c) to make the reader more sensitive   (d) to enrich our lives   (e) to make money.   5. ....

Our revels now are ended. These our actors,
As I foretold you, were all spirits, and
Are melted into air, into thin air:
And, like the baseless fabric of this vision,
The cloud-capp'd towers, the gorgeous palaces,
The solemn temples, the great globe itself,
Yea, all which it inherit, shall dissolve,
And, like this unsubstantial pageant faded,
Leave not a rack behind. We are such stuff
As dreams are made on, and our little life
Is rounded with a sleep.

6. In these lines the speaker (a) addresses the actors (b) interprets the play (c) announces the coming end of the world (d) condemns dreamers (e) fears he is going to lose the battle.   6. ....

7. The speaker predicts (a) the end of the play (b) the end of the world (c) great success (d) war (e) sleepiness.
                                             7. ....

8. The play is compared to (a) a dream (b) nature's scenery (c) life itself (d) visions (e) spirits.   8. ....

9. The speaker finds (a) life a tragedy (b) life rich and filled with significance (c) dreams worthwhile (d) life without meaning (e) plays exciting.   9. ....

10. A synonym for *sleep* as used in this selection would be (a) oblivion (b) nap (c) play (d) musing (e) imagining.
                                             10. ....

Time at End ....   *Minutes Elapsed* ....
                                     Average Time 14 *Minutes*

Answer Key for this test is on page 321:

My Score: *Number Right* ....   *Number Wrong* ....
            Average Number Right 6

Section 6   Reading For Full Comprehension

Answer Key

Third Day   Page 282

1. (d)	5. (c)	9. (c)	13. (d)	17. (e)
2. (c)	6. (b)	10. (d)	14. (d)	18. (d)
3. (a)	7. (b)	11. (b)	15. (a)	19. (a)
4. (e)	8. (e)	12. (a)	16. (b)	20. (c)

Fourth Day   Page 287

1. (a)	5. (e)	9. (b)	13. (a)	17. (d)
2. (d)	6. (e)	10. (d)	14. (c)	18. (b)
3. (d)	7. (b)	11. (c)	15. (d)	19. (e)
4. (c)	8. (d)	12. (b)	16. (e)	20. (e)

Fifth Day   Page 293

1. (d)	5. (a)	9. (c)	13. (a)	17. (b)
2. (b)	6. (c)	10. (e)	14. (d)	18. (b)
3. (e)	7. (b)	11. (c)	15. (d)	19. (e)
4. (d)	8. (c)	12. (c)	16. (c)	20. (d)

Sixth Day   Page 299

1. (e)	5. (b)	9. (e)	13. (a)	17. (a)
2. (a)	6. (a)	10. (e)	14. (b)	18. (c)
3. (c)	7. (e)	11. (d)	15. (d)	19. (b)
4. (d)	8. (c)	12. (e)	16. (e)	20. (b)

Seventh Day   Page 304

1. (b)	5. (b)	9. (c)	13. (e)	17. (e)
2. (c)	6. (d)	10. (b)	14. (b)	18. (a)
3. (d)	7. (b)	11. (e)	15. (a)	19. (b)
4. (a)	8. (a)	12. (d)	16. (c)	20. (a)

Eighth Day   Page 310

1. (e)	3. (c)	5. (d)	7. (d)	9. (d)
2. (a)	4. (a)	6. (c)	8. (e)	10. (b)

Ninth Day   **Page 312**

| 1. (b) | 3. (c) | 5. (c) | 7. (d) | 9. (b) |
| 2. (b) | 4. (a) | 6. (a) | 8. (b) | 10. (e) |

Tenth Day   **Page 314**

| 1. (c) | 3. (d) | 5. (c) | 7. (c) | 9. (e) |
| 2. (c) | 4. (d) | 6. (e) | 8. (a) | 10. (c) |

Eleventh Day   **Page 316**

| 1. (b) | 3. (c) | 5. (a) | 7. (a) | 9. (d) |
| 2. (c) | 4. (e) | 6. (b) | 8. (a) | 10. (d) |

Twelfth Day   **Page 318**

| 1. (c) | 3. (a) | 5. (a) | 7. (b) | 9. (d) |
| 2. (e) | 4. (c) | 6. (b) | 8. (c) | 10. (a) |

COMPLETING THE THOUGHT

Section 7: COMPLETING THE THOUGHT

Another integral part of most College Entrance Examinations is the section in which the task is to select, from the choices offered, the word or set of words that best completes a sentence or a group of sentences.

Although each of the verbal parts of the examination may contain only ten of these items out of a total of one hundred, the skills and knowledge involved are similar to those tested in the vocabulary and reading-comprehension questions. Therefore, by concentrating on a program to improve your mastery of the completion question, you will sharpen your ability in these related fields.

What is the extent of your present command over questions requiring that you choose the correct words to complete a thought? Take the Inventory Test that follows and find out!

First Day: Inventory Test

Time at Start ....

In the space provided, write the letter of the set of words that best completes the thought of the sentence group.

1. *Mental retardation* does not mean that the person's total being is retarded. Only his .... capacities happen to be retarded. He may have other skills and aptitudes in which he .... could excel other workers.
(a) physical ... almost   (b) social ... never
(c) limited ... certainly   (d) intellectual ... conceivably
(e) personal ... possibly   1. ....

2. He flattered himself on being a man without prejudices; and this .... itself is a very great ....
(a) statement . . . achievement   (b) pretension . . . prejudice   (c) realization . . . accomplishment
(d) fact . . . concession   (e) concept . . . feat   2. ....

3. Under our present practice in the high schools, a passing percentage mark is required for promotion to the next level of work. It is now proposed to demand much more than this: nothing short of adequate .... of the entire complex of knowledge, skill, and aptitude that is to be taught. Obviously, something less than letter-perfect learning is to be looked for, but the goal .... this limit.
(a) understanding . . . approaches   (b) mastery . . . achieves   (c) realization . . . must be   (d) learning . . . cannot reach   (e) sensing . . . could reach   3. ....

4. A .... man will select his books, for he would not wish to class them all under the sacred name of friends. Some can be accepted only as acquaintances. The best books of all kinds are taken to the heart, and cherished as his most precious possessions. Others to be chatted with for a time, to spend a few hours with and laid aside, but not ....
(a) friendly . . . studied   (b) clever . . . overlooked
(c) wise . . . forgotten   (d) shrewd . . . cherished
(e) foolish . . . put to use   4. ....

5. I do not allow myself to .... that either the convention or the league has concluded to decide that I am either the greatest or the best man in America; but rather they have concluded that it is not best to swap horses while crossing the river; and have further concluded that I am not so poor a horse that they might not make a(n) .... of it in trying to swap.
(a) demand . . . trade   (b) suggest . . . mess
(c) boast . . . attempt   (d) think . . . holocaust
(e) suppose . . . botch   5. ....

6. You, my lord, are a judge; I am the supposed culprit. I am a man; you are a man also. By a revolution of power we might change .... though we could never change ....
(a) history . . . fate   (b) places . . . characters
(c) the sentence . . . accusation   (d) circumstances . . . guilt   (e) names . . . roles   6. ....

7. .... keeps up a kind of daylight in the mind, filling it with a steady and perpetual ....

(a) Despair . . . hope   (b) Hope . . . gloom
(c) Cheerfulness . . . serenity   (d) Jealousy . . . glow
(e) Joy . . . shadow   7. ....

8. Life is a test, and this world is a place of trial. Always the problems—or it may be the same problem—will be presented to every .... in different ....

(a) man . . . areas   (b) candidate . . . elections
(c) leader . . . struggles   (d) hero . . . battles
(e) generation . . . forms   8. ....

9. Were it offered to my choice, I should have no objection to a repetition of the same life from its beginning, only asking the advantages authors have in a second edition to .... some .... of the first.

(a) correct . . . faults   (b) vindicate . . . errors
(c) erase . . . triumphs   (d) elevate . . . triumphs
(e) duplicate . . . weaknesses   9. ....

10. .... minds generally .... everything that passes their understanding.

(a) Great . . . disregard   (b) Mediocre . . . condemn
(c) First-rate . . . study   (d) Simple . . . admire
(e) Educated . . . read   10. ....

11. There's nothing in a(n) .... philosophy that says the needs of an educational elite come first, any more than the needs of an economic or a cultural or a political elite come first. A(n) .... must be struck.

(a) working . . . offender   (b) democratic . . . balance
(c) realistic . . . pose   (d) idealistic . . . compromise
(e) fascist . . . resolution   11. ....

12. Isolation from familiar groups is one of the deadliest perils. We .... our sense of identity and composure by constant reference to .... groups.

(a) create . . . new   (b) maintain . . . older
(c) uncover . . . unfriendly   (d) develop . . . unknown
(e) keep . . . friendly   12. ....

13. Good seasons and bad seasons are in the order of nature, just as the day of .... and the day of ...., the summer's warmth and the winter's snow.

(a) sunshine . . . rain   (b) happiness . . . thought
(c) pain . . . planning   (d) richness . . . poverty
(e) reckoning . . . reward   13. ....

14. A society committed to the search for truth must give protection to, and set a high value upon, the independent and original mind, however angular, however rasping, however socially .... it may be; for it is upon such minds, in large measure, that the .... search for truth depends.
(a) worthwhile ... successful   (b) worthless ... ultimate
(c) unpleasant ... effective   (d) costly ... painful
(e) undesirable ... rich   14. ....

15. Associate with men of good quality if you esteem your own reputation, for it is better to be .... than in .... company.
(a) alone ... bad   (b) snubbed ... worthless
(c) admired ... disreputable   (d) ignored ... desirable
(e) lost ... insignificant   15. ....

16. The exact measure of the progress of civilization is the degree in which the .... of the common mind has prevailed over wealth and brute force; in other words, the measure of the progress of civilization is the progress of the ....
(a) needs ... youth   (b) image ... Congress
(c) desires ... leaders   (d) intelligence ... people
(e) ambitions ... educators   16. ....

17. To limit the press is to insult a nation; to .... reading of certain books is to declare the .... to be either fools or slaves.
(a) encourage ... readers   (b) allow ... authors
(c) censure ... youth   (d) restrict ... librarians
(e) prohibit ... inhabitants   17. ....

18. He who is of a calm and happy nature will hardly feel the .... of age, but to him who is of an opposite disposition, youth and age are equally a ....
(a) coming ... pleasure   (b) pressure ... burden
(c) illnesses ... joy   (d) passage ... disturbance
(e) advantage ... compensation   18. ....

19. The same sun which gilds all nature, and .... the whole creation, does not shine upon .... ambition.
(a) enjoys ... excessive   (b) depresses ... honest
(c) exhilarates ... disappointed   (d) fulfills ... foolish
(e) enhances ... meager   19. ....

20. In the arts of life man invents ....; but in the arts of death he .... Nature herself, and produces by chemistry

and machinery all the slaughter of plague, pestilence, and famine.
(a) nothing . . . outdoes   (b) much . . . conquers
(c) little . . . defeats   (d) greatly . . . destroys
(e) equally . . . imitates   20. ....

Time at End ....   *Total Number Of Minutes Elapsed* ....

Answer Key

1. (d)	5. (e)	9. (a)	13. (a)	17. (e)
2. (b)	6. (b)	10. (b)	14. (c)	18. (b)
3. (a)	7. (c)	11. (b)	15. (a)	19. (c)
4. (c)	8. (e)	12. (e)	16. (d)	20. (a)

My Score: Number Right.............   Number Wrong.............

Comparing With Others

	Time	Number Correct
Elite	19 minutes	20
Superior	20–24 minutes	18–19
Average	25–28 minutes	15–17
Below Average	29–31 minutes	12–14
Weak	32–40 minutes	8–11

Clinch by Checking

The purpose in your taking this test was twofold: to discover your level of competency and to discover how much time you need to handle just such questions. The results become meaningful not only when you compare your efforts with those of other students, but also when you compare your present score and the amount of time spent in taking this test with the results after you have done the daily exercises that follow. No one can ask you to do better than your best! These exercises will help to bring you up to that level by giving you the day-by-day sharpening that means best results.

Second Day: Gaining Exam Know-How

Taking A Closer Look

There is no royal road toward maximum marks in reading comprehension exercises. There is no quick formula that is a substitute for daily practice in reading. So too with the completion question, the student who reads widely and regularly will achieve best. However, there are some examination hints that can help the wary reader to avoid some of the traditional pitfalls that beset the inexperienced who face this question for the first time. What are these pitfalls? Let us begin by analyzing a typical passage.

Before looking at the analysis that follows, read the exercise below and answer the accompanying questions.

To speak of democracy flourishing and being saved or advanced in war is like speaking of a fish flourishing out of water. The only air in which democracy can breathe is .... and it must be free air and abundant air, in which all ideas regardless of labels and origins can be ....

  (a) free . . . realized   (b) American . . . suppressed
  (c) healthful . . . studied   (d) peace . . . expressed
  (e) scientific . . . analyzed   Answer ....

Analysis

  (b) *American . . . suppressed* This answer is wrong because the word *suppressed* is opposite in meaning to the obvious intent of the rest of the passage.

  (c) *healthful . . . studied* The word *healthful* takes the passage out of the figurative into the literal, contrary to the intent of the writer; therefore this answer is wrong.

  (e) *scientific . . . analyzed* These choices give the second sentence a meaning that does not fit in with the intent of the first sentence; therefore this answer is incorrect.

  (a) *free . . . realized* and (d) *peace . . . expressed* remain. Both appear possible, but (d) *peace . . . expressed* gives the passage a deeper and clearer meaning. The word *peace* fits into a necessary contrast with the word *war* in the first sentence. The word *peace* actually crystallizes the meaning of the entire passage. The word *free* is weak and colorless in comparison. The word *expressed* follows logically from *free air and abundant air*. The word *realized* could possibly fit, but since it is combined with *free*, this choice is *not* the equal of the other. Therefore, your answer should be (d).

Is such careful analysis necessary? Yes! The purpose of this type of question is to test your ability to discriminate closely between meanings of words and to evaluate your ability to follow the author's pattern of thought. To do both of these, you must read with extreme care.

For Highest Marks

1. Read the passage through quickly to see whether you can follow the meaning even though words are missing. If you find the passage easy, you may even be able to supply the missing words at this point.

2. Do not jump to any conclusions! You must train yourself not to do so. Even if you are positive that you know the correct answer, do *not* skip any of the given choices. This is the point at which the careless reader loses credit. The one that you skip could so easily be the best answer!

3. Use the cues in the rest of the passage to help you eliminate the obviously wrong choices. Often one word of a pair will be nearly opposite in meaning to the word that fits logically. Thus you can eliminate a pair when one word is *not* appropriate— even though the other is.

4. If you find that you cannot select the better of two, then go on to the next passage and return to this after your mind has had a chance to go to work on the details. The better answer usually comes through with vivid clarity when you practice this type of patience.

5. Don't fill in random answers for those passages which you do not understand or for which you lack the time. Remember that the penalty for guessing on this examination can be too great. If you have been able to eliminate two or three of the five choices, then an educated guess would not be amiss. If you have, however, four or more to choose from, it is much better to leave the answer blank and to go on to the next. Later, if time permits, you can come back to this troublesome one and reread it with a different perspective.

6. Spend as much time as necessary on each passage. Don't dawdle, though. Have a sense of urgency, but not a feeling of undue pressure. If one passage seems to give you undue trouble, go on to the next, which you may find much simpler, since the passages are not arranged in any particular order of difficulty. You can always go back, if you have time.

7. Looking at the fill-in choices first is not a good idea. Some people say that by doing so they can obtain some idea of what the passage is about; however, by doing so, you can too easily try to twist the passage to fit a particular choice that struck your eye first. It is better to read the passage first.

8. Look for the internal evidence in the passage as a whole, in a sentence, or even in an explanatory phrase—for the clues that will help you to eliminate the wrong choices. Rely upon a constant rereading of the passage and *not* upon your previous knowledge.

The tests that follow will give you the practice that should lead to your achieving maximum results on the examination. Do not rush through them. Speed will come after accuracy. Your first task is to develop a technique that results in correct answers; *then* speed will follow. Analyze each of your wrong answers to try to discover why you went astray. If necessary, after an interim of a few weeks, take the same tests over again, not to recall the correct answers, but to recall the techniques that produce correct answers at your maximum rate of reading speed.

Third Day: Analysis and Practice Test

A Closer Look

Before looking at the analysis that follows, read the exercise below, and write your own answer in the space provided.

The glaring truth which nobody else has dared to say out loud is that his .... city simply cannot cope with its present .... Its housing, traffic, schools, water supply, police, and municipal finance are strained to the danger point—or beyond.

(a) unfortunate . . . factors   (b) fortunate . . . population
(c) stricken . . . overcrowding   (d) happy . . .
good fortune   (e) oversized . . . size   **Answer** ....

Analysis

Since the tone of the paragraph is one that stresses weaknesses, (b) *fortunate . . . population* and (d) *happy . . . good fortune* can be eliminated because they contain the words *fortunate, happy,* and *good fortune.*

Choices (a) *unfortunate . . . factors* and (e) *oversized . . . size* could possibly fit, but when they are compared with the more dramatic (c) *stricken . . . overcrowding*—especially since *stricken* is truly a word that summarizes the results of the overcrowding—it is clear that choice (c) must be the correct answer.

Practice Test

Time at Start ....

In the space provided, write the letter of the set of words that best completes the thought of the sentence group.

1. History has dealt harshly with short-term Presidents. If Lincoln had been struck down in his third year in office rather than in his fifth, ... might still be searching in the mid-Civil War disarray for the grand design of reunion that we now .... was there.
(a) professors . . . could recognize   (b) historians . . ; know   (c) leaders . . . saw   (d) politicians . . . hope
(e) generals . . . heard   1. ....

2. The Lincoln Memorial perhaps more than any other monument is likely to evoke a deep emotional surge in the American visitor. The memorial is experienced most profoundly at night, when the massive marble figure stands out in the darkness, just as in life Lincoln never .... his conviction or his courage in the dark days of his service as .... and war President of a torn nation.
(a) lost . . . martyr   (b) won . . . general
(c) regained . . . politician   (d) lost . . . American
(e) slackened . . . prophet   2. ....

3. The Jefferson Memorial is a monument to the man, the statesman, the thinker, and the architect. Jefferson's name has become synonymous with the fight for liberty and human decency, and his .... are used to protest against the boot of .... wherever it walks.
(a) words . . . tyranny   (b) laws . . . cruelty
(c) deeds . . . hunger   (d) hopes . . . dictatorship
(e) wishes . . . death   3. ....

4. Different societies at different historical periods have different needs, and hence demand different kinds of art. Primitive man sought to control nature by means of tools and magic.

Magic is the mental equivalent of a tool: a means of influencing and controlling nature. The clay figures and drawings of animals that we find in Stone Age caves are there to propitiate the animal world—to achieve .... over .... by means of an image.

(a) control ... others   (b) mind ... matter
(c) power ... fear   (d) mastery ... reality
(e) peace ... all

4. ....

5. The ideal role of a congressman is easy to state: to represent his constituency, by knowing its needs and aspirations—at the same time inspiring it to something better. Both functions—to represent and to lead—are indispensable if a democracy of ordinary .... is to survive .... revolutions every decade.

(a) politicians ... peaceful   (b) workers ... successful
(c) humans ... scientific   (d) dimensions ... unsuccessful
(e) power ... world

5. ....

6. Toys that teach concepts and practical lessons are as old as time. Most toys originated as tools through which young and old alike mastered themselves and learned to understand their .... The pinwheel, for example, demonstrates the way windmills work. The .... child understands and is interested in toys that the child of a generation ago would not know what to do with.

(a) jobs ... clever   (b) weaknesses ... dull
(c) world ... space age   (d) parents ... educated
(e) friends ... older

6. ....

7. The continuing education of adults is truly purposeful only to the extent that it helps the individual .... his absolute dependence upon the community. The adult must learn how to become increasingly skillful as a .... in the ever-changing stream of modern life.

(a) control ... follower   (b) increase ... listener
(c) lose ... nonparticipant   (d) keep ... leader
(e) decrease ... participant

7. ....

8. There is a certain something in the air at the beginning of a trip. One is perhaps a little more .... and aware than at any other time during the expedition, and because one is aware, somehow everything stands out in sharper focus and seemingly insignificant things are ....

(a) cautious ... evaluated   (b) alive ... important
(c) carefree ... bothersome   (d) critical ... disappearing
(e) uncritical ... observed

8. ....

9. To judge a poem or piece of prose, you apply the one test—the greatest test. You listen for the sentence sounds. If you find some of those not bookish, caught from the mouths of people, some of them striking, all of them .... and recognizable, so recognizable that with a little trouble you can place them and even name them, you know you have found a ....

(a) prosaic ... genius   (b) definite ... writer
(c) pleasant ... friend   (d) poetic ... poet
(e) startling ... modern   9. ....

10. Forgetting its revolutionary heritage, Garrison's generation believed that moral issues like political interests were matters for adjustment and that in exchange for their promise of good behavior, minorities might receive a(n) .... guarantee of fair play. This assumption meant that American democracy functioned effectively just as long as there were .... absolute moral judgments to clog the machinery.

(a) everlasting ... many   (b) republican ... ever
(c) sincere ... not many   (d) majority ... no
(e) lasting ... few   10. ....

11. Failure to unite its powerful elements on a(n) .... can be disastrous to a major political party. That is why ideological factional leaders so seldom have been ....

(a) candidate ... nominated   (b) campaign ... losers
(c) issue ... winners   (d) legal point ... heard
(e) tragedy ... successful   11. ....

12. A theater which exists primarily to serve a community, and only secondarily to make a profit, will be more apt to .... repertory. The standard of performance is apt to be higher and out-of-town visitors will be able on three successive nights, if they have a mind to, to see three .... plays.

(a) avoid ... star-studded   (b) evaluate ... mediocre
(c) offer ... different   (d) question ... unusual
(e) scorn ... good   12. ....

13. We may emphasize as often as we like that intellect is powerless when compared with .... in human life—and we shall be right! But after all there is something peculiar about this weakness; the voice of the intellect is low, but it rests not until it gets a hearing. In the end, after countless ...., it gets one after all.

(a) feeling ... victories   (b) impulse ... repulses
(c) humor ... innings   (d) tragedy ... defeats
(e) emotion ... impulses   13. ....

14. In other words, psychoanalysts relieve their patients from feeling guilty about things of which they are not ...., and leave them with the sense of guilt about things of which they really are ....

(a) concerned . . . innocent   (b) guilty . . . guilty
(c) aware . . . concerned   (d) conscious . . . conscious
(e) told . . . unaware   14. ....

15. The people who settled in New England came there for religious freedom, but religious freedom to them meant freedom for their kind of religion only. They were not going to be any more .... to others who .... with them in this new country than others had been with them in countries from which they came.

(a) liberal . . . differed   (b) acceptable . . . came
(c) intolerant . . . disagreed   (d) harsh . . . agreed
(e) tolerant . . . agreed   15. ....

Time at End ....   *Minutes Elapsed* ....
                                     Average Time 21 *Minutes*

Answer Key for this test is on page 363.

My Score: *Number Right* ....   *Number Wrong* ....
              Average Number Right 12

Fourth Day: Analysis and Practice Test

A Closer Look

Before looking at the analysis that follows, read the exercise below, and write your own answer in the space provided.

Investigations have shown that the average automobile carries in its everyday travels the equivalent of only one and a half persons. The streets of our large cities are absurdly .... with these great .... vehicles.

(a) empty . . . mechanical   (b) distorted . . . man-made
(c) covered . . . garish   (d) congested . . . empty
(e) overwhelmed . . . inefficient   Answer ....

Analysis

(a) *empty . . . mechanical*   While *mechanical* may fit, the paragraph carries too little meaning when *empty* is added.

(b) *distorted . . . man-made*   Again, one word—in this case, *man-made*—fits, but the other doesn't: a city's being distorted is not the essential idea of this paragraph.

(c) *covered . . . garish   Garish* means elaborately decorated. The paragraph does not carry this meaning for the automobiles.

(e) *overwhelmed . . . inefficient*   The paragraph stresses that inefficient use is being made of the automobiles, and not that the cars in themselves are inefficient.

(d) *congested . . . empty   Empty* develops logically from the statement in the first sentence that so few people are in each automobile. The word *absurdly* shows the logic of using *congested!* This is the correct answer because with these words, the second sentence carries the ideas in the first sentence to a conclusion.

Practice Test

Time At Start ....

In the space provided, write the letter of the set of words that best completes the thought of the sentence group.

1. Today's colleges are looking for students who have already demonstrated their eagerness and ability to .... Invariably, these eager students are ....
(a) be accepted . . . outstanding   (b) conform . . . accepted   (c) absorb . . . successful   (d) learn . . . readers
(e) grow . . . followers   1. ....

2. Since in the long run progress is more important than peace to a university, the ultimate test of the effectiveness of its president is whether he permits progress to be made fast enough and in the right direction, whether the needed .... take precedence over the .... of the institution.
(a) reforms . . . needs   (b) innovations . . . conservatism
(c) finances . . . errors   (d) adjustments . . . weaknesses
(e) leaders . . . followers   2. ....

3. We seem to be bent on the creation of the audience for the arts at the expense of the arts and the artist. In our determination to nurture the audience, we create an enthusiasm less for the .... than for being part of the right ....

(a) arts ... audience (b) artist ... group
(c) left ... wing (d) masterpiece ... technique
(e) purchaser ... element   3. ....

4. Every person is responsible for all the .... within the scope of his abilities, and for no more, and .... can tell whose sphere is the largest.

(a) power ... anyone (b) good ... none
(c) wealth ... an expert (d) thought ... he
(e) wisdom ... few   4. ....

5. We judge ourselves by what we feel capable of ...., while others judge us by what we have already ....

(a) wishing ... accomplished (b) understanding ... heard (c) saying ... seen (d) doing ... done
(e) seeing ... said   5. ....

6. Absence, like ...., sets a seal on the .... of those we love; we cannot realize the intervening changes which time may have affected.

(a) taxes ... devotion (b) chains ... thoughts
(c) death ... image (d) love ... fate (e) love ... lips
          6. ....

7. There are lying within a man a thousand .... that he does not .... till he takes up his pen to write.

(a) thoughts ... know (b) deeds ... try (c) ideals ... consider (d) ideas ... fathom (e) hopes ... desire 7. ....

8. The .... of any people for .... sake has rarely had any effect other than to fix those opinions deeper and to render

(a) trying ... justice's (b) oppression ... opinions'
(c) condemnation ... freedom's (d) freeing ... society's
(e) praising ... truth's   8. ....

9. What is to prevent .... from being made the greatest organ of social life? Books have had their day, the theaters have had their day, the temple of religion has had its day. .... can be made to take the lead of all these in the great movement of human thought and human civilization.

(a) a daily newspaper ... A newspaper (b) Congress ... A representative (c) television ... Radio
(d) advertising ... A magazine (e) fear ... Progress
          9. ....

10. A .... being is one who is capable of reflecting on his past actions and their ....; of approving of some and disapproving of others.
(a) criminal ... causes (b) kind ... effects
(c) moral ... motives (d) thinking ... results
(e) normal ... joys

10. ....

11. Every monopoly and all exclusive privileges are granted at the expense of the .... who ought to receive a fair ....
(a) owners ... compensation (b) public ... equivalent
(c) consumers ... treatment (d) victims ... sentence
(e) peasants ... wage

11. ....

12. As ten millions of circles cannot ever make a square, so the united voices of .... cannot lend the smallest foundation to ....
(a) nations ... fate (b) mankind ... truth
(c) wealth ... justice (d) myriads ... falsehood
(e) charity ... selfishness

12. ....

13. .... is to the collective body what health is to every individual body. Without health no pleasure can be tasted by man; without liberty no .... can be enjoyed by society.
(a) Liberty ... happiness (b) Peace ... food
(c) Thought ... deed (d) Employment ... day
(e) Joy ... luxury

13. ....

14. A light supper, a good night's sleep, and a fine morning have often made a(n) .... of the same man who by indigestion, a restless night, and a rainy morning would have proved a(n) ....
(a) hero ... coward (b) egotist ... tyrant
(c) leader ... follower (d) dictator ... democratic leader (e) scientist ... artist

14. ....

15. Every mind was made for ...., for knowledge; and its nature is sinned against when it is doomed to ....
(a) education ... misery (b) growth ... ignorance
(c) greatness ... folly (d) the truth ... falsity
(e) beauty ... failure

15. ....

Time at End ....   *Minutes Elapsed* ....
                                   Average Time 22 Minutes

Answer Key for this test is on page 363.

My Score: *Number Right* ....   *Number Wrong* ....
             Average Number Right 11

Fifth Day: Analysis and Practice Test

A Closer Look

Before looking at the analysis that follows, read the exercise below, and write your own answer in the space provided.

The American image of the Soviet Union is not always a(n) .... one, but when it is said here that the fate of that country is in the hands of a small, self-perpetuating group which decides not only what is to be done, but also what is to be published and read, this is a(n) .... description.

(a) honest . . . distorted   (b) distorted . . . unfair
(c) fair . . . accurate   (d) objective . . . unproved
(e) hostile . . . ridiculous   Answer ....

Analysis

The key to the understanding of this sentence lies in the clause, "that the fate of that country is in the hands of a small, self-perpetuating group which decides not only what is to be done, but also what is to be published and read." This is a statement that is not distorted, unfair, unproved, or ridiculous. On this basis we can eliminate (a) *honest . . . distorted,* (b) *distorted . . . unfair,* (d) *objective . . . unproved,* and (e) *hostile . . . ridiculous* because of the second word of each pair. Sometimes on examinations the path to a correct answer opens as quickly as did this. Even if so, do not omit the final check. In this case, (c) *fair . . . accurate* fits because both words help to complete the meaning of the passage.

Practice Test

Time at Start ....

In the space provided, write the letter of the set of words that best completes the thought of the sentence group.

1. The shadow that the possibility of nuclear war casts over the human spirit is not solely the shadow of measureless .... It is also a shadow over human self-respect and over the entire scope of human ....
(a) conquest . . . waste   (b) prospects . . . existence
(c) calamity . . . faith   (d) endeavor . . . pessimism
(e) futility . . . race   1: ....

2. If today Delacroix' subjects seem overromantic, even ...., there is no denying that his methods set the pace for much of .... art.
(a) realistic . . . past   (b) alien . . . modern
(c) amateurish . . . surrealistic   (d) artistic . . . ancient
(e) outlandish . . . forgotten

2. ....

3. With the single exception of death, mankind's classic enemy is .... All through the historical period, right up to the present moment, our best thinkers have stood .... before the problem of how to grow enough food to keep expanding populations well-fed.
(a) war . . . amazed   (b) disease . . . powerless
(c) starvation . . . gleeful   (d) hunger . . . paralyzed
(e) ignorance . . . amazed

3. ....

4. The law is made to protect the .... by punishing the ....
(a) haves . . . have-nots   (b) righteous . . . offensive
(c) offender . . . defender   (d) poor . . . influential
(e) innocent . . . guilty

4. ....

5. Accurate .... is the basis of correct opinions; the .... of it makes the opinions of many people of little value.
(a) truth . . . negation   (b) knowledge . . . want
(c) observation . . . dearth   (d) statement . . . denial
(e) aim . . . acceptance

5. ....

6. Language is the amber in which a thousand precious thoughts have been safely embedded and .... It has arrested ten thousand lightning flashes of genius which, unless thus fixed and arrested, might have been bright, but would also have been as quickly passing and perishing as the ....
(a) preserved . . . lightning   (b) lost . . . buffalo
(c) saved . . . fossil   (d) dissolved . . . brontosaurus
(e) solidified . . . wind

6. ....

7. He who learns, and makes no use of his learning, is a beast of burden with a load of books.— Does the donkey .... whether he carries on his back a .... or a bundle of faggots?
(a) question . . . man   (b) complain . . . stick
(c) starve . . . giant   (d) stagger . . . child
(e) comprehend . . . library

7. ....

8. We can all agree on the definition of the .... high school as a high school whose programs correspond to the educational needs of .... the youth of the community.
(a) old-fashioned ... 80% of   (b) modern ... none
(c) comprehensive ... all   (d) community ... many of
(e) vocational ... none of   8. ....

9. Rules of conduct, whatever they may be, are not sufficient to produce good .... unless the .... sought are good.
(a) manners ... effects   (b) children ... rewards
(c) behavior ... punishments   (d) results ... ends
(e) times ... ideas   9. ....

10. Great discoveries and improvements .... involve the .... of many minds. I may be given credit for having blazed the trail, but when I look at the subsequent developments, I feel the credit is due to others rather than to myself.
(a) invariably ... cooperation   (b) often ... thoughts
(c) never ... substance   (d) must ... integrity
(e) does ... individuality   10. ....

11. Some men give up their designs when they have almost reached the goal; while others, on the contrary, obtain .... by exerting at the last moment more vigorous .... than before.
(a) a pause ... wishes   (b) defeat ... cries
(c) victory ... efforts   (d) a prize ... complaints
(e) a draw ... actions   11. ....

12. The races of mankind would perish did they cease to aid each other. We cannot exist without .... help. All, therefore, who need aid have a right to ask for it from their fellow men; and no one who has the power of granting can refuse it without ....
(a) mutual ... guilt   (b) independent ... remorse
(c) outside ... contentment   (d) self- ... regret
(e) a leader's ... loss   12. ....

13. We are apt to .... our vocation by looking out of the way for occasions to exercise great and rare ...., and by stepping over the ordinary ones that lie directly in the road before us.
(a) anticipate ... caution   (b) mistake ... virtues
(c) overlook ... deeds   (d) anticipate ... rewards
(e) forget ... judgment   13. ....

14. The extreme of .... is that life is not worth living; the extreme of .... is that everything is for the best in the best of worlds. Neither of these is true.

(a) foolishness ... wisdom   (b) pessimism ... optimism
(c) optimism ... pessimism   (d) cowardice ... bravery
(e) despair ... thoughtfulness   14. ....

15. Peace has to be .... in order to be maintained. It is the product of Faith, Strength, Energy, Will, Sympathy, Justice, Imagination, and the triumph of principle. It will never be .... by passivity and quietism.

(a) fought for ... lost   (b) enforced ... ended
(c) created ... achieved   (d) wished for ... conquered
(e) desired ... lost   15. ....

Time at End ....   *Minutes Elapsed* ....
                                           Average Time 17 *Minutes*

Answer Key for this test is on page 363.

My Score: Number Right ....   *Number Wrong* ....
            Average Number Right 13

Sixth Day: Analysis and Practice Test

A Closer Look

Before looking at the analysis that follows, read the exercise below and write your own answer in the space provided.

The Group Plan at Claremont is an arrangement in which a number of colleges share a common campus and certain common facilities—auditorium, library, and health center—and yet maintain their own .... The .... is that the colleges can remain small and preserve their own peculiar genius.

(a) faculty ... intent   (b) self-government ... advantage
(c) facilities ... aim   (d) purposes ... disadvantage
(e) collections ... disaster   Answer ....

Analysis

The writer is obviously in favor of the plan. Therefore (d) *purposes ... disadvantage* can be eliminated because of the second word. We can also eliminate (e) *collections . . . disaster* for a similar reason, since *disaster* is a negative word.

We can eliminate (c) *facilities . . . aim* since the word *facilities* causes a contradiction in the selection.

While (a) *faculty . . . intent* and (b) *self-government . . . advantage* both seem to fit, one of these must be the better choice. Maintaining their own faculty would not give the same degree of individuality that self-government would. Therefore, (b) *self-government . . . advantage* is the correct answer.

Practice Test

Time at Start ....

In the space provided, write the letter of the set of words that best completes the thought of the sentence group.

1. A(n) .... revolution is taking place in American life today. It is a revolution in the means of producing goods and services, and it is profoundly changing the nature of the American ....

   (a) unusual . . . home (b) quiet . . . teen-ager
   (c) industrial . . . economy (d) political . . . scene   **1.** ....

2. A system of mass production cannot exist without mass consumption. What is more, as the abundance of goods and services that America can produce rises dramatically each year, this system must also generate the increase in family personal income required to .... and to .... this abundance.

   (a) manufacture . . . sell (b) buy . . . enjoy (c) need . . .
  order (d) merchandise . . . order   **2.** ....

3. Aristotle observed that democracy would flourish only when all persons share alike in the government to the utmost. America's founding fathers, two thousand years later, hopefully envisioned a nation in which citizens both assumed responsibility in .... and kept a close weather eye on .... charged with their conduct.

   (a) public affairs . . . officeholders (b) wartime : : :
  generals (c) business . . . managers
  (d) private matters . . . judges   **3.** ....

4. Americans are closest to their government through the broad program of insured protection which currently pays $15 billion yearly in social security benefits to 18½ million Americans

and provides coverage to nine out of ten workers. This blanket of .... over all of the United States is an important part of the network of .... security that makes our form of government so stable.

(a) money . . . political   (b) protection . . . personal
(c) wealth . . . economic   (d) control . . . inner   4. ....

5. If the state has the right to exact certain compliance with its demands, then it also is the right of the state to .... its people to the proper .... of such demands.

(a) elevate . . . level   (b) indoctrinate . . . acceptance
(c) compel . . . respect   (d) educate . . . understanding

5. ....

6. Vocational education has failed conspicuously to keep up with the needs of society. It has been changed little since the beginning of the century. Inadequately financed and too rigidly structured, vocational courses were training young people for .... jobs and doing little to develop skills .... in modern industry.

(a) well-paying . . . lost   (b) permanent . . . developed
(c) nonexistent . . . needed   (d) useless . . . unnecessary

6. ....

7. State and local efforts to improve schools, remarkable though they have been, have not been able to catch up to the real need. Thousands of communities and many states simply do not have the .... resources to develop a school system that would equip their .... to meet the needs of today's society.

(a) manpower . . . schools   (b) financial . . . children
(c) natural . . . teachers   (d) inner . . . cities   7. ....

8. It is only in the make-believe world of Dr. Kildare and Ben Casey that the drama ends when the medical crisis is overcome and the patient is on the road to recovery. In real life, especially if the patient is ...., an even greater .... lies ahead—that of paying a crushing hospital bill.

(a) ill . . . difficulty   (b) obstinate . . . adversity
(c) elderly . . . crisis   (d) young . . . question   8. ....

9. Preventive medicine or proper diagnosis and early treatment are the best means of health care, and much less .... than .... in a hospital.

(a) dangerous . . . diagnosis   (b) safe . . . treatment
(c) dangerous . . . confinement   (d) expensive . . .
confinement   9. ....

10. It is not in .... but in the .... which can be communicated from one to another that the civilized man shows his superiority to the savage.
(a) skill . . . knowledge   (b) speed . . . worth
(c) method . . . purpose   (d) results . . . joy   10. ....

11. No man undertakes a trade he has not yet ...., even the meanest. Yet everyone thinks himself sufficiently qualified for the hardest of all trades, that of ....
(a) mastered . . . bartering   (b) learned . . . government
(c) observed . . . warfare   (d) taught . . . education   11. ....

12. We keep on deceiving ourselves in regard to our ...., until we at last come to look upon them as ....
(a) faults . . . virtues   (b) wishes . . . deeds
(c) friends . . . enemies   (d) ideals . . . errors   12. ....

13. If you limit the search for truth and forbid men anywhere, in any way, to seek knowledge, you .... the .... force of truth itself.
(a) weaken . . . overpowering   (b) strengthen . . . eventual   (c) paralyze . . . vital   (d) kill . . . essential
                                                              13. ....

14. Were it left to me to decide whether we should have a government without newspapers, or newspapers without government, I should not hesitate a moment to .... the ....
(a) decide . . . issue   (b) prefer . . . latter
(c) condemn . . . press   (d) proclaim . . . victory   14. ....

15. Ignorance of the law excuses no man; not that all men .... the law, but, because it is an excuse, every man will .... it, and no man can tell how to refute him.
(a) respect . . . seek   (b) follow . . . ignore
(c) disobey . . . scorn   (d) know . . . plead   15. ....

Time at End ....   *Minutes Elapsed* ....
                                     Average Time 24 *Minutes*

Answer Key for this test is on page 364.

My Score: *Number Right* ....   *Number Wrong* ....
           Average Number Right 11

Seventh Day: Analysis and Practice Test

A Closer Look

Before looking at the analysis that follows, read the exercise below and write your own answer in the space provided.

The world will never know of my life if it should write and read a hundred .... The main facts of it are known, and are likely to be known, to myself alone, of all .... men.

(a) biographies ... created   (b) biographies ... unknown
(c) stories ... famous   (d) articles ... injured
(e) autobiographies ... fortunate   Answer ....

Analysis

Any one person can write only one autobiography; therefore (e) *autobiographies ... fortunate* can be eliminated.

To know a man, biographies would be the best source; therefore (c) *stories ... famous* and (d) *articles ... injured* can be eliminated.

Which is the better answer: (a) *biographies ... created* or (b) *biographies ... unknown?* The key lies, obviously, in the words *created* and *unknown.* If the main facts of his life are known, then *unknown* is not as definitive as *created.* The selection does make sense with (a) *biographies ... created.* This therefore, as proved by both the process of elimination and by a positive check, is the correct answer.

Practice Test

Time at Start ....

In the space provided, write the letter of the set of words that best completes the thought of the sentence group.

1. How can we appraise a proposal if the terms hurled at our ears can mean anything or nothing, and change their significance with the inflection of the voice? Welfare state, socialism, radical, liberal, conservative, reactionary, and a regiment of others—these terms in today's usage are generally compounds of confusion and prejudice. If our attitudes are ...., our

language is often to blame. A good tonic for clearer .... is a dose of precise, legal definition.

(a) hostile . . . legislation   (b) muddled . . . thinking
(c) mixed . . . patriotism   (d) admirable . . . hostilities
(e) unrecognizable . . . objections   1. ....

2. Men give me some credit for genius. All the genius I have lies just in this: when I have a subject in hand, I study it profoundly. Day and night it is before me. I explore it in all its bearings. My mind becomes pervaded with it. Then the effort which I make the people are pleased to call the fruit of genius. It is the fruit of .... and ....

(a) listening . . . reading   (b) talking . . . reading
(c) luck . . . chance   (d) labor . . . thought
(e) experience . . . luck   2. ....

3. People disparage knowing and the intellectual life, and urge doing. I am very content with knowing, if only I could know. That is an august entertainment, and would suffice me a great while. To .... a little would be worth the .... of this world.

(a) know . . . expense   (b) explore . . . joys   (c) do . . . troubles   (d) read . . . silliness   (e) accomplish . . . worries   3. ....

4. It is the fortuitous, sensational, and tragic events that make up the bulk of what we call "news." The dilemma is obvious. There can be no effective moral housecleaning without exposure, proof of wrongdoing, and an awakened public .... On the other hand, one wonders what the impact of this drip, drip, drip of icy criticism may be upon those of our citizens who have no sense of history. They may be tempted to say "There is none ...., no, not one"—and that is not true.

(a) indifference . . . honest   (b) power . . . indifference
(c) fear . . . innocent   (d) admiration . . . guiltless
(e) conscience . . . righteous   4. ....

5. Some men of a .... and .... life have sent forth from their closet or cloister rays of intellectual light that have agitated courts and revolutionized kingdoms—like the moon, which, though far removed from the ocean and shining upon it with a serene and sober light, is the chief cause of all those ebbings and flowings which incessantly disturb that restless world of waters.

(a) political . . . active   (b) willful . . . ambitious
(c) secluded . . . studious   (d) warlike . . . militant
(e) wise . . . distinguished   5. ....

6. The world of reality has its limits; the world of imagination is boundless. — Not being able to enlarge the one, let us .... the other; for it is from their .... that all the evils arise which render us unhappy.
  (a) expand ... incompatibility (b) contract ... difference
  (c) disregard ... likeness (d) enlarge ... similarity
  (e) develop ... inflexibility   6. ....

7. Ideas go booming through the world louder than cannons. .... are mightier than armies. ....have achieved more victories than horsemen or chariots.
  (a) Men of peace ... Teachers (b) Fears ... Diseases
  (c) Thoughts ... Principles (d) Principles ... Scientists
  (e) Leagues ... Confederations.   7. ....

8. My country owes me nothing. It gave me, as it gives every boy and girl, a chance. It gave me schooling, independence of action, opportunity for service and honor. In no other land could a boy from a country village, without .... or influential friends, look forward with unbounded ....
  (a) good looks ... promotion (b) a family ... pessimism
  (c) education ... optimism (d) inheritance ... hope
  (e) political power ... opportunity   8. ....

9. Not to know what has been transacted in former times is to be always a child. — If no use is made of the labors of past ages, the world must remain always in the .... of ....
  (a) chains ... ignorance (b) infancy ... knowledge
  (c) beginning ... progress (d) wake ... disaster
  (e) throes ... discovery   9. ....

10. To be entirely just in our estimate of other ages is not only difficult, it is impossible. Even what is passing in our .... we see but through a glass darkly. In historical inquiries the most instructed thinkers have but a limited advantage over the most illiterate. Those who know the most approach .... to agreement.
  (a) reading ... closest (b) times ... best
  (c) own estimate ... close (d) age ... not
  (e) presence ... least   10. ....

11. It is only imperfection that complains of what is imperfect. The more .... we are, the more .... and quiet we become toward the defects of others.
  (a) perfect ... gentle (b) imperfect ... resistant
  (c) gentle ... accepting (d) violent ... imperfect
  (e) passive ... annoyed   11. ....

12. There are two kinds of discontent in this world: the discontent that works and the discontent that wrings its hands. The first .... what it wants, and the second .... what it had. There is no cure for the first but success, and there is no cure at all for the second.
(a) cries for . . . gains   (b) orders . . . uses
(c) loses . . . retains   (d) gets . . . loses   (e) guesses . . .
tells   12. ....

13. To speculate without facts is to attempt to enter a house of which one has not the key, by wandering aimlessly around and around, searching the wall, and now and then peeping through the windows. .... are the ....
(a) Facts . . . key   (b Thoughts . . . rewards
(c) Men . . . losers   (d) Scientists . . . searchers
(e) Ideals . . . winners   13. ....

14. The first panacea for a .... nation is inflation of the currency; the second is .... Both bring a temporary prosperity; both bring a permanent ruin. But both are the refuge of political and economic opportunists.
(a) second-rate . . . diplomacy   (b) Communist . . . peace
(c) mismanaged . . . war   (d) modern . . . research
(e) wealthy . . . taxes   14. ....

15. Romantic plays with happy endings are almost of necessity .... in artistic values to true tragedies. Not, one would hope, simply because they end happily, but because a tragedy in its great moments can generally afford to be .... while romantic plays live in an atmosphere of ingenuity and make-believe.
(a) superior . . . unhappy   (b) weaker . . . unreal
(c) inferior . . . sincere   (d) incomparable . . . exaggerated
(e) fairer . . . alive   15. ....

Time at End ....   *Minutes Elapsed* ....
                                              Average Time 21 *Minutes*

Answer Key for this test is on page 364.

My Score: Number Right ....   *Number Wrong* ....
             Average Number Right 13

Eighth Day: Analysis and Practice Test

A Closer Look

Before looking at the analysis that follows, read the exercise below and write your own answer in the space provided.

Most of us take the .... for granted, or believe it to be .... from now to eternity; but this is an error, for the atmosphere, just like the land and sea, which make up the rest of our world, has a long history behind it and is still changing.

(a) scenery . . . unchangeable   (b) air . . . immutable
(c) earth . . . mutable   (d) universe . . . revolving
(e) oxygen . . . valuable   Answer ....

Analysis

The key to this passage is in the clause, "for the atmosphere . . . is still changing." Since the atmosphere, the land, and the sea make up the earth, the earth could not be the item taken for granted; nor could the universe which includes all of these. On this basis, therefore, (c) *earth . . . mutable* and (d) *universe . . . revolving* are eliminated because of the first word of each pair. We could eliminate (c) *earth . . . mutable* also because *mutable* would be an error.

We can eliminate (e) *oxygen . . . valuable* because if we expect life to continue, we can neither expect oxygen to change nor can we take it for granted.

We are left with (a) *scenery . . . unchangeable* and (b) *air . . . immutable*. Inasmuch as *unchangeable* and *immutable* are synonyms, we must test *scenery* and *air* for appropriateness: Since people do expect scenery to change somewhat with man's improvements, for example, we could eliminate (a) *scenery . . . unchangeable*. Then, when we test (b) *air . . . immutable*, the passage makes sense with air being that which we consider constant. Therefore (b) *air . . . immutable* is the correct answer.

Practice Test

Time at Start ....

In the space provided, write the letter of the set of words that best completes the thought of the sentence group.

1. The most certain test by which we judge whether a country is really .... is the amount of security enjoyed by ....
(a) wealthy ... workers (b) socialistic ... its president
(c) democratic ... its leaders (d) free ... minorities
(e) interesting ... visitors   1. ....

2. An egoist will always speak of .... either in praise or censure. But a(n) .... man ever shuns making himself the subject of his conversation.
(a) his deeds ... proud (b) himself ... modest
(c) others ... timid (d) his country ... patriotic
(e) no one ... educated   2. ....

3. It is always easy to begin a war, but very difficult to stop one since its .... and .... are not under the control of the same man.
(a) death ... destruction (b) cause ... effect
(c) beginning ... end (d) men ... materials
(e) cost ... burden   3. ....

4. It is more .... that even a(n) .... person should be punished without the forms of law than that he should escape.
(a) dangerous ... guilty (b) fitting ... simple
(c) worthwhile ... innocent (d) beneficial ... accused
(e) significant ... young   4. ....

5. There are other forms of culture besides physical science, and I should be profoundly .... to see the fact forgotten or even to observe a tendency to starve or cripple .... or aesthetic culture for the sake of science.
(a) pleased ... medicine (b) willing ... liberal
(c) annoyed ... chemical (d) reluctant ... art
(e) sorry ... literary   5. ....

6. We live in deeds, not years; in thoughts, not breaths; in feelings, not in figures on the dial; we should count time by heartthrobs. He most lives who thinks ...., feels the ...., acts the best.
(a) kindly ... sorrows of others (b) most ... noblest
(c) independently ... pressures (d) oftenest ... deepest
(e) often ... power   6. ....

7. It is a very easy thing to .... good laws; the difficulty is to make them ....
(a) consider ... legal (b) write ... lasting
(c) enact ... realistic (d) talk about ... reasonable
(e) devise ... effective   7. ....

8. The will of the people is the only .... foundation c
any government, and to protect its free .... should be ou
first objective.
(a) faithful . . . will   (b) considerable . . . press
(c) legitimate . . . expression   (d) specious . . . ways
(e) true . . . men   8. ....

9. Courage is doing what you are .... to do. There ca
be no courage unless you are ....
(a) told . . . ordered   (b) willing . . . bold
(c) unwilling . . . reluctant   (d) compelled . . . reliable
(e) afraid . . . scared   9. ....

10. Courage is doing what you think is ...., no matter wha
the .... You don't teach a boy to be courageous. You tr
to teach him the difference between right and wrong, and the
you tell him to do what is right.
(a) brave . . . orders   (b) sane . . . conditions
(c) courteous . . . rule   (d) right . . . consequences
(e) best . . . results   10. ....

11. The definition of the word *courage* in war and in peac
remains ...., for what is valor to one man is not to another
and what is considered courage in one era is not .... judge
similarly in another.
(a) definite . . . always   (b) mysterious . . . often
(c) elusive . . . necessarily   (d) absolute . . . ever
(e) questionable . . . frequently   11. ....

12. "The Japanese suicide pilots in World War II were ....,"
say some war heroes. "On the contrary," say others, "the
died knowingly and willingly for what they believed. The
were ...."
(a) stupid . . . courageous   (b) courageous . . . foolhardy
(c) courageous . . . stupid   (d) men . . . heroes
(e) heroes . . . children   12. ....

13. Courage is .... of the highest order, for the brave ar
prodigal of the most .... things.
(a) thinking . . . expensive   (b) patriotism . . . rare
(c) feeling . . . talked about   (d) generosity . . . precious
(e) sacrifice . . . trivial   13. ....

14. True courage is to do without .... everything that on
is capable of doing before ....
(a) thinking . . . all   (b) witnesses . . . all the world
(c) selfishness . . . thought   (d) sacrifice . . .
reaction sets in   (e) feeling . . . it is too late   14. ....

15. Often .... leave no alternative to the courageous way out. Courage can be born of ....
(a) leaders ... command   (b) duties ... fear
(c) circumstances ... desperation   (d) wishes ... hope
(e) ambitions ... medals   15. ....

Time at End ....   *Minutes Elapsed* ....
                                     Average Time 17 Minutes

Answer Key for this test is on page 364.

My Score: *Number Right* ....   *Number Wrong* ....
                    Average Number Right 12

Ninth Day: Analysis and Practice Test

A Closer Look

Before looking at the analysis that follows, read the exercise below and write your own answer in the space provided.

Our diplomatic corps is the basis of the operation of our foreign policy. Personal diplomacy is sometimes .... and the politically appointed diplomat may be successful. Yet there can be no substitute for the well-trained, ... diplomat. A nation that does not have such a corps does not have a foreign policy.

(a) a failure ... professional   (b) successful ... national
(c) effective ... devoted   (d) weak ... personal
(e) ineffective ... patriotic   Answer ....

Analysis

We can begin by eliminating (b) *successful ... national* since the term *national diplomat* has no meaning for this selection. The words *sometimes* and *successful* point to the need for a beneficial term to follow *sometimes*. Therefore we can eliminate (e) *ineffective ... patriotic*, (a) *a failure ... professional*, and (d) *weak ... personal*. Again through the process of elimination we can reach a single possible answer, but don't accept it until you have checked to prove that (c) *effective ... devoted* does fit.

Practice Test

Time at Start ....

In the space provided, write the letter of the set of words that best completes the thought of the sentence group.

1. The need for .... to prevent government from whittling away the rights of the .... was never greater. Today, as rarely before, case after case comes to the Court, which finds the individual battling to vindicate a claim under the Bill of Rights against the powers of government, federal and state.
(a) laws ... state   (b) leaders ... Court   (c) jurors ... minorities   (d) vigilance ... individual
(e) legislation ... corporations   1. ....

2. Today most Americans seem to have forgotten the ancient evils which forced their ancestors to flee to this new country and to form a government stripped of old powers used to suppress them. But the Americans who supported the Revolution and the adoption of our Constitution knew firsthand the dangers of tyrannical governments. They were familiar with the long-existing practice of English persecutions of people wholly because of their religious or political beliefs. They knew that many accused of such offenses had stood, ... to defend themselves, before .... legislators and judges.
(a) bravely ... ignorant   (b) helpless ... biased
(c) unprepared ... cruel   (d) prepared ... disinterested
(e) foolishly attempting ... weak   2. ....

3. There is no such thing as a little country. The greatness of a people is no more determined by their .... than the greatness of a man is determined by his ....
(a) weapons ... might   (b) wishes ... genius
(c) wars ... wisdom   (d) wealth ... dealings
(e) number ... height   3. ....

4. It is instructive to recall that our nation at the time of the Constitutional Convention was also faced with formidable problems. The English, the French, the Spanish, and various tribes of hostile Indians were all ready and eager to subvert or occupy the fledgling Republic. Nevertheless, in that environment, our Founding Fathers conceived a Constitution and Bill of Rights replete with provisions indicating their determination to protect human rights. There was no call for a .... state

in those times of .... peace. We should heed no such call now.

(a) democratic ... temporary   (b) warlike ... unsettled
(c) police ... lasting   (d) garrison ... precarious
(e) peaceful ... no   4. ....

5. Those who would give up essential liberty to purchase a little temporary safety deserve neither .... nor ....

(a) life ... limb   (b) liberty ... safety   (c) peace ...
security   (d) wealth ... longevity   (e) power ... comfort
                                                        5. ....

6. Is .... so dear or .... so sweet as to be purchased at the price of chains and slavery? ... I know not what course others may take, but as for me, give me liberty or give me death.

(a) life ... peace   (b) food ... drink   (c) thought ...
ideal   (d) love ... children   (e) land ... profit   6. ....

7. The liberty of the .... must be thus far limited: he must not make himself a .... to other people.

(a) employer ... model   (b) employee ... slave
(c) individual ... nuisance   (d) child ... leader
(e) leader ... dictator   7. ....

8. The shepherd drives the wolf from the sheep's throat, for which the sheep thanks the shepherd as his liberator, while the wolf .... him for the same act as the .... of liberty.

(a) denounces ... destroyer   (b) thanks ... defender
(c) praises ... protector   (d) condemns ... essence
(e) slanders ... perpetuator   8. ....

9. Democracy has another merit. It allows criticism, and if there isn't public criticism, there are bound to be hushed-up scandals. That is why I believe in the press, despite all its .... and ....

(a) costs ... omissions   (b) lies ... vulgarity
(c) news editors ... reporters   (d) facts ... figures
(e) strengths ... weaknesses   9. ....

10. Every American takes pride in our tradition of hospitality to men of all races and creeds. We must be constantly vigilant against the attacks of intolerance and injustice. We must scrupulously guard the civil rights and civil liberties of all ...., whatever their background. We must remember that any oppression, any injustice, any hatred is a wedge designed to attack our ....

(a) allies ... country   (b) minorities ... economy
(c) citizens ... civilization   (d) ages ... world
(e) offenders ... form of justice   10. ....

11. The imitator is a poor kind of creature. If the man who paints only the tree, or flower, or other surface he sees before him were a(n) ...., the king of artists would be the photographer. It is for the artist to do something beyond this: in portrait painting to put on canvas something more than the face the .... wears for one day; to paint the man, in short, as well as his features.

(a) realist . . . scenery (b) soldier . . . child
(c) photographer . . . nature (d) artist . . . model
(e) romanticist . . . countryside   11. ....

12. Autumn is full of leave-taking. In September the swallows are chattering of destination and departure like a crowd of ...., and soon they are ....

(a) school children . . . satisfied (b) dreams . . . dispelled
(c) ghosts . . . forgotten (d) daffodils . . . harvested
(e) tourists . . . gone   12. ....

13. Let no man imagine that he has no .... Whatever he may be, and wherever he may be placed, the man who .... becomes a light and a power.

(a) friends . . . smiles (b) influence . . . thinks
(c) originality . . . writes (d) worth . . . counts
(e) talent . . . tries   13. ....

14. To pardon those absurdities in ourselves which we .... in others is neither better nor worse than to be more willing to be .... ourselves than to have others so.

(a) find . . . clever (b) accept . . . childish (c) judge . . . sane (d) condemn . . . fools (e) mirror . . . poor   14. ....

15. Books without the knowledge of .... are useless; for what should books teach but the art of ....

(a) truth . . . lying (b) life . . . living (c) art . . . writing
(d) people . . . understanding (e) reading . . . learning
                    15. ....

Time at End ....   *Minutes Elapsed* ....
                    Average Time 18 *Minutes*

Answer Key for this test is on page 364.

My Score: Number Right ....   *Number Wrong* ....
        Average Number Right 11

Tenth Day: Analysis and Practice Test

A Closer Look

Before looking at the analysis that follows, read the exercise below and write your own answer in the space provided.

A nuclear submarine, not requiring air for combustion of fuel in its engines, is able to divorce itself from the earth's .... and thus is a true submarine rather than a surface ship which can .... for short periods. It is an underwater satellite.

(a) air . . . float   (b) gravity . . . surface   (c) power . . . advance   (d) atmosphere . . . submerge
(e) attraction . . . operate   Answer ....

Analysis

(a) *air . . . float* can be eliminated because *float* contradicts the meaning of the selection.

(b) *gravity . . . surface* The submarine cannot divorce itself from gravity; therefore this answer is wrong.

(c) *power . . . advance* Since *power* is a vague word and *advance* has no contrast to prove the difference between a true submarine and a surface ship, this could not be the correct answer.

(e) *attraction . . . operate* Even if *attraction* did not eliminate this as a choice, *operate* twists *true* and *surface* out of any meaning.

(d) *atmosphere . . . submerge* The sub does divorce itself from the atmosphere when it dives into the water. The nuclear sub submerges for long periods of time in contrast to surface vessels that can submerge for brief periods. This is therefore the correct answer.

Practice Test

Time at Start ....

In the space provided, write the letter of the set of words that best completes the thought of the sentence group.

1. A fast neutron reactor has several advantages over a nuclear reactor using slowed down or moderated neutrons, in which

the energy of the neutrons is reduced from a speed of 10,000 miles a second to one mile a second. One of the advantages is that about 15 per cent of fast neutrons have energy great enough to .... the otherwise nonfissionable U-238, thus providing a substantial breeding .... of 15 per cent.
(a) create ... loss   (b) split ... bonus   (c) outdo ... gain   (d) destroy ... reserve   (e) equal ... example

1. ....

2. There is a probability, astronomers believe, that once in a long while an OH radical comes near to and combines with a hydrogen atom to form an interstellar water molecule. The discovery in space of the OH radical, which constitutes two of the three atoms of the water molecule, provides the first .... that .... exists in the space among the stars.
(a) proof ... life   (b) refutation ... oxygen
(c) sign ... molecules   (d) indication ... water
(e) denial ... ether

2. ....

3. The cellular elements that carry .... information must be present in every .... cell. In addition, to account for the fact that like faithfully begets like, these elements must be capable of reproducing or dividing accurately.
(a) hereditary ... reproducing   (b) somatic ... germinating   (c) cancerous ... genetic   (d) generic ... sex   (e) health ... healthy

3. ....

4. Medical historians of human warfare are fond of pointing out the instances in which .... battles have been credited to the wrong champion by .... historians. Who defeated the barbarian hordes that besieged Rome—the Romans or malaria-carrying anophelese mosquitoes rising from the Pontine Marshes? Who turned back Napoleon and the pride of French armies when they were at Russia's gates—the Russian soldiers or body lice carrying typhus rickettsiae?
(a) famous ... ancient   (b) fantastic ... universal
(c) bloody ... modern   (d) long-lasting ... objective
(e) victorious ... social

4. ....

5. If you travel vertically upward in a helicopter, the pointer of the barometer will fall as you rise higher and higher. This is not surprising for, as we ascend, the amount of air below us .... and the air above us weighs correspondingly ....
(a) decreases ... less   (b) increases ... more
(c) stabilizes ... the same   (d) decreases ... more
(e) increases ... less

5. ....

6. The presence of distinct seasons on a planet depends on the .... of its rotational axis to its orbit around the .... as well as on the time of rotation around the sun and on its atmosphere.
(a) speed . . . universe   (b) action . . . solar system
(c) atmosphere . . . center   (d) inclination . . . sun
(e) mass . . . galaxy   6. ....

7. The eyes of frogs and alligators are lacking in ability to accommodate and are not subjected to great variations in distance. The eyes of those birds which swoop down on their prey from great heights are capable of exceptionally .... accommodation necessary in order that the prey may be held in ....
(a) rapid . . . focus   (b) wide . . . their claws
(c) narrow . . . view   (d) clear . . . a glance
(e) unusual . . . awe   7. ....

8. Plant fossils occur in many types of rock but are most familiar to us as coal. Deposits of this .... are indicative of an age when the world had an extraordinarily hot climate. During this period, the .... of the world was uniform from pole to pole.
(a) plant . . . atmosphere   (b) fuel . . . climate
(c) fossil . . . shape   (d) type . . . cover   (e) material . . ; surface   8. ....

9. In the not-too-distant past, man bore .... of a degree which would send us moderns into howls of anguish. He had to accept bitter cold, festering sores, vermin, and slow-healing wounds as a(n) .... part of life.
(a) disease . . . unusual   (b) sorrow . . . infrequent
(c) burns . . . regular   (d) wounds . . . usual
(e) pain . . . routine   9. ....

10. In the dawning age of the surgical .... there seems to be no end to the variety of daring and delicate feats that surgeons are willing to try in the hope of saving patients who would otherwise be doomed by the .... of a vital organ.
(a) genius . . . infection   (b) transplant . . . failure
(c) team . . . transplanting   (d) miracle . . . vitalization
(e) needle . . . removal   10. ....

11. Among the most baffling of all mysteries of life is the mechanism by which impulses from the brain are transmitted along nerve fibers and eventually to muscles so that thought is translated into action. Some researchers have concentrated on the chemical aspects of the ....; others have worked with

electrical circuitry. Neither group has as yet been able to offer a complete explanation of nerve-impulse ....

(a) mechanism ... transmission   (b) organism ... fibers
(c) theory ... waves   (d) experiment ... data
(e) brain ... theory   11. ....

12. Nerves will react to light, and to mechanical, thermal, chemical, or electrical stimuli; that is, any rapid change in the physical or chemical condition of the .... will .... the passage of an impulse over a nerve.

(a) stimulus ... obstruct   (b) nerve ... block
(c) patient ... start   (d) environment ... initiate
(e) light ... generate   12. ....

13. When one of the valves of the heart fails to close perfectly, a .... occurs. The seriousness of the effects on the .... depends upon the valves affected and the degree of the defect.

(a) clot ... heart   (b) leakage ... body   (c) disease ... valve   (d) problem ... thinking   (e) heart attack ... heart   13. ....

14. Sunstroke is caused by excessive exposure of the head to the heat of the sun's rays. It increases the temperature of the brain and thereby causes the cerebral arteries to dilate and the cerebral blood pressure to .... This may bring about .... of some of the vital centers in the cerebrum and medulla, especially those controlling respiration, heart action, and vasomotor action.

(a) contract ... the disappearance   (b) develop ...; pulsation   (c) increase ... paralysis   (d) lower ... collapse   (e) remain constant ... overactivity   14. ....

15. It is rather .... to explain some of the cold and warm sensations produced on the surface of the .... when neither a cold nor a warm object has come in contact with it. For example, menthol gives rise to a sensation of coldness whereas carbon dioxide causes one of warmth.

(a) difficult ... skin   (b) usual ... machine
(c) simple ... earth   (d) common ... mirror
(e) odd ... body   15. ....

Time at End ....   *Minutes Elapsed* ....
                                 Average Time 20 *Minutes*

Answer Key for this test is on page 364.

My Score: *Number Right* ....   *Number Wrong* ....
              Average Number Right 11

Eleventh Day: Test of Mastery

Time at Start ....

In the space provided, write the letter of the set of words that best completes the thought of the sentence group.

1. American Presidential nominations are essentially transfers of a political party's titular leadership from one man to another. In a party of diversified interests, geographical differences, and wide philosophical range, if that .... cannot be accomplished in a manner that leaves all the party elements reasonably satisfied, the .... must enter the general election with his coalition broken and his strength dissipated.
(a) candidate . . . President   (b) allegiance . . . individual
(c) leadership . . . party   (d) party . . . voter
(e) transfer . . . nominee   1. ....

2. He claimed that our own State Department has adopted a policy designed to frustrate the principle of freedom of .... and communication and has erected, instead, barriers between our people and the people of each nation whose government the department ....
(a) election . . . sponsors   (b) travel . . . disapproves
(c) choice . . . approves   (d) opinion . . . denies
(e) worship . . . views   2. ....

3. The sweetly mannered young people I talked to seemed most of all gripped by a poignant loyalty to the shaky present and easy past of the white South, a loyalty .... by alien facts and ideas from beyond the tight and .... little world of Mississippi.
(a) uncorrupted . . . turbulent   (b) spoiled . . . peaceful
(c) dictated . . . snug   (d) contrived . . . comfortable
(e) envied . . . noisy   3. ....

4. Despite courageous legislation, India is still deeply divided by caste. In what is probably the world's most stratified social system, the *untouchable* and the .... person must struggle against almost insuperable odds to achieve a position of dignity and economic .... for himself and his family.
(a) wealthy . . . order   (b) undesirable . . . freedom
(c) lower-caste . . . security   (d) uneducated . . . chains
(e) younger . . . power   4. ....

5. The United States is clearly committed to a policy of development in outer space for peaceful purposes with the widest

possible dissemination of the fruits of that effort. But if ....
is to proceed under a rule of law rather than under a rule of
might, all nations must agree upon and accept .... rules of
behavior governing space activities.

(a) policy . . . the UN's   (b) development . . .
international   (c) invention . . . American
(d) research . . . European   (e) man . . . national   5. ....

6. The world of military analysis is bizarre and unsettling,
where the unthinkable is thought about, sometimes with gusto;
in which every .... must be considered a reality; and where
no thermonuclear hold is ....

(a) contingency . . . barred   (b) aspect . . . exploded
(c) angle . . . considerable   (d) dream . . . a nightmare
(e) person . . . broken   6. ....

7. Meaningful .... from the Communist countries is
.... All of their production will continue to be needed
domestically for the foreseeable future and the quality of their
industrial products is not likely to be generally acceptable in
Western markets.

(a) propaganda . . . dangerous   (b) arbitration . . .
possible   (c) production . . . certain   (d) competition . . .
unlikely   (e) material . . . possible   7. ....

8. Labor arbitration is a by-product of the peculiar characteristics of the union contract. Whereas .... agreements
are usually drawn up in the calm atmosphere of a law office,
with each provision couched with respect for the niceties of legal
language, a .... agreement is hewed out of the rough-and-
tumble of collective bargaining.

(a) ordinary . . . clever   (b) foreign . . . domestic
(c) governmental . . . illegal   (d) private . . . foreign
(e) commercial . . . labor   8. ....

9. Democratic government is a .... phenomenon in history.
In ancient Greece, where the idea and practice were both invented,
democratic governments retained their .... for only about
two hundred years.

(a) common . . . youth   (b) human . . . ideals
(c) rare . . . vigor   (d) benevolent . . . growth
(e) known . . . power   9. ....

10. Most political decisions in this country are .... decisions.
In my own state, I know of no one's being elected because he

presented a better program or was a better guy. It has always been the result of some kind of "............" vote.
(a) negative ... against (b) careless ... impulse
(c) thoughtful ... hate (d) hasty ... majority
(e) social ... regional   10. ....

11. The .... road does lead somewhere as all roads do. Incessant windings, potholes, and traffic jams make it difficult to see just where it will end, but there are signs that the Congo is at last beginning to .... its way uncertainly and painfully toward a temporary equilibrium.
(a) main ... speed (b) independence ... grope
(c) motor ... sense (d) international ... wend
(e) rocky ... understand   11. ....

12. I want to be a President who responds to a problem not by hoping that his subordinates will act, but by .... them to ....
(a) commanding ... obey (b) sending ... troubled areas
(c) pleading with ... listen (d) asking ... investigate
(e) directing ... act   12. ....

13. Our strength as well as our convictions has imposed upon this nation the role of leader in freedom's cause. No role in history could be more difficult or more important. This nation was born of revolution and raised in freedom. And we do not intend to leave a(n) .... road to ....
(a) easy ... peace (b) open ... despotism
(c) difficult ... peace (d) impossible ... the future
(e) rocky ... others   13. ....

14. The United States cannot withdraw from Europe, unless and until Europe should wish us gone. We cannot distinguish its .... from our own. We cannot .... our contributions to Western security or abdicate the responsibility of power.
(a) friends ... destroy (b) enemies ... increase
(c) losses ... ignore (d) future ... equate
(e) defenses ... diminish   14. ....

15. In the long history of the world, only a few generations have been granted the role of defending .... in its hour of maximum danger. I do not shrink from this responsibility—I welcome it. I do not believe that any of us would exchange places with any other people or any other generation. The energy, the faith, the devotion which we bring to this endeavor

will light our country and all who serve it—and the glow from
that fire can truly .... the world.
  (a) our country ... delight   (b) peace ... extinguish
  (c) freedom ... light   (d) the UN ... undermine
  (e) the world ... overcome   15. ....

16. Without free speech no search for truth is possible. Without
free speech no discovery of truth is useful. Without free speech
progress is checked and the nations no longer march forward
toward the noble life which the future holds for men. Better a
thousandfold abuse of free speech than denial of free speech.
The abuse dies in a day, but the denial .... the life of the
people and .... the hope of the race.
  (a) guarantees ... remains   (b) creates ... ends
  (c) destroys ... is   (d) slays ... entombs
  (e) builds ... enlivens   16. ....

17. The equal right of all men to use the land is as clear as
their equal right to breathe air. It is a right proclaimed by
the .... of their existence. For we cannot .... that some
men have a right to be in this world and others have no right.
  (a) fact ... suppose   (b) law ... argue
  (c) judgment ... deny   (d) essence ... prove
  (e) Constitution ... justify   17. ....

18. The inherent right in the people to reform their government I do not deny; and they have another right, and that is to
resist .... laws without .... the government.
  (a) fair ... harming   (b) unconstitutional ... overturning
  (c) unjust ... disobeying   (d) moral ... injuring
  (e) foolish ... blaming   18. ....

19. It is the close observation of .... things which is the
secret of success in business, in art, in science, and in every
pursuit of life. Human knowledge is but an accumulation of
.... facts made by successive generations of men—the little
bits of knowledge and experience carefully treasured up and
growing at length into a mighty pyramid.
  (a) intrinsic ... biological   (b) trivial ... eccentric
  (c) significant ... tremendous   (d) little ... small
  (e) successful ... winning   19. ....

20. Education is the leading of human souls to what is best,
and making what is best out of them, and these two objects are
always attainable together, and by the same means; the training

which makes men .... themselves also makes them most
.... to others.
(a) displeased with ... foolish   (b) hopeful for ...
hopeless   (c) confident in ... useless
(d) ambitious for ... significant   (e) happiest in ...
serviceable   20. ....

Time at End ....   *Minutes Elapsed* ....

Answer Key for this test is on page 364.

My Score: Number Right ....   *Number Wrong* ....

Comparing With Others

	Time	Number Correct
Elite	18 minutes	20
Superior	19–23 minutes	18–19
Average	24–26 minutes	14–17
Below Average	27–30 minutes	11–13
Weak	31–38 minutes	7–10

Section 7: Completing the Thought

Answer Key

Third Day   **Page 329**

1. (b)	4. (d)	7. (e)	10. (d)	13. (b)
2. (e)	5. (c)	8. (b)	11. (a)	14. (b)
3. (a)	6. (c)	9. (b)	12. (c)	15. (a)

Fourth Day   **Page 333**

1. (d)	4. (b)	7. (a)	10. (c)	13. (a)
2. (b)	5. (d)	8. (b)	11. (b)	14. (a)
3. (a)	6. (c)	9. (a)	12. (d)	15. (b)

Fifth Day   **Page 337**

1. (c)	4. (e)	7. (e)	10. (a)	13. (d)
2. (b)	5. (b)	8. (b)	11. (c)	14. (b)
3. (d)	6. (a)	9. (d)	12. (a)	15. (c)

Sixth Day **Page 340**

1. (c)	4. (b)	7. (b)	10. (a)	13. (c)
2. (b)	5. (d)	8. (c)	11. (b)	14. (b)
3. (a)	6. (c)	9. (d)	12. (a)	15. (d)

Seventh Day **Page 344**

1. (b)	4. (e)	7. (c)	10. (e)	13. (a)
2. (d)	5. (c)	8. (d)	11. (a)	14. (c)
3. (a)	6. (b)	9. (b)	12. (d)	15. (c)

Eighth Day **Page 348**

1. (d)	4. (a)	7. (e)	10. (d)	13. (d)
2. (b)	5. (e)	8. (c)	11. (c)	14. (b)
3. (c)	6. (b)	9. (e)	12. (a)	15. (c)

Ninth Day **Page 351**

1. (d)	4. (d)	7. (c)	10. (c)	13. (b)
2. (b)	5. (b)	8. (a)	11. (d)	14. (d)
3. (e)	6. (a)	9. (b)	12. (e)	15. (b)

Tenth Day **Page 355**

1. (b)	4. (e)	7. (a)	10. (b)	13. (b)
2. (d)	5. (e)	8. (b)	11. (a)	14. (c)
3. (a)	6. (d)	9. (e)	12. (e)	15. (a)

Eleventh Day **Page 359**

1. (e)	5. (b)	9. (c)	13. (b)	17. (a)
2. (b)	6. (a)	10. (a)	14. (e)	18. (b)
3. (a)	7. (d)	11. (b)	15. (c)	19. (d)
4. (c)	8. (e)	12. (e)	16. (d)	20. (e)

CURRENT AMERICAN USAGE

Section 8: GUIDE TO AMERICAN USAGE

Usage and the College Tests

The Scholastic Aptitude Test, the morning examination given by the College Entrance Examination Board, is the one that most colleges require. The test covers two areas, Verbal and Mathematics. The Verbal section includes antonyms, sentence completion, reading comprehension, and analogies. It does *not* include questions on usage. Usage is tested directly only in certain portions of the afternoon Achievement Test on Composition and English; not many students are required to take this test.

The American College Test, on the other hand, includes an English Usage Test as the first part of the examination. A connected passage containing errors and inappropriate expressions is presented. Then the passage is reprinted in spread-out form with various words and phrases—possible error situations—set off and numbered. The candidate is asked to select from three suggested alternatives the correct or most appropriate word or phrase to replace the marked items.

The first test on the National Merit Examination also deals with English usage. The format is the same as that for the ACT. The New York State Scholarship Examination also contains questions on usage with alternative choices, but without the connected prose passage.

As you can see, a precaution is necessary. Before you begin to do the day-by-day tasks that follow, make certain that you are going to take the test in which knowledge of usage is evaluated!

For Maximum Results

1. Become familiar with the format of the question on usage in

the test that you have to take. The practice material that follows is in the forms found on usage sections of the nationwide tests. The manuals, such as those distributed by the College Entrance Examination Boards and the American College Testing Program, contain sample questions.

2. Plan for 100% mastery of the material that is found in each day's work in this Section. Use the initial tests to discover the items that require study. Concentrate on the Analysis of these items. Then take the Practice Tests that follow to evaluate your progress.

3. Take over those tests that you found difficult. The repetition will lead you to complete mastery.

4. Follow the directions carefully. If you are told to read a complete paragraph, do not look for short cuts. Save time, not by cutting corners, but through concentration and complete understanding of the task ahead.

5. When in doubt, rely upon your past training. Do not choose an alternative because it is different from what you normally say or write!

6. Look for obvious errors first. Only as a last resort decide on the over-refined as being the source of error.

7. Do not spend much time on items you already know. Use your study time to increase your area of control.

8. Daily, spaced practice is much more productive than would be one or two cram sessions.

First Day

The word *error* has a highly specialized meaning when used to describe language techniques. Since the only purpose of language is to communicate ideas, a basic error should be one that would interfere with the listener's comprehension of the intent of the speaker. However, in the language arts the word *error* is most often used to refer to specific forms of expression. Sometimes there is a logical reason for the rejection of a word or phrase. At other times, the only explanation is that "custom has so ruled!" How then can you "know" what the examiners will mark as correct? The analyses that follow each Inventory Test in this Section will give you much of the necessary mastery.

First Inventory Test

Each of the following sentences contains an italicized expression. Below each sentence are four suggested answers. Decide which answer is correct and place its number in the space provided.

1. *Flinging himself at the barricade he* pounded on it furiously.
(a) Correct as is (b) Flinging himself at the barricade, he
(c) Flinging himself at the barricade—he (d) Flinging himself at the barricade; he

1. ..... b

2. When he *begun to give us advise*, we stopped listening.
(a) Correct as is (b) began to give us advise (c) begun to give us advice (d) began to give us advice

2. ..... b✗d

3. John was the only one of the boys *whom as you know was* not eligible.
(a) Correct as is (b) who as you know were (c) whom as you know were (d) who as you know was

3. ..... b✗d

4. Why *was Jane and he* permitted to go?
(a) Correct as is (b) was Jane and him (c) were Jane and he (d) were Jane and him

4. ..... d✗c

5. *Take courage Tom: we* all make mistakes.
(a) Correct as is (b) Take courage Tom—we (c) Take courage, Tom; we (d) Take courage, Tom we

5. ..... b✗

6. How much *has food costs raised* during the past year?
(a) Correct as is (b) have food costs rose (c) have food costs risen (d) has food costs risen

6. c

7. "Will you come *too*" she pleaded?
(a) Correct as is (b) too,?" she pleaded. (c) too?" she pleaded. (d) too," she pleaded?

7. ..... b✗

8. If he *would have drank* more milk, his health would have been better.
(a) Correct as is (b) would drink (c) had drank
(d) had drunk

8. ..... c✗

9. Jack had *no sooner laid down and fallen asleep when* the alarm sounded.
(a) Correct as is (b) no sooner lain down and fallen asleep than (c) no sooner lay down and fell asleep when
(d) no sooner laid down and fell asleep than

9. ..... d✗

10. Jackson is *one of the few Sophomores, who has* ever made the varsity team.

(a) Correct as is   (b) one of the few Sophomores, who have
(c) one of the few sophomores, who has   (d) one of
the few sophomores who have   10. ....b......

Answer Key and Analysis

1. (b)

Flinging himself at the barricade is an introductory participle
phrase.   Introductory phrases are separated from the rest of
the sentence by a comma, not by a dash (c) or a semicolon (d).

2. (d)

The past participle *begun* must be preceded by a helping
verb such as *have, has,* or *had;* therefore, (a) and (c) are incorrect.   The past tense *began* must be used without an auxiliary
or helping verb, thus leaving (b) or (d) as correct.   The noun
form is *advice;* the verb form is *advise.*   Since *give* is followed
by a noun, the verb form *advise* makes (b) wrong.

3. (d)

Who is used as subject; *whom* is the object form.   In deciding
whether to use *who* or *whom,* you must disregard thrown-in expressions such as *as you know, I suspect, I believe.*   With *as you
know* out of the way, the clause becomes (*who-whom*) *was not
eligible.*   Substitute *he* for *who* and *him* for *whom.*   Since *he was
not eligible* is correct, *who* is your appropriate choice, eliminating
(a) and (c).

When *one* is involved, *was* is correct.   When more than one is
concerned, then *were* is correct.   In this clause how many were
not eligible?   The answer is only John; thus *was* is correct,
eliminating (b) as an appropriate choice.

4. (c)

The subject form is *he;* the object form is *him.*   When given a
compound subject (*Jane and he-him*), the correct form can be discovered by eliminating the other subject (*Jane and*).   We
would not say *him was permitted to go!*   Thus (b) and (d) are
wrong choices.

A plural subject requires *were;* a singular subject is followed
by *was.*   The subject in this sentence is *Jane and he,* a plural
subject.   Therefore (a) is incorrect.

5. (c)

Two complete ideas can be treated in four basic ways:

(1) they may be separated into two independent sentences; (2) they can be joined together with a comma and a conjunction; (3) one of the ideas may be subordinated to the other; and (4) if the ideas are close to each other a semicolon may be used in place of a comma and conjunction. The writer may not use a comma alone or just a mechanical running together of the two sentences.

Item 5 contains two complete ideas. (a) is wrong because a colon may not join two complete ideas. (b) is wrong because a dash may not be used to separate two complete ideas. (d) is wrong because a comma may not be used to join two ideas.

6. (c)

The form *have* is used for plural forms while *has* is used for third-person singular forms used as subjects of the verb. The subject is *costs* (not *food*), and therefore (a) and (d) are eliminated. The verb *raise* takes an object (I *raised* my hand). The verb *rise* describes a state and does not take an object (the cake has risen). Since *costs* did not raise anything and a condition is being described, *risen* is correct, rather than *raised*. The form *rose* cannot be used with a helping verb as in choice (b). Therefore (c) is the correct answer.

7. (c)

In a direct quotation, the question mark follows the question. Therefore (a) and (d) are wrong since *she pleaded* is not in question form. When a quotation in quotation marks is in question form, it is followed by the question mark which takes the place of any other mark of punctuation usually found in that place. A question mark and a comma are wrong (b). The correct form is (c).

8. (d)

The form *drank* is the past tense and may not be used with a helper. The past participle *drunk* requires a helping verb. All of the choices include a helper; therefore (a) and (c) are wrong.

After *if* in a clause that states a condition contrary to fact, the subjunctive is used. The sign of the subjunctive is *had*. The conditional *would* is the wrong helper. Therefore (a) is wrong. *If he would drink milk* is present. The rest of the sentence, *his health would have been better*, is all in the past. Thus (b) is wrong because the tenses contradict each other and form a meaningless pattern.

9. (b)

It is a rare examination that does not include the *lie-lay* confusion. Memorize: lie(rest, recline)—lying—lay—has, have lain; lay (put, place)—laying—laid—has, have laid.

In the given sentence Jack was resting, and therefore some form of *lie* is needed. Since *had* is present, *lain* is called for. Thus (a) and (d) are incorrect.

The past tense forms are *lay* and *fell*. A helping verb may not be used with either of these. The past participle forms are *lain* and *fallen*. Since the sentence contains *had*, the past participle forms must be used. Therefore (c) is wrong.

10. (d)

The word *sophomores* describes a general class and therefore is not to be capitalized ordinarily. Thus (a) and (b) are wrong.

If we exclude the clause *who (has-have) ever made the varsity team*, the rest of the sentence loses meaning. Therefore the *who*-clause is restrictive and no comma may be used to separate it from the rest of the sentence. Once again (a) and (b) are wrong! And so is alternative (c).

A plural subject calls for *have;* a singular subject calls for *has*. Which is correct in this case? The rule states that the verb following *who* is governed by the nearest noun that *who* may refer to. In this case the noun is *sophomores*, a plural form, and *who* could modify it according to the meaning of the sentence. Therefore *have* is correct. Choice (d) is doubly correct because of *sophomores* and because of *have*.

My Score: *Number Right* ....   *Number Wrong* ....

Second Day

There are many levels of appropriate speech and language patterns. Some linguists have labeled these levels as *substandard*, *slang*, *colloquial*, *standard written*, and *formal*. An expression that is appropriate on one level may be completely wrong for another. The college president does not address his children in the quiet of his home with the same language patterns that he uses when he delivers his annual message to the Board of Trustees. What level is expected of you? Since you are being tested for college-level competency, the level of language you must have mastery of is the standard written or formal. You must be able to distinguish between these levels and the colloquial and slang. The Inventory Tests in this Section will help you to gain this control.

Second Inventory Test

Each of the following sentences contains an italicized expression. Below each sentence are four suggested answers. Decide which answer is correct and place its number in the space provided to the right.

1. The general, *with all his soldiers*, *was* captured.
(a) Correct as is (b) , with all his soldier's were (c) , with all his soldiers; was (d) with all his soldiers, was 1...........

2. He is the *boy who's* poster was chosen for the contest.
(a) Correct as is (b) boy, whose (c) boy whose
(d) boy, who's 2. ....

3. Humbled by the loss of prestige, *his plans changed*.
(a) Correct as is (b) a change in his plans occurred.
(c) his plans were changed. (d) he changed his plans. 3. ....

4. We were not surprised at *him losing* his way.
(a) Correct as is (b) his losing (c) him for loosing
(d) his loosing 4. ....

5. The prize money is to be divided *among you and I*.
(a) Correct as is (b) among you and me
(c) between you and me (d) between you and I 5. ....

6. Henderson, the president of the class and *who is also captain of the team*, will lead the rally.
(a) Correct as is (b) since he is captain of the team
(c) captain of the team (d) also being captain of the team 6. ....

7. Our car has always *run good* on that kind of gasoline.
(a) Correct as is (b) run well (c) ran good
(d) ran well 7. ....

8. There was a serious difference of opinion *among her and I*.
(a) Correct as is (b) among she and I
(c) between her and I (d) between her and me 8. ....

9. "This is most unusual," said *Helen*, "*the* mailman has never been this late before."
(a) Correct as is (b) Helen, "The (c) Helen. " The
(d) Helen; "The 9. ....

372 The Handbook of College Entrance Examinations

10. The three main characters in the story are Johnny Hobart, a *teenager, his mother a widow, and* the local druggist.

   (a) Correct as is (b) teenager; his mother, a widow; and
(c) teenager; his mother a widow; and
(d) teenager, his mother, a widow and   10. ....

Answer Key and Analysis

1. (a)

The plural of nouns is usually formed by the addition of *s* or *es*. The apostrophe form shows possession. Since the *soldiers* called for in this sentence is the plural form, (b) is wrong.

The subject of the sentence is *general*. The word *general* is modified by the prepositional phrase *with all his soldiers*. The verb *was-were* must agree with the subject. Since the subject is *general* (and not general *and* his soldiers), the singular *was* is correct. Choice (b) is again eliminated.

The phrase *with all his soldiers* separates the subject *general* from the verb *was captured*. To show that it is a nonrestrictive phrase (one that can be omitted without the main thought of the sentence being changed), twin commas may be used. One comma before or after the phrase would not signal the purpose of the phrase, and thus (d) would be wrong. A comma is not paired with a semicolon, and thus (c) is wrong.

2. (c)

A favorite examination trap for the unwary is the *whose-who's* confusion. Memorize: *who's* always stands for *who is; whose* always shows possession. The sentence becomes meaningless if we substitute *who is* for *who's;* therefore, (a) and (d) are eliminated.

Should a comma separate the clause introduced by *who* from the rest of the sentence? Use the test of restrictive-nonrestrictive. If the clause may be omitted without the impairment of the meaning of the sentence, then the clause is nonrestrictive and a comma may be used. If the sentence loses almost complete meaning, then the clause is restrictive and no comma may be used. In this instance, if we omit the clause, the remainder of the sentence is *He is the boy*, a group of words that needs the clause in order to become meaningful. Therefore, no comma is needed. Choice (b) is wrong; (c) is correct.

3. (d)

Most students learn quickly to identify a dangling present

participle. We see the humor and thus catch the error in sentences similar to: *Talking aloud to himself, the wall reverberated with his anger.* We know that the participle must have in the sentence a noun or pronoun which it modifies. The wall, in the example, could not talk aloud.

You must be equally sensitive to the past participle when it is used adjectivally as in this sentence. The past participle *humbled* cannot modify *plans!* Therefore (a), (b), and (c) are wrong. In (d) the pronoun *he* is introduced as the logical word for *humbled* to modify.

4. (b)

This item contains an old favorite of examination makers: *lose-loose.* When something is untied, it is *loose;* defeat requires *lose.* Since nothing is being untied in this sentence, (a), (c), and (d) are eliminated, leaving (b) in sole sway!

The *him-his* before an -ing noun was merely a decoy. Why is *his* correct? We were not surprised at *him* but at *his losing!*

5. (c)

Among refers to more than two. *Between* is used for two or a choice between two. Therefore (a) and (b) are eliminated.

Despite the colloquial acceptance of *between you and I*, there is only one "correct" formal form, *between you and me.* Memorize the correct answer, and you will have gained your mental sustenance for this day! Why is *me* correct? *Between* is a preposition and the object of a preposition must be in the objective case. *I* is the subject form while *me* is the object form. Therefore *me* is correct in *between you and me!*

6. (c)

Parallel ideas should be in similar form in a sentence. *Henderson* is modified and explained by *the president of the class* and *who is also captain of the team.* As they are, the former is an appositive and the latter is a relative clause. They both should be either appositives or relative clauses. Therefore (c), which converts the latter into an appositive, is correct.

7. (b)

The past is *ran*, which may not be used with a helping verb. The past participle is *run*, which must be preceded by a helping verb in order to be the main verb of the sentence. Since *has* is present, (c) and (d) are eliminated.

Well has two distinct uses when in contrast to *good.* *Well*

374 The Handbook of College Entrance Examinations

describes *how* in terms of the action in the verb. *Well* also refers to health as opposed to *ill*. *Good* modifies a noun or pronoun (the *good* man); *good* may be used after a verb, but always to describe the noun or pronoun (This *apple* certainly *tastes* good!). In the test sentence, how the machine *runs* is being described, not the machine itself; therefore, *well* is correct and (a) is incorrect.

8. (d)
Among refers to more than two; *between* refers to two. Since only two are involved, (b) and (a) are eliminated.
Between is a preposition. The pronouns that follow *between* must be in the object case. *I-she* are subjects; *me-her* are objects. Therefore (c) is incorrect.

9. (c)
The quotation consists of two complete ideas: (1) *This is most unusual*, and (2) *The mailman has never been this late before.* Two ideas may not be separated by a comma as in (a) and (b). If *said Helen* had not been included, the semicolon could have been correct (d), but since the semicolon in this case would have clouded the meaning of *said Helen*, giving it equal status with the rest of the sentence, only the period and capital letter may be used (c).

10. (b)
As the sentence stands we cannot really tell whether three or five people are involved. When a sentence contains internal commas for a series, then semicolons must be used to separate the elements of the series. Confusing commas are in (a) and (d). There is a failure to use a comma to separate a noun and its appositive in (c).

My Score: *Number Right* ....   *Number Wrong* ....

Third Day

The material in the exercises usually approximates the tone and content of a high school senior's theme. Your judgment concerning the correctness or appropriateness of the underlined portions must be based on your understanding of the meaning in the selection and your knowledge of formal usage. You must, therefore, train yourself to read the exercise completely before deciding on your answer, and you must rely upon the training that your teachers have given you in recitation classes and in your directed readings.

The Inventory Test in this day's work is based on a variation in the examination type question.

Third Inventory Test

The paragraph below has ten underlined parts. Some of these are incorrect in grammar, punctuation, or usage. For each incorrect part, write your correction in the space at the right. For each correct part, place a C in the space.

Radio and television programs, along with other
media of communication, <u>helps</u> us to
            ₁
appreciate the arts and to keep informed. Music,
for example, <u>most</u> always has listening
           ₂
and viewing audiences numbering in the hundreds of
thousands. When operas are performed on radio or
television, <u>they</u> <u>effect</u> the listener
      ₃   ₄
in that after hearing them <u>he wants</u>
                  ₅
to buy recordings of the music. To <u>we</u> Americans
                       ₆
the daily news program has become important
because of <u>it's</u> coverage
           ₇
of a <u>days'</u> events. <u>In</u> schools,
     ₈
teachers <u>advice</u> their students to listen to or
         ₉
to view certain programs. In these ways we are
<u>preceding</u> toward the goal of an educated and an
  ₁₀
informed public.

1. ....
2. ....
3. ....
4. ....
5. ....
6. ....
7. ....
8. ....
9. ....
10. ....

Answer Key and Analysis

1. **help**
   The word *communication* is the object of the preposition of

and cannot be the subject word. The subject is *programs*, a plural word, and therefore *help* is correct.

2. almost
Most may be used as an adjective, as in *most men*. It cannot be used as a contraction of *almost*.

3. C
The comma is required because the sentence is introduced by an adverbial clause, *When operas are performed on radio or television.*

4. affect
In deciding between *effect* and *affect*, remember that *effect* is the noun (*the effect of*) while *affect* is the verb, as in the given sentence.

5. C
Since *he wants* refers to the *listener*, a singular form, *he*, not *they*, is called for.

6. us
This is another favorite of examination makers. To decide whether to use *we* or *us* before a noun (in apposition), block out the noun. We require an object of the preposition *To*. We would not say *To we;* but *To us* sounds correct and is correct!

7. its
If you missed this one, then you should memorize that *it's* is a contraction of *it is* while *its* shows possession. In the paragraph, *it is* coverage would not make sense.

8. day's
The phrase means *events of a day*. Since the base word *day* ends in *y*, the apostrophe form is *day's*.

9. advise
The noun form is *advice* while the verb form is *advise*. The key sentence calls for the verb form.

10. proceeding
That which *precedes*, goes before; that which *proceeds* occurs. The sense of the sentence calls for the latter form.

My Score: *Number Right* ....   *Number Wrong* ....

Fourth Day

By this time you should have evolved a working technique for handling usage questions on examinations. It is best not to approach the question positively when choices are given. Instead of looking for the correct answer, begin by eliminating the choices that you know are definitely wrong. In most instances you will soon discover that all that is left is the correct answer! By using this method, you automatically avoid hasty decisions. By using this method, if you have to guess, you increase your chances for guessing correctly by lowering the number of items to choose from. By using this method, you should achieve maximum results on the Inventory Test that follows.

Inventory Test Four

Below the selection are four suggested alternatives for each underlined part. In the space provided write the letter of the expression you consider best.

Howard was requested to leave, <u>however,</u> he insisted on staying
$\qquad$ 1

as long as he wished.

<u>Being that</u> we did not wish to create a disturbance, we <u>confers</u>
2 3

with the others and conceded to his demands.

We knew that we were offering him <u>sort of a bribe</u> to prevent
4

anything that would interfere with the success of the meeting.

<u>We were all upset, which</u> was what he had hoped would happen.
5

The thing that saved the <u>morn</u> for us was that we did not rush in-
6

to a hasty course of action. We called an emergency <u>get together</u>
7

of the program committee. The situation was explained, and

each one was allowed to express <u>their opinions</u> freely.
8

When the flurry of words <u>ended.</u> It was evident that the cool
9

heads had prevailed. We even admitted to the possibility <u>of</u>

<u>Howard being within his rights</u> when he refused to leave!
10

   1. (a) No change (b), however; (c). However;
(d); however,   1. ....

   2. (a) No change (b) Being (c) Since
(d); On account of   2. ....

   3. (a) No change (b) conferred (c) colluded
(d) would have conferred   3. ....

   4. (a) No change (b) a kind of a bribe
(c) the equivalent of a bribe (d) a sort of a bribe   4. ....

   5. (a) No change (b) We were all upset; this,
(c) Our being upset (d) We were all upset. Which   5. ....

   6. (a) No change (b) morning (c) A.M.
(d) situation on hand   6. ....

   7. (a) No change (b) get-together (c) convocation
(d) meeting   7. ....

   8. (a) No change (b) their opinion (c) themselves
(d) his opinions   8. ....

   9. (a) No change (b) ended, and it (c) ended, it
(d) ended; it   9. ....

   10. (a) No change (b) that Howard was right
(c) of Howard's being right (d) of Howard's being
within his rights   10. ....

Answer Key and Analysis

  1. (d)

However, moreover, thus, hence, and *therefore* are not conjunctions; they are conjunctive adverbs. They may not be used, therefore, to join two ideas. When placed between two ideas, a conjunctive adverb may be preceded by a semicolon and followed by a comma or preceded by a period and be capitalized. The only acceptable method of punctuation is (d).

  2. (c)

Being or *Being that* may not be used as a substitute for

Since or *Because.* **On account of** does not fit into this sentence.

3. (b)

The tense used in the passage is the past; therefore, (a) *confers* is incorrect since *confers* is the present tense, and there is no reason for a change in tense. (c) *colluded* implies conspiracy, which is not present in the context. (d) *would have conferred* changes the meaning of the sentence.

4. (c)

Kind of *a* and *sort* of *a* may not be used to mean *somewhat.* (Without the *a, this kind of* and *this sort of* are acceptable when used appropriately.) (c), which avoids the problem, is the only acceptable form.

5. (c)

The pronoun *which* must refer to a specific word in the sentence. *Which* may not be used to refer to an entire idea, as in this sentence in which *We were all upset* is the antecedent of *which.* Therefore (a) is eliminated. *This,* too, cannot refer to an entire group of words; thus (b) is wrong. (d) is wrong because it contains a sentence fragment, *Which is what he had hoped,* in addition to a misused *which.*

6. (b)

Morn is a poetic word and is inappropriate in the context. *A.M.,* when used alone, as in this case, is on the slang level. *Situation on hand* is an elegant or business term that is inappropriate in this context.

7. (d)

Get-together or *get together* would be too informal; *convocation* is much too formal.

8. (d)

Each one is singular. The pronoun referring back to *each one* must be singular. *Their* is plural; *his* is singular. *Themselves* is plural and cannot refer to *each one.*

9. (c)

An introductory adverb clause, *When the flurry of words ended,* must be followed by a comma. If it is followed by a period, the clause becomes a sentence fragment as in (a). (b) contains *and,* which converts the entire sentence into a sentence fragment!

10. (d)

What was admitted was not Howard but Howard's *being within his rights.* (c) is wrong because it changes the meaning of the sentence.

My Score: *Number Right* ....   *Number Wrong* ....

Fifth Day

Those who do best on the Usage Question use a three-pronged approach. They begin by looking for an obvious error in usage. If none of this variety is present, they then examine the possibility of an error in punctuation. Only after they have exhausted these two possibilities do they then check for words or phrases that are on an unacceptable level of usage in relation to the rest of the passage. The first group of obvious errors includes misspellings and mixed-up homonyms. The last group included wordiness, cases in which four words were used in place of one.

Practice using this approach on the Inventory Test that follows.

Fifth Inventory Test

There are four suggested alternatives for each underlined part. In the space provided, write the letter of the expression that you consider best.

I truthfully can say that I do not feel badly about what had
<u>   </u>
                                           1
happened. It was all so <u>different than</u> I had expected! My
                          2
friends all agreed that mine had been <u>a healthy</u> reaction to a
                                        3
situation that could have been most trying.

Under normal circumstances we all enjoy listening to gossip,
trying to separate truth from fancy, and <u>to evaluate</u> the worth in
                                           4
the data given. However what they had been saying was more
falsified than <u>anything</u> I had ever heard! Neither of the men
                5
being maligned <u>was</u> present in the room at the time the story was
                6
told. My reaction <u>I suppose,</u> could have been called instinctive.
                    7
At first I could not imagine <u>whom</u> they were talking about.
                               8
"You ought to be ashamed of <u>yourselves"</u> I blurted out just as I
                               9
began to realize how distorted their comments were. Everyone

in the room seemed to be staring at <u>me</u> and there was complete
10
silence for what seemed like an eternity!

  1. (a) No change (b) feel ill (c) feel bad (d) feel illy
1. ....

  2. (a) No change (b) differently than
(c) different than what (d) different from what   2. ....

  3. (a) No change (b) an healthy (c) a healthful
(d) a wholesome   3. ....

  4. (a) No change (b) evaluating (c) to discuss
(d) to discard   4. ....

  5. (a) No change (b) anything that
(c) anything else that (d) all that   5. ....

  6. (a) No change (b) were (c) is (d) are   6. ....

  7. No change (b) —I suppose, (c) , I suppose
(d) , I suppose,   7. ....

  8. No change (b) who (c) , whom (d) , who   8. ....

  9. (a) No change (b) yourselves", (c) yourselves!"
(d) yourselves!",   9. ....

  10. (a) No change (b) me: and (c) me, and
(d) me. And   10. ....

Answer Key and Analysis

  1. (c)
  We *feel ill* when we are sick. We cannot *feel illy* or *badly* when we refer to health or an inner reaction. When we are having an emotional reaction, we *feel bad*.

  2. (d)
  The correct idiom on the most formal level is *different from*.

  3. (d)
  A person is *healthy*. Something that produces health (like a diet) is *healthful*. *Wholesome* implies behavior that is sound.

4. (b)

Since *listening* and *trying* are in a construction similar to the one under question, *evaluate* should be in the *-ing* form too.

5. (c)

That which was false was not worse than anything that I had heard. Since I had heard it, it could not be worse than itself. Logically, *else* had to be added.

6. (a)

The story is in the past tense, and thus (c) and (d) are wrong since they are in the present. Since *neither* is singular when it refers to singular nouns, *was* is correct.

7. (d)

A parenthetical expression like *I suppose* is set off by twin commas.

8. (a)

By substituting *he-him*, we discover that "they were talking about *him*." Therefore *whom* is correct—as object of the preposition *about*.

9. (c)

The exclamation mark is included before the quotation marks and takes the place of the comma that is usually placed after the quotation marks.

10. (c)

The two elements of a compound sentence joined by *and* are usually separated by a comma before the *and*.

My Score: Number Right ....   *Number Wrong* ....

Practice Tests in Usage

Test Number 1

Below the selection are four suggested alternatives to each underlined part. In the space provided, write the letter of the expression you consider best.

We—my relatives together with me—had just received the
1
invitation that was to change our lives so completely. We

<u>Estermans</u> are a proud people not accustomed to surprises that
 2
could possibly embarrass. Everyone except <u>my grandparents</u>
                                               3
<u>and I</u> was prepared to ignore the note that we had received.

Now that the time of tension is <u>at its finish</u>, we can look back
                                     4
and realize how upset we had been. We had spent endless

hours <u>in the discussing of</u> what we should do as a group.
        5
Our inability to reach a unanimous decision <u>come to</u> us as a
                                  6   7
shock. Finally, it was my Uncle Bert <u>who</u> I respect greatly who
                                          8
ended the impasse. "Everyone should send <u>their</u> own reply to
                                              9
the invitation," he stated simply, <u>"we</u> must learn to act inde-
                                       10
pendently when our points of view diverge."

1. (a) No change (b) My relatives and me
(c) We—my relatives and I— (d) I and my relatives   1. ....

2. (a) No change (b) Us Estermans (c) The Ester-
mans (d) Our Estermans   2. ....

3. (a) No change (b) my grandparents' and me
(c) my grandparent's and I
(d) my grandparents and me   3. ....

4. (a) No change (b) a thing of the forgotten past
(c) over (d) complete   4. ....

5. (a) No change (b) discussing (c) in the discussion
of (d) involved with   5. ....

6. (a) No change (b) omit <u>a</u> (c) an (d) the   6. ....

7. (a) No change (b) was coming (c) had come
(d) came   7. ....

8. (a) No change (b) which (c) whom (d) he who 8. ....

9. (a) No change (b) his or her (c) there (d) his   9. ....

10 (a) No change (b) . "We (c) ; "We (d) "we   10. ....

Answer Key and Analysis are on page 389

Test Number 2

Below the selection are four suggested alternatives to each underlined part. In the space provided, write the letter of the expression you consider best.

The architect <u>not only was</u> willing but eager to show us the
            1

plans that had directed the growth of this unusual building.

<u>Being</u> one of the first commissions that he had ever had, he was
2

most defensive.

"It is I who <u>am</u> at fault," he stated simply, <u>"And</u> not the men
              3   4

who assisted me, if there are any serious flaws in the design."

"The essential factor in considering these plans <u>are</u> objectivity,"
                                       5

I replied.

"<u>During the time of</u> our conferences," he added, "I would
          6

brook no compromises. None of their comments <u>effected</u> my
                                      7

determination to make this building a reflection of me."

<u>In view of the fact that</u> he seemed so determined and <u>was so</u>
             8

<u>proud</u>, we offered only praise. As we left, we wondered whether
9

he had gained the respect of the people with whom he <u>had worked</u>
                                                10

<u>with</u>.

1. (a) No change (b) was not only (c) not only is
(d) not only has been   1. ....

2. (a) No change   (b) Being that it was
(c) Because it was   (d) Because that it was   2. ....

3. (a) No change   (b) has been   (c) is
(d) had been   3. ....

4. (a) No change   (b) . "And   (c) , "and
(d) ; "And   4. ....

5. (a) No change   (b) is   (c) may have been
(d) will be   5. ....

6. (a) No change   (b) On the occasion of
(c) Following   (d) During   6. ....

7. (a) No change   (b) effects   (c) affected
(d) would have effected   7. ....

8. (a) No change   (b) Due to the fact that
(c) For the reason that   (d) Because   8. ....

9. (a) No change   (b) was so officious   (c) proud
(d) a person of great pride   9. ....

10. (a) No change   (b) was working with
(c) had worked   (d) work with   10. ....

Answer Key and Analysis are on page 390

Test Number 3

Below the selection are four suggested alternatives to each
underlined part. In the space provided, write the letter of the
expression you consider best.

My principle objection to them claiming control of the votes in
    1   2

this district is pretty obvious. When they offer you money to
            3

pay the rent, to settle a debt, or for a trip, they are buying more
                          4

than your vote for the candidate of their choice.
 5

Lets not try to fool anyone, not even ourselves!
 6

They can exist in strength and power only because there are

people <u>like us</u> <u>who</u> find nothing wrong with their digging into the
      7   8

public coffers to line their own pockets!

Whenever anyone wishes to buy a commodity, <u>they have</u> to
                                       9

pay a definite <u>price, however</u> when a person sells his vote, he is
                     10

selling himself into slavery!

1. (a) No change   (b) principal   (c) sole
(d) singular   1. ....

2. (a) No change   (b) they're   (c) there   (d) their   2. ....

3. (a) No change   (b) sure   (c) (omit *pretty*)
(d) definitely   3. ....

4. (a) No change   (b) paying for a trip
(c) to pay for a trip   (d) for the joy of a trip   4. ....

5. (a) No change   (b) than just   (c) then only
(d) then just   5. ....

6. (a) No change   (b) Lets us   (c) Lets'   (d) Let's 6. ....

7. (a) No change   (b) like we   (c) as we   (d) as us 7. ....

8. (a) No change   (b) , who   (c) , which
(d) whom   8. ....

9. (a) No change   (b) you have   (c) one must
(d) he has   9. ....

10. (a) No change   (b) ; However,   (c) . However
(d) , however,   10. ....

Answer Key and Analysis are on page 391

Test Number 4

Below the selection are four suggested alternatives to each
underlined part. In the space provided, write the letter of the
expression you consider best.

I plan to <u>gather together</u> all of the letters that he had written to
         1

his former students. I am especially <u>anxious</u> to have those that
                             2

he had sent to his eager readers. <u>Describing</u> the sights and
3
sounds that enthralled him during his trips through Europe.

This <u>later</u> material about the wonders to be found in foreign
4
countries <u>were</u> so exciting to the receivers that <u>us New Yorkers</u>
5   6
had spent endless hours reading and rereading his glowing
descriptions.

<u>The parties who were the recipients of</u> his notes on foreign
7
travel had all attended Lafayette High School. <u>A public institu-</u>
8
tion in the area called Bensonhurst.

He brought them <u>in</u> contact with so many foreign places.
9
<u>Liege,</u> Grachen, Gris, Altmaar—were just a few!
10

1. (a) No change (b) amass together (c) gather
d) collect together   1. ....

2. (a) No change (b) enthusiastic (c) eager
(d) desirous   2. ....

3. (a) No change (b) describing (c) descriptive of
(d) , describing   3. ....

4. (a) No change (b) These later (c) These latter
(d) This latter   4. ....

5. (a) No change (b) was (c) could have been
(d) had been   5. ....

6. (a) No change (b) New Yorkers (c) We New
Yorkers (d) we New Yorkers   6. ....

7. (a) No change (b) The citizens who had gotten
(c) The fortuitous recipients of
(d) Those who received   7. ....

8. (a) No change (b) , a (c) ; a (d) : a   8. ....

9. (a) No change (b) (omit *in*) (c) into (d) into a 9. ....

10. (a) No change   (b) , Liege,   (c) ; Liege,
(d) : Liege   10. ....

Answer Key and Analysis are on page 392

Test Number 5

Below the selection are four suggested alternatives to each underlined part. In the space provided, write the letter of the expression you consider best.

Athletes <u>who have had no instruction</u> develop many super-

1
fluous movements. <u>Which</u> hamper their progress toward

2
maximum results from maximum efforts. The bad habits of a

<u>self taught</u> athlete are very hard to eradicate. <u>If they ever can</u>

3   4
<u>be gotten rid of.</u>

5

<u>It says in an article that I had read</u> <u>somewheres</u> that the least

6   7
expense is that of hiring a professional to give a beginner the

correct form and approach.

What the author had to say was so interesting that I could not

<u>lay</u> the magazine down until I had completed the entire selection.

8
<u>This kind of an</u> article can make a reader of even the most

9
reluctant.

No one knows better <u>than me</u> how costly the lack of training

10
can be to an athlete!

1. (a) No change   (b) —who have had no instruction   (c) ,
who have had no instruction,   (d) —who had had no
instruction,   1. ....

2. (a) No change   (b) , which   (c) ; which
(d) which   2. ....

3. (a) No change   (b) selftaught   (c) self-taught
(d) self taut   3. ....

4. (a) No change   (b) : if   (c) ; if   (d) —if   4. ....

5. (a) No change   (b) eliminated   (c) gotten rid
(d) overturned   -   5. ....

6. (a) No change   (b) I had read   (c) They state in
an article that I had read (d) An article that I read says 6. ....

7. (a) No change   (b) somehow   (c) somewhere
(d) anyhow   7. ....

8. (a) No change   (b) sit   (c) lie   (d) lain   8. ....

9. (a) No change   (b) These kind of   (c) This kind
of a   (d) This kind of   9. ....

10. (a) No change   (b) then me   (c) than I
(d) then I   10. ....

Answer Key and Analysis are on page 394

Practice Tests in Usage

Answer Keys and Analyses

Test Number 1:   Page 382

1. (c)
We is the subject.   *My relatives and I* is an appositive which must be in the subject case, the same case as we.

2. (a)
This is another example of an appositive to be found on many examinations.   To test whether *we* or *us* is appropriate, omit the noun in apposition (*Estermans*).   We would not say, "*Us are a proud people!*"   We is the subject of *are*.

3. (d)
There is no possession shown by *grandparents;* therefore the apostrophe form is uncalled for [(b) and (c)] .   After the preposition *except* we need the objective form (except *me*).

4. (c)
(b) is too wordy.   (d) changes the meaning of the sentence. (c) states in fewer words and with the same tonal values what is said in (a).   (c) is, therefore, more appropriate.

5. (b)
(a) is wordy. (b) states what is said in (a) but in fewer words. (c) is just as wordy as (a) and much more formal. (d) changes the meaning of the sentence.

6. (a)
We use *a* rather than *an* before a word that begins with the *you*-sound.

7. (d)
The past tense form is *came*, not *come*. Since the event was completed, the progressive *was coming* is inappropriate. Since the event occurred within the time of the narrative, the past perfect *had come* is inappropriate.

8. (c)
Substituting *he-him*, we find that the expression is *I respect him greatly*; therefore, *whom* is necessary. *Which* is inappropriate since *which* cannot refer to people when used as a pronoun. (d) is wrong because *he* is not necessary.

9. (d)
Another contact with an examination favorite! *Everyone* is followed by *his*.

10. (b)
Each sentence in a quotation must be preceded by a period and must begin with a capital letter!

My Score: *Number Right* ....   *Number Wrong* ....

Superior Results	9-10 *Correct*
Average Results	7-8 *Correct*
Poor Results	*Below* 6 *Correct*

Test Number 2:   Page 384

1. (b)
Since *not only ... but also* balance *willing* and *eager*, the conjunctions must precede the words that they modify.

2. (b)
Being and *being that* may not be used in place of *because*. (d) is wrong because *that* is unnecessary.

3. (a)
The verb after *who* depends on the noun or pronoun that

who refers to (*I*); therefore since we say I *am, am* is correct.

4. (c)
The conjunction *and* introduces the rest of the predicate nominative (It is *I and not the men*). Therefore the comma is required.

5. (b)
Plans is not the subject; *factor is.*

6. (d)
(d) is correct because *during* carries the intended meaning of the sentence and is less wordy than (a) or (b). (c) changes the meaning of the sentence.

7. (c)
The verb form, *affect*, is required in this sentence.

8. (d)
(d) *Because* carries the intended meaning of the sentence and is least wordy.

9. (c)
Parallel structure is required: *so determined* and *so proud* give us two adjective constructions.

10. (c) *With* has already been expressed in the sentence (*with whom*). There is no need for the *with* that ends the sentence.

My Score: *Number Correct* ....   *Number Wrong* ....

Superior Results	9-10 *Correct*
Average Results	6-7 *Correct*
Poor Results	*Below 5 Correct*

Test Number 3:   Page 385

1. (b)
Principle is always a noun. The head of a school is a *principal*; the main or important aspect is a *principal* aspect. *Sole* and *singular* change the meaning of the sentence.

2. (d)
Their shows possession; *they're* means they are; *there* shows direction or begins a sentence. The writer is not objecting to *them* but to *their claiming.*

3. (c)
Pretty and *sure* when used as adjectives are not acceptable. *Definitely* changes the meaning of the sentence. Something is either *obvious* or *not obvious;* the *pretty* did not add to the meaning of *obvious.*

4. (c)
We need a parallel structure: to pay the rent, to settle a debt, or *to pay for a trip.*

5. (a)
Than is used in comparisons (more). *Then* refers to time.

6. (d)
Let's means let us; *lets* is the form that follows he, she, or it. There is no meaning to the form *lets'.* (b) *lets us* does not make sense in this sentence.

7. (a)
When *like* is a preposition, it is followed by the object form *us.*

8. (a)
When we substitute *they-them,* we find that we need the subject form *they* (find nothing); therefore, *who* is required. Since the clause is necessary to the meaning of the sentence, the comma may not be used.

9. (d)
Anyone is singular, and so we need the singular form *he has.* (b) and (c) change the meaning of the sentence.

10. (c)
However may not be used to join two ideas with a comma. The only acceptable forms are . However and ; however.

My Score: Number Right ....   *Number Wrong* ....

Superior Results	10 *Correct!*
Average Results	7-9 *Correct*
Poor Results	*Below 6 Correct*

Test Number 4:   Page 386

1. (c)
Gather means to *bring together; together* need not be repeated. (b) and (d) change the meaning of the sentence.

2. (c)
Anxious has an unpleasant connotation. *Desirous* and *enthusiastic* change the intent of the sentence.

3. (d)
Describing begins an adjective phrase modifying *those*. The phrase cannot be treated as a sentence; it must be separated by a comma to show that *readers* is not being described. *Descriptive of* is an elegant phrase that does not fit in with the style of the rest of the selection.

4. (d)
Later refers to time; *latter* refers to position. Since material is singular, *this* must be used.

5. (b)
Material is singular and therefore *was* is needed. (c) and (d) change the meaning of the sentence.

6. (d)
Since *we had spent* is appropriate when *New Yorkers* is omitted, we discover that *New Yorkers* is in the subject form and the appositive pronoun, *we*, must be in the same form. There is no reason to capitalize *we*.

7. (d)
(a) is too wordy. (b) changes the meaning of the sentence. (c) contains a misused word (fortuitous). (d) is the simplest, most direct.

8. (b)
A public institution is in apposition with *Lafayette High School*. (b) is the only correct form.

9. (c)
The colloquial idiom is *into* contact with.

10. (a)
The last group beginning with *Liege* is a complete sentence and should be treated as such.

My Score: *Number Right* ....   *Number Wrong* ....

Superior Results	9-10 *Correct*
Average Results	6-8 *Correct*
Poor Results	*Below* 5 *Correct*

Test Number 5:   Page 388

1. (a)
Since *who have had no instruction* is necessary to the meaning of the sentence, it is a restrictive clause and is not set off by commas or dashes.

2. (d)
Since *Which hamper their progress toward maximum results*, etc., modifies *movements*, this clause cannot stand as a separate sentence.

3. (c)
When *self* is attached to another word, the two words are separated (or joined) by a hyphen.

4. (d)
Since *If they ever can be gotten rid of* is an added thought, the dash is the correct mark of punctuation.

5. (b)
The more appropriate expression is *eliminated.*

6. (b)
It says, they say are expressions to be avoided when referring to something written in an article, because *it* and *they* are without a noun or pronoun to which they refer.

7. (c)
(b) and (d) change the meaning of the sentence. *Somewheres* is an unacceptable form.

8. (a)
Since *put* is the synonym, *lay* is needed.

9. (d)
The idiom is *this kind of.*

10. (c)
Than is used in comparisons. When deciding which form of the pronoun to use in a comparison, complete the sentence by adding the missing verb or other words. In this case *No one knows better than I do.*

My Score:	*Number Right*	*Number Wrong* ....
	Superior Results	*8-10 Correct*
	Average Results	*5-7 Correct*
	Poor Results	*Below 5 Correct*

Part II

Mathematics

MATHEMATICS

The purpose of any College Entrance Examination is to afford a reliable prediction of your probable success once you meet courses on the college level. The examination includes the fundamental operations of arithmetic, per cents, algebra, geometry, and modern trends.

Basic to success in any area of mathematics is the ability to add, subtract, multiply, and divide with accuracy. It is axiomatic that your chances of reaching a correct solution in the algebra or geometry are slim indeed if you are "error-prone" in the arithmetic processes. Therefore, we composed Section 9 as a thorough review of the skills that you need for speed and accuracy in computation. *Don't skip this section!* If you already have the necessary accuracy, then use this section to gain in speed. If, however, you are *not* sure of your fundamentals, then the short cuts and devices included will assure such mastery.

One of the topics stressed in College Entrance Examinations but usually overlooked by students is that of dealing with per cents. Yet a knowledge of the operations with them is just as important as knowing how to add, subtract, multiply, and divide. Thus, we have also included, in Section 10, a thorough review of the essentials of per cents which you should have under control before you enter the examination.

The College Entrance Examinations may be counted on to include algebra and geometry questions too. So both the algebra and geometry sections (Sections 11 and 12) of this book contain practice drills of all the operations that you need to review in order to solve the problems found on the examinations.

Section 13, on modern topics in mathematics, must not be overlooked! It covers those new developments that are finding their way into math examinations. The exercises in this section will prepare you for the type of thinking necessary in the handling of such problems.

In using this book, in order to achieve maximum results, plan for accuracy rather than for speed at first. In order to do this, you must approach each section systematically. The first thing that you must discover is what you know and what you *don't* know. The Inventory Tests will help you with this. Since you are working to achieve 100 per cent, you must concentrate in your practice sessions on eliminating your weaknesses as revealed by these Inventory Tests. Spaced, daily practice is far better than occasional cram sessions for bringing you up to your maximum level of efficiency.

Section 9: FUNDAMENTAL OPERATIONS

The first step toward maximum scores in the mathematical sections of the College Entrance Examinations is through speed and accuracy in arithmetic computation. Since there is no partial credit allowed, one careless miscalculation in addition, subtraction, division, or multiplication can cause a student who knows how to solve a problem to be penalized for wrong work and a wrong answer.

Let us begin with a word of warning. While speed is important, too much of it can lead to disaster. It little avails to be the first one to finish—with a very low mark. For that reason, the primary purpose of this section is to lead you to greater accuracy. Once you have begun to achieve on this level, *then* let speed become a major factor. Work to develop a sense of *controlled* pressure along with urgency for accuracy!

How good are you in handling the four basic operations of arithmetic computation? Take the Inventory Test that follows and find out!

First Day: Inventory Test

Time at Start............

In the space provided, write the correct answer to the problem. Do *not* use scrap paper. Do all your computations in the margins and blank spaces on the page.

1. Add: 53
          23
          34
          ——   1. ....

2. Add: 879
        513
        647
        315   2. ....

3. Subtract: 607
             72   3. ....

4. Subtract: 703
             47   4. ....

5. Subtract: 1547
             568   5. ....

6. From 3,285 take 479.   6. ....

7. Multiply: 327
             49   7. ....

8. Find the product of 835 and 57.   8. ....

9. Divide 1,896 by 79.   9. ....

10. Divide 21,504 by 56.   10. ....

11. Add: 26
         47
         25   11. ....

12. Add: 532
         649
         851
         603   12. ....

13. Subtract: 836
              724   13. ....

14. Subtract: 523
              397   14. ....

15. From 1,532 take the sum of 825 and 231.   15. ....

16. Multiply: 803
              46   16. ....

17. Find the product of 230 and 57.   17. ....

18. Divide 25,748 by 82.   18. ....

19. Divide 83,224 by 206.   19. ....

20. Divide the product of 437 and 22 by 16.   20. ....

Time at End............   *Total Number of Minutes Elapsed*............
                    Average Time 18 *Minutes*

Answer Key

1. 110	6. 2,806	11. 98	16. 36,938
2. 2,354	7. 16,023	12. 2,635	17. 13,110
3. 535	8. 47,595	13. 112	18. 314
4. 656	9. 24	14. 126	19. 404
5. 979	10. 384	15. 476	20. 600⅞

My Score: Number Right............   Number Wrong............
            Average Number Right 17

Clinch by Checking

If you missed any of questions 1, 2, 11, or 12, you need practice in addition. Every time you see problems involving addition in the sections that follow, be extra careful in your work.

If you missed any of questions 3, 4, 5, 6, 13, 14, or 15, you need practice in subtraction.

If you missed any of questions 7, 8, 16, or 17, you need practice in multiplication.

If you missed any of questions 9, 10, 18, 19, or 20, you need practice in division.

Second Day: Inventory Test

Being able to do the four fundamental operations is not sufficient to insure maximum scores. See how well you can do on this Inventory Test involving verbal problems. Then check your answers and methods of solution with those given.

Time at Start............

In the space provided, write the letter of the correct answer to the problem.

1. The value of $8 + 4 \times 2 - 3 \times 4$ is
   (a) 0   (b) 28   (c) -48 (d) 4   (e) none of these   1. ....

2. The sum of $\frac{1}{2} + \frac{1}{3} + \frac{1}{4}$ equals
   (a) $\frac{3}{14}$ (b) $\frac{1}{14}$ (c) 1   (d) $\frac{13}{12}$ (e) none of these   2. ....

3. The value of $\dfrac{\frac{1}{3} + \frac{1}{6}}{\frac{1}{5} + \frac{1}{10}}$ is
   (a) $\frac{9}{10}$ (b) $\frac{10}{9}$ (c) $\frac{9}{10}$ (d) $\frac{5}{3}$ (e) none of these   3. ....

4. The product $(.00016)(.01)(.4)$ is equal to
   (a) .00064   (b) .000064   (c) .0000064   (d) .00000064
   (e) .000000064
                                                                4. ....

5. Kool Katt read from page 203 to page 404 inclusive in his history book. How many pages did he read?
   (a) 199   (b) 200   (c) 201   (d) 202   (e) 203   5. ....

6. Mickey Moose needs $\frac{2}{3}$ of the votes cast to be elected Head Moose. If 1,133 ballots are cast, what is the minimum number of votes that Mickey Moose needs to be elected?
   (a) 752   (b) 753   (c) 754   (d) 755   (e) 756   6. ....

7. If one cubic foot equals .028 meters, how many meters are there in one cubic yard?
   (a) $\frac{28}{27,000}$ (b) $\frac{28}{2,700}$ (c) .756   (d) .765   (e) none of these
                                                                7. ....

8. Which one of the following numbers is divisible by 9 and 11?
   (a) 1,395   (b) 4,785   (c) 1,579   (d) 7,821   (e) 6,381
                                                                8. ....

9. Given a number that equals $29 \times 27 \times 23 \times 12 \times 5 \times 4 \times 1$. This number is divisible by
              (I) 4   (II) 36   (III) 81   (IV) 25   (V) 16
   (a) only I is correct   (b) only II is correct   (c) I, II, and III are correct   (d) only I, II, III, and IV are correct   (e) only I, II, III, and V are correct
                                                                9. ....

10. Which of these fractions has the largest value if d and n are positive integers?

   (a) $\dfrac{n+1}{d}$ (b) $\dfrac{n-1}{d}$ (c) $\dfrac{n}{d}$ (d) $\dfrac{n}{d+1}$ (e) $\dfrac{n+1}{d+1}$

Time at End...........   *Total Number of Minutes Elapsed*...........
                             Average Time 25 minutes

Answer Key with Analysis

ANSWERS	ANALYSIS

1. (d)
The value of $8 + 4 \times 2$
$\quad - 3 \times 4$
is $8 + (4 \times 2) - (3 \times 4)$
which is $8 + 8 - 12$
or $16 - 12$
or 4.

1. Remember the key phrase: "Pity My Days at School." The words' first letters give the order of operations:
P—powers, roots
M—multiply
D—divide
A—add
S—subtract

2. (d)
l.c.d. is 12
$\frac{1}{2} + \frac{1}{3} + \frac{1}{4}$ equals
$\frac{6}{12} + \frac{4}{12} + \frac{3}{12}$ which is
$\frac{6+4+3}{12}$ or
$\frac{13}{12}$

2. Choose a lowest common denominator, in this case, 12. Change each fraction to twelfths; then combine.

3. (d)
l.c.d. is 30
$\frac{\frac{1}{3} + \frac{1}{6}}{\frac{1}{5} + \frac{1}{10}}$
$= \frac{\frac{10}{30} + \frac{5}{30}}{\frac{6}{30} + \frac{3}{30}}$
$= \frac{\frac{15}{30}}{\frac{9}{30}}$
$= (\frac{15}{30})(\frac{30}{9})$
$= \frac{15}{9}$
$= \frac{5}{3}$

3. In dealing with complex fractions, select a common denominator for the fractions involved. Change every fraction to this denominator; then simplify through division.

4. (d)
$16 \times 1 \times 4 = 64$
$(.00016)(.01)(.4)$
$\quad = .000\ 000\ 64$

4. To multiply decimals, multiply the digits involved. Then add the number of decimal places in each of the numbers multiplied. This sum is the number of decimal places in your answer. Supply zeros as needed.

5. (d)

$$404$$
$$-$$
$$203$$
$$\overline{201}$$
$$+$$
$$1$$
$$\overline{202}$$

5. The number of pages *between* the first and last is their difference. Then add one to include the first page.

6. (e)
$\frac{2}{3} \times 1133$
$= \frac{2266}{3}$
$= 755\frac{1}{3}$
So the answer is 756.

6. If we round off to the nearest vote, the 755 votes would *not* provide the $\frac{2}{3}$ needed. Therefore we must use the next highest number of votes, or 756.

7. (c)
1 cubic foot
$= .028$ meters
1 cubic yard
$= 27$ cubic feet
1 cubic yard
$= .028 \times 27$ meters
$= .756$ meters

7. 1 linear yard
$= 3$ linear feet
1 square yard
$= 3 \times 3$ square feet
$= 9$ square feet
1 cubic yard
$= 3 \times 3 \times 3$ cubic feet
$= 27$ cubic feet

8. (d)

$$
\begin{array}{r}
869 \\
9)\overline{7821} \\
72 \\
\overline{62} \\
54 \\
\overline{81} \\
81 \\
\overline{0}
\end{array}
\qquad
\begin{array}{r}
711 \\
11)\overline{7821} \\
77 \\
\overline{12} \\
11 \\
\overline{11} \\
11 \\
\overline{0}
\end{array}
$$

8. Actually, it is not necessary to try dividing each choice, since there are simple tests for divisibility by each number. See fourth day's work.

9. (e)
There is a 4 in the factor 12.
There is a 36:
    Note that $9 \times 4 = 36$.
    There is a 9 in the 27 and a 4 in the 4.
There is an 81: 27 in 27
                 3 in 12.

9. Numbers can always be broken down into their prime factors. For example, if we have a 27 and are seeking a 9, we may also express the 27 as 9×3 and then may say that 27 is divisible by 9.

There is only one 5, and
thus no 25.

There is a 16:   4 in 4

                         4 in 12.

10. (a)

    The largest numerator is
$n + 1$.

    The smallest denominator
is d.

    The largest fraction is
therefore $(n + 1)/d$.

10. A fraction has its largest
value when its numerator is
as large as possible and its
denominator is as small as
possible.

My Score: Number Right............   Number Wrong............

                  Average Number Right 6

Third Day: Fractions

What You Should Know

1. To combine fractions with the *same* denominator, keep the
denominator and perform the indicated operation—addition
or subtraction—in the numerator.

$$\frac{2}{5} + \frac{1}{5} = \frac{2+1}{5} = \frac{3}{5}$$

2. To combine fractions with *unlike* denominators:

  (a) Find a number into which *all* the denominators divide
evenly: a common denominator. There will always be
more than one such denominator. The smallest of these
is called the lowest common denominator: the l.c.d.

  (b) Multiply *both* the numerator and the denominator of
each fraction by the quotient of this common denominator
divided by the denominator of the fraction.

PROBLEM: Find $\frac{1}{2} - \frac{1}{3} + \frac{3}{4}$.

ANALYSIS: A number into which all of these denominators divide
evenly is $2 \times 3 \times 4 = 24$. The l.c.d., however, is
12, which is easiest to use.

             Multiply the first fraction, top and bottom, by $\frac{12}{2}$,
or 6. Multiply the second fraction, top and bottom,
by $\frac{12}{3}$, or 4, etc.

Thus $\frac{1}{2} = \frac{6}{12}$, $\frac{1}{3} = \frac{4}{12}$, $\frac{3}{4} = \frac{9}{12}$. The answer is $\frac{6 - 4 + 9}{12} = \frac{11}{12}$.

Practice Test

Time at Start...........10:35 PM

In the space provided, write the letter of the correct answer to the problem.

1. When the fractions $\frac{1}{3} + \frac{2}{5} - \frac{1}{6}$ are combined, the result is
(a) $\frac{11}{30}$ (b) $\frac{21}{30}$ (c) $\frac{23}{30}$ (d) $\frac{17}{30}$ (e) 1
1. ....

2. Find the value of $\dfrac{2\frac{1}{3}}{3\frac{1}{4} + 5\frac{1}{2}}$.

(a) $\frac{28}{79}$ (b) $\frac{4}{15}$ (c) $\frac{28}{100}$ (d) $\frac{4}{17}$ (e) none of these
2. ....

3. Find the value of $\dfrac{1/a + 1/b}{1/ab}$ when $a = \frac{1}{3}$ and $b = \frac{1}{4}$.

(a) 11 (b) $\frac{7}{12}$ (c) 7 (d) $\frac{4}{11}$ (e) none of these 3. ....

4. Three heirs are to share evenly in $\frac{5}{9}$ of an estate. Each heir is to receive what fractional part of the estate?
(a) $\frac{5}{27}$ (b) $\frac{5}{7}$ (c) $\frac{5}{9}$ (d) $\frac{15}{9}$ (e) $\frac{1}{3}$
4. ....

5. Four-thirds is how many more eighteenths than $\frac{7}{12}$?
(a) $22\frac{1}{2}$ (b) $13\frac{1}{2}$ (c) 10 (d) $\frac{11}{12}$ (e) this problem cannot be done
5. ....

6. Simplify: $\dfrac{\dfrac{1}{a} + \dfrac{1}{b}}{\dfrac{1}{ab}}$

(a) $a \oplus b$ (b) $a - b$ (c) $(a \oplus 1)/ab$ (d) a/b (e) none of these
6. ....

7. The value of $\dfrac{\frac{1}{3} + \frac{1}{4}}{\frac{1}{5} + \frac{1}{6}}$ is

(a) $\frac{35}{22}$ (b) $\frac{35}{27}$ (c) $\frac{35}{66}$ (d) $\frac{7}{11}$ (e) $\frac{27}{35}$ 7. ....

8. A man spent ⅜ of his money and had $80 left. How much did he start with?

   (a) $640 (b) $320 (c) $128 (d) $213.33 (e) $135

8. ....

9. The fraction $(a + b)/b$ where $b \neq 0$ has the same value as

   (a) $a + 1$ (b) a (c) $(a/b) + b$ (d) $(a/b) + 1$ (e) none of these

9. ....

10. The fraction a/b where $b = 0$ is

   (a) 0 (b) 1 (c) b/a (d) 2 (e) undefined

10. ....

Time at End............   *Minutes Elapsed*............
Average Time 25 Minutes

Answer Key for this test is on page 417.

My Score: *Number Right*............   *Number Wrong*............
              Average Number Right 5

Fourth Day: Fractions and Divisibility

What You Should Know

VOCABULARY

   digits: the counting numbers 1, 2, 3, 4, 5, 6, 7, 8, 9, and 0
   even numbers: numbers ending with even digits 2, 4, 6, 8, or 0
   odd numbers: numbers ending with odd digits 1, 3, 5, 7, or 9

PROBLEM: Find the value of $\dfrac{1}{1 + \dfrac{1}{2 + \frac{1}{3}}}$.

ANALYSIS: This type of problem is best solved by beginning at the end, and working towards the top.

$$\frac{1}{1 + \dfrac{1}{2 + \frac{1}{3}}} = \frac{1}{1 + \dfrac{1}{\frac{7}{3}}} = \frac{1}{1 + \frac{3}{7}} = \frac{1}{\frac{10}{7}} = \frac{7}{10}$$

1. The more readily used tests for divisibility are as follows:

A number is exactly divisible by	*if*
2	the number ends with an even digit.
3	the sum of the digits is divisible by 3.
4	the number formed by the last two digits is divisible by 4.
5	the number ends with a 5 or a zero.
6	the number is divisible by 2 and by 3.
8	the number formed by the last three digits is divisible by 8.
9	the sum of the digits is divisible by 9.
10	the number ends with a zero.

PROBLEM: Test 8,461,620 for divisibility by 3, 4, and 9.

ANALYSIS: The sum of the digits is $8 + 4 + 6 + 1 + 6 + 2 + 0 = 27$, which is divisible by 3 and by 9; therefore the number is divisible by 3 and by 9.

The last two digits form a number, 20, which is divisible by 4; therefore the seven-digit number is divisible by 4.

Practice Test

Time at Start ....

In the space provided, write the letter of the correct answer to the problem.

1. Find the value of $\dfrac{1}{\dfrac{1}{1+3}}$.

 (a) ¼   (b) ⅓   (c) 4   (d) 3   (e) 7   1. ....

2. Find the value of $\dfrac{1}{\dfrac{2}{1+¼} \div 1}$.

 (a) ¹³⁄₅   (b) ⁵⁄₁₃   (c) ¹²⁄₅   (d) ⁵⁄₁₂   (e) ⅚   2. ....

3. Find the value of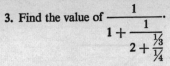

(a) $\frac{3}{10}$ (b) $\frac{13}{10}$ (c) $\frac{10}{3}$ (d) $\frac{10}{13}$ (e) none of these

3. ....

4. Which of the following numbers is divisible by 4 and by 5?
(a) 41,235 (b) 27,140 (c) 43,230 (d) 91,990 (e) none of these

4. ....

5. Given the five-digit number 64,98k. In order for this number to be divisible by 2, 3, and 9, k must be

(a) 0 (b) 1 (c) 4 (d) 6 (e) 9

5. ....

6. Given the six-digit number 828,75p. In order for this number to be divisible by 18, p must be

(a) 4 (b) 5 (c) 6 (d) 7 (e) 8

6. ....

7. A boy can divide his marbles into piles of 3, 4, or 5 and have none left over each time. The smallest total number of marbles that he might have is

(a) 10 (b) 15 (c) 20 (d) 30 (e) 60

7. ....

8. Given that $n!$ means $n(n-1)(n-2) \ldots (3)(2)(1)$, so that 6! means $6 \times 5 \times 4 \times 3 \times 2 \times 1$, then the number 21! is divisible by

(I) 3 (II) 10 (III) 17 (IV) 105

(a) only I is correct (b) only I and II are correct (c) only I, II, and III are correct (d) I, II, III, and IV are all correct (e) none of the above is correct

8. ....

9. The number $23 \times 21 \times 19 \times 17 \times 15 \times 3 \times 1$ is not divisible by

(a) 2 (b) 3 (c) 5 (d) 9 (e) 63

9. ....

10. A man wishes to fold a strip of cardboard into any of the three shapes shown at the right. In each figure, the segments are of equal length. Each segment contains an integral number of units in length. Then the shortest length of cardboard he must have is

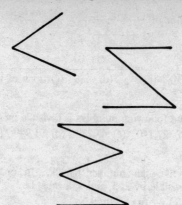

   (a) 5 units (b) 10 units (c) 25 units (d) 30 units (e) 60 units

                                                                    10. ....

Time at End............   *Minutes Elapsed*............
                                                     Average Time 30 Minutes

Answer Key for this test is on page 417.

My Score: *Number Right*............   *Number Wrong*............
               Average Number Right 6

Fifth Day: Intervals and Spaces

What You Should Know

VOCABULARY

   inclusive: includes the first and the last
   minimum: least number possible
   maximum: largest number possible
   integer: whole number such as −3, −2, −1, 0 1, 2, 3
   circumference: perimeter of a circle

1. To find the number of even integers between and including
   two even numbers, or to find the number of odd integers
   between and including two odd numbers,
    (a) subtract the smallest number from the largest one,
    (b) divide this result by 2,
    (c) add 1.

PROBLEM: How many even integers are there between 2 and 6?

ANALYSIS: $\dfrac{6-2}{2} + 1 = \dfrac{4}{2} + 1 = 2 + 1 = 3$ (They are 2, 4,

and 6.)

2. If there are n telephone poles on a straight line, then there are $n-1$ spaces between them.

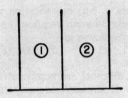

3 poles, 2 spaces

3. If there are n telephone poles on a circle, there are n spaces between them.

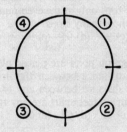

4 poles, 4 spaces

Practice Test

Time at Start...........

In the space provided, write the letter of the correct answer to the problem.

1. The value of $(2 \times 8^2) - (4 \times 3) + 1$ is
(a) 112   (b) 115   (c) 117   (d) 245   (e) 361   **1.** ....

2. Sam Student is running for president of the Alpha Club. If there are 23 members in the club and ¾ of the votes are needed for election, find the minimum number of votes Sam needs.
(a) 9   (b) 15   (c) 17   (d) 18   (e) 19   2. ....

3. Ben Bore reads from page 202 to page 302 inclusive in a boring book. How many pages does Ben read?
(a) 51   (b) 99   (c) 100   (d) 101   (e) 102   3. ....

4. A worker takes a 3-month vacation every fourth year. If he took six of these 3-month vacations and the last one was in 1961, then his first one was in
(a) 1945   (b) 1941   (c) 1937   (d) 1933   (e) 1929   4. ....

5. The rooms of a school are numbered consecutively from 101 to 581 inclusive. How many odd-numbered rooms are there?
(a) 340   (b) 240   (c) 241   (d) can be done, but answer is not given   (e) cannot be done with the given information

5. ....

6. The bus stations in Dodgerville are on every street corner from First Street to 191st Street. An express bus is put into service to make its stops only at the even-numbered streets. This express bus makes how many stops?
(a) 82   (b) 92   (c) 93   (d) 95   (e) 96   6. ....

7. Sixty-one telegraph poles are placed along a straight highway such that the distance between the first and last poles is 3,660 feet, and the distance between any two consecutive poles is the same. How many feet apart are any two successive poles?
(a) 59   (b) 60   (c) 61   (d) 62   (e) 63   7. ....

8. A circle has a circumference of 60 feet. Thirty spots are to be marked on this circle so that the distances between the spots are equal. This can be done by placing the spots how many feet apart?
(a) $^{60}/_{29}$ (b) $^{60}/_{30}$ (c) $^{60}/_{31}$ (d) can be done, but the answer is not given   (e) cannot be done with the given information

8. ....

9. How many more five-digit numbers are there than four-digit numbers?
(a) 100   (b) 1,000   (c) 10,000   (d) 81,000   (e) 90,000
9. ....

10. A man has 5,000 dozen pencils. He inspects them and discovers that one out of every 12 is defective. How many pencils are defective?

(a) 5,000   (b) 60,000   (c) 500   (d) 50,000   (e) none of these

10. ....

Time at End............   *Minutes Elapsed*............
                                      Average Time 30 Minutes

Answer Key for this test is on page 418.

My Score: *Number Right*............   *Number Wrong*............
               Average Number Right 6

Sixth Day: Averages

What You Should Know

1. To find the average of a number of marks, heights, weights, etc., divide the sum of the items by the number of items.

$$\text{Average} = \frac{\text{sum of items}}{\text{number of items}}$$

2. If the average of a definite number of items is known and one of the items is unknown, the numerical value of the missing item can be found by multiplying the number of items by the average and subtracting the sum of the known items.

PROBLEM: Steve has an average of 86 in three exams. What mark does he need on the next exam so that his average will be 88?

ANALYSIS: Altogether there are four exams. Using the formula in (2) above, we get

$$(4 \times 88) - (3 \times 86) = 352 - 258 = 94$$

You may also reason that Steve needs to raise his mark two points on each of the three exams he has already taken to reach the 88 per cent. Thus, his fourth mark should be $88 + (3 \times 2)$, or 94.

3. The value of any fraction remains unchanged if the numerator and denominator are multiplied by the same nonzero number.

$$\frac{3}{5} = \frac{5 \times 3}{5 \times 5} = \frac{7 \times 3}{7 \times 5}$$

4. If two or more fractions are positive and if they have the same denominator, the one with the largest numerator is the largest in value.

5. If two or more fractions are positive and have the same numerator, the one with the smallest denominator is the largest in value.

Practice Test

Time at Start............

In the space provided, write the letter of the correct answer to the problem.

1. A six-man football team has players whose weights in pounds are 204, 195, 175, 180, 195, and 155. The average weight of the players on this team is how many pounds?
   (a) 200   (b) 193   (c) 186   (d) 184   (e) 190   1. ....

2. The heights of the basketball players on the Pottsville High School team are 6'0", 5'11", 6'2", 6'3", and 6'6". Find the average height of the players on the team.
   (a) 6'0"   (b) 6'2"   (c) 6'3"   (d) 6'4"   (e) 6'5"   2. ....

3. Which of the following fractions is greater than $\frac{3}{4}$ but less than $\frac{7}{8}$?
   (a) $\frac{5}{7}$ (b) $\frac{10}{11}$ (c) $\frac{9}{16}$ (d) $\frac{15}{24}$ (e) $\frac{11}{13}$ 3. ....

4. If x is a positive integer, which of the following fractions has the smallest value?
   (a) $11x/18$ (b) $13x/18$ (c) $15x/18$ (d) $3x/5$ (e) $4x/5$
                                                          4. ....

5. Which of the following fractions has the largest value?
   (a) $\frac{8}{9}$ (b) $\frac{9}{10}$ (c) $\frac{10}{11}$ (d) $\frac{11}{12}$ (e) $\frac{12}{13}$ 5. ....

6. New York City had 6 snowstorms averaging 6 inches of snow. Three of these storms averaged 3 inches each, two of the storms averaged 5 inches each. How deep was the sixth storm?

(a) 12 inches   (b) 13 inches   (c) 25 inches   (d) 15 inches
(e) 17 inches   6. ....

7. A football team consists of 4 backs and 7 linemen. The Princeton football team averaged 20 pounds more than that of Yale. If the 4 backs of the Princeton team averaged 15 pounds a man more than the Yale backs, by how much did the average weight of the Princeton lineman exceed that of Yale?

(a) 20 pounds   (b) 22 pounds   (c) 22⁶⁄₇ pounds   (d) 25 pounds
(e) 24²⁄₇ pounds   7. ....

8. Find the average of the 15 odd numbers beginning with 3.
(a) 3   (b) 15   (c) 17   (d) 19   (e) none of these is correct
                                                           8. ....

9. Find the average of all numbers from one to 100 that end in 4.
(a) 50   (b) 49   (c) 48   (d) cannot be done from the given information   (e) can be done, but the answer is not given
                                                           9. ....

10. Mackerel has marks of 80, 75, 70, and m on four tests. If his average for these four marks is t, express m in terms of t.
(a) $4m - 225$ (b) $225 - 4m$ (c) mt (d) $225 - 4t$
(e) $4t - 225$ 10. ....

11. The age of Mr. Nelson is n, which is ⅘ the combined ages of his three children. If his children are 9, 8, and t years old, express n in terms of t.
(a) $t = ⅘n$ (b) $17 - t = n$ (c) $n = ⅘(t ⊹ 17)$
(d) $n + 17 = t$ (e) $n = ¾(t ⊹ 17)$ 11. ....

Time at End............   *Minutes Elapsed*............
                                 Average Time 35 Minutes

Answer Key for this test is on page 418.

My Score: *Number Right*............   *Number Wrong*............
              Average Number Right 5

Seventh Day: Test of Mastery

Time at Start............

In the space provided, write the letter of the correct answer to the problem.

1. The houses on Sandwich Street are numbered from 103 to 203 inclusive. How many houses are there on this street?

(a) 50   (b) 51   (c) 100   (d) 101   (e) none of these 1. ....

2. There are 11 markers on a straight line. The distance between marker one and marker two is one foot. If the distance between each pair of markers is the same, find the distance between markers one and eleven.

(a) 9 feet   (b) 10 feet   (c) 11 feet   (d) can be done, but the answer is not given   (e) cannot be done from the given information

2. ....

3. Find the average of the even integers starting with 2 and ending with 61.

(a) 30   (b) 31   (c) 32   (d) 33   (e) none of these   3. ....

4. Bart received a mark of 5% on each of three examinations. What mark must he receive on the fourth examination so that his average will be t?

(a) $15 + 4t$ (b) $15 - 4t$ (c) $4t$ (d) $4t - 15$ (e) $15/4t$

4. ....

5. By how much is the maximum value of a/b more than the minimum value of a/b if a has values between 10 and 50, and b has values between 40 and 70?

(a) $^{38}/_{28}$ (b) $^{31}/_{280}$ (c) $^{40}/_{31}$ (d) $^{31}/_{28}$ (e) $^{13}/_{28}$ 5. ....

6. How many more even numbers are there from 1 to 1,000 inclusive than odd numbers from 1 to 99 inclusive?

(a) 450   (b) 440   (c) 449   (d) 44   (e) 420   6. ....

7. Find the value of $\dfrac{3\frac{1}{2}}{2\frac{1}{3} + 3\frac{1}{4}}$.

(a) $^{14}/_{27}$ (b) $^{42}/_{67}$ (c) $^{27}/_{14}$ (d) $^{67}/_{42}$ (e) none of these

7. ....

8. Which of the following fractions is not between $\frac{3}{4}$ and $\frac{4}{5}$?

(a) $^{31}/_{40}$ (b) $^{49}/_{60}$ (c) $^{63}/_{80}$ (d) $^{79}/_{100}$ (e) none of these

8. ....

9. A man spent $\frac{1}{2}$ of his share of a business in which he owns $\frac{1}{3}$. His share of the business is $800. What is the entire estate worth?

(a) $1,200   (b) $1,600   (c) $2,400   (d) $2,800   (e) $4,800

9. ....

10. A man spent $\frac{2}{5}$ of his share of a small savings account. He has \$90 left. What was his share of the savings account worth?
(a) \$225 (b) \$200 (c) \$150 (d) \$125 (e) \$100 10. ....

11. Which of the following numbers is divisible by 3?
(a) 22 (b) 2,222 (c) 22,222 (d) 222,222 (e) none of these
11. ....

Time at End........... *Minutes Elapsed*...........
Average Time 25 *Minutes*

Answer Key for this test is on page 419.

My Score: *Number Right*........... *Number Wrong*...........
Average Number Right 8

Section 8: Fundamental Operations

Answer Key with Hints

Third Day Page 405

1. (d) Use 30 as a lowest common denominator. Change each fraction to thirtieths and combine.
2. (b) First change the mixed numbers to improper fractions. Then change to twelfths. Then combine and simplify.
3. (b) Substitute as indicated for *a* and *b*. Remember: $\frac{1}{\frac{1}{3}} = 3.$
4. (a) Divide $\frac{5}{9}$ of the estate by 3.
5. (b) Set up a simple equation: $\frac{4}{3} = \frac{7}{12} + x/18.$
6. (a) Use l.c.d. of *ab*. Then simplify as indicated.
7. (a) Use 60 as l.c.d. Change to sixtieths; then simplify.
8. (c) Remember that $\frac{3}{8}$ is the part *spent*; $\frac{5}{8}$ is left. Then $\frac{5}{8}x = \$80.$
9. (d) Divide both the *a* and *b* in the numerator by *b*.
10. (e) Division by zero is not allowed in mathematics.

Fourth Day Page 407

1. (c) Remember: $1/\frac{1}{4}$ equals 4.
2. (b) Again start at the bottom, by simplifying $1 + \frac{1}{4}$.

3. (d) Once you get $\frac{\frac{1}{3}}{\frac{1}{4}}$, simplify this to $\frac{4}{3}$.

4. (b) See appropriate tests under "What You Should Know" on page 377.

5. (a) The sum of $6 + 4 + 9 + 8$ is already 27, which is divisible by 3 and by 9.

6. (c) To test for divisibility by 18, test for 9 and 2.

7. (e) Since 3, 4, and 5 have no common factor, their l.c.d. must be $3 \times 4 \times 5 = 60$. See definition of l.c.d.

8. (d) Since 21! means $21 \times 20 \times 19 \times \ldots \times 5 \times 4 \times 3 \times 2 \times 1$, it clearly contains factors of 3, 10, and 17. Breaking 105 down into the product of 15 and 7 reveals that 105, too, is present in 21!.

9. (a) It is obvious that there is no even factor in the given number, hence no divisibility by 2.

10. (d) In order for there to be integral segments, the unit length of the cardboard strip must be a multiple of 2, 3, and 5, or 30.

Fifth Day   Page 410

1. (c) Group your operations: $(2 \times 64) - (4 \times 3) + 1$.

2. (d) Three-fourths of 23 is $17\frac{1}{4}$; round off to the next highest number, since 17 is less than $\frac{3}{4}$ of the vote.

3. (d) Subtract 202 from 302 and remember to add 1.

4. (b) Just count backwards from 1961 by 4's.

5. (c) Subtract 101 from 581; divide by 2; then add 1.

6. (d) We are looking for the number of even integers between 2 and 190 inclusive. Subtract, divide by 2, and add 1.

7. (c) Sixty-one poles in a straight line give 60 spaces.

8. (b) On a circle, 60 spots give 60 spaces.

9. (d) The number of five-digit numbers is $99,999 - 10,000 + 1$. The number of four-digit numbers is $9,999 - 1,000 + 1$.

10. (a) Remember that one out of 12 is the same as one per dozen.

Sixth Day   Page 413

1. (d) Use the standard method of finding an average: add the items and divide by the number of items.

2. (b) When we add the inches, we get 22. Remember that this is the same as 10 inches and 1 additional foot.

3. (e) If we change each fraction to its decimal equivalent (by dividing denominator into numerator), we can see which fraction is not in the range from .75 to .875.

4. (d) The x has no effect on the problem since it is contained in the numerator of each fraction. If we change all the fractions to 90ths, we have a means of comparison.

5. (e) Subtract each fraction from 1. The fraction with the smallest difference is the answer. (See rule 5.)

6. (e) The total snowfall was 36 inches; the first three total 9 inches; the second two total 10 inches. The remaining amount is $36 - 19 = 17$ inches.

7. (c) The total weight difference is $11 \times 20 = 220$. The backs make up 60 pounds. The linemen make up the other 160. Divide 160 pounds by 7.

8. (c) The first odd number is 3, the last is 31. Since the numbers have a common difference between them, the average can be found by adding the first and last number and dividing by 2. $(3 + 31)/2 = 17$.

9. (b) The numbers are 4, 14, 24, 34, 44, ..., 84, 94. $(94 + 4)/2 = 49$.

10. (e) $(225 + m)/4 = t$.

11. (c) $n = \frac{4}{5}(t + 17)$.

		More of this type can be found in the work of day
Seventh Day	**Page 415**	
1. (d)	Take $203 - 103 = 100$ and add 1.	5
2. (b)	Eleven markers in a straight line give 10 spaces.	5
3. (b)	The first is 2, the last is 60. Take $(60 + 2)/2$.	6
4. (d)	$t = \dfrac{3(5) + x}{4}$. Solve for x.	6
5. (d)	A fraction is a maximum when its numerator is largest, denominator smallest—in this case, $\frac{50}{40}$. Its minimum value involves the reverse—in this case, $\frac{10}{70}$. Then subtract the two fractions.	6
6. (a)	Even numbers: $(1,000 - 2)/2 = 499$. Odd numbers: $(99 - 1)/2 = 49$.	5
7. (b)	After changing each mixed number to an improper fraction, multiply top and bottom by a common denominator, 12.	4

8. (b) Take ¾ and ⅘ and change to fortieths, sixtieths, eightieths, etc. 3

9. (c) If ⅓ of the business is $800, the entire business is worth 3 × $800 = $2,400. The ½ has no bearing on this problem. 3

10. (c) If he spent ⅖, he has ⅗ left. Thus, ⅗ of the account is $90; ⅕ is $30; 5/5 is $150. 3

11. (d) The sum of the digits must be a multiple of 3. 4

HANDLING PER CENT

Section 10: HANDLING PER CENT

Many of the problems that we face in everyday life involve the ability to handle per cent. Taxes, interest, dividends, discounts, comparison statistics in economics, all involve per cent tables.

Because problems in this area are so widespread, a significant number of the questions that you meet on the College Entrance Examinations include fundamental operations in handling per cent. How can you make certain that you will get maximum results when you meet such problems? The first and most important step is to make certain that you know the table of per cents found in the second day's work of this section. Make sure that you have it memorized before doing any of the other work in the section. This will give you the speed and accuracy that you need for best results.

How well can you handle fundamental operations involving per cents? Take the Inventory Test that follows and find out!

First Day: Inventory Test

Time at Start............

In the space provided, write the letter of the correct answer to the problem.

1. What fraction is equal to $87\frac{1}{2}\%$?
   (a) $\frac{1}{8}$ (b) $\frac{3}{8}$ (c) $\frac{5}{8}$ (d) $\frac{7}{8}$ (e) $\frac{5}{6}$ **1.** ....

2. What number is 20% of 20?
   (a) 1 (b) 4 (c) 6 (d) 20 (e) 400   **2.** ....

3. A jeweler had 24 watches. He sold 12½% of them. How many did he have left?
   (a) 21   (b) 18   (c) 15   (d) 12   (e) 3   3. ....

4. One is what per cent of 20?
   (a) 1%   (b) 5%   (c) 20%   (d) 10%   (e) 12½%   4. ....

5. What per cent of 6 is .03?
   (a) 3%   (b) 6%   (c) ½%   (d) 5%   (e) ⅙%   5. ....

6. Eighteen is 9% of what number?
   (a) 50   (b) 100   (c) 150   (d) 200   (e) 250   6. ....

7. What per cent of a is b?
   (a) b/a (b) a/b (c) $100b/a$ (d) $100a/b$ (e) $a/100b$ 7. ....

8. m is 20% of what number?
   (a) m (b) $20m$ (c) $5m$ (d) $3m$ (e) $16m$ 8. ....

9. In a class of 25 men and 15 women, what per cent of the class is female?
   (a) 20%   (b) 37½%   (c) 40%   (d) 44%   (e) 48%   9. ....

10. A man sold a radio for $56 after giving a discount of 12½% from the list price. What was the list price?
    (a) $53   (b) $50   (c) $60   (d) $63   (e) $64   10. ....

Time at End.............   *Total Number of Minutes Elapsed.............*
                            Average Time 20 Minutes

Answer Key with Analysis

ANSWERS	ANALYSIS

1. (d)
   $87\frac{1}{2}\% = \frac{175}{2} \div 100$
   $= \frac{175}{200}$
   $= \frac{7}{8}$

1. Although the answer can be worked out as shown at the left, it will be to the student's advantage to memorize the per cent table in the second day's work of this section.

2. (b)
   $20\% = \frac{1}{5}$
   $(\frac{1}{5})(20) = 4$

2. Again, we may use 20% as $\frac{20}{100}$, but it is to your advantage to memorize the per cent table.

3. (a)
⅛ of 24 is 3. Thus, the jeweler had 24 − 3, or 21, watches left.

3. The use of $12\frac{1}{2}\%$ as ⅛ avoids any long, complex multiplication in the problem.

4. (b)
$1 = (x/100)(20)$
$100 = 20x$
$5 = x$

4. The key here is the word-for-word translation from English into symbols (see third day's work).

5. (c)
$(x/100)(6) = .03$
$6x = 3$
$x = \frac{3}{6} = \frac{1}{2}$

5. Again we use direct translation of the words *per* and *cent* to get our equation.

6. (d)
$18 = \frac{9}{100}x$
$1800 = 9x$
$x = 200$

6. No new difficulties arise here.

7. (c)
$(x/100)(a) = b$
$ax = 100b$
$x = 100b/a$

7. Even though the problem uses letters in place of numbers, we still follow the same pattern of translation.

8. (c)
$m = \frac{1}{5}x$
$5m = x$

8. The reader by now should see that there is not too much variation in these problems. All require translations.

9. (b)
women: 15
class: 40(25 + 15)
$\frac{15}{40} = \frac{3}{8} = 37\frac{1}{2}\%$

9. To figure a per cent, we place the number of women over the total number of class members, and reduce to lowest terms. The per cent table tells us that $\frac{3}{8} = 37\frac{1}{2}\%$.

10. (e)
x = list price
$\frac{1}{8}x$ = discount
$x - \frac{1}{8}x = 56$
$8x - x = 448$
$7x = 448$
$x = 64$

10. The list price — discount = selling price. Express the discount as a per cent of the list price.

My Score: Number Right............   Number Wrong............
Average Number Right 6

Second Day: Per Cent—Fraction Relationships

What You Should Know

While many problems can be done the long way, you can save much time by memorizing the basic relationships shown in the following table.

eighths	sixths	thirds	fourths
$12\frac{1}{2}\% = \frac{1}{8}$	$16\frac{2}{3}\% = \frac{1}{6}$	$33\frac{1}{3}\% = \frac{1}{3}$	$25\% = \frac{1}{4}$
$37\frac{1}{2}\% = \frac{3}{8}$	$83\frac{1}{3}\% = \frac{5}{6}$	$66\frac{2}{3}\% = \frac{2}{3}$	$50\% = \frac{1}{2}$
$62\frac{1}{2}\% = \frac{5}{8}$			$75\% = \frac{3}{4}$
$87\frac{1}{2}\% = \frac{7}{8}$			

and these, too:

$$100\% = 1$$
$$150\% = 1\frac{1}{2}$$
$$250\% = 2\frac{1}{2}$$
$$\tfrac{1}{2}\% = .005$$

Practice Test

Time at Start............

In the space provided, write the correct answer to the problem.

1. $\frac{1}{2} = ...\%$ 1. ....

2. $\frac{1}{4} = ...\%$ 2. ....

3. $83\frac{1}{3}\% = ...$ 3. ....

4. $250\% = ...$ 4. ....

5. $150\% = ...$ 5. ....

6. $87\frac{1}{2}\% = ...$ 6. ....

7. $\frac{1}{3} = ...\%$ 7. ....

8. $\frac{3}{8} = ...\%$ 8. ....

9. $12\frac{1}{2}\% = ...$ 9. ....

10. $125\% = ...$ 10. ....

11. $\frac{1}{4}$ of $1\% = ...$ 11. ....

12. ⅗ = ...%   **12.** ....

Time At End..............   *Total Number of Minutes Elapsed*..............
                                Average Time 6 Minutes

Answer Key for this test is on page 431.

My Score: Number Right..............   *Number Wrong*..............
                Average Number Right **11**

Third Day: Ratio and Proportion

What You Should Know

VOCABULARY

ratio: a comparison of two quantities by division
proportion: a statement maintaining that two ratios are equal

PROBLEM: Do the ratios 2/3 and 4/9 form a proportion?

ANALYSIS: Since the two ratios are unequal, they do not form a
proportion.

1. In the proportion $\frac{a}{b} = \frac{c}{d}$, *b* and *c* are called "means," while
a and *d* are called "extremes."

2. In a proportion, the product of the means equals the product
of the extremes.

PROBLEM: Solve for *x*: 2/3 = 15/*x*.

ANALYSIS: Since the product of the means must equal the product
of the extremes, the 2*x* = 45, or *x* = 22½.

Practice Test

Time At Start..............

In the space provided, write the letter of the correct answer
to the problem.

1. Which pair of ratios forms a proportion?
(a) 1/3, 2/7 (b) 2/7, 3/10 (c) 4/7, 12/21 (d) 1/4, 2/7
(e) 3/4, 7/10   **1.** ....

2. If $x/3 = 6/7$, then x equals
(a) 2/7 (b) 18/7 (c) 21/6 (d) 6/21 (e) 14   2. ....

3. If 4 books cost 6 dollars, the cost of 5 books in dollars is
(a) 6.30 (b) 7 (c) 7.20 (d) 7.40 (e) 7.50   3. ....

4. If $(x + 3)/4 = 3$, then x is
(a) 1 (b) 4 (c) 7 (d) 9 (e) 10   4. ....

5. If a books cost b dollars, then c books cost how many dollars?
(a) bc/a (b) ab/c (c) ac/b (d) $(a + c)/b$ (e) $(a + b)/c$
      5. ....

6. If Ina types 30 pages in 45 minutes, how many pages can she type in 3 hours working at the same rate of speed?
(a) 40 (b) 70 (c) 90 (d) 120 (e) 150   6. ....

7. If $385/4 = 11/x$, then x is
(a) 31/5 (b) 4/35 (c) 7/4 (d) 35/4 (e) 4/31   7. ....

Time at End............   *Minutes Elapsed*............
                                  Average Time 15 Minutes

Answer Key for this test is on page 432.

My Score: *Number Right*............   *Number Wrong*............
                 Average Number Right 5

Fourth Day: Translating Per Cents

What You Should Know

VOCABULARY

of: usually means "multiplied by"
per cent: *per* means "divided by"
          cent means "one hundred"
what number: usually translated by the letter "*x*"
is: translated by "equals"

Thus, "what per cent" would be represented by

$$x \rightarrow \text{what}$$
$$\overline{} \rightarrow \text{per}$$
$$100 \rightarrow \text{cent}$$

PROBLEM: Seven is what per cent of 28?

ANALYSIS: $7 = \dfrac{x}{100} \div 28$

$$7 = \frac{28x}{100}$$

$$700 = 28x$$
$$25 = x$$

PROBLEM: Change $\frac{1}{2}\%$ to a decimal.

ANALYSIS: $\frac{1}{2}\% = \dfrac{\frac{1}{2}}{100} = \dfrac{1}{200} = .005$

Practice Test

Time at Start............

In the space provided, write the letter of the correct answer to the problem.

1. Fifteen is 20% of what number?
(a) 3   (b) 30   (c) 50   (d) 75   (e) 100   1. ....

2. Fifteen is $p\%$ of what number?
(a) $15p/100$ (b) $1500/p$ (c) $15/p$ (d) $p/15$ (e) none of these   2. ....

3. Fifteen is 250% of what number?
(a) 5   (b) 6   (c) 10   (d) 12   (e) 25   3. ....

4. What is 3% of m?
(a) $3m/100$ (b) $100/3m$ (c) $3m$ (d) $1/3m$ (e) none of these   4. ....

5. What number is $a\%$ of b?
(a) $ab/100$ (b) $b/100a$ (c) $a/100b$ (d) $100/ab$ (e) a/b 5. ....

6. A man saved $24. This is $37\frac{1}{2}\%$ of his salary. How much does he earn?
(a) $24   (b) $37   (c) $56   (d) $64   (e) $72   6. ....

7. Eight is what per cent of 2?
(a) 25%   (b) 100%   (c) 200%   (d) 300%   (e) 400%   7. ....

8. In a group of 250 men, 38% are above 21 years of age. How many are above 21 years of age?
(a) 75   (b) 95   (c) 100   (d) 112   (e) none of these   8. ....

9. a is $37\frac{1}{2}\%$ of what number?
(a) $3a/8$ (b) $3/8a$ (c) $8/3a$ (d) $8a/3$ (e) $3a$ 9. ....

10. Fifteen per cent of what number is p?
(a) $15p$ (b) $3p/8$ (c) $20p/3$ (d) $3p/20$ (e) none of these
10. ....

Time at End............   *Minutes Elapsed*............
                                              Average Time 25 Minutes

Answer Key for this test is on page 432.

My Score: *Number Right*............   *Number Wrong*............
                Average Number Right 5

Fifth Day: Verbal Problems in Per Cent

What You Should Know

1. There are two fundamental relationships that exist in problems dealing with selling:

(a) selling price = cost + profit

(b) list price − discount = selling price (The list price is sometimes designated as the marked price.)

PROBLEM: A book sells for $4.80. This represents a profit of 20% on the cost. Find this cost. (NOTE: Profit is *usually* considered as a per cent of the selling price unless otherwise indicated.)

ANALYSIS: This particular problem specifies that the profit is stated as a per cent of the *cost*. Thus, if x represents the cost, $20\%x$, or $\frac{1}{5}x$, or $x/5$ represents the profit. Using formula (a) above:

$$4.80 = x + x/5$$
$$24 = 5x + x$$
$$24 = 6x$$
$$4 = x$$

2. If no base figure is given in the problem, we can always choose a number. Thus, if a problem talks about a sum of money doubling, for example, we may choose $3 and $6, or $1 and $2, or $100 and $200.

Practice Test

Time at Start............

In the space provided, write the letter of the correct answer to the problem.

1. The selling price of a chair is $50. This represents the cost plus a profit of 10% on the selling price. Find the cost.
(a) $40 (b) $45 (c) $50 (d) $51.50 (e) none of these
1. ....

2. A man bought some stock on Monday for $50. On Tuesday it went up 10%; on Wednesday it went down 10%; on Thursday it went up 10%. Find the value of the stock after Thursday.
(a) $60 (b) $59 (c) $54.45 (d) $53.35 (e) none of these
2. ....

3. John Q. Bookworm pays $6 for a book after receiving a discount of 20%. What is the list price of the book?
(a) $5 (b) $6 (c) $6.85 (d) $7.50 (e) $9.25   3. ....

4. A tailor buys a dress for $90. He wishes to resell it at a profit of 10% on the selling price. What should he sell it for?
(a) $90 (b) $81.00 (c) $100 (d) $95.50 (e) $99 4. ....

5. Mr. Blic saved $28 last week. This represented 25% of his week's salary. Find his week's salary.
(a) $35 (b) $97.33 (c) $109.50 (d) $80 (e) $112 5. ....

6. Mr. Super Salesman earns a basic salary of $5,500 a year, plus 5% commission on all sales over $20,000. His sales for last year were $30,000. Find his salary last year.
(a) $5,700 (b) $5,800 (c) $5,500 (d) $6,000 (e) $6,500
6. ....

7. A TV set sells for $198. This represents a profit to the dealer of 10% based on his cost. Find this cost.
(a) $180 (b) $185 (c) $190 (d) $198 (e) $200   7. ....

8. Joe buys a desk for $72 after receiving a discount of 20% of the marked price. What was the marked price of the desk?
   (a) $75 (b) $95 (c) $90 (d) $100 (e) $79.80   8. ....

9. A man buys a dress for $60. He wishes to give a discount of 10% on the marked (list) price, and still to make a profit of 10% on the selling price. Find the list price to the nearest dollar.
   (a) $65 (b) $72 (c) $74 (d) $75 (e) $80   9. ....

10. A man drove his car from *A* to *B* at a speed that was 10% above the posted limit. His speedometer read 55 miles per hour. Find the posted limit.
   (a) 45 mph (b) 50 mph (c) 52 mph (d) 55 mph
   (e) none of these   10. ....

11. Find the single discount that is equivalent to two successive discounts of 10% and 20%.
   (a) 30% (b) 15% (c) 10% (d) 28% (e) none of these
   11. ....

Time at End............   *Minutes Elapsed*............
    Average Time 30 *Minutes*

Answer Key for this test is on page 432.

My Score: *Number Right*............   *Number Wrong*............
    Average Number Right 5

Sixth Day: Test of Mastery

Time at Start............

In the space provided, write the letter of the correct answer to the problem.

1. What fraction is equivalent to $62\frac{1}{2}\%$?
   (a) $\frac{1}{8}$ (b) $\frac{3}{8}$ (c) $\frac{5}{8}$ (d) $\frac{1}{6}$ (e) $\frac{5}{6}$ 1. ....

2. Eight per cent of 8 is sixteen per cent of what number?
   (a) 4 (b) 6 (c) 8 (d) 16 (e) 32   2. ....

3. A man spent 75% of his salary. He had $37.50 left. What was his salary?
   (a) $50 (b) $75 (c) $112.50 (d) $150 (e) $175   3. ....

4. Seven is what per cent of 56?
   (a) $\frac{1}{8}\%$ (b) 3% (c) 8% (d) 10% (e) $12\frac{1}{2}\%$ 4. ....

5. What per cent of a foot is a yard?
(a) $\frac{1}{2}\%$ (b) $33\frac{1}{3}\%$ (c) 100% (d) 200% (e) 300%

5. ....

6. What is 5% of 40g?
(a) 2 (b) 9 (c) 2g (d) 9g (e) 45g

6. ....

7. What is m% of n?
(a) $n/100m$ (b) $m/100n$ (c) $100mn$ (d) $mn/100$
(e) $100/mn$

7. ....

8. A jeweler sold some watches for $33 each. This included a profit of 10% on the cost. Find the cost of each watch.
(a) $29.70 (b) $30 (c) $33 (d) $35 (e) $36.30

8. ....

9. In a 200-pound shipment of corn oil, 20% was spoiled in transit. How many pounds were left?
(a) 180 (b) 40 (c) 120 (d) 160 (e) 100

9. ....

10. Eighteen boys passed an arithmetic test in Mr. Johnson's class. This represents 60% of the total number of boys in his class. How many boys are there in Mr. Johnson's class?
(a) 28 (b) 30 (c) 48 (d) cannot be done from the given information (e) can be done, but answer is not given.

10. ....

Time at End............   *Minutes Elapsed*............
                                    Average Time 30 *Minutes*

Answer Key for this test is on page 433.

My Score: *Number Right*............   *Number Wrong*............
                   Average Number Right 8

Section 9:   Handling Per Cent

Answer Key with Hints

Second Day   Page 424

1. 50%   7. $33\frac{1}{3}\%$
2. 25%   8. $37\frac{1}{2}\%$
3. ⅚   9. ⅛
4. 2½   10. 1¼
5. 1½   11. .0025
6. ⅞   12. 60%

Third Day   Page 425

1. (c) $4/7 = 12/21$; $4 \times 21 = 12 \times 7$.
2. (b) $x/3 = 6/7$; $7x = 18$; $x = 18/7$.
3. (e) $4/6 = 5/x$; $4x = 30$.
4. (d) $(x + 3)/4 = 3/1$; $x + 3 = 12$.
5. (a) $a/b = c/x$; $ax = bc$; $x = bc/a$.
6. (d) $30/45 = x/180$; $2/3 = x/180$.
7. (b) $385/4 = 11/x$; $35/4 = 1/x$.

Fourth Day   Page 426

1. (d) $20\% = \frac{1}{5}$.   The equation is: $15 = \frac{1}{5}x$.
2. (b) Use the equation: $15 = px/100$.
3. (b) $250\% = \frac{5}{2}$.
4. (a) The phrase "3% of *m*" may be written as $\frac{3}{100}m$.
5. (a) $x = (a/100)(b)$.
6. (d) Remember that the $37\frac{1}{2}\%$ is what he *saves*.
7. (e) You might notice that 8 is 4 times 2.
8. (b) There is no shortcut for 38%.   Multiply .38 by 250.
9. (d) $a = 3x/8$.
10. (c) Again a direct translation: $\frac{15}{100}x = p$.

Fifth Day   Page 428

1. (b) The profit is 10% of the selling price of $50, or $5
2. (c) Careful on this one—in each case we are taking 10% of a different number.
3. (d) Use the equation: $x - x/5 = 6.00$ where x = list price.
4. (c) Selling price = cost + profit. Thus, $x = 90 + x/10$.
5. (e) If x represents his salary, then $28 = \frac{1}{4}x$.
6. (d) His salary is $5,500 + 5\%$ of the $10,000, or ($30,000 − $20,000).
7. (a) Equation: $198 = x + x/10$.
8. (c) Equation: $x - x/5 = 72$ (where x = marked or list price).
9. (c) There are really two stages to this problem. In the first one, we can find the selling price by: $x - x/10$ = s. p. Then, using the selling price as $9x/10$, we get our answer by the equation $9x/10 = 60 + (\frac{1}{10})(9x/10)$.
10. (b) Speed limit + 10% (speed limit) = 55.

11. (d) Use 100 as a base. If the discounts are 20% and 10%, you pay 80% and 90% respectively. Thus, you pay $(.80)(.90) = .72$ altogether. Your discount is therefore $100\% - 72\% = 28\%$.

More of this type can be found in the work of day

Sixth Day   Page 430

1. (c) See the chart under the second day's work   2
   of this section.
2. (a) $(\frac{8}{100})(8) = \frac{16}{100}x$.   4
3. (d) Remember that the $37.50 he has left is   4
   25% of the salary.
4. (e) $7 = (x/100)(56)$.   4
5. (e) Remember that 1 yard = 3 feet.   4
6. (c) Equation: $x = (\frac{1}{20})(40g)$.   4
7. (d) Equation: $x = (m/100)(n)$.   4
8. (b) If x = his cost, then $33 = x + x/10$.   5
9. (d) If 20% was spoiled, then 80% (or $\frac{4}{5}$)   5
   remained.
10. (b) Equation: $18 = \frac{2}{5}x$.   5

THE ABCs OF ALGEBRA

Section 11: THE ABCs OF ALGEBRA

Mastery of algebraic operations is as essential to your success as knowing how to add, subtract, multiply, and divide. The purpose of this section is to help you evaluate and improve on the degree to which you are able to manipulate algebraic symbols. The short cuts and techniques included in each day's work should give you the speed, accuracy, and understanding you will need. Remember, most of the problems on your College Entrance Examinations will involve algebraic techniques. While it is true that some of these may be solved arithmetically, the algebraic solution is the better one for achieving speed and accuracy.

Use the Inventory Test to discover just where you must concentrate your efforts. For best results, plan your review time in daily units, not in one or two cram sessions. The Test of Mastery will help you to evaluate your gain in control over the operations of algebra.

First Day: Inventory Test

Time at Start............

In the space provided, write the letter of the correct answer to the problem.

1. The result obtained when -6 is subtracted from -4 is
(a) -10 (b) $+10$ (c) $+24$ (d) -2 (e) $+2$ 1. ....

2. If $ax + d = e$, $a \neq 0$, x is equal to
(a) $d - e - a$ (b) $e - d - a$ (c) $e + a - d$
(d) $(e - d)/a$ (e) $(d - e)/a$ 2. ....

434

3. Solve for $r : r^2 = 9r$
(a) 9 (b) 0 (c) 0, 9 (d) 11, 9 (e) 3, 9   3. ....

4. If $\sqrt{x} = -2$, x is
(a) 4 (b) 2 (c) −4 (d) −2 (e) none of these   4. ....

5. If $x + y = a$, $x - y = b$, xy is
(a) $a^2 + b^2$ (b) $(a^2 - b^2)/4$ (c) $(a^2 + b^2)/4$
(d) $(a^2 - b^2)/2$ (e) $(a^2 + b^2)/8$ 5. ....

6. A student bicycles to school at 6 miles per hour, and after school he returns home at 3 miles per hour. The average rate for the round trip in miles per hour is
(a) 4 (b) 4½ (c) 14 (d) 5 (e) 3   6. ....

7. If 10 ounces of an $x\%$ solution of disinfectant are mixed with 20 ounces of a $y\%$ solution of disinfectant, the percent of disinfectant in the final solution is
(a) $(.1y + .2x)/30$ (b) $(.1x + .2y)/30$ (c) $(x + 2y)/30$
(d) $(.x + 2y)/3$ (e) $(x + 2y)/3$ 7. ....

8. A man has 25 coins in nickels and dimes, the total value being $2.25. How many dimes does the man have?
(a) 5 (b) 20 (c) 15 (d) 10 (e) 4   8. ....

9. The tens digit of a two-digit number is represented by t, and the units digit is represented by u. The number with its digits reversed is represented by
(a) tu (b) ut (c) $10t + u$ (d) $t + 10u$ (e) $10u + 10t$
                                        9. ....

10. A boy can do a job in 4 hours; his father can do the same job in 2 hours. The number of hours it will take both of them working together to do the job is
(a) 3 (b) 1½ (c) 1⅓ (d) 1¼ (e) 1⅕   10. ....

Time at End............   *Total Number of Minutes Elapsed*.............
                            Average Time 30 Minutes

Answer Key with Analysis

ANSWERS

1. (e)
$$-4$$
$$-$$
$$\underline{-6}$$
$$+2$$

ANALYSIS

1. When subtracting signed numbers, change the sign of the bottom one and apply the rules for addition.

2. (d)
$$ax + d = e$$
$$ax = e - d$$
$$x = (e - d)/a \quad (a \neq 0)$$

2. Subtract d from both sides of the equation; then divide by a.

3. (c)
$$r^2 = 9r$$
$$r^2 - 9r = 0$$
$$r(r - 9) = 0$$
$$r = 0 \quad r - 9 = 0$$
$$\qquad\qquad r = 9$$

3. Bring all terms onto one side of the equation. Set this side equal to zero, factor, set each factor equal to zero and solve for r.

4. (e)
$$\sqrt{x} = -2$$
no root

4. The symbol $\sqrt{}$ stands for the *positive* square root only; $\sqrt{x}$ could never be a negative number.

5. (b)
(1) $x + y = a$
(2) $x - y = b$
$$2x = a + b$$
$$x = (a + b)/2$$
$$2y = a - b$$
$$y = (a - b)/2$$
$$xy = (a + b)(a - b)/(2)(2)$$
$$\quad = (a^2 - b^2)/4$$

5. Add equations (1) and (2) and solve for x. Subtract equation (2) from equation (1) and solve for y. Then multiply x by y.

6. (a)
Average rate
$$= \frac{\text{total distance}}{\text{total time}}$$

$$= \frac{18 + 18}{6 + 3} = \frac{36}{9} = 4$$

6. Assume a convenient distance (18). Then use the formula for average rate.

7. (b)
$$\frac{(10)(.01x) + (20)(.01y)}{10 + 20}$$
$$= (.1x + .2y)/30$$

7. Use the equation
% disinfectant =
$$\frac{\text{amount pure disinfectant}}{\text{amount solution}}$$

8. (b)

	Number of coins	×	Value in cents	=	Total value
Nickels	25 − x		5		5(25 − x)
Dimes	x		10		10x
Total	25				225

$$5(25 - x) + 10x = 225$$
$$125 - 5x + 10x = 225$$
$$5x = 100$$
$$x = 20$$

8. A table helps to tabulate our information about the coins. The basic relationship is value of nickels + value of dimes = total value.

9. (d)
   t: tens digit
   u: units digit
   Original number: $10t + u$
   Number with digits reversed: $10u + t$

9. The number is represented by $10t + u$, so the number with digits reversed must be $10u + t$.

10. (c)
   Let x be the number of hours it will take the boy and his father working together.
   $(x/4) + (x/2) = 1$
   $x + 2x = 4$
   $3x = 4$
   $x = 1\frac{1}{3}$

10. In 1 hour, the boy and his father will do $\frac{1}{4}$ and $\frac{1}{2}$ of the job, respectively; in x hours they will do $x/4$ and $x/2$.

My Score: Number Right............   Number Wrong............
            Average Number Right 6

Second Day: Signed Numbers

What You Should Know

VOCABULARY

quotient: the result whenever one number is divided by another
parentheses: a symbol of inclusiveness used in grouping

signed numbers: numbers with a + or − in front. A temperature of 7° above zero can be represented as +7; a temperature of 7° below zero can be represented as −7. A gain of $4 can be represented as +$4; a loss of $4 can be represented as −$4.

absolute value of a number: the number's magnitude, denoted by two vertical bars: $|+7| = 7$; $|-7| = 7$; $|-\frac{1}{2}| = \frac{1}{2}$.

1. To add signed numbers:
  (a) if the signs are the same, add absolute values and repeat the sign.
  (b) if the signs are different, take the difference of the absolute values of the numbers and use the sign of the number having the larger absolute value.

2. To subtract signed numbers, change the sign of the bottom one and follow the rules for addition.

3. The product or quotient of two numbers having the same sign is positive.

4. The product or quotient of two numbers having different signs is negative.

Practice Test

Time at Start............

In the space provided, write the letter of the correct answer to the problem.

1. When +5 and −6 are added, the result is
(a) 1   (b) −1   (c) 11   (d) −11   (e) −30   1. ....

2. When −3 and −8 are added, the result is
(a) +5   (b) −5   (c) +11   (d) −11   (e) +30   2. ....

3. Subtract: +4
           −5
(a) 9   (b) −9   (c) −1   (d) 1   (e) −20   3. ....

4. When −5 is subtracted from +8, the result is
(a) −3   (b) 3   (c) −13   (d) 13   (e) −40   4. ....

5. $(-3)(-7)$ equals
(a) -10 (b) 10   (c) 21   (d) -21 (e) -4 5. ....

6. The result obtained from the multiplication $(-4)(+\frac{1}{2})(-6)$ is
(a) $-10\frac{1}{2}$ (b) $10\frac{1}{2}$ (c) 12   (d) -12 (e) 48   6. ....

7. The sign of the quotient $+8 \div -3$ is
(a) $+$ (b) $-$ (c) either $+$ or $-$ (d) cannot be done from the given information   (e) none of these   7. ....

8. When $(+3)(-6)(-2) - (-3)$ is simplified, the result is
(a) -2 (b) -33 (c) 33   (d) -8 (e) 39   8. ....

9. When $(+3) + (-5) - (-2)$ is simplified, the result is
(a) 0   (b) -4 (c) 10   (d) 8   (e) 13   9. ....

10. When $(+8) - (-6)(+3)$ is simplified, the result is
(a) 30   (b) 6   (c) 42   (d) 26   (e) -10 10. ....

Time at End............   *Minutes Elapsed*............
                                   Average Time 10 *Minutes*

Answer Key for this test is on page 460.

My Score: *Number Right*............   *Number Wrong*............
                     Average Number Right 7

Third Day: Simple Equations

What You Should Know

VOCABULARY

equation: a statement of equality, for example, $3x = 9$, $x + 1 = 3$, $a = a$

identity: an equation true for all values of the unknown(s), for example, $x + 1 = x + 1$, $x + y = x + y$, $x = x$, $4 = 4$

PROBLEM: Solve for x: $3x + 2 = 8$.

ANALYSIS: Subtract 2 from both sides of the equation, yielding $3x = 6$. Then divide both sides by 3 to obtain $x = 2$.

PROBLEM: Solve for x: $ax + b = c$ where $a \neq 0$.

ANALYSIS: Subtract b from both sides of the equation, yielding $ax = c - b$. Then divide both sides by a where $a \neq 0$ to obtain $x = (c - b)/a$.

PROBLEM: Solve for x: $.035x + .245 = 1.295$

ANALYSIS: Multiply both sides of the equation by 1000 (move decimal points three places to the right).
$$35x + 245 = 1295$$
$$35x = 1050$$
$$x = 30$$

PROBLEM: Solve for x and y: $3x + 2y = 5; 2x + 7y = 9$.

ANALYSIS: (1) $3x + 2y = 5$
(2) $2x + 7y = 9$

Method 1: Multiply equation (1) by 2 and equation (2) by 3.
$$6x + 4y = 10$$
$$6x + 21y = 27$$

Now subtract the bottom equation from the top.
$$-17y = -17$$
$$y = 1$$

Substitute in equation (1) to get x.
$$3x + 2(1) = 5$$
$$3x = 3$$
$$x = 1$$

Method 2: Solve equation (1) for y.
$$3x + 2y = 5$$
$$2y = 5 - 3x$$
$$y = (5 - 3x)/2$$

Substitute this value in equation (2).
$$2x + [7(5 - 3x)/2] = 9$$

Now multiply by 2.
$$4x + 7(5 - 3x) = 18$$
$$4x + 35 - 21x = 18$$
$$-17x = -17$$
$$x = 1$$

Substitute in equation (2) to get y.
$$2(1) + 7y = 9$$
$$7y = 7$$
$$y = 1$$

Practice Test

Time at Start............

In the space provided, write the letter of the correct answer to the problem.

1. If $3x + 9 = 11$, x equals
(a) $-\frac{3}{2}$ (b) $-1\frac{1}{3}$ (c) $\frac{2}{3}$ (d) -2 (e) $\frac{3}{2}$ **1.** ....

2. If $bx = c$ and $b \neq 0$, then x equals
(a) $c - b$ (b) $b - c$ (c) b/c (d) bc (e) c/b **2.** ....

3. Solve for y: $ay = by + c, a \neq b$.
(a) $a + b - c$ (b) $c/(a - b)$ (c) $(a + b)/c$ (d) $(a - b)/c$
(e) $c/(a + b)$ **3.** ....

4. Solve for u: $u - 3(u - 1) = -1$.
(a) $u = 2$ (b) $u = 1$ (c) $u = -1$ (d) $u = -2$
(e) $u = 0$ **4.** ....

5. If $t/3 + t/4 = 1$, find t.
(a) $\frac{1}{2}$ (b) $1\frac{1}{8}$ (c) $\frac{7}{12}$ (d) $\frac{8}{11}$ (e) $1\frac{2}{7}$ **5.** ....

6. If $3/(3 - x) + \frac{1}{2} = 2$, find x.
(a) $\frac{1}{2}$ (b) $\frac{3}{4}$ (c) 1 (d) $\frac{5}{4}$ (e) $\frac{3}{2}$ **6.** ....

7. If $.03x = 9$, x equals
(a) $.33$ (b) 30 (c) 300 (d) 3000 (e) 3 **7.** ....

8. Solve for x: $1 + .2x = 1.010$.
(a) $.00005$ (b) $.0005$ (c) $.005$ (d) $.05$ (e) $.5$ **8.** ....

9. Find x and y: $x + y = 9; x - y = 5$.
(a) $7; 2$ (b) $2; 7$ (c) $6; 3$ (d) $3; 6$ (e) $5; 4$ **9.** ....

10. If $x + y = 6a$, $x - y = 8b$, then y is
(a) $12ab$ (b) $a - 4b$ (c) $a + 4b$ (d) $3a - 4b$
(e) $4b - 3a$ **10.** ....

Time at End............   *Minutes Elapsed*............
                              Average Time 25 *Minutes*

Answer Key for this test is on page 461.

My Score: *Number Right*............   *Number Wrong*............
            Average Number Right 7

Fourth Day: Quadratic Equations

What You Should Know

VOCABULARY

quadratic equation: an equation that can be put into the form $ax^2 + bx + c = 0$ where $a \neq 0$ and a, b, and c are independent of x. Examples are $x^2 + 3x = 0$, $x^2 = 16$, $x^2 - 3x = -2$.

1. Every quadratic equation has two roots.

2. $\sqrt{b}$ means the positive square root of b. For example, $\sqrt{9} = +3$, $\sqrt{16} = +4$.

PROBLEM: Solve for x: $x^2 = 9$.

ANALYSIS: Take the square root of each side: $x = \pm\sqrt{9} = \pm 3$ or $x = +3, -3$. Both signs, $+$ and $-$, are necessary since $\sqrt{9}$ alone would mean the positive square root only.

PROBLEM: Solve for x: $x^2 = 2x$.

ANALYSIS: Bring all terms to one side of the equation: $x^2 - 2x = 0$. Factor: $x(x - 2) = 0$. Then set each factor equal to zero: $x = 0$; $x - 2 = 0$, $x = 2$. The solution is therefore $x = 0, 2$.

PROBLEM: Solve for x: $x^2 - 5x = 6$.

ANALYSIS: Bring all terms to one side of the equation: $x^2 - 5x - 6 = 0$. Factor: $(x - 6)(x + 1) = 0$. Then set each factor equal to zero: $x - 6 = 0$, $x = 6$; $x + 1 = 0$, $x = -1$. The solution is therefore $x = 6, -1$.

3. The sum of the roots $(r_1 + r_2)$ of the equation $ax^2 + bx + c = 0$ where $a \neq 0$, is equal to $-b/a$; the product of the roots $(r_1 r_2)$ is equal to c/a.

PROBLEM: Find both the sum and the product of the roots of the equation $2x^2 - 7x = 3$.

ANALYSIS: Bring all terms to one side of the equation: $-2x^2 + 7x + 3 = 0$. Now $r_1 + r_2 = -b/a = -7/-2 = 7/2$; $r_1 r_2 = c/a = 3/-2 = -3/2$.

4. In an equation whose solution requires that both sides be squared or cubed, it is imperative that results be checked in the original equation.

5. Remember that when a binomial is squared, we get a trinomial (3 terms).
$$(2 - x)^2 = (2 - x)(2 - x) = 4 - 4x + x^2$$

PROBLEM: Solve for x: $\sqrt{x} = -7$.

ANALYSIS: Method 1: $\sqrt{x}$ must be either a positive number or equal to zero. Since it could never be -7, a negative number, the equation has no root.

Method 2: Square both sides of the equation.
$$(\sqrt{x})^2 = (-7)^2$$
$$x = 49$$
Since we have squared our equation in solving, we must check our result by substituting it in the original equation. This yields $\sqrt{49} = -7$, which is incorrect since $\sqrt{49} = +7$. Therefore the equation has no root.

PROBLEM: Solve for x: $\sqrt{x - 2} + x = 2$.

ANALYSIS: Isolate the radical: $\sqrt{x - 2} = 2 - x$. Square both sides: $(\sqrt{x - 2})^2 = (2 - x)^2$; $x - 2 = 4 - 4x + x^2$. Combine like terms, factor, and solve in the usual way: $x^2 - 5x + 6 = 0$; $(x - 3)(x - 2) = 0$; $x = 3, 2$. Now check these tentative roots in the original equation:

First, $x = 3$
$$\sqrt{3 - 2} + 3 \overset{?}{=} 2$$
$$\sqrt{3 - 2} \overset{?}{=} 2 - 3$$
$$\sqrt{1} \overset{?}{=} -1$$
This is incorrect since $\sqrt{1} = +1$. Therefore 3 is not a root.

Next, $x = 2$
$$\sqrt{2 - 2} + 2 \overset{?}{=} 2$$
$$\sqrt{2 - 2} \overset{?}{=} 2 - 2$$
$$\sqrt{0} \overset{?}{=} 0$$
$$0 = 0$$
Since there is no contradiction here, $x = 2$ is a root, and the only one.

PROBLEM: Solve for x: $2\sqrt{2x+1} - 3\sqrt{x} = 0$.

ANALYSIS: Separate the radicals: $2\sqrt{2x+1} = 3\sqrt{x}$.   Square both sides: $4(2x+1) = 9x$. This yields $x = 4$ as a tentative root.   Now check it in the original: $2\sqrt{2 \times 4 + 1} - 3\sqrt{4} \overset{?}{=} 0$; $2\sqrt{9} - 3\sqrt{4} \overset{?}{=} 0$; $2 \times 3 - 3 \times 2 \overset{?}{=} 0$; $0 = 0$. Since it leads to no contradiction, $x = 4$ is a root of the equation.

Practice Test

Time at Start............

In the space provided, write the letter of the correct answer to the problem.

1. If $x^2 = 16$, the solution(s) for x is (are)
(a) 4   (b) 2, 8   (c) 0, 4   (d) 4, -4 (e) none of these
1. ....

2. Solve for x: $x^2 - 10 = 0$.
(a) 5   (b) 2, 5   (c) $\pm\sqrt{10}$ (d) $\sqrt{10}$ (e) none of these
2. ....

3. The root(s) of $3\sqrt{2x+5} = -5$ is (are)
(a) 0   (b) 2   (c) 0, 5   (d) -5 (e) this equation has no roots
3. ....

4. The root(s) of $x^2 = 3x$ is (are)
(a) 1   (b) 0   (c) 3, 0   (d) -3 (e) $-3, 0$
4. ....

5. Solve for x: $x^2 + bx = 0$.
(a) b (b) 0, $-b$ (c) 0, b (d) 0   (e) b^2
5. ....

6. The solution(s) of $x^2 + 4x = 12$ is (are)
(a) $-6, 2$ (b) 6, -2 (c) 6   (d) -1 (e) 1
6. ....

7. Solve for x: $3\sqrt{x-5} - 2\sqrt{x} = 0$.
(a) 9   (b) -9 (c) 0, 9   (d) 0, -9 (e) this equation has no roots
7. ....

8. The solution(s) of $\sqrt{x-7} - x = -9$ is (are)
(a) 11, 8   (b) 8   (c) 10   (d) 11   (e) this equation has no roots
8. ....

9. The sum of the roots of $ax^2 - c = 0$, $a \neq 0$, is
(a) c/a (b) 0   (c) $-c/a$ (d) a/c (e) $-a/c$
9. ....

10. If one of the roots of $3x^2 - 9x + k = 0$ is 2, k is
(a) 1 (b) -2 (c) $+2$ (d) -6 (e) 6   10. ....

Time at End............   *Minutes Elapsed*............
          Average Time 30 *Minutes*

Answer Key for this test is on page 481.

My Score: *Number Right*............   *Number Wrong*............
          Average Number Right 6

Fifth Day: More on Equations

What You Should Know

PROBLEM: If $x/3 = \frac{1}{6}$, then what does $x/2$ equal?

ANALYSIS: Multiply by 6 and solve for x: $2x = 1$; $x = \frac{1}{2}$.
Now simply divide this result by 2: $x/2 = \frac{1}{2}/2 = \frac{1}{4}$.

PROBLEM: If $a = 33$, $b = 333$, $c = 3333$ and $x = b - a$, $y = c + b$, $z = 3b - a$, find the numerical value of $x + y - z$.

ANALYSIS: $x + y - z = (b - a) + (c + b) - (3b - a)$
          $= b - a + c + b - 3b + a$
          $= c - b$
          $= 3333 - 333$
          $= 3000$

PROBLEM: If $1/x = 3$ and $1/y = 4$, find the numerical value of $(x + y)/xy$.

ANALYSIS:
$(x + y)/xy = (x/xy + y/xy = 1/y + 1/x = 3 + 4 = 7$

Practice Test

Time at Start............

In the space provided, write the letter of the correct answer to the problem.

1. If $x/9 = \frac{1}{5}$, then $x/6$ is
(a) $\frac{54}{5}$ (b) $\frac{5}{54}$ (c) $\frac{10}{7}$ (d) $\frac{3}{10}$ (e) $\frac{10}{3}$ 1. ....

2. If $3x + 2 = -4$, then $(x + 1)/3x$ is
(a) $1/6$ (b) $-1/6$ (c) $-1/2$ (d) $1/2$ (e) $1/3$ 2. ....

3. Solve for x: $\left(\frac{x}{2} - \frac{x}{3}\right)^{13} = \left(\frac{1}{6}\right)^{13}$.
(a) 1 (b) 2 (c) -1 (d) -2 (e) $1/2$ 3. ....

4. If $x + y = k$ and $x = y$, then $(xy)^2$ equals
(a) $k^4/12$ (b) $k^4/4$ (c) $k^8/16$ (d) $k^4/16$ (e) $k^{16}/16$
4. ....

5. If $x + l = m$, $x - l$ is
(a) $m + l$ (b) $m - 2l$ (c) $m + 2l$ (d) $m - l$ (e) $m + 3l$
5. ....

6. If $a = 72$, $b = 14$, $c = 21$ and $Q = b - 2c$, $R = a - c$, $T = b - 3c + a$, then $Q + R - T$ is
(a) 6,594 (b) 22 (c) $7/22$ (d) 0 (e) -4 6. ....

7. If $1/x = 2$, $1/y = 3$, then $(x - y)/(x + y)$ is
(a) 0 (b) -6 (c) $1/56$ (d) $-1/6$ (e) $1/5$ 7. ....

8. If $(x^2 + 9)/9 = k$, $(x/3)^2$ is
(a) 11 (b) $k - 2$ (c) $k - 1$ (d) $k + 1$ (e) $k + 2$
8. ....

9. If $a + b = k$ and $ab = s$, then $a^2 + b^2$ is
(a) k^2 (b) $3k^2 + 2$ (c) $3k^2 - 1$ (d) $k^2 - 2s$ (e) $k^2 + 2s$
9. ....

10. If $a - b = k$ and $ab = s$, then $(1/a^2) + (1/b^2)$ is
(a) $2s/k$ (b) k^{3s}/s^2 (c) $(k^2 - 2s)/s^2$ (d) $(k^2 - 2)/s$
(e) $(k^2 + 2s)/s^2$ 10. ....

Time at End........... *Minutes Elapsed*...........
Average Time 30 *Minutes*

Answer Key for this test is on page 452.

My Score: *Number Right*........... *Number Wrong*...........
Average Number Right 7

Sixth Day: Work and Digit Problems

What You Should Know

1. For work problems:

$$\text{Part of job completed} = \frac{\text{time actually worked}}{\text{time usually taken}}$$

PROBLEM: Davey Jones usually completes a job in 5 days. After working for 2 days he is joined by Billy Smith and they finish the job together in 1 day. How long does the job usually take Billy alone?

ANALYSIS: Let x represent Billy's usual time in days.

$$\underset{1 \text{ (the whole job)}}{\underline{\begin{array}{c}\text{part of job Davey does} \\ + \text{ part of job Billy does}\end{array}}}$$

$$\frac{\text{Actual time:}}{\text{Usual time:}} \quad \frac{2+1}{5} + \frac{1}{x} = 1$$

$$3x + 5 = 5x$$
$$5 = 2x$$
$$x = 2\tfrac{1}{2}$$

The job would therefore take Billy $2\tfrac{1}{2}$ days working alone.

PROBLEM: It takes 3 men 5 days to assemble 30 cars. How long will it take 2 men to assemble 6 cars?

ANALYSIS: 3×5 or 15 man-days: 30 cars
3 man-days: 6 cars
3 man-days $= (2 \text{ men})(x \text{ days})$
$$x = 1\tfrac{1}{2}$$

It would therefore take 2 men $1\tfrac{1}{2}$ days to assemble 6 cars.

2. For digit problems: since *tu* and *ut* in algebra both mean *t* multiplied by *u*, we represent a two-digit number by $10t + u$, and the number with its digits reversed by $10u + t$.

Practice Test

Time at Start............

In the space provided, write the letter of the correct answer to the problem.

1. Mr. Strongback can do a job in 5 days, while his friend, Mr. Weakmind, needs 10 days to complete the same job. How long will the job take if both men work together?
(a) 3 days (b) $3\tfrac{1}{3}$ days (c) 7 days (d) $2\tfrac{1}{2}$ days
(e) 5 days   1. ....

2. Farmer Alfalfa can sweep his barn in d hours. How much of the job is completed in m hours, d being greater than m?
   (a) md (b) $m - d$ (c) d/m (d) $m + d$ (e) m/d 2. ....

3. Mrs. Page does her dishes in 15 minutes, while her daughter Ann needs twice as long to do the same dishes. If they work together, how many minutes will the job take them?
   (a) 5   (b) 7   (c) $7\frac{1}{2}$ (d) 10   (e) 30   3. ....

4. Two pipes can fill a swimming pool in 5 hours and 12 hours respectively. A third pipe can empty the pool in 4 hours. If the caretaker makes a mistake and leaves all three pipes open, how many hours will it take to fill the pool?
   (a) $3\frac{1}{3}$ (b) 15   (c) 30   (d) 45   (e) 60   4. ....

5. Mr. Snow can build a tool shed in 6 hours. Mr. Snow works alone for 2 hours, and is then called away. His partner, Mr. Hale, then finishes the job in 5 hours. How many hours would it take Mr. Hale alone to do the job?
   (a) 7   (b) $7\frac{1}{2}$ (c) 8   (d) 13   (e) 15   5. ....

6. If 3 Boy Scouts can build 30 shelters in 4 hours, how many hours will it take 2 Boy Scouts to build 10 shelters at the same rate?
   (a) 2   (b) $2\frac{1}{2}$ (c) 6   (d) 12   (e) 1   6. ....

7. If 3 men clean a garden in 6 days, how long would it take q men to do the same job?
   (a) $6q$ days   (b) $18q$ days   (c) $(18 - q)$ days   (d) $6/q$ days
   (e) $18/q$ days   7. ....

8. If 3 men can build a tree house in 5 days and 7 boys can build the same house in 10 days, how long will it take if the 3 men and 7 boys work together?
   (a) 3 days   (b) $3\frac{1}{3}$ days   (c) $3\frac{1}{2}$ days   (d) 12 days
   (e) 10 days   8. ....

9. If r represents the tens digit of a two-digit number and s represents the units digit, by how much does the number with its digits reversed exceed the sum of the digits?
   (a) $9s$ (b) $9r$ (c) $9s + r$ (d) $9r + s$ (e) $9(s + r)$
                                                        9. ....

10. The sum of the digits of a two-digit number is 11. If the digits are reversed, the new number exceeds the original number by 27. Find the tens digit of the original number.

(a) 4 (b) 7 (c) 6 (d) 8 (e) 9   10. ....

Time at End............   *Minutes Elapsed*............
                                 Average Time 35 Minutes

Answer Key for this test is on page 462.

My Score: *Number Right*............   *Number Wrong*............
               Average Number Right 7

Seventh Day: Motion Problems

What You Should Know

1. Motion problems usually involve three basic formulas easily remembered by the following:

$$\text{"how far"} \quad D = R \times T$$
$$\text{"how fast"} \quad R = D/T$$
$$\text{"how long"} \quad T = D/R$$

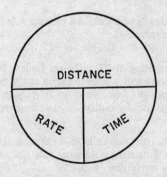

2. Remember that average rate is *not* the sum of two rates divided by two. It is the total distance divided by the total time.

PROBLEM: A man drives 60 miles to a nearby town at 20 miles per hour and returns the same distance at 30 miles per hour. Find his average rate for the entire trip.

ANALYSIS:

$$\text{Time going} = \frac{60}{20} = 3$$

$$\text{Time returning} = \frac{60}{30} = 2$$

$$\text{Average rate} = \frac{\text{total distance}}{\text{total time}} = \frac{60 + 60}{3 + 2} = \frac{120}{5} = 24$$

His average rate was therefore 24 miles per hour.

Practice Test

Time at Start............

In the space provided, write the letter of the correct answer to the problem.

1. Dr. Killemoff leaves for a convention at 10:15 A.M. and arrives at 3:45 P.M. If he stopped for one hour for lunch and traveled at a uniform rate of 30 miles per hour, how far away in miles is the convention?
(a) 135   (b) 165   (c) 75   (d) 195   (e) none of these
1. ....

2. A man walks ⅓ of a mile in 4 minutes. At how many miles per hour did he travel?
(a) 5   (b) 12   (c) 4   (d) 1⅓   (e) 20   2. ....

3. A plane traveling at 600 miles per hour is 30 miles from an airport. How long will it take to arrive at the airport?
(a) 15 minutes   (b) 3 minutes   (c) 20 minutes   (d) cannot be done from the given information   (e) can be done, but the answer is not given   3. ....

4. Joe Speedy runs one mile in 4 minutes. He runs the first ¾ of a mile in 2 minutes. At what rate (in miles per minute) must he run the remaining ¼ mile?
(a) ¹⁄₁₆   (b) ⅛   (c) ¼   (d) ⅝   (e) 7½   4. ....

5. Two men start driving from the same city in the same direction at 40 miles per hour and 50 miles per hour respectively. How soon are they 30 miles apart?
(a) 3 hours   (b) 1½ hours   (c) 2 hours   (d) 81 minutes
(e) none of these   5. ....

6. A man travels for 3 hours at 30 miles per hour, then increases his speed to 45 miles per hour for 2 hours. Find his average rate for the entire trip.

(a) 30 mph   (b) 35 mph   (c) 15 mph   (d) 45 mph
(e) 36 mph   6. ....

7. If a man goes *t* miles in *h* hours, what is his rate in miles per hour?

(a) h/t (b) t/h (c) $h \div t$ (d) $h - t$ (e) $2t - h$ 7. ....

8. A jet airliner makes a round trip between cities *A* and *B*, 2,000 miles apart. If the rate of the plane going from *A* to *B* is 500 miles per hour and the average rate for the round trip is 400 miles per hour, at what rate in miles per hour did the airliner return?

(a) 300   (b) 320   (c) $333\frac{1}{3}$ (d) $369\frac{2}{3}$ (e) 380   8. ....

9. A man goes downstream in his motorboat for 10 miles, then returns. How much time did he spend on the round trip?

(I) He travels downstream at 15 miles per hour.

(II) The stream flows at the rate of 2 miles per hour.

To do this problem,

(a) the given information and statement I are enough   (b) the given information and statement II are enough   (c) the given information and statements I and II are enough   (d) the given information and statement I or statement II are enough   (e) the given information and statements I and II are not enough

9. ....

10. A cable car travels up a Swiss mountainside at *m* miles per hour for *c* hours, then returns the same distance at *d* miles per hour. Express the average rate in miles per hour in terms of *m*, *c*, and *d*.

(a) md/c (b) mc/d (c) $2md/(d + m)$
(d) $2mcd/(mc + cd)$ (e) none of these   10. ....

Time at End.............   *Minutes Elapsed*............
                                              Average Time 25 Minutes

Answer Key for this test is on page 463.

My Score: *Number Right*............   *Number Wrong*............
               Average Number Right 7

Eighth Day: Mixture Problems (Chemical)

What You Should Know

VOCABULARY

evaporate: to remove water or some other liquid
dilute: to make a solution weaker by adding water or some other liquid

1. If A is some substance in solution,
Amount of pure A = % of pure A in solution (written as decimal) × total amount of solution

PROBLEM: In 1,000 gallons of a 10% solution of salt, how much salt is present?

ANALYSIS: Amount salt = % salt × total amount solution
= .10 × 1000 gallons
= 100 gallons

2. If A is some substance in solution,

$$\% \text{ of pure } A \text{ in solution} = \frac{\text{amount of pure } A}{\text{total amount of solution}}$$

PROBLEM: How many gallons of water must be added to 40 gallons of a 15% solution of salt water in order to obtain a 10% solution of salt water?

ANALYSIS: Let x represent the necessary number of gallons.

$$\% \text{ salt} = \frac{\text{amount salt}}{\text{total amount solution}}$$

$$\frac{10}{100} = \frac{.15(40)}{40 + x}$$

$$\frac{1}{10} = \frac{6}{40 + x}$$

$$40 + x = 60$$
$$x = 20$$

Practice Test

Time at Start............

In the space provided, write the letter of the correct answer to the problem.

1. An orange-drink manufacturer uses 25% pure orange juice in the manufacture of orange drink. If the manufacturer makes 1 million gallons of orange drink, how many gallons of pure orange juice does he need?
   (a) 750,000   (b) 250,000   (c) 200,000   (d) 275,000
   (e) none of these   1. ....

2. A cola manufacturer uses carbonated water and cola flavoring in the manufacture of a bottled drink. If 16% of the drink is cola flavoring and each bottle holds 32 ounces, how many ounces of carbonated water are there in each bottle?
   (a) 2   (b) 5.12   (c) 30   (d) 27.88   (e) none of these
                                                  2. ....

3. A solution contains x ounces of $p\%$ pure alcohol. The number of ounces of pure alcohol in the solution is
   (a) px (b) $10px$ (c) $100p/x$ (d) $.1px$ (e) $.01px$ 3. ....

4. Thirty ounces of a $p\%$ solution of dye are mixed with 50 ounces of a 10% solution of dye. The percentage of dye in the final solution is
   (a) $(.03p + 5)/80$ (b) $(.05p + 3)/80$ (c) $(.3p + 5)/80$
   (d) $(.3p + 5)/35$ (e) $(.05p + 3)/35$ 4. ....

5. A solution contains 10 ounces of a 1% solution of iodine. If p ounces of iodine are added, the percentage of iodine in the solution is
   (a) $(.1 + p)/(10 + p)$ (b) $(.01 + p)/(10 - p)$
   (c) $(.1 + p)/10$ (d) $p/100$ (e) $(.001 + p)/10$ 5. ....

6. How many ounces of pure acid must be added to 20 ounces of a 9% solution in order to make it a 12% solution?
   (a) $\frac{1}{2}$ (b) $\frac{3}{8}$ (c) $\frac{15}{22}$ (d) $\frac{7}{11}$ (e) none of these   6. ....

7. How many pounds of water must be added to 96 pounds of a 10% solution of salt water in order to dilute the solution so that it contains 6% salt?
   (a) 59   (b) 62   (c) 64   (d) 65   (e) none of these   7. ....

8. How many pounds of copper must be alloyed with 100 pounds of pure silver to form sterling silver which is 88 parts silver to 12 parts copper?
   (a) 13   (b) 13⁷⁄₁₁   (c) 14   (d) 14⁷⁄₁₁   (e) none of these

8. ....

9. How many gallons of water must be evaporated from 200 gallons of a 6% solution of salt in order to leave a 10% solution?
   (a) 80   (b) 90   (c) 100   (d) 101½   (e) none of these

9. ....

10. An automobile radiator contains 10 gallons of a solution which is 20% alcohol and 80% water. How many gallons of the solution must be drained off and replaced by alcohol in order to make the solution 60% alcohol?
   (a) 3   (b) 3¾   (c) 4½   (d) 5   (e) 6

10. ....

Time at End............   *Minutes Elapsed*............
                                             Average Time 30 *Minutes*

Answer Key for this test is on page 464.

My Score: *Number Right*............   *Number Wrong*............
             Average Number Right 6

Ninth Day: Mixture Problems (Nonchemical)

What You Should Know

VOCABULARY

principal: the amount of money with which an investor starts

1. Principal × rate of interest (expressed as decimal) = amount of interest, or $PR = I$

PROBLEM: A man has $2,000 invested at 4½% interest per year. How much money in interest does he receive at the end of one year?

ANALYSIS: $$PR = I$$
                    $$(\$2000)(.045) = I$$
                    $$\$90 = I$$

2. The total value of a mixture equals the sum of the values of its individual components.

PROBLEM: How many pounds of coffee worth 50 cents a pound must be mixed with 20 pounds of coffee worth 80 cents a pound in order to make a mixture worth 60 cents per pound?

ANALYSIS: Use a tabular arrangement like the one below:

	Number of pounds	Value per pound in pennies	Total value in mixture
	20	80	20(80)
	x	50	$x(50)$
Total	$20 + x$	60	$(20 + x)60$

$$20(80) + 50x = 60(20 + x)$$
$$1600 + 50x = 1200 + 60x$$
$$-10x = -400$$
$$x = 40$$

The required number of pounds is therefore 40.

Practice Test

Time at Start............

In the space provided, write the letter of the correct answer to the problem.

1. How many pounds of candy worth 32 cents a pound must be mixed with 40 pounds of candy worth 50 cents a pound to produce a mixture worth 36 cents a pound?
   (a) 120   (b) 125   (c) 135   (d) 140   (e) none of these

1. ....

2. A woman bought steak and liver totaling 10 pounds, for which she collected 74 Duke Dan trading stamps. If she got 8 trading stamps per pound for the steak and 6 per pound for the liver, how many pounds of steak did she buy?
   (a) 3   (b) 7   (c) 4   (d) 6   (e) none of these

2. ....

3. A man has $5,000 invested in a mortgage that pays 5%. He buys some bonds paying $2\frac{1}{2}$%, after which his total investment pays him 3% annually. How much has he invested in bonds?
  (a) $15,000   (b) $18,000   (c) $20,000   (d) $23,000
(e) none of these

3. ....

4. A man invested $6,000 in two businesses. At the end of one year he found he had gained 6% on one of the sums invested and had lost 4% on the other. His profit for the year was $160. How much did he invest in the business which paid 6%?
  (a) $4,000   (b) $2,000   (c) $3,000   (d) $5,000
(e) none of these

4. ....

5. A man has 20 coins consisting of silver dollars and quarters. Altogether he has $8. How many quarters does he have?
  (a) 17   (b) 16   (c) 15   (d) 14   (e) none of these   5. ....

6. If e pounds of coffee worth c cents a pound are mixed with f pounds of coffee worth d cents a pound, how much is the mixture worth in cents per pound?
  (a) $ed + fc$ (b) $ec + fd$ (c) $(ed + fc)/(e + f)$
(d) $(ec + fd)/(e + f)$ (e) none of these

6. ....

7. Jolly Joe has n coins consisting of nickels and dimes. If he has p dollars altogether, how many nickels does he have?
  (a) $(10n - p)/5$ (b) $(10n + p)/5$ (c) $2n - 20p$
(d) $n + p$ (e) none of these

7. ....

8. A student has 3 times as many dimes as quarters. If his dimes and quarters total $2.20, the number of dimes he has is
  (a) 4   (b) 6   (c) 8   (d) 10   (e) 12   8. ....

9. A storekeeper mixed candy costing 12 cents per pound with candy costing 30 cents per pound. If the mixture totals 60 pounds and is worth 18 cents per pound, how much candy worth 12 cents a pound is present?
  (a) 10 pounds   (b) 15 pounds   (c) 20 pounds
(d) 30 pounds   (e) 40 pounds

9. ....

Time at End............   *Minutes Elapsed*............
                                   Average Time 30 *Minutes*

Answer Key for this test is on page 465.

My Score: *Number Right*............   *Number Wrong*............
               Average Number Right 6

Tenth Day: More Verbal Problems

What You Should Know

VOCABULARY

reciprocal: The reciprocal of a number is the number 1 divided by that number. For example, the reciprocal of 3 is $\frac{1}{3}$; the reciprocal of $\frac{2}{3}$ is $\frac{1}{\frac{2}{3}}$; or $\frac{3}{2}$

1. The product of a number and its reciprocal is 1. For example,

$$3\cdot\frac{1}{3} = 1; \frac{2}{3}\cdot\frac{3}{2} = 1.$$

PROBLEM: The reciprocal of $1/c(c \neq 0)$ is $d/3$. Express d in terms of c.

ANALYSIS:
$$(\text{number})(\text{reciprocal}) = 1$$
$$(1/c)(d/3) = 1$$
$$d/3c = 1$$
$$d = 3c$$

PROBLEM: A man rents a car for d days, d being greater than 5. He pays x dollars a day for the first 5 days and $x/2$ dollars for each additional day. Find the cost of renting the car.

ANALYSIS: Cost for first 5 days: $5x$ dollars
Cost for additional $(d - 5)$ days: $(x/2)(d - 5)$ dollars
Total cost: $5x + (x/2)(d - 5)$ dollars

PROBLEM: If 3 brums = 8 tums and if 7 tums = 9 lums, find the value of $31\frac{1}{2}$ brums in terms of lums.

ANALYSIS: Multiply the given equations by 7 and 8 respectively:
$$21 \text{ brums} = 56 \text{ tums}$$
$$56 \text{ tums} = 72 \text{ lums}$$
It is clear that 21 brums = 72 lums. Now just add half this new equation to itself:

$$\begin{array}{r} 21 \text{ brums} = 72 \text{ lums} \\ 10\frac{1}{2} \text{ brums} = 36 \text{ lums} \\ \hline 31\frac{1}{2} \text{ brums} = 108 \text{ lums} \end{array}$$

Practice Test

Time at Start............

In the space provided, write the letter of the correct answer to the problem.

1. The reciprocal of cx is ab where a, b, and $c \neq 0$. The value of x is

  (a) cb/a (b) ca/b (c) c/ab (d) a/bc (e) $1/abc$ 1. ....

2. A couple rents an apartment. They agree to pay nothing for the first 3 months of occupancy and d dollars a month thereafter. What is the total rent paid for m months of occupancy if m is greater than 12?

  (a) md (b) $d(m + 12)$ (c) $d(m - 12)$ (d) $d(m - 3)$
  (e) $d(m + 3)$ 2. ....

3. A boy receives d dollars as an allowance. His father agrees to raise this allowance c cents every 6 months. In 20 months, the boy's allowance in cents is

  (a) $d + 3c$ (b) $3d + c$ (c) $100d + c$ (d) $100d + 3c$
  (e) $c(d - 3)$ 3. ....

4. If $6x = 11y$ and $12y = 21a$, find the value of $24x$ in terms of a.

  (a) $61a$ (b) $70a$ (c) $77a$ (d) $79a$ (e) $81a$ 4. ....

5. A man is twice as old as his brother. In 9 years the man will be ⅔ as old as his brother will be in 9 years. How old will his brother be in 4 years?

  (a) 9 (b) 11 (c) 13 (d) 15 (e) 17   5. ....

6. A homeowner wishes to spray his lawn with g gallons of a certain chemical. How many gallons should he buy of an insecticide containing 5% of this chemical?

  (a) $5g$ (b) $20g$ (c) $.5g$ (d) $.05g$ (e) $200g$ 6. ....

7. Ed is 4 times as old as Holly is now. If Holly will be y years old in 4 years, how old is Ed now?

  (a) $4y - 16$ (b) $4y - 4$ (c) $4y - 2$ (d) $4y$ (e) $2y - 8$
                                    7. ....

8. A salesman earns weekly $60 plus a 5% commission on all sales over $4,000. How much must his total sales be for a week in order for the salesman to earn $125?

  (a) $3,250 (b) $4,500 (c) $4,900 (d) $5,300 (e) $5,800
                                    8. ....

9. On a transatlantic cruise there are 1,220 passengers. There are 20 more men than women and 20 more adults than children. How many women passengers are on this ship?
(a) 300   (b) 320   (c) 370   (d) 450   (e) 600   9. ....

10. A man is 12 years older than his friend. But *b* years ago, the man was twice as old as his friend. If the friend is *x* years old now and *x* is greater than *b*, the numerical value of $x - b$ is
(a) 12   (b) 13   (c) 14   (d) 15   (e) 16   10. ....

Time at End............   *Minutes Elapsed*............
                                             Average Time 25 Minutes

Answer Key for this test is on page 467.

My Score: *Number Right*............   *Number Wrong*............
               Average Number Right 7

Eleventh Day: Test of Mastery

Time at Start............

In the space provided, write the letter of the correct answer to the problem.

1. The result obtained when -6 is subtracted from -8 is
(a) -14 (b) -2 (c) $+2$ (d) $+14$ (e) $+48$ 1. ....

2. Solve for *x*: $(x/3) + (x/2) = 1$.
(a) ⅚   (b) 5   (c) ⅚   (d) ⅕   (e) $\sqrt{6}$ 2. ....

3. Find the solution(s) for *p* if $p^2 + 11p = 0$.
(a) -11 (b) $0, -11$ (c) 1   (d) $0, 11$ (e) $1, -11$ 3. ....

4. If $2x + y = a$ and $x - 2y = b$, the value of $3x - y$ is
(a) $b - a$ (b) $2a - b$ (c) $2b - a$ (d) $a - b$ (e) $b + a$ 4. ....

5. Bob drives to his friend's house 120 miles away at the rate of 40 miles per hour and returns at the rate of 60 miles per hour. His average rate for the round trip in miles per hour is
(a) 42   (b) 44   (c) 46   (d) 48   (e) 50   5. ....

6. James is twice as old as Joe is now. In 5 years, Joe will be *y* years old. How old is James now?
(a) $2y - 10$ (b) $2y - 5$ (c) $2y - 3$ (d) $2y - 1$ (e) $2y$ 6. ....

7. Sharon and Robert pool their money to buy a gift for their friend Nancy. They have 30 coins consisting of half dollars, quarters, and dimes. If the number of quarters is half the number of dimes and the amount of money they have is $9.75, the number of quarters they have is
   (a) 5   (b) 10   (c) 15   (d) 20   (e) 25   7. ....

8. A professional laundry has *m* ounces of a 20% solution of bleach. How many ounces of water must they add in order to make the solution 10% bleach?
   (a) .5*m*   (b) .7*m*   (c) .8*m*   (d) .9*m*   (e) *m*   8. ....

9. A store manager receives a salary of $100 a week plus 3% of the store sales over $15,000. If the store takes in $*x* one week (*x* greater than 15,000), the manager receives in dollars a salary of
   (a) $100 + 3x$ (b) $100 + .03(15,000 - x)$
   (c) $100 + .003(x - 15,000)$ (d) $100 + .03(15,000x)$
   (e) $100 + .03(x - 15,000)$ 9. ....

10. Bob can paint a fence alone in 5 hours. He and Jim work at the job together for 2 hours, and then Bob is called away. Jim then takes 2 additional hours to finish. In how many hours can Jim do the job working alone?
   (a) $4\frac{1}{2}$ (b) 5   (c) 6   (d) $6\frac{2}{3}$ (e) 8   10. ....

Time at End.............   *Minutes Elapsed*.............
                                    Average Time 30 *Minutes*

Answer Key for this test is on page 468.

My Score: *Number Right*.............   *Number Wrong*.............
                Average Number Right 7

Section 10: The ABCs of Algebra

Answer Key with Hints

Second Day   Page 438

1. **(b)** The difference of the absolute values (5 and 6) is 1. Use the sign of the number having the largest absolute value (−6).

2. **(d)** Add absolute values (8 + 3 = 11) and repeat the sign.

3. (a) Change the sign of the bottom number and follow the rules for addition $(4 + 5 = 9)$.
4. (d) $8 - (-5) = 8 + 5 = 13$.
5. (c) The product of two numbers having the same sign is positive.
6. (c) $(-4)(\frac{1}{2})(-6) = (-2)(-6) = 12$.
7. (b) The quotient of two numbers having different signs is negative.
8. (e) $(+3)(-6)(-2) - (-3) = (-18)(-2) - (-3)$
   $= 36 - (-3) = 36 + 3 = 39$.
9. (a) $(+3) + (-5) - (-2) = +3 - 5 - (-2)$
   $= (-2) - (-2) = -2 + 2 = 0$.
10. (d) $(+8) - (-6)(+3) = (+8) - (-18)$
   $= +8 + 18 = +26$.

Third Day   Page 441

1. (c) $3x + 9 = 11$; $3x = 2$; $x = \frac{2}{3}$.
2. (e) Simply divide both sides by $b \neq 0$.
3. (b) $ay = by + c$; $ay - by = c$; $y(a - b) = c$. Since $a \neq b$, then $a - b \neq 0$ and we can divide by it, yielding $y = c/(a - b)$.
4. (a) $u - 3(u - 1) = -1$; $u - 3u + 3 = -1$;
   $-2u = -4$; $u = 2$.
5. (e) Multiply both sides of the equation by 12:
   $4t + 3t = 12$; $7t = 12$; $t = \frac{12}{7}$.
6. (c) Multiply both sides of the equation by $2(3 - x)$:
   $3(2) + 1(3 - x) = 2(2)(3 - x)$;
   $6 + 3 - x = 4(3 - x)$; $9 - x = 12 - 4x$;
   $3x = 3$; $x = 1$.
7. (c) Multiply through by 100: $3x = 900$; $x = 300$.
8. (d) Multiply through by 1000: $1000 + 200x = 1010$;
   $200x = 10$; $x = \frac{10}{200} = \frac{5}{100} = .05$.
9. (a) First add the equations, yielding $2x = 14$; $x = 7$. Now substitute this value of x back in one of the original equations to solve for y.
10. (d) Subtract the second equation from the first:
   $2y = 6a - 8b$; $y = 3a - 4b$.

Fourth Day   Page 444

1. (d) $x^2 = 16$; $x = \pm\sqrt{16} = \pm 4$.
2. (c) $x^2 = 10$; $x = \pm\sqrt{10}$.

3. (e) The left side of this equation is always positive and
4.   can never equal the right side, which is negative. The
        equation therefore has no roots.

   (c) $x^2 - 3x = 0$; $x(x - 3) = 0$; $x = 0$; $x - 3 = 0$;
       $x = 3$.

5. (b) $x(x + b) = 0$; $x = 0$; $x + b = 0$; $x = -b$.

6. (a) $x^2 + 4x - 12 = 0$; $(x + 6)(x - 2) = 0$; $x = -6$,
       2.

7. (a) $3\sqrt{x - 5} = 2\sqrt{x}$; $9(x - 5) = 4x$; $x = 9$.

8. (d) $\sqrt{x - 7} = x - 9$; $x - 7 = x^2 - 18x + 81$;
       $x^2 - 19x + 88 = 0$. This equation yields $x = 8$
       and $x = 11$ as tentative roots, but $x = 8$ does not
       check in the original equation.

9. (b) $0/a = 0$.

10. (e) Since 2 is a root of the equation, the equation must
        hold true when we substitute 2 for x. Therefore
        $3(2)^2 - 9(2) + k = 0$; $3(4) - 18 + k = 0$;
        $12 - 18 + k = 0$; $k = 6$.

Fifth Day   Page 445

1. (d) $5x = 9$; $x = \%$; $x/6 = \frac{9}{30} = \frac{3}{10}$.

2. (a) $x = -2$; $(x + 1)/3x = -1/-6 = \frac{1}{6}$.

3. (a) $(3x - 2x)/6 = \frac{1}{6}$; $3x - 2x = 1$; $x = 1$.

4. (d) $x = k/2$; $y = k/2$; $(xy)^2 = (k^2/4)^2 = k^4/16$.

5. (b) Subtract $2l$ from both sides: $x - l = m - 2l$.

6. (d) $Q + R - T = b - 2c + (a - c) - (b - 3c + a)$
                  $= b - 2c + a - c - b + 3c - a$
                  $= 0$

7. (e) $x = \frac{1}{2}$; $y = \frac{1}{3}$; $x - y = \frac{1}{2} - \frac{1}{3} = \frac{1}{6}$; $x + y$
       $= \frac{1}{2} + \frac{1}{3} = \frac{5}{6}$; $\dfrac{x - y}{x + y} = \dfrac{\frac{1}{6}}{\frac{5}{6}} = (\frac{1}{6})(\frac{6}{5}) = \frac{1}{5}$.

8. (c) $(x^2 + 9)/9 = x^2/9 + \frac{9}{9} = (x/3)^2 + 1$; $(x/3)^2 + 1$
       $= k$; $(x/3)^2 = k - 1$.

9. (d) $(a + b)^2 = k^2$; $a^2 + 2ab + b^2 = k^2$; $a^2 + b^2$
       $= k^2 - 2ab = k^2 - 2s$.

10. (e) $(1/a^2) + (1/b)^2 = (b^2 + a^2)/a^2b^2$; $(a - b)^2$
        $= a^2 - 2ab + b^2 = k^2$; $a^2 + b^2 = k^2 + 2s$;
        $(b^2 + a^2)/a^2b^2 = (k^2 + 2s)/s^2$.

Sixth Day   Page 447

1. (b) Let x represent the number of days they work
       together. Then $(x/5) + (x/10) = 1$; $x = 3\frac{1}{3}$ days.

2. (e) In one hour he sweeps $1/d$ of the barn; in m hours he sweeps m/d.

3. (d) Let x represent the number of minutes they work together. Then $(x/15) + (x/30) = 1$; $x = 10$ minutes.

4. (c) Let x represent the number of hours taken to fill the pool. Then the equation is $(x/5) + (x/12) - (x/4) = 1$; $x = 30$ hours.

5. (b) Let x represent the number of hours taken by Mr. Hale working alone. The equation is $(2/6) + (5/x) = 1$.

6. (a) 12 Boy Scout–hours: 30 shelters
       4 Boy Scout–hours: 10 shelters
   Let x represent the number of hours it takes 2 Scouts to build 10 shelters. Then $2x = 4$; $x = 2$.

7. (e) Let x represent the desired number of days. Then $(q \text{ men})(x \text{ days}) = 18$ man-days; $x = 18/q$.

8. (b) Let x represent the number of days it will take working together. Then $(x/5) + (x/10) = 1$. Note that the number of men and boys is irrelevant to the solution here.

9. (a) Number with digits reversed: $10s + r$
   Sum of digits: $r + s$
   Difference: $(10s + r) - (r + s) = 10s + r - r - s = 9s$

10. (a) $t + u = 11$; $10u + t = 10t + u + 27$; $9u - 9t = 27$; $u - t = 3$.

$$
\begin{array}{r}
t + u = 11 \\
-t + u = 3 \\
\hline
2t \quad\;\; = 8 \\
t = 4
\end{array}
$$

Seventh Day   **Page 450**

1. (a) $R \times T = D$; $30 \times 4\frac{1}{2} = D$; $D = 135$.

2. (a) $\dfrac{\frac{1}{3}}{4} = \dfrac{x}{60}$; $4x = 20$; $x = 5$.

3. (b) $T = D/R = {}^{30}\!/_{600} = \frac{1}{20}$. It will therefore take $\frac{1}{20}$ of an hour, or 3 minutes.

4. (b) Joe does the last $\frac{1}{4}$ mile in 2 minutes. His rate is therefore $\frac{1}{8}$ mile per minute.

5. (a) Let t be the number of hours it takes for the men to be 30 miles apart. Then the distances they covered are

$40t$ and $50t$ respectively. **Use the equation**
$50t - 40t = 30;$ $10t = 30;$ $t = 3.$

6. (e) Average rate = (total distance)/(total time)

Average rate = $\dfrac{(3 \times 30) + (2 \times 45)}{3 + 2} = {}^{180}\!/_5 = 36$

7. (b) $R = D/T = t/h.$

8. (c) Let x represent the number of hours the return trip took.

Average rate = (total distance)/(total time)

Average rate = $\dfrac{2000 + 2000}{4 + x}$

$4000/(4 + x) = 400;$ $x = 6.$ If it took 6 hours to return, the airline must have been traveling at 2000/6, or $333\frac{1}{3}$, miles per hour.

9. (c) If we are given the distance, we must determine the rate in order to solve for the time $(T = D/R)$. Using statements I and II, we can find that going downstream the man travels at $15 + 2$ or 17 miles per hour, and that returning he travels at $15 - 2$ or 13 miles per hour.

10. (c) Average rate = (total distance)/(total time)

Average rate = $\dfrac{me + mc}{c + mc/d} = \dfrac{mcd + mcd}{cd + mc} = \dfrac{2\,md}{d + m}$

Eighth Day   Page 452

1. (b) $.25(1,000,000) = 250,000.$

2. (e) If 16% is cola flavoring, then 84% is carbonated water. Therefore $.84(32) = 26.88,$ which is not among the choices.

3. (e) Remember: $p\% = .01p.$

4. (c) % dye = $\dfrac{\text{amount pure dye}}{\text{amount solution}} = \dfrac{(.01p)(30) + .10(50)}{30 + 50}$

$= \dfrac{.3p + 5}{80}$

5. (a) % iodine = $\dfrac{\text{amount pure iodine}}{\text{amount solution}} = \dfrac{(.01)(10) + p}{.10 + p}$

$= \dfrac{.1 + p}{10 + p}$

6. (c) $\dfrac{(.09)(20) + x}{20 + x} = \dfrac{1.8 + x}{20 + x} + \dfrac{12}{100};$

$180 + 100x = 240 + 12x;$ $88x = 60;$

$x = {}^{60}\!/_{88} = {}^{15}\!/_{22}.$

7. (c) $\dfrac{(.01)(96)}{96 + x} = \dfrac{6}{100}$.

8. (b) $\dfrac{100}{100 + x} = \dfrac{88}{100}$.

9. (a) $\dfrac{.06(200)}{100 + x} = \dfrac{10}{100}$.

10. (d) Let x represent the amount of solution drained off. Note that this equals the amount of alcohol added. Also, remember that when x ounces of solution are removed, .2x ounces of this is alcohol. The equation is therefore $\dfrac{(.20)(10) - .2x + x}{10} = \dfrac{60}{100}$.

Ninth Day   Page 454

1. (d)

	Number of pounds	Cents per pound	Total value in cents
	40	50	40(50)
	x	32	32x
Total	40 + x	36	36(40 + x)

$$40(50) + 32x = 36(40 + x)$$

2. (b)

	Number of pounds	Stamps per pound	Total stamps
Steak	x	8	8x
Liver	10 − x	6	6(10 − x)
Total	10		74

$$8x + 6(10 - x) = 74$$

3. (c)

	Principal	% interest as decimal	Interest per year
Mortgage	5000	.05	.05(5000)
Bonds	x	.025	.025x
Total	5000 + x	.03	.03(5000 + x)

$$.05(5000) + .025x = .03(5000 + x)$$

4. (a)

	Principal	% interest as decimal	Interest per year
	x	.06	$.06x$
	$6000 - x$	$-.04$	$-.04(6000 - x)$
Total	6000		160

$$.06x - .04(6000 - x) = 160$$

5. (b)

	Number of coins	Value in cents per coin	Total value in cents
Quarters	x	25	$25x$
Dollars	$20 - x$	100	$100(20 - x)$
Total	20		800

$$25x + 100(20 - x) = 800$$

6. (d)

	Number of pounds	Value in cents per pound	Total value in cents
	e	c	ec
	f	d	fd
Total	$e + f$	x	$x(e + f)$

$$ec + fd = x(e + f)$$

7. (c)

	Number of coins	Value in cents per coin	Total value in cents
Nickels	x	5	$5x$
Dimes	$n - x$	10	$10(n - x)$
Total	n		$100p$

$$5x + 10(n - x) = 100p$$

8. (e)

	Number of coins	Value in cents per coin	Total value in cents
Dimes	3x	10	10(3x)
Quarters	x	25	25x
Total	4x		220

$$10(3x) + 25x = 220$$

9. (e)

	Number of pounds	Value in cents per pound	Total value in cents
	x	12	12x
	60 − x	30	30(60 − x)
Total	60	18	60(18)

$$12x + 30(60 - x) = 60(18)$$

Tenth Day   Page 457

1. (e) (number)(reciprocal) = 1; $(cx)(ab) = 1$; $x = 1/abc$.

2. (d) If the couple stays for m months, they pay rent for $(m - 3)$ months. Simply multiply this by the cost per month, which is d dollars.

3. (d) In 20 months, the boy's allowance will have been raised 3 times, or 3c cents. His total allowance must therefore be, in cents, $100d + 3c$.

4. (c) Multiply the equations by 12 and 11 respectively, which yields

$$72x = 121y$$
$$121y = 231a$$

Thus $72x = 231a$. Divide by 3 in order to get 24x. Note that $24x = (231/3)a = 77a$.

5. (c)

	Age now	Age in 9 years
Man	2x	2x + 9
Brother	x	x + 9

$$2x + 9 = \tfrac{3}{2}(x + 9)$$
$$x = 9$$
$$x + 4 = 13$$

6. (b) Let x represent the number of gallons of insecticide needed. Then $.05x = g$; $x = 20g$.

7. (a)

	Age now	Age in 4 years
Ed	$4(y - 4)$	
Holly	$y - 4$	y

8. (d) Let x represent the total sales for a week. Then $125 = 60 + .05(x - 4000)$.

9. (a) Let x represent the number of women passengers; then $x + 20$ represents the number of men. Since the total number of adults is $2x + 20$, the number of children, which is 20 less, must be $2x$. The equation now is $(2x + 20) + (2x) = 1220$.

10. (a)

	Age now	Age b years ago
Man	$x + 12$	$x + 12 - b$
Friend	x	$x - b$

$x + 12 - b = 2(x - b)$
$x + 12 - b = 2x - 2b$
$12 = x - b$

More of this type can be found in the work of day

Eleventh Day   Page 459

1. (b) $(-8) - (-6) = -8 + 6 = -2.$ 2
2. (c) Multiply by 6: $2x + 3x = 6$; $x = \frac{6}{5}$.   3
3. (b) $p(p + 11) = 0$; $p = 0$; $p + 11 = 0$;   4
   $p = -11$.
4. (e) Simply add the two equations.   5
5. (d)   7
   Average rate = (total distance)/(total time)
   $= (120 + 120)/(3 + 2)$
   $= \frac{240}{5}$
   $= 48$

6. (a)

	Age now	Age in 5 years
James	$2(y - 5)$	
Joe	$y - 5$	y

7. (a)

	Number of coins	Value in cents per coin	Total value in cents
Half dollars	$30 - 3x$	50	$50(30 - 3x)$
Quarters	x	25	$25x$
Dimes	$2x$	10	$10(2x)$
Total	30		975

$$50(30 - 3x) + 25x + 10(2x) = 975$$

8. (e) $\dfrac{.2m}{m + x} = \dfrac{10}{100};\ \ x = m.$ 8

9. (e) If x dollars are taken in, the manager   10
receives $\$100 + 3\%$ of $(x - 15,000)$.

10. (d) Let x represent the number of hours it   6
takes Jim working alone. Then $(\frac{2}{5}) +$
$(4/x) = 1.$

GEOMETRY

Section 12: Geometry

In most high-school geometry courses, emphasis is placed on the reasoning behind the theories and formulas. Teachers usually stress the derivation of the fundamental ideas. However, those problems in geometry that are included in College Entrance Examinations do *not* test your ability to derive a formal proof. Rather, the emphasis is on application of such proofs. For example, you most likely will not be asked to explain *how* we arrive at πr^2 as the formula for the area of a circle. However, it is highly probable that you will be given the diameter of a circle and be asked to find the numerical area of the circle.

The best approach to this section is the same for students who have just completed a course in geometry, or completed the course a year or so ago, or have never taken a course in the subject. The College Entrance Examination that you will take *usually* lists the formulas that you may be called on to use in the geometry problems. Unless you are fully aware, however, of how to apply them, you will waste too much time. Therefore, use the Inventory Test that follows to discover any weaknesses in your background. Concentrate on memorizing basic formulas. Space your study time. Concentrate on accuracy and then speed will follow. Use the Test of Mastery to check your progress.

First Day: Inventory Test

Time at Start............

In the space provided, write the letter of the correct answer to the problem.

470

1. A street light is on top of a pole 24 feet high. How long must a wire be to extend from the top of the pole to a point on the ground that is 10 feet from the base of the pole?

   (a) 13 feet   (b) 18 feet   (c) 26 feet   (d) 30 feet   (e) 10 feet

                                         1. ....

2. In the diagram, *AB*, *CD*, and *EF* are all straight lines. If angle 4 = 60°, find the number of degrees in the sum of angles 1, 2, 3, 4, and 5.

   (a) 360°   (b) 200°   (c) 240°   (d) 280°   (e) 300°   **2.** ....

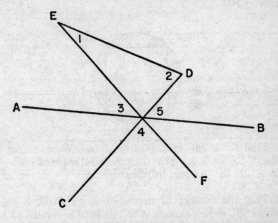

3. Three isosceles triangles are placed as shown. The vertex angles are respectively 10°, 20°, and 30°. Find the number of degrees in angle *x*.

   (a) 40   (b) 60   (c) 75   (d) 90   (e) none of these   **3.** ....

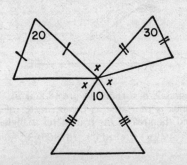

4. A man spent 25% of his income on his rent. If we wish to represent his income by means of a circle graph, how many degrees will there be in the sector that represents his rent?

(a) ¼   (b) 90   (c) 360   (d) cannot be done because we don't know the actual income   (e) can be done, but the answer is not given

4. ....

5. A square is inscribed in a circle whose diameter is $10\sqrt{2}$. Find the area of the shaded portion.

(a) 100   (b) 50π (c) $100 - 50\pi$ (d) $100 + 50\pi$
(e) $50\pi - 100$

5. ....

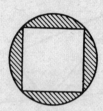

6. Find the length of an arc of a circle whose radius is 12 inches, if the arc is intercepted by a central angle of 120°.

(a) π (b) 8π (c) 16π (d) 24π (e) 30π 6. ....

7. Find the number of degrees in angle *BCD*, if angle *B* contains 50°, angle *D* contains 65°, and *AB* is parallel to *DE*.

(a) 115   (b) 130   (c) 195   (d) cannot be done
(e) can be done, but the answer is not given   7. ....

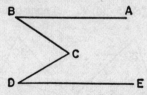

8. The diagonals of a rhombus are 18 and 24. The perimeter of the rhombus is the same as the perimeter of an equilateral triangle. Find the area of the equilateral triangle.

(a) $25\sqrt{3}$ (b) $49\sqrt{3}$ (c) $81\sqrt{3}$ (d) $100\sqrt{3}$ (e) $400\sqrt{3}$

8. ....

9. The angles of a triangle are in the ratio 1:2:3. If the largest side of the triangle is 12, find the area of the triangle.

(a) 16   (b) 72   (c) $36\sqrt{3}$ (d) $18\sqrt{3}$ (e) $9\sqrt{3}$ 9. ....

10. The cistern in Mike Farmer's back yard is shaped like a right circular cylinder whose height is twice its diameter. If the radius of the base is 7 units, find the volume of the cistern in cubic units.

(a) 2,156   (b) 4,312   (c) 308   (d) 5,212   (e) none of these
                                                           10. ....

11. Find the length of the line segment that joins the points whose coordinates are (2,3) and (7,6).

(a) $\sqrt{8}$ (b) $\sqrt{34}$ (c) $\sqrt{18}$ (d) 81   (e) none of these is correct
                                                           11. ....

Time at End............   *Total Number of Minutes Elapsed............*
                              Average Time 30 Minutes

Answer Key with Analysis

ANSWERS   ANALYSIS

1. (c)   1. Since this is a right tri-
$$10^2 + 24^2 = x^2$$ angle, we can use the
$$100 + 576 = x^2$$ Pythagorean Theorem. If,
$$676 = x^2$$ however, we recognize
$$26 = x$$ the 5–12–13 triplet, the
                                    problem is more easily
                                    solved.

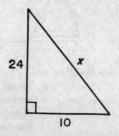

2. (e)
Since
$$\angle 1 + \angle 2 + \angle 4 = 180°$$
and
$$\angle 3 + \angle 5 + \angle 4 = 180°$$
we have
$$\angle 1 + \angle 2 + \angle 3 + \angle 4$$
$$+ \angle 4 + \angle 5 = 360°$$
$$\underline{- \angle 4 \qquad\qquad -60°}$$
$$\angle 1 + \angle 2 + \angle 3$$
$$+ \angle 4 + \angle 5 = 300°$$

2. Three theorems are used in this problem: vertical angles are equal; the sum of the interior angles of a triangle is 180°; the sum of the angles about a point on one side of a line is 180°. Since we get two $\angle 4$'s in our equation, we must subtract one $\angle 4$, which contains 60°, from both sides of the equation.

3. (e)
$$\angle 1 = \frac{180° - 20°}{2}$$
$$= 80°$$
$$\angle 2 = \frac{180° - 30°}{2}$$
$$= 75°$$
$$10° + 80° + 75° = 165°$$
$$3x = 360° - 165° = 195°$$
$$x = 195°/3 = 65°$$

3. Again we need three theorems: the sum of the angles of a triangle is 180°; the base angles of an isosceles triangle are equal; the sum of the angles about a point equals 360°.

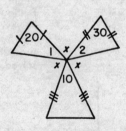

4. (b)
$$¼(360°) = 90°$$

4. Since $25\% = ¼$ of his income, and since the entire circle contains 360°, we take ¼ of 360°.

5. (e)

Area of circle $= \dfrac{\pi d^2}{4}$

$= \dfrac{200\pi}{4}$

$= 50\pi$

Area of square $= \dfrac{d^2}{2}$

$= \dfrac{(10\sqrt{2})^2}{2}$

$= 100$

5. We can apply two little-used formulas in this problem: that for the area of a circle in terms of its diameter, and that for the area of a square in terms of its diagonals (see work of fifth and sixth days).

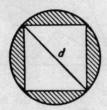

Difference in areas:
$50\pi - 100$

6. (b)

$\dfrac{120°}{360°} = \dfrac{x}{2 \cdot \pi \cdot 12}$

$\frac{1}{3} = x/24\pi$

$x = 8\pi$

6. We compare the circumference of a circle to the length of an arc.

7. (a)

angle $1 = 50°$

angle $2 = 65°$

angle $BCD = 115°$

7. It is a common practice to draw a third line parallel to the other two in this type of diagram, and then use the alternate interior angles.

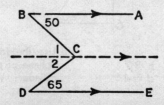

8. (d)
$9^2 + 12^2 = x^2$
$15 = x$
Perimeter of rhombus
   $= 60$
Side of equilateral triangle
   $= {}^{60}\!/_3 = 20$
Area of equilateral triangle
   $= s^2\sqrt{3}/4$
Area of $\triangle = 20^2\sqrt{3}/4$
Area of $\triangle = 100\sqrt{3}$

8. This is a two-stage problem. First, use the fact that the diagonals of a rhombus bisect each other and are perpendicular in order to get a side; then the formula for the area of an equilateral triangle.

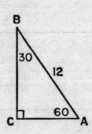

9. (d)
$x + 2x + 3x = 180°$
$6x = 180°$
$x = 30°$
$AC = 6$
$BC = 6\sqrt{3}$
Area $= \frac{1}{2}$ product of legs
Area $= \frac{1}{2} \times 6 \times 6\sqrt{3}$
Area $= 18\sqrt{3}$

9. Use the fact that the sum of the angles of a triangle is 180° to show that this is a right triangle. Then use the 30°-60°-90° relationships to find the legs and then the area.

10. (b)
$V = \pi r^2 h;\quad r = 7$
$d = 14$

10. Use the formula for the volume of a right circular cylinder: $V = \pi r^2 h$. Re-

$$h = 28$$
$$V = \frac{22}{7} \times 7^2 \times 28$$
$$V = 22 \times 7 \times 28$$
$$V = 4{,}312$$

member that in this example the height is twice the *diameter* of the base, or 2×14.

11. (b)
$$d =$$
$$\sqrt{(x_2 - x_1)^2 + (y_2 - y_1)^2}$$
$$d = \sqrt{(7 - 2)^2 + (6 - 3)^2}$$
$$d = \sqrt{25 + 9}$$
$$d = \sqrt{34}$$

11. Use the formula for distance (see eighth day's work). No tricks involved.

My Score: Number Right............ Number Wrong............
Average Number Right 5

Second Day: Angle Sums and Special Angles

What You Should Know

1. The sum of the interior angles of a triangle is 180°.
2. The sum of the angles about a point on one side of a line is 180°.
3. The sum of the angles about a point is 360°.
4. Base angles of an isosceles triangle are equal.
5. Consecutive angles on the same side of a transversal are supplementary if the lines are parallel.
6. Alternate interior angles of parallel lines are equal.
7. Corresponding angles of parallel lines are equal.

PROBLEM: Find the exterior angle at the base of an isosceles triangle whose vertex angle is 70°.

ANALYSIS: By (1) above, the sum of angles B and ACB is 110°.
By (4) above, angle B = angle ACB = 55°.
By (2) above, angle x = 125°.

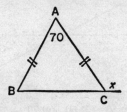

Practice Test

Time at Start............

In the space provided, write the letter of the correct answer to the problem.

1. The angles of a triangle are in the ratio of 1:2:3. The triangle is

(a) isosceles (b) equilateral (c) right (d) cannot be determined from the given information   (e) can be determined, but the answer is not given   1. ....

2. Three isosceles triangles are labeled as shown. Find the number of degrees in angle x if angle $A = 40°$, angle $B = 50°$, angle $C = 30°$.

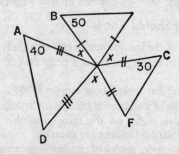

(a) 10 (b) 20 (c) 30 (d) 50 (e) 60   2. ....

3. Find the number of degrees in angle A if angle $B = 90°$, angle $D = 100°$, and $DC = DE$.

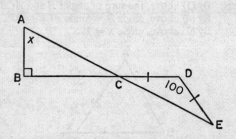

(a) 10 (b) 30 (c) 50 (d) 60 (e) 70   3. ....

4. In triangle *RST*, the exterior angles at the base are 120° and 150° as shown. Find the number of degrees in angle *S*.

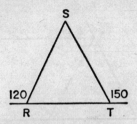

(a) 30   (b) 60   (c) 90   (d) 120   (e) 150   4. ....

5. If angle *r* = 50°, angle *u* = 50°, then find the number of degrees in angle *w*.

(a) 80   (b) 70   (c) 60   (d) cannot be determined from the given information   (e) can be determined, but the answer is not given   5. ....

6. Angle *EGH* = 80° and angle *B* = angle *C* = 40°. At what angle does *CD* meet *EF*?

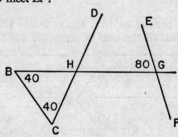

(a) 40°   (b) 70°   (c) 80°   (d) they do not meet
(e) they meet at an angle that is not given   6. ....

7. If *AD* is parallel to *BC*, *AB* = *AC*, and angle 1 = 80°, find angle *EAD*.

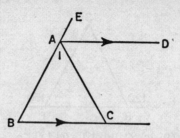

(a) 50° (b) 80° (c) 100° (d) 130° (e) none of these

7. ....

8. If triangle *RST* is an equilateral triangle and *SR* is perpendicular to *UV* at *R*, find the number of degrees in angle *x* when *WT* is a straight line.

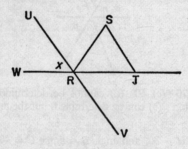

(a) 30 (b) 60 (c) 90 (d) 120 (e) 150   8. ....

9. If *AB* is parallel to *CD*, angle *AFE* = 120°, and angle *CGE* = 110°, find the number of degrees in angle *FEG*.

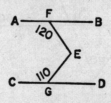

(a) 10 (b) 60 (c) 70 (d) 100 (e) 130   9. ....

10. If *BCE* is perpendicular to *ACD* at *C* and if angle *A* contains *y*°, then the number of degrees in angle *B* is

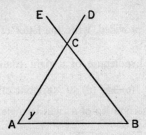

(a) *y* (b) 90 − *y* (c) 90 + *y* (d) 180 − *y* (e) 180 + *y*

10. ....

Time at End............ *Minutes Elapsed*............

Average Time 25 Minutes

Answer Key for this test is on page 502.

My Score: *Number Right*............ *Number Wrong*............

Average Number Right 6

Third Day: Sides of Special Right Triangles

What You Should Know

1. In right triangles, the "hypotenuse" is defined as the side of the triangle opposite the right angle. The other two sides are called "legs."

2. In a right triangle, $(\text{leg})^2 + (\text{leg})^2 = (\text{hypotenuse})^2$, usually expressed as $a^2 + b^2 = c^2$.

3. If $a^2 + b^2 = c^2$, then the triangle is a right triangle.

4. Remember that the largest of the three numbers *must* be the hypotenuse. Since certain combinations of numbers occur frequently in working with right triangles, it is to your advantage to memorize them:

    3–4–5
    5–12–13
    8–15–17
    7–24–25

    or any multiples thereof.

Practice Test

Time at Start............

In the space provided, write the letter of the correct answer to the problem.

1. Find the hypotenuse of a right triangle whose legs are 16 and 30.
   (a) 8   (b) 17   (c) 34   (d) 40   (e) none of these   1. ....

2. Find the second leg of a right triangle if the first is 5 and the hypotenuse is 12.
   (a) 13   (b) $\sqrt{109}$ (c) $\sqrt{119}$ (d) 109   (e) 119   2. ....

3. Find the second leg of a right triangle if the first is 40 and the hypotenuse is 41.
   (a) 1   (b) 9   (c) 21   (d) 81   (e) none of these   3. ....

4. In the diagram below showing two right triangles, find the value of *x*.

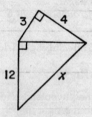

   (a) 5   (b) 12   (c) 13   (d) 26   (e) 8   4. ....

5. Find the diagonal of a rectangle whose length is 15 and whose width is 12.
   (a) $\sqrt{41}$ (b) 9   (c) $3\sqrt{41}$ (d) $\sqrt{379}$ (e) none of these   5. ....

6. A man has 7 circular tables whose diameters in feet are 12, 13, 14, 15, 16, 17, and 18. He wants to bring some of them into his shop, but his doorway is only 8 feet wide and 12 feet high. How many tables can he bring in?
   (a) 2   (b) 3   (c) 4   (d) 5   (e) 1   6. ....

7. A pole 20 feet high has a wire attached to its top. The pole stands vertically on level ground, and the wire hits the ground at

a spot that is 15 feet from the base of the pole. Find the length of the wire.

   (a) 25 feet   (b) 26 feet   (c) 23 feet   (d) 35 feet
(e) 22 feet   7. ....

   8. A man travels due east for 8 miles, then due south for 8 miles, then due east again for 7 miles. How far from his starting point is he now?

   (a) $\sqrt{65}$ miles   (b) 17 miles   (c) $4\sqrt{20}$ miles   (d) 9 miles
(e) none of these   8. ....

   9. In the diagram, AB is parallel to CD. If $GE = 25$, $GF = 7$, and GF and EF are angle bisectors, find the length of EF.

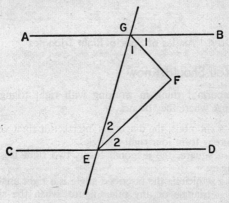

   (a) 32   (b) 18   (c) 24   (d) can be done, but answer is not given
(e) cannot be done from given information   9. ....

   10. In the diagram, at the top of page 454, all four small triangles are right, with the right angles as shown. Find the value of x.

   (a) 17   (b) $\sqrt{176}$ (c) 12   (d) 10   (e) 34   10. ....

Time at End............   *Minutes Elapsed*............
                                          Average Time 25 Minutes

Answer Key for this test is on page 503.

My Score: *Number Right*............   *Number Wrong*............
                  Average Number Right 6

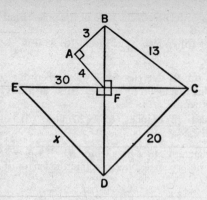

Fourth Day: Angles of Special Right Triangles

What You Should Know

1. An important thing in working with right triangles is to recognize where they occur:

   (a) In a rhombus, the diagonals intersect at right angles and thereby form four right triangles.

   (b) In a square, the diagonal forms two right isosceles triangles.

   (c) In a semicircle the inscribed angle is a right angle.

   (d) In a triangle or any other figure, when the altitude is drawn it forms right angles with the base.

2. In a 45°–45°–90° triangle: the leg = ½(hypotenuse)($\sqrt{2}$)
                                    the hypotenuse = (leg)($\sqrt{2}$)

3. In a 30°–60°–90° triangle: the side opposite 30° = ½(hypotenuse)

                                    the side opposite 60° = ½(hypotenuse)($\sqrt{3}$)

                                    the hypotenuse = twice the side opposite 30°

                                    the hypotenuse = twice the side opposite 60° divided by $\sqrt{3}$

PROBLEM: In triangle *ABC*, altitude *CD* is drawn dividing angle *C* as shown. Find the length of *AB*.

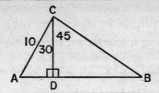

ANALYSIS: Since we have right angles at D, triangle ACD is a 30°–60°–90° triangle. Thus $AD = 5$, $CD = 5\sqrt{3}$. But triangle CBD is a 45°–45°–90° triangle having one leg equal to $5\sqrt{3}$. Thus BD, which is the other leg, must also equal $5\sqrt{3}$.

Practice Test

Time at Start...........

In the space provided, write the letter of the correct answer to the problem.

1. The diagonals of a rhombus are 12 and 16. Find one side of the rhombus.
   (a) $\sqrt{112}$ (b) 10   (c) 11   (d) $\sqrt{110}$ (e) 9   1. ....

2. In the circle, RS is a diameter, angle $R = 30°$, and $ST = 12$. Find the radius of the circle.

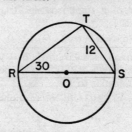

   (a) 12   (b) 24   (c) $6\sqrt{3}$ (d) 6   (c) $6\sqrt{2}$ 2. ....

3. The altitude of an equilateral triangle is 5. Find the side of the triangle.
   (a) 10   (b) $5\sqrt{3}$ (c) $5/\sqrt{3}$ (d) $10/\sqrt{3}$ (e) $4\sqrt{2}$ 3. ....

4. The diagonal of a square is 18. Find a side of the square.

(a) $9\sqrt{2}$ (b) $\sqrt{27}$ (c) 9   (d) $6\sqrt{2}$ (e) $18\sqrt{2}$ 4. ....

5. The angles of a triangle are in the ratio 1:2:3. Find the ratio of the largest side to the smallest side.

(a) 3:1   (b) 3:2   (c) 2:1   (d) $\sqrt{3:1}$ (e) none of these

5. ....

6. In the diagram at the right, *RSTU* is a rectangle with $RS = 20$ and $RU = UV = VT$. Find the diameter of the circle.

(a) $10\sqrt{2}$ (b) $20\sqrt{2}$ (c) $5\sqrt{2}$ (d) 10   (e) 20   6. ....

7. The hypotenuse of a right triangle is 24, and the legs are in the ratio $\sqrt{3}:1$. Find the longer leg of the triangle.

(a) 12   (b) $8\sqrt{3}$ (c) $12\sqrt{3}$ (d) $24\sqrt{3}$ (e) 8   7. ....

8. The diagonal of a rhombus is 12 and equals one of its sides. Find the other diagonal of the rhombus.

(a) $\sqrt{216}$ (b) $2\sqrt{108}$ (c) $6\sqrt{3}$ (d) $12\sqrt{3}$ (e) $\sqrt{108}$

8. ....

9. The perimeter of a right isosceles triangle is $12 + 6\sqrt{2}$. Find the hypotenuse.

(a) 3   (b) $3\sqrt{2}$ (c) 6   (d) $6\sqrt{2}$ (e) 12   9. ....

10. In the diagram on page 457, angle $B = 90°$, angle $A = 30°$, $AC = 24$. Find the length of CD if BD is perpendicular to AC and if DE is perpendicular to BC.

(a) 12   (b) $8\sqrt{3}$ (c) $12\sqrt{3}$ (d) 6   (e) none of these

10. ....

Time at End.............   *Minutes Elapsed*.............
                                             Average Time 30 *Minutes*

Answer Key for this test is on page 504.

My Score: *Number Right*.............   *Number Wrong*.............
                 Average Number Right 6

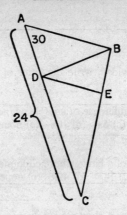

Fifth Day: Circles

What You Should Know

1. The number π has a value close to 3.14 or $22/7$. In general, use whichever is easier for the problem.

2. To find the length of a circle (its perimeter or circumference):
$$C = 2\pi r \quad \text{where } r = \text{radius}$$
$$\text{or} \qquad d = \text{diameter}$$
$$C = \pi d$$

3. To find the area of a circle:
$$A = \pi r^2 \quad \text{where } r = \text{radius}$$
$$\text{or} \qquad d = \text{diameter}$$
$$A = \pi d^2/4$$

4. To find the length of an arc:
$$n/360 = l/C \quad \text{where } n = \text{number of degrees in the central angle}$$
$$l = \text{length of the arc}$$
$$C = \text{circumference of the circle}$$

5. To find the area of a sector:
$$n/360 = A/\pi r^2 \quad \text{where } r = \text{radius}$$
$$n = \text{number of degrees in the central angle}$$
$$A = \text{area of the sector}$$

6. Note that using the number of degrees in the central angle for n is equivalent to using the number of degrees in its intercepted arc, since these two quantities are equal.

Practice Test

Time at Start............

In the space provided, write the letter of the correct answer to the problem.

1. Find the circumference of a circle whose radius is 5.
(a) 25   (b) 25π (c) 5π (d) 10π (e) none of these
1. ....

2. Find the area of a circle whose circumference is 14π.
(a) 14   (b) 49   (c) 14π (d) 49π (e) none of these
2. ....

3. Find the area of a circle whose diameter is 12.
(a) 36π (b) 144π (c) 24π (d) 12π (e) none of these
3. ....

4. In the accompanying diagram, the circle is inscribed in a square. If a side of the square is 9, find the area of the circle.

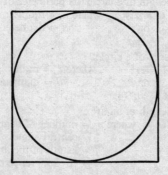

(a) 81π (b) $81\pi/4$ (c) 9π (d) can be done, but the answer is not given   (e) cannot be done from the given information
4. ....

5. The figure consists of a square whose sides are the diameters of four semicircles. Find the area of the entire figure if a side of the square is 8.

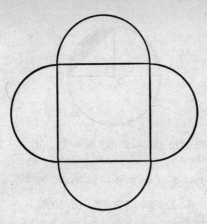

(a) $64\pi + 64$ (b) $64 + 32\pi$ (c) $32\pi + 12$ (d) $32 + 16\pi$
(e) $16 + 32\pi$ 5. ....

6. Given two concentric circles as shown in the diagram. If the radius of the smaller circle, *OA*, is 4 and *AB* = 2, find the area of the shaded portion.

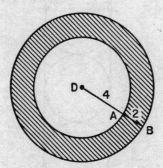

(a) 36π (b) 26π (c) 20π (d) 16π (e) 4π 6. ....

7. Find the length of an arc of 30° in a circle whose radius is 24.
(a) 24π (b) 16π (c) 12π (d) 8π (e) 4π 7. ....

8. Find the area of the shaded part if the central angle is 90° and *OB* = 6.

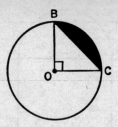

(a) $18 - 9\pi$ (b) $18\pi - 9$ (c) $9\pi - 18$ (d) $9 - 18\pi$
(e) none of these   8. ....

9. If the radius of a circle is increased by 50%, the area is increased by
(a) 125%   (b) 225%   (c) 250%   (d) 300%
(e) none of these   9. ....

10. If three equal circles can be cut from a rectangular piece of tin 12 inches by 4 inches as shown, find the amount of waste tin to the nearest square inch.

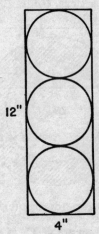

(a) 10   (b) 36π (c) 36   (d) 10π (e) none of these
                                                    10. ....

Time at End............   *Minutes Elapsed*............
                                             Average Time 30 *Minutes*

Answer Key for this test is on page 505.

My Score: *Number Right............*   *Number Wrong............*
                Average Number Right 7

Sixth Day: Areas

What You Should Know

VOCABULARY

polygon: a closed geometric figure composed of straight lines
area of a polygon: the number of square units in the region
                        bounded by the polygon

PROBLEM: Find the area of a rectangle whose sides are 8 and 10.

ANALYSIS: In a rectangle, two adjacent sides are the base and
height.

$$\boxed{A = b \times h}$$
$$A = 8 \times 10$$
$$A = 80$$

PROBLEM: Find the area of a square whose diagonal is 3.

ANALYSIS: We may use either of two formulas for the area of a
square:

$$\boxed{A = s^2} \quad \text{(where } s \text{ is the side)}$$

$$\boxed{A = d^2/2} \quad \text{(where } d \text{ is the diagonal)}$$

Substituting in the second, we get

$$A = 3^2/2$$
$$A = 9/2 = 4\tfrac{1}{2}$$

PROBLEM: Find the area of a parallelogram whose base is 6 and
whose altitude is 8.

ANALYSIS:

$$\boxed{A = b \times h}$$
$$A = 6 \times 8$$
$$A = 48$$

Note: In a parallelogram the height is usually *not* equal to the sides adjacent to the base.

PROBLEM: The base of a rhombus is 6 and its diagonals are 9 and 8. Find the altitude.

ANALYSIS: $\boxed{A = dd'/2}$ (where d and d' are the two unequal diagonals)

$$A = (9 \times 8)/2$$

$$A = 72/2$$

$$A = 36$$

Since a rhombus is also a parallelogram,

$$\boxed{A = b \times h}$$

$$36 = 6h$$

$$6 = h$$

Practice Test

Time at Start............

In the space provided, write the letter of the correct answer to the problem.

1. What is the area of a rectangle whose sides are 12 and 6?
   (a) 18   (b) 6   (c) 12   (d) 72   (e) none of these   **1.** ....

2. Find the area of a square whose side is 5.
   (a) 5   (b) 10   (c) 25   (d) 20   (e) none of these   **2.** ....

3. A square has an area of 24. Find in simplest form a side of the square.
   (a) 576   (b) $2\sqrt{6}$ (c) 6   (d) 12   (e) none of these   **3.** ....

4. A parallelogram has a base of 9 and an altitude of 4. Find its area.
   (a) 36   (b) 13   (c) 18   (d) 26   (e) none of these   **4.** ....

5. A rhombus has diagonals of 7 and 9. Find its area.
   (a) 63   (b) 31.5   (c) 16   (d) 8   (e) none of these   **5.** ....

6. The sides of a parallelogram are 6 and 10. The included angle is 30°. What is its area?
   (a) 60   (b) 30   (c) 16   (d) 32   (e) none of these   **6.** ....

7. The diagonal of a rectangle is 13. One side is 5. Find the area.
   (a) 65   (b) 60   (c) 156   (d) 128   (e) none of these   **7.** ....

8. The area of a rhombus is 64. Find the numerical value of the product of the diagonals.

(a) 8　(b) 116　(c) 32　(d) 16　(e) 128　　　8. ....

9. The diagonal of a square is 9. Find the area.

(a) $9\sqrt{2}$　(b) 40.5　(c) 81　(d) 18　(e) 36　　　9. ....

Time at End............　　　　　*Minutes Elapsed*............
　　　　　　　　　　　　　　　Average Time 15 *Minutes*

Answer Key for this test is on page 506.

My Score:　*Number Right*............　*Number Wrong*............
　　　　　Average Number Right 6

Seventh Day: Areas II

What You Should Know

PROBLEM:　The bases of a trapezoid are 8 and 14, and the altitude is 5. Find the area.

ANALYSIS:

$$A = \tfrac{1}{2}h(b + b')$$

$A = \tfrac{1}{2} \times 5 \times (8 + 14)$
$A = \tfrac{1}{2} \times 5 \times 22$
$A = 5 \times 11$
$A = 55$

A trapezoid having two equal legs is known as "isosceles." When doing problems with the isosceles trapezoid, draw two altitudes from the end points of the shorter base as shown below.

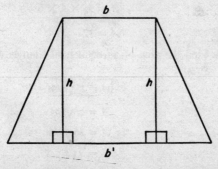

PROBLEM: The leg of an isosceles trapezoid is 5, and the bases
are 9 and 17. Find the area.

ANALYSIS: (a) Because the trapezoid is isosceles, $ED = AF$
(by $\cong$ triangles).
(b) $BCEF$ is a rectangle. Therefore $BC = EF = 9$.

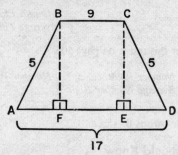

(c) $AF + ED = 8$, so $AF = 4$.
(d) Using right triangle AFB, we get $h = 3$.

(e)
$$\boxed{A = \tfrac{1}{2}h(b + b')}$$

$A = \tfrac{1}{2} \times 3 \times (9 + 17)$
$A = \tfrac{1}{2} \times 3 \times 26$
$A = 3 \times 13$
$A = 39$

PROBLEM: The base of a triangle is 4 and the altitude drawn to
that base is 6. Find the area of the triangle.

ANALYSIS:
$$\boxed{A = \tfrac{1}{2}bh}$$

$A = \tfrac{1}{2} \times 4 \times 6$
$A = \tfrac{1}{2} \times 24$
$A = 12$

PROBLEM: Find the area of an equilateral triangle whose side
is 6.

ANALYSIS:
$$\boxed{A = s^2\sqrt{3}/4}$$

$A = 6^2\sqrt{3}/4$
$A = 36\sqrt{3}/4$
$A = 9\sqrt{3}$

PROBLEM: Find the area of a right triangle whose legs are 5 and 6.

ANALYSIS: The area of a right triangle equals half the product of the legs.

$$\boxed{A = \tfrac{1}{2}ll'}$$

$$A = \tfrac{1}{2} \times 5 \times 6$$
$$A = \tfrac{1}{2} \times 30$$
$$A = 15$$

Practice Test

Time at Start............

In the space provided, write the letter of the correct answer to the problem.

1. Find the area of a trapezoid whose bases are 9 and 10, and whose altitude is 10.
(a) 450   (b) 29   (c) 14.5   (d) 95   (e) 900   1. ....

2. Find the altitude of an isosceles trapezoid whose bases are 10 and 20 and whose legs are each 13.
(a) 5   (b) 12   (c) 13   (d) 113   (e) 1,300   2. ....

3. Find the base of a trapezoid whose area is 84, whose altitude is 4, and one of whose bases is 25.
(a) $\frac{42}{25}$ (b) 2   (c) 17   (d) 46   (e) 21   3. ....

4. Find the area of a triangle whose base is 8 and whose altitude drawn to that base is 10.
(a) 80   (b) 20   (c) 18   (d) 40   (e) none of these   4. ....

5. The area of a triangle is 24; the base is 12. Find the altitude.
(a) 2   (b) 4   (c) 6   (d) 8   (e) cannot be done from the given information   5. ....

6. Two sides of a triangle are 8 and 12. The altitude drawn to the side that is 12 is 6. Find the altitude drawn to the side that is 8.
(a) 4   (b) 16   (c) 9   (d) 72   (e) 36   6. ....

7. The area of an equilateral triangle is $36\sqrt{3}$. Find a side of the triangle.
(a) 12   (b) 18   (c) 6   (d) 36   (e) none of these   7. ....

8. The side of an equilateral triangle is 8. Find the area.
(a) 4   (b) 32   (c) $16\sqrt{2}$ (d) $16\sqrt{3}$ (e) none of these

8. ....

9. The legs of a right triangle are 9 and 10. Find the area.
(a) 90   (b) 19   (c) 13   (d) $\sqrt{19}$ (e) none of these   9. ....

10. The legs of a right triangle are 8 and 15. What is the altitude to the hypotenuse?
(a) 120   (b) 60   (c) $120/17$ (d) $60/17$ (e) none of these

10. ....

Time at End............   *Minutes Elapsed*............
                                 Average Time 25 Minutes

Answer Key for this test is on page 506.

My Score: *Number Right*............   *Number Wrong*............
              Average Number Right 7

Eighth Day: Coordinate Geometry

What You Should Know

In coordinate geometry we use two basic formulas.

1. *midpoint:* $x_m = (x_1 + x_2)/2$
                             $y_m = (y_1 + y_2)/2$

This formula is often used:
(a) to find the coordinates of the midpoint of a line segment when the ends are given,
(b) to find the second end point of a line segment when the midpoint and the first end point of the segment are given, and
(c) to find the center of a circle when the end points of a diameter are given.

PROBLEM: Given $A(5,2)$ and $B(3,6)$. Find the midpoint of line AB.

ANALYSIS: $x_m = (x_1 + x_2)/2 = (5 + 3)/2 = 8/2 = 4$
            $y_m = (y_1 + y_2)/2 = (2 + 6)/2 + 8/2 + 4$
            Thus the midpoint is (4,4).

2. *distance:* $\qquad d = \sqrt{(x_2 - x_1)^2 + (y_2 - y_1)^2}$

This formula is often used:

(a) to find the length of a line segment when given its end points,

(b) to find the radius of a circle,

(c) to find the missing side of a triangle, and

(d) to find the distance between two points.

PROBLEM: Find the radius of a circle whose center is (8,11) and which passes through the point (2,3).

ANALYSIS: Using the formula above,

$$x_2 - x_1 = 8 - 2 = 6$$
$$y_2 - y_1 = 11 - 3 = 8$$
$$d = \sqrt{(x_2 - x_1)^2 + (y_2 - y_1)^2}$$
$$d = \sqrt{6^2 + 8^2}$$
$$d = \sqrt{36 + 64}$$
$$d = \sqrt{100}$$
$$d = 10$$

Practice Test

Time at Start............

In the space provided, write the letter of the correct answer to the problem.

1. Find the midpoint of line segment *AB* if *A* has coordinates (3,5) and *B* has coordinates (5,7).

(a) (3,5) (b) (5,7) (c) (8,12) (d) (2,2) (e) (4,6) **1.** ....

2. Triangle *ABC* with a right angle at *C* is inscribed in a circle. If the coordinates of *A* are (6,2) and the coordinates of *B* are (4,8), find the coordinates of the center of the circle.

(a) (5,5) (b) (10,10) (c) (6,2) (d) cannot be done from the given information (e) can be done, but the answer is not given

2. ....

3. The coordinates of *M*, the midpoint of line *AB*, are (5,7). If the coordinates of *A* are (3,1), find the coordinates of *B*.

(a) (2,0) (b) (2,6) (c) (4,4) (d) (7,13) (e) none of these

3. ....

4. Find the length of the line joining (3,6) and (5,8).

(a) $\sqrt{20}$ (b) $\sqrt{8}$ (c) $\sqrt{260}$ (d) 2   (e) none of these

4. ....

5. The center of a circle is $O(3,2)$. The circle passes through the point $O(-2,-3)$. Find the radius of the circle.

(a) 0   (b) $\sqrt{50}$ (c) $\sqrt{5}$ (d) $\sqrt{2}$ (e) cannot be done from the given information

5. ....

6. How far is it on a map from $A(12,10)$ to $B(4,4)$?

(a) 16 units   (b) 22 units   (c) 10 units   (d) $\sqrt{282}$ units   (e) none of these

6. ....

7. Find the longest side of triangle RST if the coordinates of R are $(9,7)$, of S are $(1,1)$, and of T are $(9,16)$.

(a) RS (b) ST (c) RT (d) cannot be done from the given information   (e) can be done, but the answer is not given

7. ....

8. Triangle ABC is shown at the right. Each box on the X axis represents 2 units. If the area of the triangle is 36 square units, how many units are represented by one box on the Y axis?

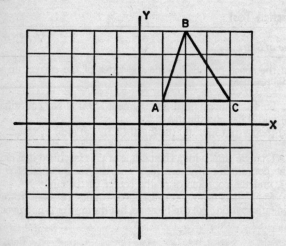

(a) 1   (b) 2   (c) 3   (d) 4   (e) 5

8. ....

Answer Key for this test is on page 507.

My Score: *Number Right.............*   *Number Wrong............*
                Average Number Right 5

Ninth Day: Solid Geometry

What You Should Know

1. In a rectangular or cubic solid, there are:
   (a) 6 faces (front, rear, right, left, top, bottom),
   (b) 12 edges (the lines where faces meet),
   (c) 8 vertices (the points where edges meet).

2. The volume of a rectangular solid equals the area of the base
($l \times w$) multiplied by the height (h).

3. In a cube, all dimensions are equal.

4. The volume of most any regular solid figure equals the area
of the base multiplied by the height. Thus,
      Volume of a cube = $B \times h = e^2 \times e = e^3$
      Volume of a right circular cylinder = $B \times h = \pi r^2 h$

5. Volumes of similar solids are to each other as the cubes of
the corresponding sides:
$$\frac{V}{V'} = \frac{s^3}{s'^3}$$

Practice Test

Time at Start............

In the space provided, write the letter of the correct answer
to the problem.

1. The base of a right circular cylinder has a radius of 4. The
height of the cylinder is 10. Find the volume of the
cylinder.
   (a) 40π (b) 160π (c) 28π (d) 14π (e) 640   **1.** ....

2. The edge of a cube is 6 inches. Find its volume in cubic
inches.
   (a) 36   (b) 27   (c) 96   (d) 216   (e) none of these   **2.** ....

3. A right circular cylinder has a volume of 100π and a height of 4. Find the diameter of the base.

(a) 5   (b) 10   (c) 5π (d) 25π (e) none of these   3. ....

4. A piece of wire 48 inches long is used to form a cube. Find the surface area of this cube in square inches.

(a) 96   (b) 64   (c) 72   (d) 8   (e) 24   4. ....

5. The surface area of a cube equals 54 square inches. Find the volume of the cube in cubic inches.

(a) 54   (b) 153   (c) 421   (d) 729   (e) 27   5. ....

6. The edges of two rectangular solids are in the ratio 3:4. If the solids are similar, find the ratio of their volumes.

(a) 9:16   (b) 27:64   (c) 9:64   (d) cannot be done from the given information   (e) can be done, but the answer is not given

6. ....

7. The ratio of the surface areas of two cubes is 4:9. Find the ratio of their edges.

(a) 4:9   (b) 2:4   (c) 2:3   (d) 9:4   (e) 8:18   7. ....

8. Find the length in inches of the largest rod that can be packed into a wooden rectangular box whose length is 8 inches, width is 6 inches, and height is 24 inches.

(a) 13   (b) 24   (c) 26   (d) 512   (e) 1,152   8. ....

9. The ratio of the surface areas of two cubes is 4:9. Find the ratio of their volumes.

(a) 16:81   (b) 64:729   (c) 2:3   (d) 8:27   (e) none of these

9. ....

10. A face diagonal of a cube is $4\sqrt{2}$. Find the space diagonal of the cube.

(a) 8   (b) $16\sqrt{2}$ (c) $4\sqrt{2}$ (d) $8\sqrt{2}$ (e) $4\sqrt{3}$ 10. ....

Time at End............   *Minutes Elapsed*............
                                            Average Time 30 *Minutes*

Answer Key for this test is on page 507.

My Score: *Number Right*............   *Number Wrong*............
                Average Number Right 5

Tenth Day: Test of Mastery

Time at Start............

In the space provided, write the letter of the correct answer to the problem.

1. If angles *a*, *b*, and *c* are in the ratio 1:3:2, find the number of degrees in angle *b*.

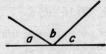

(a) 30 (b) 60 (c) 90 (d) 120 (e) 180   1. ....

2. A man travels due north for 8 miles, then due east for 6 miles. Find the distance the man is from his starting point.

(a) 2 miles (b) 6 miles (c) 8 miles (d) 10 miles
(e) 14 miles   2. ....

3. The diagonals of a rhombus are 16 and 30. Find the perimeter of the rhombus.

(a) 17 (b) 46 (c) 60 (d) 68 (e) none of these   3. ....

4. Find a side of an equilateral triangle whose altitude is $9\sqrt{3}$.

(a) 6 (b) 9 (c) 18 (d) $18\sqrt{3}$ (e) none of these 4. ....

5. Square *ABCD* is inscribed in circle *O* as shown. If $AB = 9\sqrt{2}$, find the circumference of the circle in terms of π.

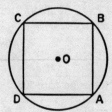

(a) 9π (b) 18π (c) $9\sqrt{2}\pi$ (d) $18\sqrt{2}\pi$ (e) 27   5. ....

6. Central angle *AOB* contains 45°. If $AO = 8$, find the area of the sector *AOB*.

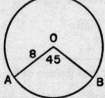

(a) 8π (b) 16π (c) 32π (d) 64π (e) none of these
        6. ....

7. A rhombus is equal in area to a rectangle whose base is 12 and whose altitude is 6. If one diagonal of the rhombus is 18, find the other.

(a) 4   (b) 23   (c) 9   (d) 16   (e) 8   7. ....

8. Find the area of an equilateral triangle whose perimeter is the same as a square of side 6.

(a) 8   (b) $16\sqrt{3}$ (c) $64\sqrt{3}$ (d) $12\sqrt{3}$ (e) 16   8. ....

9. The legs of a right triangle are 6 and 8. Find the altitude to the hypotenuse.

(a) 2.4   (b) 3.6   (c) 4.8   (d) 6.8   (e) none of these   9. ....

10. Find the length of the line joining (6,8) and (4,−2).

(a) $\sqrt{110}$ (b) $\sqrt{162}$ (c) $\sqrt{40}$ (d) $\sqrt{200}$ (e) none of these

10. ....

11. Find the midpoint of the line segment joining (5,3) and (7,−1).

(a) (5,2)   (b) (12,2)   (c) (6,1)   (d) (8,6)   (e) (12,4)

11. ....

12. Find the space diagonal of a cube whose edge is 7.

(a) 7   (b) $7\sqrt{2}$ (c) $7\sqrt{3}$ (d) $3.5\sqrt{2}$ (e) none of these

12. ....

Time at End............   *Minutes Elapsed*............
                                     Average Time 35 Minutes

Answer Key for this test is on page 508.

My Score: *Number Right*............   *Number Wrong*............
               Average Number Right 7

Section 11: Geometry

Answer Key with Hints

Second Day   Page 477

1. (c) Use the fact that the sum of the angles of a triangle is 180°.

2. (b) Since 30°, 40°, and 50° are base angles of isosceles triangles, the vertex angles are respectively 120°, 100°, and 80°. Then our equation is $3x + 300 = 360$.

3. (c) Since triangle *BCE* is isosceles, angle *BCE* = 40° = angle *ACB*.

4. (c) The exterior angles are the supplements of the interior angles.

5. (d) Since angles *r* and *u* both equal 50°, they are vertical angles. We must be given one more angle in order to solve the problem.

6. (d) The two 40° angles leave 100° for the missing angle of the triangle as well as for the vertical angle *DHG*. Therefore *HD* and *GE* are parallel since the sum of the consecutive interior angles is 180°.

7. (a) Since the triangle is isosceles, angle *B* = 50°. Moreover, since angle *B* and the angle we want are corresponding angles of parallel lines, angle *EAD* also equals 50°.

8. (a) The angle formed by perpendicular lines is 90°; the angle of the triangle is 60°.

9. (e) Draw another parallel line through *E*. Then use alternate interior angles.

10. (b) The perpendiculars give us an angle of 90°. Thus angle *B* is the complement of angle *y*.

Third Day   Page 481

1. (c) This presents a special right triangle (8-15-17), each side of which has been multiplied by 2.

2. (c) This is *not* a special triplet since the 12 is the hypotenuse. We must therefore use the equation $5^2 + x^2 = 12^2$.

3. (b) This is not listed as a triplet, but the equation $a^2 + b^2 = c^2$ yields an integral solution.

4. (c) The top triangle has a missing side of 5 (3-4-5). This can be used as a leg in the lower triangle (5-12-13).

5. (c) This is not a special triplet. The Pythagorean Theorem yields $\sqrt{369}$, but this can be factored into $\sqrt{9} \times \sqrt{41}$, which is $3\sqrt{41}$.

6. (b) The theorem $a^2 + b^2 = c^2$ gives us a diagonal of $\sqrt{208}$, which is some number between 14 and 15. The man can thus bring in only the tables with diameters of 12, 13, and 14 feet.

7. (a) We have a $(3 \times 5) - (4 \times 5) - (5 \times 5)$ special right triangle.

8. (b)

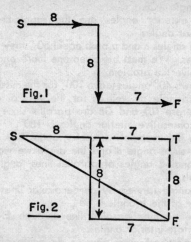

Fig. 1

Fig. 2

In triangle *STF*, *ST* = 15, *FT* = 8. Thus hypotenuse *SF* = 17.

9. (c) Since consecutive interior angles of parallel lines are supplementary, $\angle 1 + \angle 2 = 90°$, so that $\angle F = 90°$. We thus have a 7-24-25 right triangle.

10. (e) We first find that *BF* is 5 (3-4-5); next *CF* = 12 (5-12-13); then *DF* = 16 (3-4-5); finally *DE* = 34 (8-15-17).

Fourth Day   Page 484

1. (b) The triangle formed is a right triangle whose legs are half the diagonals. We thus have a 3-4-5 right triangle.

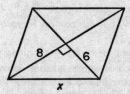

2. (a) Angle *T* must equal 90° since it is inscribed in a semicircle. Thus diameter *SR* = 24.

3. **(d)** We are given the side opposite 60° in a 30°-60°-90° triangle. To find the hypotenuse, double and divide by $\sqrt{3}$.

4. **(a)** The triangle is a 45°-45°-90° isosceles triangle.

5. **(c)** Using the fact that the sum of the angles of a triangle is 180°, we obtain a 30°-60°-90° triangle.

6. **(a)** Since this is a rectangle, $UT = 20$, $UV = 10$, $RU = 10$, diameter $RV = 10\sqrt{2}$.

7. **(c)** If the legs are in the ratio $\sqrt{3}:1$, we have a 30°-60°-90° triangle whose hypotenuse equals 24.

8. **(d)** Triangle *ABC* is equilateral, so angles *CBA* and *CAB* both equal 60°. Thus $BE = 6\sqrt{3}$, diagonal $BD = 12\sqrt{3}$.

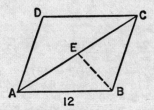

9. **(d)** $2x + x\sqrt{2} = 12 + 6\sqrt{2}$. Therefore the hypotenuse is $6\sqrt{2}$ and each leg is 6.

10. **(d)** Since *ABC* is a 30°-60°-90° triangle, $AC = 24$, $AB = 12\sqrt{3}$. But *ABD* is a 30°-60°-90° triangle, so $AD = 18$. Thus $CD = 6$.

Fifth Day   Page 487

1. **(d)** The circumference equals $2\pi r$, where *r* is 5.

2. **(d)** $C = 14\pi = 2\pi r$. Thus $r = 7$. Then $A = \pi r^2$ where $r = 7$.

3. **(a)** $A = \pi r^2$; $r = 6$.

4. (b) $A = \pi d^2/4$ where d is a side of the square.
5. (b) The area of the square is 64. The four semicircles are equivalent to two circles, with $r = 4$.
6. (c) large circle: 36π; small circle: 16π
7. (e) $30°/360° = (n/2) \times \pi \times 24$.
8. (c) $90°/360° = (x/\pi) \times 6^2$.
9. (a) The original area is πr^2. The new area is $\pi(3r/2)^2 = (9/4)\pi r^2$, which is an *increase* of $1\frac{1}{4}$, or 125%.
10. (a) Rectangle: $12 \times 4 = 48$
    Diameter of one circle: $(\frac{1}{3})(12) = 4$
    Area of one circle: $\pi r^2 = 4\pi$
    Area of three circles: 12π

Sixth Day   Page 491

1. (d) $A = bh = 12 \times 6 = 72$.
2. (c) $A = s^2 = 5^2 = 25$.
3. (b) $A = s^2$; $24 = s^2$; $\sqrt{24} = s$; $\sqrt{4}\sqrt{6} = s$; $s = 2\sqrt{6}$.
4. (a) $A = bh = 9 \times 4 = 36$.
5. (b) $A = dd'/2 = (7 \times 9)/2 = 63/2 = 31\frac{1}{2}$.
6. (b) $A = bh$. To find h, use the 30°-60°-90° triangle. $A = 10 \times 3 = 30$.
7. (b) $A = bh$. The diagonal and two adjacent sides form a right triangle; use this fact to find the missing side (12). Then $A = 12 \times 5 = 60$.
8. (e) $A = dd'/2$; $dd' = 2A$; $dd' = 2 \times 64 = 128$.
9. (b) $A = d^2/2 = 81/2 = 40.5$.

Seventh Day   Page 493

1. (d) $A = \frac{1}{2}h(b + b')$; $A = \frac{1}{2} \times 10 \times (9 + 10) = 5(19) = 95$.
2. (b) Use 5-12-13 triangle.

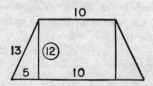

3. (c) $A = \frac{1}{2}h(b + b')$; $84 = \frac{1}{2} \times 4 \times (25 + b')$; $84 = 2(25 + b')$;   dividing by 2, $42 = 25 + b'$; $b' = 17$.

4. (d) $A = \frac{1}{2}bh = \frac{1}{2} \times 10 \times 8 = \frac{1}{2} \times 80 = 40.$

5. (b) $A = \frac{1}{2}bh;$ $24 = \frac{1}{2} \times 12 \times h;$ $24 = 6h;$ $h = 4.$

6. (c) $A = \frac{1}{2}bh;$ $A = \frac{1}{2} \times 12 \times 6 = \frac{1}{2} \times 72 = 36.$
      $36 = \frac{1}{2} \times 8 \times h;$ $36 = 4h;$ $h = 9.$

7. (a) $A = s^2\sqrt{3}/4;$ $36\sqrt{3} = s^2\sqrt{3}/4;$ $36 = s^2/4;$
      $s^2 = 144;$ $s = 12.$

8. (d) $A = s^2\sqrt{3}/4 = 8^2\sqrt{3}/4 = 64\sqrt{3}/4 = 16\sqrt{3}.$

9. (e) $A = \frac{1}{2}(\text{leg})(\text{leg}) = \frac{1}{2} \times 9 \times 10 = \frac{1}{2} \times 90 = 45.$

10. (c) Use 8-15-17 right triangle: $A = \frac{1}{2} \times 8 \times 15$
      $= 4 \times 15 = 60;$ $A = \frac{1}{2} \times h \times 17;$ $60 = \frac{1}{2} \times h$
      $\times 17;$ $120 = 17h;$ $^{120}/_{17} = h.$

Eighth Day   Page 496

1. (e) Use the midpoint formula.

2. (a) Use the midpoint formula since AB will be a diameter.

3. (d) Use the midpoint formula.

4. (b) Use the distance formula: $8 - 6 = 2;$ $5 - 3 = 2.$

5. (b) Use the distance formula: $2 - (-3) = 5;$
                              $3 - (-2) = 5.$

6. (c) Use the distance formula: $10 - 4 = 6; 12 - 4 = 8.$

7. (b) Apply the distance formula three times: $RS = 10;$
      $RT = 9;$ $ST = 17.$

8. (d) Base: 3×2 units $= 6$ units
      Let u be the number of units represented by one box
      on the Y axis.
      Altitude: $3u$ units
      $A = \frac{1}{2}bh;$ $36 = \frac{1}{2} \times 6 \times 3u.$

Ninth Day   Page 499

1. (b) Substitute in the formula $V = \pi r^2 h$, where we know r
      and h.

2. (d) The volume of a cube is e^3.

3. (b) This time we know the volume and the height. Use the
      formula to obtain r, the radius.

4. (a) Since a cube has 12 edges, divide the 48 by 12. Each
      surface is a square, and there are 6 such square
      surfaces (faces).

5. (e) Divide 6 (faces) into 54. Thus each square face is 9,
      each edge is 3.

6. (b) Volumes have the same ratio as the cubes of edges.

7. (c) The edges are to each other as the square roots of the
      areas.

8. (c) This is asking for the "space diagonal" of the box. The face diagonal of the 6 by 8 rectangle is 10. Use this to obtain a 10-24-26 triangle.

9. (d) First take the relationship back to the edges (i.e., 2:3). Then the volumes are to each other as the cubes of edges.

10. (e) If the face diagonal is $4\sqrt{2}$, then the edge is 4. $4^2 + (4\sqrt{2})^2 = x^2$, where x is the space diagonal. $48 = x^2$; $x = 4\sqrt{3}$.

More of this type can be found in the work of day

Tenth Day   Page 500

1. (c) $x + 3x + 2x = 180$.   2
2. (d) Use the 6-8-10 right triangle.   3
3. (d) The 8-15-17 right triangle gives 17 as a side of the rhombus.   3
4. (c) When the altitude is drawn, a 30°-60°-90° triangle is formed.   4
5. (b) Diagonal AC is the hypotenuse of a 45°-45°-90° triangle and is also a diameter of the circle.   5
6. (a) $45°/360° = A/\pi 8^2$.   5
7. (e) The area of the rectangle is $12 \times 6 = 72$. The area of the rhombus is $18x/2$. $18x/2 = 72$.   6
8. (b) The perimeter of the square is $4 \times 6 = 24$. Thus a side of the triangle is 8. $A = s^2\sqrt{3}/4$.   7
9. (c) The area of the triangle is ½(leg)(leg) $= 24$. Its area is also ½bh. So ½bh = 24. Now we have a 6-8-10 right triangle. ½ × 10 × h = 24.   7
10. (e) Use the distance formula: $x - x_1 = 6 - 4 = 2$; and $y - y_1 = 8 - (-2) = 10$.   8
11. (c) $x_m = (x_1 + x_2)/2 = (5 + 7)/2$; and $y_m = (y_1 + y_2)/2 = (3 - 1)/2$.   8
12. (c) The edge is 7, the face diagonal is $7\sqrt{2}$, and the space diagonal is $7\sqrt{3}$.   9

MODERN TRENDS IN MATHEMATICS

Section 13: MODERN TRENDS IN MATHEMATICS

Here is one of the most important sections in this book! Much of the material in this section is not taught in mathematics courses in high school. However, the topics are sometimes included on College Entrance Examinations as a test of your ability to think mathematically. Since the material is so varied, use the Inventory Test to discover where you should concentrate your efforts. Certainly, to give you needed practice in facing "new" problems, do not skip any of the units in the section.

Be systematic and the results will be worth it.

First Day: Inventory Test

Time at Start............

In the space provided, write the letter of the correct answer to the problem.

1. If $3x - 6 > 30$, find the values of x.
   (a) $x > 10$ (b) $x < 10$ (c) $x > 12$ (d) $x < 12$
   (e) none of these   1. ....

2. If $x \boxminus y$ means $x^3 - y^2$, so that $4 \boxminus 3$ means $4^3 - 3^2 = 64 - 9 = 55$, find the value of $2 \boxminus (-1)$.
   (a) 5   (b) 6   (c) 7   (d) 8   (e) 9   2. ....

3. On a football squad of 20 men, there are 8 who can play quarterback and 9 who can play end, including 5 men who can play both. How many can play neither?
   (a) 3   (b) 5   (c) 6   (d) 7   (e) 8   3. ....

509

4. A man has a calendar from the year A, which is a leap year. What is the probability that February 29 will be a Saturday in the year A?
(a) $\frac{1}{28}$ (b) $\frac{1}{29}$ (c) $\frac{1}{5}$ (d) $\frac{1}{7}$ (e) $\frac{1}{365}$ 4. ....

5. Susie knows that x is an integer greater than 4 but less than 9. Billy knows that x is an integer less than 12 but greater than 6. If Billy and Susie get together, between them they know that
(a) x can be figured exactly (b) x can have any one of two values (c) x can have any one of three values (d) x can have any one of four values (e) x cannot be determined   5. ....

6. In our number system which uses the base ten, we have symbols from 0 to 9 to express all of our numbers. If 3426 is a number in some base other than ten, what is the lowest number that could serve as base for this number?
(a) two (b) five (c) seven (d) eight (e) nine   6. ....

7. In a darkened room, a box contains 7 red socks and 7 blue socks. What is the minimum number of socks that I must take out into the light to be certain I have a pair—that is, 2 socks of the same color?
(a) 2 (b) 3 (c) 8 (d) 9 (e) cannot be determined

7. ....

8. A man has 4 jackets and 3 ties. How many different outfits can he wear if each outfit is composed of one jacket and 1 tie?
(a) 1 (b) 3 (c) 4 (d) 7 (e) 12   8. ....

9. In a certain number system, two numbers are considered "equal" if they give the same remainder when divided by a given integer. For example, 5 and 11 both give 2 as a remainder (R) when divided by 3, and thus are equal in the system. Which of the following numbers equals 7 with respect to division by 4?
(a) 12 (b) 11 (c) 10 (d) 9 (e) 8   9. ....

10. If $5 \wedge 3$ means $5^3 = 5 \times 5 \times 5 = 125$, find the value of $2 \wedge (3 \wedge 2)$.
(a) 4 (b) 8 (c) 256 (d) 320 (e) none of these 10. ....

Time at End............   *Total Number of Minutes Elapsed*............
Average Time 30 *Minutes*

Answer Key with Analysis

ANSWERS	ANALYSIS

1. (c)
$$3x - 6 > 30$$
$$3x > 36$$
$$x > 12$$

1. Inequalities may be handled in the same manner as equalities (with minor exceptions). There is no trick involved here; merely add 6 to both sides and then divide by 3.

2. (c)
$$2 \boxminus (-1) = 2^3 - (-1)^2$$
$$= 8 - 1 = 7$$

2. Problems that introduce a new symbol are easy if you follow the examples given.

3. (e)
$$\begin{pmatrix} \text{men who play} \\ \text{quarterback} \\ \text{only} \end{pmatrix}$$
$$+ \begin{pmatrix} \text{men who play} \\ \text{quarterback} \\ \text{and end} \end{pmatrix}$$
$$+ \begin{pmatrix} \text{men who} \\ \text{play end} \\ \text{only} \end{pmatrix}$$
$$= \begin{pmatrix} \text{quarterbacks} \\ \text{and ends} \end{pmatrix}$$

3. Draw a circle diagram; then overlapping can be used to represent the 5 men who play both end and quarterback. This allows us to examine the actual number of men involved.

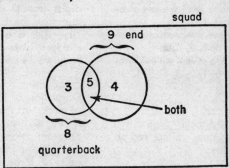

$$3 + 5 + 4 = 12$$

squad — (quarterback + ends)

$$= \begin{pmatrix} \text{men playing} \\ \text{neither} \\ \text{position} \end{pmatrix}$$

$20 - 12 = 8$

4. (d)

$$\frac{\text{favorable}}{\text{total}}$$

$$\frac{1 \text{ day (Saturday)}}{7 \text{ days (a week)}}$$

$\frac{1}{7}$

4. There are only seven possible days that the extra day in February can be!

5. (b)
Susie knows that x may be 5, 6, 7, or 8; Billy knows that x may be 7, 8, 9, 10, or 11. Thus between them they know that x may be either 7 or 8.

5. This is a problem more in common sense than in any mathematical operation.

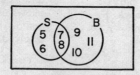

6. (c)
In base two, we use symbols 0, 1.
In base five, we use symbols 0, 1, 2, 3, 4.
In base seven, we use symbols 0, 1, 2, 3, 4, 5, 6.

6. The base we choose has digits from 0 up to one less than the base itself. Thus, if 8 is a digit, the smallest base we could have would be nine.

7. (b)
First sock: red
Second sock: blue
Third one: either red or blue

7. Regardless of the number of socks in the drawer, if there are only two different colors, the third sock drawn must give a pair. If three colors are involved, the fourth sock gives a pair.

8. (e)
$4 \times 3 = 12$

8. With each jacket, the man has a choice of three ties. Thus he has three choices with the first jacket, three with the second, etc.

9. (b)

$$7 \div 4 = \frac{7}{4}$$
$$= 1 \text{ with } R \text{ of } 3$$
$$12 \div 4 = \frac{12}{4}$$
$$= 3 \text{ with } R \text{ of } 0$$
$$11 \div 4 = \frac{11}{4}$$
$$= 2 \text{ with } R \text{ of } 3$$

9. The best way to attempt a "which of the following" question is to try the choices in order.

10. (e)
$3 \wedge 2 = 3^2 = 9$
We thus want the value of $2 \wedge 9$, which is 2^9, which is 512.

10. Always simplify expressions contained in parentheses first—in this case, $3 \wedge 2$.

My Score: Number Right............ Number Wrong............
Average Number Right 5

Second Day: Inequalities and Probability

What You Should Know

SYMBOLS

$x > y$: x is greater than y
$x < y$: x is less than y

1. For solution purposes, inequalities may be handled in the same manner as linear equations, with two exceptions:
   (a) If you multiply by a negative number, reverse the order of the inequality.
   (b) If you divide by a negative number, reverse the order of the inequality.

PROBLEM: Find the range of values for x if $3x \oplus 2 > 17$.

ANALYSIS: $3x \oplus 2 > 17$
$3x > 15$
$x > 5$

PROBLEM: Find the range of values of x for which $5 - 3x < 20$.

ANALYSIS: $5 - 3x < 20$
$-3x < 15$
$x > -5$

2. Probability is defined as the fraction:

$$\frac{\text{Successful events}}{\text{Total events}}$$

PROBLEM: What is the probability that a card drawn from a deck of 52 playing cards be an ace?

ANALYSIS: There are 4 aces in the deck, thus 4 chances for success. The probability is therefore $\frac{4}{52}$, or $\frac{1}{13}$.

Practice Test

Time at Start............

In the space provided, write the letter of the correct answer to the problem.

1. Find the range of values for x such that $5x - 7 > 13$.
(a) $x > 4$ (b) $x < 4$ (c) $x > \frac{6}{5}$ (d) $x < \frac{6}{5}$
(e) $x > \frac{5}{6}$ 1. ....

2. Find the values of x that satisfy the inequality $11 - 2x < 9$.
(a) $x > 1$ (b) $x < 2$ (c) $x > 10$ (d) $x < 10$
(e) none of these   2. ....

3. Solve for x: $x/3 + 6 > 10$.
(a) $x > 48$ (b) $x < 48$ (c) $x > 12$ (d) $x < 12$
(e) none of these   3. ....

4. Solve for the range of values of x: $25 - (x/2) > 16$.
(a) $x > 18$ (b) $x < 18$ (c) $x > 9$ (d) $x < 9$
(e) none of these   4. ....

5. A drawer contains 7 red socks and 7 blue socks. If I draw one sock from the drawer, what is the probability that it is a red sock?
(a) $\frac{1}{7}$ (b) $\frac{1}{14}$ (c) $\frac{1}{2}$ (d) cannot be done from given information   (e) can be done, but answer is not given
                                              5. ....

6. What is the probability that March 5 in the year X will be a Sunday?
(a) $\frac{1}{52}$ (b) $\frac{7}{52}$ (c) $\frac{52}{365}$ (d) $\frac{7}{30}$ (e) $\frac{1}{7}$ 6. ....

7. If we draw one card from a standard deck of 52 playing cards, what is the probability that it will be a spade?
(a) $\frac{1}{4}$ (b) $\frac{1}{13}$ (c) $\frac{1}{3}$ (d) $\frac{4}{7}$ (e) none of these 7. ....

8. There are 9 boys in a club, the Vikings. There will be a drawing among the boys for 2 circus tickets. What is the probability that John, the oldest of the Vikings, will win one of the tickets?
(a) $\frac{1}{9}$ (b) $\frac{2}{9}$ (c) $\frac{1}{3}$ (d) $\frac{2}{3}$ (e) none of these 8. ....

9. What is the probability that a house number chosen at random from a box of digits will begin with a 5?
(a) $\frac{1}{5}$ (b) $\frac{1}{9}$ (c) $\frac{1}{7}$ (d) $\frac{2}{9}$ (e) none of these 9. ....

10. Solve for a: $3a + b > c$.
(a) $a > (b + c)/3$ (b) $a < (b - c)/3$ (c) $a > 3c - b$
(d) $a > (c - b)/3$ (e) $a > c - 3b$ 10. ....

Time at End............ *Minutes Elapsed*............
Average Time 30 *Minutes*

Answer Key for this test is on page 529.

My Score: *Number Right*............ *Number Wrong*............
Average Number Right 7

Third Day: **Graphing the Solutions to Inequalities**

What You Should Know

1. The *number line* on which we show solutions is a straight line which extends indefinitely in two directions and of which each point corresponds to a real number. The middle of the line is usually labeled "zero."

2. We will indicate only integers along this number line, although the fractions and irrational numbers may also be found there.

3. A solid dot (●) indicates a point that is included in a solution; an open dot (○) indicates that the point is excluded.

PROBLEM: The solution of $2x - 3 = 5$ is represented by (?).

ANALYSIS: If we solve the equation algebraically, we obtain the solution set $x = 4$. This is represented by:

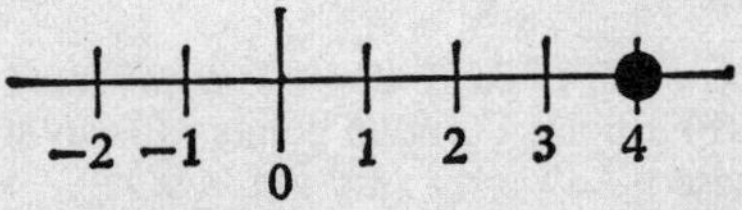

PROBLEM: The solution of $4x > 8$ is represented by (?).

ANALYSIS: If we solve the expression algebraically, we obtain the solution set $x > 2$. This is represented by:

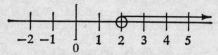

The arrow indicates that the solution extends indefinitely in one direction (to the right). The open dot at 2 indicates that 2 *is not* part of the solution set.

PROBLEM: The solution of $y \leq 3$ is represented by (?).

ANALYSIS: Since we must include 3 in our solution set, we use the solid dot.

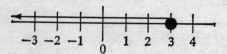

PROBLEM: The positive, integral solutions of $2x < 8$ are represented by (?).

ANALYSIS: If we solve algebraically, we obtain the solution set consisting of integers greater than zero, but less than 4. These are 1, 2, and 3.

Practice Test

Time at Start............

In the space provided, write the letter of the correct answer to the problem.

1. The solution set of $3x \nleftrightarrow 8 = 8$ is represented by
(a) a line   (b) a point   (c) two points   (d) an arrow
(e) none of these   1. ....

2. The solution of $3y + 6 = 12$ is represented by

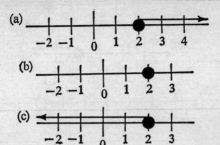

(a)

(b)

(c)

(d) none of these is correct (e) the solution cannot be
represented on a number line   2. ....

3. The solution set of $2x > 4$ is represented by

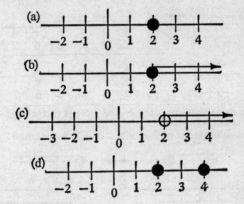

(a)

(b)

(c)

(d)

(e) none of these   3. ....

4. The solution set of $2x + 3 < 9$ can be represented by

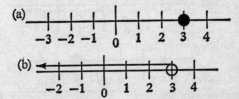

(a)

(b)

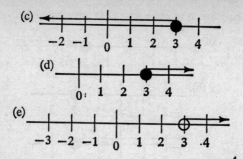

(c)

(d)

(e)

4. ....

5. The solution set of $6 > x > 2$ can be represented by

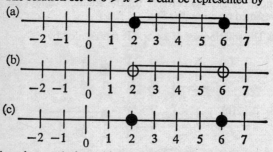

(a)

(b)

(c)

(d) there is no solution   (e) none of these is correct   5. ....

6. The solution set of $2 > x > 2$ can be represented by

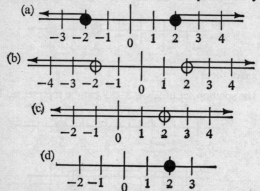

(a)

(b)

(c)

(d)

(e) there is no solution

6. ....

7. The positive integral solutions of $2x < 9$ may be represented by

(a)

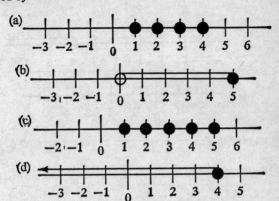

(b)

(c)

(d)

(e) none of these

7. ....

8. Represent the values of x such that $2x \geq 10$.

(a)

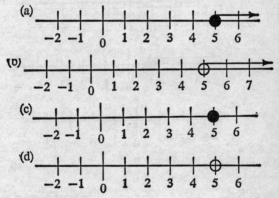

(b)

(c)

(d)

(e) none of these

8. ....

9. The solution set of $3x - 1 \geq 19 - 2x$ is represented by

(a)

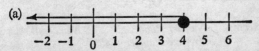

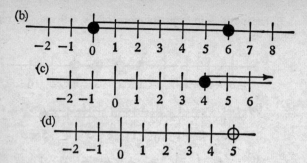

(e) none of these

9. ....

10. The solution set of $3 - 2x > 5$ can be represented by

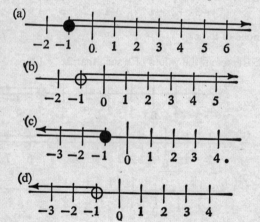

(e) none of these

10. ....

Time at End............

Minutes Elapsed............
Average Time 25 Minutes

Answer Key for this test is on page 530.

My Score: *Number Right*............   *Number Wrong*............
          Average Number Right 6

Fourth Day: The Language of Sets

What You Should Know

VOCABULARY

set: a collection of objects called "elements." The set (1, 2, 3, 4)
    has four elements.

empty or *null set:* the set having no elements. Thus if we take
        the set of odd members of the set (2, 4, 6, 8,
        10), we get the empty set. It is denoted by the
        symbols "$\emptyset$" and "( )."

subset: a set having all its members chosen from a set either
    larger than itself or of the same size.

union of two sets: a set consisting of the *combined* members of
        the two sets. It is denoted by the symbol
        "$\cup$." Thus,

$$(1, 2, 3, 4) \cup (3, 4, 5) = (1, 2, 3, 4, 5)$$

intersection of two sets: a set consisting of those elements
        common to the two sets. It is denoted
        by the symbol "$\cap$." Thus,

$$(1, 3, 5, 7) \cap (2, 4, 7, 8) = (7)$$

Practice Test

Time at Start............

In the space provided, write the letter of the correct answer
to the problem.

1. Find $(1, 2, 3) \cup (2, 4, 6)$.
  (a) (1, 2, 3) (b) (2, 4, 6) (c) (1, 2, 3, 4, 6) (d) (2)
(e) none of these   1. ....

2. Find $(1, 2, 3) \cap (2, 4, 6)$.
  (a) (1, 2, 3) (b) (2, 4, 6) (c) (1, 2, 3, 4, 6) (d) (2)
(e) none of these   2. ....

Questions 3 through 7 refer to the sets $A = (1, 2)$, $B = (2, 4, 6)$,
$C = (1, 2, 3, 4, 5, 6, 7)$, and $D = (2, 4)$.

3. Find $A \cup C$.
  (a) (1, 2) (b) (1, 2, 3, 4, 5, 6, 7) (c) (2, 4) (d) (2)
(e) cannot be done   3. ....

4. Find $A \cap C$.
  (a) (1, 2) (b) (1, 2, 3, 4, 5, 6, 7) (c) (2, 4) (d) (2)
(e) none of these   4. ....

5. Find $B \cap D$.
(a) A (b) B (c) C (d) D (e) cannot be done from the given information   5. ....

6. Find $A \cup B \cup D$.
(a) (2, 4, 6)   (b) (1, 2, 4, 6)   (c) (1, 2)   (d) (2, 4)
(e) none of these   6. ....

7. Find $C \cup A \cup D$.
(a) A (b) B (c) C (d) D (e) none of these   7. ....

8. Find the set (2, 4, 6, 8) $\cap$ (1, 3, 5, 7).
(a) (1, 3, 5, 7)   (b) (2, 4, 6, 8)   (c) (1, 2, 3, 4, 5, 6, 7, 8)
(d) ( )   (e) none of these   8. ....

Time at End.............   *Minutes Elapsed.............*
                                             Average Time 30 *Minutes*

Answer Key for this test is on page 530.

My Score: *Number Right.............*   *Number Wrong.............*
               Average Number Right 4

Fifth Day: Solving Problems in Sets with Venn Diagrams

What You Should Know

A Venn diagram (named for the mathematician Jacob Venn) can be used when relationships between sets are involved. The first part of a Venn diagram is a rectangle representing the entire "universe" of things we are discussing. Circles are then placed within this rectangle to indicate the subsets of the basic universe.

PROBLEM: If A represents the set (1, 2, 3, 4, 5, 6, 7, 8) and B represents the set (5, 7, 9, 11), then how do we represent the intersection of A and B?

ANALYSIS: The rectangle represents all the numbers in our universe. The first circle, A, represents set A. The second one, B, represents set B. The overlapping part of A and B represents their intersection.

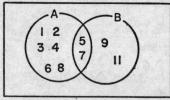

PROBLEM: There are 12 trains that pass through towns P and Q. One-half of these stop at P; one-third stop at Q; one-fourth stop at both P and Q. How many stop at neither?

ANALYSIS: We let our rectangle represent the 12 trains. $(\frac{1}{2})(12) = 6$; $(\frac{1}{3})(12) = 4$; $(\frac{1}{4})(12) = 3$. Then circle P represents the 6 that stop at P, circle Q the 4 that stop at Q. The area of overlap represents the trains common to both sets.

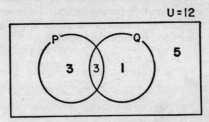

Since there are 3 trains stopping at both P and Q, we have only 3 others stopping at P alone, and only 1 other stopping at Q alone. Thus we have only discussed $3 + 3 + 1$ or 7 trains, leaving 5 that must stop at neither P nor Q.

PROBLEM: Joe and Ann gave a party and invited 20 people. At the party, 12 people had sandwiches, 7 had cokes, and 5 had both. How many had neither?

ANALYSIS: Since there are 5 people who had both, we place a 5 in the intersection of the circles.

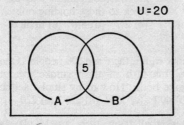

Now, we need only fill in the remainders (7 others in circle A for sandwiches, and 2 others in circle B for cokes).

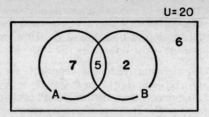

Notice that this still shows 12 people having sandwiches and 7 having cokes. However, the total
number of people involved is 7 ⊕ 5 ⊕ 2, or 14.
Therefore, 6 people had neither.

Practice Test

Time at Start...........

In the space provided, write the letter of the correct answer
to the problem.

1. On the Hawks, a professional baseball team, there are 18
men not counting the pitchers. If 7 of these can play outfield, 3
can play first base, and 2 can play both, how many men play
neither the outfield nor first base?
(a) 6   (b) 7   (c) 10   (d) 18   (e) none of these   1. ....

2. There are 10,000 stockholders in XYZ International
Corporation and 14,000 in ABC Local Company. If 6,000
people own stock in both companies, find the ratio of those
holding only XYZ stock to those holding only ABC stock.
(a) 1:2   (b) 5:7   (c) 2:7   (d) 5:6   (e) none of these

2. ....

3. In a trailer camp, there are 500 people. One-tenth of these
smoke cigars, one-fifth of them smoke cigarettes, and one-
twentieth smoke both. How many smoke neither?
(a) 450   (b) 400   (c) 375   (d) 325   (e) 220   3. ....

4. On a basketball team, there are 15 players. Of these, 7
play guard, 8 play forward, and 3 play neither. How many can
play both positions?
(a) 3   (b) 4   (c) 5   (d) 7   (e) 10   4. ....

5. On a menu in a certain restaurant, there are 7 dinners involving a main course of sea food, 5 dinners involving meat, and 3 dinners involving neither. If 2 dinners involve both meat and sea food, how many dinners are listed on the entire menu?

  (a) 17 (b) 15 (c) 13 (d) 11 (e) 9   5. ....

Time at End.............   *Minutes Elapsed*............

                                        Average Time 20 *Minutes*

Answer Key for this test is on page 531.

My Score: *Number Right*............   *Number Wrong*............

              Average Number Right 3

Sixth Day: New Symbolism

What You Should Know

The College Entrance Examination you take may test your ability to adjust to brand new situations. The questions will define an unusual symbol that you have never seen before. Then you will be asked to do a problem using the new symbol.

PROBLEM: If $x \frown y$ means $x^3 - 3y$, so that $3 \frown 2$
$= 3^3 - (3 \times 2) = 27 - 6 = 21$, find $2 \frown 1$.

ANALYSIS: $x \frown y = x^3 - 3y$
$2 \frown 1 = 2^3 - (3 \times 1)$
$= 8 - 3$
$= 5$

PROBLEM: If $P \oslash Q = PQ - (P \oplus Q)$, find $(3 \oslash 2) \oslash 2$.

ANALYSIS: The solution consists of two parts:
(a) $3 \oslash 2 = 3 \times 2 - (3 \oplus 2)$
$= 6 - 5$
$= 1$
Substituting 1 for $(3 \oslash 2)$, the expression $(3 \oslash 2) \oslash 2$ simplified becomes $1 \oslash 2$.
(b) $1 \oslash 2 = 1 \times 2 - (1 \oplus 2)$
$= 2 - 3$
$= -1$

Practice Test

Time At Start...........

In the space provided, write the letter of the correct answer to the problem.

1. If $R \diagdown S$ means $R \oplus 1/S$, so that $3 \diagdown 2 = 3 \oplus \frac{1}{2} = 3\frac{1}{2}$, find $2 \diagdown 3$.

(a) $3\frac{1}{2}$ (b) $2\frac{1}{3}$ (c) $1\frac{2}{3}$ (d) 2   (e) 1   1. ....

2. If $\begin{vmatrix} M \\ P \end{vmatrix} = MP - 2M$, find $\begin{vmatrix} 5 \\ 3 \end{vmatrix}$.

(a) 15   (b) 2   (c) 5   (d) 10   (e) 8   2. ....

3. If $\diagup z \diagdown \atop x - y$ means $x \oplus y - z$, so that $\diagup 5 \diagdown \atop 3 - 4 = 3 \oplus 4 - 5$

$= 7 - 5 = 2$, find the value of $\diagup 2 \diagdown \atop 2 - 2$.

(a) 0   (b) 2   (c) −2   (d) 8   (e) none of these   3. ....

4. If $\begin{vmatrix} a & b \\ c & d \end{vmatrix} = ad - bc$, find $\begin{vmatrix} 2 & 5 \\ 3 & 1 \end{vmatrix}$.

(a) −6   (b) 6   (c) 13   (d) −13   (e) none of these

4. ....

5. If $s \diamondsuit q \atop r \atop p$ means $p \oplus r - (s \oplus q)$, so that $1 \diamondsuit 3 \atop 4 \atop 2 =$

$(2 \oplus 4) - (3 \oplus 1) = 6 - 4 = 2$, find $2 \diamondsuit 4 \atop 3 \atop 1$.

(a) 2   (b) −2   (c) −3   (d) 4   (e) none of these   5. ....

6. If $P \boxtimes Q = P^2 \dotplus 1/Q$, find the value of $3 \boxtimes 2$:
(a) $\frac{3}{13}$ (b) $\frac{5}{3}$ (c) $\frac{5}{2}$ (d) $13\frac{1}{3}$ (e) $19\frac{1}{2}$ 6. ....

7. If $\begin{vmatrix} a & b \\ c & d \end{vmatrix} = ad - bc$, find the value of x so that $\begin{vmatrix} 3 & 2 \\ x & 4 \end{vmatrix}$ will be equal to 0.

(a) 3 (b) 5 (c) 0 (d) 4 (e) 6   7. ....

8. If $\underset{x\;-\;y}{\overset{z}{\diagdown\!\diagup}}$ means $x \oplus y - z$, find $\underset{3\;-\;4}{\overset{5}{\diagdown\!\diagup}} + \underset{3\;-\;4}{\overset{5}{\diagdown\!\diagup}}$.

(a) 19 (b) 4 (c) 3 (d) 9 (e) 12   8. ....

9. If $x \oslash y = x^y - (x \oplus y)$, find $3 \oslash 4$.

(a) 0 (b) 74 (c) 81 (d) 20 (e) −5   9. ....

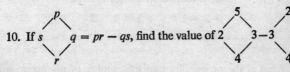

10. If $s \diamond q = pr - qs$, find the value of $2 \diamond 3 - 3 \diamond 1$.

(a) 10 (b) 7 (c) 5 (d) 9 (e) 2   10. ....

Time at End.............   *Minutes Elapsed.............*
                                              Average Time 30 Minutes

Answer Key for this test is on page 532.

My Score: *Number Right.............*   *Number Wrong.............*
               Average Number Right 5

Seventh Day: Test of Mastery

Time at Start.............

In the space provided, write the letter of the correct answer to the problem.

1. Find the range of values for p such that $3p - 2 > 7$.
(a) $p > 9$ (b) $p < 9$ (c) $p > 3$ (d) $p < 3$
(e) none of these   1. ....

2. The solution set of $6x \div 2 = -10$ can be represented by

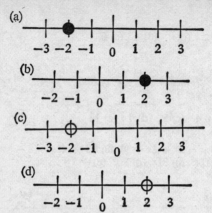

(a)

(b)

(c)

(d)

(e) none of these   2. ....

3. What is the probability that the number of my house will end with an odd digit?

(a) ⅑ (b) ⅓ (c) ⅕ (d) 5/9 (e) ½   3. ....

4. Find the number of members in the set which represents the intersection of $A(1, 2, 3)$ and $B(3, 4, 5)$.

(a) 1 (b) 2 (c) 3 (d) 5 (e) 6   4. ....

5. If A represents the number of boys in a seventh-grade class and B represents the number of boys in an eighth-grade class, how many members are there in the set $A \cap B$?

(a) 1 (b) 2 (c) 3 (d) cannot be done from the given information (e) none of these   5. ....

6. At Smithington College there are 250 seniors taking their midyear exams. There are 125 of them taking mathematics exams and 145 taking language exams. If 30 seniors are taking neither the mathematics nor the language ones, how many seniors are taking both?

(a) 15 (b) 25 (c) 30 (d) 50 (e) none of these   6. ....

7. If there are 30 people at the meeting of the PQR Club, and 20 drink soda, 17 drink coffee, and 14 drink both, how many drink neither?

(a) 9 (b) 7 (c) 5 (d) 3 (e) none of these   7. ....

8. If $5 \boxtimes 3$ means $5 \times 3 + (5 - 3) = 15 + 2 = 17$, find the value of $4 \boxtimes 2$.

  (a) 10   (b) 12   (c) 8   (d) 6   (e) none of these   8. ....

9. If $\begin{vmatrix} p & q \\ r & s \end{vmatrix}$ means $ps - qr$, so that $\begin{vmatrix} 3 & 5 \\ 6 & 4 \end{vmatrix}$ means $3 \times 4 - 5 \times 6$

$= -18$, find the value of $\begin{vmatrix} 3 & 5 \\ 6 & 7 \end{vmatrix}$.

  (a) 9   (b) -9 (c) 17   (d) -17 (e) none of these

                                                    9. ....

10. If $x \oslash y$ means $x^2 - y$, so that $5 \oslash 3$ means $5^2 - 3 = 22$, find the value of $4 \oslash (3 \oslash 2)$.

  (a) 7   (b) 167   (c) 9   (d) 49   (e) none of these   10. ....

Time at End............   *Minutes Elapesd*............
                                                       Average Time 25 Minutes

Answer Key for this test is on page 533.

My Score: *Number Right*............   *Number Wrong*............
              Average Number Right 7

Section 13: Modern Trends in Mathematics

Answer Key with Hints

Second Day   **Page 513**

1. (a) Add 7 to both sides; then divide by 5.
2. (a) Subtract 11 from both sides; then divide by -2. Remember to reverse the order of the inequality.
3. (c) Subtract 6 from both sides; then multiply by 3.
4. (b) Subtract 25 from both sides; then multiply by -2 and change the order of the inequality.
5. (c) Since there are 14 socks (total possibilities) and 7 are red (favorable), we get $\frac{7}{14}$, or $\frac{1}{2}$.
6. (e) There are 7 days to choose from (total possibilities), and only one of these (Sunday) is favorable.
7. (a) A standard deck contains 4 suits: hearts, diamonds, clubs, and spades.

8. (b) The fact that John is the oldest has no bearing on the problem. There are two prizes (favorable) and nine drawings (total possibilities).

9. (b) There are only nine digits to choose from (house numbers won't begin with digit 0), and only one is favorable (the 5).

10. (d) We treat this literal inequality the same as a numerical one. First subtract b from both sides, then divide through by 3.

Third Day   Page 515

1. (b) The algebraic solution of $3x + 8 = 8$ is $x = 0$, one point.

2. (b) The algebraic solution of $3y + 6 = 12$ is $y = 2$, one point.

3. (c) The algebraic solution of $2x > 4$ is the set of all x greater than 2, but not including 2.

4. (b) The algebraic solution of $2x + 3 < 9$ is the set of values for x less than 3, but not including 3.

5. (b) The line representing values greater than 2 but less than 6 cannot include the 2 and 6.

6. (e) There can be no values of x, since there is no number that is *both* greater than 2 and less than 2.

7. (a) The algebraic solution of the inequality gives us the set of values less than $4\frac{1}{2}$; we want only positive *integers*.

8. (a) Since the solution set consists of all values greater than or equal to 5, we must include the 5 on our graph.

9. (c) The algebraic solution of $3x - 1 \geq 19 - 2x$ consists of all values of x greater than or equal to 4. Thus 4 is included on the graph.

10. (d) In solving this inequality algebraically, we obtain $3 - 2x > 5$; $-2x > 2$; $x < -1$. Remember to reverse the order!

Fourth Day   Page 521

1. (c) Combine all the different elements from each set.

2. (d) The only element common to both given sets is 2.

3. (b) Since C contains all elements of A, then C itself represents the union.

4. (a) Since C contains all the elements of A, then A itself is the intersection.

5. **(d)** Since *D* is a subset of *B*, it must contain all the elements common to both sets.

6. **(b)** $A \cup B = (1, 2, 4, 6)$. This already contains the elements of *D*.

7. **(c)** Since *C* contains all the elements of both *A* and *D*, it represents the union, or the combined elements of all three sets.

8. **(d)** The two given sets have no elements in common, so their intersection must contain no elements and thus be the empty or null set.

Fifth Day   Page 522

1. **(c)**

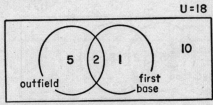

$5 + 2 + 1 = 8$
$18 - 8 = 10$

2. **(a)**

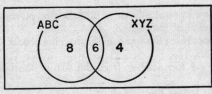

4:8, or 1:2

3. **(c)**

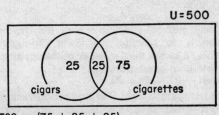

$500 - (75 + 25 + 25)$

4. (a)

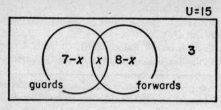

$(7 - x) + x + (8 - x) + 3 = 15$
$x = 3$

5. (c)

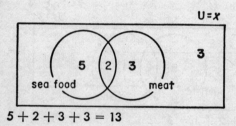

$5 + 2 + 3 + 3 = 13$

Sixth Day   Page 525

1. (b) The new symbol tells us to add the first number to the reciprocal of the second.
2. (c) Subtract twice the top number from the product of both numbers.
3. (b) Take the top number from the sum of the horizontal ones.
4. (d) Simply follow the model.
5. (b) $(1 + 3) - (2 + 4) = 4 - 6 = -2$.
6. (e) $3^2 + \frac{1}{2} = 9\frac{1}{2} = \frac{19}{2}$.
7. (e) $12 - 2x = 0;\quad x = 6$.
8. (b) The only method yielding one of the choices as a solution is to simplify the lower "triangle" first, obtaining 6 as the third member of the upper triangle. Evaluate each one separately.
9. (b) $3^4 = 81;\quad 81 - 7 = 74$.
10. (d) Work from left to right. The first set of numbers gives $20 - 6 = 14$; then the second set gives $8 - 3 = -5$. Evaluate each one separately.

More of this
type can be
found in the
work of day

Seventh Day   **Page 527**

1. (c) Add 2 to both sides; then divide by 3.   2
2. (a) The solution set consists of just one point,   3
        −2.
3. (e) There are 5 odd digits—1, 3, 5, 7, 9—and   2
        10 possible digits—1, 2, 3, 4, 5, 6, 7, 8,
        9, 0.
4. (a) The two sets have only one member in   4
        common.
5. (e) The two classes can have no members in   4
        common.

6. (d)   5

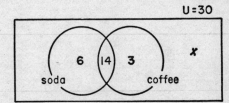

$$125 - x + 145 - x + x + 30 = 250$$

7. (b)   5

U=30

soda 6 14 3 coffee x

$$6 + 14 + 3 + x = 30$$

8. (a) $4 \times 2 + (4 - 2)$ 6
9. (b) $3 \times 7 - 5 \times 6$ 6
10. (c) Work with the parentheses first; $3 \oslash 2$ 6
        $= 7$. Then $4 \oslash 7$ means $4^2 - 7 = 16 - 7$
        $= 9$.

Part III

Exams: Getting into the
Competitive Line-up

EXAMS: GETTING INTO THE
COMPETITIVE LINE-UP

This section contains five practice tests covering verbal areas and ten dealing with mathematics. The average time and analysis of scores should help you to evaluate your own ability to face the pressures ahead. To increase your speed, do each of these tests several times. To increase your score, analyze your results, discover the areas of weakness, and then turn to the appropriate section in Parts I and II of this book. If you are limited in time, then take one examination at each session. Otherwise alternate verbal and mathematics, taking three examinations at any one time. Remember, the College Boards are usually three hours long and contain approximately five sections: two or three of verbals, and two or three of mathematics.

VERBAL AND MATHEMATICS TESTS

Test Number 1

Time at Start............

In the space provided, write the letter of the correct answer to the problem.

1. In right triangle *ABC*, the right angle is at *A*, and *D* is a point on line *AC* between *A* and *C*. If *BC* = 15, *BD* = 13, and *AB* = 12, find the length of segment *CD*.

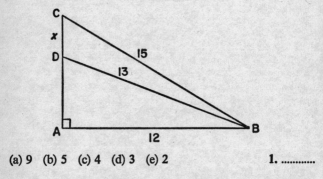

(a) 9 (b) 5 (c) 4 (d) 3 (e) 2   1. ....

2. It takes 8 men 3 days to do a job. At the same rate, how long would it take 6 men to do the job?
(a) 3 days (b) 4 days (c) 6 days (d) 8 days (e) 10 days
2. ....

3. The legs of a right triangle are a and $a/3$ as shown. How many such triangles would be necessary to form a square?

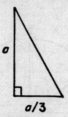

(a) 2   (b) 4   (c) 6   (d) 8   (e) 10   3. ....

4. Two numbers are related such that 5 times the first equals 2 times the second. What is the ratio of the first to the second?
   (a) 2:5   (b) 5:2   (c) 7:2   (d) 7:5   (e) none of these
                                                        4. ....

5. If a $3\frac{1}{2}$-pound box of cookies costs \$2.10, how much per pound are the cookies?
   (a) 60c   (b) 70c   (c) \$1.05   (d) \$1.20   (e) \$7.35   5. ....

6. Mr. Jones received \$1,400 as his share of a business in which he owns $\frac{2}{7}$ of the stock. How much should his partner receive for the other $\frac{5}{7}$?
   (a) \$2,800   (b) \$3,000   (c) \$3,500   (d) \$4,900
(e) none of these   6. ....

7. The Twelfth Boy Scout Unit had 20 troops, each made up of 30 scouts. After the summer, the Unit lost 100 scouts. If the Unit still has 20 troops, how many scouts are in each troop now?
   (a) 20   (b) 25   (c) 30   (d) cannot be done from the given information   (e) can be done, but the answer is not given
                                                        7. ....

8. If apples weigh about 5 pounds per dozen, approximately how much in pounds will 59 apples weigh?
   (a) 300   (b) 100   (c) 50   (d) 25   (e) 10   8. ....

9. On the *Bigtime* professional basketball team, the center is 6'11", the guards are 5'10" and 6'2", while the forwards are 6'3" and 6'6". What is the average height of the *Bigtime* players?
   (a) 6'1"   (b) 6'2"   (c) 6'3"   (d) 6'4"   (e) none of these
                                                        9. ....

10. Right angle *ABC* is at the center of circle *B* as shown. If *BD* bisects angle *ABC*, find the number of degrees in angle *DCB*.

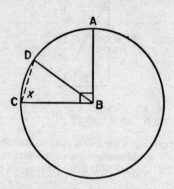

(a) 45   (b) 60   (c) 67½   (d) 72½   (e) 90   10. ....

11. If $x \otimes y = x^2 - xy$, find the value of $5 \otimes 4$.
(a) 25   (b) 20   (c) 10   (d) 5   (e) none of these   11. ....

12. Find the difference between the sum of the numbers from 21 to 40 and the sum of the numbers from 1 to 20.
(a) 40   (b) 400   (c) 444   (d) 450   (e) none of these
                                                          12. ....

13. Two tests each contain 25 different questions. If the first 5 from test *A* are placed at the end of test *B* and the first 5 from test *B* are placed at the end of test *A*, each test then has 30 questions. How many questions will be the same on both tests, assuming they began with no questions in common?
(a) 5   (b) 10   (c) 15   (d) cannot be determined
(e) can be determined, but the answer is not given   13. ....

14. For what positive integral value of *y* will $\sqrt{5y/4}$ be a whole number?
(a) 20   (b) 16   (c) 5   (d) 4   (e) no such value exists
                                                          14. ....

15. A cotton shirt that costs $3 must be washed and ironed at a commercial laundry at a cost of 25 cents. A wash-and-wear shirt costs $5, but can be laundered at home at no cost. How

much money could be saved in 25 wearings of the wash-and-wear shirt as compared with 25 wearings of the cotton shirt?

(a) $4.25   (b) $9.25   (c) $6.25   (d) there would be no savings (e) none of these   15. ....

16. A bar of copper alloy contains copper, zinc, and lead in the ratio of 2:3:7. How much zinc is there in 60 pounds of the alloy?

(a) 10 pounds   (b) 15 pounds   (c) 35 pounds   (d) 40 pounds (e) none of these   16. ....

17. If $x^2 - a^2 = y^2 - b^2$ and $a > b > 0$, which of the following may be concluded?

(a) $x^2 > y^2$ (b) $x^2 = y^2$ (c) $x^2 < y^2$
(d) $x^2 + a^2 > y^2 + b^2$ (e) $a^2 < b^2$ 17. ....

18. A man has 8 sacks, each containing the same number of coins. He spends 24 coins and finds that he has 72 left. How many coins were in each sack at the start?

(a) 6   (b) 9   (c) 12   (d) 16   (e) 24   18. ....

19. A man buys 60 transistor radios for $180. He wishes to make a profit of $16\frac{2}{3}\%$ on his investment. At what price should he sell each radio?

(a) $3.16   (b) $3.32   (c) $3.30   (d) $3.50
(e) none of these   19. ....

20. Margaret takes 18 minutes to do the dishes. Her mother can do them in 9 minutes. How long would it take them if they worked together?

(a) $4\frac{1}{2}$ minutes   (b) 5 minutes   (c) 6 minutes
(d) $6\frac{1}{2}$ minutes   (e) none of these   20. ....

Time at End............   *Minutes Elapsed*............
                                            Average Time 30 *Minutes*

Answer Key for this test is on page 604.

My Score: Number Right............   *Number Wrong*............

Comparing With Others

	Number Correct
Top 1%	19–20
Top 10%	16–18
Average	12–15
Low Average	9–11
Below Average	0–10

Test Number 2

Time at Start............

A. Antonyms

In the space provided, write the letter of the word that is most nearly opposite in meaning to the first word.

1. PARSIMONIOUS   (a) willing   (b) lavish
(c) venerable   (d) wary   (e) fraught   1. ....

2. GARNER   (a) scatter   (b) sell   (c) gain
(d) order   (e) arrest   2. ....

3. IGNOBLE   (a) dogmatic   (b) felicitous
(c) splendid   (d) regal   (e) common   3. ....

4. EXTENUATE   (a) order   (b) excel   (c) recall
(d) retract   (e) blame   4. ....

5. JOCULAR   (a) immature   (b) ripe   (c) regional
(d) domestic   (e) grave   5. ....

6. FIASCO   (a) success   (b) completion   (c) struggle
(d) penalty   (e) loss   6. ....

7. NEOPHYTE   (a) client   (b) dealer   (c) loser
(d) expert   (e) teen-ager   7. ....

8. EUPHONIOUS   (a) ill   (b) harsh   (c) slow
(d) recent   (e) hilly   8. ....

9. LARGESS   (a) pettiness   (b) locality
(c) weakness   (d) tiniest   (e) stinginess   9. ....

10. DIFFIDENT   (a) similar   (b) timely   (c) bold
(d) borrowed   (e) exceptional   10. ....

B. Sentence Completion

In the space provided, write the letter of the set of words that best completes the sentence.

11. The exercise of .... power by whatever means is .... and should not be tolerated.
   (a) limited...fascism   (c) benevolent...democracy
   (b) irresponsible....tyranny   (d) irrational....foolish

                                                         11. ....

12. By .... the smallest states thrive; by .... the greatest are destroyed.

(a) rivalry...cooperation   (c) union...discord

(b) commerce...competition   (d) wisdom...enemies

12. ....

13. Opinions founded on .... are always sustained with the greatest violence.

(a) prejudice   (c) reality

(b) folly   (d) willingness   13. ....

14. Although the wound was ...., it was so painful that the doctor had to give the patient a sedative.

(a) ostensible   (c) sustained

(b) dormant   (d) superficial   14. ....

15. We shall do everything within our powers to .... this costly error.

(a) justify   (c) exonerate

(b) conciliate   (d) rectify   15. ....

16. Those who never .... their opinions love themselves more than they love ....

(a) defend...life   (c) express...their neighbors

(b) deny...liberty   (d) retract...truth

16. ....

17. To be conscious that you are .... is a great step to ....

(a) wrong...power   (c) alive...greatness

(b) ignorant...knowledge   (d) suspected...achievement

17. ....

18. There are binding on the human subject no laws that assault the .... or violate the ....

(a) people...Constitution   (c) body...conscience

(b) rights...privileges   (d) mind...regulations

18. ....

19. Only a .... would be so .... to the cries of a people suffering from the effects of disastrous floods and fires.

(a) tyrant...oblivious   (c) villain...alert

(b) fool...responsive   (d) misanthrope...callous

19. ....

20. .... lies not in being strong but in the right use of
....
(a) Folly...force   (c) Greatness...strength
(b) Wisdom...experience   (d) Violence...trickery

20. ....

C. Analogies

In the space provided, write the letter of the set of words
that best completes the analogy.

21. LAUNCH : EMBARK UPON :: (a) treaty : attack
(b) motor : sail   (c) career : venture   (d) ship : restriction
(e) man : work   21. ....

22. OVERTURE : PREAMBLE :: (a) last : first
(b) first : last   (c) conclusion : beginning   (d) score :
summary   (e) music : speech   22. ....

23. PROLOGUE : POEM :: (a) foreword : preface
(b) induction : office   (c) innovation : old-fashioned
(d) initiation : vote   (e) child : infant   23. ....

24. EVOLVE : ACCUMULATE :: (a) ramble : ripen
(b) more : less   (c) internal : external   (d) boom : mature
(e) slow : fast   24. ....

25. RANK : LUSH :: (a) more : less   (b) slowly :
quickly   (c) mature : young   (d) uncontrolled : thick
(e) natural : fertilized   25. ....

26. DRAFT : BANK :: (a) depth : boat   (b) check :
depositor   (c) call : army   (d) salary : worker   (e) land :
estate   26. ....

27. BALL-POINT : FOUNTAIN :: (a) pen : pencil
(b) modern : ancient   (c) fine : blunt   (d) cheap :
expensive   (e) paste : liquid   27. ....

28. INSIGNIA : RANK :: (a) decoration : medal
(b) weight : burden   (c) reading : culture   (d) blue :
sadness   (e) red : danger   28. ....

29. DESIGNER : DRESS :: (a) carpenter : cabinet
(b) house : builder   (c) contractor : dam   (d) mayor : city
(e) architect : house   29. ....

30. MARS : VENUS :: (a) Earth : moon   (b) nearest :
farthest   (c) Jupiter : sun   (d) war : love   (e) Greek :
Roman   30. ....

D. Reading Comprehension

Read the selection, and in each space provided, write the letter of the set of words that best completes the statement.

What we have inherited from our fathers and mothers is not all that "walks in us." There are all sorts of dead ideas and lifeless old beliefs. They have no tangibility, but they haunt us all the same and we cannot get rid of them. Whenever I take up a newspaper I seem to see ghosts gliding between the lines. Ghosts must be all over the country, as thick as sands of the sea.

31. The ghosts the author talks about (a) appear to everyone who is sensitive (b) injure those whom they visit (c) are the same for all people (d) originate with our parents (e) are not valid for present-day living.   31. ....

32. The author (a) reveres tradition (b) dislikes parental influences (c) is optimistic about chances of eliminating the ghosts (d) tries to be a critical thinker (e) is a man of action.
                                                        32. ....

33. The danger involved in these ghosts is that (a) we fear them (b) we are not fully aware of them (c) we can do nothing about them (d) they influence our life in the wrong direction (e) they are undemocratic.   33. ....

34. An example of such a ghost would be (a) the belief that knocking on wood can prevent bad luck (b) the hope that the future will be better (c) faith in democratic processes (d) faith in the ability of the UN to promote world betterment (e) desire to seek self-betterment.   34. ....

35. The one suggestion among the following that is not a possible antidote is (a) reading widely (b) becoming aware of one's own prejudices (c) developing a willingness to listen to others (d) developing a willingness to view one's own attitudes objectively (e) looking for objective proofs to substantiate statements.
                                                        35. ....

No more fatuous chimera ever infested the brain of man than that you can control opinions by law or direct belief by statute, and no more pernicious sentiment ever tormented the human heart than the barbarous desire to do so. The field of inquiry should remain open, and the right of debate must be regarded as a sacred right. I look upon those who would deny others the right to urge and argue their position, however irksome or pernicious they may seem, as intellectual and moral cowards.

36. The main topic discussed by the author in this selection is (a) freedom of the press (b) freedom from want (c) freedom of opinion (d) freedom of speech (e) follies of man.

36. ....

37. The author would defend (a) refusing to allow a known Communist to address a meeting in the local town hall (b) a political candidate's refusing to meet his opponent on a television program (c) passing a law to prohibit the drinking of alcoholic beverages (d) keeping the public square open to anyone who would want to speak there (e) having students sign a pledge of allegiance to the local form of government.

37. ....

38. According to the author, people who suppress the opinions of others do so because (a) they want to protect their children (b) they are afraid to defend their own points of view (c) they fear physical violence (d) they know that they are in the wrong (e) they want to protect their way of life.

38. ....

39. The author does not (a) use logic (b) express his point of view clearly (c) have faith in the ability of people to defend their points of view (d) resort to name-calling (e) sound sincere.

39. ....

40. To promote change, the author would (a) try to have laws passed (b) disregard laws (c) publicize his beliefs (d) organize his followers (e) write to his congressman, urging support.

40. ....

Time at End............   *Minutes Elapsed*............
                                    Average Time 40 *Minutes*

Answer Key for this test is on page 606.

My Score: *Number Right*............   *Number Wrong*............

Comparing With Others

	Number Correct
Top 1%	38–40
Top 10%	35–37
Average	30–34
Low Average	26–29
Below Average	0–25

Test Number 3

Time at Start............

In the space provided, write the correct answer to the problem.

1. If $^{14}\!/_{364} = 7/x$, x equals
(a) $3\frac{5}{7}$ (b) 4   (c) 181   (d) 182   (e) 81   1. ....

2. If 1 bam = 2 lams and 3 lams = 8 nams, then 6 bams equal
(a) 16 nams   (b) 24 nams   (c) 6 nams   (d) 32 nams
(e) none of these   2. ....

3. The value of $\dfrac{2}{2 + \dfrac{1}{2 + \frac{1}{2}}}$ is

(a) $\frac{2}{3}$ (b) $\frac{5}{6}$ (c) $\frac{7}{8}$ (d) $\frac{8}{9}$ (e) $\frac{9}{10}$ 3. ....

4. If 4 men can do $\frac{1}{3}$ of a job in half a day, how many days will it take them to do the whole job?
(a) $\frac{2}{3}$ (b) 1   (c) $\frac{3}{2}$ (d) $\frac{4}{3}$ (e) $\frac{5}{4}$ 4. ....

5. A 6-ounce container of a dehydrated substance is diluted by adding 3 containers of water. The percentage of the substance in the diluted mixture is
(a) 18   (b) 21   (c) 23   (d) 25   (e) 27   5. ....

6. In the diagram at the right, AB is parallel to CD, points E and H are on line AB. points F and G are on line CD. If the area of triangle EFG is 68, $HG = 9$, and $HF = 16$, then the area of triangle HFG is

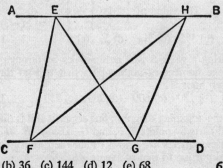

(a) 72   (b) 36   (c) 144   (d) 12   (e) 68   6. ....

7. The number of four-digit integers is
(a) 8,998   (b) 8,999   (c) 9,000   (d) 9,001   (e) 9,002

7. ....

8. If $1/ab = 3$ and $1/cd = 9$, then $(ab \oplus cd)/abcd$ equals
(a) 12   (b) 243/4   (c) 9/2   (d) 4/9   (e) 9/4   8. ....

9. A man decided to tile a 2-foot-wide border around his rectangular swimming pool. If the dimensions of the pool are 14 feet by 18 feet, then the area of the border in feet is
(a) 48   (b) 64   (c) 144   (d) 96   (e) 168   9. ....

10. *L, M,* and *N* are centers of 3 tangent circles of radius 1. The area of the shaded portion is

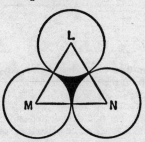

(a) $\sqrt{3}/4 - \pi/2$ (b) $\sqrt{3} - \pi/2$ (c) $2\pi/3 - \sqrt{3}$
(d) $\pi/2 - \sqrt{3}/4$ (e) $\sqrt{3} - \pi/3$ 10. ....

11. For *a* and *b* integers, the symbol $\left\{ a \oplus \genfrac{}{}{0pt}{}{}{b} \right\}$ is defined to be $ab/(a \oplus b)$. The value of $\left\{ 5 \oplus \genfrac{}{}{0pt}{}{}{3} \right\} + \left\{ (-5) \oplus \genfrac{}{}{0pt}{}{}{(-3)} \right\}$ is
(a) $^{15}\!/_{8}$ (b) $^{15}\!/_{4}$ (c) $^{8}\!/_{15}$ (d) $^{4}\!/_{7}$ (e) 0   11. ....

12. During a week 50,400 automobiles go through a tunnel. The average number of automobiles that will go through the tunnel in an hour is
(a) 300   (b) 150   (c) 600   (d) 200   (e) 250   12. ....

13. In the adjoining diagram, line segment *AD* is divided into four equal parts by points *E, F,* and *G*. Using *AE, AF, AG,* and *AD* as bases, squares are drawn. Find the ratio of the area of the shaded portion to that of square *ABCD*.

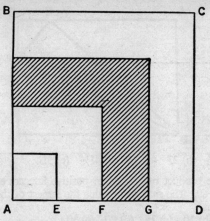

(a) 3/16   (b) 1/4   (c) 5/16   (d) 3/8   (e) 7/16   13. ....

14. Four is what per cent of f?
(a) $25/f$ (b) $f/25$ (c) $400/f$ (d) $f/400$ (e) $(f \oplus 4)/100$

14. ....

15. In the diagram, O is the center of the circle, point D is on line AC extended. The number of degrees in angle ECD is

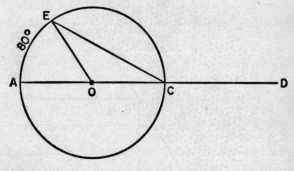

(a) 100   (b) 120   (c) 130   (d) 140   (e) 150   15. ....

16. Given rectangle $ABCD$, $AB = 12$, $BC = 9$, points E and F on AB and BC respectively so that $EB = BF = 3$. The area of triangle DEF is

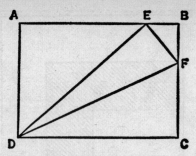

(a) $22\frac{1}{2}$ (b) 27   (c) 35   (d) $41\frac{1}{2}$ (e) 51   16. ....

17. The product of 3 unequal positive integers each greater than 1 is 60. The maximum value the largest of these integers can have is

(a) 5   (b) 10   (c) 15   (d) 20   (e) 30   17. ....

18. The sum of any 12 consecutive odd integers is always

(a) odd   (b) divisible by 8   (c) divisible by 12
(d) divisible by 16   (e) divisible by 20   18. ....

19. In the diagram at the right, point P lies in the shaded portion of the graph to the left of line AB. For all positions of point P,

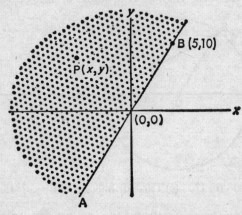

(a) $x > y$ (b) $2x > y$ (c) $y > 2x$ (d) $y > 3x$
(e) $3x > y$ 19. ....

20. Given $A = 2\sqrt{1 \times 1}$, $B = \sqrt{3}$, $C = \sqrt[4]{10}$. The correct arrangement, in order of increasing magnitude, of A, B, and C is
  (a) B, C, A (b) C, B, A (c) A, C, B (d) A, B, C
  (e) C, A, B 20. ....

Time at End............   *Minutes Elapsed*............
                                   Average Time 30 *Minutes*

Answer Key for this test is on page 606.

My Score: *Number Right*............   *Number Wrong*............

Comparing With Others

	Number Correct
Top 1%	19–20
Top 10%	16–18
Average	12–15
Low Average	9–11
Below Average	0–10

Test Number 4

Time at Start............

In this test, each problem will be followed by two statements numbered I and II. You do not have to compute the answers to the problems. Instead, you must decide whether sufficient information has been given to obtain the answer. In the space to the right of each question, mark the letter
  (a) if statement I alone is sufficient to solve the problem, but statement II alone is not sufficient,
  (b) if statement II alone is sufficient to solve the problem, but statement I alone is not sufficient,
  (c) if statements I and II together are sufficient to solve the problem, but neither statement I nor II alone is sufficient,
  (d) if both statements I and II are each sufficient,
  (e) if both statements I and II together are not sufficient to solve the problem.

PROBLEM: What is the average daily income on the carousel in an amusement park for the month of August, if the capacity of the carousel is 100 people per ride?
  (I) A ride begins every 15 minutes from 6 P.M. until 10 P.M. during July and August.
  (II) The cost of a ride is 25 cents.

ANALYSIS: From statement (I), we can calculate the number of
rides during the month of August. Even though statement (II) tells us the cost per ride per person, we do
not know how many people are on each ride. Thus
the correct answer is (e)—both statements together
are not sufficient to solve the problem.

1. How many times have the Sioux beaten the Apaches?
    (I) The Sioux have won $\frac{2}{3}$ of their games.
    (II) Six games have ended in ties.   1. ....

2. How long would it take to fill container Q?
    (I) Container Q is rectangular in shape, $5'' \times 4'' \times 13''$.
    (II) Container Q fills at the rate of 0.4 cubic inches per
        second.   2. ....

3. Which is greater, x or y?
    (I) $y - x$ is positive.
    (II) $y = x + z$.   3. ....

4. What is the ratio of the areas of two unequal circles?
    (I) The ratio of their radii is 1:2.
    (II) The radius of the smaller circle is 5.   4. ....

5. On what date will Thanksgiving in the year X occur?
    (I) In the year X, November 1 is a Wednesday.
    (II) In the year X, November 2 is a Thursday.   5. ....

6. A triangle is inscribed in a circle of radius 4. Is the triangle
   a right triangle?
    (I) One of its sides goes through the center of the circle.
    (II) One of its sides equals 8.   6. ....

7. Is either P or Q equal to zero?
    (I) $P^2 + Q^2 = (P + Q)^2$.
    (II) $nP + kQ = kP + nQ$.   7. ....

8. If Paul, James, and Mary have 95 cents between them, how
   much has Paul?
    (I) Paul has twice as much as James, who has 10 cents more
        than Mary.
    (II) James has 20 cents less than Paul, who has three times
        as much as Mary.   8. ....

9. A special deck of cards is being used in a game. How many
   cards are there in this deck?
    (I) There are 15 cards in each suit of the deck.
    (II) Any 7 cards *must* contain 2 cards of the same suit,
        but this is not true of less than 7 cards.   9. ....

10. How many dollars was Joe's salary raised?
   (I) His pay per week is now $85, after a raise of 5%.
   (II) He used to receive a salary of $75 a week.   10. ....

11. Mr. Jones wishes to buy a set of chairs. He has $100. How much more money does he need?
   (I) Chairs are $8 each.
   (II) There are 16 chairs in a set.   **11.** ....

12. Find the numerical value of $x^2 - y^2$.
   (I) $x - y = y + 2$.
   (II) $x - y = 1/(x + y)$.   **12.** ....

13. How many rooms of a house can one man paint in a day?
   (I) One man working alone takes three days to do one room.
   (II) Three men do three rooms in three days.   **13.** ....

14. What are the relative values of a knife and a gun?
   (I) A knife can be traded for three blankets.
   (II) Seven blankets can be traded for one gun.   **14.** ....

15. How many people in a given classroom were born in the same month?
   (I) There are 15 people in the classroom.
   (II) John and Paul were born in January.   **15.** ....

16. Find the area of triangle *ABE* inscribed in the rectangle as shown.

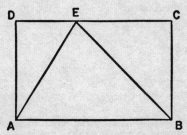

   (I) The rectangle has a perimeter of 48 inches.
   (II) The area of the rectangle is 48 square inches.

                                        16. ....

17. Find the volume of a right circular cylindrical pail.
   (I) The radius of the pail is 14 inches.
   (II) The height of the pail is twice the diameter of the base.
                                   17. ....

18. Find the length of the space diagonal of a cube.
 (I) An edge of the cube is 8 inches.
 (II) The diagonal of a face of the cube is $8\sqrt{2}$ inches.

18. ....

19. Is $x > y$?
 (I) $x^2 > y^2$.
 (II) $x^3 > y^3$.

19. ....

20. How many rangas make a vanga?
 (I) Two rangas make a langa.
 (II) Three picas make a vanga.

20. ....

Time at End.............   *Minutes Elapsed.............*
                                             Average Time 30 Minutes

Answer Key for this test is on page 609.

My Score: Number Right.............   Number Wrong.............

Comparing With Others

	Number Correct
Top 1%	19–20
Top 10%	16–18
Average	12–15
Low Average	9–11
Below Average	0–10

Test Number 5

Time at Start.............

A. Antonyms

In the space provided, write the letter of the word that is most nearly opposite in meaning to the first word.

1. FROWSY   (a) intelligent   (b) active   (c) clean
(d) sluggish   (e) smooth
1. ....

2. IMPLACABLE   (a) lenient   (b) wild   (c) childish
(d) imperial   (e) democratic
2. ....

3. AVARICE   (a) fear   (b) praise   (c) gentleness
(d) generosity   (e) envy
3. ....

4. CIRCUMVENT   (a) cover   (b) promote
(c) remove   (d) fly   (e) spend   4. ....

5. CORPULENT   (a) fallow   (b) exemplary
(c) godly   (d) dogmatic   (e) lean   5. ....

6. RELEGATE   (a) drive   (b) order   (c) extend
(d) invite   (e) descend   6. ....

7. SERRATED   (a) mountainous   (b) low
(c) smooth   (d) talkative   (e) quiet   7. ....

8. DESECRATE   (a) redress   (b) petrify
(c) anticipate   (d) relieve   (e) honor   8. ....

9. FELICITOUS   (a) mature   (b) awkward   (c) noisy
(d) pedantic   (e) piquant   9. ....

10. GLEAN   (a) scatter   (b) beat   (c) accept
(d) abominate   (e) dim   10. ....

B. Sentence Completion

In the space provided, write the letter of the set of words that best completes the sentence.

11. With great care, the editor .... the final copy of the corrected ....
   (a) permeated...letter   (c) perused...manuscript
   (b) emended...conclave   (d) surmised...volume
                                        11. ....

12. I shall never .... to your committing an act of injustice.
   (a) mediate   (c) indulge
   (b) acquiesce   (d) debase   12. ....

13. Did he tell you the main .... upon which he plans to .... the dispute?
   (a) criterion...mediate   (c) contraband...interfere in
   (b) approbation...settle   (d) diadem...redress
                                        13. ....

14. ...., as far as it is able, follows nature as a pupil imitates his master; thus your .... must be, as it were, God's grandchild.
   (a) Goodness...goodness   (c) Art...art
   (b) Mastery...mastery   (d) Science...research
                                        14. ....

15. If the .... lead the ...., both shall fall into the ditch.
(a) ignorant...wise
(c) deaf...blind
(b) blind...blind
(d) foolish...deaf

15. ....

16. Books are .... erected in the great .... of time.
(a) monuments...periods
(c) lighthouses...sea
(b) quirks...deserts
(d) barriers...shoals

16. ....

17. I count him braver who overcomes his own .... than him who overcomes his ....
(a) emotions...enemies
(c) wishes...temptations
(b) friends...enemies
(d) hatred...objections

17. ....

18. Everything in nature is a .... from which there flows some ....
(a) present...obligation
(c) cause...effect
(b) obligation...reward
(d) effect...cause 18. ....

19. It is a good thing to learn .... by the .... of others.
(a) order...command
(c) obedience...threats
(b) caution...misfortunes
(d) wisdom...actions

19. ....

20. Industrial .... imply social .... and necessitate political ....
(a) advances...evils...deals
(c) failures...progress
...adjustment
(b) revolutions...upheaval
...conquest
(d) changes...changes
...changes 20. ....

C. Analogies

In the space provided, write the letter of the set of words that best completes the analogy.

21. DOLPHIN : SHARK :: (a) hoodlum : gangster
(b) king : subject   (c) whale : elephant   (d) squirrel : rodent   (e) monkey : tiger   21. ....

22. ALLIGATOR : SWAMP :: (a) student : school
(b) penguin : Antarctica   (c) seal : aquarium
(d) seminary : monk   (e) engineer : laboratory   22. ....

23. PARTNER : SPOUSE :: (a) groom : bride
(b) wife : matron   (c) affianced : betrothed   (d) squaw :
helpmate   (e) bachelor : divorcee   23. ....

24. SIBLING : HEIR :: (a) son : daughter
(b) brother : son   (c) minor : urchin   (d) father : child
(e) tyke : cherub   24. ....

25. ANCESTOR : POSTERITY :: (a) predecessor :
forefather   (b) parent : antecedent   (c) was : will be
(d) has been : is   (e) could have been : had been   25. ....

26. SCOOT : SUDDENLY :: (a) dash : quickly
(b) lope : gallop   (c) trot : high speed   (d) scurry :
long distance   (e) dart : scamper   26. ....

27. *SEÑORA* : *MADEMOISELLE* :: (a) married :
single   (b) unmarried : unmarried   (c) single : married
(d) married : married   (e) male : female   27. ....

28. PICKLE : SALT :: (a) sharp : zesty   (b) sugar :
jam   (c) wet : dry   (d) jelly : gelatin   (e) necessity :
luxury   28. ....

29. SNARE : DRUM :: (a) fret : tuba
(b) harpsichord : piano   (c) bow : violin   (d) accordion :
key   (e) clef : note   29. ....

30. GALLEY : COOK :: (a) carrier : aircraft
(b) bridge : captain   (c) deck : stoker   (d) hold : cargo
(e) passenger : cabin   30. ....

D. Reading Comprehension

Read the selections below; and in each space provided, write
the letter of the word or words that best completes the statement.

It is the power of the reiterated suggestion and consecrated
platitude that at this moment has brought our entire civilization
to imminent peril of destruction. The individual is as helpless
against it as the child is helpless against the formulas with which
he is indoctrinated. Not only is it possible by these means to
shape his tastes, his feelings, his desires, and his hopes; but it is
possible to convert him into a fanatical zealot, ready to torture
and destroy and to suffer mutilation and death for any obscene
faith, baseless in fact, and morally monstrous.

31. The writer would hold as responsible for the coming of a Hitler (a) our moral upbringing (b) our childishness
(c) fanaticism (d) poverty (e) slogans.   31. ....

32 The author does not tell us (a) how effective suggestion can be (b) how strong beliefs in such suggestions can be (c) how to indoctrinate people (d) how to overcome such suggestions (e) why such suggestions may be dangerous.

32. ....

If we work upon marble, it will perish. If we work upon brass, time will efface it. If we rear temples, they will crumble to dust. But if we work upon men's immortal minds, if we imbue them with high principles, with the just fear of God and the love of their fellow men, we engrave on those tablets something which no time can efface, and which will brighten and brighten to all eternity.

33. Of all of man's works, that which will last longest is (a) education (b) bridges (c) tunnels (d) books
(e) corporations.   33. ....

34. The tablets referred to in the selection are (a) pages of books (b) minds of men (c) religious beliefs
(d) doors of temples (e) laws.   34. ....

35. The time element referred to is (a) twenty-five years (b) one hundred years (c) one thousand years
(d) centuries (e) eternity.   35. ....

36. The type of education preferred by the writer is (a) scientific training (b) moral values (c) sectarianism (d) atheism
(e) religious.   36. ....

The whole fury and might of the enemy must very soon be turned on us. Hitler knows that he will have to break us in this Island or lose the war. If we can stand up to him, all Europe may be free and the life of the world may move forward into broad, sunlit uplands. But if we fail, then the whole world, including the United States, all that we have known and cared for, will sink into the abyss of a new Dark Age, made more sinister and perhaps more protracted by the lights of perverted science.

Let us therefore brace ourselves to our duties, and so bear ourselves that, if the British Empire and its Commonwealth last for a thousand years, men will still say, "This was their finest hour."

37. The writer advocates (a) attack   (b) courage   (c) fear
(d) one world   (e) freedom.   37. ....

38. This selection was written (a) before World War I
(b) after World War II   (c) during the Korean War
(d) during the Civil War   (e) during World War II.   38. ....

39. In failure, the author sees (a) slavery   (b) the end of the
world   (c) success for science   (d) the end of Hitler
(e) a step backward for all mankind.   39. ....

40. The writer is confident that (a) the English will do their
best   (b) Hitler will be defeated   (c) the United States will
suffer   (d) Europe will be free
(e) science is being misused by the enemy.   40. ....

Time at End............   *Minutes Elapsed*............
                                      Average Time 45 Minutes

Answer Key for this test is on page 611.

My Score: *Number Right*............   *Number Wrong*............

Comparing With Others
	Number Correct
Top 1%	38–40
Top 10%	35–37
Average	30–34
Low Average	26–29
Below Average	0–25

Test Number 6

Time at Start............

In the space provided, write the letter of the correct answer to the problem.

1. In the accompanying diagram, the perimeter of square *ABCD* is 28. Find the total area of the figure. Use $\pi = \frac{22}{7}$

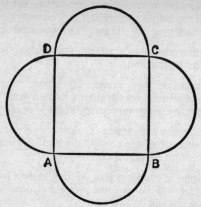

(a) 154   (b) 77   (c) 203   (d) 308   (e) none of these

1. ....

2. Six adults or 8 children can be served from a gallon of ice cream. If 10 gallons are bought and 45 adults are served first, how many children can be served?

(a) 7½   (b) 8   (c) 20   (d) 32   (e) none of these   **2.** ....

3. In Booth City, ⅙ of the high-school graduates go into the armed forces. Of these, ½ go to Officers Candidate School. Of these, ⅘ become officers. How large a graduating class would be needed to produce 60 officers?

(a) 600   (b) 750   (c) 800   (d) 850   (e) 900   **3.** ....

4. In the accompanying figure, *ABCD* is a rectangle. Points *A* and *B* are used as centers of circles of which *ADE* and *BCE* are quadrants. Find the area of the shaded portion.

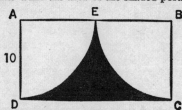

(a) 200 − 50π   (b) 200 − 100π   (c) 400 − 50π
(d) 400 − 100π   (e) none of these   **4.** ....

5. In right triangle *RST*, *RS* = n/3 and *ST* = n/4. Find hypotenuse *RT*.

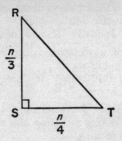

(a) $n/5$ (b) $5/n$ (c) $5n/12$ (d) $7n$ (e) none of these

5. ....

6. A man has a broken alarm clock. The clock keeps good time, but will ring only at 2 P.M. The man retires at midnight and wishes to be awakened at 7:30 A.M. What time should he turn the hands of the clock to read before retiring?

(a) 6 A.M.   (b) 6:30 A.M.   (c) 7 A.M.   (d) 7:30 A.M.
(e) 8 A.M.

6. ....

7. Lollipops come in 5 different flavors. A mother wishes to buy enough to assure herself of having 3 of at least 1 flavor. What is the least number of lollipops she should buy to be certain of this?

(a) 3   (b) 7   (c) 10   (d) 11   (e) 15

7. ....

8. On a 100-mile highway, 50 miles per hour is permitted where no construction is taking place, but only 20 miles per hour where there is construction. If 40 miles of the road are under construction, what is the average speed for the entire highway?

(a) 35 mph   (b) 70 mph   (c) $33\frac{3}{4}$ mph   (d) $51\frac{1}{2}$ mph
(e) $31\frac{1}{4}$ mph

8. ....

9. A man buys some stock. On Monday it goes up 10%; on Tuesday it goes down 20%; on Wednesday it goes up 10%. By what per cent does the price now differ from when first bought?

(a) up 3.2%   (b) down 3.2%   (c) no change
(d) up 1%   (e) down 1%

9. ....

10. Nine per cent of what number equals 18?

(a) 2   (b) 200   (c) 20   (d) 180   (e) none of these   10. ....

11. Given the series 12, 13, 15, 18, 22, x. Find the value of x.

(a) 27   (b) 23   (c) 24   (d) 40   (e) 36   11. ....

12. How many 3-gallon cans of paint are needed to paint a room that requires twelve 2-gallon cans?

(a) 8   (b) 9   (c) 12   (d) 24   (e) none of these   12. ....

13. The length of a rectangle is $2x + 3$ and its area is $2x^2 + 11x + 12$. Find its width.

(a) $2x^2 + 9x + 9$ (b) $12x + 4$ (c) $2x + 4$ (d) $x + 4$
(e) none of these   13. ....

14. A girl has 2 skirts, 3 sweaters, and 4 pairs of shoes. In how many different outfits consisting of a skirt, a sweater, and a pair of shoes can she dress?

(a) 9   (b) 3   (c) 10   (d) 12   (e) 24   14. ....

15. The perimeter of an isosceles triangle is 60. Each of the equal legs is twice the base. How long is one leg?

(a) 12   (b) 16   (c) 24   (d) 32   (e) none of these   15. ....

16. Paul and John have to make 75 book covers. Paul can make 6 an hour, but John works only $\frac{2}{3}$ as fast. How long will it take the two together to finish the job?

(a) 7 hours   (b) $7\frac{1}{2}$ hours   (c) 8 hours   (d) 9 hours
(e) $9\frac{1}{2}$ hours   16. ....

17. A man sells $1\frac{1}{2}$ shares of the 6 shares he has in a business. What per cent of the 6 shares does he retain?

(a) 25   (b) 50   (c) 75   (d) 100   (e) none of these   17. ....

18. $(\frac{1}{2})(\frac{1}{3})(4)$ is $\frac{1}{8}$ of what number?

(a) 5   (b) 3   (c) 2   (d) 8   (e) $5\frac{1}{3}$ 18. ....

19. $33\frac{1}{3}\%$ of what number equals $12\frac{1}{2}\%$ of 24?

(a) 8   (b) 9   (c) 3   (d) 6   (e) none of these   19. ....

20. The figure below is composed of 5 equal squares. If the area of the figure is 125, find its perimeter.

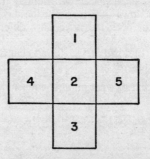

(a) 60 (b) 100 (c) 30 (d) cannot be done from the given information (e) can be done, but the answer is not given

20. ....

Time at End............ *Minutes Elapsed............*

Average Time 30 Minutes

Answer Key for this test is on page 611.

My Score: *Number Right............* *Number Wrong............*

Comparing With Others

	Number Correct
Top 1%	19–20
Top 10%	16–18
Average	12–15
Low Average	9–11
Below Average	0–10

Test Number 7

Time at Start............

In the space provided, write the letter of the correct answer to the problem.

1. If $a = b/9$, the value of b/a is
(a) $\frac{1}{8}$ (b) $\frac{1}{9}$ (c) $\frac{8}{1}$ (d) $\frac{9}{1}$ (e) none of these **1.** ....

2. The average of $\frac{1}{5}$ and $\frac{1}{7}$ is
(a) $\frac{1}{6}$ (b) $\frac{6}{35}$ (c) $\frac{2}{13}$ (d) $\frac{3}{17}$ (e) $\frac{12}{35}$ **2.** ....

3. If $4y = 7z$, then $7z/4y$ is
(a) 4 (b) 7 (c) $\frac{4}{7}$ (d) 1 (e) none of these **3.** ....

4. In the diagram, a, b, and c are the sides of a right triangle, whose right angle is at B. If K represents the area of the triangle, then K is

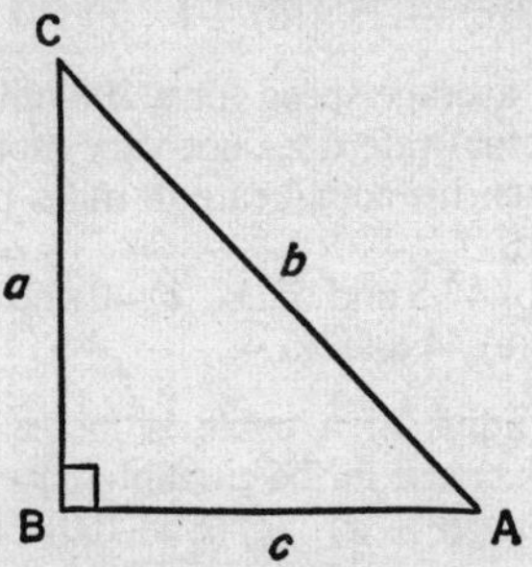

(a) *ab*   (b) *ab/2*   (c) *ac*   (d) *ac/2*   (e) *bc/2*   4. ....

5. If *x* nails cost *p* cents, find the cost in cents of *y* nails.
(a) *py*   (b) *xy/p*   (c) *x/py*   (d) *pxy*   (e) *py/x*   5. ....

6. If $.7y = 7\%$, then $y =$
(a) 70   (b) 10   (c) .1   (d) 1   (e) 0.01   6. ....

7. In the figure below, *GH* is parallel to *FE*. If angles 1, 2, and 3 are as shown, their sum is

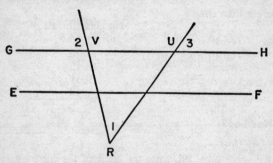

(a) 70°   (b) 150°   (c) 180°   (d) 360°
(e) cannot be determined from the given information   7. ....

8. $(2x - 2y)/(y - x)$ is equivalent to
(a) $x - y$ (b) $y - x$ (c) $(2x/y) - (2y/x)$ (d) 1
(e) none of these   8. ....

9. A man buys stock in the XYZ Corporation. During the month of April the stock rises 5%, and during the month of May it drops 5%. The net change in per cent over the 2-month period is
(a) 0   (b) +.25   (c) −.25   (d) +1   (e) −1   9. ....

10. A motorist's average speed for a 200-mile trip is 50 miles per hour. If his actual rate does not vary more than 5% from his average rate, then his actual rate in miles per hour must be between the limits of
(a) 45 and 55   (b) 47.5 and 52.5   (c) 40 and 60
(d) 42.5 and 57.5   (e) 44 and 56   10. ....

11. The *r*-inch radius of a circle is increased by *x* inches. The percentage of increase in the circumference is
(a) *x/r*   (b) $(r - x)/(r + x)$ (c) $(r/x)(100)$ (d) $100x/r$
(e) $(2\pi r - x)/r$ 11. ....

12. A circular wading pool of radius 3 feet is partially filled. As a result of a rainstorm, the depth of the pool is increased by 2 inches. The amount of rainfall in cubic feet caught in the pool is

(a) 4π (b) $\pi/36$ (c) 18π (d) $3\pi/2$ (e) $\pi/4$ 12. ....

13. The average of 3 unequal positive integers is 72. The largest possible value that any one of these integers can have is

(a) 69 (b) 70 (c) 139 (d) 40 (e) 213   13. ....

14. Ten ounces of a 20% solution of bleach are added to 15 ounces of water. The per cent of bleach in the solution now is

(a) 4 (b) 6 (c) 8 (d) 10 (e) none of these   14. ....

15. In the triangle ABC, $AB = AC$. If line AD is drawn from A to any point on BC, then

(a) $AB > BC$ (b) $AB < BC$ (c) $BD = DC$
(d) $AC < AD$ (e) $AC > AD$ 15. ....

16. Which one of the following equations has no real root?

(a) $x^8 = 1$ (b) $x^2 = 9$ (c) $x = \sqrt{7}$
(d) $(x + 1)/(x - 1) = 3$ (e) $x^2 + 16 = 0$ 16. ....

17. If $P \times S$ is defined to equal $(P + S)/(P \times S)$ where P and S are unequal, positive, rational numbers, then the value of $(P \times S)^2$ where $P = 3$ and $S = 4$ is

(a) -7 (b) $\sqrt{3}$ (c) $\sqrt{7}$ (d) -3 (e) 7 17. ....

Questions 18, 19, and 20 will each be followed by two statements numbered I and II. You do not have to compute the answers to the problems. Instead, you must decide whether sufficient information has been given to obtain the answer. In the space to the right of each question, mark the letter

    (a) if statement I alone is sufficient to solve the problem, but statement II alone is not sufficient,

    (b) if statement II alone is sufficient to solve the problem, but statement I alone is not sufficient,

    (c) if statements I and II together are sufficient to solve the problem, but neither statement I nor II alone is sufficient,

    (d) if both statements I and II are each sufficient,

    (e) if both statements I and II together are not sufficient to solve the problem.

18. Find the numerical value of *ab*, where *a* and *b* are not equal to zero.
   (I) $a = b/7$.
   (II) $a - b = 0$.   18. ....

19. *ABCD* is a square circumscribed about a circle whose center is *O*. Find the area of the shaded portion.

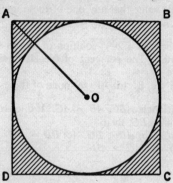

   (I) A side of the square is 4.
   (II) *OA* is $2\sqrt{2}$.   19. ....

20. Find the average rate in miles per hour for a trip from *A* to *B*, and then to *C*.
   (I) The rate going from *A* to *B* is *x* miles per hour.
   (II) The rate going from *B* to *C* is *y* miles per hour.
                                                              20. ....

Time at End.............   *Minutes Elapsed*.............
                                              Average Time 30 *Minutes*

Answer Key for this test is on page 613.

My Score: *Number Right*.............   *Number Wrong*.............

Comparing With Others

	Number Correct
Top 1%	19–20
Top 10%	16–18
Average	12–15
Low Average	9–11
Below Average	0–10

Test Number 8

Time at Start............

A. Antonyms

In the space provided, write the letter of the word that is most nearly opposite in meaning to the first word.

1. TACITURN   (a) discernible   (b) talkative
(c) piquant   (d) mean   (e) foolish   **1.** ....

2. EXTRICATE   (a) instruct   (b) learn   (c) allow
(d) follow   (e) hamper   **2.** ....

3. MOTLEY   (a) warlike   (b) uniform   (c) variegated
(d) ignorant   (e) seasonal   **3.** ....

4. INGENUOUS   (a) clever   (b) clear
(c) sophisticated   (d) tragic   (e) whining   **4.** ....

5. MISCREANT   (a) judge   (b) accused   (c) famous
(d) hero   (e) boor   **5.** ....

6. EXACERBATE   (a) freeze   (b) elevate   (c) cancel
(d) express   (e) soothe   **6.** ....

7. EXCORIATE   (a) dissemble   (b) cure   (c) extol
(d) extend   (e) retract   **7.** ....

8. FOIBLE   (a) oral   (b) nonfiction   (c) consecutive
(d) strong   (e) virtue   **8.** ....

9. POTENTATE   (a) influential   (b) ability   (c) slave
(d) king   (e) selection   **9.** ....

10. ACCOMPLICE   (a) enemy   (b) suspect
(c) officer   (d) craven   (e) optimist   **10.** ....

B. Sentence Completion

In the space provided, write the letter of the set of words that best completes the sentence.

11. The .... merchant was .... of contributing to every cause that was called to his attention.
(a) deleterious...jocular   (c) omniscient...quizzical
(b) mendacious...weary   (d) affluent...chary

     11. ....

12. The child tried in vain to .... candy money from her mother.
(a) disparate   (c) mediate
(b) wheedle   (d) extirpate   12. ....

13. No man ever yet became .... by ....
(a) maudlin...choice   (c) cryptic...stealth
(b) great...imitation   (d) carnivorous...hunger
                                                    13. ....

14. The absent are never without ...., nor the present without ....
(a) fault...excuse   (c) forbearance...pillage
(b) artifice...poultice   (d) innocence...guilt
                                                    14. ....

15. I am bound to furnish my .... with arguments, but not with ....
(a) friends...intelligence   (c) antagonists...comprehen-
                                   sion
(b) enemy...causes   (d) children...money
                                                    15. ....

16. Character is much easier .... than ....
(a) acquired...lost   (c) kept...recovered
(b) maligned...rationalized   (d) desecrated...sanctified
                                                    16. ....

17. A life spent worthily should be measured by ...., not ....
(a) thoughts...deeds   (c) accomplishments...
                                   actions
(b) deeds...years   (d) ideals...ideas 17. ....

18. Democracy is a ...., not a static condition. It is becoming, rather than being. It can easily be lost, but never is fully won. Its essence is eternal ....
(a) revolution...strife   (c) fluctuation...peace
(b) state...change   (d) process...struggle
                                                    18. ....

19. From principles is derived ...., but truth or certainty is obtained only from ....
(a) probability...facts   (c) faith...ideas
(b) heresy...deeds   (d) leadership...obedience
                                                    19. ....

20. Eternal .... is the condition not only of .... but of
everything which as civilized men we hold dear.
(a) suspicion...guilt   (c) satisfaction...profit
(b) happiness...justice   (d) vigilance...liberty

20. ....

C. Analogies

In the space provided, write the letter of the set of words that
best completes the analogy.

21. OXYGEN : AIR :: (a) hydrogen : water
(b) notes : music   (c) salt : sea water   (d) grain : wood
(e) stalk : plant   21. ....

22. CINEMA : SCENARIO :: (a) actor : scene
(b) author : text   (c) play : script   (d) angle : photography
(e) television : commercial   22. ....

23. AUTHOR : PLAYWRIGHT :: (a) iron : ironmonger
(b) piano : tuner   (c) sound : noise   (d) science : dentist
(e) technician : draftsman   23. ....

24. BRIDE : SPINSTER :: (a) woman : worker
(b) groom : bachelor   (c) marriage : fishing
(d) ceremony : practicality   (e) present : future   24. ....

25. BEAM : AIRPLANE :: (a) conscience : man
(b) horse : trail   (c) law : infraction   (d) penalty :
criminal   (e) knob : door   25. ....

26. MICROTOME : BIOLOGIST :: (a) thermometer :
doctor   (b) saw : lumberjack   (c) scale : chemist
(d) wheel : automobile   (e) string : guitarist   26. ....

27. FURY : ENTHUSIASM :: (a) wastrel : conservative
(b) evil : worthy   (c) windy : ideal   (d) action : deed
(e) jealousy : happiness   27. ....

28. EDUCATION : PREJUDICE :: (a) treasure : wealth
(b) teacher : ignorance   (c) bulb : shadows   (d) reading :
pleasure   (e) driving : distance   28. ....

29. CALENDAR : YEAR :: (a) watch : day   (b) clock :
12 hours   (c) watch : minute   (d) clock : time
(e) hourglass : week   29. ....

30. MILLSTONE : GRIND :: (a) drill : hole
(b) saw : wood   (c) microscope : focus   (d) awl : bore
(e) electricity : power   30. ....

D. Reading Comprehension

Read the selections below; and then in each space provided, write the letter of the word or words that best complete the statement.

Can honor set a leg? no: or an arm? no: or take away the grief of a wound? no. Honor hath no skill in surgery, then? no. What is honor? a word. What is that word honor? air. Who hath it? he that died o'Wednesday. Doth he feel it? no. Doth he hear it? no. It is insensible, then? Yes, to the dead. But will it not live with the living? no. Therefore I'll none of it. Honor is a mere scutcheon; and so ends my catechism.

31. The speaker is (a) frightened   (b) sarcastic
(c) sentimental   (d) realistic   (e) idealistic.   31. ....

32. His basic conclusion about honor is that (a) only the dead respect it   (b) a man cannot live without it   (c) all men should avoid it   (d) he is envious of those who have it
(e) it is not worth his dying for.   32. ....

33. The honor he discusses is the honor of (a) soldiers
(b) thieves   (c) lovers   (d) one's country   (e) kings.
        33. ....

One cool judgment is worth a thousand hasty councils. The thing to do is to supply light and not heat. At any rate, if it is heat it ought to be white heat and not sputter, because sputtering heat is apt to spread the fire. There ought, if there is any heat at all, to be that warmth of the heart which makes every man thrust aside his own personal feeling, his own personal interest, and take thought of the welfare and benefit of others.

34. The light suggested is (a) sunlight   (b) cooperation
(c) reasonableness   (d) reasoning   (e) intellectualism.
        34. ....

35. By "sputtering heat" the author suggests (a) false thinking
(b) wrong ideas   (c) anger   (d) vague direction
(e) intense flame.   35. ....

36. The best type of decision is made (a) for self-advancement
(b) for the good of all   (c) unemotionally   (d) sentimentally
(e) with sympathy   36. ....

If it's near dinner time, the foreman takes out his watch when the jury has retired and says: "Dear me, gentlemen, ten minutes to five, I declare! I dine at five, gentlemen." "So do I," says everybody else except the two men who ought to have dined at three, and seem more than half disposed to stand out in consequence. The foreman smiles, and puts up his watch. "Well, gentlemen, what do we say? Plaintiff, defendant, gentlemen? I rather think so far as I am concerned, gentlemen—I say I rather think—but don't let that influence you—I rather think the plaintiff's the man." Upon this two or three other men are sure to think so too—as of course they do; and then they get on very unanimously and comfortably.

37. The purpose of the writer is to (a) defend democracy (b) expose weaknesses in trial by one's peers (c) attack our definition of justice (d) demand a reform in our trial proceedings (e) prove that men are selfish.   37. ....

38. To prove his contention, the author (a) uses satire (b) presents examples (c) offers proof (d) cites authorities (e) appeals to reason.   38. ....

39. The process of thinking in members of the jury (a) concerns itself with the evidence on hand (b) revolves around the abstractions of justice (c) involves the cautions presented by the judge (d) is filled with bribery and corruption (e) ignores the interchange of interpretation of evidence presented.

39. ....

40. The author suggests (a) that we do away with trial by jury (b) that jurors be trained to sift evidence (c) that meals be served to jurors (d) that a competent man be made foreman of the jury (e) none of the above.   40. ....

Time at End............   *Minutes Elapsed*............
                                        Average Time 45 *Minutes*

Answer Key for this test is on page 614.

My Score: Number Right............   *Number Wrong*............
Comparing With Others

	Number Correct
Top 1%	38–40
Top 10%	35–37
Average	30–34
Low Average	26–29
Below Average	0–25

Test Number 9

Time at Start............

In the space provided, write the letter of the correct answer to the problem.

1. If $45 = \frac{5}{9}x$, then $x =$
(a) 25   (b) 35   (c) 60   (d) 72   (e) 81   1. ....

2. Four is what per cent of 25?
(a) 10   (b) 12   (c) 16   (d) 20   (e) 24   2. ....

3. In the figure below, AB is parallel to CD and BC is parallel to AD. If angle $A = x°$ and angle $B = (2x - 30)°$, then $x =$

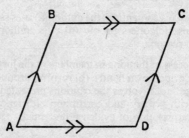

(a) 30   (b) 40   (c) 50   (d) 60   (e) 70   3. ....

4. Three men take 8 days to complete half a job. If 5 more men are added after the eighth day, how many days will it take to complete the job? (Assume that all the men work at the same rate of speed.)
(a) 3   (b) 4   (c) 5   (d) 11   (e) 12   4. ....

5. The diameter of a circle is increased by 50%. The increase in the area is
(a) 100%   (b) 125%   (c) 300%   (d) 400%   (e) 500%   5. ....

6. The houses on street S are numbered consecutively from 315 to 747 inclusive. If a census is taken in one out of every three homes, the number of homes visited on street S is
(a) 143   (b) 144   (c) 145   (d) 146   (e) 147   6. ....

7. If $3a = 5b$, then $b/a =$
(a) $\frac{8}{3}$ (b) $\frac{5}{3}$ (c) $\frac{3}{5}$ (d) $\frac{3}{8}$ (e) $\frac{2}{5}$ 7. ....

8. In the diagram below, $AB = AC = 8$. If $60 < x < 90$, the range of values for side BC is

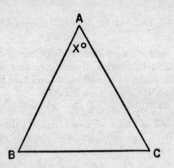

(a) 0 to 8   (b) 8 to $8\sqrt{2}$ (c) 8 to $8\sqrt{3}$ (d) 8 to 16

(e) $8\sqrt{3}$ to $16\sqrt{3}$ 8. ....

Questions 9 and 10 refer to the diagram about types of boats built

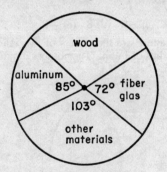

Type of Boats Built

9. If 20% of all the boats made from Fiberglas can seat more than 2 passengers, then the per cent of all boats that are both made of Fiberglas and able to seat more than 2 passengers is

(a) 4   (b) 8   (c) 12   (d) 16   (e) 20   9. ....

10. If x boats are built, then by how many 72nds does the fraction of boats made from wood and aluminum exceed those built from Fiberglas and all other materials?

(a) $1x$ (b) $2x$ (c) $3x$ (d) $4x$ (e) $5x$ 10. ....

11. *AB* is the diameter of circle *O*. If the coordinates of point *A* are $(7,-8)$ and of point *O* are $(8,11)$, then the coordinates of point *B* are
(a) $(7.5,1.5)$ (b) $(7.5,-1.5)$ (c) $(9,30)$ (d) $(9,14)$
(e) $(9,-14)$ 11. ....

12. A candy vendor mixes 20 pounds of candy costing him 35 cents a pound with 40 pounds of candy costing him 50 cents a pound. How many cents a pound must he charge for the mixture in order to make a 10% profit on his cost?
(a) $42\frac{1}{2}$ (b) 44   (c) $46\frac{1}{2}$ (d) 48   (e) $49\frac{1}{2}$ 12. ....

13. If $x + y = 1/a$ and $x - y = 1/b$, the value of a/b is
(a) 2   (b) $(x+y)/(x-y)$ (c) $(x-y)/(x+y)$
(d) 0   (e) $(1+y)/(1-y)$ 13. ....

14. If $\begin{pmatrix} a & b \\ & c & \end{pmatrix}$ is defined as being equal to $ac - bc$, the value of
$$\left(\begin{pmatrix} 1 & 2 \\ & 3 & \end{pmatrix} \begin{pmatrix} 4 & 5 \\ & 6 & \end{pmatrix} \atop \begin{pmatrix} 3 & 1 \\ & 0 & \end{pmatrix} \right)$$ is

(a) 0   (b) -3 (c) -6 (d) 8   (e) -8 14. ....

15. Points *O* and *P* are the centers of two intersecting circles each having a radius of 1 unit. The number of units in the length of arc *AOC* is

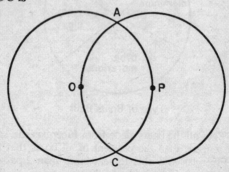

(a) $\pi/6$ (b) $\pi/3$ (c) $2\pi/3$ (d) $3\pi/4$ (e) π 15. ....

16. Any two consecutive odd integers and any two consecutive even integers are added together. The sum is always divisible by
(a) 2   (b) 5   (c) 7   (d) 10   (e) none of these will always work
                                                                          16. ....

17. The graphs of $y = 3x$ and $y = -5x$ are drawn on a coordinate axis. The regions in the figure are such that $3x < y < -5x$ are

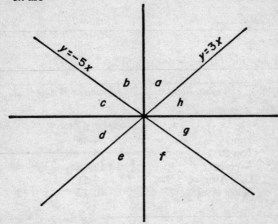

(a) d, e, f, g, h (b) a, b (c) c, d (d) e, f, g (e) h, a

17. ....

Questions 18, 19, and 20 will each be followed by two statements numbered I and II. You do not have to compute the answers to the problems. Instead, you must decide whether sufficient information has been given to obtain the answer. In the space to the right of each question, mark the letter

(a) if statement I alone is sufficient to solve the problem, but statement II alone is not sufficient,

(b) if statement II alone is sufficient to solve the problem, but statement I alone is not sufficient,

(c) if statements I and II together are sufficient to solve the problem, but neither statement I nor II alone is sufficient,

(d) if both statements I and II are each sufficient,

(e) if both statements I and II together are not sufficient to solve the problem.

18. Is the number abc divisible by 25?

(I) abc is divisible by 15.

(II) abc is divisible by 10.   18. ....

19. Find the shorter diagonal of a rhombus.

(I) The perimeter of the rhombus is 15.

(II) The longer diagonal is 6.   19. ....

20. *A* and *B* are positive integers. Which one is greater?
   (I) $AC > BC$.
   (II) $C < 0$.   20. ....

Time at End............   *Minutes Elapsed*............:
                                          Average Time 30 *Minutes*

Answer Key for this test is on page 615.

My Score: *Number Right*............   *Number Wrong*............

Comparing With Others

	Number Correct
Top 1%	19–20
Top 10%	16–18
Average	12–15
Low Average	9–11
Below Average	0–10

Test Number 10

Time at Start............

In the space provided, write the letter of the correct answer to the problem.

1. The product $(\frac{1}{2})(\frac{1}{3})(\frac{1}{4})$ is *x* less than 1. Then *x* is
   (a) $\frac{8}{9}$ (b) $\frac{1}{24}$ (c) $\frac{1}{9}$ (d) $\frac{11}{12}$ (e) $\frac{23}{24}$ 1. ....

2. A fruit punch is made with the following ingredients: 4 cups of pineapple flavoring, 6 cups of orange flavoring, 8 cups of grape flavoring, 2 cups of sugar, and 20 cups of water. The per cent of water in the punch is
   (a) 40   (b) 50   (c) 60   (d) 70   (e) 80   2. ....

3. What is the minimum number of rectangles as shown necessary to form a square?

$$\frac{x}{6}$$

x

   (a) 2   (b) 4   (c) 6   (d) 8   (e) 12   3. ....

4. Twenty-one telegraph poles lie in a straight line. The poles are evenly spaced and the distance between the first and twenty-

first poles is 2,000 feet. The distance in feet between the first and fifth poles is

  (a) 400   (b) $8000\!/21$ (c) 100   (d) 550   (e) 600   4. ....

5. How many odd integers are there between 1 and 12 (excluding 1) which have no factors besides 1 in common with 12?

  (a) 1   (b) 2   (c) 3   (d) 4   (e) 5   5. ....

6. The triangle below is divided into four regions by lines AB and CD. If one more line is drawn, the maximum number of additional regions created is

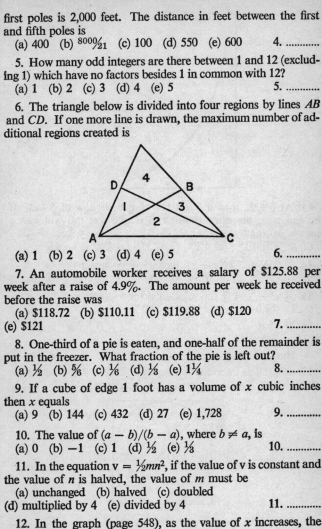

  (a) 1   (b) 2   (c) 3   (d) 4   (e) 5   6. ....

7. An automobile worker receives a salary of $125.88 per week after a raise of 4.9%. The amount per week he received before the raise was

  (a) $118.72   (b) $110.11   (c) $119.88   (d) $120
(e) $121   7. ....

8. One-third of a pie is eaten, and one-half of the remainder is put in the freezer. What fraction of the pie is left out?

  (a) ½   (b) ⅝   (c) ⅙   (d) ⅓   (e) 1¼   8. ....

9. If a cube of edge 1 foot has a volume of x cubic inches then x equals

  (a) 9   (b) 144   (c) 432   (d) 27   (e) 1,728   9. ....

10. The value of $(a - b)/(b - a)$, where $b \neq a$, is

  (a) 0   (b) −1   (c) 1   (d) ½   (e) ⅓   10. ....

11. In the equation $v = ½mn^2$, if the value of v is constant and the value of n is halved, the value of m must be

  (a) unchanged   (b) halved   (c) doubled
(d) multiplied by 4   (e) divided by 4   11. ....

12. In the graph (page 548), as the value of x increases, the value of y

  (a) increases   (b) decreases and then increases
(c) increases and then decreases   (d) remains unchanged
(e) decreases   12. ....

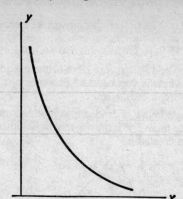

13. At 3 P.M., a man 6 feet tall casts a shadow of 5 feet. If the sun is in the same position, a man 5 feet tall will cast a shadow of length
(a) 4′ (b) 4′1″ (c) 4′2″ (d) 4′3″ (e) 4′4″   13. ....

14. If $x + y = 2/(x - y)$, then $x^2 - y^2$ equals
(a) 1   (b) 2   (c) 3   (d) 4   (e) 5   14. ....

15. If $x^2 - x = 0$, the solution(s) for x is(are)
(a) 1   (b) 0   (c) −1   (d) 1, 0   (e) 0, −1   15. ....

16. If $[rs] = r \times s - (r/s)$ where $s \neq 0$, the value of $[(4)(3)] - [(3)(4)]$ is
(a) $\frac{7}{12}$ (b) $-\frac{7}{12}$ (c) 24   (d) 0   (e) $\frac{25}{12}$ 16. ....

17. A circle is inscribed in a square. If O is the center of the circle and $AOB = 16$, the area of the square is

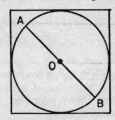

(a) 64   (b) 16   (c) 128   (d) 256   (e) 144   17. ....

18. If the surface area of a cube is 216 square feet, its volume in cubic feet is
(a) 4   (b) 46   (c) 64   (d) 216   (e) 256   18. ....

19. A number is divisible by 9 if the sum of its digits is divisible by 9. Which one of the following numbers is divisible by 18?
(a) 34556181   (b) 434932031   (c) 135979128
(d) 79891111431   (e) 3697166135522   19. ....

20. If $x + 2$ is odd, which one of the following is even?
(a) $x + 4$ (b) x (c) $3x + 6$ (d) $2x + 2$ (e) $x - 2$
                                                          20. ....

Time at End............   *Minutes Elapsed*............
                                  Average Time 30 *Minutes*

Answer Key for this test is on page 617.

My Score: Number Right............   Number Wrong.............

Comparing With Others

	Number Correct
Top 1%	19–20
Top 10%	16–18
Average	12–15
Low Average	9–11
Below Average	0–10

Test Number 11

Time at Start............

A. Antonyms

In the space provided, write the letter of the word that is most nearly opposite in meaning to the first word.

1. ALLAY   (a) intensify   (b) enemy   (c) weakness
(d) force   (e) wealth   1. ....

2. STALWART   (a) brisk   (b) compatible   (c) rabid
(d) stainless   (e) weak   2. ....

3. TOXIC   (a) bent   (b) solid   (c) poisonous
(d) harmless   (e) unharmed   3. ....

4. DISTRAIT   (a) prosaic   (b) quiescent
(c) articulate   (d) rude   (e) alert   4. ....

5. DEBACLE   (a) triumph   (b) downpour
(c) drought   (d) oration   (e) selection   5. ....

6. EBULLIENT   (a) enthusiastic   (b) flowing
(c) dispirited   (d) afar   (e) droll   6. ....

7. PUNGENT   (a) shot   (b) absent   (c) deterrent
(d) bland   (e) fiery   7. ....

8. TACIT   (a) expressed   (b) silent   (c) ostensible
(d) prodigious   (e) perfect   8. ....

9. CRAVEN   (a) weak   (b) citizen   (c) traitor
(d) boastful   (e) ugly   9. ....

10. ACCOST   (a) profit   (b) employ   (c) devise
(d) shun   (e) tease   10. ....

B. Sentence Completion

In the space provided, write the letter of the set of words that best completes the sentence.

11. Can one who has .... the heady draughts of leadership assume a .... role when the tides of fortune change?
(a) honed...decrepit   (c) indicted...destitute
(b) imbibed...mundane   (d) depleted...dank
                                                         11. ....

12. The .... will never forgive the .... child who had laughed aloud at her attempts to catch the attention of the young men.
(a) philanthropist...coy   (c) coquette...ingenuous
(b) crony...fastidious   (d) gossamer...insatiable
                                                         12. ....

13. Since I had already accepted the invitation before I had learned that Phyllis was not being invited, I am really in a(n) ....
(a) anathema   (c) defection
(b) tumbrel   (d) quandary   13. ....

14. Logical consequences are the .... of fools and the .... of wise men.
(a) scarecrows...beacons   (c) fears...joys
(b) guides...results   (d) unknowns...proofs
                                                         14. ....

15. Whenever there is a conflict between .... rights and .... rights, ... rights must prevail.

(a) political...social...
political

(b) human...property...
human

(c) men's...women's...
neither's

(d) political...national...
individual

15. ....

16. Man is a(n) .... He is committed by his .... not to conform.

(a) animal...needs

(b) conservative...fears

(c) thinker...make-up

(d) rebel...biology

16. ....

17. No .... ought ever to be converted into a(n) ....

(a) affect...effect

(b) debt...flight

(c) quarrel...policy

(d) argument...discussion

17. ....

18. Toward no crimes have men shown themselves so cold-bloodedly .... as in punishing differences of ....

(a) logical...ideals

(b) cruel...belief

(c) determined...color

(d) wrong...parties

18. ....

19. Simple as it seems, it was a great discovery that the key of .... could turn both ways, that it could open, as well as lock the door of .... to the many.

(a) knowledge...power

(b) wealth...the future

(c) power...wealth

(d) language...com-
munication   19. ....

20. What greater or better gift can we offer the .... than to teach and instruct our ....?

(a) enemy...ambassadors

(b) future...elders

(c) republic...youth

(d) children...hearts

20. ....

C. Analogies

In the space provided, write the letter of the set of words that best completes the analogy.

21. SIGH : BREATH :: (a) snivel : cold   (b) laugh :
voice   (c) smile : lips   (d) tear : sight   (e) wheeze : asthma

21. ....

22. PUBLISHER : EDITOR :: (a) manager : owner
(b) movie : scenery   (c) people : voters   (d) producer :
director   (e) mayor : council   22. ....

23. MOLEST : TOUCH :: (a) irk : pester   (b) gall :
taste   (c) heckle : sound   (d) nag : sight   (e) jest : tease
23. ....

24. POUT : FROWN :: (a) resent : rage   (b) bitter :
fume   (c) bark : growl   (d) storm : madden   (e) stare :
yell   24. ....

25. NOVEL : ESSAY :: (a) fiction : opinion   (b) plot :
action   (c) fiction : truth   (d) story : truth   (e) one :
series   25. ....

26. HUTCH : RABBITS :: (a) cot : goats   (b) bee :
hive   (c) sty : cows   (d) burrow : fox   (e) lair : horses
26. ....

27. PRINCIPAL : FACULTY :: (a) admiral : war college
(b) president : university   (c) governor : the state
(d) President : cabinet   (e) general : army   27. ....

28. DESSERT : APPETIZER :: (a) antipasto : ice cream
(b) fish : meat   (c) cold : hot   (d) cold : cold
(e) cooky : salad   28. ....

29. INTEGER : FRACTION :: (a) dividend : divisor
(b) ordinal : Arabic   (c) whole number : decimal
(d) prime number : product   (e) numerator : sum   29. ....

30. FLOOR : STOCK MARKET :: (a) shipping room :
wholesaler   (b) showroom : dressmaking   (c) lobby :
industry   (d) salesroom : manufacturing   (e) cage : banking
30. ....

D. Reading Comprehension

Read the selections below; and in each space provided, write
the letter of the word or words that best completes the statement.

For true philosophers, who are only eager for truth and
knowledge, never regard themselves as already so thoroughly
informed, but that they welcome further information from
whomsoever and from whencesoever it may come; nor are they
so narrow-minded as to imagine any of the arts or sciences
transmitted to us by the ancients, in such a state of forwardness
or completeness, that nothing is left for the ingenuity and industry
of others. Very many, on the contrary, maintain that all we know
is still infinitely less than all that still remains unknown; nor do

philosophers pin their faith to others' precepts in such wise that they lose their liberty, and cease to give credence to the conclusions of their proper senses. Neither do they swear such fealty to their mistress Antiquity, that they openly, and in the sight of all, deny and desert their friend Truth.

31. The scholars described in this selection would (a) become impatient with those who attempt to contradict them   (b) use suspended judgment   (c) be easy prey to the ideas of a dictator (d) place their trust in proven facts   (e) experiment rather than read books.   31. ....

32. The truth these philosophers search for (a) is eternal (b) is popular   (c) is based on the knowledge discovered in the past   (d) changes   (e) is verifiable in the laboratories.
                                                                      32. ....

33. These thinkers do *not* (a) accept ideas coming from those who disagree with them   (b) accept ideas on faith   (c) disregard the past   (d) claim that what they know is the whole truth (e) ignore the findings of present-day research.   33. ....

I believe that that community is already in process of dis-solution where each man begins to eye his neighbor as a possible enemy, where nonconformity with the accepted creed, political as well as religious, is a mark of disaffection; where denunciation without specification or backing takes the place of evidence; where orthodoxy chokes freedom of dissent; where faith in the eventual supremacy of reason has become so timid that we dare not enter our convictions in the open lists to win or lose. Such fears as these are a solvent which can eat out the cement that binds the stones together; they may in the end subject us to a despotism as evil as any that we dread and they can be allayed only in so far as we refuse to proceed on suspicion, and trust one another until we have tangible ground for misgiving.

34. The writer advocates (a) dictatorships   (b) trusting our ability to direct others   (c) that our judgments be based on our backgrounds   (d) that we should overcome the advantages of others   (e) none of the above.   34. ....

35. The author believes that (a) we must never doubt our neighbors   (b) we must always trust our neighbors   (c) all must conform   (d) we must rely on reason, not custom (e) we must avoid orthodoxy.   35. ....

36. When a social group condemns one of its members it must do so on the basis of (a) national emergency (b) suspicions (c) differences in political beliefs (d) opposition to accepted school policies (e) none of the above.   36. ....

One thing has struck me as very strange, and that is the resurgence of the one-man power after all these centuries of experience and progress. It is curious how the English-speaking peoples have always had this horror of one-man power. They are quite ready to follow a leader for a time, as long as he is serviceable to them; but the idea of handing themselves over, lock, stock, and barrel, body and soul, to one man, and worshiping him as if he were an idol—that has always been odious to the whole theme and nature of our civilization.

37. The writer has (a) faith in the ability of one man to lead well (b) a distaste for the English-speaking people (c) a distrust for rule by one man (d) fears for the future (e) admiration for men like Hitler.   37. ....

38. The English-speaking people have (a) never trusted their leaders (b) always rebelled against their leaders (c) distrusted hero worship (d) progressed because of their aggressiveness (e) learned their lessons through bitter experience.   38. ....

The most influential books, and the truest in their influence, are works of fiction. . . . They repeat, they rearrange, they clarify the lessons of life; they disengage us from ourselves, they constrain us for the acquaintance of others; and they show us the web of experience, but with a singular change—that monstrous consuming ego of our being, for the once, struck out.

39. The type of book that has the greatest effect on others is the (a) biography (b) encyclopedia (c) textbook (d) collection of poetry (e) collection of short stories.   39. ....

40. The most influential books do *not* (a) force us to meet others (b) allow us to look at life objectively (c) emphasize lessons to be learned from life (d) allow us to view ourselves objectively (e) avoid experience.   40. ....

Time at End..........   *Minutes Elapsed*..........
                                 Average Time 50 Minutes

Answer Key for this test is on page 620.

My Score: Number Right..........   *Number Wrong*..........

Comparing With Others

	Number Correct
Top 1%	38–40
Top 10%	35–37
Average	30–34
Low Average	26–29
Below Average	0–25

Test Number 12

Time at Start............

In the space provided, write the letter of the correct answer to the problem.

1. The value of $\dfrac{2\frac{1}{4}}{3\frac{1}{2} + 2\frac{1}{4}}$ is

(a) $\frac{2}{7}$ (b) $\frac{27}{64}$ (c) $\frac{7}{2}$ (d) $\frac{9}{23}$ (e) $\frac{4}{11}$ 1. ....

2. A salesman's weekly salary is $73.50 after a raise of 5%. His salary before the raise was
(a) $69.82   (b) $69.83   (c) $69.28   (d) $70   (e) $70.75

2. ....

3. A postman has a delivery route consisting of the odd-numbered houses from 105 to 703, inclusive. The number of houses on the route is
(a) 299   (b) 300   (c) 301   (d) 302   (e) 298   3. ....

4. The five squares in the diagram below are equal in area. If the total area of the figure is 720 square units, the number of units in a side of any one square is

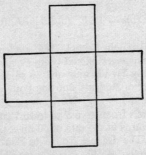

(a) 12   (b) 16   (c) 230   (d) 7   (e) 18   4. ....

5. Given four points A, B, C, and D on the circumference of a circle. The number of triangles that can be formed by connecting any of the points is

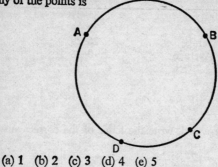

(a) 1   (b) 2   (c) 3   (d) 4   (e) 5   5. ....

6. In the figure, a pair of parallel lines is

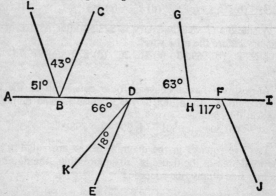

(a) $LB \parallel GH$ (b) $BC \parallel DE$ (c) $LB \parallel FJ$ (d) $CB \parallel DK$
(e) $GH \parallel FJ$ 6. ....

7. At Central High School, 156 students study foreign languages, the languages offered being French and Spanish. If 100 students study French only and 30 students study Spanish only, the number of students studying both languages is
(a) 86   (b) 26   (c) 96   (d) 43   (e) 40   7. ....

8. A man travels from town S to town T at a rate of 60 miles per hour. He returns at the rate of 50 miles per hour, taking 52 minutes longer. The distance from S to T in miles is
(a) 260% (b) 260   (c) 270   (d) 290   (e) 300   8. ....

9. A circle is divided into 15 parts with the divisions numbered consecutively starting at zero. If an arrow points to number 10 and then moves 5 spaces, it now points to
    (a) 5   (b) 5 or 13   (c) 5 or 14   (d) 5 or 0   (e) 5 or 1

9. ....

10. One-half of one-third is equal to which of the following?
    (a) ⅙%   (b) 16⅔%   (c) 20%   (d) ⅕%   (e) 25%

10. ....

11. A man was left with ⅝ of his money after spending $48. The amount of money he had initially was
    (a) $108   (b) $96   (c) $72   (d) $192/9   (e) $36   11. ....

12. In the figure, both triangles are isosceles, angle $QMP = x°$, $QL = QM$, $PM = PN$, and LMN is a straight line. The number of degrees in the sum of angles 1 and 2 is

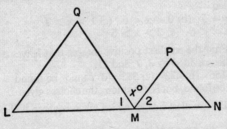

    (a) x (b) $180 - 2x$ (c) $90 - x$ (d) $180 - 2x$
    (e) $180 - x$ 12. ....

13. In the figure, BC is an arc of the circle with center at A. If $AB = 2$ and AB is perpendicular to AC, the perimeter of the shaded portion is

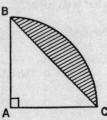

    (a) $2 + \pi$ (b) $2\sqrt{2} + 4\pi$ (c) $2\sqrt{3} + 4\pi$ (d) $2\sqrt{2} + \pi$
    (e) $2\sqrt{3} + \pi$ 13. ....

14. What is the maximum integer that will divide evenly into the average of any 3 consecutive even integers?
   (a) 2   (b) 3   (c) 4   (d) 5   (e) 6   14. ....

15. Two partners divide $1,600 so that one man receives 60% and the other receives 40% of the money. The difference in dollars in their shares is
   (a) 320   (b) 300   (c) 1,220   (d) 200   (e) 230   15. ....

16. The area of a sector of a circle is equal to ⅛ of the area of the circle. The central angle of the sector contains
   (a) 15°   (b) 20°   (c) 25°   (d) 35°   (e) 40°   16. ....

17. The difference in the sum of the integers from 3 to 40 divisible by 3 and the sum of the integers from 41 to 78 divisible by 3 is
   (a) 507   (b) 745   (c) 749   (d) 751   (e) 761   17. ....

18. If two sides of a triangle are each 3 and x is the third side, then
   (a) $x = 5$ (b) $0 < x < 6$ (c) $1 > x > 7$
   (d) $2 < x < 6$ (e) $2 > x > 6$ 18. ....

19. Find the smallest positive integer that leaves a remainder of 1 when divided by 3, 7, and 11.
   (a) 1156   (b) 432   (c) 385   (d) cannot be found
   (e) can be found, but is not among the choices given   19. ....

20. The smallest integer which when squared will be less than 10 is
   (a) 0   (b) 1   (c) 2   (d) cannot be found
   (e) can be found, but is not among the choices given   20. ....

Time at End..............   *Minutes Elapsed*..............
                                      Average Time 30 Minutes

Answer Key for this test is on page 620.

My Score: *Number Right*..............   *Number Wrong*..............

Comparing With Others

	Number Correct
Top 1%	19–20
Top 10%	16–18
Average	12–15
Low Average	9–11
Below Average	0–10

Test Number 13

Time at Start............

In the space provided, write the letter of the correct answer to the problem.

1. If $\frac{5}{8}x = 400$, then x is
   (a) 640   (b) 10   (c) 250   (d) $\frac{5}{8}$ (e) 1,992   1. ....

2. A man's salary decreases by 10% one week and increases by 20% the next week. The total change in the man's salary over the 2-week period is
   (a) +5%   (b) +7%   (c) ∓8%   (d) +10%   (e) +12%
                                                           2. ....

3. Straight lines *AD* and *CF* meet at *G*, and *BG* and *GE* have been drawn. If angle 1 = 70° and angle 2 = 80°, find the number of degrees in angle 3.

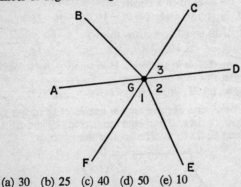

   (a) 30   (b) 25   (c) 40   (d) 50   (e) 10   3. ....

4. Which of the following intervals contains the largest number of integers that are divisible both by 2 and by 3? (Consider the first and last numbers as part of each interval.)
   (a) 6–23   (b) 7–22   (c) 8–24   (d) 12–30   (e) 13–35
                                                           4. ....

5. The value of $(.1 + .01)(.1 - .01)$ is
   (a) .01   (b) .001   (c) .09   (d) .0099   (e) .00099   5. ....

6. Two trains 420 miles apart start towards each other at 3 P.M. If the rate of one train is 5 miles more per hour than that of the second and they meet after 4 hours, find the rate in miles per hour of the faster train.
   (a) 45   (b) 50   (c) 55   (d) 52½   (e) 57½   6. ....

7. If $\frac{5}{8}$ of a number is 16, then $187\frac{1}{2}\%$ of the number is

(a) 44   (b) 48   (c) $112\frac{4}{5}$ (d) $222\frac{2}{5}$ (e) $271\frac{1}{5}$ 7. ....

8. If $a = c - b$, the value of a^2 is

(a) $c^2 - b^2$ (b) $c^2 + b^2$ (c) $c^2 - b^2 - 2bc$

(d) $c^2 + b^2 + 2bc$ (e) $c^2 + b^2 - 2bc$ 8. ....

9. A man goes to a movie with his wife and two children. The price of admission for each child is half the price of admission for each adult. If the man pays a total of $4.20, find the total cost for both children.

(a) 70c   (b) $1.40   (c) $1.80   (d) $2   (e) $2.10   9. ....

10. Given a square, a rectangle, a circle, an equilateral triangle, and a regular pentagon. If the areas of each of the above figures are known, the perimeters of how many can be found?

(a) 1   (b) 2   (c) 3   (d) 4   (e) 5   10. ....

11. If $(x + 1)^2 = x^2$, then x equals

(a) 0   (b) 0, $\frac{1}{2}$ (c) 0, $-\frac{1}{2}$ (d) 0, -1 (e) $-\frac{1}{2}$ 11. ....

12. Three-fourths equal how many thirds?

(a) 2   (b) $2\frac{1}{4}$ (c) $2\frac{1}{2}$ (d) 3   (e) $3\frac{1}{2}$ 12. ....

13. A man runs 22 feet in a second. How many miles would he cover traveling at this rate for an hour?

(a) 15   (b) 18   (c) 21   (d) 24   (e) 27   13. ....

14. BC, DE, FG, and HA are arcs of circles of radius 4; CD and HG are both horizontal and equal to 6; and AB and EF are both vertical and equal to 5. The area of the figure is

(a) $182 - 8\pi$ (b) $182 - 16\pi$ (c) $196 - 8\pi$

(d) $196 - 16\pi$ (e) $182 + 8\pi$

          14. ....

15. Parallel lines *AB* and *CD* intersect transversal *MN* in *E* and *F* respectively. The bisectors of angles 1 and 2 meet at *G*. The number of degrees in angle 3 is

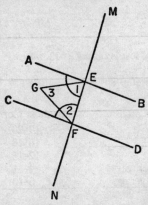

(a) more than 30 and less than 60   (b) 60   (c) more than 60 and less than 90   (d) 90   (e) more than 90 and less than 180

15. ....

16. If *n*! is defined as $n(n-1)(n-2)(n-3)\ldots 1$, then 7! is divisible by

         (I) 21   (II) 8   (III) 11

(a) I only   (b) II only   (c) I and II only
(d) I and III only   (e) I, II, and III   16. ....

17. A man spends ⅙ of his weekly salary on food and ⅓ of the remainder on shelter. He then has $45 left. His weekly salary is

   (a) $80   (b) $81   (c) $86   (d) $90   (e) $95   17. ....

18. If $u = v^2$, $u^2 = v^4$, and $u^3 = 1$, the value of u^{262} is

   (a) v (b) v^2 (c) v^3 (d) v^4 (e) 1   18. ....

19. The lines $y = 2x$, $y = -2x$, and $y = 5$ form a triangle whose area is

   (a) $^{25}\!/\!_2$ (b) $2\frac{1}{2}$ (c) $18\frac{3}{4}$ (d) 25   (e) $31\frac{1}{4}$ 19. ....

20. The numerator of a fraction is the sum of three consecutive even integers, and its denominator is the sum of three consecutive odd integers. Then

   (a) the numerator is divisible by 4 and the denominator by 5
   (b) the numerator is divisible by 4 and the denominator by 3

(c) the numerator is divisible by 6 and the denominator by 3
(d) the numerator is divisible by 6 and the denominator by 5
(e) the numerator is divisible by 2 and the denominator by 5

20. ....

Time at End............   *Minutes Elapsed*............
                                  Average Time 30 *Minutes*

Answer Key for this test is on page 623.

My Score: *Number Right*............   *Number Wrong*............

Comparing With Others

	Number Correct
Top 1%	19–20
Top 10%	16–18
Average	12–15
Low Average	9–11
Below Average	0–10

Test Number 14

Time at Start............

A. Antonyms

In the space provided, write the letter of the word that is most nearly opposite in meaning to the first word.

1. DISBURSE (a) extract (b) collect (c) praise
(d) dream (e) orate   1. ....

2. STRIDENT (a) shrill (b) soft (c) modern
(d) spurious (e) abridged   2. ....

3. CONDOLENCE (a) superiority (b) adversary
(c) wish (d) importance (e) congratulation   3. ....

4. ASSAIL (a) on foot (b) on land (c) defer
(d) defend (e) redress   4. ....

5. LOATH (a) desirable (b) eager (c) love
(d) additional (e) superficial   5. ....

6. SINUOUS (a) straight (b) open (c) healthful
(d) alert (e) weak   6. ....

7. REDOUBTABLE (a) enjoyable (b) certain
(c) admired (d) envied (e) regrettable   7. ....

8. GERMANE (a) aseptic (b) spoiled (c) detailed
(d) truthful (e) unrelated   8. ....

9. SALUBRIOUS (a) pure (b) unctuous
(c) unhealthy (d) impossible (e) trivial   9. ....

10. AUGUST (a) daily (b) receptive (c) fond
(d) undignified (e) unkind   10. ....

B. Sentence Completion

In the space provided, write the letter of the set of words that best completes the sentence.

11. Who will assume the .... task of purchasing all the supplies that we shall need for the hike?
  (a) sententious   (c) onerous
  (b) lugubrious   (d) complacent   11. ....

12. When the flood waters threatened to .... the valley, a group of volunteers worked endlessly to strengthen the walls of the dam.
  (a) overwhelm   (c) extricate
  (b) incarcerate   (d) inundate   12. ....

13. He was foolish enough to .... his energies on trifles• and when the .... moment arrived, he was incapable of sustained action.
  (a) annihilate...exotic   (c) dissipate...decisive
  (b) detonate...derelict   (d) deplete...authentic
                          13. ....

14. Man is the .... animal. He has but begun to explore, and the universe lies before him.
  (a) unsatisfied   (c) tamed
  (b) gregarious   (d) thinking   14. ....

15. Gratitude is a duty which ought to be paid, but which .... have (has) a right to ....
  (a) none...expect   (c) all...demand
  (b) some...give   (d) none...request
                          15. ....

16. In a free world, if it is to remain free, we must maintain, with our lives if need be, but surely by our lives, the .... for a man to learn ....
  (a) privilege...science   (c) necessity...the facts
  (b) right...history   (d) opportunity...anything
                          16. ....

17. Governments exist to protect the rights of .... The loved and the rich need no ....—they have many friends and few enemies.

(a) the majority...influence   (c) minorities...protection
(b) all...privilege   (d) the few...weakness

17. ....

18. .... must work through the brains and the arms of good and brave men, or they are no better than ....

(a) Ideas...dreams   (c) Discoveries...nightmares
(b) Advances...evils   (d) Improvements...the past

18. ....

19. The sentiment of .... is so natural and so universally accepted by all mankind, that it seems to be .... of all law, all party, all religions.

(a) patriotism...above   (c) brotherhood...parent
(b) justice...independent   (d) rebellion...the source

19. ....

20. Perfect .... is effected only when the .... is permitted to form, to express, and to employ its own convictions of truths on all subjects, as it chooses.

(a) peace...intelligence   (c) harmony...child
(b) democracy...enemy   (d) emancipation...mind

20. ....

C. Analogies

In the space provided, write the letter of the set of words that best completes the analogy.

21. TAPE : RECORDER :: (a) memory : man
(b) tube : radio   (c) audio : video   (d) phonograph : record   (e) cover : radiator

21. ....

22. CRAFTSMAN : HANDICRAFT :: (a) grocer : food   (b) government : politician   (c) tactician : trickery   (d) artist : taste   (e) diplomat : affairs of state

22. ....

23. ABBEY : MONK :: (a) knight : castle   (b) cave : hermit   (c) regiment : soldier   (d) manuscript : writer
(e) nest : eagle

23. ....

24. CURTAIN : WINDOW :: (a) tapestry : wall
(b) safe : combination   (c) door : room   (d) book : cover
(e) fold : drapery

24. ....

25. TOURNEY : KNIGHT :: (a) goals : hockey players
(b) series : baseball players   (c) pennant : American League
(d) league : college   (e) umpire : goalie   25. ....

26. ACCOUNT EXECUTIVE : ADVERTISING ::
(a) narrator : play   (b) adviser : investing   (c) manager :
store   (d) consumer : purchasing   (e) plant : foreman
                                                      26. ....

27. POD : RIND :: (a) alike : shelf   (b) bean : cheese
(c) pea : turtle   (d) orange : lima bean   (e) vegetable :
paint   27. ....

28. SONG : LYRICS :: (a) tune : baritones   (b) opera :
libretto   (c) author : novels   (d) symphony : composers
(e) soprano : arias   28. ....

29. TYRO : NEOPHYTE :: (a) ancient : modern
(b) corporal : lieutenant   (c) apprentice : novice
(d) sage : sagacity   (e) Swiss : Grecian   29. ....

30. CONNOISSEUR : DILETTANTE :: (a) deep :
shallow   (b) much : least   (c) carpenter : sculptor
(d) turnip : grape   (e) attempt : achievement   30. ....

D. Reading Comprehension

Read the selections below; and then in each space provided,
write the letter of the word or words that best completes the
statement.

The chief wrong which false prophets do to their following is
not financial. The real harm is on the mental and spiritual plane.
There are those who hunger and thirst after higher values which
they feel wanting in their humdrum lives. They live in mental
confusion or moral anarchy and seek vaguely for truth and
beauty and moral support. When they are deluded and then
disillusioned, cynicism and confusion follow. The wrong of these
things, as I see it, is not in the money the victims part with half
so much as in the mental and spiritual poison they get. But
that is precisely the thing the Constitution put beyond the reach
of the prosecutor, for the price of freedom of religion or of
speech or of the press is that we must put up with, and even
pay for, a good deal of rubbish.

31. The false prophets do not (a) fill the minds of their followers with dangerously false ideas   (b) break laws   (c) drain

money from their supporters (d) appeal to prejudice and ignorance (e) claim that theirs is the best way.

31. ....

32. People are willing to listen to such leaders because (a) they are dissatisfied with democracy (b) they dislike their neighbors (c) they do not want to know the truth (d) they want to improve their own lives (e) they want to become rich. 32. ....

33. One result of following such a leader *not* mentioned by the writer is (a) the followers lose their ability to hope (b) the followers spend their money on unproductive causes (c) the leaders hinder democratic growth (d) the leaders become very influential (e) the followers clutter up their minds with nonsense.

33. ....

34. The solution implied by the writer is that (a) the Constitution should be changed (b) such leaders should be jailed (c) such leaders must be protected (d) such leaders should be exposed (e) we must support such leaders.

34. ....

35. Such type of poison (a) must be expected (b) must be eradicated (c) spoils our youth (d) leads to Hitlerism (e) endangers the UN. 35. ....

To be honest, to be kind—to earn a little and to spend a little less, to make upon the whole a family happier for his presence, to renounce when that shall be necessary and not be embittered, to keep a few friends but these without capitulation—above all, on the same grim condition to keep friends with himself—here is a task for all that a man has of fortitude and delicacy.

36. Man's courage and inner controls of conscience should be used (a) to protect his family (b) to defend his country (c) to build one world (d) to meet daily needs (e) to fight hypocrisy. 36. ....

37. The author does not mention the necessity of (a) living within one's income (b) respecting one's own self (c) control of one's temper (d) compromise (e) standing up for one's principles. 37. ....

38. The author differs with most people on the definition of (a) friends (b) self-image (c) courage (d) surrender (e) honesty. 38. ....

This country, with its institutions, belongs to the people who inhabit it. Whenever they shall grow weary of the existing Government, they can exercise their constitutional right of amending it, or their revolutionary right to dismember or overthrow it. I cannot be ignorant of the fact that many worthy and patriotic citizens are desirous of having the National Constitution amended. While I make no recommendations of amendments, I fully recognize the rightful authority of the people over the whole subject, to be exercised in either of the modes prescribed in the instrument itself; and I should, under existing circumstances, favor rather than oppose a fair opportunity being afforded the people to act upon it.

39. The writer is opposed to (a) changing the Constitution (b) democracy   (c) adopting the Constitution (d) opposing the will of the people   (e) revolution.   39. ....

40. The writer is (a) a Communist   (b) a conservative   (c) a revolutionary   (d) tired of our present form of government (e) none of the above.   40. ....

Time at End............   *Minutes Elapsed*............
                                    Average Time 45 Minutes

Answer Key for this test is on page 625.

My Score: *Number Right*............   *Number Wrong*............

Comparing With Others

	Number Correct
Top 1%	38–40
Top 10%	35–37
Average	30–34
Low Average	26–29
Below Average	0–25

Test Number 15

Time at Start............

In the space provided, write the letter of the correct answer to the problem.

1. Pencils cost a storekeeper 10 cents per dozen. The storekeeper sells them at 2 for 5 cents. His profit in cents per dozen is

(a) 1½   (b) 1⅙   (c) 15   (d) 20   (e) 12   1. ....

2. A watch "loses" a second a minute. In a week the watch loses

(a) 16.8 minutes   (b) 168 minutes   (c) 168 seconds
(d) 100 minutes   (e) 16.8 seconds

2. ....

3. If p and q are positive integers, not equal to 1, then
(a) $p/(q+2) > p/(q+1)$ (b) $q/p < (q-1)/p$
(c) $p/q > (p+1)/(q+1)$ (d) $p/q < p/(q-1)$
(e) $q/p < (q-1)/(p+1)$

3. ....

4. A boy has 8 different-colored pairs of socks in a drawer. If the pairs of socks become separated and the boy cannot see into the drawer, the minimum number of socks he must take out in order to assure a matched pair is

(a) 2   (b) 9   (c) 3   (d) 11   (e) 15

4. ....

5. The area of triangle *ABC* is 24 square units. If each division of the *X* axis is 1 unit, then each division of the *Y* axis is

(a) 2 units   (b) 4 units   (c) 6 units   (d) 10 units
(e) 12 units

5. ....

6. The average of the 7 consecutive even integers a, b, c, d, e, f, and g is

(a) d (b) b (c) $2d$ (d) e (e) $3e$

6. ....

7. The sum of all the integers from 3 to 89 inclusive is
(a) $(91)(43)$ (b) $(92)(44)$ (c) $(92)(43)$ (d) $(46)(87)$
(e) $(91)(87)$

7. ....

8. If $n! = n(n - 1)(n - 2) \ldots 1$ (e.g., $8! = 8 \times 7 \times 6 \times 5 \times 4 \times 3 \times 2 \times 1$), then the number $14!$ is
(a) equal to $9! + 5!$ (b) divisible by 2 but not by 18
(c) divisible by 3 but not by 24   (d) divisible by 5 and by 17
(e) divisible by 6 and by 13   8. ....

9. The number of square units in *ABCD* is

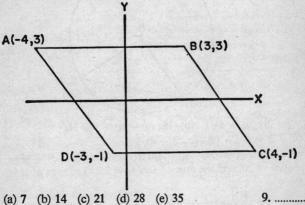

(a) 7   (b) 14   (c) 21   (d) 28   (e) 35   9. ....

10. *ABCD* is a rectangle with $AB = 20$ feet and $BC = 16$ feet. Twenty squares of side 2 are drawn as shown. The combined area of the squares represents what per cent of the area of the rectangle?

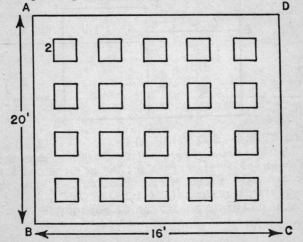

(a) 25   (b) 17   (c) 20   (d) 10   (e) 35   10. ....

11. Point O is the center of the circle, and AO = chord AB = 4. The area of the shaded portion is

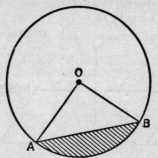

(a) $(8\pi/6) - 4\sqrt{3}$ (b) $(16\pi/6) - 4\sqrt{3}$ (c) 16π
(d) $16\pi - 4\sqrt{3}$ (e) $(8\pi/6) - 4\sqrt{3}$

11. ....

12. $ABCD$, $DEFG$, and $AMNG$ are squares. The area of $ABCD$ = 16, and the area of $DEFG$ = 25. The area of $AMNG$ is

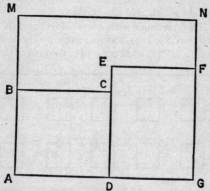

(a) 41   (b) 9   (c) 82   (d) 81   (e) 42   12. ....

13. Three circles of equal radius are tangent to each other as shown (p. 571). Lines PMN and MQ are drawn tangent to circles L and S, and line MQ is extended through Q to R, the center of the third circle. If $PM = 2$, MR equals

(a) 4   (b) $4\sqrt{2}$ (c) $2 + 2\sqrt{2}$ (d) $2 + 2\sqrt{3}$ (e) 6

13. ....

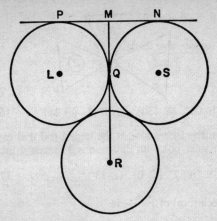

14. At 3:30 P.M., the hands of the clock form an angle
(a) of 90°   (b) between 80° and 90°   (c) between 70° and 80°
(d) between 90° and 100°   (e) between 100° and 110°

14. ....

15. Angle *ABC* = angle *DBE* = 45°. The equation(s) that fully describe the graphs of *AB* and *DB* is(are)

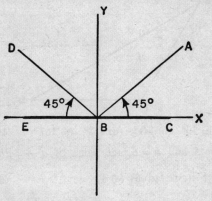

(a) $y = x$ (b) $y = x, x > 0; y = -x, x < 0$
(c) $y = -x$ (d) $y = -x, x > 0; y = x, x < 0$
(e) $y = x; y = -x$

15. ....

16. If triangles 1, 2, and 3 are equilateral (page 572), angle *x* + angle *y* + angle *z* =

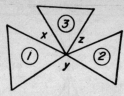

(a) 60°   (b) 90°   (c) 150°   (d) 180°   (e) 240°   16. ....

17. How many inches long is the largest rod that can be put into a rectangular box with dimensions 3 inches, 4 inches, and 12 inches?

(a) 5   (b) 9   (c) 7   (d) 10   (e) 13   17. ....

18. The reciprocal of $\dfrac{a}{b - \frac{1}{2}}$ is

(a) $(2b - 1)/a$ (b) $(1 + 2b)/2a$ (c) $a/(2b - 1)$
(d) $(2b + 1)/a$ (e) $(2b - 1)/2a$ 18. ....

19. In triangle *ABC*, angle $C = 130°$. Which of the following could not be the sum of any two angles of the triangle?

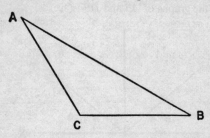

(a) 45°   (b) 50°   (c) 141°   (d) 152°   (e) 167°   19. ....

20. If $a = 5$ and $b = 6$, the value of $a^4 - 4a^3b + 6a^2b^2 - 4ab^3 + b^4$ is

(a) 0   (b) 1   (c) 2   (d) 3   (e) 4   20. ....

Time at End............   *Minutes Elapsed*............
                                  Average Time 30 *Minutes*

Answer Key for this test is on page 626

My Score: Number Right............   *Number Wrong*............

Comparing With Others

	Number Correct
Top 1%	19–20
Top 10%	16–18
Average	12–15
LoG Average	9–11
Below Average	0–10

Test Number 16

Time at start.............

Directions: Each of the following questions consists of two quantities, one in Column A and one in Column B. Compare the two quantities and mark

   A if the quantity in Column A is the greater;
   B if the quantity in Column B is the greater;
   C if the two quantities are equal;
   D if the relationship cannot be determined from the information given.

Notes: Information concerning one or both of the quantities to be compared may be between the two columns.

A symbol that appears in both columns represents the same thing in Column A as it does in Column B.

Letters such as x, y and a stand for real numbers.

	Column A		Column B	
1.	$\dfrac{\frac{1}{4} + \frac{1}{4} + \frac{1}{4}}{\frac{1}{2} + \frac{1}{2}}$		$\dfrac{\frac{1}{3} + \frac{1}{3} + \frac{1}{3}}{\frac{1}{2} + \frac{1}{2}}$	1. ....
2.	a	$a > b > c$	c	2. ....
3.	a^2	$a > b$	b^2	3. ....
4.	2	$5y = 10$	y	4. ....
5.	$3x + 1$	$x = y + 2$	$3y + 7$	5. ....
6.	$x + y$		80	6. ....

m < C = 90°

(Test Number 16 continues on p. 629)

ANSWERS TO VERBAL AND MATHEMATICS TESTS

Answer Key with Hints

Test Number 1: Page 538

More of this type can be found in the work of Section—Day

1. (c) *ABC* is a 9-12-15 triangle; *ABD* is a 5-12-13 triangle.   12   3

2. (b) It takes (8)(3), or 24, man-days to do the job; 6x = 24.   11   6

3. (c) a/3   12   4

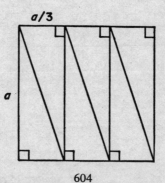

4. (a) Let $5x = 2y$; then solve for x/y. — —

5. (a) Use a proportion: $\dfrac{7/2}{\$2.10} = \dfrac{1}{\$x}$. 10 3

6. (c) If $\frac{2}{7}$ are worth \$1,400, then $\frac{1}{7}$ is worth \$700, and $\frac{5}{7}$ is worth (5)(\$700), or \$3,500. 9 3

7. (b) Originally there are 20×30, or 600, scouts. After 100 are lost, 500 remain to be divided into 20 troops. 9 1

8. (d) 59 apples approximate 5 dozen. 10 3

9. (d) The sum of the heights is $31'8''$; divide this by 5. 9 6

10. (c) Since radii BD and BC are equal, triangle BCD is isosceles and its base angles are equal. 12 2

11. (d) $5^2 - 5 \times 4 = 25 - 20 = 5$. 13 6

12. (b) Each number in the first set differs from the corresponding number in the second set by 20, e.g., — —

$$1 \text{ and } 21,$$
$$2 \text{ and } 22,$$
$$3 \text{ and } 23,$$
$$\ldots$$
$$20 \text{ and } 40.$$

So take $20 \times 20 = 400$.

13. (b) The first 5 questions of A and B now appear on each test, making a total of 10 questions in common. — —

14. (a) The y must contain a 4 to cancel the denominator, and a 5 to make the numerator a perfect square; thus choose 5×4 which is 20. 11 4

15. (a) The cotton shirt costs $25 \times 25c + \$3$, or \$9.25. The wash-and-wear shirt costs \$5. — —

16. (b) $2x + 3x + 7x = 60$. 10 3

17. (a) Since $a > b$ and a and b are positive,   10   4
$a^2 > b^2$. Thus a larger number is subtracted from the x^2, which must therefore be a larger number to start with.

18. (c) If the man spent 24 coins and has 72 left,   —   —
he began with 96 coins. Divide 96 by 8.

19. (d) The 60 radios cost $3 each. A profit of   9   2
$16\frac{2}{3}\%$, or $\frac{1}{6}$, is 50 cents.

20. (c) $(x/9) + (x/18) = 1$.   10   6

Answer Key

Test Number 2: Page 542

A. Antonyms

1. (b)	3. (c)	5. (e)	7. (d)	9. (e)
2. (a)	4. (e)	6. (a)	8. (b)	10. (c)

B. Sentence Completion

11. (b)	13. (a)	15. (d)	17. (b)	19. (d)
12. (c)	14. (d)	16. (d)	18. (c)	20. (c)

C. Analogies

21. (c)	23. (b)	25. (d)	27. (e)	29. (e)
22. (e)	24. (c)	26. (b)	28. (e)	30. (d)

D. Reading Comprehension

31. (e)	33. (b)	35. (a)	37. (d)	39. (a)
32. (d)	34. (a)	36. (c)	38. (b)	40. (c)

Answer Key with Hints

Test Number 3: Page 547

More of this
type can be
found in the
work of
Section—Day

1. (d) $\frac{14}{364} = 7/x$; $\frac{2}{364} = 1/x$; $\frac{1}{182} = 1/x$;   9   3
$x = 182$.

2. (d) Multiply the given equations by 6 and 4   10   10
respectively, yielding 6 bams = 12 lams
and 12 lams = 32 nams. From this we
get 6 bams = 32 nams.

3. (b) $\dfrac{2}{2 + \dfrac{1}{2 + \frac{1}{2}}} = \dfrac{-2}{2 + \frac{5}{2}} = \dfrac{2}{2 + \frac{2}{5}}$ 8   4
etc.

4. (c) Four men do $\frac{1}{3}$ of the job in $\frac{1}{2}$ day;   9   3
4 men do $3(\frac{1}{3})$ of the job in $3(\frac{1}{2})$ days.

5. (d) $\dfrac{\text{Amount of substance}}{\text{Amount of mixture}} \times 100$ 10   8

$= \dfrac{6}{6 + 18} \times 100 = 25.$

6. (e) The lengths of HG and HF are irrelevant   11   7
here. Triangles EFG and HFG have the
same base (FG) and the same altitude
(since E and H are both on AB, which is
parallel to the base). Therefore the triangles are equal in area.

7. (c) The 4-digit integers range from 1,000 to   8   5
9,999; take the difference (8,999) and
add 1 (9,000).

8. (a) $\dfrac{ab + cd}{abcd} = (1/cd) + (1/ab) = 3 + 9$ 8   3
$= 12.$

9. (c) $22(18) - 18(14) = 18(22 - 14)$ —   —
$= 18(8)$
$= 144$

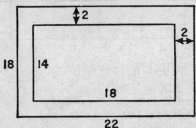

10. (b) Area of shaded part = area of equilateral triangle — area of 3 sectors
$= (\sqrt{3}) - 3(\pi/6) = (\sqrt{3}) = \pi/2$

                                 11   7

11. (e) $\left\{ \begin{matrix} 5 \\ + \\ 3 \end{matrix} \right\} = (5)(3)/(5+3)$;

                                 12   6

    $\left\{ \begin{matrix} (-5) \\ + \\ (-3) \end{matrix} \right\}$

         $= (-5)(-3)/(-5 + -3)$;
$(^{15}\!/_8) + (-^{15}\!/_8) = 0.$

12. (a) 1 day = 24 hours; 7 days = 168 hours.
Average number per hour

                                  8   6

$$= \frac{\text{total number}}{\text{number of hours}} = \frac{50,400}{168} = 300.$$

13. (c) Let $AD = 4x$. Then the area of the
shaded portion is $x(3x) + x(2x)$, or
$5x^2$, and the area of $ABCD$ is $(4x)^2$, or
$16x^2$. $5x^2/16x^2 = ^5\!/_{16}.$

                                 11   6

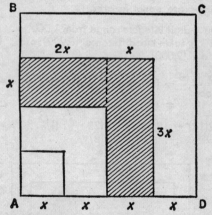

14. (c) $4 = (x/100)(f)$; $x = 400/f.$

                                  9   4

15. (d) Angle $ECA = \frac{1}{2}(80°) = 40°$;
angle $ECD + $ angle $ECA = 180°$;
angle $ECD = 140°.$

                                 11   5

16. (b) Area of triangle DEF = area of ABCD   12   **7**
   — area of triangles 1, 2, and 3 = 108
   — $\frac{1}{2}[(9 \times 9) + (3 \times 3) + (6 \times 12)]$
   = $108 - \frac{1}{2}(81 + 9 + 72)$
   = $108 - \frac{1}{2}(162) = 108 - 81 = 27.$

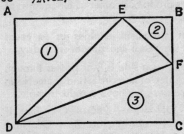

17. (b) Since the numbers must be more than 1   9   **4**
   and unequal, the following trios are
   impossible: (30,2,1); (15,2,2); (15,4,1).
   The correct trio is (10,3,2).

18. (c) Call the integers $x - 10, x - 8, x - 6,$ 9   **5**
   $x - 4, x - 2, x, x + 2, x + 4, x + 6,$
   $x + 8, x + 10, x + 12.$ Then their sum
   is $12x + 12,$ or $12(x + 1),$ which is
   always divisible by 12.

19. (c) Since the line passes through (0,0) and   —   **—**
   (5,10), its equation is $y = 2x.$ For all
   points "above" the line, $y > 2x.$

20. (a) Since the original numbers are positive,   —   **—**
   raising each to the fourth power will not
   change the numerical order of the mag-
   nitudes. $A^4 = 2^4 = 16; B^4 = (\sqrt{3})^4 = 3^2$
   $= 9; C^4 = 10.$ Therefore $B < C < A.$

Answer Key with Hints

Test Number 4:   Page 551

More of this
type can be
found in the
work of
Section—Day

1. (e) Neither statement gives us any actual   —   **—**
   numbers to use.

2. (c) The first statement enables us to find the container's volume; the second tells us at what rate it fills.   11   9

3. (a) $y = x + z$, but perhaps z is negative.   10   2

4. (a) Areas are to each other as the squares of radii.   11   5

5. (d) Either statement enables us to count until we reach the proper Thursday.   —   —

6. (d) As long as a side is 8 or passes through the center of the circle (the diameter in both cases), we have a right triangle.   11   4

7. (a) $(P + Q)^2 = P^2 + 2PQ + Q^2$. Thus, if $(P + Q)^2$ also equals $P^2 + Q^2$, then $2PQ$ must $= 0$; P and/or $Q = 0$.   10   2

8. (d) We can use either statement to set up a linear equation.   10   10

9. (c) Statement I gives us the number of cards in a suit; statement II tells us the number of suits (6).   —   —

10. (a) We can set up an equation: $x + 5\%x = 85$.   9   4

11. (c) Statement I tells us the cost per chair; statement II tells us how many chairs.   8   1

12. (b) Simply multiply both sides by $(x + y)$.   10   2

13. (d) Either statement enables us to find that one man paints a third of a room daily.   10   6

14. (c) The "common denominator"—a blanket —enables us to solve.   —   —

15. (e) We get no help from either statement.   —   —

16. (b) The area of the rectangle is bh; the area of the triangle is $\frac{1}{2}bh$.   11   6

17. (c) To find the volume, we need the base radius and the height.   11   9

18. (d) Either statement enables us to find the edge, the face diagonal, and then the space diagonal.   11   9

19. (b) If $x = -3, y = -2$, then $x^2 > y^2$, but $x < y$.   10   2

20. (e) We would need a relationship between   11   10
langas and picas to solve the problem.

Answer Key

Test Number 5:   Page 554

A. Antonyms

1. (c)	3. (d)	5. (e)	7. (c)	9. (b)
2. (a)	4. (b)	6. (d)	8. (e)	10. (a)

B. Sentence Completion

11. (c)	13. (a)	15. (b)	17. (a)	19. (b)
12. (b)	14. (c)	16. (c)	18. (c)	20. (d)

C. Analogies

21. (e)	23. (c)	25. (c)	27. (a)	29. (b)
22. (b)	24. (b)	26. (a)	28. (d)	30. (b)

D. Reading Comprehension

31. (e)	33. (a)	35. (e)	37. (b)	39. (e)
32. (d)	34. (b)	36. (e)	38. (e)	40. (a)

Answer Key with Hints

Test Number 6:   Page 559

More of this
type can be
found in the
work of
Section—Day

1. (e) A side of the square is 7; a radius of the   11   6
semicircle is $\frac{1}{2}$; four semicircles are
equivalent to two circles.

2. (c) Forty-five adults consume $7\frac{1}{2}$ gallons of ——   ——
ice cream. This leaves $2\frac{1}{2}$ gallons, which
will serve $2\frac{1}{2} \times 8$, or 20, children.

3. (e) $(\frac{2}{3})(\frac{1}{2})(\frac{1}{6})(x) = 60.$ 9   3

4. (a) The width of the rectangle is equal to a   12   5
radius of the circle, which is 10. The two
quadrants add up to a semicircle.

5. (c) This is not a 3-4-5 right triangle! Use   12   3
$a^2 + b^2 = c^2$.

6. (b) The man wants $7\frac{1}{2}$ hours of sleep. Count   —   —
back $7\frac{1}{2}$ hours from 2 p.m.

7. (d) If she takes 10, she may have 2 of each   13   2
flavor. The eleventh does it!

8. (e) $\dfrac{\text{Total distance}}{\text{Total time}} = \dfrac{100}{\frac{40}{20} + \frac{60}{50}}.$ 11   7

9. (b) Use 100 as a base and work each   10   5
part separately.

10. (b) $\frac{9}{100}x = 18.$ 10   4

11. (a) The differences form the series 1, 2, 3, 4.   —   —
So take $22 + 5 = 27$.

12. (a) Twelve 2-gallon cans give 24 gallons.   —   —

13. (d) Simply divide $(2x^2 + 11x + 12)$ by   12   6
$(2x + 3)$.

14. (e) Multiply $2 \times 3 \times 4$.   13   2

15. (c) Let the base be x, the legs $2x$, the   12   2
perimeter $2x + 2x + x$.

16. (b) In an hour John makes $(\frac{2}{3})(6)$, or 4, book-   11   6
covers. Thus together they complete
$6 + 4$, or 10, per hour.

17. (c) $1\frac{1}{2}/6 = \frac{1}{4} = 25\%$; this leaves 75%.   10   4

18. (e) $(\frac{1}{2})(\frac{1}{3})(4) = \frac{1}{8}x.$ 9   3

19. (b) $12\frac{1}{2}\%$ of 24 is 3; $\frac{1}{3}x = 3$; $x = 9$.   10   2

20. (a) The area of each square is 25; therefore   12   6
a side is 5.

Answer Key with Hints

Test Number 7:   Page 563

More of this
type can be
found in the
work of
Section—Day

1. (d) Use a proportion: $a/1 = b/9$.   10   3

2. (b) $\frac{1}{5} + \frac{1}{7} = \frac{12}{35}$; now divide by 2.   9   6

3. (d) Any quantity except 0 divided by its —   —
equal is 1.

4. (d) The area of a right triangle equals half   12   7
the product of the legs.

5. (e) Use a proportion: $\dfrac{x \text{ nails}}{p \text{ cents}} = \dfrac{y \text{ nails}}{c \text{ cents}}$.   10   3

6. (c) $.7y = 7/100$; $7y = 70/100$;   10   4
$y = 10/100 = .1$.

7. (c) Use vertical angles at 2 and 3, then   12   2
determine the sum of the angles of
triangle *UVR*.

8. (e) $\dfrac{2x - 2y}{y - x} = \dfrac{2(x - y)}{-1(x - y)} = -2$.   —   —

9. (c) Let $100 be the original value. Then the   10   5
April rise makes the value $105, and the
May drop makes it $99.75.

10. (b) Take 5% of 50; then add this to and   11   7
subtract it from 50.

11. (a) $\dfrac{\text{New} - \text{original}}{\text{Original}} = \dfrac{2\pi(r + x) - 2\pi r}{2\pi r}$.   12   5

12. (d) $V = \pi r^2 h = (\pi)(3^2)(\frac{1}{6})$.   12   9

13. (e) The numbers must total 3(72), or 216. If   9   6
two of them are 1 and 2, this leaves 213
for the third one.

14. (c) $\dfrac{(.20)(10)}{15 + 10} = \dfrac{2}{25} = 8\%.$ 11   8

15. (e) Angle ADC is greater than angle ABD,   12   2
and therefore greater than angle ACD.

16. (e) Since x^2 is positive when x is real,   11   4
$x^2 + 16$ cannot equal zero.

17. (e) $P \times S = (P + S)/(P \times S)$; cross-multi-   13   6
ply to obtain $(P \times S)^2 = P + S.$

18. (e) If $a - b = 0$, then $a = b$. Then $b = \dfrac{b}{7},$ —   —
or $b = 0.$

19. (d) Either statement can be derived from the   12   5
other.

20. (e) The average rate depends on the dis-   11   7
tance between A and B, and between
B and C.

Answer Key

Test Number 8:   Page 567

A. Antonyms

1. (b)	3. (b)	5. (d)	7. (c)	9. (c)
2. (e)	4. (c)	6. (e)	8. (e)	10. (a)

B. Sentence Completion

11. (d)	13. (b)	15. (c)	17. (b)	19. (a)
12. (b)	14. (a)	16. (c)	18. (d)	20. (d)

C. Analogies

21. (c)	23. (e)	25. (a)	27. (e)	29. (b)
22. (c)	24. (b)	26. (b)	28. (b)	30. (d)

D. Reading Comprehension

31. (d)	33. (a)	35. (d)	37. (b)	39. (e)
32. (e)	34. (d)	36. (c)	38. (a)	40. (e)

Answer Key with Hints

Test Number 9:   Page 572

More of this
type can be
found in the
work of
Section—Day

1. (e) $5/9x = 45; x/9 = 9; x = 9 \times 9 = 81.$ 11   5

2. (c) Translate as follows: $4 = (x/100)(25).$ 10   4

3. (e) In this parallelogram, angle A + angle 12   2
$B = 180°.$

4. (a) The job takes 48 man-days. If 3 men 11   6
work 8 days, this is 24 man-days. Then 8
men take 3 days to finish.

5. (b) $\left(\dfrac{new - old}{old}\right)100 =$ 12   5

$$\left(\frac{\dfrac{\pi(3d/2)^2}{4} - \dfrac{\pi d^2}{4}}{\dfrac{\pi d^2}{4}}\right)100.$$

6. (c) $747 - 315 = 432;\quad 432 \div 3 = 144;$ 9   5
$144 + 1 = 145.$

7. (c) If $3a = 5b$, then $3/5 = b/a.$ 10   3

8. (b) Since triangle ABC is isosceles, it is equi- 12   4
lateral if angle $x = 60°$, and a 45°-
45°-90° triangle if x is a right angle.
Side BC will therefore vary from 8 to
$8\sqrt{2}.$

9. (a) $72° = (1/5)(360°)$; take $(1/5)(1/5)(100)$ to 10   5
get the desired per cent.

10. (b) $\dfrac{(85 + 100)x}{360} - \dfrac{(72 + 103)x}{360}$ —   —

$$= 10x/360 = 2x/72.$$

11. (c) $8 = (x + 7)/2$; $11 = (y - 8)/2$.   11   8

12. (e) The total value of the mixture is   10   9
 $(20 \times 35¢) + (40 \times 50¢)$, or \$27. To
 make a 10% profit on his cost, the vendor
 must collect \$27 + \$2.70, or \$29.70.
 Divide this by 60 to get the price per
 pound.

13. (c) $1/(x + y) = a$; $x - y = 1/b$. There-   —   —
 fore $a/b = (x - y)/(x + y)$.

14. (a) Since $3\!\!\!\diagdown\!\!\!1 = C$, the value will $= 0$.   12   6

15. (c) Draw OP, OA, AP, PC, CO. Since radii   11   5
 of the same circle are equal, $OP = OA$
 $= AP = PC = CO = 1$. Therefore
 angles APO and OPC both equal 60°,
 and arc AOC equals 120°. Let x represent the length of arc AOC in units.
 $120°/360° = x/2\pi r$.

16. (a) Let the odd integers be represented by   —   —
 $2x - 1$ and $2x + 1$, and the even
 integers by $2y - 2$ and $2y$. Their sum is
 then $4x + 4y - 2$, or $2(2x + 2y - 1)$,
 which is always divisible by 2.

17. (c)   —   —

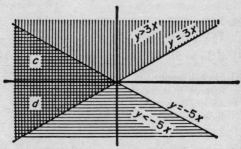

The crosshatched region satisfies both
inequalities.

18. (e) If a number is divisible by 25, it is   8   4
 divisible by 5×5. From statement I we

know the number is divisible by 5; from statement II we know it is divisible by a second 5 ($10 = 5 \times 2$). However, a number such as 30 satisfies both (I) and (II), but does not work.

19. (c) The shorter diagonal can be found using **11**   **3**
both statements and the following: the diagonals of a rhombus are perpendicular and bisect each other; the sides of a rhombus are equal.

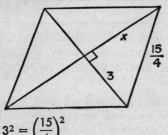

$$x^2 + 3^2 = \left(\frac{15}{4}\right)^2$$

20. (c) We must know whether C is positive or   —   —
negative. For instance, $5(-3) < 4(-3)$; but $5 > 4$.

Answer Key with Hints

Test Number 10:   Page 576

More of this
type can be
found in the
work of
Section—Day

1. (e) $(\frac{1}{2})(\frac{1}{3})(\frac{1}{4}) = \frac{1}{24}$; $1 - \frac{1}{24} = \frac{23}{24}$.   —   —

2. (b) Per cent water = $\dfrac{\text{amount water}}{\text{amount punch}}$ **9**   **5**

$$= \frac{20}{20 + 4 + 2 + 6 + 8}$$

$$= 1/2 = 50\%.$$

3. (c)   12   4

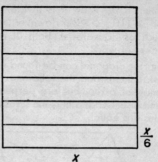

$\dfrac{x}{6}$

x

4. (a) Twenty-one poles give 20 intervals;   9   5
5 poles give 4 intervals; $(\frac{4}{20})(2000)$
= 400.

5. (c) Factors of 12 not equal to 1 are 2, 3, and   9   5
12. The only odd integers between 1
and 12 (excluding 1) not having any of
these factors are 5, 7, and 11.

6. (c)   —   —

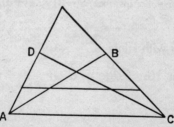

7. (d) $x + .049x = 125.88$.   Multiply   both   10   5
sides of the equation by 1000, and solve:
$x = 120$.

8. (d) If $\frac{1}{3}$ is eaten, $\frac{2}{3}$ remains. $\frac{1}{2} \cdot \frac{2}{3}$, or $\frac{1}{3}$ is   9   3
put in the freezer, leaving $\frac{1}{3}$ outside.

9. (e) 1 foot = 12 inches;   (1 foot)³ = (12   12   9
inches)³ = 1,728 cubic inches.

10. (b) $(a - b)/(b - a) = (a - b)/-(a - b)$ —   —
$= 1/-1 = -1$.

11. (d) When *n* is halved, $v = \frac{1}{2}m(\frac{1}{2}n)^2 = \frac{1}{2}m\frac{1}{4}n^2$. So the value of *m* must be multiplied by 4 in order for v to remain the same (i.e., $\frac{1}{2}mn^2$).

12. (e) As x increases, y approaches the X axis, or decreases.

13. (c) $6/5 = 5/x$; $6x = 25$; $x = 4\frac{1}{6}$.   10   3

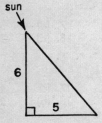
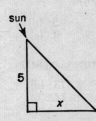

14. (b) $(x + y)/1 = 2/(x - y)$;
$(x + y)(x - y) = 2$; $x^2 - y^2 = 2$.

15. (d) $x^2 - x = 0$; $x(x - 1) = 0$; $x = 0$;   11   4
$x - 1 = 0, x = 1$.

16. (b) $[4 \times 3 - \frac{4}{3}] - [(3 \times 4 - \frac{3}{4})]$ 13   6
$= -\frac{4}{3} + \frac{3}{4} = -\frac{7}{12}$.

17. (d) Area $= (16)^2 = 256$.   12   5

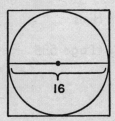

18. (d) Surface area of cube $= 6e^2$; $216 = 6e^2$;   12   9
$e^2 = 36$; $e = 6$. Volume of cube $= e^3$
$= 6^3 = 216$.

19. (c) A number divisible by 18 must be divis-   9   4
ible by 9 and by 2.

20. **(d)** $2x + 2$, which factors into $2(x + 1)$, —   —
must be an even integer since it contains
the factor 2.

Answer Key

Test Number 11:   Page 579

A. Antonyms

1. (a)	3. (d)	5. (a)	7. (d)	9. (d)
2. (e)	4. (e)	6. (c)	8. (a)	10. (d)

B. Sentence Completion

11. (b)	13. (d)	15. (b)	17. (c)	19. (a)
12. (c)	14. (a)	16. (d)	18. (b)	20. (c)

C. Analogies

21. (d)	23. (c)	25. (a)	27. (d)	29. (c)
22. (d)	24. (c)	26. (d)	28. (e)	30. (d)

D. Reading Comprehension

31. (b)	33. (c)	35. (d)	37. (c)	39. (e)
32. (d)	34. (e)	36. (e)	38. (c)	40. (e)

Answer Key with Hints

Test Number 12:   Page 585

More of this
type can be
found in the
work of
Section—Day

1. **(d)** $\dfrac{2\frac{1}{4}}{3\frac{1}{2} + 2\frac{1}{4}} = \dfrac{\frac{9}{4}}{\frac{7}{2} + \frac{9}{4}} = \dfrac{9}{14 + 9} = \dfrac{9}{23}.$ 8   3

2. **(d)** Let x represent the man's original salary   9   5
in dollars. $x + .05x = 73.50;$ $105x$
$= 7350;$ $x = 70.$

3. (b) Number of homes   9   5
$= (703 - 105)/2 + 1 = 300.$

4. (a) Area of one square $= 720/5 = 144;$ 12   6
$s^2 = 144; \quad s = 12.$

5. (d)   —   —

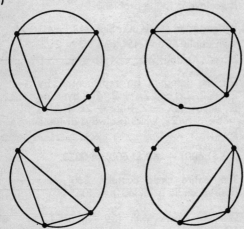

6. (e) Angle $GHF = 180° - 63° = 117°;$ 12   2
$GH \parallel FJ;$ alternate interior angles of
parallel lines are equal.

7. (b) Let x represent the number of students 13   5
studying both languages; $100 + 30 + x$
$= 156; \quad x = 26.$

8. (b) Let t represent the time going in hours; 12   7
then $60t$ represents the distance going.
It follows that $t + {}^{52}\!/_{60}$ represents the
time coming and $50(t + {}^{52}\!/_{60})$ represents
the distance coming. The two distances
are equal: $60t = 50(t + {}^{52}\!/_{60}).$

9. (d) Remember that the arrow can move for- —   —
wards or backwards. Moving forward 4
spaces would bring us to number 14; a
fifth space leaves us at zero.

10. (b) $\frac{1}{2} \cdot \frac{1}{3} = \frac{1}{6}; \quad \frac{1}{6} = 16\frac{2}{3}\%.$ 10   2

11. (a) The man spent $1 - \frac{5}{9}$, or $\frac{4}{9}$, of his — —
money. $4x/9 = 48$; $x = 108$.

12. (e) Angle 1 + angle 2 + $x° = 180°$; angle   11   2
1 + angle 2 = $(180 - x)°$. Note that
the fact that both triangles are isosceles
is irrelevant to the problem.

13. (d) Perimeter = $BC + \overset{\frown}{BC}$. Since $AB = AC$,   11   5
then angle $ACB = 45°$, and $BC = 2\sqrt{2}$.
$\overset{\frown}{BC} = (90/360)(2 \times \pi \times 2) = \pi$.

14. (a) Let the integers be represented by — —
$2x - 2$, $2x$, and $2x + 2$. The average
is then $(2x - 2 + 2x + 2x + 2)/3$
$= 6x/3 = 2x$, which is always divisible
by 2.

15. (a) $.60(\$1,600) - .40(\$1,600) = \$320$.   9   5

16. (e) The entire circle contains $360°$; the — —
desired angle is $\frac{1}{9}(360°) = 40°$.

17. (a) We can work with $(39-3)$ $3+1$, or   8   5
13 differences, each amounting to 39.
For instance,

$$42 - 3 = 39,$$
$$45 - 6 = 39,$$
$$48 - 9 = 39,$$
etc.

The total difference is therefore $(13)(39)$.

18. (b) The third side of a triangle must be less — —
than the sum of the other two (6) and
more than the difference between the
other two (0). $0 < x < 6$.

19. (e) Since $3 \times 7 \times 11$ is the smallest positive   8   4
integer divisible by 3, 7, and 11, we can
use $3 \times 7 \times 11 + 1$ to give us a
remainder of 1.

20. (e) The smallest integer would be -3, which — —
when squared gives a result of 9.

Answer Key with Hints

Test Number 13:   Page 589

More of this
type can be
found in the
work of
Section—Day

1. (c) $8x/5 = {}^{400}\!/_1$; $8x = 2000$; $x = 250$.   10   5

2. (c) Regard the original salary as 100%; then after the first week it is 90%. A 20% increase on this is equivalent to $(.90)(.20)$ or 18% of the original, so that after the second week the man's salary is $90\% + 18\%$, or 108%. This represents a total increase of $108\% - 100\%$, or 8%.   9   5

3. (a) Angle 1 + angle 2 + angle 3 = 180°; $70° + 80° +$ angle 3 = 180°; angle 3 = 30°.   11   2

4. (d) Note that for 12–30, the first and last numbers of the interval are divisible by 6.   8   5

5. (d) $(.1 + .01)(.1 - .01) = (.1)^2 - (.01)^2$ $= .01 - .0001 = .0099$.   —   —

6. (c) Let r represent the rate of the slower train. Then $4(r + 5) + 4r = 420$; $r = 50$ and $r + 5 = 55$.   10   7

7. (b) Let x be the number. Then $5x/8 = 16$, $x = 16(8)/5$. $187\frac{1}{2}\% = 1 + \frac{7}{8} = \frac{15}{8}$; $\dfrac{15}{8} \cdot \dfrac{16 \times 8}{5} = 48$.   9   4

8. (e) Simply expand $(c - b)$.   —   —

9. (b) Let x represent the cost per adult; then $x/2$ represents the cost per child. $x + x + 2(x/2) = 4.20$; $3x = 4.20$; $x = 1.40$, which is the cost for *two* children.   —   —

10. (d) The only perimeter which cannot be found   11   6
is that of the rectangle ($P = 2L + 2W$).
In the regular pentagon, a relationship
could be found between the side and
apothem.

11. (e) $(x + 1)^2 = x^2 + 2x + 1 = x^2;$ 10   4
$2x + 1 = 0;$ $x = -\frac{1}{2}.$

12. (b) Use a direct proportion: $\frac{3}{4} = x/3;$ 8   3
$4x = 9;$ $x = 2\frac{1}{4}.$

13. (a) Remember: 60 miles per hour   9   3
                = 88 feet per second
        15 miles per hour
                = 22 feet per second.

14. (b) Complete the figure as shown.   11   5
$A = (14)(13) - 4(\frac{1}{4})\pi(4)^2$

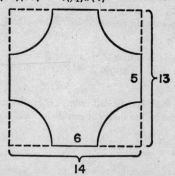

15. (d) If 2 lines are parallel, then angles on the   11   2
same side of a transversal are supple-
mentary: angle 1 + angle 2 = 180°.
Since these angles are bisected, we have

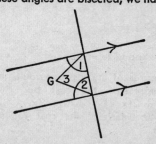

$$\frac{\text{angle } 1}{2} + \frac{\text{angle } 2}{2} = \frac{180°}{2} = 90°.$$

16. (c) $7! = 7 \times 6 \times 5 \times 4 \times 3 \times 2 \times 1.$ 8   4
Since 7! contains a 7 and a 3, it is divisible by 21. Since 7! contains a 4 and a 2, it is divisible by 8. 11 is not, however, contained in 7!.

17. (b) Let x represent the man's weekly salary.   8   3
If $\frac{1}{6}$ is spent on food, $\frac{5}{6}$ is left. Therefore $(\frac{1}{3})(\frac{5}{6})$, or $\frac{5}{18}$, is spent on shelter. $1 - \frac{1}{6} - \frac{5}{18} = \frac{18}{18} - \frac{3}{18} - \frac{5}{18} = \frac{10}{18} = \frac{5}{9}$. Therefore \$45 is $\frac{5}{9}$ of his weekly salary. Form a proportion to find his weekly salary, x. $\frac{5}{9} = 45/x$; $5x/9 = \$45$; $x = \$81$.

18. (b) $v^{262} = (v^3)^{87}v^1 = (1)^{87}v^1 = v^1 = v^2.$ —   —

19. (a) $A = \frac{1}{2}(5)(5).$ —   —

20. (c) Let the even integers be represented by   —   —
$2x - 2$, $2x$, and $2x + 2$. Let the odd integers be represented by $2x - 1$, $2x + 1$ and $2x + 3$. By summing, we get $6x$ for the numerator and $3(2x + 1)$ for the denominator. These are always divisible by 6 and 3, respectively.

Answer Key

Test Number 14:   Page 592

A. Antonyms

1. (b)	3. (e)	5. (b)	7. (c)	9. (c)
2. (b)	4. (c)	6. (a)	8. (e)	10. (d)

B. Sentence Completion

11. (c)	13. (c)	15. (d)	17. (c)	19. (b)
12. (d)	14. (a)	16. (d)	18. (a)	20. (d)

C. Analogies

21. (a)	23. (b)	25. (b)	27. (b)	29. (c)
22. (e)	24. (a)	26. (c)	28. (b)	30. (a)

D. Reading Comprehension

31. (b)	33. (c)	35. (a)	37. (e)	39. (d)
32. (d)	34. (d)	36. (d)	38. (c)	40. (e)

Answer Key with Hints

Test Number 15:   Page 597

More of this type can be found in the work of Section—Day

1. (d) Selling price per dozen — cost per — —
dozen = profit per dozen; 30¢ — 10¢
= 20¢.

2. (b) The watch loses 1 second per minute, or — —
60 seconds per hour, or 24 minutes per
day, or $7(24) = 168$ minutes per week.

3. (d) A fraction will increase its value if its — —
denominator decreases while its nu-
merator increases or remains the same,
provided we are working with positive
integers. Choice (d) satisfies these
conditions.

4. (b) If the boy picks out 9 socks, 2 must belong   12   2
to one pair since there are only 8
different pairs.

5. (b) Let x represent the number of units in   11   6
each division of the Y axis. Then the
area of the triangle is $\frac{1}{2}(4)(3x)$.
$24 = \frac{1}{2}(4)(3x)$; $x = 4$.

6. (a) Let the integers a through g be repre-   8   6
sented by $2x - 6, 2x - 4, 2x - 2, 2x$,
$2x + 2$, $2x + 4$, and $2x + 6$. Their
sum is then $14x$; $14x/7 = 2x$ (which was
used to represent d).

7. (d) There are $[(89 - 3 + 1)/2]$ pairs of   8   5
numbers whose sum is 92: e.g.,
$$3 + 89 = 92,$$
$$4 + 88 = 92,$$
$$5 + 87 = 92,$$
$$\text{etc.}$$
The answer is therefore $(92)\dfrac{(87)}{2}$ or $(46)(87)$

8. (e) Since $14!$ contains a 2 and a 3, it is   8   4
divisible by 6. $14!$ also contains a 13
and is therefore divisible by that number
also.

9. (d) $A = bh = (7)(4) = 28.$ 11   8

10. (a) $\dfrac{\text{Area of squares}}{\text{Total area}} \times 100$ 11   6

$$= \frac{80}{20 \times 16} \times 100 = 25.$$

11. (b) Triangle AOB is equilateral.   11   5
Area of shaded part
$= $ area of sector $-$ area of triangle
$= (16\pi/6) - 4^2\sqrt{3}/4$
$= (16\pi/6) - 4\sqrt{3}.$

12. (d) $AB = 4, DG = 5, AG = 9$; area $= 81.$ 11   6

13. (d) Since tangents to a circle from a given   11   5
outside point are equal, $MN = MQ$
$= MP = 2$. Draw SN, SQ, and SR.
$SN = MQ = 2$, so $LQ = 2$ (since all
the circles are equal), and $LR = 4$. This
makes $QR = 2\sqrt{3}$. Finally, $MR = MQ$
$+ QR = 2 + 2\sqrt{3}.$

14. (c) At 3:30 p.m., the hour hand is midway   —   —
between the 3 and 4 (page 598); there-
fore angle $x = 30° + 30° + 15° = 75°$.

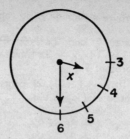

15. (b) Simply try each of the choices.   —   —

16. (d) Remember: the sum of the angles about   11   2
    a point is 360°. Therefore angle
    x + angle y + angle z + 180° = 360°,
    and then angle x + angle y + angle
    z = 180°.

17. (e) The largest rod will equal the diagonal   11   9
    of the solid.

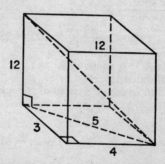

18. (e) The reciprocal is $(b - \frac{1}{2})/a$, which equals   —   —
    $(2b - 1)/2a$.

19. (a) If the sum of two angles of the triangle   11   2
    (A and B) were 45°, the sum of all three
    angles would be 175°, which is impos-
    sible.

20. (b) $a^4 - 4a^3b + 6a^2b^2 - 4ab^3 + b^4$ —   —
    $= (a - b)^4 = (5 - 6)^4 = 1.$

(Test Number 16 continued from p. 603)

7.   **AB**   10   7. ....

8. x $|x| = 5$ -4 8. ....
                 Note $|x| = x \quad x \geq 0$
                        $= -x \quad x < 0$

9. $x^2 - 4x + 4$ 0   9. ....

10. A diagonal of a square   An altitude of   10. ....
     with side S an equilateral
                                     triangle with
                                     side S

11. A man finishes $\frac{1}{3}$ of a job in $\frac{1}{2}$ 11. ....
     $\frac{2}{3}$ of a day. At the same rate
     the fraction of the job he
     does in one day

12. $\dfrac{x - y}{x}$ $\dfrac{x + y}{x} = \dfrac{7}{4}$ $\frac{1}{8}$ 12. ....

13. a^3 $a > b$ b^3 13. ....

14. $a + b + c$ $a + b = 3$ 6   14. ....
                    $b + c = 4$
                    $c + a = 5$

15. The greatest   The least in-   15. ....
     integer less   teger greater
     than $14\frac{1}{9}$ than $10\frac{10}{11}$

16. Two numbers a and b are related such that the product of 5
     and a is equal to the product of 11 and b.
         $\dfrac{a}{b}$ $\dfrac{5}{11}$ 16. ....

17.

17. ....

CB   45

Circle with center 0, $\overline{AB}$ diameter;
$AC = 14$, $CO = 25$

18. $rst = 105$ and r, s, t are   3   18. ....
positive integers. Number
of integers r, s and t that
are odd

19.   3 P is a prime   The number   19. ....
number   of factors of
P^3 (include 1)

Cube box with side S

20. Length of space   20. ....
diagonal $\overline{BE}$
                                          $2S$

Answer Key with Hints

More of this
type can be

Test Number 16:   Page 603

found in the
work of
Section—Day

1. B $\dfrac{\frac{1}{3} + \frac{1}{3} + \frac{1}{3}}{\frac{1}{2} + \frac{1}{2}} = \dfrac{1}{1}$, $\dfrac{\frac{1}{4} + \frac{1}{4} + \frac{1}{4}}{\frac{1}{2} + \frac{1}{2}} =$ 9   3

$\dfrac{\frac{3}{4}}{1} = \dfrac{3}{4}$.

2. A $a > b > c$ implies $a > c$.   13   2

3. **D**   If both a and b are greater than zero,   13   2
$a > b$ implies $a^2 > b^2$. However, consider
the following: $2 > -4$ but $(2)^2 < (-4)^2$
and $-2 > -10$ but $(-2)^2 < (-10)^2$.

4. **C** $5y = 10$ implies $\dfrac{5y}{5} = \dfrac{10}{5}$ implies $y = 2$.   11   3

5. **C**   The binomial $3x + 1$ is equivalent to   —   —
$3(y + 2) + 1$ or $3y + 7$.

6. **A**   The sum of the measures of the angles of a   12   2
triangle is 180. Therefore, $x + y + 90 =$
180 or $x + y = 90$.

7. **B**   Since the sum of the measure of the angles   12   2
of a triangle is 180, $m < B = 70$. In a
triangle the shortest side is opposite the
smallest angle. Therefore $AB < 10$.

8. **D**   The $|x| = 5$ implies $x = 5$ or $-x = 5$;   —   —
so $x = 5$ or -5.

9. **D**   The trinomial $X^2 - 4X + 4 = (X - 2)^2$.
Recall that the square of a real number is
greater than OR equal to zero. This implies
that
$$X^2 - 4X + 4 \geq 0.$$

10. **A**   12   4

$s^2 + s^2 = d^2$ $h^2 + \dfrac{s^2}{4} = s^2$

$2s^2 = d^2$ $h^2 = \dfrac{3s^2}{4}$
$s\sqrt{2} = d$

$\sqrt{2} = 1.414$ $h = \dfrac{s\sqrt{3}}{2}$
$1.414s \approx d.$

$\sqrt{3} \approx 1.732$
$h \approx .8660s.$

11. C A man finishes $\frac{1}{3}$ of a job in $\frac{2}{3}$ of a day   — —
or $(\frac{1}{3})(\frac{3}{2})$ of a job in $(\frac{2}{3})(\frac{3}{2})$ of a day or
$\frac{1}{2}$ of a job in one day.

12. B Note that $\dfrac{x + y}{x} = \dfrac{x}{x} + \dfrac{y}{x} = 1 + \dfrac{y}{x}.$ 10   3

Then $1 + \dfrac{y}{x} = \dfrac{7}{4}$ or $\dfrac{y}{x} = \dfrac{3}{4}.$ Similarly

$\dfrac{x - y}{x} = 1 - \dfrac{y}{x} = 1 - \dfrac{3}{4} = \dfrac{1}{4}.$

13. A Recognize that the cube of a negative   13   2
integer is negative; e.g. $-2 > -3$ im-
plies $(-2)^3 > (-3)^3$ or $-8 > -27.$

14. C Add the three equations   11   3
$2a + 2b + 2c = 12$ or $a + b + c = 6.$

15. C The greatest integer less than $\frac{14}{9}$ is 1. The   — —
least integer greater than $\frac{10}{11}$ is 1.

16. A $5a = 11b$ or $\dfrac{a}{b} = \dfrac{11}{5}.$ 11   10

17. A Since the measure of an angle inscribed   12   3
in a semicircle is 90, the $m < ABC$ is 90.
The diameter of the circle is 2(25) or 50.
Recall that if 7-24-25 are sides of a right
triangle then $2(7) - 2(24) - 2(25)$ are
also sides of a right triangle and $CB =
2(24) = 48.$

18. C When 105 is factored the results are   — —
(3)(5)(7) or (105)(1)(1). In each case the
three integers are odd.

19. B The factors of P^3, P prime, are 1, P, P^2, P^3.   — —

20. B $s^2 + (s\sqrt{2})^2 = d^2$ 12   9
$3s^2 = d^2$
$s\sqrt{3} = d$
$2s > s\sqrt{3}.$